Handbook of Blockchain Law

Handbook of Blockchain Law

A Guide to Understanding and Resolving the Legal Challenges of Blockchain Technology

Edited by

Matthias Artzt
Thomas Richter

Wolters Kluwer

Published by:
Kluwer Law International B.V.
PO Box 316
2400 AH Alphen aan den Rijn
The Netherlands
E-mail: international-sales@wolterskluwer.com
Website: lrus.wolterskluwer.com

Sold and distributed in North, Central and South America by:
Wolters Kluwer Legal & Regulatory U.S.
7201 McKinney Circle
Frederick, MD 21704
United States of America
Email: customer.service@wolterskluwer.com

Sold and distributed in all other countries by:
Air Business Subscriptions
Rockwood House
Haywards Heath
West Sussex
RH16 3DH
United Kingdom
Email: international-customerservice@wolterskluwer.com

Printed on acid-free paper.

ISBN 978-94-035-1763-6

e-Book: ISBN 978-94-035-1815-2
web-PDF: ISBN 978-94-035-1863-3

Printed in the United Kingdom.

Editors

Dr Matthias Artzt is a certified lawyer and senior legal counsel at Deutsche Bank AG since 1999. Prior to joining Deutsche Bank, he worked as a lawyer at a law firm in Stuttgart, Germany. He has been practising data protection law for many years and was particularly involved in the implementation of the General Data Protection Regulation (GDPR) within Deutsche Bank AG. He advises internal clients globally regarding data protection issues as well as complex international outsourcing agreements involving data privacy related matters and regulations. He is a graduate of the University of Tübingen, Germany, where he obtained his Doctor of Law degree. Moreover, he is a member of the International Association of Privacy Professionals (IAPP) and since January 2018, a Certified Information Privacy Professional/Europe (CIPP/E). Since January 2020, he is also a member of the European Advisory Board of the IAPP. Matthias is the author of numerous articles on data protection law. Further, he is a regular panel speaker on various national and international conferences, seminars and webinars, e.g., at the Central Bank of Brazil in 2018. He has an in-depth knowledge of the GDPR and its interfaces with other topics, such as Cloud Computing, Big Data, AI, Blockchain, US-Cloud Act and PSD2.

Thomas Richter is a technology and bank regulatory lawyer and senior counsel at Germany's leading bank in Frankfurt. Prior to that, Thomas was an associate at the global law firm, White & Case, in their Frankfurt offices for several years. He is qualified to practice in Germany (*Rechtsanwalt*) and England & Wales (*Solicitor*). Thomas has more than ten years of experience in advising on complex multinational outsourcing and cloud transactions, including on the regulatory aspects. He also frequently advises on digitalization projects and innovative financial solutions. He has particular knowledge on the regulatory aspects of blockchain and crypto assets and is a frequent speaker and panelist on these questions. Thomas has extensive international experience and holds a law degree from the University of Tübingen, Germany, and a Master of Laws in Commercial and Financial law from King's College, London. He has also obtained a Certificate in Transnational law from the University of Geneva. Last year, he had been seconded to Singapore for a period of three months. In his legal training, he worked, *inter alia*, for leading law firms in Munich and Brussels.

Contributors

Prof Dr Lothar Determann practices and teaches international data privacy, technology, commercial and intellectual property law. At Baker McKenzie in San Francisco and Palo Alto, he has been counselling companies since 1998 on data privacy law compliance and taking products and business models international. Admitted to practice in California and Germany, he has been recognized as one of the top ten Copyright Attorneys and top twenty-five Intellectual Property Attorneys in California by the San Francisco & Los Angeles Daily Journal and as a leading lawyer by Chambers, Legal 500, IAM and others. For more information, *see* www.bakermckenzie.com. Contact: ldetermann@bakermckenzie.com. Prof Dr Determann has been a member of the Association of German Public Law Professors since 1999 and teaches Data Privacy Law, Computer Law and Internet Law at Freie Universität, Berlin (since 1994), University of California, Berkeley School of Law (since 2004), Hastings College of the Law (since 2010), Stanford Law School (2011) and University of San Francisco School of Law (2000–2005). He has authored more than 150 articles and treatise contributions as well as five books, including Determann's Field Guide to Data Privacy Law (3d ed. 2017, also available in Chinese, German, Japanese, Portuguese, Russian and Turkish) and California Privacy Law – Practical Guide and Commentary (3d ed. 2018). Recent papers include Healthy Data Protection (http://ssrn.com/abstract=3357990); Electronic Form over Substance (http://ssrn.com/abstract=3436327); No one owns data (https://ssrn.com/abstract=3123957).

Chris Ewing is a solicitor at Warner Bros., a global leader in the creation, production, distribution, licensing and marketing of all forms of entertainment. As part of the Corporate Legal team in London, he provides support to all affiliates' offices across EMEA for non-theatrical distribution, technical operations and general commercial matters, including technology and strategic sourcing. Prior to working at Warner Bros., Chris was an associate in the intellectual property practice group of global law firm, White & Case.

Matthias Goetz (LL.M. Cambridge) is an associate in the intellectual property practice group of global law firm, White & Case. He is qualified to practise in England and Wales as well as in Germany. Matthias advises national and international clients in the areas of data protection and privacy, information technology (IT) and intellectual property (IP). In the area of data protection, he advises on matters such as cross-border data transfers, data breach responses, implementing privacy policies and general data protection compliance issues. Matthias has published several articles on data protection topics and notably co-authored the Jurisdiction Chapter on the United Kingdom in the International Comparative Legal Guide (ICLG) to: Data Protection 2019. For further details, *see*: www.linkedin.com/in/matthiasgoetz.

Dave Hirsch J.D., CFE, is senior counsel in the US Security and Exchange Commission's Division of Enforcement. He is a graduate of the UCLA School of Law, Los Angeles, California, and clerked for Judge Edward J. Schwartz in the United States District Court for the Southern District of California. Prior to his service with the SEC, Dave was a litigator with the law firm of McDermott, Will & Emery, and later he co-founded and ran a private investigation firm focused on securities fraud investigations. Dave is the Cyber Liaison in the Fort Worth Regional Office and is a member of the SEC Digital Ledger Technology Working Group and the Dark Web Working Group. He received the SEC Staff Excellence Award in 2018.

Andreas Holzwarth-Rochford has practiced intellectual property law for nearly twenty years and has prosecuted numerous IP applications and pled in numerous litigation hearings in the areas of physics and mechanical and electrical engineering, as well as software-implemented inventions. Andreas has significant technical experience in optics, laser technology, and new technologies, especially artificial intelligence, machine learning and blockchain applications, wireless data communications and network engineering. In addition to advising on the prosecution and enforcement of patent rights, Andreas supports M&A deals regarding IP due diligence, including freedom to operate (FTO) analysis. He also advises on the economic enhancement of R&D departments, especially regarding efficient patent document surveillance systems and service invention reporting systems, and supports clients in their efforts to find avoidance solutions for third-party rights. He provides counsel to start-up companies on the establishment of patent portfolios and strategies. Andreas has been elected as a delegate of the Federal Association of German Patent Attorneys (Bundesverband Deutscher Patentanwälte e.V) since January 2013. He is also a member of the European Practice Committee of the Intellectual Property Owners Association (IPO), the GRUR, the VPP, the LES, the Federal Association of German Patent Attorneys, the European Patent Litigators Association (EPLIT), the Institute of Professional Representatives before the European Patent Office (epi), and the Interdisciplinary Center for IP of the University of Mannheim.

Dr Michael Juenemann, Co- Head of international Finance and Financial Regulation Group at Bird & Bird, understands the intricacies of the legal frameworks around FinTech and is one of the few to integrate the knowledge of technology with capital markets law. Michael has extensive experience in financial markets and payment services regulation, which he combines with dedicated expertise in disruptive technologies and a deep commitment to innovation in the FinTech sector. Michael regularly expands his network through sector specific events and is a founding member of the International RegTech Association (IRTA). Ranked by Chambers and Partners Fintech and as a legal influencer by Lexology underlines his insightful and helpful knowledge in today's area in Cryptocurrency, Blockchain and FinTech.

William Long is a global co-leader of Sidley's highly ranked Privacy and Cybersecurity practice and also leads the EU Data Protection practice. William advises international clients on a wide variety of GDPR, data protection, privacy, information security, social media, e-commerce and other regulatory matters. William has been a member of the European Advisory Board of the International Association of Privacy Professionals (IAPP) and on the DataGuidance panel of data protection lawyers. He is also on the editorial board of e-Health Law & Policy and also assists with dplegal ('data privacy' legal), a networking group of in-house lawyers in life sciences companies examining international data protection issues. Representative matters have included: advising numerous international companies on the GDPR; advising companies on data privacy issues with Big Data, Internet of Things and profiling; advising a global e-commerce company in dealing with an international data security breach; and assisting a global manufacturing company with a global data protection project, including implementation of Binding Corporate Rules.

William was previously in-house counsel to one of the world's largest international financial services groups. He has been a member of a number of working groups in London and Europe looking at the EU regulation of e-commerce and data protection and spent a year at the UK's Financial Law Panel (established by the Bank of England) as an assistant to the chief executive working on regulatory issues with online financial services. William is recognized in *Chambers UK* 2020 for Data Protection and Information Law, with sources telling the publication, he is 'extremely knowledgeable, not just about what the law requires but also about what the regulators think, and about the landscape of the market.' In the 2019 edition, he was described as bringing 'a broad depth of knowledge on the key areas of law,' whilst in the 2017 edition, clients cite him as 'very knowledgeable, very practical and always solution-driven.' He is recognized in the *LMG Life Sciences Guide* 2014 for Intellectual Property and *Who's Who Legal* 2017 for TMT. He has also been listed in *Best Lawyers* 2020 for Privacy & Data Protection Law and *Who's Who Legal: Data* 2020. William is recognized for both Data Protection, Privacy & Cybersecurity and Pharmaceuticals & Biotechnology in *The Legal 500* UK 2017, with clients noting that his 'forward-thinking and proactive approach keeps him ahead of the curve' and describing his advice as 'thorough, timely and on the leading edge.' He is also included in the 2018 edition of *Best Lawyers* for Privacy & Data Protection and is listed in the Data chapter of *Who's Who Legal: Thought Leaders – Global Elite* 2020. William is also the author of a new book on the EU GDPR and a contributor to a number of books on data protection, including leading legal textbooks published by BNA in the area of privacy, cloud computing and the use of health data. William has been interviewed widely for his thought leadership, including in such leading publications as the international *New York Times, Financial Times* and *The Guardian* and writes for a number of publications including *Data Protection Law & Policy, Computer Weekly, Cloud Pro* and *CIO Today.*

Jay Modrall is a partner in the Antitrust and Competition practice of Norton Rose Fulbright LLP and head of its Brussels office. With over thirty years of experience, Jay is a leading advisor for EU and international competition and regulatory work. His competition law work includes the review and clearance of international mergers and acquisitions, advising on potentially restrictive agreements and abuses of dominant positions and the review and approval of State aid under EU law. Jay has written extensively on EU competition law and is a frequent speaker at EU law conferences, in particular, in relation to the policy and enforcement implications of digitization of the economy.

Sandra Ro, Chief Executive Officer, Global Blockchain Business Council. Sandra is an avid proponent for 'human-centric tech'. She left a career in investment banking and currency markets to focus on blockchain for social impact and is an early investor in and advocate of cryptocurrencies. Sandra currently serves as the CEO of the Global Blockchain Business Council (GBBC), a Swiss-based non-profit as well as an angel investor, Board member, advisor, and cofounder of several start-ups, including Gro Markets, focusing on helping rural, small shareholder farmers and another, Proof of Art, helping independent artists remove business frictions. Whilst at CME Group, she founded and led Digitization, architected the CME CF Bitcoin pricing indices and CME Bitcoin Futures. Previously, she was a derivatives banker at Morgan Stanley and Deutsche Bank, based in London. She holds an MBA from London Business School, studied Computer Science at Columbia University, School of Continuing Studies and earned a double BA degree from Yale University. Sandra was named to the Innovate Finance, Women in Fintech 2016 Power List and holds further directorships on industry, government, and philanthropic boards.

Dr Philip Trillmich is a partner in the intellectual property practice group of global law firm, White & Case. He is qualified to practise in England and Wales as well as in Germany. Philip advises on complex and often cross-border technology transactions, both on a stand-alone basis and in connection with joint ventures, strategic collaborations, mergers and acquisitions, restructurings, business separations and spin-offs. He has a special focus on the digital transformation of industries and the resulting innovative services and business models, in particular, in the areas of financial technology (fintech), digital health and smart technologies. For further details, *see*: https://www.linkedin.com/in/ptrillmich/

Jake van der Laan is a Canadian lawyer and computer scientist with decades of experience in technology and the law. He is currently the Chief Information Officer and Director of Information Technology and Regulatory Informatics at the New Brunswick Financial and Consumer Services Commission (FCNB) in New Brunswick, Canada. He was previously its Director of Enforcement, a position he held for twelve and a half years. Prior to joining FCNB, he was a trial lawyer for twelve years, acting primarily as plaintiff's counsel. He is a regular speaker and teacher with respect to emerging technology-related issues, particularly in the context of financial services and consumer protection regulation. *See* his LinkedIn page for more details at https://www.linkedin.com/in/jakevanderlaan/.

Summary of Contents

Table of Contents

Foreword

Bitcoin, the grandfather of all blockchains to follow, was the very first and remains the most prolific cryptocurrency. However, the story of this strange yet paradigm shifting technology proliferates significantly from this point onwards.

It moved from the cyberpunk chat rooms and subreddits of eclectic technologists to obscure pubs and underground meet ups of London traders, staunch libertarians, risk takers, and anti-establishment, anti-wall street folk in the early 2010s. That is when I first learned about 'this fascinating technology which could supposedly disintermediate many industries' and create new processes and systems. It was quite crude and rudimentary in those early days, and frankly, the rest of the world did not care. We were still reeling from the aftermath of the Great Recession of 2008.

Matthias and I first met in Brasilia at the Banco Central do Brasil's International Seminar on Digital Innovation in Financial Markets, June 2018. We discussed not only the blockchain research work that the Central Bank had been doing but also the crossover of private sector technology companies into traditionally financial institution / bank / central bank roles. How does a government manage to promote innovation of blockchain technology while protecting consumers and providing sufficient regulatory guard rails? Many questions ensued.

In a world where technology is taking data and turning it into 'value' or 'currency', how do central banks and regulators deal with innovations that don't fit neatly into existing legal frameworks? Regulation usually lags behind technology; in the case of blockchain, certain use cases, like a social network issuing digital tokens for commerce, have serious implications for global financial stability and markets.

This is a BIG problem. We must close the gaps.

Fast forward to 2020, we have a decade of technological evolution, from payments or stores of value to use cases covering identity, supply chain track and tracing, (any) record verification and validation, stablecoins, central bank digital currencies, capital formation (initial coin offerings, security token offerings, initial exchange offerings, etc.). From bitcoin's humble origins exploded a plethora of use cases for blockchain technology and digital assets across every industry.

Blockchain technology necessarily requires collaboration – in such spirit, Matthias Artzt & Thomas Richter have brought together in this 'blockchain law' reference book many of the brightest legal minds to cover topics as critical as information security to capital markets implications and data privacy considerations.

This book fulfils a critical need for a blockchain law reference guide and will serve as the bedrock for future additions as this technology continues to evolve. We have just gotten started; thank you for joining us on this fascinating journey into a technology that is impacting people, governments and industries around the world.

To human ingenuity, to human collaborative spirit and to decades of innovation to come. Welcome to the world Handbook of Blockchain Law, Version 1.0.

Sandra Ro
Chief Executive Officer, Global Blockchain Business Council

Preface

Blockchain became known as the technology behind Bitcoin. Inevitably, the pertinent legal discussion was also very Bitcoin-centric over the first number of years. But now, blockchain technology has emancipated itself from Bitcoin and is recognized as a multi-faceted generic technology which may be beneficial in a large variety of potential use cases. We are convinced that the legal aspects of blockchain also need such emancipation, towards a comprehensive and systematic legal assessment of it as a generic technology rather than a narrow use case-based approach. This handbook features such a broader approach and should provide an excellent foundation for conducting detailed legal analyses of specific blockchain use cases.

With that, a key prerequisite in the blockchain journey will be a reliable and robust legal and regulatory framework for blockchain users. Blockchain poses significant legal and regulatory challenges as applications and agreements enabled by that technology are not necessarily easy to reconcile with existing legal norms and regulatory principles.

The innovative artefacts of blockchain technology are essentially decentralization, pseudonymity/anonymity, immutability/finality and – particularly in the context of smart contracts – automation. These characteristics are often the root cause of difficult legal questions. For example, in large-scale blockchain networks, it may be difficult to determine who the actors in the network are, where they are located, and what their actions have been. That can make it challenging to assign legal responsibility and achieve compliance with existing laws and regulations.

This handbook showcases many points of tension between blockchain technology and regulatory or legal requirements, such as the new data protection regime in the European Union (GDPR). One of the key benefits of this book is that the authors, all of them experts and practitioners, carefully lay out and explore these various areas of tension and provide valuable insights into how these might be resolved. Many of these areas of friction arise from fundamental properties of blockchain protocols, which are built on decentralized paradigms. Those are conceptually different from the more centralized approaches that are currently the norm. For instance, in a typical digital platform today, a single entity acts as a 'gate keeper' of that platform and offers a wealth of services to the users. Centrally controlled servers process information and validate data, whereas in the 'new world' of blockchain-based decentralized networks of validating nodes – usually spread all over the world – data validation consensus is reached via an automated protocol and, most importantly, without any third-party authority. Decentralized digital environments may spark questions, such as who is legally responsible for the network and for the actions taken by the applicable blockchain or distributed ledger protocol.

This handbook also takes up the latest debates on how to get the existing legal and regulatory framework aligned with blockchain technology. It starts with a comprehensive functional overview aiming to foster a better understanding of the blockchain and its features. The subsequent chapters build on this understanding and cover specific legal areas closely associated with technological aspects of the blockchain.

We hope that this handbook will be a helpful guide for anybody who is interested in the legal frameworks around blockchain: lawyers, in-house legal counsel, lawmakers, data privacy professionals, data protection officers and authorities, blockchain associations, law schools, universities, blockchain developers and IT experts who typically encounter blockchain in their daily work and are interested in legal questions stemming from the use of that technology.

The authors of this handbook are all experienced practitioners and distinguished blockchain experts, and their expertise and deep understanding make it so valuable. The final editorial work of this book took place while the COVID-19 crisis reached its peak in Europe and in the US, and when other things took priority for all of us. We would like to thank all authors for their continued dedication to the book, even in these difficult times.

Dr Matthias Artzt
Thomas Richter
Frankfurt, 20 April 2020

List of Abbreviations

2WP	2-way Peg
ABI	Application Binary Interface
ACID	Atomicity Consistency Isolation Durability
AI	Artificial Intelligence
AML	Anti-money-Laundering
API	Application Programming Interface
ArbnErfG	German Act on Employee Inventions
ARIPO	African Regional Intellectual Property Organization
ARM	Advanced RISC Machines
ASCII	American Standard Code for Information Interchange
ASIC	Application Specific Integrated Circuit
ATM	Automated Teller Machine
B2C	Business-to-Consumer
BaaS	Blockchain-as-a-Service
BaFin	Germany Federal Financial Supervisory Authority
BCH	Bitcoin Cash
BFT	Byzantine Fault Tolerance
BGBl.	Bundesgesetzblatt
BIP	Bitcoin Improvement Proposal
bona fide	In Good Faith, Covenant of Good Faith and Fair Dealing
BSA	Bank Secrecy Act
BTC	Bitcoin
Cal. Civ. Code	California Civil Code
CAP	Consistency, Availability, Partition (Tolerance)
CCPA	California Consumer Privacy Act
CD	Community Design

CDS	Central Securities Depositary
CEA	Commodity Exchange Act
CFAA	Computer Fraud and Abuse Act
CFT	Countering the Financing of Terrorism
CFTC	US Commodities Futures Trading Commission
CII	Computer Implemented Inventions
CIS	Collective Investment Schemes
CJEU	Court of Justice of the European Union
CJN	EC Consolidated Jurisdictional Notice under the EUMR
CNIL	Commission Nationale Informatique & Libertes
CNMV	Spanish Stock Market Commission
Consob	Italian Supervisory Authority
CPU	Central Processing Unit
CRM	Customer Relationship Management
CRUD	Create Read Update Delete
CSA	Canadian Securities Administrators
CVC	'Convertible' Virtual Currency
DAG	Directed Acyclic Graph
DAO	Decentralized Autonomous Organization
dApp	Distributed Application
DDoS	Distributed Denial-of-Service
DEX	Decentralized Exchange
DLT	Distributed Ledger Technology
DPA	Data Protection Authority
DPIA	Data Privacy Impact Assessment
DPO	Data Protection Officer
DPoS	Delegated Proof of Stake
DTO	Guide to Digital Token Offerings
e.g.	Lat. example gratia = for example – yet to start
EAPO	Eurasian Patent Organization
EC	European Commission
ECC	Elliptic Curve Cryptography
EDPB	European Data Protection Board
EDPS	European Data Protection Supervisor
EEA	European Economic Area
EFD	Essential Facilities Doctrine
EFSA	Estonian Financial Supervisory Authority
EIP	Ethereum Improvement Proposal
EOA	Externally Owned Account
EPC	European Patent Convention
EPO	European Patent Office

ERC	Ethereum Requests for Comments
erga omnes	Lat. towards all
ESMA	European Securities and Markets Authority
ETC	Ethereum Classic
ETH	Ether
EU	European Union
EUIPO	European Union Intellectual Property Office
EUMR	EU Merger Regulation
EVM	Ethereum Virtual Machine
FAQ	Frequently Asked Questions
FBA	Federated Byzantine Agreement
FinCEN	US Financial Crimes Enforcement Network
FIN-FSA	Finnish Financial Supervisory Authority
FINMA	Swiss Financial Market Supervisory Authority
FINRA	US Financial Industry Regulatory Authority
FinTRA	Financial Transactions and Reports Analysis Centre of Canada
FISA	Federal Intermediated Securities Act
FMA	Austrian Financial Market Authority
FM-GWG	Financial Markets Anti-money Laundering Act
FRAND	Fair, Reasonable and Non-discriminatory
GAAP	Generally Accepted Accounting Principles
GB	Gigabyte
GCCPO	Patent Office of the Cooperation Council for the Arab States of the Gulf
GDPR	General Data Protection Regulation
GPTO	German Patent and Trademark Office
GUI	Graphical User Interface
HTLC	Hashed Time Lock Contract
i.e	Lat. id est = that is
ICO	Initial Coin Offering
IDE	Integrated Development Environment
IEO	Initial Exchange Offering
IF	Investment Firm
IFMs	Investment Fund Managers
IFRS	International Financial Reporting Standard
IMEI	International Mobile Equipment Identity
inter alia	Lat. among other things
inter se	Lat. among or between themselves
IoT	Internet of Things
IP	Internet Protocol

IP	Intellectual Property
IP Address	Internet Protocol Address
IPRP	International Preliminary Report on Patentability
IPRs	Intellectual Property Rights
IRS	US Internal Revenue Service
IT	Information Technology
ITO	Initial Token Offering
ITS	Token Sale ITS
JVM	Java Virtual Machine
KMG	Capital Markets Act
KWG	German Banking Act (*Kreditwesengesetz*)
KYC	Know Your Customer
LCL	Last Closed Ledger
lege lata	Lat. the law as it exists
Liechtenstein FMA	Financial Market Authority of Liechtenstein
LMV	Spanish Securities Market Act (*Ley del Mercado de Valores)*
LN	Lightning Network
MAC	Media Access Control
MAR	Market Abuse Regulation
MAS	Monetary Authority of Singapore
MB	Megabyte
MFN	Most Favoured Nation
MiFID II	Markets in Financial Instruments Directive II
MPEP	Manual of Patent Examining Procedure
MSB	Money Services Business
MTF	Multilateral Trading Facility
NDA	Non-disclosure Agreements
nemo dat	Lat. nemo dat quod non habet = no one can give what they do not have
NIST	National Institute of Standards and Technology U.S. Department of Commerce
OAPI	African Intellectual Property Organization
obiter	Lat. by the way
opt-in model	Closed-Loop Email Authentication
OSC	Ontario Securities Commission
OTF	Organized Trading Facility
P2P	Peer to Peer
PACTE	Plan d'Action pour la Croissance et la Transformation de l'Entreprise
PCT	Patent Cooperation Treaty
PFSA	Polish Financial Supervision Authority

PoET	Proof of Elapsed Time
PPC	Peercoin Cryptocurrency
PRIIP	Packaged Retail and Insurance-Based Investment Products
PS Act	Payment Services Act 2019
PSD2	Payment Services Directive 2
PTAB	Patent Trial and Appeal Board
Quid	Lat. one or another
RAM	Random Access Memory
RCD	Registered Community Design
REACT	California Regional Enforcement Allied Computer Team
RISC	Reduced Instruction Set Computer
RPCA	Ripple Protocol Consensus Algorithm
RPM	Resale Price Maintenance
SARs	Suspicious Activity Reports
SEC	Securities and Exchange Commission
SFA	Securities & Futures Act of Singapore
SGX	Software Guard Extensions
SHA (256)	Secure Hash Algorithm (Generating a 256 bit Hash Digest)
SIM	Mobile Phone Identity, Which Is Stored on a SIM Card
SMA	Finnish Securities Markets Act
SQL	Structured Query Language
SRO	Self-Regulatory Organization
SSS	Securities Settlement System
STO	Security Token Offering
TCP	Transmission Control Protocol
TEE	Trusted Execution Environment
TFEU	Treaty on the Functioning of the European Union
TGE	Token Generation Event
TOR	The Onion Router Network
TPS	Transactions Per Second
TVTG	Tokens and TT Service Provider Act
TXID	Transaction ID
UK	United Kingdom
UK ICO	UK Information Commissioner's Office
UKJT	UK Jurisdiction Taskforce
UNICODE	Computing Industry Standard for the Encoding, Representation, and Handling of Text
UNL	Unique Node List
UPC	Unified Patent Court
USPTO	US Patent and Trademark Office

UTXO	Unspent Transaction Output
VBER	EU Vertical Block Exemption Regulation
VCP	Finnish Act on Virtual Currency Providers
vice versa	Lat. by the other way around
WAG	Austrian Securities Supervision Act
WIPO	World Intellectual Property Organization
WTO	World Trade Organization
XML	Extensible Markup Language
XRP	Ripple Cryptocurrency

CHAPTER 1

Understanding Blockchain

Jake van der Laan

§1.01 INTRODUCTION

Blockchain and distributed ledger technology (DLT),[1] including functionality such as *smart contracts*, have in the past few years been identified as potential solutions for a variety of business problems. Many of its proponents point to the benefits of removing centralized trusted intermediaries, the immutability[2] of the data, and/or potential improvements in the efficiency of existing business processes as bases for implementing these technologies.[3] Some suggest it will enable a whole new business functionality altogether. There are also others who remain quite sceptical.[4] This chapter is not intended to support either camp, or to otherwise pass any sort of judgement on the merits of blockchain and its related technologies. It simply seeks to explain how it all works. A good understanding of these technologies is important to anyone considering implementing blockchain-based solutions, or anyone rendering advice with respect to them.

This chapter sets out a pathway to understanding blockchain and its related technologies in an iterative manner suitable for non-technical professionals with little or no background in math or computer science. Necessary core concepts and some key components are explained first. With that foundation, the functionality of a blockchain is explained. This then, in turn, enables the exploration of subsequent innovations

1. These are not the same thing. A blockchain is a *type* of distributed ledger technology.
2. The inability to change data after it has been committed to the blockchain.
3. Amazon lists over 7,000 titles after a search for 'blockchain book'. *See* https://www.amazon.ca/s?k=blockchain+book&ref=nb_sb_noss_1 (accessed 27 Dec. 2019).
4. *See*, for instance, Robinson, J., '*BitCoin: The Naked Truth about Bitcoin*' Amazon Digital Services 26 (2014): 149; Gerard, D., '*Attack of the 50 Foot Blockchain: Bitcoin, Blockchain, Ethereum & Smart Contracts*' (2017); and Popper, N., '*Digital Gold: The Untold Story of Bitcoin*' (2015).

such as smart contracts, other distributed data structures, and additional consensus mechanisms.

This approach to explaining blockchain is rooted in observations made after having sought to explain blockchain and DLTs to many hundreds of non-technical people over the past number of years. That experience revealed the critical importance of explaining the various underlying technical building blocks in detail first. It also made it clear that for many people certain aspects of the blockchain, such as hashing functions and Proof of Work difficulty, are more difficult to grasp than others. Additional time is therefore spent on setting out how these things work by breaking them down into understandable pieces.

Most of the core concepts in this chapter are explained in the context of the Bitcoin blockchain, as it is the oldest and most used blockchain at the time of writing. A solid understanding of the Bitcoin blockchain is a good foundation for delving into more intricate topics, such as the Ethereum blockchain, smart contracts, and other consensus mechanisms and related concepts.

§1.02 CORE CONCEPTS

[A] Record-Keeping

Humans have been record keepers for thousands of years.[5] Record-keeping has served throughout time to crystalize human memory to ensure that obligations or entitlements were not only tracked but also *provable*.

Not surprisingly, record-keeping methodologies were quickly adopted to enable tax assessment and collection, and also became a backbone of the banking system. Over time sophisticated record-keeping mechanisms and accounting systems were developed for these purposes, which today are embodied in standards such as GAAP and IFRS (*see* https://en.wikipedia.org/wiki/Accounting_standard).[6]

Records have been traditionally kept by the individuals or parties seeking to benefit from the recorded state of something which such records provide. Businesses use them to track their various revenues and expenses, inventory, goods sold, etc. Banks use them to maintain records of the various entitlements and obligations of their customers. Governments use them to track tax obligations and many other bits of data about the citizenry, among other things to track budgets and inform public policy. Today, much of this record-keeping is entrusted with computers running sophisticated database systems and has been centralized[7] within the organizations maintaining them.

The accuracy and reliability of records maintained in this manner are traditionally accepted on the basis of trust in the record keeper itself. To bolster such trust,

5. *See*, for instance, https://www.metmuseum.org/art/collection/search/329081 (accessed 15 Dec. 2019).
6. https://www.ifrs.org/ (accessed 15 Dec. 2019).
7. It must be noted that within such organizations there usually exist robust back up and redundancy systems to safeguard these records.

ethical obligations have over time been imposed on these record keepers through legal duties and standards, as well as explicit regulation.[8]

Blockchain offers a novel way of record-keeping which seeks to shift this traditional trust away from the record keeper *to the record-keeping systems themselves. This is achieved* by virtue of the addition of what are essentially 'data storage tricks' which ensure that what is stored can be relied upon to not have been altered once it has been committed to the blockchain.[9]

The building blocks of these 'storage tricks' have been well known for some time. It is the combination of them by Satoshi Nakamoto in his famous 2008 paper[10] that has spawned the current interest in blockchain as a potential alternative record-keeping solution for businesses and governments.

Let's now review some of blockchain's technical building blocks as well as some basic computational concepts to lay the foundation for understanding how blockchain and other emerging DLTs work.

[B] How Computers Encode Data

Many of blockchain's underlying concepts, ideas and operational components include the use of things like digital keys, digital signatures and numerical addresses. In seeking to understand these, it is helpful to have a basic idea of how computers handle data and information.

At its most basic level, a computer uses electronic switches, or transistors, to store data. A switch has only two settings, or states, off or on, which are traditionally used to represent the number 0 or 1.[11]

Two switches (or 'bits' as they are known to computer scientists) can, for example, be used to represent – through their various combinations of either off or on – the numbers, or values, from 0 to 3 (Figure 1.1).

8. *See*, for instance, the extensive record-keeping standards with which Canadian Chartered Public Accountants must comply, available at: https://www.cpacanada.ca/en/business-and-accounting-resources/cpa-canada-handbook-the-standards-and-guidance-collection (accessed 15 Dec. 2019).
9. Some will argue that the blockchain eliminates the need for trust, but it is submitted that is not the case. Trust is actually *shifted* to the various methodologies employed in the blockchain, including its various human-controlled aspects, such as programming of the applicable blockchain software and software applications used to access the blockchain.
10. https://bitcoin.org/bitcoin.pdf (accessed 15 Dec. 2019).
11. A switch can also be used to represent other binary type states, such as yes/no, true/false, etc.

Figure 1.1 Binary Form of the Numbers 0 to 3

	Bit A	Bit B
0	0	0
1	0	1
2	1	0
3	1	1

With three switches, or bits, one can increase the storage capacity to any of the numbers from 0 through 7. With 4 bits, it is possible to capture 16 numbers, and so on.

As one adds another bit, the number of combinations increases by a power of 2 each time. A set of 8 bits (referred to as an *octet* or a *byte*[12]) can thus represent 2^8, or 256 different things, such as the numbers 0 to 255.

These various combinations of sets of bits can be used to encode complete sets of characters like the alphabet. This makes the digitization of text possible. To that end, and very early on in the development of computers, it was agreed among computer scientists that certain characters would be represented by certain combinations of bits in an octet or byte. These agreements are known as *encoding standards*. Two very popular and often used encoding standards are ASCII[13] and UNICODE. The latter has several different standards for representing all the different characters used by the languages of the world.[14]

Encoding standards, together with the ability to place many billions of very small transistors on silicon storage devices or magnetically represent zeroes and ones on magnetic tapes or drives, enable the storage of very large volumes of text and data in digital form.

[C] How Computers Store Large Numbers

In our day-to-day interaction, the base-10 system is used for counting and representing mathematical values. A base-10 counting system is a methodology to represent a specific quantity by way of a sequence digits between 0 and 9. The set of digits in a base-10 number represent different powers of 10, in sequence, with the smallest power always on the right. For example, the number 123 is really a short way of saying 3 x (10^0) + 2 x (10^1) + 1 x (10^3) = 3 + 20 + 100 = 123. (Note that any number raised to the power 0 (zero) is always 1.)

A computer is limited to only using zeroes and ones to represent a number, given that it is built on switches which can only represent two states. The number system which uses only 2 states (0 and 1) is called base-2 or the *binary* system of counting.

12. It is likely better to use octet as there is no ambiguity that it references 8 items. Some implementations of a byte have used 7 bits.
13. The *American Standard Code for Information Interchange* was initially based on using only 7 bits.
14. https://home.unicode.org (accessed 15 Dec. 2019).

Like the base-10 system, each location in the base-2 number represents a power of the base, and thus allows one to count incrementally by adding up the sequence of the number of times the various powers of 2 occur in the number. For example, in the case of the binary number 1011, this works as follows: (again, counting from right to left): $1 \times (2^0) + 1 \times (2^1) + 0 \times (2^3) + 1 \times (2^4) = 1 + 2 + 0 + 8 = 11$.

Compare the numbers 0 through 9 in both base-10 and base-2 (Figure 1.2).

Figure 1.2 The Numbers 0 Through 9 in Base-10 and Base-2 (Binary)

0	00000000
1	00000001
2	00000010
3	00000011
4	00000100
5	00000101
6	00000110
7	00000111
8	00001000
9	00001001

Many computer programs use base-16 (commonly referred to as *hexadecimal*, or 'hex') to represent numbers in half byte (4 bit) segments.[15] When representing these numbers in writing, it was agreed to add the letters *a* through *f* to the above table to denote the base-2 values of 1010 through 1111 (which are the base-10 values of 10 through 15) (Figure 1.3).

Figure 1.3 The Numbers 10 Through 15 in Hexadecimal and Binary

a	00001010
b	00001011
c	00001100
d	00001101
e	00001110
f	00001111

As an example, here is the number 123,456,789 in binary and base-16:

Binary: 111010110111100110100010101
Hex: 75BCD15

To indicate that a particular number is in hexadecimal, it is customary to place 0x in front of it. The above hex example number 75BCD15 can thus also be written as 0x75BCD15. Likewise, a binary number may be preceded by '0b' for the same purpose.

15. Because one can create 16 different combinations of zeroes and ones with 4 bits. Note that the first four bits in the above example are all zeroes for the first 16 hex numbers.

As will be seen later, many of the components of blockchain use the hex format to represent various important numbers.

Some other components (such as some public key addresses) may use yet another form of numeric encoding called base-58 which was designed to avoid confusion between digits which look the same.[16]

[D] Computer Programming

A computer, at the most basic level, performs two core functions: data storage and data manipulation. A computer is really nothing more than a very fast data manipulator.

The storage function involves the placing of programming code and data contemplated for manipulation by that programming code on one or more storage devices, such as a hard drive and random-access memory (RAM).

The manipulation function involves the retrieval of data from RAM or a storage device and doing something with, or to, that data based on rules set out in programming code, before re-storing it back into a memory location or a section of a hard drive storage device.

Modern programming languages permit the manipulation of data using several logical building blocks which can be combined in an unlimited manner to create very detailed logical sequences. These logical sequences, also known as programs, can perform complex operations or automate many processes and workflows which involve manipulation of data or information.

It is helpful to gain a basic understanding of some of the building blocks of a computer program, particularly in anticipation of the later explanation of smart contracts.

[1] Variables

A variable is a certain amount of storage space (a quantity of bytes) reserved in the computer's RAM which can be accessed (for retrieval or modification) by referencing the name of the variable.[17]

A variable is sometimes further described by the kind of data that should be put in the reserved memory location. For example, a variable may be 'typed' as an integer, which means that the memory space's content will be interpreted as being an integer.[18]

16. Base-58 uses the numbers 1–9 as well as both upper- and lower-case letters but skips characters prone to confusion, such as the letter Oh and the number Zero, as well as the letters I, L and the number One.
17. The programming language looks after translating the variable name to the actual memory location in order to make it easier for the programmer.
18. Which will also mean that if one tries to put something into the memory location which cannot be an integer, such as the letter 'D', the computer will let us know that an error has occurred. This type of error is very common in programming and is called a 'type mismatch'.

Most program languages have many different types of variables available for use[19] and most allow the creation of custom variable types as well.[20]

[2] Control Structures

A control structure examines and compares variables retrieved from memory and directs program flow based on that comparison. The most often used control structure is the *if ... then ... else* statement which allows branching based on the value of variables used in the *if ... then ... else* statement. For example, the following code uses such a statement to display different messages based on the age of a person[21] (Figure 1.4).

Figure 1.4 An Example of If ... Else Statement[22]

```
if (age < 20 AND age > 12) then
{
        print "this person is a teenager"
        }
else
        {
        print "this person is not a teenager"
        }
```

Another often used control structure is the *while loop* which allows the repeated execution of a section of logic for as long as a condition is true. Here is a *while loop* example which displays an integer variable as it is being incremented from 1 to 10 (Figure 1.5).

19. Usually referred to as *primitive* data types. *See*, for example, the taxonomy for such built in primitive variable data types in the Java programming language, available at: https://www.javatpoint.com/java-data-types (accessed 15 Dec. 2019).
20. Particularly so in the case of programming languages which follow the object-oriented paradigm to programming, where very complex objects with many different attributes can be created as effectively 'super variables'.
21. Note that in many programming languages, the code which is executed together as part of a branch from a control structure is placed between two 'squirrely' brackets ({and}).
22. Note that most computer programming languages use the reserved word 'print' to generate output to a display. This is a leftover from the days when output was actually generated by a physical printer.

Figure 1.5 An Example of While Statement

```
        integer variable = 1
while (integer variable < 11)
        {
                print integer variable
                integer variable = integer variable + 1
                }
```

Control structures can be used to build ever more complex functionality from very basic building blocks,[23] which can then be stored as *functions* or routines and re-used in other computer programs. For example, it is very easy to build a multiplication function (seeking to multiply x and y) if a programming language only had a simple addition function, by simply adding y to y, x number of times. Once such a multiplication function is created and can be accessed as a function (or a *callable* set of code), it can then be used to create another function to calculate the power of a number, and so on.

All programming languages have developed extensive sets of complex functions, procedures and reusable code, called *libraries*. Libraries can be accessed, or called, by any computer program written in the applicable programming language, without having to 're-invent the wheel'. This is one of the most important features of modern programming – the ability to re-use and build on existing code.

In many cases, sets of libraries for a particular program are combined to create an *Application Program Interface* or API, which then allows other programming languages, and in some cases devices with programmatic functionality, to interact with programs written in the language for which the API is available.[24]

[3] Data Structures

Data structures are methods of storing data in computer memory in a certain way, to enable certain capabilities for manipulating that data, which would be (much) more difficult or not possible without that data structure.

In many instances, data structures incorporate or enable certain relationships between data elements which then facilitate indexing, sorting, editing, or other functionality, including certain kinds of calculations. Data structures in many cases also help with the efficient access and manipulation of data stored in memory.

---

23. Which build on the very basic capacities of the core circuitry of a computer's Central Processing Unit or CPU. A CPU has only a limited set of core functionalities, including addition and multiplication. The power of a CPU is in being able to do billions of these basic operations per second.
24. *See*, for instance, the API for the Java programming language at: https://docs.oracle.com/javase/7/docs/api/ (accessed 15 Dec. 2019).

[a] The Array

An *array* is an example of a simple data structure, which is simply a list of items in order. Here is an example of an array containing the months of the year (Figure 1.6).

Figure 1.6 An Array of the Months of the Year

Jan	Feb	Mar	Apr	May	Jun	Jul	Aug	Sep	Oct	Nov	Dec
0	1	2	3	4	5	6	7	8	9	10	11

The location of an element in an array is referred to as its *index*, displayed above, below each month.[25]

An array is useful if one wants to relate a specific location in that array with the ranked order of the data items stored. In the above example, the months of the year are thus listed in the order in which they occur.

Another example is the list of ingredients in packaged food, usually found on its label. This array is usually required to be listed in the order of prevalence of the ingredients listed. The ingredient with the highest percentage of content goes first, the ingredient with the next highest goes next, and so on. The structure of the array thus embodies a sorted list without needing to do anything further.

[b] The Linked List

The *linked list* is another example of a data structure. A linked list is a set of data objects where each data object, in addition to storing some data value, keeps track of the location of the next item in the list by way of a pointer (usually pointing to the memory address of the next item in the list) (Figure 1.7).

Figure 1.7 A Linked List

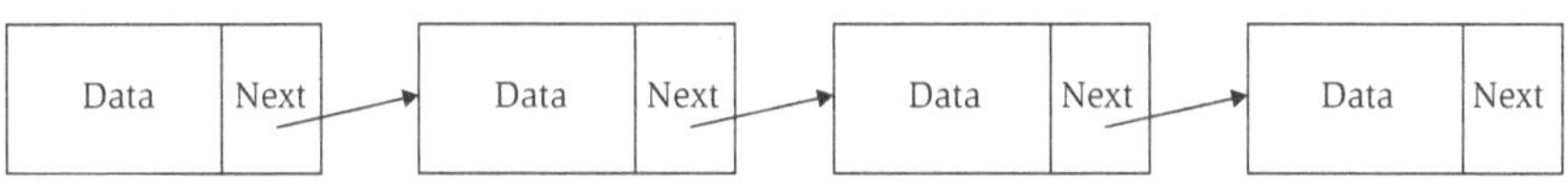

Linked lists are very useful for maintaining an ordered list because it is very easy to insert or remove elements from the list. For example, to insert a new element in an ordered list, one only needs to update the pointer of the previous ordered item in the list. Compare this to an array where one would need to shift all subsequent list members over one location to the right.

The core idea behind the linked list (tying data elements together with a pointer) is also used in a slightly different way in a blockchain.

25. Note that many programming languages start the index at 0, which is perhaps a bit counterintuitive but makes it easier for the computer, which deems 0 to be just as good a number as 1.

[4] Syntax

The syntax of a programming language is the set of rules for translating a logical process or workflow into a sequence of instructions which the computer can understand and execute.

When writing a program in a specific language, it is very important to fully understand that language's syntax. Any misunderstanding of the syntax can lead to errors in the instructions which may go unnoticed in the final implementation of a program until a set of conditions arises which causes the execution of the program to go awry. These types of errors are often referred to as 'bugs' and no computer program is without them.[26]

It should be noted at this point that bugs or errors in how computer programs run can occur not only from syntax errors in the code but also from such things as:

- Errors in the operating system software of the computer, for instance how the operating manages its memory.
- Errors in the hardware configuration of the computer, for instance how data traffic is managed on the motherboard of the computer.
- Logical errors in the code which fail to contemplate the full range of possible values for input variables to programmatic control structures and may thus cause unintended program flow and/or memory overflows[27] as a result.

No computer program of any complexity is without some bugs.

[5] From Program Code to Machine Code

A computer language, such as Java, Python or Visual Basic, is actually a large computer program written to make programming of computers easier for humans. These higher-level languages use simple English words to represent their syntax, and many have complex integrated editing tools with a great deal of features.[28]

The product of these high-level programming languages is a relatively easy-to-read text file, compliant with the structural formatting and syntax requirements of the specific programming language used. This file is not directly usable by the computer for execution, however, and must first be converted to *machine code* interpretable by the Central Processing Unit (CPU)[29] of the computer on which the code is to be executed.

The type of machine code required depends on the architecture of the CPU in question. Machine code for an Intel processor[30] is different from that for an ARM

26. With the exception perhaps of the code written to power the lunar missions in the late 1960s and early 1970s.
27. For instance, by placing a value in a memory location which is too large for the reserved space, which can then result in overwriting the next memory location.
28. Referred to as Integrated Development Environments, or IDEs.
29. The 'brains' of the computer, which contains hardwired circuitry which can execute basic computer instructions at a very high rate.
30. Found in most desktop computers.

processor,[31] for example. The required machine code is determined by the *instruction set* for the CPU, which can be thought of as the complete list of available instructions which can be issued to the CPU by a computer program.

The program which translates the program language specific text file into machine code is called a *compiler*.[32] The product of a compiler is a long string of zeroes and ones called a *bitstream*, which in the case of a computer program is usually referred to as a *binary*.

In some cases, an intermediary code interpreter, called a *virtual machine*, *process virtual machine*, or *runtime environment*, sits between the programming language and the CPU.

Such a virtual machine is used to create the ability to execute a particular program on any CPU for which a virtual machine exists.[33] The Java programming language uses the *Java Virtual Machine*, or JVM, exactly for this purpose, and it is one of the reasons why this language is so popular: it can run on many different types of hardware.

In the case of the JVM, the compiler does not generate binary code, but rather a *bytecode* file, which the JVM then converts to machine code usable by the specific hardware being used.

In many cases, the binary or bytecode is transmitted to a computer or virtual machine for execution using hex encoding. As we will see, this is also how smart contracts are encoded and transmitted to the blockchain.

§1.03 THE MATHEMATICS OF BLOCKCHAIN

[A] The Hash Function

A function is a mathematical recipe for turning an input into a desired output based on a clearly articulated formula or algorithm. For example, the addition function 'C = A + B' takes the variables A and B as inputs and generates the desired output C by adding A and B together.

One group of functions relevant to understanding blockchain is the set of *hash functions*. Hash functions are used to convert a usually large input of data into a much smaller, fixed-length output to create a unique 'signature' of the larger input.

A hash function thus maps the input data to a numerical key. This key is usually referred to as the *hash value* or *hash digest*, or just the *hash* (Figure 1.8).

31. Advanced RISC Machines, which is used in many mobile and embedded devices.
32. This is a dramatic oversimplification of what a compiler does, but it is sufficient for our limited purposes.
33. A virtual machine thus allows a programming language to become *multi-platform*.

Figure 1.8 A Hash Function

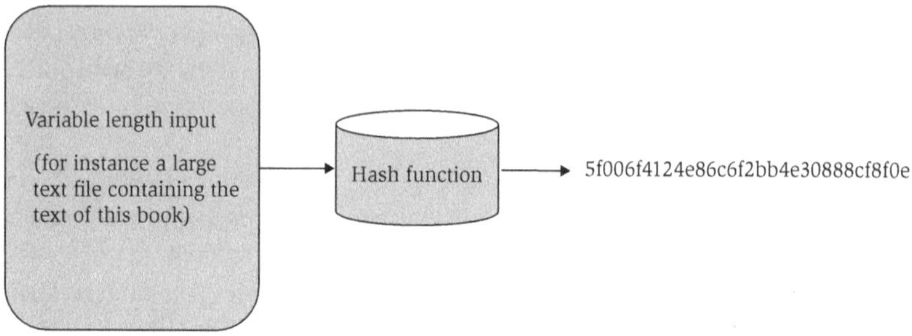

Most hash functions work by taking the input data, chopping it up into smaller sections and then applying certain functions to those smaller chunks. The division and remainder - or *modulo* - function is often used in this process, which gives a hash function a 'one-way' property. It is not possible to recreate the original input from the eventual hash generated by the function.[34]

These hash functions then shuffle and/or combine the outputs from these smaller chunks in a predefined manner and reapply the modulo, or some variant, again. This process is continued until a single output of the desired length is achieved.

The output of a hash function is often written in hex. For example, the very popular hashing algorithm SHA256[35] (which is used in the Bitcoin blockchain) will output a 64-bit hash digest which might look like this:[36]

5e884898da28047151d0e56f8dc6292773603d0d6aabbdd62a11ef721d1542d8

Note that this hex value is the following very large number in base-10:

42,758,200,014,260,304,871,795,218,010,112,217,441,437,394,933,425,264, 440,882,844,866,153,524,052,696[37]

34. Further discussed *infra*. Appreciate that the remainder function is very helpful in creating a 'one-way' function, given that the same remainder can arise for many different divisions. For example, 10 divided by 3 leaves remainder 1. 16 divided by 5 also leaves remainder 1. A specialized implementation building on this property, which is often used in public key encryption, is the *elliptic curve* function, available at: https://blog.cloudflare.com/a-relatively-easy-to-understand-primer-on-elliptic-curve-cryptography/ (accessed 15 Dec. 2019).
35. *See* https://csrc.nist.gov/csrc/media/publications/fips/180/4/archive/2012-03-06/documents/fips180-4.pdf (accessed 15 Dec. 2019) for the standard description of this algorithm. It is a complicated process.
36. Available at: https://www.fileformat.info/tool/hash.htm (accessed 15 Dec. 2019).
37. This is a 77-digit number and one of the 2^{256} possible outputs from the SHA256 hashing algorithm. Note that the number of digits of that number can be determined by calculating n log 2, in this case 256 log 2 which equals 77.

Hash functions are used in many applications dealing with the storage and indexing of large data sets. More refined hashing functions are used to assist in ensuring that data is not corrupted or has been changed.

[B] The Cryptographic Hash Function

One specific type of hash function is particularly relevant to our understanding of blockchain: the *cryptographic hash function*. Like a regular hash function, the cryptographic hash function takes a data input of variable length and generates a fixed-length hash digest as its output.

A cryptographic hash function has some specific and very useful properties which the blockchain takes advantage of.

[1] The 'Always the Same' Property

A cryptographic hash function will always generate the same hash value for the same input. This is usually described by computer scientists and mathematicians as the 'deterministic' property. A function which is non-deterministic will generate different outputs because a certain amount of randomness exists in how the function works. An example of a non-deterministic function is the rolling of a set of dice.

[2] The 'Digital Signature' Property

A cryptographic hash function also uses a formula which ensures (with an extremely high level of confidence[38]) that the hash digest will be *unique*. A hash digest thus becomes a *digital signature* of the input data and can be used to determine whether an input has been modified or not.

In the use of a cryptographic hash function, the smallest possible change (i.e., one bit or character) in the input data will generate a completely different output digest (Figure 1.9).

38. Particularly in the case of *structured data*, i.e., data which follows a pattern, such as the grammar of a language. This property is sometimes also referred to as the function having 'strong collision resistance'.

Figure 1.9 An Example of How a Minimal Change in Input Generates a Completely Different Hash Digest

Input text	SHA256 hash digest
This is sample text submitted to the SHA256 hashing algorithm. We will change it just a little bit by adding a period to the end of this sentence below	bbadbf8c5138b8c9ced5c5197082ff5b3 6c9128f009bbb4cb450389c626c0214
This is sample text submitted to the SHA256 hashing algorithm. We will change it just a little bit by adding a period to the end of this sentence below.	9d2f5d3b509a0334e752a0aaa0fe468f3 4affdddcc1c1912aeeee75321117514

This is a very valuable feature which enables a cryptographic hash function to serve several useful purposes. For example, this property is exploited when transmitting digital files over the internet to ensure they arrive on the receiver's computer in identical form to that sent by the sender. That process works as follows:

- The sender feeds the digital file (of any size) to one of a number of available cryptographic hashing functions[39] and generates a hash digest, usually somewhere between 32 and 128 bits in length.
- The sender transmits the digital file to the recipient over the internet and also sends particulars of the cryptographic hash function used, together with the generated hash digest.
- The receiver feeds the received digital file to the cryptographic hash function generating a hash digest.
- If the receiver's hash digest matches the hash digest sent by the sender, then we must conclude that the received file is identical to the one transmitted by the sender.
- If the hash digests do not match, then there was an error in transmission, and the file needs to be resent.

[3] The 'No Reverse Engineering' Property

A cryptographic hash function is also a 'one-way function' which means it is not possible to recreate or 'reverse engineer' the original file from the hash digest.

One might think that calculating all possible permutations of the input data and then looking for the digest in that list to find the original input data is an option. This is, however, computationally prohibitive – it would require more computational power

39. For further review and testing with a number of these hashing algorithms: https://www.tools4noobs.com/online_tools/hash/ (accessed 15 Dec. 2019).

and time than that is reasonably possible to obtain - particularly with large input data sets of different sizes.[40]

One-way functions are very useful in many applications, including public-private key encryption.

[C] The Hash List

One application of a cryptographic hash function is the *hash list.* The hash list is used a lot in peer-to-peer (P2P) file sharing systems (discussed *infra*) to ensure that the various distributed pieces of a file come together to reconstitute the original file without errors. In that context, a hash list (Figure 1.10) functions as follows:

- The file being shared is broken up into several smaller pieces, called data blocks, which are sufficiently small to enable easy transmission over the internet as packets or groups of packets.
- Each block is hashed, and the hash value added to a separate hash list.
- Once all block hashes have been added, the hash list file is itself hashed and a *top hash* generated.
- The top hash file is kept by a trusted authority.
- Anyone wishing to obtain the file from the P2P network will first obtain the top hash file from the trusted source.[41]
- With that file in hand, the hash list can then be obtained from any other source (i.e., any other sharing user on the P2P network) for comparison with the top hash.
- If the hash of the hash list file matches the top hash, the user can proceed to download the various data blocks from any of the other users on the network who have those blocks available.
- Every block's hash is compared with the hash value for that block in the confirmed hash list file, and if it matches, it is accepted as genuine.

40. These types of problems are called *intractable* which means they cannot be solved within the bounds of our foreseeable computational capacity, *see* https://en.wikipedia.org/wiki/Computational_complexity_theory#Intractability (accessed 15 Dec. 2019).
41. In the case of BitTorrent, this file actually contains both the top hash as well as the hash values for all the data blocks for the file being shared.

Figure 1.10 A Hash List

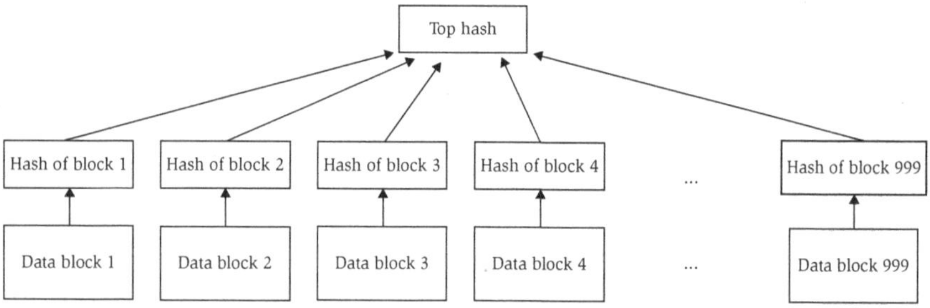

Given the properties of the cryptographic hash function, one is assured that if the hash of a received data block is not the same as the hash found in the hash list, a change or corruption is present in that block of data, necessitating a retransmission or obtaining the block from another source.

Using a hash list to verify the integrity of a file in blocks has another advantage in that it is much easier to determine where data errors exist than if one simply hashed the whole file. Fixing 'bad data' is thus much easier and faster.

[D] The Merkle Tree

A Merkle tree (also sometimes referred to as a *binary hash tree* or just *hash tree*) takes the ideas behind the hash list a step further, for even better data integrity.

Rather than creating a simple list of hashes of data blocks, a Merkle tree incorporates data hashes into an upside down tree type structure, much like one might organize a family tree for a genealogy project. The individual elements in the tree are referred to as *nodes* and every node has two children and one parent.

At the bottom of the tree are the various data block nodes (sometimes referred to as *leaves*[42]), which are hashed individually, and their hash digests are then combined in pairs and hashed together again to create a parent hash. These parent hashes are, in turn, paired together and hashed again to create 'grandparent' hashes, and so on.

The Bitcoin blockchain uses a Merkle tree to organize and verify integrity for every individual transaction contained in a block of transactions. To that end, the content of a leaf is limited to only one transaction. Hashes are combined using the above approach until there is only one hash at the top of the tree.

This top hash is called the *Merkle root* (Figure 1.11).

42. Leaves are not stored in the Merkle tree.

Figure 1.11 A Simple Merkle Tree

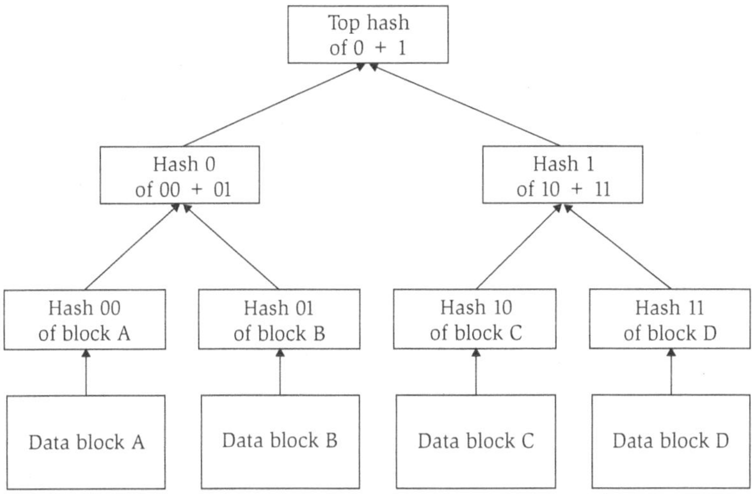

The Merkle trees used in the Bitcoin blocks use the double-SHA256 hashing algorithm.[43]

[E] Public-Private Key Encryption

The ability to successfully encode, or encrypt, a message into a form which can only be read by the intended recipient, and no one else, has been something which mankind has pursued for centuries.[44]

Until the 1970s or so, the only solution was any of a number of different variants of *symmetric key* approaches (Figure 1.12), where the key for encryption was the same as the key used to decrypt the message. An encryption key converts the original message into gibberish using some sort of predefined, usually complex, algorithm.[45]

43. Applying SHA256 twice.
44. For a short overview of the history of cryptography, *see* https://pdfs.semanticscholar.org/938a/24139dbf089d4d8a43118445c471e1e7f0aee.pdf (accessed 15 Dec. 2019).
45. An encryption key is used to convert the original message into gibberish using some sort of predefined usually complex algorithm. An example of such an algorithm is AES, the Advanced Encryption Standard, available at: https://en.wikipedia.org/wiki/Advanced_Encryption_Standard (accessed 15 Dec. 2019).

Figure 1.12 Symmetric Key Encryption

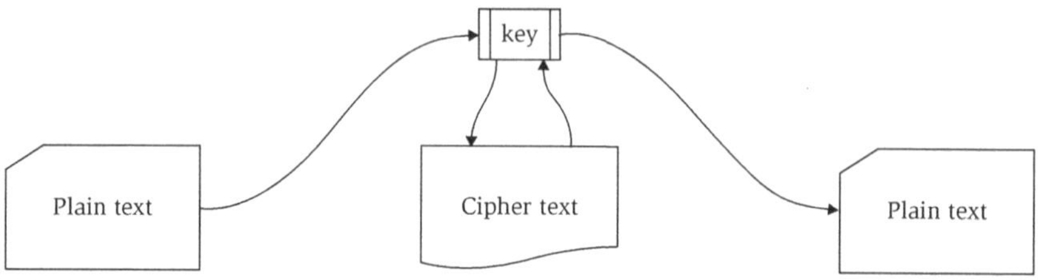

A very simple encryption key is the *substitution cypher* for which a key might look like this (Figure 1.13).

Figure 1.13 A Simple Substitution Cypher

A	B	C	D	E	F	G	H	I	J	K	L	M	N	O	P	Q	R	S	T	U	V	W	X	Y	Z
Q	W	Z	A	R	K	B	J	C	L	S	D	X	E	Y	U	H	T	P	G	V	N	F	M	O	I

Using this cypher, the phrase 'blockchain is simple' encrypts as 'wdyzsxjqe cp pcxudr'.

With symmetric key encryption, both the sender and the receiver use the same key, which they must also *both* keep secret. In addition, a cypher must be resistant to any of a number of potential decryption attacks.[46] Achieving both of these conditions is not always easy.

Over the centuries many intricate systems were developed with the intent of recreating and safeguarding this common key and making it resistant to decryption attacks, sometimes changing it daily via a predetermined formula or mechanical aid.

The most famous example of creating and managing the common key in a very complex manner is the Enigma machine used by the Germans in World War II. Enigma used an elaborate system of changing codes and rotary dial settings to generate the same key for both the sender and the receiver of a message, based on the time the message was sent.[47]

The need for these types of elaborate strategies in the context of protecting confidential communications largely disappeared with the invention of *public-private key encryption* (or public key cryptography) in the 1970s.[48]

Public-private key encryption does not require that the sender and the receiver both keep a single (encryption and decryption) key secret.

46. There are many different methodologies for this, starting with simple frequency and message structure analysis. For example, in the example given, the presence of a two-character word is an opportunity to explore the limited set of two-character words which might work, to give some insight into what the replacement key values might be.
47. An online version is available at: https://cryptii.com/pipes/enigma-machine (accessed 15 Dec. 2019).
48. That is not to say that symmetric key encryption disappeared. It too has evolved and continues to be used in many different forms today, for other situations where encryption is required.

Instead, every participant in a secret communication channel now has two keys: a *private* key which that person keeps secret and a *public* key (Figure 1.14) which is published to the world. The beauty of this approach is that no elaborate mechanism needs to be designed to share a common key. Implementation is thus much easier.

The manner in which these keys are used to encrypt messages involve the use of 'one-way functions' which make it easy to generate an encrypted output, but impossible[49] to reverse engineer the input from that output, if only the public key is known.[50] If one knows the private key, however, decrypting the message is trivial.

Figure 1.14 Basic Public Key Encryption

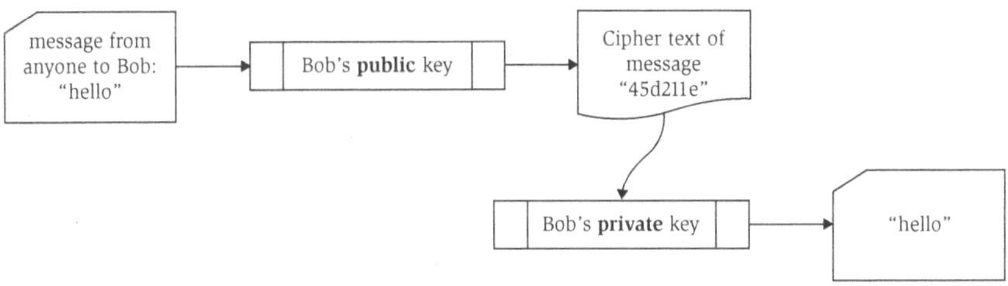

Likewise, a message signed with a sender's private key can be authenticated by decrypting it with the public key. The ability to so decrypt it confirms that the message was in fact sent by the sender, assuming the sender has been able to keep the private key completely secret.

This type of a public-private key encryption application is usually referred to as a 'digital signature' process and is used in a number of authentication processes online (Figure 1.15).

49. This impossibility relies in many cases on the fact that factoring sufficiently large integers is not possible with our current or foreseeable computational capabilities. Determining whether two factors combine to produce a large integer (the one-way aspect of factorization), however, is a trivial exercise.

50. The 'one-way' function used in most encryption methodologies exploits the fact that it is quite easy to multiply very large prime numbers together but very difficult (i.e., computationally infeasible) to find the originating prime factors from the resulting product.

Figure 1.15 Digital Signatures: Using Public Key Encryption to Authenticate a Message

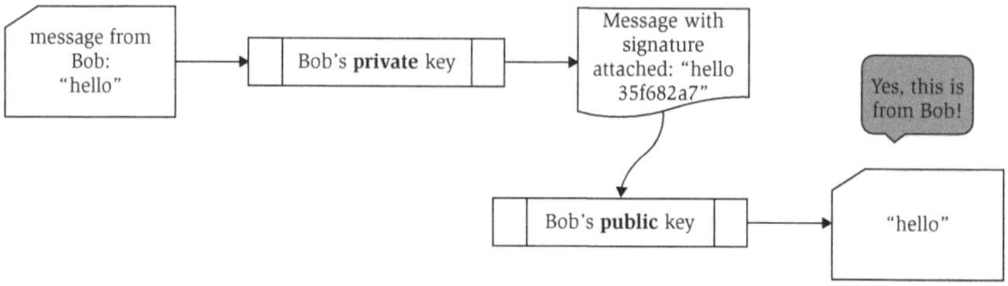

Public-private key encryption is used in the Bitcoin blockchain to validate the authenticity of transactions submitted to the blockchain.[51]

Anyone wishing to participate on the Bitcoin network must create a private key (which is just a random number between 0 and 2^{256}) and then derive a public key from that number using the (one-way) ECC (elliptic curve multiplication) function, which can be easily done with most programming languages.[52]

Once a public key has been created, it can be given to someone who wants to send Bitcoin to that person, for inclusion in the intended transaction.[53]

Typing in private and public keys can be difficult and is prone to errors. For this reason, some public-private key encryption systems will include a *checksum* in their addresses, which can then be used to validate that a particular key is properly constituted. For example, Bitcoin addresses include a 4-bit checksum which can be used to programmatically confirm that a specific address does not have a typo.[54]

The Ethereum blockchain addresses do not contain a checksum, which has resulted in many a misconfigured, but confirmed, transaction resulting in inaccessible and thus lost cryptocurrency.

§1.04 DATABASE CONCEPTS

A database is a large set of data digitally organized in a manner consistent with a database standard. A database standard is a specific design approach to make the storage and retrieval of usually large volumes of data and information convenient and efficient. Numerous different database standards and design approaches have been created to meet the specific data analysis needs of data owners.

51. Some participants in the blockchain space will suggest that the blockchain itself is encrypted. In the case of Bitcoin this is not the case.
52. Or online at a site like https://www.bitaddress.org (accessed 15 Dec. 2019).
53. *See* below for what all goes into a Bitcoin transaction. Also note that in some cases, a *hash* of the public key may be included instead.
54. A similar approach is used to provide a rudimentary check on the constitution of such things as credit card and social security or social insurance numbers.

A database standard will embody the concepts and techniques for the management of the data in the database, as well as the *data model* used, that is, how the various types of data within the database relate to each other.

A popular database data model is the *Relational Model* which seeks to articulate data as tables with relationships inside and among them.[55] For example, in the case of a school, one might store information about a student in a student table, with the various attributes, or properties, of that student, stored as elements of that table (Figure 1.16).

Figure 1.16 An Example of Student Database Table

Student ID	Name	Date of Birth
1434	John Smith	2 August 1998
1675	Peter Jones	5 July 2001
3221	Mary Hynes	6 April 1999

One could then also store courses taught in a separate table (Figure 1.17).

Figure 1.17 An Example of Course Database Table

Course ID	Course Name	Semester Offered	Instructor
225	Math 1103	Fall 2018	K. Friedman
674	Physics 2106	Fall 2018	J. Fung
609	Computer Science 4407	Winter 2019	P. Kirby

And list grades for courses taken by students in yet another table, simply referencing the IDs from the other two tables (Figure 1.18).[56]

Figure 1.18 An Example of Grades Database Junction Table

Student ID	Course ID	Grade
1434	225	65
1675	225	77
1675	674	76
3221	609	88
3221	225	90

A Relational Model is often used where the data being stored is structured, i.e., it is known in advance what the various bits of data (attributes or properties) are. An example of a Relational Model based database standard is the *Structured Query Language* or SQL.[57]

55. Traditionally these relationships are of three kinds: one to one, one to many, or many to many.
56. This type of table is usually referred to as a *junction table*.
57. https://en.wikipedia.org/wiki/SQL (accessed 15 Dec. 2019).

Another popular data model is the *Extensible Markup Language* or XML, which is used extensively to represent semi-structured data (i.e., data entities which may have attributes or properties that are different or perhaps not fully known at the time of the database design).

An example of data suitable for modelling with XML is a text message (Figure 1.19). It is likely that one might want to add additional attributes or properties to a text message in the future (such as audio or video files perhaps).

Figure 1.19 An Example of XML Representation of a Text Message

```
< text message >
        < to > Peter < /to >
        < from > Jake < /from >
        < heading > Hi! < /heading >
        < body > How are you? < /body >
        < emoji > smiley < /emoji >
< /text message >
```

[A] Database Operations

All commercial databases enable the manipulation of data with four key operations (usually referred to as CRUD):

(i) CREATE a new record (based on the implementation of a data model).
(ii) READ a stored record.
(iii) UPDATE a stored record (i.e., change a value associated with a particular entity or attribute of an entity).
(iv) DELETE a stored record.

Many software programs store the data they use in a database in order to exploit the far superior abilities of a database to index and search data, particularly where larger volumes are concerned. To facilitate this, many databases provide interface functionality through which programs can connect to them. Many online databases also provide such interfaces, usually referred to as *web services*, to enable the making of search requests and the obtaining of the results over the internet.

[B] A Transaction Log Distinguished from a Database

It is worthwhile pointing out the difference between a transaction log and a database.

A transaction log, of which the blockchain is an example, is a chronological record to which new records are added by appending them to the end of the log.

An 'append-only' transaction log does not meet the definition of a traditional database because it is not possible to perform all four of the CRUD operations. It is only able to perform two operations: CREATE (and then only by adding data to the end of the file) and READ.

The absence of the capacity to UPDATE and DELETE has several impacts on the ability to efficiently deal with information kept solely in a transactional log. These include:

- The transaction log continuously gets larger. It is not possible to 'clean up' the data by eliminating updated entries.
- The efficiency of finding information stored becomes more difficult as the log grows larger. This requires the use of separate databases (which do have CRUD functionality) to quickly finding the right data, such as that required to determine a particular address's entitlement reflected in a blockchain.

[C] Database Transactions: The ACID Properties

A database is changed through one or more of the CRUD transactions. To maintain database integrity, these transactions must comply with what are commonly referred to as the *ACID principles* or properties:

- *A – Atomicity*. The entire database transaction either takes place or does not take place at all.[58] Partial completion of a transaction, such as only the debit of one account without a credit to another is not permitted.
- *C – Consistency*. The database must be consistent both before and after the transaction. In other words, the data contained in the database is persistently correct. For example, a transaction which transfers a balance from one account to another, once completed, maintains the correct total balance of funds in both accounts.
- *I – Isolation*. Transactions do not interfere with each other and are completed independently. Intermediate states are not visible to the rest of the database. For example, in the case of a transfer between two accounts, the database only sees the before and after states of the transaction.
- *D – Durability*. Changes to the database because of a successful transaction persist in the event of a system or power failure. This usually requires that they have been successfully written to a non-volatile storage state.

There is an active academic discussion on the extent to which these principles are achievable in and/or applicable to a blockchain.[59]

58. This principle is sometimes also referred to as the 'all or nothing' rule.
59. *See*, for instance, Tai, S., Eberhardt, J. and Klems, M., *Not ACID, Not BASE, but SALT*, Proceedings of the 7th International Conference on Cloud Computing and Services Science. SCITEPRESS-Science and Technology Publications, Lda, 2017, available at: http://www.ise.tu-berlin.de/fileadmin/fg308/publications/2017/2017-tai-eberhardt-klems-SALT.pdf (accessed 15 Dec. 2019).

§1.05 NETWORKING FUNDAMENTALS

The ability of two computers to connect and exchange data is the backbone of the internet. It is helpful to have a basic understanding of how this works, on our path towards understanding the blockchain.

Computers communicate by sending long strings of zeroes and ones to each other over high-speed wires connecting them together. To enable these zeroes and ones to take on meaning, certain standards – known as *protocols* – have been developed which allow a sending computer to put together a string of zeroes and ones on one end, which are interpretable and make sense to the computer on the other end.

A well-known protocol for sending data over the internet in this way is the Internet Protocol (or IP).[60] The IP protocol transmits data between computers in packets, which are just long strings of zeroes and ones with a predefined structure.

The IP protocol also includes standards for identifying every computer uniquely on the network, with what is known as an *IP address*. The IP address is used much in the same way as an address for a residence – to send something to the right destination.[61]

IP addresses are denoted as sets of numbers separated by dots, such as 144.101.65.131[62] or FE80:0000:0000:0000:0202:B3FF:FE1E:8329.[63]

Under the IP protocol, a sending computer will put together a long string of zeroes and ones in a manner consistent with the standard template set out in the IP protocol specification.

A receiving computer will look for a specific pattern of zeroes and ones to denote the start of a packet and then start parsing out the various components of the packet after that based on the rules of the applicable protocol specification.

The two main components of an IP packet are the *header* and the *payload*. The header contains various administrative type information such as the version of the protocol used, the IP address of the sending computer, the length of the packet etc. The payload is usually raw data to be used by another application program on the destination computer.

The way in which data is packed for transmission over the internet is not dissimilar to how it is stored in blocks in a blockchain.

[A] P2P Networks

A P2P network is a network of computers which can share resources, like the storage of files, processing capacity or bandwidth. These resources are available to each of the peers (members) of the network via a protocol specific to the P2P network.

60. Successful data transmission over the internet requires the use of another protocol as well, the Transmission Control Protocol or TCP, but for the purpose of explaining network communications, it is not necessary to delve too far.
61. At the local network level an IP address is tied to the physical hardware identifier of a computer known as a MAC, or Media Access Control, address.
62. This format is known as IP4.
63. This format is known as IP6. Note the use of hexadecimal again!.

Unlike a traditional client-server model of networking, a P2P network does not have a centralized host or authority which controls the network's activity – every peer thus acts as both a server and a client.

Any necessary controls to enable the network to function without a centralized server-type authority are embedded in the P2P software being run on each of peers (or nodes) on the network.

One of the earliest P2P networks was Napster – created in 1999 – which was used to (illegally) share music files over the internet.[64]

P2P networks are prevalent today and are used in a wide array of applications,[65] including blockchain.

A P2P network is a form of *distributed* computing, which effectively is a group of computers connected together to achieve a common goal.

A common problem in many distributed computing applications is ensuring that they have a common set of identical data elements, for example, a ledger or a price list, to reference. This challenge of ensuring data consistency in a distributed system containing data which is regularly changed or updated is known as the *consensus* problem.

In the case of a ledger of entitlements or obligations, keeping a copy of the same ledger up to date on many computers connected over the internet creates a significant consensus challenge. How does one keep them all consistent?

The Bitcoin blockchain has an ingenious[66] way of achieving this.

§1.06 CORE BLOCKCHAIN FUNCTIONALITY

With a good grasp of some of the key underlying concepts and ideas, it is now possible to move on to exploring the actual functionality of a blockchain.

First, it is important to appreciate that a blockchain is nothing more than a large file comprised of blocks of transactions, arranged in a chronological order. It is, at its root, and as noted previously, nothing more than *a sequential 'append-only' transaction log* with some 'special' features.

These blocks of transactions are linked together using a few tricks based on the core concepts outlined above to prevent them from being altered or tampered with. Let's dig a bit deeper into how this works by examining the Bitcoin block chain as an example.

In order to help understand the Bitcoin blockchain, think of the blockchain file as a long train – locomotive and wagons – with the wagons individually sealed and also

64. Napster still exists, although it has now transformed into a legitimate music streaming service, available at: https://napster.com (accessed 15 Dec. 2019).
65. For example, BitTorrent, a very popular file sharing application, is used for much of the illegal file sharing of media around the world. An example for a more legitimate use, Microsoft uses peer-to-peer functionality to distribute software updates to the vast number of computers running the Windows 10 operating system.
66. This is not to suggest that the Bitcoin blockchain approach to reaching consensus is perfect. It is not. As we will see, it has a high cost and has significant scaling issues.

connected together in a particular way so that the wagons cannot be separated, or the contents in the individual wagons changed (Figure 1.20).

Figure 1.20 The Blockchain Train

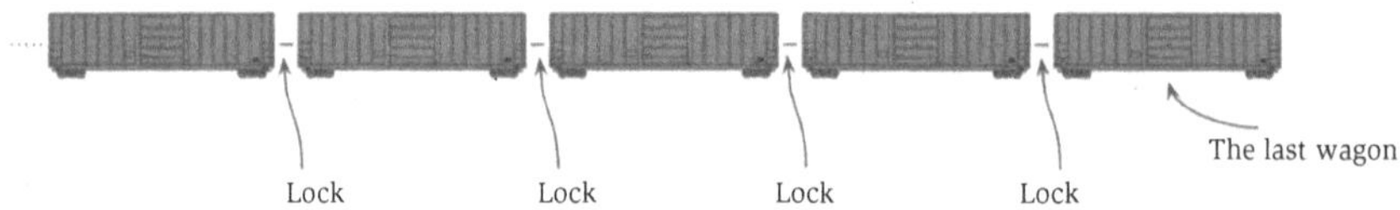

In this train analogy, the locomotive wagon contains the first transactions in the blockchain (sometimes referred to as the *genesis* block), and the wagons that follow contain bundles of transactions which have each been subsequently added in a chronological order. The last wagon of the train contains the most recently added set of transactions.

Every wagon in the train is like a *block* in the blockchain, where each block contains a series of transactions which have been added.

In the case of the Bitcoin blockchain, this block is around 1 MB in size, which represents around 2,000–2,500 transactions per block, on average.[67]

[A] Tying Blocks Together to Prevent Tampering

As explained above, a cryptographic hash function can be used to confirm that an input data set has not been altered. If a reapplication of the cryptographic hash function to a (copy of the) data set generates the same hash digest, then it is certain that the data set has not been altered and/or that the copy of the data is the same as the original.

This neat little trick can be used to extend this functionality over a *series* of data sets by including the hash of one block *into the content* of the next block.

Applying that idea to the train example, the following process is followed for each block, or wagon, of the train, starting with the first block (the locomotive) (Figure 1.21):

- The data (sets of new transaction information) to be added is placed in a block, to which the cryptographic hash function is applied, generating a unique hash digest for that block.
- This unique hash digest is next placed *inside* the data set for the following block (together with whatever transactions will be part of the following block), and this data set (i.e., the hash digest from the previous block together with the transaction data) is subjected to the same cryptographic hash function again, generating another unique hash digest for this second block.
- This second unique hash digest is, in turn, placed inside the data to be hashed for the third block, and so on.

67. At the time of the writing of this chapter. This amount does fluctuate. *See* https://www.blockchain.com/en/charts/n-transactions-per-block?timespan = all (accessed 15 Dec. 2019).

Figure 1.21 Forward-Embedding Hash Digests

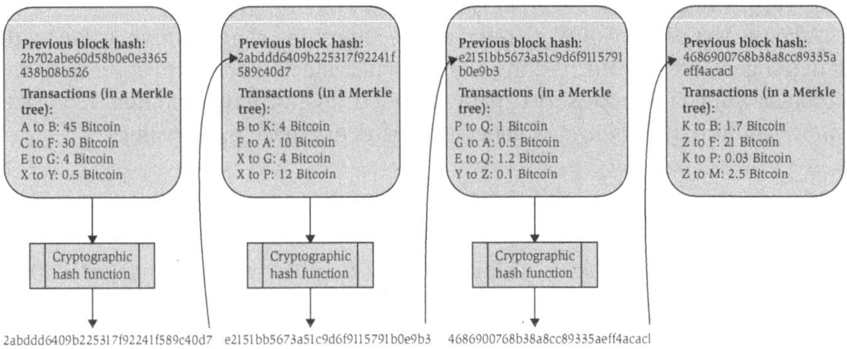

With this approach of embedding the hash digest from one block *inside the data* to be hashed for the next block, a couple of important outcomes are achieved:

(i) The integrity of *all the data* contained in all the sequential blocks is now tied together in an immutable chain of forward-embedded hash digests. In other words, any alteration of any data in a block will immediately change the hash digest for that block, which will then no longer match the embedded hash digest at the beginning of the next block, signalling a loss of integrity of the data.

(ii) It is easy to verify the integrity of the data in any block (wagon) at any time, by recalculating the hash digest of every block in the chain and comparing it with the hash digest embedded in the data for the next block.[68] If anywhere along the line a mismatch is encountered, then the data in that block (wagon) has been altered. To identify which specific transaction was altered, one simply examines the Merkle tree hash consistency within the block data itself.

[B] Adding a Time Cost

The above approach of tying together blocks with forwardembedded hash digests has a weakness. If one can control the storage of the whole blockchain, it is possible to make an alteration and then simply recalculate all the hashes for all the blocks. Such a successful alteration and recalculation would still present in a manner consistent with the above tamper-proof strategy.

68. Note that changing the hash digest in the second block to match the hash digest generated from the altered first block, so as to hide the alteration, will not work, as this change of the second block will change the forward-embedded hash digest in the third block, and so on.

To eliminate this weakness, Satoshi Nakamoto ingeniously added a *time cost* to the process of adding a block to the blockchain, in order to make any such recalculation process very difficult. This invention is known as *Proof of Work*.[69]

A key aspect of Proof of Work relies on the imposition of a *maximum value* for the hash digest generated by the hashing of a particular block. In order to appreciate how that process works, it is necessary to gain an understanding of two additional concepts: the *nonce* and the *probabilities* of generating particular hash digest values.

[1] The Nonce

A *nonce* is a *number used once*. Think of it as a number which is changed without repeating a value, for example, by incrementing it like a counter.

[2] The Probabilities of Generating a Particular Hash Value

[a] Randomness

The first idea to understand is that of *randomness*, which is the quality of an event lacking any sort of pattern of occurring. Rolling a dice[70] is a random event because any of the 6 outcomes is equally likely to occur.

Rolling a weighted dice is not a random event. One of the potential outcomes is more likely to occur than the other five.

An event which has the property of randomness is called a *random variable*.

[b] Sample Space

A *sample space* is the range of all possible values for a random variable. It can be thought of as a complete list of all the possible ways that the random variable event could happen. For example, if a particular random variable generates a number between 0 and 101, then the sample space is all the numbers from 1 to 100.

The sample space also has a size. Mathematicians call it a *cardinality*, which in the case of the above example of 100 possible outcomes is 100.

Knowledge of the sample space cardinality allows the determination of certain probabilities about that random variable. The roll of dice is a good example to illustrate this point.

A dice has six sides, and there are therefore six ways that the event of the roll of a dice can happen (its sample size is six). The chance, or probability, of getting any one of those sides is the prevalence of that event within the size of the sample space. In the case of the dice, that is one divided by six – one-sixth – or 0.166666666666.

69. Sometimes also referred to as Nakamoto Consensus.

70. Some might argue one should use 'die' as a singular, but some Googling suggests it is now acceptable to use 'dice' as the singular instance as well.

Likewise, pulling a *specific* card from a well-shuffled deck of cards (which has a sample space of 52) is 1/52 or 0.01923076923.

[3] Not Replacing Generated Events

Something interesting happens to the probability of an event if an event is removed from the sample space after it has been generated. In the case of a shuffled deck of cards from which one seeks to select a specific predetermined card, this is achieved by not replacing a card drawn from a deck after drawing it.

Note how the probability of drawing the desired card changes as the sample space gets smaller (Figure 1.22).

Figure 1.22 Change in Probability in a Shrinking Sample Space

# of cards drawn	Remaining sample space	Probability of drawing the desired card
1	51	1/51 = 0.0196
10	42	1/42 = 0.0238
20	32	1/32 = 0.0312
30	22	1/22 = 0.0454
45	7	1/7 = 0.1428
50	2	½ = 0.5000

The critical nuance to appreciate is what happens to the probability of the desired event if generated (or drawn) events are not replaced *and* the desired event is not a specific item in the sample space (such as a card) but is satisfied if one selects (or draws) an event *within a particular range* within the sample space (such as, for instance, if the desired event is a black card below 5).

Let's explore that question with the example of generating a random number less than or equal to 10 in a sample space of all numbers from 1 to 1,000. It should be obvious that the first attempt at generating a number less than or equal to 10 from a sample space of the first 1,000 numbers is 10/1000 or 0.01.

Note what happens to this probability as more numbers are drawn from the sample space without finding one less than or equal to 10 (Figure 1.23).

Figure 1.23 Probability of Generating a Number in a Subset

Numbers drawn	Remaining sample space	Probability of generating a number less than or equal to 10
1	999	10/999 = .01001
10	990	10/990 = 0.0101
100	900	10/900 = 0.0111
300	700	10/700 = 0.0142
500	500	10/500 = 0.0200

As more events are drawn from the sample space, the probability of getting a number less than or equal to 10 steadily increases. There comes a point, usually after a significant number of selections from the sample space, where the probability of finding a number within the desired range becomes close to certain.

[4] A Cryptographic Hash Function Behaves Like a Random Variable

Recall from the discussion of the SHA256 hash function that it generates a 64-bit hash digest (which is really just a large number in hex format).

It turns out that the hash digest generated by a particular input file behaves very much like a random variable. In other words, the likelihood of generating a particular hash digest number[71] within the SHA256 sample space is for all intents and purposes *equal* for all numbers within that space.

The input to the hashing function can be changed by adding a nonce to the input data and changing it (for instance, by incrementing it) after each hash. This will generate a new unique - and random - hash digest each time (Figure 1.24).

Figure 1.24 Different Nonces Generate Different Hash Digests

Data	Nonce	SHA256 hash digest
This is some text we are hashing		a2d973f3bf58343a27a3d3f95704b9567d7e534af876c575db5d450ea5e277d3
This is some text we are hashing	1	30c6f072dd5dc63871ee254f994a3ed52f2c1e4a2545910aa288ccca03831b2d
This is some text we are hashing	2	dc275df4716b2c207cb06cb4a2e7809bfdfc6c9ad4cedf45f3482327b3e40f3e
This is some text we are hashing	3	c3da9d7ceab0d66a20b1e290db1af09115f63e7370a1924e8e9d63837506b38a
This is some text we are hashing	4	7425946654639d5c6719620e64e46ba0221875ddfb198878627b1de9bdb25bd8
This is some text we are hashing	5	c3e6f7c957240b39750653863a53b38908b0f730fd4184671f0d858b0914c53f
This is some text we are hashing	6	427e922f9af5b0586268e867323ac6d71e087881b53e2c2b9b957a7197a8a76c

The sample space for the SHA256 hash digest is *very* large: it comprises all numbers between 0 and 2^{256}, a number with 77 digits.[72]

The current hash rate of the Bitcoin network is around 100 million trillion[73] hashes per second. Even if that network was committed solely to generating all possible hashes for SHA256, it would still take *trillions* of years to do so. The likelihood of generating a *specific number* as a hash digest for a particular input file with a changing nonce is very unlikely.

Recall that with a random variable, as the sample space gets smaller, the probability of generating a specific event increases consistently. It goes without saying that at some point - as the sample space gets smaller - the desired event will be generated (assuming it is possible to generate all possible events within a reasonable amount of time).

As noted, with SHA256 this is not feasible if one is looking for a single number. However, if instead, the task is to find a hash digest *below a certain value*, in other

71. Recall that a hash digest is just a long number.
72. 2^{256} is 115,792,089,237,316,195,423,570,985,008,687,907,853,269,984,665,640,564,039, 457,584,007,913,129,639,936.
73. 100,000,000 x 10^{12} or 100,000,000,000,000,000,000.

words within a small subset of the sample space, then the time required to find a valid hash digest decreases to reasonable levels.

It is this correlation between computational capacity and the size of the subset of the sample space which Proof of Work exploits to impose a cost on the hashing process for each block.

The core idea is to force the commitment of significant computational resources to the finding of a particular nonce, which is predictable to take a certain amount of time, so as to impose a significant *time cost* on adding a new wagon to the train, or block to the blockchain.

[5] Requiring a Hash Value Below a Certain Value

It turns out that it is possible to estimate – with a great deal of certainty – how long a computational resource (in terms of trillions of hashes per second in the case of the Bitcoin network) will take to find a hash value below a certain threshold value using the above 'change the nonce' process repeatedly.

It is also then quite easy to adjust that threshold to keep that time requirement reasonably constant should the computational capacity to hash (the hash rate) change.[74]

Satoshi Nakamoto decided that this time constant should be around 10 minutes and developed a formula for calculating the threshold (the *target hash*) every 2016 blocks (or every two weeks) based on the hash rate of the Bitcoin network.

Bitcoin hashing difficulty is expressed as a number. Its value on 3 October 2019 was 12,759,819,404,409.[75] This number represents how many times more difficult it is to find a number below the threshold than to generate any hash value in SHA256's sample space.

As of October 2019, the target hash for Bitcoin required a successful hash digest to have at least 18 leading zeroes, like this one for block 597707:

0000000000000000000110bbc354868a8849aa01ff271877500e0e2aa869c69f

[C] The Proof of Work Process

Taking advantage of the predictable time within which one is highly certain to find a hash digest below the target hash, it is now possible to proceed as follows:

(1) Set the target hash consistent with ten minutes of computation to find a valid hash digest below the target hash.

74. Given that these two variables are correlated.
75. The current difficulty level is available at: https://www.coinwarz.com/difficulty-charts/bitcoin-difficulty-chart (accessed 15 Dec. 2019).

(2) Take a data set (in our case a series of transactions and the hash digest from the previous block) and combine it with a nonce value.
(3) Submit this to the SHA256 algorithm and examine the hash digest:
  (a) If the hash digest is above the target hash, change the nonce and repeat step 2 (remember that after about ten minutes of this, one is highly likely to have found a winning hash).
  (b) If the hash digest is below the target hash, then eureka! – the Proof of Work is considered complete (what happens after that will be discussed further below).

Note what this process does for the immutability of the blockchain.

First, the ability to verify the various hashes of the data to confirm the integrity of the blockchain is not affected. Recalculating a few hashes and comparing them is a trivial exercise, and it is easy to recalculate all hashes in all blocks in the blockchain within a reasonable amount of time.

Second, falsifying and recalculating the whole blockchain has now become much more difficult. If one wanted to change a transaction in a block, a recalculation will now take ten minutes per block. The further back a block is in the blockchain, the more time it will take to recalculate it and thus the more secure it becomes. Note that if one wanted to change the blockchain from a very early block in the blockchain onwards, it would take about as much time as the age of that block.[76]

It should now be clear how a blockchain creates and maintains immutability of the blocks of transactions it contains. The next step towards a complete understanding of the blockchain is an appreciation of how it maintains internal consistency of the transactional data itself. This is of course critically important if a blockchain is used for tracking such things as cryptocurrency balances for their owners.

§1.07 TRANSACTIONS ON THE BITCOIN BLOCKCHAIN

Ownership of a bitcoin on the Bitcoin blockchain is stored as a confirmed entitlement entry somewhere in the blockchain. This entitlement entry is called a *transaction*, and it has several components:

- A link to a previous transaction or transactions in the blockchain which hold certain entitlement amounts which are the source for the entitlement created in the particular transaction at hand. These are referred to as the *inputs* to the new transaction (and as *outputs* from the old transaction).

76. Admittedly recalculating the earlier blocks would take less time today than it took when these were initially created, as the target hash was much larger then, given the much lower hashing rate of the network.

- An encryption mechanism to validate that the person entitled to the output(s) has authorized the transaction.[77] This mechanism is referred to as the Script-PubKey or the *locking script*. Think of the transaction having been digitally signed by the person sending the Bitcoin to someone else.
- The value that the transaction holds, to be spent/claimed by the new holder in a future transaction. As noted, this value is referred to as the *output* of the transaction.
- A unique identifier called a TXID (Transaction ID), which is created by hashing the transaction data (above) twice with the SHA256 cryptographic hash function.[78] It is this TXID by which a subsequent transaction will identify this transaction as an input.

Note that the blockchain transaction does not store any information about the person who holds the entitlement. Also, the transaction data in the Bitcoin blockchain is not encrypted and is easily viewable by anyone.[79]

[A] Bitcoin Scripting

It is possible to impose some limited decision-making logic upon transactions on the Bitcoin blockchain, for instance, to require the authorization of a transaction by a third party. These are referred to as 'scripted transactions'. Such a control which assigns spending authority to multiple persons is referred to as a *multi-signature* transaction.[80]

[B] Entitlement Tracking

All bitcoin entitlement arises because of one or more transactions which have been previously committed to the blockchain. Entitlement entries can thus be traced back – through time – to some point when new entitlement was created for the first time (on the Bitcoin blockchain new entitlement is created as a result of the *mining reward*, discussed *infra*).

In order to make this sequential entitlement tracking process work properly, it is necessary to explicitly track any residual entitlement if an amount *less than the output* entitlement from a specific transaction existing in the blockchain is being transmitted to another person. To illustrate this nuance, assume Jim has an output transaction on the blockchain with a value of 0.5 BTC, and he wishes to transmit 0.1 BTC of that to

77. These are configurable in any of a number of different ways, incorporating quite complex logic if desired.
78. Recall that this will generate a unique ID given the highly reliable collision resistance of SHA256. A quirky bug of the Bitcoin blockchain places this ID on the blockchain in reverse order, which necessitates that one search for the reverse of the TXID to find it. Most transaction search tools make this requirement opaque to the user.
79. The suggestion by some that the Bitcoin blockchain is encrypted is thus incorrect, and it is usually a clear indication that the person suggesting the same does not have a full understanding of how the Bitcoin blockchain works.
80. This functionality becomes very useful in the use of sidechains, as will be discussed in section §1.18[B], *infra*.

Larry. To properly record this activity, *two* output transactions need to be created: one to transmit 0.1 BTC to Larry and another to transmit 0.4 BTC *back* to Jim (this can be thought of as the 'change' one might receive in a store when paying for a small item with a bill larger than the cost).[81]

Once a transaction's outputs have been claimed as inputs for future transactions, that transaction is deemed to have been 'spent', to guard against double spending.

Any transaction which has an unclaimed output is known as an *Unspent Transaction Output* or UTXO.

[C] The UTXO Database

The UTXO database is maintained alongside the Bitcoin blockchain to keep track of all currently available unspent outputs on the Bitcoin blockchain. This separate database is necessary to maintain an appropriate level of efficiency in processing transactions. Having to retrieve outputs from the blockchain every time one wants to verify an output entitlement would require a full read-through of the ever growing blockchain file (currently well in excess of 200 GB) which is prohibitively difficult and time consuming to do.[82]

Given a basic understanding of how the Bitcoin blockchain protects against tampering as well as how it ensures internal integrity of the various balances recorded, the next step is to explore how this all works in a distributed P2P network. This not only provides additional benefits but also raises some new issues which require some more trickery to resolve.

§1.08 THE DISTRIBUTED BLOCKCHAIN

[A] The Bitcoin Network

The Bitcoin network is made up of thousands of computers connected together over the internet. As in many other P2P networks, each of these computers is referred to as a *node*.[83]

Every node runs a copy of the Bitcoin blockchain software[84] which allows it to do a couple of things (among other administrative stuff) in relation to the Bitcoin blockchain:

---

81. On the Bitcoin network if this second transaction is not created, any change is claimed as a transaction fee, and thus effectively lost to its holder.
82. The UTXO database stores this data and indexes it for easy access in a file of about 3 to 4 GB.
83. On the Bitcoin network, there are different kinds of nodes which perform different aspects of the workflow of the network. A node which can do all the different processes is referred to as a full node. To keep things simple, a reference to a node here means a full node.
84. Which is available as open source, *see* https://bitcoin.org/en/download (accessed 15 Dec. 2019).

    The open source availability of the Bitcoin code has given rise to many 'copycat' cryptocurrencies which function largely the same way as Bitcoin with minor adjustments to certain parameters. The best example of this is likely Litecoin, *see* https://litecoin.org/ (accessed 15 Dec. 2019).

- Maintain a copy of the Bitcoin blockchain file[85] and verify and add new blocks to that copy.
- Maintain a copy of the UTXO database to verify that transactions have the required inputs to be added to the blockchain.
- Grab transactions from the *memory pool* (explained below) to create a candidate block.
- Repeatedly hash a candidate block (with an included nonce) to try and find a hash digest below the target hash.

The general 'workflow' within the Bitcoin network is as follows:

(1) A person holding some amount of Bitcoin submits a transaction to (a node of) the Bitcoin network for confirmation to the blockchain.
(2) The transaction is verified as valid (i.e., the outputs have valid inputs, and it complies with the various formatting requirements and a bunch of other constraints).
(3) The transaction is added to a 'transaction holding area' called the *memory pool.*
(4) The various computers (nodes) in the Bitcoin P2P network each select a group of (different) transactions from the memory pool to fill a new block, called a *candidate block*, which that node is going to try to add to the blockchain.
(5) Nodes then compete to be the first to find a hash digest below the target hash for their candidate block.[86] This hash digest finding exercise is commonly referred to as *mining.*
(6) The first node to find a valid hash digest broadcasts that fact, as well as a copy of the candidate block used to find it (including the nonce), to all other nodes on the network.
(7) The other nodes very quickly verify[87] that the block transactions and the hash digest are valid, and if so, add this block to their copy of the blockchain.
(8) Once 51 % of all active nodes on the network have confirmed the validity of the block in this manner, the block is considered to be officially confirmed on the blockchain, and the official ledger embodied in the blockchain is expanded to now include the transactions in this latest block.[88] This critical step, together with the initial transaction validation (which prevents selecting an input which has already been spent), avoids running into the *double spending problem* (covered in more detail *infra*). Sometimes a

85. Which as of the writing of this chapter was approaching 250 GB in size. It grows by approximately 150 MB per day or around 1 GB each week.
86. To be clear, every node's candidate block contains a unique set of different transactions obtained from that node's memory pool.
87. Remember, it only takes one execution of the hash algorithm to confirm.
88. This is a bit of an oversimplification of this process. *See* the heading called 'Adding a Mined Block' for more detail.

winning hash is found by two nodes at almost the same time, which leads to groups of nodes accepting different new blocks into their version of the blockchain (there are rules for resolving this, discussed *infra*).

(9) The winning node gets a reward for finding the winning hash value. This value was 'pre-recorded' at the beginning of the winning block (at the time of its composition before the mining process was started) in what is known as the *coinbase transaction*.[89]

(10) As soon as a node accepts a new block on its blockchain, it will discard any block it was working on and select a new set of transactions from the memory pool and start the process at step 3 above anew. (This can lead to some issues if a node quickly finds a subsequent valid block connected to a prior valid block which it has added to its blockchain, but which has not (yet) been accepted by 51 % of the network, and may by then conflict with another blockchain version on the network. How this is resolved is discussed in the Adding a Mined Block section *infra*.)

(11) When all nodes on the network have converged to a common longest blockchain, there is then consensus about the confirmation of the included transactions.

A closer examination of some of these components is helpful.

[B] The Memory Pool

The memory pool is a database which contains transactions received by a node from Bitcoin holders who are looking to have these transactions confirmed on the blockchain. The memory pool is like a 'waiting room' for transactions.

There are rules about which transactions should be selected first. Transactions which refer to older outputs on the blockchain or which transfer larger amounts are prioritized.

This waiting room also has a priority queue, in that bitcoin holders who want to have their transactions chosen for inclusion in a candidate block can incentivize the node to pick their transaction by including a transaction fee (more on that below).

[C] Adding a Mined Block

The primary rule by which the main blockchain is maintained is that it must be the chain of blocks of transactions which has the *highest amount of cumulative difficulty* associated with it. This usually matches the chain with the highest number of blocks, but not always. Things can get a bit challenging if several blocks are successfully mined by different nodes at almost the same time.

89. Or generation transaction. Transaction fees, discussed below, are also tracked here. There is a specific place in the block for this transaction.

In order to handle this effectively, a node may, in addition to a block recently added to its copy of the blockchain, maintain additional blocks which have been successfully mined in that they also validly extend the local copy of the blockchain, but have not (yet) been confirmed by a majority of the nodes. These blocks may have been received from other nodes.

These different paths for growing the blockchain are referred to as *secondary chains*. If a block mined after a block in a secondary chain causes the cumulative difficulty to be the highest, then that will result in a change in the official blockchain – as maintained by that node – within the two latest blocks of the official block chain. The node will then start selecting new candidate blocks to proceed from this new longest blockchain onwards.

It may also happen that mined blocks are received out of order, in that an intermediate block is missing. This is usually the case if the previous block hash digest reference in the received block is non-existent in the blockchain. A node will hold on to these 'orphan' blocks for a few block mining cycles to see if the missing block shows up. If it does, it will assess whether its inclusion changes its 'greatest difficulty' version of the blockchain.

The creation of such alternate potential longest chains within the Bitcoin network is known as 'forking' of the blockchain.[90] In the Bitcoin network, one block length forks occur somewhat regularly, but to date, they have all resolved with the receipt of the following block, which then causes the blockchain to converge to a common stable version.

There is a relationship between the incidence of forks and the length of the confirmation time dictated by the Proof of Work for a particular block chain: the shorter (in terms of time) that the required Proof of Work time cost is, the higher the likelihood of forks occurring. This has been one of the considerations weighing against the desire by some to shorten the Proof of Work time requirement of Bitcoin in order to speed up confirmation of transactions.

[D] The Double Spending Problem

A fundamental challenge in creating a distributed ledger without a centralized authority is solving the double spending problem. It should be evident by now that three core aspects of the distributed Bitcoin blockchain process virtually eliminate[91] any chance of double spending:

- The validation of unspent entitlement (an unspent output on the blockchain) before any transaction is even considered for addition to the ledger.
- The forward-embedded cryptographic hash digest tracking system which ensures that the ledger data is verifiably immutable.

90. There are blockchain forks which are more consequential, as a result of software upgrades to the blockchain software. *See* the discussion under Blockchain Forks, section §1.09, *infra*.
91. But not absolutely. *See* the section on the 51% attack, §1.08[G], *infra*.

- The Proof of Work barrier to prevent someone from going back and redoing number 2.

[E] The Mining Reward

As noted, every successfully mined block accepted by 51 % of the nodes creates a new entitlement to bitcoin, usually claimed by the owner of the successful node.

This reward is recorded in a special section of the winning block called the *generation* or *coinbase transaction*. Because this entitlement is created out of nothing, it does not have a pointer to a previous output transaction on the blockchain.

The generation transaction has some features of note:

- It has a place for the mining node to insert notes. Nodes now use this area to store an additional nonce for the purpose of pursuing a Proof of Work hash digest.[92] This space is also sometimes used to identify that a block was mined by a group of miners. Other miners have used it for all kinds of (sometimes bizarre) messages.[93]
- A block reward cannot be spent for 100 blocks (or around sixteen hours). This is to ensure that a potential blockchain fork does not invalidate the entitlement.

The Bitcoin reward halves every 210,000 blocks, or about every four years. In 2009, when the Bitcoin blockchain was started, this reward was 50 bitcoin. This was halved to 25 bitcoin in November 2012 and halved again to 12.5 bitcoin in July 2016. It will halve once more to 6.75 bitcoin in May 2020.[94]

[F] Mining Pools

As the price of bitcoin started to increase in 2011, more and more individuals and organizations became interested in mining bitcoin for profit. This, in turn, grew the pool of nodes as well as the global hashing power of the Bitcoin network.

This hashing race was fuelled even more in 2013 with the development of hardware specifically designed to perform very high rates of block hashing.[95]

In order to yet further improve their chances of finding the winning hash first, many node operators joined forces by establishing mining pools, through which they coordinated the mining of new blocks at ever increasing hashing speeds. Mining pools

92. This became necessary as a result of the capacity of mining hardware growing to the point that all possible permutations of the nonce memory space were exhausted in less than a second. A second is a barrier as the timestamp (which is also tracked in the block) changes every second.
93. Explore: http://www.bitcoinstrings.com/ (accessed 15 Dec. 2019), to see these messages.
94. This halving will continue until 2140 at which time no more bitcoin will be created, at least according to the current rules.
95. The processors used by these 'mining rigs' are called *Application Specific Integrated Circuits* or ASICs.

distribute mining rewards to their various participants using a methodology usually specified in the mining pool membership agreement.

Many of these mining pools are made up of hundreds of thousands of participants all over the world. Commercial mining pools, or hashing farms, started to enter the network after 2013 as well. By 2013, it had become quite unrealistic for an individual miner to expect to be able to compete against these mining pools and find a winning hash with any probability.

[G] The 51% Attack

Given that it takes a 51% majority of miners to confirm the longest Bitcoin blockchain, this also means – in theory – that this same majority can compromise that blockchain. Such a group could exploit the rule that the longest/most difficult chain is the valid one, by creating intentional forks of longer length than – say – the last 4 or 5 blocks of the blockchain, thereby undoing what would otherwise be an irreversible set of transactions. This longer chain would then be adopted as the correct blockchain by virtue of this foundational Bitcoin blockchain principle.

A theoretical malicious actor, who had access to 51% of the hash capacity of the Bitcoin blockchain, could thus cause his or her previously confirmed payment to another person to be redirected or reversed or introduce double spend transactions into the blockchain going forward.

A 51% attack's likelihood of succeeding diminishes significantly as the transactions being sought to be manipulated are further back in the blockchain.

It is not actually necessary to have 51% of the hashing power to be able to successfully execute this type of attack (although at 51% such an attempt is *guaranteed* to succeed). Some suggest as little as 30% will do the trick.[96]

The chance of a 51% attack succeeding on the Bitcoin blockchain, given the size of the network and volume of miners, is highly unlikely, but cannot be ruled out. The fact that much of the hashing power is now increasingly centralized with a small group of hashing farms/pools does not abate this risk.

In the case of a smaller or differently constructed blockchain, this risk may be much higher, as has been evident from several such attacks on smaller cryptocurrencies in 2018.[97] Most notably, the Ethereum Classic blockchain appears to have been the victim of a 51% type of attack in January 2019.[98]

96. Available at: https://www.oreilly.com/library/view/mastering-bitcoin/9781491902639/ch08.html (accessed 27 Dec. 2019).
97. Saad M., et al., *Exploring the Attack Surface of Blockchain: A Systematic Overview* (arXiv preprint arXiv:1904.03487, 2019), available at: https://arxiv.org/pdf/1904.03487.pdf (accessed 15 Dec. 2019).
98. https://bravenewcoin.com/insights/etc-51-attack-what-happened-and-how-it-was-stopped (accessed 15 Dec. 2019).

Much like any complex computer-based system, a blockchain has a number of other potential vulnerabilities at the various stages of its workflow life cycle, which are beyond the scope of this chapter.[99]

§1.09 BLOCKCHAIN FORKS

The software which runs on the nodes of a blockchain network is updated from time to time to add new features or to make changes in how the blockchain functions.

These code changes are considered adopted when a majority of nodes on the network install and start using an updated version of the blockchain software. These code updates or changes to the blockchain code are referred to as *forks* (Figure 1.25).

Figure 1.25 A Blockchain Fork

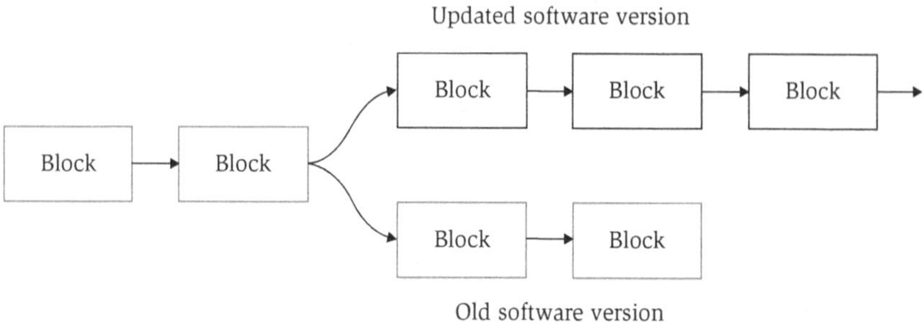

There are two types of forks with different impacts on the blockchain.

[A] The Soft Fork

Updates which are backwards compatible with prior versions of the blockchain software are known as *soft forks*. A node running an old version of the software will still be able to submit transactions and participate in the blockchain but may not benefit from some of the new features offered by the newer blockchain software version. Nodes on a blockchain usually seek to install updated software for that reason.

[B] The Hard Fork

Blockchain software updates which are *not* backwards compatible with older versions of the blockchain software are called *hard forks*.

99. *See* Saad et al., *supra* n. 97, at note 64; Chen, H., et al., *A Survey on Ethereum Systems Security: Vulnerabilities, Attacks and Defenses* (arXiv preprint arXiv:1908.04507, 2019), available at: https://arxiv.org/pdf/1908.04507.pdf (accessed 15 Dec. 2019); Alkhalifah, A., et al., *A Taxonomy of Blockchain Threats and Vulnerabilities*, available at: https://www.preprints.org/manuscript/201909.0117/v1/download (accessed 15 Dec. 2019).

Hard fork changes are usually significant and change fundamental aspects of how a blockchain functions, such as the block size, hashing algorithm used, or how consensus is reached.

In some cases, the blockchain running on the older version of the software, or rather, the persons behind the nodes who may disagree with the rationale for the hard fork or the effects of it, may break off and continue as a separate blockchain. This event is referred to as a *contentious hard fork*. The 2016 DAO hack[100] of the Ethereum network resulted in a contentious hard fork after a large number of node owners disagreed with a rollback of the blockchain in order to reclaim a large amount of ether[101] lost due to the hack. As a result, Ethereum split into two blockchains: Ethereum and Ethereum Classic.

The Bitcoin network has also experienced three hard forks so far, largely as a result of a fundamental agreement over how Bitcoin should function or evolve:

- Bitcoin Cash, which hard forked from Bitcoin at block 478558 on 1 August 2017.
- Bitcoin Gold, which hard forked from Bitcoin at block 491407 on 24 October 2017.
- Bitcoin SV, which hard forked at block 556766 on 15 November 2018.

A quirk of a contentious hard fork is that anyone having an entitlement in the blockchain before the hard fork will end up with entitlement in *both* blockchains after the hard fork.

A hard fork may also be initiated because of the planned evolution of the blockchain network itself. The Ethereum blockchain software has proceeded, and continues to proceed, along a planned path of soft and hard forks which makes incremental planned changes to the fundamental functionality of that blockchain.[102]

§1.10 BLOCKCHAIN AS A PLATFORM

[A] Ethereum

Ethereum is a blockchain-based platform which launched in 2015 following Vitalik Buterin's 2013 publication of a white paper laying out its intended functionality.[103]

Like Bitcoin, Ethereum tracks transactions on a blockchain.

The key evolution of Ethereum was the addition of the ability to store program code on the blockchain and then to be able to run that code within the Ethereum

100. The SEC report on its investigation of the DAO gives a good overview of this event, available at: https://www.sec.gov/litigation/investreport/34-81207.pdf (accessed 15 Dec. 2019).
101. The Ethereum cryptocurrency, *see* section §1.10.
102. https://docs.ethhub.io/ethereum-basics/history-and-forks/ (accessed 15 Dec. 2019).
103. https://www.weusecoins.com/assets/pdf/library/Ethereum_white_paper-a_next_generation_smart_contract_and_decentralized_application_platform-vitalik-buterin.pdf (accessed 15 Dec. 2019).

network to manipulate the state of variables stored on the blockchain. Ethereum thus seeks to implement the blockchain as a distributed computer.

The cryptocurrency used on the Ethereum platform is called *ether*.[104] The Ethereum platform also uses another cryptocurrency called *gas*[105] for the purpose of providing 'fuel' to contract accounts on Ethereum.

In general terms, the Ethereum blockchain works very much like the Bitcoin blockchain, with a few notable differences:

- The Ethereum block confirmation time is around 15 seconds, compared to 10 minutes for Bitcoin.
- Ethereum does not use a UTXO approach to tracking transactions and entitlement, but rather uses something called *state transitions*. More on that below.
- The Ethereum mining reward is relatively constant and does not halve on a schedule like Bitcoin. The block reward is currently around 2 ether per block.
- The Ethereum Proof of Work uses a different hashing function called Ethash. The Ethash function has evolved since 2015 and now incorporates a Proof of Stake scheme every 50 blocks, designed to thwart the effect of ASIC-based mining rigs gaining too strong a foothold in the Ethereum mining ecosystem. The goal of the Ethereum Foundation is to (eventually) eliminate Proof of Work as a consensus mechanism and replace it with Proof of Stake. When this will happen is not clear.
- The Ethereum blockchain has no block size limit. Instead, it has a 'gas' limit.

[1] Gas: Limiting How Long a Program Can Run

A poorly written piece of code running forever on a blockchain-based distributed computer has to be avoided, as it would grind the whole system to a halt.[106] This is a significant problem, as it is not possible to determine generally, based on a program's code and the input to that code, whether a program will execute and stop or whether it may run on forever.[107]

The solution to this problem is to simply automatically terminate any code (or program) which runs out of a predefined resource associated with that particular program. On the Ethereum platform, this solution is implemented by requiring every computational transaction to have a certain amount of computational fuel, or *gas*, associated with it, which terminates execution if it runs out before the program has

104. There is a whole hierarchy of terms for various quantities of ether: https://gwei.io (accessed 15 Dec. 2019).
105. The exchange rate from ether to gas can be viewed at: https://ethgasstation.info (accessed 15 Dec. 2019).
106. This is particularly so in the case of Ethereum, which cannot execute code in parallel but only in series, one program, or smart contract, after another.
107. This is known as the Halting Problem, which was conclusively proven (using a contradiction proof) by Alan Turing in 1936.

finished running.[108] The downside of this approach is that a program which has run out of gas will end execution and will not result in any state change to the blockchain.

Every Ethereum transaction must be accompanied by gas for this purpose. The benefit of the use of gas goes to the mining nodes as payment for their work confirming the transaction.

[2] An Ethereum Transaction

An Ethereum transaction has the following components:

- An *Ethereum address* to which the transaction is being sent.
- A *digital signature* confirming that the transaction validly emanates from a valid Ethereum account.
- A sequence number called a *nonce*, but with a different purpose than the Proof of Work process used by the Bitcoin blockchain. On the Ethereum blockchain, a nonce is a running sequential number reflecting the series of transactions confirmed for the digitally signed destination, i.e., Ethereum address. This number helps ensure that transactions sent are processed (executed) in the order intended by the sender and that every transaction is unique.[109]
- A *gas price*, which is the exchange rate the sender is willing to pay to get gas for the transaction, expressed in an amount of ether per gas unit.
- A *gas limit*, which is the maximum gas the sender is prepared to buy to have the transaction processed. The sender of the transaction must have a credit balance in excess of the amount of ether this represents, in order for the transaction to be processed.
- A *value*, which is the amount of ether being sent.
- *Data*, or the variable references and values to be used by any contract to which the transaction has been sent.

Given the very short block confirmation time of Ethereum, it is almost impossible to cancel an Ethereum transaction once it has been submitted to the memory pool. One strategy which may be successful in a rare case is the very fast resubmission of a transaction with more gas using the same nonce.[110]

Multi-signature transactions are implemented with a smart contract (explained *infra*) which contains code requiring incoming transactions from all authorizing signatories before completing a particular transaction.

108. A program's gas cost depends on how the logic inside it executes. Some code sections or components may be more expensive to run than others.
109. The Ethereum network code checks that any new transaction arriving and about to be processed is the next in line from the Ethereum address referenced in that transaction, by comparing its nonce to the last nonce associated with that address on the blockchain.
110. Similar strategies for cancelling a memory pool submitted bitcoin transaction exist, which involve submitting another transaction to the memory pool with a higher fee.

[3] Ethereum Transaction Account Types

Activity on the Ethereum blockchain is tracked through two types of accounts:

(1) Externally Owned Accounts (EOA).
(2) Contract accounts.

[a] The EOA

An EOA is similar to a Bitcoin user account, in that it is comprised of a public-private key pair which provides a means to access ether entitlement, as well as manage and run code stored on the Ethereum blockchain.

Ethereum tracks entitlements in a different way from Bitcoin. Instead of the Bitcoin UTXO model, Ethereum uses an *account state* model, which is essentially a running balance associated with a particular public key address that is updated as transactions are processed and confirmed on the Ethereum blockchain.[111]

[b] The Contract Account

A contract account is an account, referenced by its public address, which contains executable program code. It is created as a special type of transaction sent to the Ethereum blockchain *zero address*. This address can only be used as a destination in a transaction which seeks to add a new contract account to the Ethereum blockchain.

Programs stored on the Ethereum blockchain in this manner are usually referred to as 'smart contracts'. These programs are accessed by sending a transaction containing data to the contract account's public address. The contract is then executed via the Ethereum Virtual Machine, or EVM.

[4] The Ethereum Virtual Machine

As noted previously, a virtual machine is a 'runtime environment' which acts as a bridge between a specific programming language and the hardware and architecture on which code in that programming language is sought to be executed.

The EVM works in the same way, except that there is no underlying hardware or operating system where code and data are stored and manipulated. With Ethereum, all of that is done using the computational capacity of the nodes on the network and the code and data stored on the blockchain.

111. It should be noted that in the event a transaction references a public key address not previously referenced on the blockchain, a new EOA account is 'opened' and the incoming balance recorded and added to the public key address identified in the transaction. If this happens as a result of having entered the public key address in error, any ether contained in the transaction is lost, once confirmed, as there exists no corresponding private key with which to update the account.

The EVM does require that the program code be in a particular form of bytecode which it can interpret. It is this bytecode that is stored on the blockchain inside the smart contract.

§1.11 SMART CONTRACTS

Smart contracts on the Ethereum blockchain, or any of a number of similar implementations,[112] are neither smart nor (legal) contracts.[113] They are simply bits of computer code committed to the Ethereum or similar blockchain.[114] Smart contracts are nothing more than a series of programmed steps, like any other computer program, and are not imbued with any specific properties just because they are called 'smart'. The perception by many that these program code snippets have some sort of artificial intelligence capability, particularly now that artificial intelligence is top of mind for many, is unfortunate.

Smart contracts only run when they are 'called' by a particular incoming transaction, and always execute sequentially, in the order in which the transactions are added to the blockchain. Two smart contracts cannot be executed in parallel, i.e., run at the same time.[115]

A smart contract can use a number of programmatic components found in programming languages such as control structures, data types and certain data structures. A smart contract can also call other smart contracts and pass data to them.

As with any program, a smart contract will execute exactly as it is coded, which does not mean it will necessarily perform the intended functionality of its designer and coder. Smart contracts on the blockchain have bugs and many have execution errors. If a smart contract is committed to the blockchain with code errors which cause execution to fail or halt, then any desired state changes will not be committed to the blockchain. Any committed gas will, however, be spent.

A smart contract can hold a balance of ether and can also transfer out ether.

If the programmer includes certain self-destruction functionality in a smart contract when adding it to the blockchain, then that smart contract can be subsequently deleted and rendered inoperable. If self-destruction code is not included, an Ethereum smart contract cannot be deleted. Nothing will happen if a transaction is sent to the address of a deleted smart contract.

The available sophistication of smart contracts is significantly limited by the distributed nature of the EVM. Smart contract code simply cannot run as efficiently as

112. There is not a great deal of difference in the core structure of what a smart contract is and how it is generally implemented in a particular blockchain. Some use different programming languages and have some additional features, but a good understanding of how smart contracts work in Ethereum readily translates to an understanding of an implementation in another blockchain platform.
113. But the term has stuck, nonetheless. This is regrettable as it continues to fuel the perception that smart contracts have certain magical properties when in fact, they are no different than any other computer code.
114. Which cannot be changed, other than by replacing it with a new 'smart contract'.
115. This is another limitation imposed by the fact that a blockchain is a sequential, append-only log.

it would on a single computer where data is stored in very fast RAM. This severely limits the complexity of smart contracts.

[A] Programming Smart Contracts

Smart contracts can be written in any of several languages before being compiled into bytecode. The most popular language for programming Ethereum contracts is Solidity.[116]

An Ethereum contract program, once compiled, will store information with respect to how to interact with the smart contract in a file called the Application Binary Interface. This file provides details on the available functionality and required input data for such functionality. In the case of Solidity, this file is generated by the compiler for use by anyone wishing to use a particular smart contract. This file is not stored on the blockchain.

[B] Oracles

In order to maintain the integrity of a distributed blockchain, every piece of code contained in a smart contract stored on the blockchain *must* execute the same exact way each time – in other words, it must give the same result for every node which runs it.

This is not a problem if the variables which are inputs to the code are constant and set out in the transaction. It becomes a problem, however, when:

- the contract code requires some form of randomness, for instance if the contract codifies a game of chance like a lottery or a card game;
- inputs to the contract vary depending on the time of execution, for instance as a result of varying prices of a commodity with respect to the sale of which the contract is programmed to perform some function.

Ethereum solves this problem by allowing the creation of trust relationships upon which a smart contract can rely in receiving data from certain external (i.e., off-chain) sources covered by such a trusted relationship. These trusted sources are hard coded, or embedded, in a smart contract. Such hard coding allows the smart contract to retrieve trusted data when required and use it.

Smart contracts which embed trust in external sources are called *oracles*. An oracle ensures that all other executions of the same contract (by other nodes) will use the same inputs for whatever data the oracle is trusted to provide.

An oracle can update the value it is trusted to provide, for instance in the case of the price of the commodity, by maintaining a historical list of data values within the contract. If the data being tracked is large, a hash may be stored instead, to verify the correctness of any large data set retrieved from a separate 'off-chain' resource.

116. An overview of the language, as well as its code, may be found at: https://github.com/ethereum/solidity (accessed 15 Dec. 2019).

Oracles may also be used to perform computationally intensive calculations off-chain, for instance where the gas cost of such computations exceed the block gas limit.[117]

Oracles are often centralized and therefore a single source of data. It is important that 'trust-ability' be confirmed before incorporating an oracle into a smart contract.

[C] Decentralized Applications

Decentralized applications, or dApps, are smart contracts, or a set of smart contracts, which interact with an off-chain interface to enable applications which users can access, usually through a browser-based interface.

In the case of Ethereum, this can be achieved by installing a browser extension called Metamask.[118] A dApp combines 'on-chain' core functionality of an application (the 'back end') with 'off-chain' interface functionality ('the front end'). The front-end portion of a dApp can, in turn, be maintained on one of several separate distributed networks created for that purpose.[119] Any required dApp messaging can also be off-loaded to yet another distributed network like Whisper.[120]

DApps have been developed to enable blockchain-based application functionality for gaming,[121] token marketplaces[122] and gambling.[123] The most popular dApp to date is Cryptokitties,[124] a game application which allows users to create and breed digital pet cats. This game went viral for a period of time in late 2017, severely impacting the ability of the Ethereum network to function due to the volume of transactions being submitted to the network. This event exposed a number of Ethereum's functional complexity and scalability limitations.[125]

There now exist several Ethereum-like platforms which offer smart contract and dApp functionality, including EOS,[126] NEO,[127] Waves,[128] TRON,[129] Lisk,[130] Factom[131] and Stratis.[132]

---

117. Which is a number that changes based on the combined input from Ethereum mining nodes, who can change this limit within a certain range. To see the current gas limit, go to: https://etherscan.io/blocks (accessed 15 Dec. 2019) and look for the 'Gas Limit' column.
118. https://metamask.io/ (accessed 15 Dec. 2019).
119. https://ethersphere.github.io/swarm-home/ (accessed 15 Dec. 2019).
120. https://github.com/ethereum/wiki/wiki/Whisper (accessed 15 Dec. 2019).
121. *See*, for example, https://www.mycryptoheroes.net (accessed 15 Dec. 2019).
122. Usually referred to as 'exchanges', which is somewhat problematic as that term is attributed to regulated exchanges in many jurisdictions. *See* the discussion under Initial Coin Offerings, *infra*. An example of an exchange DApp is available at: https://idex.market/eth/idex (accessed 15 Dec. 2019).
123. *See*, for example, https://etheroll.com/#/about (accessed 15 Dec. 2019).
124. https://www.cryptokitties.co (accessed 15 Dec. 2019).
125. https://diar.co/volume-2-issue-22/#4 (accessed 15 Dec. 2019).
126. https://eos.io (accessed 15 Dec. 2019).
127. https://neo.org (accessed 15 Dec. 2019).
128. https://wavesplatform.com (accessed 15 Dec. 2019).
129. https://tron.network (accessed 15 Dec. 2019).
130. https://lisk.io (accessed 15 Dec. 2019).
131. https://www.factom.com (accessed 15 Dec. 2019).
132. https://stratisplatform.com (accessed 15 Dec. 2019).

§1.12 TOKENS ON THE BLOCKCHAIN

The most prevalent use of Ethereum and similar platforms has to date been the creation of *tokens*. Tokens are 'smart contract'-based encapsulated 'entitlement tracking' functionality for a particular purpose.

Contract-based tokens allow the use of a distributed ledger for record-keeping without the necessity to create a new and separate blockchain. Some proposed[133] uses of tokens include:

- Tracking entitlement of a virtual medium of exchange (cryptocurrencies).
- Tracking game credits or cloud-storage entitlement.
- Maintaining a digital registry for land titles.
- Keeping an index of birth certificates or marriage data.
- Tracking voting or collecting census data.

Token balances are separate and distinct from ether and gas balances on the Ethereum platform. Token balances are created and stored *within smart contracts* and not explicitly on the Ethereum blockchain, as is the case with ether.

Standards have been developed for the creation of Ethereum tokens at the smart contract level. The most often used standard is ERC-20[134] discussed in more detail below. Some other standards relating to token smart contracts are:

- ERC-223: Intended to protect against accidental smart contract transfers.
- ERC-721: A standard for non-fungible tokens ('deeds').[135]
- ERC-809: Used to 'rent' non-fungible tokens.
- ERC-1238: A standard for non-transferable tokens ('badges').

[A] The ERC-20 Token Standard

This standard sets out a minimum set of functionalities which every compliant Ethereum-based token smart contract must have.[136] Every ERC-20 compliant token smart contract must have (among others):[137]

- A *totalSupply* function which returns the total number of tokens in existence.
- A *balanceOf* function which returns the token balance for a particular address.

133. Although there is a great deal of enthusiasm about these use cases, actual commercially successful implementations remain elusive.
134. ERC stands for Ethereum Request for Comments. A full list of ERC standards is available at: https://eips.ethereum.org/all (accessed 15 Dec. 2019). An ERC is a step in the process for Ethereum platform improvements. *See* the discussion on Ethereum governance, section §1.13[B] *infra*.
135. Tokens which cannot be interchanged with each other or divided.
136. A number of other blockchain platforms have also adopted the ERC-20 token standard for their blockchains.
137. The full specification is available at: https://theethereum.wiki/w/index.php/ERC20_Token_Standard (accessed 15 Dec. 2019).

- A *transfer* function which allows a sender to transfer tokens to a designated address.

An ERC-20 compliant token smart contract will also have the functionality to track information of tokens issued and their ownership, through two lists:

- Token entitlement by owner.
- Delegation of spending authority (an 'allowance') by an owner.

These two lists inform and support two default types of token transactions within the token contract:

- Transfers by a person who is a holder of a quantity of tokens within the contract to another person.
- Delegated transfers on behalf of a person who is a holder of tokens, to another person.

The second type of transaction enables the exercise of control over token distribution by a centralized entity (such as an Initial Coin Offering (ICO) issuer) or a third-party intermediary (such as a token marketplace[138]).

These functionalities enable a certain level of interoperability between token smart contracts which comply with the standard.

[B] Crowdfunding on the Blockchain

The most prevalent use of ERC-20 compliant blockchain tokens to date has been as a means of crowdfunding for novel technology-related projects (many of them seeking to leverage blockchain in some new way).

Unlike traditional crowdfunding, tokenized crowdfunding offers the added feature that crowdfunding tokens can - in many cases - be traded on a secondary market almost immediately.[139]

This blockchain-based crowdfunding and subsequent secondary trading are done in several slightly different ways. It is helpful to briefly describe each. Their legal implications will be discussed in later chapters.

[1] Initial Coin Offerings

An Initial Coin Offering (ICO) (or Initial Token Offering or ITO) is the process by which a new, usually ERC-20 compliant, token is released for purchase and subsequent trading on a blockchain-based platform like Ethereum.

138. Sometimes referred to as an 'exchange' as noted previously. *See* the discussion with respect to Initial Exchange Offerings, section §1.12[B][3] *infra*.
139. Which raises a host of consumer-protection concerns.

The ICO process generally[140] works as follows:

- A 'white paper' is prepared detailing the venture with respect to which a token is to be issued for fundraising purposes.
- A smart contract for a token sale is written and added to a tokenization platform like Ethereum.[141]
- A website is created describing the venture and listing the individuals behind the venture. The white paper is also made available for download from this website. The website will also list the period of time during which the ICO will be active, i.e., when tokens may be purchased by sending transactions to the token smart contract.
- The venture may seek the listing of its token on any of several marketplaces or 'exchanges',[142] so as to enable secondary trading after the ICO is completed.
- A promotional campaign is undertaken by advertising the ICO on social media platforms and forums.
- Once the ICO launches, tokens are purchased by sending transactions to the token smart contract.
- After the ICO is completed, tokens may become tradeable if they have been accepted for listing on an exchange. At this point in time, the underlying venture will also take the proceeds from the ICO and use them to fund the venture.[143]

As of the writing of this chapter, more than 5,500 ICOs have been either completed, are in progress or are slated for launch in the near future.[144]

A sizable ecosystem has developed around the creation of, trading in, and speculation with ICO tokens. This includes hundreds of exchanges,[145] ICO consulting and promotion companies, token rating agencies, token custodians, etc.

[2] Token Generation Events

A Token Generation Event, or TGE, is the same as an ICO from a functional perspective.

140. It must be noted that there is no defined ICO process methodology. The enumerated steps are not always followed and then not always in the order set out here.
141. It is possible to launch an ICO completely on its own blockchain and network as well, but this is rarely done given the significantly increased resources required.
142. The use of the term 'exchange' in the context of the trading of tokens is somewhat problematic, given that this term is – in many jurisdictions – a term of art meant to identify a securities marketplace, which after meeting a large set of regulatory requirements, is recognized by a regulatory authority as a regulated 'exchange'. In the financial markets, an organization recognized as an exchange carries with it a certain level of professional *gravitas*, which in many cases is not justified in the cryptocurrency and token markets. Nonetheless, the term has stuck, and marketplaces will thus be referred to herein as 'exchanges' for the sake of consistency with the practice in the cryptocurrency space.
143. Which in many cases requires conversion of the proceeds from a cryptocurrency into some sort of fiat currency.
144. *See*, for example: https://icobench.com/ (accessed 15 Dec. 2019).
145. *See*, https://coinmarketcap.com/rankings/exchanges/ (accessed 15 Dec. 2019).

Some differentiate a TGE on the basis that the underlying functionality is more in the nature of a 'utility' or that the token is affiliated with a dApp.

[3] Initial Exchange Offerings

An Initial Exchange Offering, or IEO, is effectively an ICO underwritten by an exchange. A venture seeking to raise funds approaches an exchange offering this option[146] and seeks to comply with their requirements to complete an IEO. Once accepted, the token issuance for the venture is managed through the exchange.

In order to buy into an IEO, a purchaser will first need to create an account with the exchange which is offering or underwriting the IEO.[147] Once an account has been set up,[148] the user can proceed to purchase the IEO tokens through the exchange's trading platform.

Note that in the case of an IEO, token ownership may not be tracked on a blockchain but rather in the accounting system of the exchange.

There is a general expectation that an exchange which is offering an IEO has conducted a certain level of due diligence with respect to the IEO before offering it.[149]

Secondary trading in purchased tokens is straightforward, given the fact that they are already tradeable on the exchange underwriting the IEO.

[4] Security Token Offerings

A Security Token Offering, or STO, is very similar to an ICO from a functional perspective but differs in one material (legal) aspect: an STO token tracks ownership of some real-world underlying asset, such as shares in a company.

STOs are therefore presumed by their issuers to be securities offerings.

[5] A Note on Token Fungibility

'Fungibility' is the property of *interchangeability* of a commodity or good. For example, one barrel of crude oil is as good as another. Fungibility is usually thought of as one of the fundamentally useful properties of paper money.

Fungibility of a particular entitlement to a cryptocurrency or token stored on a blockchain might become *tainted* by the history of ownership of that particular token if any prior transactions were connected to illegal or otherwise suspect conduct.

146. *See*, for example https://launchpad.binance.com/ (accessed 15 Dec. 2019).
147. The exchange may pre-purchase a large number of tokens for distribution on its platform and may also charge fees to the token issuer for the services it provides.
148. Which on a proper exchange should include Know Your Client (KYC) and Anti Money Laundering (AML) compliance procedures.
149. This due diligence may be more focused on ensuring that the IEO will be successful rather than protecting investors.

Given the use of bitcoin as the primary medium of exchange on the Dark Net, this poses a particular problem for that cryptocurrency.[150] Law-enforcement agencies as well as a number of private firms have assembled databases tying bitcoin addresses to a variety of illegal activities.[151]

Several 'privacy coins' attempt to prevent these types of connections from being made.[152]

§1.13 BITCOIN AND ETHEREUM GOVERNANCE

Bitcoin and Ethereum blockchain functionality are wholly controlled by the blockchain code running on each of the nodes of these networks. No component of its operation is controlled by any human discretion. There is thus, at least in theory, no need for governance like one might find in other types of P2P networks, such as Wikipedia.[153]

However, in the absence of an operational governance structure, it is still necessary to make changes to the blockchain network code from time to time, to address security issues or add enhancements, for instance. Processes have been developed for this purpose.

[A] The Bitcoin Governance Process

The primary groups who influence the code base of the Bitcoin network are the Bitcoin Core development group and the group of miners operating Bitcoin nodes.

The Bitcoin Core development group is a small group of software developers who have rights to update the core Bitcoin software. This group is currently led by Wladimir van der Laan.[154]

The core code, or *code base*, for Bitcoin is maintained in a Github[155] software repository available online.[156] Github is a company which provides online hosting of code repositories using the Git open source version control software. Git uses a Merkle tree structure to ensure the integrity of a particular code repository or 'repo' and to track all changes made.

Anyone can interact with a Github-hosted repository in several ways:

150. One investigation suggested that almost half of all Bitcoin addresses are associated with some form of illegal activity, available at: https://www.independent.co.uk/life-style/gadgets-and-tech/news/bitcoin-price-fall-criminals-blockchain-anonymous-cryptocurrency-zcash-monero-dash-a8174716.html (accessed 15 Dec. 2019).
151. *See*, for example: https://www.elliptic.co/ and https://www.chainalysis.com (both accessed 15 Dec. 2019).
152. *See* Berg, A., *The Identity, Fungibility, and Anonymity of Money* (10 Jul. 2018), available at: https://ssrn.com/abstract=3211011 or http://dx.doi.org/10.2139/ssrn.3211011 (both accessed 15 Dec. 2019).
153. *See* https://wiki.p2pfoundation.net/Peer_Governance (accessed 15 Dec. 2019).
154. No relation to the author.
155. https://github.com (accessed 15 Dec. 2019).
156. https://github.com/bitcoin/bitcoin (accessed 15 Dec. 2019).

- 'Forking a repo'. This process allows anyone to build on top of an existing set of programming code. Forking involves copying an existing repo, making changes and then publishing this updated code.
- 'Pull requests'. Anyone who has forked a repo and thinks that the added code would be great to incorporate into the original project repo can ask the owners of the original project to consider incorporating the forked repo into the original project.
- Networking. One of Github's ecosystem's primary benefit is the communication and collaboration among software developers that it enables.[157]

[1] Bitcoin Improvement Proposals

A change to the Bitcoin protocol is mediated through a Bitcoin Improvement Proposal or a 'BIP'. The BIP process was created in 2011 and took a page from the Python Enhancement Proposal process for improving the Python programming language.[158]

A Github repository tracking the status of all BIPs is maintained online.[159] There are three general categories of BIPs:

- A *Standard Track BIP*, which proposes a structural or functional change to the Bitcoin protocol as embodied in the code base.
- An *Informational BIP*, which provides clarity or information to the community but does not propose any new feature or change.
- A *Process BIP*, which proposes a change which does not directly impact the code base, but may suggest new procedures, changes to decision making in development, or changes to tools used in developing Bitcoin.

A BIP generally proceeds as follows:[160]

- Anyone seeking a change in the Bitcoin protocol first raises the issue on the Bitcoin protocol discussion mailing list[161] to gauge interest and receive preliminary input.
- If there is interest, the BIP is submitted to the BIP Git repository as a pull request and assigned a number.
- An assessment is made whether the change requires a soft fork or a hard fork.
- The proponent of the BIP or someone else who supports it (sometimes referred to as the 'champion') writes the code to implement the proposed change.
- The code is examined, tested and discussed in a 'peer-review' type process.

157. It is possible to also use Git and Github to manage version control for any types of files, not just software code, as well as conduct project management: https://github.com/features/project-management/ (accessed 15 Dec. 2019).
158. https://www.python.org/dev/peps/pep-0001/ (accessed 15 Dec. 2019).
159. https://github.com/bitcoin/bips (accessed 15 Dec. 2019).
160. This a high-level summary. *See* BIP002 for a full description, available at: https://github.com/bitcoin/bips/blob/master/bip-0002.mediawiki (accessed 15 Dec. 2019).
161. https://lists.linuxfoundation.org/mailman/listinfo/bitcoin-dev (accessed 15 Dec. 2019).

- Once there appears to be sufficient support, a date for the roll out of the software is proposed.

The adoption of the change then depends on how many of the nodes on the network actually install the updated version. A soft fork BIP requires 'clear miner majority' which means that 95% of miner nodes must upgrade their software to include the BIP. A hard fork BIP requires that the 'entire community' adopt it by installing an update that includes the BIP. This is a difficult and uncertain threshold. As a result there have been no hard fork BIPs to date.

The most discussed and controversial BIP was likely BIP141 dealing with the 'Segregated Witness' soft fork proposal. It deserves a bit of further discussion.

[2] Segwit

As noted previously, the Bitcoin block size was limited to 1 MB at the time the Bitcoin network was launched. This 1 MB block size limitation is a significant scalability barrier for Bitcoin as it permits only a limited number of transactions to be processed every ten minutes.

The combination of the small block size and the ten-minute Proof of Work requirement limits the number of transactions which can be processed on the Bitcoin network to somewhere between four and five transactions per second (TPS). Compare this to the capacity of the VISA network to process up to 56,000 TPS.[162]

Prior to Segwit, the Bitcoin network was vulnerable to a potential weakness in the Bitcoin transaction process, known as *transaction malleability*, which could be exploited to change transaction ownership information before transactions were confirmed within a particular block.

In order to attempt to cram more transactions into a block as well as eliminate the transaction malleability problem, a proposal was made to store the transaction signature data[163] for a particular block *outside* the main Bitcoin blockchain, but still on the same network, using a *sidechain*.[164]

This proposed process of 'segregating the witness' to block transactions became known as Segwit and was first proposed in BIP141. Segwit was activated by way of a soft fork in August 2017. Some members of the Bitcoin community did not agree with this change and hard forked a new blockchain which they named Bitcoin Cash (BCH).[165]

Another Segwit proposal, known as Segwit2X,[166] was subsequently made with a view to doubling the Bitcoin block size to 2 MB. This (hard fork-based) proposal was controversial and was not adopted.

162. The VISA network takes about twelve seconds to process the total *daily* volume of transactions processed by Bitcoin.
163. Which usually takes up about 65% of the storage space for an average transaction.
164. Sidechains are covered in more detail under section §1.18[B] *infra*.
165. https://www.bitcoincash.org/ (accessed 15 Dec. 2019).
166. https://en.bitcoin.it/wiki/SegWit2x (accessed 15 Dec. 2019).

These Segwit proposals illustrate the difficulties often encountered in governing a distributed blockchain protocol without any central authority.[167] It is a slow, arduous and frustrating process.

[B] Ethereum Governance

Ethereum is currently governed through a consensus-based code update process called the Ethereum Improvement Proposal, or EIP.[168] It functions largely in the same manner as a BIP but does have a more extensive proposal documentation requirement. Ethereum also has a more formalized issue discussion protocol known as the Ethereum Request for Comment, or ERC, as discussed previously. An ERC can turn into an EIP.

[C] Off-Chain and On-Chain Governances

Both the BIP and EIP processes are referred to as 'off-chain governance' in that the approval process for changes is not tracked or executed on the blockchain.

Another approach to managing proposed changes to a blockchain's protocol is through 'on-chain' governance, where the rules and processes for change are encoded in the blockchain protocol itself.

On-chain governance usually uses a (node-based) voting mechanism process of some sort to achieve consensus regarding proposed changes. EOS[169] and TEZOS[170] are blockchains seeking to follow this model. Both have been fraught with discontent.[171]

There is the possibility that Ethereum may adopt some form of on-chain governance with a future hard fork.[172]

§1.14 MOVING BEYOND ETHEREUM

By 2015, and with the relative success[173] of Bitcoin and Ethereum, additional blockchain-based projects were being created.

These projects generally followed two approaches to blockchain implementation described as *public* and *private* blockchains.[174] In addition, with the advent of a

167. For a more detailed description of Segwit and all the consensus challenges encountered, *see* https://bitcoinmagazine.com/articles/long-road-segwit-how-bitcoins-biggest-protocol-upgrade-became-reality (accessed 15 Dec. 2019).
168. A list of EIPs is available at: https://github.com/ethereum/EIPs (accessed 15 Dec. 2019).
169. *See* the EOS white paper: https://github.com/EOSIO/Documentation/blob/master/TechnicalWhitePaper.md#governance (accessed 15 Dec. 2019).
170. *See* the TEZOS white paper: https://tezos.com/static/white_paper-2dc8c02267a8fb86bd67a108199441bf.pdf (accessed 15 Dec. 2019).
171. https://www.coindesk.com/soon-chain-governance (accessed 15 Dec. 2019).
172. https://docs.ethhub.io/ethereum-basics/governance/ (accessed 15 Dec. 2019).
173. In the sense that the value of a bitcoin had increased dramatically.
174. There are others who parse the different types of block chains using additional criteria, such as whether the blockchain is permissioned or not. Given that a public blockchain is usually permissionless and a private blockchain usually permissioned, this additional distinction is not significant from a functional perspective.

number of other distributed ledger and shared database-related technologies, the term *DLTs* emerged. Before exploring the details of some of these projects in more detail, it is helpful to have a general understanding of what these three terms mean.

[A] Public (Permissionless) Blockchains

This type of blockchain allows anyone to participate *without a specific identity*. Like Bitcoin and Ethereum, many of these blockchains require the use of a native cryptocurrency combined with a Proof of Work or similar consensus mechanism to stand in the place of a centralized trusted authority.

Trust in public blockchains is usually created and enforced with mathematical/ algorithmic structures.

Due to these requirements, public permissionless blockchains are in many cases slow and energy intensive.[175]

[B] Private (Permissioned) Blockchains

This type of blockchain is used among a set of *identified participants*, usually in the context of a commercial relationship of some sort where a common record among the participants is beneficial or desirable. Permissioned private blockchains are also sometimes referred to as 'consortium' blockchains.

Many of these types of blockchains do not use a Proof of Work and/or cryptocurrency approach to consensus but rely instead on simpler and less-resource intensive consensus mechanisms.

Given the fewer participants (and therewith nodes), a private blockchain is likely to be more centralized than a public blockchain. Quorum[176] and Tendermint[177] are examples of private blockchain platforms. Most enterprise blockchains (discussed below) are private blockchains.

Trust in private blockchains is usually enforced by contract or reputation.

[C] Distributed Ledger Technologies

This term emerged to describe a broader group of technologies which pursue some form of distributed ledger solution on the basis of a wide variety of storage modalities, P2P network topologies and consensus mechanisms.

As is often said, 'every blockchain is a DLT, but not every DLT is a blockchain'. Some of the more novel DLTs do in fact not use a blockchain to store the ledger data, but instead rely on other data structures, such as directed graphs or even traditionally secured distributed databases.

175. For example, the Bitcoin blockchain's energy consumption exceeds that of many countries, https://digiconomist.net/bitcoin-energy-consumption and https://digiconomist.net/bitcoin-energy-consumption (both accessed 15 Dec. 2019).
176. https://www.goquorum.com/ (accessed 15 Dec. 2019).
177. https://tendermint.com/ (accessed 15 Dec. 2019).

Before examining some examples of DLTs and other consensus mechanisms, it is helpful to gain a bit of insight into some theoretical aspects of distributed consensus seeking networks, which inform an understanding of some of the challenges and limitations of distributed ledger systems.

§1.15 DISTRIBUTED SYSTEM CONSENSUS THEORY

Establishing consensus among a distributed network of computers is not a new problem and has been studied from a theoretical perspective for decades.

Given that in today's world there is often the need to synchronize the same data among computers in many different locations, research and development of consensus algorithms is fundamental to many areas of applied computing.

Research in this area has generated many helpful insights into some key attributes and limitations of a distributed consensus seeking network which should inform the design of these systems. A brief overview of some core concepts and theory follows.

[A] Synchronous Versus Asynchronous Processes

A *synchronous* process involves sequential steps in a process that are connected and completed in order. No subsequent step is started until the previous step is finished. An example of a synchronous process is a queue at a theatre's ticket window - every customer must be served in order.

Synchronous processes require clear messaging with respect to when a specific step is completed, in order to avoid the process halting indefinitely.

Asynchronous processes have steps which are not connected and may be completed out of order. An example of an asynchronous process is servicing a set of tables at a restaurant. People sitting at these tables can place orders and receive food independent from each other and without any sequencing requirement.

Most consensus processes will only work if they are *asynchronous* as any synchronous process will stop if a particular step fails to complete (for instance, as a result of an unresponsive, uncooperative or malicious[178] node).

An asynchronous consensus system introduces additional challenges.

[B] The FLP Impossibility Result

In 1983, three computer scientists proved mathematically that consensus is not guaranteed in any distributed asynchronous system where even one host, or node, may fail.[179] This is commonly known as the *FLP Impossibility Result*.[180]

178. For example, a node seeking to change the value with respect to which consensus is sought.
179. Primarily because it is not possible to distinguish between an unavailable and a crashed node.
180. FLP stands for Fischer, Lynch and Patterson, the last names of the three authors of the seminal paper: Michael J. Fischer, Nancy A. Lynch, and Michael S. Paterson, *Impossibility of*

To solve this problem, consensus mechanisms must have methodologies for dealing with bad nodes (whether malicious or not) and/or slow networks.

This is usually achieved by imposing some sort of time limit on the consensus reaching process.

[C] Consensus Mechanism Properties

Any process for achieving fault tolerant[181] consensus among a distributed set of computers with respect to the state of a certain database or other record-keeping system must have mechanisms to achieve *termination*, *agreement* and *validity*:

- *Termination* (or *liveness*) means that all nodes on the network follow a (multi-stage) process which ends, i.e., it eventually decides on a value of something with respect to which consensus is sought.[182]
- *Agreement* (sometimes also called *consistency* or *safety*) means that some majority of valid nodes can reach an agreement on the same value.
- *Validity* means that the value proposed for consensus is introduced by a process agreed upon within the network.

This is not always easy to do.

[1] The CAP Theorem

Another important aspect of a distributed consensus network is the practical interplay between three physical aspects of such a network: its *consistency*, *availability* and *partition tolerance*, or CAP for short:

- *Consistency* is to what extent all nodes on a network have the same data.
- *Availability* is the extent to which the nodes on the network are accessible by users of the network.
- *Partition tolerance* is the extent to which the connections between the nodes in the network persist, i.e., are active and working.

Distributed Consensus with One Faulty Process, 32 J. ACM 2 (April 1985), 374–382. DOI = http://dx.doi.org/10.1145/3149.214121. *See also* https://groups.csail.mit.edu/tds/papers/Lynch/jacm85.pdf (both accessed 15 Dec. 2019).

181. Meaning it will still function if a number of nodes fail or are unreachable.

182. In a database, liveness requires that a transaction either abort or commit, usually within the bounds of some time constraint.

The CAP Theorem[183] states that in the event of partition within a distributed network, the users of the network must choose to have either consistency *or* availability, but cannot have both. An example will make this clear.[184]

Assume a network of five automatic teller machines (ATMs) for a bank. Each ATM maintains and stores a copy of a ledger containing the bank balances of the bank's customers.

The five ATMs are connected on a network, and the network operates some sort of consensus process to ensure each ATM's copy of the ledger is identical to those maintained by the other ATMs.

As long as the network functions correctly and all five ATMs are connected – i.e., there are no *partitions* (some ATM or ATMs whose version of the ledger is not up to date due to a network connectivity problem), then the ATMs can all be consistent and available.

However, if for some reason the network fails or is unavailable for two of the ATMs, then the balances at those ATMs may not be up to date, that is they are at risk of being *inconsistent*, which means that making them *available* to consumers may result in inconsistent ledgers within the network (new transactions on the disconnected ATMs not being present on those which maintain connectivity).

A choice needs to be made to either:

- keep the ledgers consistent while the partition exists, by making the two ATMs unavailable to consumers (risking discontent of consumers); or
- risk the inconsistency of the ledger by keeping the ATMs available for the users, risking consistency of the ledger (to the chagrin of the bank).

In today's complex distributed systems, the three CAP attributes are not binary – yes or no – type states. They should be thought of as *levels* within a particular system. In other words, a desired increased level of consistency in a system with a certain level of partitioning will result in a decreased level of availability.

The CAP Theorem is a material barrier to the usability of any distributed consensus network.

§1.16 OTHER DLT AND CONSENSUS APPROACHES

[A] Byzantine Fault Tolerance (BFT)-Based Networks

There are now many blockchains or DLTs which explore the use of consensus mechanisms quite differently from the Proof of Work approach used by Bitcoin and Ethereum.

---

183. This is a bit of an oversimplification, which is appropriate for our purposes. *See* https://fenix.tecnico.ulisboa.pt/downloadFile/1126518382178117/10.e-CAP-3.pdf for a more detailed description of the theorem as well as references to the related papers (accessed 15 Dec. 2019).

184. An additional and more detailed, but somewhat technical, example is available at: https://mwhittaker.github.io/blog/an_illustrated_proof_of_the_cap_theorem/ (accessed 15 Dec. 2019).

Many of these are evolutions of more traditional consensus algorithms used in distributed databases, which find their root in a family of algorithms commonly referred to as the *Paxos protocols*.[185] These protocols generally follow an iterative multi-phase, *voting-based* methodology to confirm transactions rather than some manner of random delegation of confirmation to a particular node (as is the case with Proof of Work).

In the context of DLTs, these types of approaches are usually referred to as 'Byzantine Fault Tolerance' consensus mechanisms. Byzantine refers to the 'Byzantine Generals Problem', a famous consensus theory problem involving (potentially) untrustworthy members of a group reaching consensus on a common decision.[186]

Many blockchain purists do not consider BFT-based ledger systems to be true blockchains, given that many of these ledger networks require a degree of centralization of certain aspects or components of the consensus process.

Two often referenced examples of the BFT approach to consensus are Ripple[187] and Stellar.[188]

[1] Ripple

At the use case level, Ripple aims to be a global currency exchange network with (close to) real-time settlement. It operates much like *Hawala*, a delegated and distributed money transfer system used in the Middle East and Asia.[189]

Ripple employs *Ripple Gateways* to create the ability for any user to send money to another Ripple user on the network. A Gateway is usually some banking or financial services entity which acts as a credit intermediary on the network by sending and receiving currency entitlements to addresses on the Ripple ledger.[190]

The Ripple cryptocurrency, XRP, is used as a liquidity mechanism within the network. Every Ripple transaction also involves the charging of a small amount of XRP as a transaction fee which is then 'burned' with the completion of that transaction.[191]

XRP tokens are 'pre-mined' and are not used as part of any token incentivized consensus mechanism.[192] Instead, Ripple consensus uses the *Ripple Protocol Consensus Algorithm* (RPCA).[193]

185. *See* https://en.wikipedia.org/wiki/Paxos_(computer_science) (accessed 15 Dec. 2019).
186. *See* this 1982 computer science paper, discussing this problem in the context of computerized consensus: https://people.eecs.berkeley.edu/~luca/cs174/byzantine.pdf (accessed 15 Dec. 2019).
187. https://www.ripple.com/ (accessed 15 Dec. 2019).
188. https://www.stellar.org/ (accessed 15 Dec. 2019). Stellar was created by Jed McCaleb, a co-founder of Ripple.
189. https://en.wikipedia.org/wiki/Hawala (accessed 15 Dec. 2019).
190. For a more detailed explanation, *see* https://xrpl.org/payment-system-basics.html (accessed 15 Dec. 2019).
191. With the idea being that this destruction enhances the value of an individual XRP token by virtue of a decreasing supply of them.
192. There are currently 100 billion XRP tokens.
193. *See* https://xrpl.org/consensus.html#introduction for a detailed explanation of the RPCA (accessed 15 Dec. 2019).

The RPCA uses a 'Byzantine fault tolerant agreement protocol over collectively trusted subnetworks'[194] to guard against double spending and achieve consensus.

The Ripple consensus protocol generally works as follows:

(1) Every node maintains a copy of the shared ledger of XRP transactions, known as the *last-closed ledger* or LCL.
(2) Every node maintains a *unique node list* (UNL) of other (trusted) nodes from which it will receive messages (called proposals) regarding transactions proposed to be added to the ledger. Every node will have a different UNL determined by whoever controls the node.
(3) The Ripple organization maintains[195] a list of default, or recommended, nodes which can be selected by consensus seeking nodes for inclusion in their UNL.[196]
(4) In addition to the proposals received from its UNL, every node is also able to accept new transactions proposed to be added to the LCL, similar to the memory pool in Bitcoin.
(5) The RPCA now kicks in and proceeds in *rounds* as follows:
    - Each node assembles valid transactions submitted to that node and which have not been previously included in the LCL, into a list known as the 'candidate set'.
    - Each node collects the proposals from all the nodes on whose UNL it appears and votes to confirm the transactions in them where a proposal transaction matches a candidate transaction.
    - Once a transaction achieves 50% of the votes from nodes on the UNL, it is transmitted to the network as a proposal to other servers.
    - Another round takes place and this time the vote requirement is upped to 60%, and then 70% and finally 80%.
    - Rounds continue to be repeated until the consensus timer runs out.[197] All transactions in the candidate set which have votes of 80%[198] of the UNL or more are now added to the LCL. Any transactions with insufficient votes are discarded.

Much like Bitcoin and Ethereum, Ripple ties together LCL versions (similar to blocks in Bitcoin and Ethereum) by incorporating a hash digest of the previous version in the header information of the next.[199]

Given the very rapid LCL commitment time, Ripple can process many more transactions than Bitcoin or Ethereum. Its current capacity is about 1,500 TPS.

194. https://arxiv.org/pdf/1802.07242.pdf (accessed 15 Dec. 2019).
195. Nodes cannot select nodes which have not been approved by Ripple. Ripple is often criticized as not being truly decentralized because of this fact.
196. https://minivalist.cinn.app/validators (accessed 15 Dec. 2019).
197. Which is about 3.5-4 seconds.
198. This threshold is usually referred to as the *quorum* parameter.
199. *See* https://xrpl.org/img/ledger-changes.png for a graphical representation of this component of the Ripple consensus process (accessed 15 Dec. 2019).

[2] Stellar

Stellar uses a consensus model called *Federated Byzantine Agreement* (FBA), which is similar to the RPCA used by Ripple with one important difference. Unlike Ripple, the Stellar model does not have a centralized recommended validator node list maintained by a centralized authority. Instead, each node individually decides which other nodes it trusts. As a result, the Stellar approach finds more favour with blockchain purists seeking a highly, if not completely, decentralized ledger system.

This node-specific list of trusted nodes is called a *quorum slice*. Quorum slices on the network overlap and via that overlap engage in the process of a voting round not unlike that used by Ripple.[200]

[B] Proof of Stake-Based Networks

Proof of Stake is yet another consensus mechanism sometimes used in cryptocurrency-based blockchains. It is notable that the Ethereum project has plans to transition to Proof of Stake with a hard fork at some point.[201]

Peercoin[202] is a good example of a blockchain which implemented a Proof of Stake consensus mechanism.[203]

[1] Peercoin

In 2012 Peercoin became the first blockchain to use Proof of Stake as a consensus mechanism.[204]

In Peercoin's model, owners of Peercoin's token (PPCoin or PPC) pursue a 'minting' process to confirm transactions to be added to the Peercoin blockchain.[205]

This minting process is based on the idea of 'coin age', which is simply a number generated by multiplying the number of coins held by a particular user by the number of days since they were last transacted.

A small reward is paid to anyone who stakes their coinage to confirm a new block to the blockchain. Minting generates approximately a 1% return annually for anyone who participates in this process.

Minting works largely like the Bitcoin mining process, with the following important differences:

200. For a detailed, but somewhat technical, explanation of quorum slices and how they work, *see* https://etale-cohomology.github.io/stellar-tutorials/blog1.html (accessed 15 Dec. 2019).
201. This plan is known as Casper. It is plagued by delays.
202. https://www.peercoin.net/ (accessed 15 Dec. 2019).
203. *See also* Tendermint by Cosmos, Dfinity, Nxt, BlackCoin, NuShares/NuBits and Qora for similar implementations.
204. The Peercoin white paper is available at: https://www.peercoin.net/whitepapers/peercoin-paper.pdf (accessed 15 Dec. 2019).
205. The general functionality of the Peercoin blockchain has a great deal of similarity to the Bitcoin blockchain as it is based on the Bitcoin open source code.

- The intended node user installs a wallet client program which has a unique address and permits connection to the Peercoin network. The node user adds PPC to the wallet by sending transactions to this unique address.[206]
- Once PPC coins are added to the wallet, they 'age' as long as no transactions are conducted with those coins. Once coins have aged thirty days, they can be used as a stake in the block confirmation process.
- The block confirmation process uses a hashing process like Bitcoin, but with a much smaller sample space. In addition, the difficulty of finding the target hash is reduced in proportion to the size of the coin age of a particular node. As a result, the likelihood of a particular node finding the winning hash is greatly increased if it has a large coin age. Nodes with the largest coin age thus have the highest probability of 'winning' a block.
- A winning node includes its stake in the confirmed block and retransmits its stake back to its wallet (thus reducing the coin age to zero and starting the aging process for those tokens over again).
- The validating node is incentivized to confirm only valid transactions as any fraudulent transaction inside a confirmed block will result in the node forfeiting its stake.[207]
- The official blockchain is identified by participating nodes accepting the blockchain with the highest cumulative coin age as the official version.[208]

[C] Delegated Proof of Stake-Based Networks

Delegated Proof of Stake (DPoS) is a variant of Proof of Stake, developed in 2013, where token holders do not seek to individually compete to validate blocks, but rather delegate their stake or vote to delegates to do the validation on their behalf.

DPoS can be thought of as a way to introduce the Bitcoin mining pool concept into a Proof of Stake network.

A purported advantage of DPoS is faster confirmation time due to a smaller set of delegated validators participating in the validation process.

A disadvantage is that the system is more decentralized (given the limited number of confirming nodes) and that delegated nodes must maintain a high level of availability on the network.

DPoS was first implemented on the BitShares network.[209]

206. Note that Peercoin also initially had a Proof of Work-based mining process which enabled the creation of users who held PPC, which they could then use in the minting process.
207. The integrity of the blockchain is separately verified to this end by validation software running on the nodes of the network.
208. Recall that in the Bitcoin blockchain this is done by seeking the longest blockchain, i.e., the one with the highest cumulative difficulty.
209. Other examples are Lisk, Steem, EOS and Tezos.

[1] BitShares

In the BitShares network, delegated validators are called *witnesses*.[210]

BitShares token holders hold votes in proportion to the number of tokens they hold. In turn, witnesses hold votes in proportion to the size of the stake they represent (which includes their own stake as well as any stakes held by nodes who delegated to, or voted for, that particular witness). In the case of BitShares, the number of witnesses must be between 20 and 101 nodes.[211]

The BitShares DPoS algorithm generally works as follows:

- A schedule of block confirmation processes is maintained, with one confirmation slated every three seconds.
- Every witness is assigned a future time slot for which it will complete the confirmation process.
- A voting process among the witnesses is followed (in the same manner as that of a regular Proof of Stake process) until two-third plus one of the witnesses have voted to confirm.

DPoS-based systems appear to have the potential to process transactions at a very high rate, approaching those achieved by centralized systems, such as Visa or Mastercard, although an actual working implementation at those rates remains elusive at the time of writing.

[D] Directed Acyclic Graph-Based Networks

A directed acyclic graph, or DAG, is yet another proposed approach to a decentralized ledger.

The DAG-based mechanism is quite different from the approaches covered so far. To understand how it works, a quick review of graph theory basics is in order.

[1] Graph Basics

In mathematics, a graph is a data structure which maps certain relationships, usually in the context of some sort of network (e.g., friend relationships on Facebook or computers on a network which have direct connections).

A graph is made up of *vertices* or *nodes* which are connected with *edges* or *links* (Figure 1.26).

210. Or block producers.

211. Other DPoS networks may use different ranges. For instance, EOS and Steemit use 21 as the upper bound.

Figure 1.26 A Simple Graph

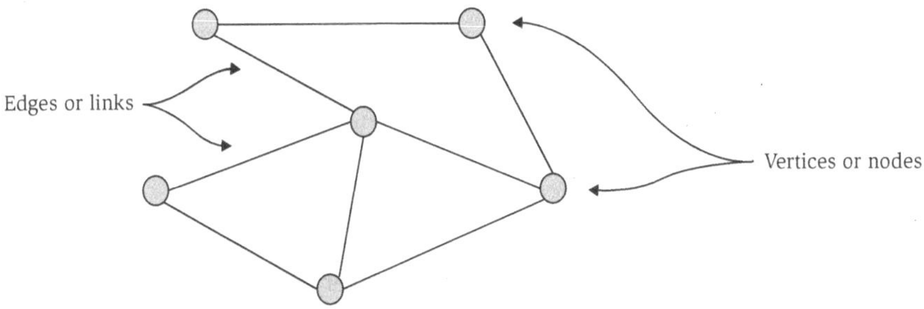

Edges may have directions and thus represent the nature of the relationship between two vertices or nodes. If a graph is structured in such a way that the relationships in the graph can only flow in one way, that is without any loops allowing a circling back, then the graph is referred to as a *directed acyclic graph* (Figure 1.27).[212]

Figure 1.27 A Sample Directed Acyclic Graph

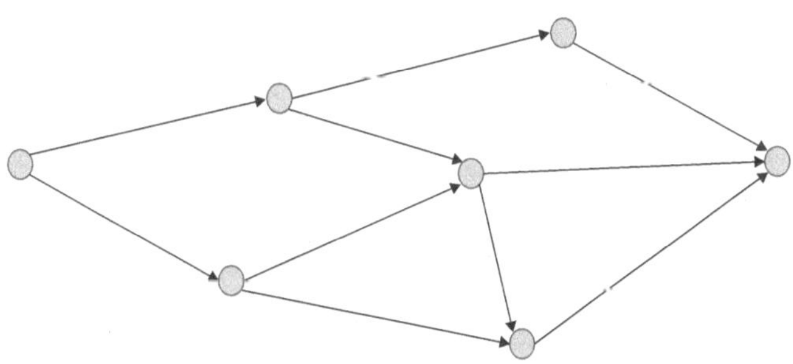

An example of a directed acyclic graph is a river system which only flows in one direction and merges with tributaries as one proceeds along with its flow from source to sea.

[2] Using a DAG as a Ledger

A DAG can also point backwards and thus create an authorization system for sequential transactions, where a particular node or vertex represents a transaction, and later vertices approve the state of previous transactions by creating a link to vertices. Links thus represent approval.

A potential key advantage of this approach is the possibility of allowing multiple transactions to be validated simultaneously.

212. Sometimes also called a *digraph*.

IOTA[213] is an early example of a DAG-based consensus algorithm.

[3] IOTA

The IOTA DAG-based consensus algorithm is called Tangle[214] and was first proposed in 2018 (Figure 1.28). Tangle is open source, feeless and permissionless.

It generally functions as follows:[215]

- All tokens for the system are created and instantiated in the first (*genesis*) vertex/node of the DAG.[216]
- Unapproved transactions are called *tips*, given that they are ends without approving nodes on the graph. Approved transactions are called *sites*.
- In order to become a candidate for confirmation, each new tip needs to identify, and link to, two previously approved transactions in the graph. This can be done directly (i.e., node A is approved by nodes B and C) or indirectly (i.e., node A is approved by B which in turn is approved by C).

Figure 1.28 IOTA Tangle Detail

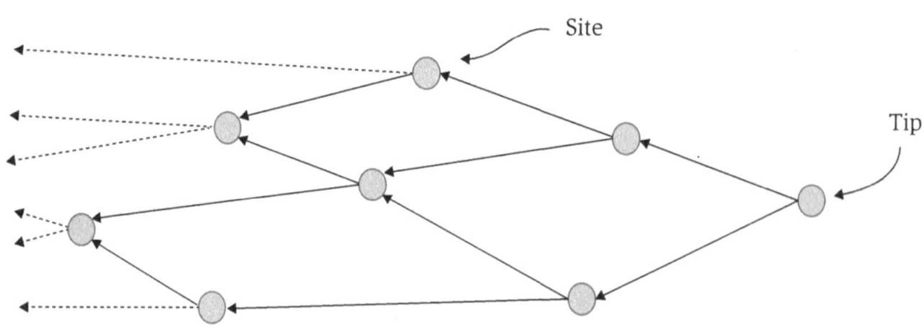

- Each transaction tracks the number of subsequent tips that have approved it. This value is called its *weight* or *cumulative weight*. As the weight increases, the confidence in the transaction increases.
- A candidate tip will select two existing tips in the network to confirm. This is done randomly.
- In order to approve these two current tip transactions (behind it in the DAG), the node seeking to add its tip will first confirm that the transactions to which it intends to link (and thereby confirm) are non-conflicting in the DAG, i.e., that they do not constitute a double spend.

213. https://www.iota.org/ (accessed 15 Dec. 2019).
214. Some also refer to the IOTA DAG generally as 'the Tangle'.
215. This is a simplified overview. For a detailed description, *see* the Tangle white paper, available at: https://assets.ctfassets.net/r1dr6vzfxhev/2t4uxvsIqk0EUau6g2sw0g/45eae33637ca92f85dd9f4a3a218e1ec/iota1_4_3.pdf (accessed 15 Dec. 2019).
216. Note that therefore there is no mining in a DAG-based ledger.

- Once that is confirmed, a hash algorithm is applied to the linking transactions and the hash stored in the tip, so as to connect these transactions together and make them immutable (this is similar to the forward embedding of hash values used in the Bitcoin blockchain).
- The cumulative weight of the confirmed tips (which are now no longer tips but sites) is adjusted upwards.
- The process carries on in this manner and more tips are continually added to the Tangle.
- The cumulative weight of confirmed transactions continues to increase as more tips are added, and once the cumulative weight of a particular transaction (site) reaches a certain level as a percentage of all subsequent tips which have approved the transaction, the transaction can be accepted as confirmed.[217]

IOTA and other DAG-based distributed ledgers are still in their infancy and have not been tested in large production environments. It will be interesting to see how this type of DLT will evolve.

§1.17 ENTERPRISE BLOCKCHAIN PLATFORMS

[A] Hyperledger

In 2015, the Linux Foundation started the development of an open source blockchain incubator with a view to creating blockchain platform technologies for enterprise use. This project was christened 'Hyperledger'.[218]

Since then, several large companies have joined the project, including IBM, Intel and Cisco. Hyperledger aims to become a reference architecture for enterprise blockchain implementations.[219]

The Hyperledger project includes several different initiatives, which are currently progressing through defined development states – proposal, incubation and active – set out by the project.

The most substantive initiatives pursued by Hyperledger to date are Fabric and Sawtooth.

217. *See* https://blog.iota.org/the-tangle-an-illustrated-introduction-79f537b0a455 for a detailed description of this step (accessed 15 Dec. 2019).
218. https://www.hyperledger.org/ (accessed 15 Dec. 2019).
219. *See* https://www.hyperledger.org/wp-content/uploads/2017/08/Hyperledger_Arch_WG_Paper_1_Consensus.pdf and https://hyperledger-fabric.readthedocs.io/en/release-1.4/architecture.html (both accessed 15 Dec. 2019). A short slide deck summarizing Hyperledger is available at: https://events.static.linuxfound.org/sites/events/files/slides/%28OSF_Mr.%20Dan%20O%27Prey%29Hyperledger%20-%20Open%20Source%20Forum.pdf (accessed 15 Dec. 2019).

[1] Fabric

Fabric is a permissioned blockchain framework[220] initiated by IBM with the goal of creating modular blockchain functionality which can be combined to create (or generate) solutions to enterprise problems. Fabric includes functionality to encrypt transactions and partition data on a blockchain for the purpose of enabling compliance with various privacy and data protection obligations of enterprise uses.

Fabric also supports smart contracts, which it calls *chaincode*.[221]

[2] Sawtooth

Sawtooth is a blockchain project[222] started by Intel which seeks to provide a flexible and modular architecture for enterprise DLT solutions. Sawtooth can be implemented in both permissioned and permissionless states and can implement a variety of consensus algorithms.

Two innovations pursued by the Sawtooth project deserve mention: The Proof of Elapsed Time (or PoET) consensus algorithm and the idea of *transaction families*.

[3] Proof of Elapsed Time Consensus

Both the Proof of Work and Proof of Stake consensus mechanisms select one node in the network to complete the validation of the next block on a blockchain, in a manner not dissimilar to a lottery. In the case of Proof of Work, it is the first node which finds the (largely random) target hash. In the case of Proof of Stake, it is the node with the largest coin age (which also follows a random pattern).

PoET is yet another approach to selecting a node to be responsible for validating the next block of transactions on a blockchain on the basis of randomness.

PoET was invented by Intel and is novel in that it is the first consensus mechanism which uses specialized computer CPU functionality to enable it. This functionality is a new instruction set for the execution of code called Intel Software Guard Extensions, or SGX. SGX is incorporated in most Intel CPUs manufactured after 2015.

SGX adds a new set of security-focused capabilities to any CPU on which it is enabled, including the ability to encrypt a portion of a computer's memory (called an *enclave*) and completely segregate the code and data placed in that enclave from view

220. The source code for Fabric is available at: https://github.com/hyperledger/fabric (accessed 15 Dec. 2019).
221. *See* https://hyperledger-fabric.readthedocs.io/en/release-1.4/chaincode.html for a technical reference (accessed 15 Dec. 2019).
222. Sawtooth source code is available at: https://github.com/hyperledger/sawtooth-core (accessed 15 Dec. 2019).

and access by the rest of the computer.[223] Intel calls this a Trusted Execution Environment, or TEE.

The instruction set for the TEE permits it to provide an *attestation* confirming that the code loaded into the TEE has been correctly initiated and has not been altered or otherwise compromised and can therefore be reliably executed.

This functionality is used in the PoET consensus approach, as follows:

- A new node seeking to join the consensus network downloads the network's specific PoET consensus code and loads it into its TEE. The consensus code contains a timer object which can generate a timer instance of random duration.
- The TEE provides a signed attestation confirming that the consensus code is properly installed and loaded. The attestation enables the node to initiate a 'join' request to the other nodes on the network.
- If a majority of nodes accept the attestation, the node is added to the network as a consensus participant.

The consensus process then proceeds, in rounds, as follows:

- At the start of the round, each node receives a timer instance of random duration from its TEE, and the timer starts running.
- The node whose timer expires first is the 'winner', and it transmits a signed certificate to the network proving and confirming its timer time, together with the block it seeks to confirm.
- Other nodes confirm the winning timer time, accept the winner and add the winner's confirmed block to their local copy of the blockchain.

PoET is a very efficient consensus mechanism and scales easily. It is an easy method to create and enforce a desirable time cost for every block, without the need for a cryptocurrency or the large resource cost of the mining process in a Proof of Work-based blockchain. PoET also does not tie up the network nodes' entitlements, as is required in a Proof of Stake implementation.

On the downside, it is dependent on a proprietary technology which runs afoul of the precept of placing trust only in the distributed network. If the desire for a completely distributed blockchain is less pressing (i.e., if the focus is on ensuring a common immutable ledger among a private group of parties), PoET would appear to be a more usable consensus solution for such a permissioned (private) blockchain.

223. Some recent reports suggest that SGX may not be as secure as suggested, available at: https://www.theregister.co.uk/2019/02/12/intel_sgx_hacked/ and https://en.wikipedia.org/wiki/Foreshadow_(security_vulnerability) (both accessed 15 Dec. 2019).

[4] Transaction Families

The transaction family concept takes smart contract infrastructure one step further by creating the ability to use *purpose specific* instruction sets and runtime functionalities in the implementation of a blockchain for a defined purpose.[224]

A blockchain designer can select only those functionalities it deems necessary to run the blockchain. This reduces the footprint of the blockchain code and further reduces the attack surface for a potential attack on the blockchain.

§1.18 SCALING THE BLOCKCHAIN

Blockchains, particularly those which rely on Proof of Work, have significant scalability issues, primarily with respect to the speed of processing transactions and the requirement to store a large amount of data about the state of the ledger embodied in the blockchain.

Increasing the block size and reducing the hash time go some way to improving these. Some of the alternative consensus mechanisms discussed above also help improve scalability further, but no combination of these options has yet been revealed as a *panacea* to blockchain's scalability challenges.

As a result, the search for other solutions to this problem continues. A couple of potential approaches to making blockchain more scalable, currently in early development stages, are worth examining.

[A] Sharding

One approach to dealing with the scalability problem is to adopt the *sharding* process used in traditional distributed database systems. The Ethereum foundation is considering this option as a potential scaling solution for the Ethereum network.

Sharding involves separating a database into distinct partitions or *shards*, usually consistent with some available logical way of splitting the dataset itself. For example, in a database of customers, one might shard the database based on the customers' geographic location and place data from different geographic areas on separate servers.

Applying this idea to a blockchain involves breaking up a blockchain into segments, for instance, based on the numerical value of the addresses with entitlements in the ledger. Each of these segments is then assigned a set of nodes responsible for confirming transactions for that segment only.[225] Such a set of nodes is called a

224. *See* https://sawtooth.hyperledger.org/docs/core/releases/1.1/transaction_family_specifications.html for a detailed specification (accessed 15 Dec. 2019).

225. Wang, G., et al., *SoK: Sharding on Blockchain* Article 4, 21, 1st ACM Conference on Advances in Financial Technologies, AFT 2019, 21–23 Oct. 2019, Zurich, Switzerland. ACM, New York, NY, USA, available at: https://doi.org/10.1145/3318041.3355457 (accessed 15 Dec. 2019). A number of universities are collaborating in this area, *see* https://www.computerworld.com/article/3334542/mit-stanford-and-others-to-build-blockchain-payments-network-to-rival-visanet.html (accessed 15 Dec. 2019).

committee. Committees confirm blocks for their shard, which once confirmed are added to a separate master chain, which is usually called the *beacon chain*.

A sharded blockchain can theoretically process transactions in parallel (to the degree of the number of shards) and thereby improve the transaction speed of the whole blockchain.

Implementing a sharded blockchain is not easy, however, as it brings additional challenges with respect to security and resolving cross-shard communications.

With respect to security, a small set of 60–80 networked nodes is clearly more susceptible to attack than a large distributed network of thousands of nodes, like the Bitcoin and Ethereum networks.[226] It thus becomes much easier to corrupt a shard, which in turn can corrupt a beacon chain. Ongoing research has suggested some possible solutions to this problem, including rotating the membership of the committee for a shard confirmation cycle each round (which is referred to as an *epoch*), as well as having certain trusted nodes act as quality control samplers of transactions.

As it relates to cross-shard communication, a mechanism is needed to resolve transactions which have effects in distinct shards (such as an account entitlement tracked in Shard 1 being transferred to an account tracked in Shard 2). This is proposed to be achieved with a *receipts exchange* process which at a high level works as follows:

- Person A in Shard 1 wants to send an amount to Person B in Shard 2.
- Shard 1 creates a receipt for the transaction, in essence setting the money aside subject to confirmation from Shard 2.
- The receipt is sent to Shard 2, which verifies the receipt and credits Person B and then sends a confirmation back to Shard 1 to confirm the reduction in the balance of Person A.

Test implementations of this asynchronous approach demonstrate that there is a risk of an in-atomic transaction[227] occurring if there is a high volume of cross shard transactions taking place and there are dishonest nodes participating in the validation process. At the time of writing, the problem of solving cross-shard communications is an active area of research and the reader is encouraged to conduct additional online research to identify new developments in this area.

The first blockchain to seek to implement a form of sharding was Zilliqa in 2017.[228] Zilliqa shards only the transaction processing component of the blockchain and not its state storage, and for that purpose creates a new shard every 600 nodes. Its test network demonstrated the ability to process 2,500 TPS.[229]

[B] Sidechains

Another approach to improving the scalability challenge is the use of a *sidechain*.

226. Given that much less hash power is required to dominate a committee than the whole network.
227. For example, only one of the two required steps in the transaction completing.
228. https://zilliqa.com/ (accessed 15 Dec. 2019).
229. https://cointelegraph.com/tags/zilliqa (accessed 15 Dec. 2019).

A sidechain is simply another, usually differently structured blockchain or DLT, to which transaction processing is off-loaded. Sidechains are thought to be a feasible solution to enable consumer payments functionality with respect to cryptocurrency blockchains, such as Bitcoin, where small transactions are not practical, either due to the length of the confirmation time or the fees involved.

A side chain generally works as follows:

- A quantity of entitlement is locked on the main blockchain.
- The same quantity of entitlement is created and unlocked on the sidechain.
- Transactions are performed with the entitlement on the sidechain.
- Once the sidechain transactions are completed or the owner wishes to update the main blockchain, the sidechain entitlement is locked (or in some cases made unusable or *burned*) and the main blockchain entitlement updated and unlocked again.

This paired locking and unlocking between a blockchain and a sidechain is referred to as a *2-way peg* or 2WP. The reliability of 2WP is key, as any weakness in its implementation impacts the reliability and integrity of both the blockchain *and* the sidechain. Specifically, the 2-way peg must ensure *settlement finality*[230] on *both* blockchains to be reliable.

There is also a *one-way peg*, in which the lock and transfer only happens in one direction. Once this one transfer is completed, the entitlement on the transferring blockchain is rendered useless or burned.

[1] The Lightning Network

The best-known example of a sidechain implementation is the Lightning Network or LN. The LN was first proposed in 2016 as a potential solution to the Bitcoin scaling problem discussed previously.[231]

The idea behind the LN is to temporarily move a certain amount of bitcoin entitlement off-chain into a 'payment channel' on the LN, where day-to-day transactions can then be completed.

After a particular period of time, or at the option of the payment channel owners, the payment channel is closed and the blockchain updated to reflect any entitlement adjustments as a result of the transactions completed in the payment channel.

The LN is made up of nodes, much like a blockchain network. Each node can communicate with other nodes, hold a balance of entitlement transferred from the blockchain, and establish payment channels with other nodes to facilitate the exchange of entitlement between or via node owners.

230. That is, not subject to being reversed.
231. *See also* the Lightning Network white paper, available at: https://lightning.network/lightning-network-paper.pdf (accessed 15 Dec. 2019).

In order to engage in a payment transaction, two nodes must either have established a direct payment channel or have existing payment channels through other nodes which create a path between the two nodes wishing to transact.

Creating and using a payment channel on the LN between two nodes is proposed to work as follows:

- The two nodes create a multi-signature address on the blockchain (in essence, functionality which requires both their (digital) approvals to complete a transaction), and each makes a deposit of entitlement to the address.
- The multi-signature address also has functionality (using scripting or a smart contract) which creates an approved, but unsubmitted 'commitment transaction'. This commitment transaction returns the initial deposits back to the respective nodes.
- As the two nodes engage in transactions in their payment channel, they create updated commitment transactions signed by both nodes and which they both store (but not on the main blockchain). As long as there is entitlement in the payment channel to fund a transaction, unlimited transactions can be completed there.
- Either node can close the payment channel at any time by broadcasting its latest commitment transaction to the blockchain, as a result of which the respective entitlements of the nodes are then updated on the blockchain.

Nodes with open payment channels are connected to enable transactions between parties which do not have a (direct) payment channel open between them. The communications between nodes are encrypted in layers, to prevent a paying node from seeing the payment channels through which the receiving node is reached.[232] The network seeks to find the shortest path between two nodes in order to optimize the time to complete a transaction.

As it relates to a specific individual transaction inside a payment channel with multiple hops, it proceeds as follows:

- The intended beneficiary A of the transaction issues an invoice to the intended payor C through intermediary node B, which includes a hash value of a random number (called the *pre-image*), generated by A.
- C sends back a signed transaction to B, together with the hash value sent by A. The logic in the transaction will not transmit any funds from B to C, unless B is provided with the original random number generated by A (from which the hash value was derived).
- B submits a transaction to C with the hash value received from A.
- C provides the original number to B, which authorizes the transaction from C to B.
- B now can unlock the transaction from B to A, and the transaction is complete.

232. This is done in a manner similar to the Tor network and is beyond the scope of this chapter. For a good explanation of how this works, *see* https://2019.www.torproject.org/about/overview.html.en (accessed 15 Dec. 2019).

In some cases, a period of time is specified within which this process must complete. This is called a *Hashed Time Lock Contract*, or HTLC.

The LN model is being slowly implemented but is not without its problems.[233] It remains to be seen whether this approach will become usable for the average consumer.

[C] Multilayer Blockchains

Another approach to addressing the scalability issues of public blockchains is to use a 'multilayer' blockchain, where various layers of the transactional workflow, each with their own blockchain, are optimized to provide scalability or other benefits (such as enhanced privacy) to a specific operational component.

For example, one might layer together three blockchains as follows:

- Layer 1: A public blockchain to track a currency entitlement.
- Layer 2: A private blockchain to store smart contracts based on business logic.
- Layer 3: A public blockchain to enable communications between users.

Each of the various blockchains within such a system are connected together with a 2WP or a similar type of locking logic, in order to maintain immutability and transaction finality between the various layers within the system.

There are several projects seeking to explore the use of multilayer blockchain in the context of the Internet of Things (or IoT) where instead of users, devices are connected in the third layer.[234]

Taking this approach one step further, researchers are proposing many distinct functional layers in a blockchain architecture as a potential solution to solving the various operational challenges to using only one blockchain. For example, a recent (Summer 2019) paper[235] by some Canadian researchers lays out an approach for the implementation of a multilayer blockchain framework for managing mobility data, using the following layers:

- Identification layer
- Privacy layer
- Contract layer
- Communication layer

233. For example, nodes need to be online at all times in order to transact, difficulties in finding the shortest path between nodes if the network gets large, and the inbound capacity problem, available at: https://blog.muun.com/the-inbound-capacity-problem-in-the-lightning-network/ (accessed 15 Dec. 2019).

234. *See*, for example, Badr, S., Gomaa, I. and Abd-Elrahman, E., '*Multi-tier Blockchain Framework for IoT-EHRs Systems*' Procedia Computer Science 141 (2018): 159–166 available at: https://www.sciencedirect.com/science/article/pii/S187705091831812X/pdf?md5=a019303c3f8b4d28728c53bbbe80807f&pid=1-s2.0-S187705091831812X-main.pdf (accessed 15 Dec. 2019).

235. Lopez, D. and Farooq, B., *A Multi-layered Blockchain Framework for Smart Mobility Data-Markets* (arXiv preprint arXiv:1906.06435, 2019), available at: https://arxiv.org/pdf/1906.06435.pdf (accessed 15 Dec. 2019).

- Consensus layer
- Incentive layer.

Much of the work with respect to multilayer blockchains and frameworks is still experimental. It will be interesting to see if this approach will deliver solutions to the various operational barriers of a single blockchain.

§1.19 BLOCKCHAIN AS A SERVICE

With the current level of maturity of cloud platforms, many companies have started to provide Blockchain as a Service (BaaS) solutions for enterprise customers. A simple online search for 'BaaS' will reveal the various vendors in this space.

FURTHER READING

Andreas M. Antonopoulos. 2017, Mastering Bitcoin: Programming the Open Blockchain (2nd ed.) O'Reilly Media, Inc.

Andreas M. Antonopoulos. 2018, Mastering Ethereum, available at: https://github.com/ethereumbook/ethereumbook/blob/develop/book.asciidoc (accessed 15 December 2019).

Imran Bashir. 2018, Mastering Blockchain (2nd ed.) Packt Publishing.

Siraj Raval. 2016, Decentralized Applications, O'Reilly Media, Inc.

CHAPTER 2
Blockchain and Information Security

Dave Hirsch

The technologies that make blockchain possible and useable represent elegant technological solutions to previously intractable challenges.[1] They have led to the creation of entirely new industries and inspired changes in pre-existing systems. But because the blockchains, supporting systems, and users all interact electronically, these innovations are intertwined with issues of information security. Average and even experienced users of blockchain systems face a significant risk of loss due to theft, hacking, malware, and user error, among other things. These risks have direct negative impacts on the rate at which blockchain technologies achieve widespread use and adoption.

This chapter addresses the information security implications of blockchain systems, with a particular focus on 'useable security'.[2] Usable security has been described as 'the idea that secure computing should be easy to do right, and hard to do wrong'.[3] With computer technology generally, and new technologies even more so, there is often a lag between its introduction and when it becomes predictably safe for an average user. That has been and remains true for blockchain systems, although there have also been notable advances in information security features and offerings.

Individuals, enterprises, policymakers, and developers all must consider prior information security failures in order to make informed decisions about how to use, regulate, structure, and protect blockchain systems going forward. It is equally

1. The Securities and Exchange Commission disclaims responsibility for any private publication of any SEC employee or Commissioner. This chapter expresses the author's views and does not necessarily reflect those of the Commission, the Commissioners, or other members of the staff.
2. Bryan D. Payne and W. Keith Edwards, *A Brief Introduction to Usable Security* (Georgia Institute of Technology Published by the IEEE Computer Society, May/June 2008).
3. Trail of Bits Blog, *Ten Rules for the Secure Use of Cryptocurrency Hardware Wallets* (27 Nov. 2018), available at: https://blog.trailofbits.com/2018/11/27/10-rules-for-the-secure-use-of-cryptocurrency-hardware-wallets/ (accessed 7 Dec. 2019).

important to consider the potential remedies, or lack thereof, for these failures should recur in the future.

This chapter analyses information security primarily through reference to digital assets stored on blockchain, and notable failures, breaches, thefts and losses. The author chose this focus because the vast majority of blockchain-related information security failures to date have involved digital assets. Information security failures typically involve an attacker or perpetrator who identifies and exploits a vulnerability. Why have most such attacks related to blockchains targeted digital assets? As the punchline to the old joke: 'why do people rob banks?' explains, because that is where the money is. Someone who obtains digital assets by breaching information security can immediately and relatively anonymously convert those assets to other digital assets or fiat currency. The payoff for breaching the security of a blockchain technology unrelated to digital assets is much less certain and direct.

This chapter first presents notable information security vulnerabilities. The focus on vulnerabilities and losses is not intended to be alarmist or to advocate against ownership of digital assets because of the security concerns. Most owners of digital assets likely never suffer an information security-related loss. However, those that do can lose all their assets quickly and irreversibly. This review of notable failures will hopefully educate and remind owners, prospective owners, and policymakers about the need for caution in this emerging confluence of technology and stored value. This chapter next discusses some useable security advances that have made owning and storing digital assets safer than in the recent past.

§2.01 RISKS AND VULNERABILITIES

This section addresses the many ways in which information security failures occur in blockchain applications. The Bitcoin blockchain, because of its wide adoption and influence as an inspiration for many solutions that followed, will be the primary blockchain addressed in this chapter. The first two paragraphs of the Bitcoin White-paper, published in October 2008 amidst a worldwide financial crisis and decreasing faith in financial intermediaries, explained that the goal of the Bitcoin protocol was to create a system in which strangers could directly exchange digital value on a peer-to-peer basis.[4] Removing intermediaries and central authorities was the explicit goal. The Bitcoin protocol combined different technologies to solve a difficult computer science and economics problem – how to create a functioning decentralized and trustless financial platform. Trustless, in this context, meaning that strangers can transact without knowing the person with whom they are transacting, nor having a trusted intermediary as recourse if the transaction goes awry.

That promise of a functioning system for the trustless exchange of value has in many ways been realized. The Bitcoin blockchain and other blockchains that followed allow strangers to trust in the integrity of the information contained in the blockchain,

4. Nakamato, S., *Bitcoin: A Peer-to-Peer Electronic Cash System*, available at: https://bitcoin.org/bitcoin.pdf (accessed 7 Dec. 2019).

rather than the trustworthiness of a known counterparty. The use of an encryption algorithm, numerous and geographically dispersed nodes that maintain accurate and immutable copies of all data, and an incentive structure that supports the investment of computer power and electricity expense ('Proof of Work') needed to confirm blocks and earn fees and block rewards, all combine to make the major blockchains quite secure.

However, while a blockchain itself may be secure,[5] the use of a blockchain continues to carry information security risks. The first risk relates to the access and control of private keys. Digital assets exist only as information. That information represents value, which typically can be redeemed or spent by whoever can transfer it. Within the Bitcoin protocol, private keys are the exclusive method for transferring or controlling the bitcoins associated with any public key address. There is no system within the Bitcoin protocol itself for recreating lost private keys or resolving ownership disputes. If a user loses, or a thief illicitly obtains, the private key, that user may lose all assets associated with that key.[6] There are dramatic information security implications for a single point of failure[7] vulnerability that carries a 100% loss potential.

To date, much of the development focus of blockchain technology has been on digital assets, which has also seen the broadest adoption by individuals. For purposes of this chapter, digital assets include (1) cryptocurrencies, such as Bitcoin, and (2) digital asset securities, which may be defined as securities by the issuer or a regulator.[8] This section analyses information security issues primarily as they apply to digital assets because digital assets explicitly represent value. The lure of that value attracts bad actors who seek to compromise information security vulnerabilities, and the loss of that value is typically the result of information security failures.[9] It is not surprising that the most costly information security failures related to blockchain have occurred in the context of digital assets.

5. There have been some notable attacks on smaller digital asset blockchains, including some successful 51% attacks. But as discussed in greater detail below, to date most information security failures for blockchain projects have occurred not in the underlying blockchains themselves, but in applications that utilize those blockchains, such as digital wallets, and exchanges.
6. In part because Bitcoin functions based exclusively on computer code, the ability to perform a function, such as transferring value using an illicitly obtained private key, is separate from the legal authority to perform that act.
7. Single point of failure, sometimes denoted as SPOF, is a concept that exists across disciplines but with particular importance to the IT community. The idea is that systems should be built with redundancies and safeguards such that one error or failure does not result in catastrophic or fatal damage to a system.
8. Various courts, regulators, and commentators have analysed the distinctions between cryptocurrencies and digital asset securities, but this chapter does not address the distinctions between these categories and instead addresses only the combined category of digital assets.
9. However, information security concerns pervade the blockchain space, beyond simply digital assets. Deloitte released its 2019 Global Blockchain Survey in which 28% of respondents identify 'potential security threats' as their projects' barrier to increasing adoption and scale in blockchain technology. This concern is one percentage behind the most frequently identified concerns: implementation and regulatory issues. *See* Deloitte, *Global Blockchain Survey* 8 (2019), available at: https://www2.deloitte.com/content/dam/Deloitte/se/Documents/risk/DI_2019-global-blockchain-survey.pdf (accessed 7 Dec. 2019).

This section illustrates the information security issues by reference to incidents in which a vulnerability was exposed and a discussion of the facts surrounding each incident. This is followed by a discussion of the legal issues raised by the incidents, and then potential policy or legislative solutions that may minimize future impacts.

The overarching theme of this section is that while blockchains themselves may be secure from an information security perspective, they are used by humans who invariably introduce vulnerabilities and risk as they adopt and adapt technologies.[10] One of the great advances provided by Bitcoin and the blockchains that followed is that they empower individuals to control valuable assets without the need of a trusted intermediary. However, this independence often comes at a price. Investor and entrepreneur Ouriel Ohayon described the issue:

> Yes, you are in control of your own assets, but the price to pay is that you are in charge of your own security. And since most people are not security experts, they are very much often exposed – without knowing. I am always amazed to see around me how many people, even tech savvy ones, don't take basic security measures.[11]

Unfortunately, after a loss or theft of digital assets, it is often impracticably difficult to recover what has been lost. Even though the major cryptocurrency blockchains keep a public record of every transaction, that information often is insufficient to track illicitly obtained cryptocurrency to the human who possesses it. Most digital assets are transferred anonymously, or pseudonymously. It is easy and relatively inexpensive for criminals to obscure the ultimate ownership of illicitly obtained cryptocurrency using various means, including multiple digital asset addresses, mixing services, unregulated digital asset exchanges, and peer-to-peer transfers.[12] The market for digital assets is global, which increases the chances that individuals who profit from a breach of information security are jurisdictionally remote, even if the victims or legal authorities could identify them. Thus, even if private individuals can track where stolen digital assets are transferred, the chances of recovering them are uncertain at best. That makes robust information security processes and practices especially important. If the prospects for recovering lost assets are dim, then preventing the loss is that much more important.

---

10. For blockchain, as in cybersecurity generally, '[e]very aspect of securing, defending, and attacking has a human element, an element that profoundly affects all the other components and guarantees there can be no silver bullet in cybersecurity'. Safran, R. and Desai, U., *Cybersecurity and the Human Element: We're All Fallible* (Dark Reading, 12 Feb. 2019), available at: https://www.darkreading.com/careers-and-people/cybersecurity-and-the-human-element-we re-all-fallible-/a/d-id/1333789 (accessed 6 Feb. 2020).
11. https://cointelegraph.com/news/six-tools-used-by-hackers-to-steal-cryptocurrency-how-to-pro
tect-wallets (accessed 6 Feb. 2020).
12. This reality does not diminish the notable successes international law enforcement have achieved tracing digital assets back to the criminals who transacted them. But for most individuals, once their digital assets are lost, the chances of recovery are quite small.

[A] Private Keys: A Single Point of Failure

To transfer bitcoins requires a private key that controls the public key address where the bitcoins are stored. There are a number of ways to generate private keys, which rely on the SHA256 algorithm (*see* Chapter 1, section §1.06[C]). The primary attribute of a private key is that it allows the holder to transfer bitcoins held at the associated public address. Because of the encryption algorithm, the private key cannot be derived by analysing or 'reverse engineering' the corresponding public key.

[1] Lost Private Keys Typically Means a Total Loss of Bitcoins Held at the Associated Public Key Address

As a rule, if the private key is lost, so too are all the bitcoins associated with the corresponding public key. The bitcoins associated with that address become essentially 'locked' with no ability to unlock them. As described in section §2.01, anyone can send bitcoins to any public address. But for the owner of the receiving address to be able to subsequently transfer the bitcoins requires a private key linked to the receiving address. Without the private key, those bitcoins will remain in place indefinitely.

This risk is not theoretical. Digital asset forensics company Chainalysis estimated that at the lower bound, 2.3 million bitcoins are locked in addresses, presumably because the owners lost control of the associated private keys.[13] Chainalysis estimated that approximately 200,000 bitcoins have been lost due to 'misdirected transactions or loss of private keys'. To put that in perspective, this represents approximately 1% of all the bitcoins that will ever exist, and approximately USD 1.44 billion in permanently lost bitcoins based on the closing price of bitcoin on 1 January 2020.[14]

One of the most famous instances of a lost key resulting in a lost fortune involves James Howells. Howells, a Welsh IT Specialist, began mining bitcoins in February 2009. That was so soon after the launch of the Bitcoin protocol that Howells claims there were only five other people in the world also mining it then.[15] Over the course of a week he mined 7,500 bitcoins,[16] but soon gave up mining because his girlfriend objected to the noise his computer made. At that time, Bitcoin was still quite new and there was not yet an established trading or commercial market. There were no

13. https://blog.chainalysis.com/reports/money-supply as of 8 Jun. 2018 (accessed 6 Feb. 2020). One central assumption in this report was that 'wallets that contain bitcoin with an average age prior to 2014 and that have not spent any bitcoin since the start of 2014 are lost'.
14. Throughout this chapter, loss estimates and digital asset prices, unless otherwise stated, are based on the closing price of the digital asset on the arbitrarily selected date 1 Jan. 2020, according to www.coinmarketcap.com (accessed 6 Feb. 2020).
15. https://www.theguardian.com/technology/2013/nov/27/hard-drive-bitcoin-landfill-site (accessed 6 Feb. 2020); https://nypost.com/2018/05/26/i-accidentally-threw-away-60m-worth-of-bitcoin/ (accessed 6 Feb. 2020).
16. With a new block confirmed approximately every ten minutes, there are 1,440 blocks per day, and 10,080 blocks created in a week. The block reward was 50 bitcoins in 2009. So out of a total of 504,000 bitcoins rewarded for confirming blocks in a week in 2009, Howells contends that he claimed approximately 1.4% of that total. What was the block reward in 2009 when he was mining?

exchanges and no established value for bitcoins. Howells kept the private key associated with those 7,500 bitcoins on the hard drive of the same computer he used for mining bitcoins. He disposed of the computer in 2010 after spilling lemonade on it, but he retained the hard drive for future use. In the summer of 2013, he decided to throw away the hard drive. At that time, the 7,500 bitcoins were worth approximately USD 500,000. Howells did not realize what he had done until 22 November 2013, when Bitcoin was in the news because the price of bitcoin was rapidly increasing. By then a bitcoin was trading at approximately USD 1,000, making the bitcoins Howells had mined worth USD 7.5 million.

After realizing his mistake, Howells researched to identify the landfill where his garbage, including the discarded hard drive, was ultimately deposited. He went to the landfill and workers showed him to an area roughly the size of a soccer pitch, piled high with trash. The landfill employee told Howells that garbage from three to four months earlier would be 'about three or four feet down'.[17] Howells asked if they could dig to find his hard drive. He was told that to excavate the site would require a team of fifteen people plus two diggers and safety equipment to protect the workers. Disturbing trash that old could lead to noxious gaseous emissions and fires. Howells said in 2013 that 'for me to fund that, it's not possible without the guarantee of money at the end'. Howells did not know if he could find the hard drive in a trash pile that large, and there was no way to know if the data on the drive could be recovered even if it was found. Because he was not willing to pay for the search, Howells never determined whether the landfill would have allowed him to try. Howells publicly acknowledged that someone else could find the hard drive and keep the bitcoins for themselves, though he later claimed that the hard drive was encrypted, such that whoever recovered it would need Howells to decrypt it and access the private key. In 2013, as a result of press interviews with Howells, the public learned of a potential USD 7.5 million windfall buried in the landfill. The town, through a spokeswoman, said that treasure hunters would not be allowed at the landfill.

In December 2017, Howells sought approval from the town council to try to retrieve the hard drive from the landfill. His locked bitcoins were then worth more than USD 75,000,000. The town council declined to permit Howells to attempt to excavate the landfill in search of the hard drive.[18] Howells claimed that it would have been the first such landfill excavation in the United Kingdom (UK) unrelated to a criminal investigation. He offered to self-fund the excavation, and grant the town 10% of any recovered bitcoins, but the town council refused citing legal restrictions and the potential environmental and health impacts. There have been no subsequent announcements indicating that the Howell's hard drive or missing bitcoin private key has been recovered by anyone.

17. https://www.theguardian.com/technology/2013/nov/27/hard-drive-bitcoin-landfill-site (accessed 6 Feb. 2020).
18. https://www.wired.co.uk/article/bitcoin-lost-newport-landfill (accessed 6 Feb. 2020).

[a] *Legal Implications of Lost Private Keys*

This raises the legal issue of who owns the private key and the associated bitcoins if the hard drive is found and restored by someone other than Howells. In practical terms, the finder of a private key can transfer any associated bitcoins to his or her own exclusive control. But does the ability to transfer bitcoins to his or her own address equate to legal ownership? As with many legal issues surrounding bitcoins, the answer likely can be found by analogy rather than a blockchain-specific legal solution.

Whether Howells or a subsequent possessor of the hard drive owns it, and its valuable contents, turns first on whether Howells abandoned or lost the hard drive. In the United States (US), an ownership dispute like this would be governed by state law. An appeals court in Indiana addressed whether personal property placed in a dumpster for disposal is considered abandoned, and reviewed rulings on that issue from various states. All of the cited decisions supported the 'widely held and long-standing doctrine that personality [personal property] discarded as waste is considered abandoned'. In Indiana, abandonment has been described as 'the relinquishment of a right by the owner with the intention to forsake and desert it'.[19] Thus, there is a strong argument that Howells abandoned the hard drive when he intentionally put it in the trash and allowed it to be transported to a landfill for disposal. It appears this result is consistent across multiple jurisdictions. For example, in Germany, section 959 of the Civil Code addresses abandonment of ownership and states 'A movable thing becomes ownerless if the owner, in the intention of waiving ownership, gives up the possession of the thing.'[20]

The fact that because of his abandonment Howells no longer owns the hard drive only partially answers the question of whether someone who finds it in the landfill can establish legal ownership. Whoever found the hard drive would have to prove why his or her claim is superior to the claim of the landfill owner where the property was found. If the finder entered the landfill without permission, his or her claim is likely inferior to an ownership claim by the landfill. This result too depends on jurisdiction and is nuanced, as some jurisdictions require the landowner to undertake a search or exercise diligence in an effort to acquire possession of the abandoned property.

There is also an added wrinkle to this question of who owns what may be the world's most valuable trash. Howells acknowledged intentionally placing the hard drive in the trash. He has not disputed that he knew this action would result in permanent loss of the hard drive and its contents, which presents a strong argument that he abandoned the device. But it is somewhat less clear from the public record whether he knew the private keys were on the hard drive when he disposed of it. Howells, years after the fact, said that he had two hard drives in the same desk drawer,

19. *Long v. Dilling Mechanical Contractors, Inc.*, 705 NE 2d 1022, 1025 (Ind: Court of Appeals 1999), citing decisions from Illinois, Arkansas, and New York that personal property placed in the trash for disposal is considered abandoned.
20. https://germanlawarchive.iuscomp.org/?p=615 (accessed 6 Feb. 2020). Civil Code in the version promulgated on 2 Jan. 2002 (Federal Law Gazette [Bundesgesetzblatt] I page 42, 2909; 2003 I page 738), last amended by Art. 1 of the statute of 27 Jul. 2011 (Federal Law Gazette I page 1600).

and he inadvertently disposed of the one with the private keys rather than the empty one, as he intended.[21]

If true, in some jurisdictions this would change the outcome in a hypothetical ownership dispute between Howells and a subsequent finder of the hard drive. 'Mislaid property is that which is intentionally put in a certain place and later forgotten ... [P]roperty is abandoned when the owner, intending to relinquish all rights to the property, leaves it free to be appropriated by any other person.'[22] In the State of Illinois, for example, if Howells could prove that he did not know the private keys were on the hard drive that he threw out, the private keys may be considered mislaid property. 'A finder of property acquires no rights in mislaid property, is entitled to possession of lost property against everyone except the true owner, and is entitled to keep abandoned property.'[23] In that hypothetical dispute, the subsequent possessor might get to keep the hard drive but have to return the private key to Howells.

[b] Policy Considerations

A dispute as to who owns the bitcoins controlled by a lost private key likely can adequately be resolved with existing laws. The same principles apply to private keys as to ownership of other types of abandoned, mislaid or disputed personal property. There is nothing so unique about blockchain technology that requires a brand new set of laws to address private key or underlying asset ownership disputes.

From a policy perspective, the owner of the private key is well positioned to prevent its accidental loss and any resulting ownership disputes. Owners of private keys can cheaply make copies, although secure storage can sometimes be challenging. Anyone who suffers a loss of a private key did so presumably knowing he or she was participating in a system without a trusted intermediary where the loss of a private key could result in a permanent loss. If users want to participate in a system in which lost private keys can be recovered or regenerated, there are digital assets with these features and Bitcoin private key generation and storage solutions that offer this feature.

Perhaps most importantly, and this is a theme that recurs throughout this chapter, a special set of laws, in this case to more clearly establish legal ownership, will not be of much practical benefit. The Bitcoin protocol is a set of computer-based rules that operates without regard to whether a court has declared that someone does or does not have the legal authority to transfer bitcoins. Possession of a private key, not a legal determination of ownership, is all that matters. If someone found Howells' hard drive, recovered the private key, and transferred the related bitcoins, a judgment establishing that Howells is the legal owner would not help him unless he could both identify the subsequent possessor and they were subject to that court's jurisdiction. By removing trusted intermediaries, Bitcoin creates some efficiencies and offers some privacy benefits. But that disintermediation also removes the third party, such as a bank or

21. https://nypost.com/2018/05/26/i-accidentally-threw-away-60m-worth-of-bitcoin/ (accessed 6 Feb. 2020).
22. *Michael v. First Chicago Corp.*, 139 Ill. App. 3d 374, 382 (Ill. App. Ct. 1985).
23. *Ibid.*

brokerage house in traditional financial systems, that typically can be relied on to honour a court's determinations about ownership.

If loss of private keys is a problem of sufficient magnitude to require a policy solution, the most effective policy response may be to educate users about the risks and suggested methods for protecting against loss.

[2] Death: Risks Associated with Digital Asset Inheritance

Owners of digital assets must keep their private key information confidential to protect against theft. As described in the prior section, lost private keys can result in a total and permanent loss of all assets associated with those private keys. A robust system for ensuring the secrecy of private keys is a benefit during the life of the owner, but can be devastating in the event of his or her death. If the owner of private keys dies or is incapacitated without having created a process for transferring private keys to his or her estate, the digital assets associated with the decedent's private keys may be lost forever.

For example, Matthew Mellon, scion of the Mellon banking family, was an early investor in XRP, a digital asset developed by Ripple Labs.[24] Mellon claimed that he made USD 2 million early investment in XRP that grew to be worth USD 1 billion at XRP's peak value in 2018. He also said in an interview that he kept the digital keys to his XRP locked in cold storage[25] in other people's names at various locations around the US. In April 2018, Mellon died suddenly of a heart attack at the age of 54 on his way to a drug rehabilitation facility in Mexico. Following his death, it was widely reported that Mellon's heirs did not have access to his private keys, cold storage locations, nor the underlying XRP.[26]

A similar problem arose for the heirs of Matthew Moody, who was an early Bitcoin miner.[27] He died in 2013 in a plane crash at the age of 26. Moody's father found that Matthew had used an Internet-based wallet to store his private keys, but his father could not access the contents without a decryption password or a copy of the private keys. He believes Matthew may have owned a substantial amount of bitcoin, but his father could not confirm that or access the bitcoins.

24. https://www.forbes.com/sites/nathanvardi/2018/04/19/the-last-days-of-banking-heir-matthew-mellon/#74427ea75d52 (accessed 6 Feb. 2020).
25. 'Cold storage' in this context means a storage system for private keys that has never been connected to the Internet. It is designed to protect against loss from hacking, malware and other Internet-based threats. Cold storage is discussed in greater detail below in section §2.02[A][1].
26. https://www.nzherald.co.nz/world/news/article.cfm?c_id=2&objectid=12037373 (accessed 6 Feb. 2020).
27. Wilmoth, J., CCN, *Humans Die, Cryptocurrencies Don't: Why Cryptocurrency Investors Need to Begin Estate Planning Immediately*, available at: https://www.ccn.com/humans-die-cryptocurrencies-dont-why-cryptocurrency-investors-need-to-begin-estate-planning-immediately/ (accessed 7 Dec. 2019).

[a] *Legal Implications of Dying Without a Plan to Transfer Private Keys*

For Mellon, Moody, and untold others, their digital assets may be permanently unavailable to their heirs because they failed to establish an estate plan.[28] The ability to inherit cryptocurrency, like any other non-physical personal property, is not controversial under the law. But without a clear plan to pass access and control to one's heirs, the digital assets of the decedent may be lost forever. As UK-based attorneys Simon Goldring and Elysa Jacobs wrote: 'it is important to take precautionary steps to avoid one's cryptocurrency being inaccessible at a time when it may be needed the most and including clauses relating to digital assets either within a Will itself or as part of an ancillary Letter of Wishes is becoming increasingly popular'.[29]

[b] *Policy Implications*

Estate planning attorneys recommend various practices to ensure the assets are available for the deceased's estate.[30] There are also a variety of third-party and electronic solutions available to assist with digital asset estate planning. It is important in considering how to prepare for post-death transfers to also consider the information security implications of the proposed solution. The benefits of establishing a plan for inheritance greatly diminish if the execution of that plan makes private keys vulnerable during life. However, there have not been reports of significant losses due to estate plans gone awry, and the greater risk appears to be a failure to establish a plan. Many digital asset investors are young and less likely to have a will or other estate plan. If policymakers are concerned with losses due to death, education campaigns highlighting the risk of permanent loss targeted at digital asset communities or social media may be the most effective solution.

[3] ***Stolen Keys: Beware of Hacking, Malware, and Man-in-the-Middle Attacks***

Digital asset owners typically transact using a computer or mobile device connected to the Internet. It is possible to transact digital assets directly using code, but this is cumbersome and often beyond the technical ability of digital asset owners. Most owners of digital assets instead use a software or hardware solution that automates the record-keeping and transfer of digital assets. These tools are known as wallets.

---

28. https://www.americanbar.org/groups/real_property_trust_estate/publications/probate-property-magazine/2019/july-august/estate-planning-cryptocurrency/, https://www.thinkadvisor.com/2018/10/22/4-key-steps-for-estate-planning-with-cryptocurrenc/?slreturn=20190913175124 (accessed 6 Feb. 2020).
29. https://www.natlawreview.com/article/cryptocurrency-current-investment-future-inheritance (accessed 6 Feb. 2020).
30. There are a wide range of legal and technical experts who offer advice and computer-based solutions to address digital asset inheritance issues. This handbook does not recommend any particular method, but does encourage users to create an inheritance plan and to counsel others to do so.

Although the technology and format vary, most wallets have several features in common, including (1) they store private keys, (2) they track the balances of the public addresses associated with those private keys, (3) through a software interface they allow users to create transactions to transfer digital assets to addresses specified by the user, and (4) they use the stored private keys to 'sign' the transaction and complete a transfer of digital assets.

Information security threats targeting wallets have resulted in thefts of private keys and losses of digital assets. These vulnerabilities impact the entire market for digital assets. A survey conducted by US law firm Foley & Lardner LLP in 2018 found that 71% of responders reported that hackers and security breaches resulting in the theft of cryptocurrency posed strong to very strong risks to 'the viability and growth of the cryptocurrency industry'.[31] The successful thefts from digital asset wallets typically occur due to hacking, phishing, malware, or a combination of these threats.

One vulnerability results from the fact that public key addresses are long and difficult to accurately type into a website or wallet application. A mistyped character or inadvertent swapping of a lowercase letter for an uppercase, or vice versa, is sometimes known as a 'fat finger' error.[32] Because sending bitcoins to an unintended address cannot be undone and may result in a total loss, copying and pasting of addresses, rather than typing them, is often considered a best practice. However, this convenience is not without risk. Hackers have developed malware, known as CrypToCurrency Clipboard Hijackers, that surreptitiously replace cryptocurrency addresses pasted into apps or websites with an address of the hacker's choosing.

One example of this was part of the All-Radio 4.27 Portable malware package that was detected in Windows computers in June 2018.[33] The clipboard hijacking component of this malware installed and ran in the background, such that a typical Windows user would not be aware that it had infected his or her computer and was active. The malware included a database of 2.3 million Bitcoin addresses. If a user whose computer was infected with this malware attempted to copy one of those 2.3 million Bitcoin addresses and paste it into any text input box, including a website or a wallet application, the infected computer instead would paste a wallet address pre-specified by whoever deployed the malware. Unless the user carefully compared the address he or she copied to what actually appeared when he or she pasted it, the user would unintentionally send bitcoins to the hacker instead of his or her intended recipient.

Another recurring threat is known as a 'man-in-the-middle attack', in which an attacker intercepts or modifies information being sent to a third party. Multiple cryptocurrency wallet providers have been accused of leaving their users vulnerable to

31. *See* https://www.foley.com/files/uploads/Foley-Cryptocurrency-Survey.pdf, 2018 at page 9 (accessed 6 Feb. 2020). The survey reported results from sixty-two cryptocurrency professionals, who were primarily based in the United States.
32. https://hackernoon.com/common-mistakes-that-crypto-beginners-make-77b5a5b6d7ec, 25 Jan. 2018 (accessed 6 Feb. 2020).
33. *See* https://www.bleepingcomputer.com/news/security/clipboard-hijacker-malware-monitors-23-million-bitcoin-addresses/, 30 Jun. 2018 (accessed 6 Feb. 2020). The author also recorded a video that shows the actual operation of the malware, available at: https://youtu.be/Ty-_IjavYH4 (accessed 6 Feb. 2020).

theft from man-in-the-middle attacks. It is unclear how much individual cryptocurrency holders have lost due to this type of attack, but it is a significant risk if wallet software providers do not adequately protect against this vulnerability.

In February 2018, a group of researchers reported a security vulnerability associated with the Ledger cryptocurrency hardware wallet and desktop application.[34] The Ledger wallet creates a new 'receive' public key address for each transaction. Thus every time a user wants to receive digital assets, the wallet generates a new public address that the user can provide to a sender. This is not uncommon. The theory is that using new addresses helps provide anonymity because reusing addresses creates a larger transaction history that may allow others to trace an address back to a specific user. The Ledger wallet software generates the new receive addresses automatically without any intervention or supervision from the user. The security report claimed that because the Ledger desktop software relies on JavaScript code running on the user's computer, if the computer had been infected with malware, it could replace the Ledger generated new receive address with an address of the malware's choosing. Thus users infected with this malware would think they were providing a newly generated receive address that the users controlled. Unbeknownst to them, they would actually provide an address controlled by whoever deployed the malware. Essentially, the users would direct a sender to transfer bitcoin to a hacker instead of themselves. The researchers claimed that to exploit the vulnerability only one line of code needed to be replaced by malware, which 'can be achieved with less than ten lines of python code'.[35]

In February 2019, Warith Al Maawali, a security and cryptocurrency researcher, reported a security vulnerability with the Coinomi cryptocurrency wallet desktop app.[36] Al Maawali reported that Coinomi provided a wallet recovery process, through which users could enter a previously generated twelve-word recovery phrase to regain access to their wallets.[37] However, Coinomi failed to disable a Google spellcheck feature so that anyone able to intercept web traffic could capture the recovery phrase as plain text and take over the user's Coinomi wallet and all its contents. Al Maawali claimed to have lost between USD 60,000 and USD 70,000 in digital assets from his

34. *See* https://www.docdroid.net/Jug5LX3/ledger-receive-address-attack.pdf (accessed 6 Feb. 2020).
35. *Ibid.*, at page 2. The Ledger desktop interface did have a button users could press to simultaneously display the address on their hardware wallet. By verifying that the addresses match, users could confirm they were validly provided by Ledger. But there was no prompt or requirement that users do so before providing third parties with an address that could have been tampered with.
36. *See* https://www.zdnet.com/article/cryptocurrency-wallet-caught-sending-user-passwords-to-googles-spellchecker/ (accessed 6 Feb. 2020).
37. Many wallets offer a recovery feature based on a multi-word passphrase. Then if the device containing the software wallet is stolen or otherwise unavailable, users can still regain access to the private keys associated with that wallet, as long as they have the recovery phrase. In theory, and generally in practice, this is more secure than keeping private keys on only one device, which as James Howells discovered, may lead to an unrecoverable loss. However, if the recovery passphrase falls into the wrong hands, whoever obtains it may be able to use that to gain access to all the private keys associated with that wallet.

Coinomi wallet, but he was not able to prove that this plain text spellcheck flaw was responsible.[38]

[a] Legal Implications

The hacking and use of malware described in this section likely represents criminal violations of federal laws in the US and might also constitute crimes in the state in which the victim and/or perpetrator resides. The US Congress enacted the Computer Fraud and Abuse Act (CFAA) in 1986 and has amended it several times in the years since as technologies have evolved. One such amendment in 2008 eliminated a prior requirement that the defendant's action must result in a loss exceeding USD 5,000 and created a felony offence if the damage affects ten or more computers.[39] That amendment also made it a crime to conspire to commit a computer hacking offence.

Prosecutors may also charge a defendant for wire fraud or money laundering based on similar conduct to that which is prohibited by the CFAA.[40] The elements of a violation of 18 U.S.C. § 1030(a)(4) are (1) knowingly accessing a protected computer without or in excess of authorization; (2) with the intent to defraud; (3) the access furthered the intended fraud; and (4) the defendant obtained anything of value. A protected computer is any computer engaged in 'interstate commerce'. This has been read quite broadly by courts to include essentially all computers that touch the Internet.[41]

The US Stored Communications Act is similar to the CFAA except it is focused on stored electronic communications and data, including email, text messages, social media communications and data in the cloud.[42] Various states in the US have also enacted statutes that criminalize the unauthorized accessing of data from another's computer.

In the UK, the hacking and use of malware described in this section are also crimes. The Computer Misuse Act (CMA) (1990) is the primary UK legislation addressing hacking and malware offences. Prosecutors have jurisdiction if there is 'at least one significant link with' England or Wales.[43] There were only forty-seven

38. Coinomi fixed the vulnerability and contested the researcher's findings and whether it was responsible for his losses.
39. *See* https://www.justice.gov/sites/default/files/criminal-ccips/legacy/2015/01/14/ccmanual.pdf (accessed 6 Feb. 2020).
40. *Ibid.*, at 26–27.
41. *See, Continental Group, Inc. v. KW Property Management.*, LLC, 622 F. Supp. 2d 1357 (S.D. Fla. 2009) (noting a split of authority but holding '[a] connection to the internet is "affecting interstate commerce or communication"'). Citing 18 U.S.C. § 1030(e)(2)(B).
42. *See* 18 U.S.C. §§ 2701, et seq., which lays out the elements and potential punishments of this offence. *See also Ehling v. Monmouth-Ocean Hospital Service Corp.*, No. 2:11-cv-3305 (WMJ) (D.N.J. 20 Aug. 2013), which held that the Stored Communications Act applies to social media including a Facebook wall post that had been set to 'private'.
43. https://www.cps.gov.uk/legal-guidance/cybercrime-prosecution-guidance (accessed 6 Feb. 2020).

convictions under this act in 2017, a period in which law firm RPC estimated there were 1.7 million cyber-related crimes.[44]

The violations described in this subsection not only subject perpetrators to criminal prosecution but also may support civil suits by victims. For example, the CFAA provides for civil remedies for private litigants. As long as a victim suffers at least USD 5,000 in loss, a violator can be ordered to pay a victim compensatory, injunctive or other equitable damages.[45]

[b] Policy Considerations

In many jurisdictions, existing laws that criminalize the unauthorized access of digital data, coupled with civil legal remedies, provide a workable framework to legally protect blockchain end users. For example, if a bad actor steals cryptocurrency through the unauthorized access of an owner's digital data, existing laws empower courts to jail and fine the perpetrators. The victim may also be able to successfully sue the perpetrators for a return of their digital data, or its equivalent value. This is not to suggest that these remedies are always, or even often, successful. Hackers can exploit information security vulnerabilities and access systems from across the globe, including from jurisdictions unlikely to extradite or recognize the criminal or civil court findings of the jurisdiction in which the victim resides. Additionally, perpetrators who steal cryptocurrencies or digital assets using these illegal methods may be sophisticated enough to anonymize those assets or store them in jurisdictions unlikely to honour seizure orders or civil judgments.

Thus, the primary policy concern posed by hackers is not the sufficiency of legal remedies, but rather the practical limitations inherent in applying those remedies. Or said another way, a conviction in absentia or civil judgment that would not be honoured can have some impact, but is unlikely to be a strong deterrent or offer satisfying redress for victims. To better protect owners of digital assets, policymakers may be best served promoting international treaties and cooperation agreements, rather than drafting new internally focused legislation. However, in jurisdictions that lack significant resources to detect, track, and identify the individuals behind unauthorized intrusions, policymakers should also consider investing in training and technology supporting the investigative resources of the law enforcement and regulatory agencies with primary responsibility of protecting their citizens' electronic data.

[4] Compromised Keys: Digital Assets Are Only as Secure as the Keys That Control Them

There is no evidence that the major digital asset blockchains themselves, for example Bitcoin and Ethereum, have ever suffered an information security failure. The process

44. https://www.itpro.co.uk/it-legislation/28174/what-is-the-computer-misuse-act (accessed 6 Feb. 2020).
45. 18 U.S.C. § 1030(g).

for ensuring that only valid transactions are confirmed as outlined in Chapter 1 has protected against that. But vulnerabilities in the process of generating private-public key pairs have allowed people to essentially guess the private keys associated with a large volume of public addresses. The result likely is not surprising. If someone can guess the private key associated with an address, they will do so, and quickly transfer away any digital assets to a new address controlled by the thief.

The Bitcoin protocol makes it easy to generate public key addresses with a user-specified password or passphrase. This method of creating a private-public key pair is known as a 'brain wallet'. There are numerous websites that generate private-public key pairs using a word or phrase supplied by the user. The encryption algorithm for Bitcoin operates such that using a specific word or phrase always generates the same key pair. Thus, users of a brain wallet do not need to save electronic or hard copies of a private key to maintain control of their digital assets. They simply need to remember the password or phrase used to initially generate the key pair, to be able to regenerate the identical key pair including the private key.

This protects against the loss of an irreplaceable private key, but comes with some significant risk. Security researcher Ryan Castellucci revealed in July 2015 ahead of that year's DEFCON hackers conference that bitcoin brain wallets were vulnerable to what can be described as a guessing attack. He estimated that within a single day a botnet[46] could 'check every possible eight character ASCII password and [combination of five common english words] against every Bitcoin address that has ever received funds'.[47] White-hat hackers typically try to reveal vulnerabilities privately, to allow a fix to be implemented before alerting the public at large, and to avoid identifying unpatched vulnerabilities that can still be exploited by bad actors. However, Castellucci revealed this brain wallet vulnerability even though there is no way to fix the vulnerability posed by brain wallets generated with guessable roots. Extremely fast guessing engines will find any such public addresses, determine if it has assets, and then drain it. So Castellucci publicized the vulnerability to convince people to simply stop using brain wallets. Castellucci said that 'the usual bitcoin private key is long enough that no one is going to guess it before the sun burns out … But if they just have to guess your passphrase, they're going to do it, because people are terrible random number generators'.[48] Marie Vasek, a computer scientist, later quantified the losses suffered by brain wallet users. As of 2017, a total of 98% of identified brain wallets containing a collective 2,846 bitcoins had been drained at least once due to insufficient brain wallet password complexity.[49]

46. A botnet is a network of computers infected by malware and under the control of an individual or group. A malicious user can surreptitiously use the computing power of the infected computers within the botnet to carry out large-scale and computationally intense attacks or processes.
47. https://www.defcon.org/html/defcon-23/dc-23-speakers.html#Castellucci (accessed 6 Feb. 2020).
48. https://www.wired.com/2015/07/brainflayer-password-cracker-steals-bitcoins-brain/ (accessed 6 Feb. 2020).
49. Vasek, M., *Measuring Bitcoin-Based Cybercrime* 68 (University of Tulsa Graduate School, 2017), available at: https://tylermoore.ens.utulsa.edu/thesis/vasek.pdf (accessed 6 Feb. 2020).

Ethereum key pairs are also vulnerable to automated private key guessing, but due to a different root cause.[50] Adrian Bednarek, a security analyst and researcher, designed a methodology to identify weak or guessable private keys for Ethereum addresses and found more than seven hundred vulnerable wallets. The same address was used to drain at least twelve of those weakly protected wallets of more than 4,000 ETH. As of April 2019, the ETH had not moved since being sent to that address. Bednarek estimates that the likelihood of someone randomly picking the same private key is like finding a grain of sand on a beach, throwing it back, then having a friend find that identical grain of sand out of an impossibly large number of beaches. But if the key generation process breaks down, it becomes computationally trivial to guess the private key. The research was not able to isolate whether the vulnerabilities were due to a weakness in wallet software, a hardware device involved in generating random numbers, or some other flaw.

Particularly for non-brain wallet related vulnerabilities, it is unclear how someone with a weak private key could have known in advance of the vulnerability. This appears to be a rare problem, as the 700 keys that Bednarek identified represent an insignificant percentage of the total number of Ethereum private keys. But even if the occurrence is rare, having a very difficult to detect vulnerability that could result in 100% loss presents a difficult information security challenge.

[a] Legal Implications

Those who successfully guess private keys and then drain the associated wallets of value commit theft. In Texas, it is an offence to unlawfully appropriate property with the intent to deprive the owner of the property.[51] It is quite clear that someone who takes digital assets they know belongs to someone else commits a crime. Most jurisdictions provide a legal framework for pursuing claims of theft through criminal prosecution, and the victim may also have a claim through civil litigation. Furthermore, it is possible that victims of theft may have a civil claim against their wallet software provider if the victim can prove that a flaw in that software leads to the loss.

[b] Policy Implications

It is not clear that new or updated legislation is needed to address losses caused by insufficiently secure private keys. Existing laws give prosecutors and victims methods to pursue claims related to theft. Additionally, new legislation may not help because as previously discussed, having good local legal remedies does not typically lead to a

50. Ethereum used to be more vulnerable to brain wallet exploits before a protocol update. An early Ethereum developer, James Levy, received a 40,000 ETH endowment from the Ethereum Foundation for his development work. He was an experienced blockchain developer, but even he was vulnerable to personal information security failures. Levy stored the tokens from the endowment in a brain wallet generated by a weak password, and someone guessed the private key and stole his ETH. https://medium.com/taptrust/frozen-the-story-of-the-largest-wallet-burglary-in-ethereums-history-a-massive-mystery-and-a-1b0a81f3ee88 (accessed 6 Feb. 2020).
51. Texas Penal Code, Chapter 7, section 31.03.

return of lost digital assets. The perpetrator is often unknown and could reside outside that locality's effective jurisdiction.

If we assume that remediation after a theft is extremely difficult given the technologies in use, then the policy focus should again be on prevention. To date, most countries have not attempted through legislation or regulation to mandate specific security features in wallets or other blockchain-related software. Many blockchains are essentially software projects created by entrepreneurs and developers. There is a significant risk of creating bad policy or unintended consequences if individual governments dictate blockchain-related software design elements, particularly for projects that span international jurisdictions. However, to the extent that blockchains seek to have recognized status within regulatory frameworks, it is reasonable to expect that the developers will provide a minimal level of security protection against weak private keys, or at least offer users advance notice of the risks.

[5] Kidnapping Seeking Digital Assets: The Intersection of Physical and Information Security

There have been several widely reported kidnappings of people known to have significant holdings in digital assets. In these cases, digital information security risks are compounded by security risks in the physical world. The financial motive is clear. With digital assets, an individual or group can identify one target who possesses portable information, i.e. private keys, worth millions of dollars or more that can be converted instantly and nearly anonymously into easily transferrable value. And potential victims may unwittingly identify themselves to criminals. Prominent Bitcoin early adopters and advocates are often active on social media. It is possible for criminals to use Facebook, Instagram, Twitter, Reddit, and YouTube to identify people who bought or mined bitcoin in the early years following its introduction when bitcoin was significantly less expensive and mining rewards were larger. These same Bitcoin social media personalities may also volunteer information about the scope of their holdings, which are often substantial due to the significant rise in the price of Bitcoin since its launch. Criminals can also use these social media sites to learn when and where prominent Bitcoin personalities are travelling, including internationally. There is enough value at stake to motivate criminals to invest a significant amount of time and resources to plan crimes against those wealthy early adopters or industry advocates. Effectively preventing such attacks is more complicated.

Two examples of kidnappings highlight the risks. In New York on 4 November 2017, Louis Meza planned and executed the kidnapping of an associate with the specific purpose of stealing that associate's ETH. After Meza dined with his victim at a Ruby Tuesday's restaurant in Times Square, his victim planned to take a train home. Meza directed him instead to a minivan that Meza claimed was an Uber that he had hired to drive the victim. The minivan was not an Uber. It was driven by one of Meza's co-conspirators, and concealed another co-conspirator hidden in the back of the vehicle. The victim entered the van, and during the drive, the man in the back of the vehicle emerged from his hiding place and pointed what appeared to be a firearm at the victim. The armed man made the victim give up his wallet, keys, and mobile phone. They also made the victim reveal the location of a twenty-four-word passphrase to access his Ledger Nano S digital currency hardware wallet.

The co-conspirators then gave Meza the victim's keys. Meza let himself into the victim's apartment, while the co-conspirators drove the victim around for two hours, held against his will. Meza stole the victim's hardware wallet from his apartment. His victim eventually escaped into a deli, but by then Meza had used the passphrase and wallet to transfer what was then USD 1.8 million worth of ETH from the victim's wallet to an address that Meza controlled.

Meza was caught due to a couple of fairly basic mistakes. The first occurred in the physical world when Meza apparently failed to notice the surveillance cameras in his victim's apartment building. Meza did not try to conceal his identity or avoid being recorded entering and leaving the victim's apartment on the night in question. According to some reporting, Meza also was heard shortly thereafter bragging about having become a player in the cryptocurrency market.[52] The second error that lead to his arrest was digital. Meza transferred his victim's ETH into an address that Meza had at a US-based cryptocurrency exchange.[53] The police traced the transactions from the victim's address to an address associated with the exchange, contacted the exchange, and the exchange identified Meza as the account holder who received the assets from the victim's address.

Meza was indicted just over a month after his crime by the New York Attorney's Manhattan office.[54] By then Meza had already converted the ETH into Bitcoin and at least one altcoin. Prosecutors were able to seize the digital assets because Meza had stored them at a US cryptocurrency exchange that responded to legal service by the prosecutors.[55] The seized assets were 84 bitcoins and 269,000 SALT lending tokens, which as of 1 January 2020 have a combined value of approximately USD 618,000.[56]

Approximately six weeks after the kidnapping in New York, another kidnapping to obtain digital assets occurred on the other side of the planet. On 26 December 2017, Pavel Lerner, an Analytics Manager for the digital asset exchange EXMO, was abducted in Kyiv, Ukraine. At the time, Lerner was a 40-year-old Russian citizen with start-up businesses in Ukraine, in addition to his work with the UK-based EXMO. Lerner was kidnapped by as many as six men who obscured their identities with dark clothes and balaclavas.

52. https://www.newsbtc.com/2018/02/02/hightech-kidnapping-botched-old-fashioned-stupidity/ (accessed 6 Feb. 2020).
53. https://fortune.com/2018/02/01/bitcoin-kidnapping-cryptocurrenccy/ (accessed 6 Feb. 2020).
54. https://www.manhattanda.org/da-vance-man-indicted-stealing-18-million-cryptocurrency/ (accessed 6 Feb. 2020).
55. https://fortune.com/2018/02/01/bitcoin-kidnapping-cryptocurrenccy/ (accessed 6 Feb. 2020).
56. Historical and current digital asset prices obtained from https://coinmarketcap.com/ (accessed 6 Feb. 2020). Meza stole ETH worth USD 1.8 million, but since then the value of ETH has fallen by 50%. The recovered assets are worth more than 66% of the stolen ETH if all the assets are measured in prices as of 1 Jan. 2020. This is an unusually large recovery of stolen digital assets.

It was initially unclear why Lerner was abducted.[57] At the time, EXMO had more than 900,000 client accounts and was quick to push back against reporting that Lerner had access to EXMO client funds.[58] EXMO expressed concern for Lerner's safety and claimed to have undertaken efforts to locate him.[59] But EXMO also emphasized that the 'nature of Pavel's job at EXMO doesn't assume access either to storages or any personal data of users. All user funds are absolutely safe'.[60] Lerner had described himself as EXMO's Managing Director on his Facebook page. Reporting in the Telegraph, while Lerner was still a captive, described him as EXMO's chief executive. It is possible that Lerner's abductors thought Lerner could pay a ransom that included digital assets belonging to EXMO's clients. Lerner later said that his abductors initially requested 10,000 BTC as ransom, indicating either a lack of experience with Bitcoin or a belief that to ensure Lerner's safety, his colleagues could deliver what was then approximately USD 150 million worth of Bitcoin on short notice.[61] After being held for approximately three days, Lerner eventually paid a ransom of 102 bitcoins, which at the time was worth about USD 1.5 million, and he was then freed.

Approximately eighteen months after his release, in what has been described as his first interview following his abduction, in July 2019 Lerner said that his attackers had not yet been identified or caught.[62] He did not expect that they ever would be. As part of the Ukrainian police investigation, officers showed Lerner postings from dark websites that offered to pay for the identity of digital asset millionaires. Based on that list and his discussion with Ukrainian police, Lerner was identified on a list of more than twenty names from one of these posts, and he was not the first on the list to be kidnapped for ransom. This illustrates a significant tension for people actively pursuing projects associated with digital assets. Their work requires them to be in the public eye as a face of their project, provide biographical information to establish their bona fides, and offer details about their experience in the industry. But early involvement with digital assets, such as Bitcoin, may also identify them as someone likely to have significant holdings in those assets. The same publicity that is necessary for entrepreneurs and technologists to promote their businesses also makes them more vulnerable to being targeted.

In his July 2019 interview, approximately eighteen months after his release from captivity, Lerner offered some advice about dealing with the threat of kidnapping.[63] 'Anyone can be abducted and robbed. It's just a question of price and time. Your objective is to make it clear to all criminals: it's easier to rob twenty shops and drive

57. https://bitcoinist.com/bitcoin-rocked-exmos-pavel-lerner-kidnapped-kiev-update-ransom-paid/ (accessed 6 Feb. 2020).
58. https://www.dw.com/en/russias-bitcoin-expert-pavel-lerner-freed-after-kidnapping/a-41975644 (accessed 6 Feb. 2020).
59. https://exmo.me/en/news_view?id=2031&year=2017&month=12 (accessed 6 Feb. 2020).
60. https://www.telegraph.co.uk/technology/2017/12/28/bitcoin-exchange-chief-executive-kidnapped-leaves-work/ (accessed 6 Feb. 2020).
61. https://bitcoinist.com/exmo-crypto-analyst-pavel-lerner-on-his-kidnapping-and-life-afterwards/ translated from Russian https://forklog.com/pervoe-intervyu-posle-pohishheniya-pavel-lerner-o-bezopasnosti-i-novoj-rabote/ (both accessed 6 Feb. 2020).
62. *Ibid.*
63. *Ibid.*

away on a fire truck than to abduct you.'[64] He also recommended personal security devices such as a locator beacon in a ring that can automatically transmit a distress signal and your location. Lastly, he recommended spending money on qualified attorneys who in his telling can help resolve problems with criminals and governmental authorities, alike.

[a] Legal Implications of Kidnapping for Ransom

There are certain legal issues associated with the rise of targeted kidnappings seeking digital assets. However, there is also a well-developed body of law to address this crime. In most countries, kidnapping for ransom is already a criminal violation. It does not appear that new legislation is required to prohibit this conduct.

There is less uniformity in laws relating to how victims and their families try to resolve kidnappings. Several countries, including Venezuela, Colombia, and Italy, have banned ransom payments entirely.[65] Regardless of where in the world a US citizen is kidnapped, the US Federal Bureau of Investigation has jurisdiction to investigate.[66] Both the US and UK official policy is to discourage ransom payments, for fear of encouraging more kidnappings.[67] But reporting on the topic indicates that '97 percent of kidnappings handled by professional negotiators are successfully resolved through the payment of ransom.' The remaining small percentage of victims are either rescued or killed. Kidnapping has been so common that there is an established international kidnapping and ransom insurance practice, which has been offering policies since the 1930s.[68]

The recovery of the victim's assets from Meza poses another unsettled legal issue. Meza had converted some of the victim's ETH to SALT tokens, whose value increased dramatically, but briefly, after Meza kidnapped his victim. The price of SALT went from USD 2.53 on 4 November 2017 to USD 17.68 on 29 December 2017 following Meza's arrest, before falling to a trading price of USD 0.0472 in January 2020. The price of BTC has not been as volatile as the less used SALT, but has changed from approximately USD 7,250 on 4 November 2017 to a high close to USD 20,000, followed by lows below USD 3,500. The value of what Meza stole has swung from USD 1.8 million on the day of the kidnapping to more than USD 6 million at peak values, to less than USD 650,000 in January 2020. If the assets were to be returned on the day of their peak value, it is unclear if Meza's victim could recover the value on the day of the theft, the value of his ETH as of the day of recovery, or the entire amount, even though it was worth much more than the assets Meza stole. If the victim is entitled to something less than the total recovered from Meza, it is also unclear who should receive the

64. *Ibid.*
65. Vannini, M., Detotto, C. & Mccannon, B., *Ransom Kidnapping* (2015) In: Backhaus, J. (eds) Encyclopedia of Law and Economics, Springer NY.
66. https://www.fbi.gov/news/stories/how-the-fbi-responds-to-international-kidnappings-050119 (accessed 6 Feb. 2020).
67. https://www.theguardian.com/news/2019/jan/25/business-of-kidnapping-inside-the-secret-world-of-hostage-negotiation-ransom-insurance (accessed 6 Feb. 2020).
68. *Ibid.*

remainder. It would be plainly unjust and counterproductive to allow Meza or any other criminal to keep the difference and thereby profit from their crime because of asset price fluctuations.

[b] Policy Implications

It is not clear who is most qualified to offer policy suggestions on how to resolve the tension between governments' desire to forbid or discourage the payment of ransom to deter kidnappings and the desire of victims and their families to have broad options to respond, including the payment of ransoms, to maximize the likelihood that the kidnapped victim will be safely returned.

As to the important, but ideally not life and death, secondary issue of when and how to liquidate digital currencies recovered from criminals, including kidnappers, there are some policy best practices. The decision of when to sell seized digital assets can have a dramatic, but unpredictable, impact on the amount of victim recovery. Most courts likely are not optimized to successfully predict market movements in the price of digital assets, and thus should not be made responsible for trying to time liquidations to maximize victim recoveries. Instead, the decision to convert likely should be made based on objectively measurable events unrelated to digital asset prices.

For example, a rule that seized or recovered digital assets be converted to fiat currency upon a guilty plea being entered or a civil judgment being recorded may be workable. So too would be a rule that sought to return assets in the form in which they were taken, such that if the perpetrator stole or received ETH as ransom, and still held the assets as ETH, then ETH could be returned to the victim. If there has been no conversion into different assets, but the value of the assets at the time of return has dropped during the time they were improperly held by the perpetrator, there is a strong argument that the victim's recovery should be limited to return of the assets. The victim may have a civil claim against the perpetrator if he can produce convincing evidence that the victim would have liquidated or converted the assets and avoided the losses if not for the perpetrator's unlawful acquisition of his or her assets. But without such additional evidence, it does not seem appropriate to hold the perpetrator responsible for gyrations that occur in a digital asset market contemporaneous to his or her commission of a crime.

Complexities multiply, however, if the recovery involves multiple victims, multiple types of assets stolen, if the perpetrator converts assets, as Meza did, or if the perpetrator uses or spends assets. In each of those situations, a pro rata distribution based on the average daily value of the assets over time may be the fairest way to proceed. Each claim would be based on the type and amount of asset taken by theft or ransom, converted to its average daily value from the time of loss to the date of court-ordered return. Then the total assets recovered can be split pro rata among claimants, with each claimant's portion calculated based on the average daily value of what they lost. This system may adequately address ensuring victims are treated fairly and violators are held responsible for the losses they caused, regardless of whether the assets appreciated or depreciated along the way.

[6] SIM Swapping: Exploiting Vulnerabilities in Digital Identities

Criminals have increasingly been exploiting a vulnerability built into much of our digital lives – the use of phone numbers as identifiers and password recovery tools. The practice of taking control of a victim's mobile phone number, known as SIM swapping, takes direct aim at individuals' digital identities and has been used to steal at least tens of millions of dollars in cryptocurrency.[69] For most people in the US and Europe, tech companies interact with their customers in part using the customers' phone numbers, as identifiers, password recovery contacts, or through two-factor authorization[70] ('2FA'). This provides not only a great deal of convenience but also a vulnerable attack vector that criminals have actively been exploiting for the last several years. The use of SIM swapping to target digital asset owners has been well documented in the US, and SIM swapping is also a problem in Europe.[71]

The process is surprisingly simple and gained popularity among criminals in a uniquely digital way. Young people using the encrypted messaging application Discord began discussing how to take over social media accounts that could then be sold for difficult to trace digital assets. Social media handles indicating that someone was among the first users of a particular platform and thus able to secure a particularly desirable unique identifier, sometimes known as 'OG' social media handles, such as 'A' or '@evil', began selling for significant sums of money.[72] For example, hackers claimed the Instagram handle '@t' sold for USD 40,000 in bitcoins. Erin West, a prosecutor in Santa Clara, California, who has successfully prosecuted SIM swapping cases, believes that these social media handle bandits may have inadvertently stumbled on cryptocurrency belonging to one of their SIM swap victims and then word spread that digital assets were a more lucrative goal to pursue than social media handles.[73] This lead to a rash of SIM swap crimes specifically targeting digital assets and the people who own them.

To accomplish a SIM swap, the criminal must gain access to a user's mobile phone identity, which is stored on a SIM card.[74] Criminals can get a user's SIM card transferred to a phone they control by impersonating the true owner of the card, a

69. https://hackernoon.com/sim-jacking-attacks-are-on-the-rise-for-crypto-holders-829899dab2f8, https://nypost.com/2019/04/13/hackers-are-stealing-millions-in-bitcoin-and-living-like-big-shots/ (accessed 6 Feb. 2020).
70. Two-factor authorization is a process through which a company will text a multi-digit code to a user at the phone number on file, to confirm that the individual requesting service is the owner of the account. As long as the customers actually control their phone, this is more secure than allowing users access with a password alone.
71. https://elpais.com/elpais/2019/06/04/inenglish/1559634688_625364.html (accessed 6 Feb. 2020).
72. Website www.ogusers.com (accessed 6 Feb. 2020) is a popular site for buying and selling social media handles, and users of the site have discussed SIM swapping as a main tool for obtaining valuable handles, *see also* https://www.vice.com/en_us/article/vbqax3/hackers-sim-swapping-steal-phone-numbers-instagram-bitcoin (accessed 6 Feb. 2020).
73. https://nypost.com/2019/04/13/hackers-are-stealing-millions-in-bitcoin-and-living-like-big-shots/ (accessed 6 Feb. 2020).
74. SIM card stands for subscriber identification module and is a physical piece of hardware that typically contains the user's unique identification number, phone number, and other user data, *see* https://www.lifewire.com/what-are-sim-cards-577532 (accessed 6 Feb. 2020).

process known as social engineering. To do this, the criminals may search social media and other sites to identify biographical information about their intended victim.[75] They can also search databases of stolen personally identifiable information available on the dark web to identify address, date of birth, phone number, and their intended victim's social security number. Using this information, the SIM swapper contacts the victim's phone company customer service or visits a retail store, claims to be the victim, and says that his or her SIM card has been lost or damaged. Then they get the customer service employee to link the phone number to a new SIM card that the criminal possesses. Once this is done, the criminal controls the victim's phone number. Calls or texts to the victim will instead be routed to the criminal's phone.

In addition to social engineering, which depends on effective deception, SIM swappers also target corrupt or corruptible telephone company employees. SIM swappers may bribe these employees, or the employees may do SIM swaps on their own. For example, in April 2019, the US Department of Justice indicted two former AT&T contract employees and one former Verizon employee for their role in SIM swapping that lead to the theft of cryptocurrency.[76] One employee allegedly assisted with twelve SIM swaps in exchange for less than USD 600 and another employee allegedly received USD 3,500 for assisting in SIM swaps. Another T-Mobile employee told a reporter that a would-be SIM swapper found him using Instagram and offered him USD 100 per target.

Regardless of how they gain control of the SIM card, once criminals control a victim's phone, they can quickly take over that victim's digital life. Using the stolen phone number, the criminal can reset the victim's email passwords, because password reset links often can be directed via text message to the victim's phone number. Then, with control of the victim's email address and phone, the SIM swapper can begin resetting passwords and access methods at a variety of websites, including cryptocurrency exchanges to gain control and transfer out the victim's digital assets.

Two such criminals who were successful at turning unauthorized phone access into millions of dollars in stolen digital assets were 20-year-old Joel Ortiz and 19-year-old Xzavyer Narvaez. Joel Ortiz was a high school valedictorian and Boston College student who lived with his mom. He was also a successful thief who used SIM swapping to steal millions of dollars in digital assets from his victims. One such victim was Mitch Liu, a Silicon Valley tech company executive. Ortiz SIM swapped Liu's cell phone and used the control of Liu's phone number to reset the passwords to Liu's email accounts and gain access to his email. Ortiz used that access to reset the passwords in Liu's cryptocurrency exchange accounts and steal USD 10,000 worth of digital assets from those accounts. He also tried to victimize Liu's friends by posing as Liu and sending text messages to Liu's contacts, asking them to send him digital assets as a temporary loan.

Even though the USD 10,000 stolen from Liu did not represent a large monetary loss, the Regional Enforcement Allied Computer Team (REACT), Santa Clara County,

75. https://www.digitaltrends.com/mobile/sim-swap-fraud-explained/ (accessed 6 Feb. 2020).
76. https://www.vice.com/en_us/article/d3n3am/att-and-verizon-employees-charged-sim-swapping-criminal-ring (accessed 6 Feb. 2020).

California, began investigating. Phone companies have the ability to identify the phone that is using a specific SIM card on their network. The investigators subpoenaed AT&T to obtain cell phone tower information for the phone used to log in to Liu's accounts and traced it to the Boston area.[77] Investigators also got from AT&T the IMEI[78] (International Mobile Equipment Identity) number associated with the phone being used by the SIM swapper to pose as Liu. The investigators then contacted Google and Apple and asked for any records associated with accounts accessed using that same IMEI number.

In reviewing those records from Google and Apple, the investigators identified an email address linked to Joel Ortiz, who lived in the Boston area. That location was consistent with the cell tower access information the investigators had already developed from AT&T. The investigators then obtained the contents of Ortiz's email account, which revealed a lot of information about him and his crimes. Ortiz's emails included a picture of him holding his Massachusetts photo id, which he had provided to a bank to verify his identity. With computer crimes, it can sometimes be difficult to conclusively attribute actions taken on the Internet to specific individuals in the real world.[79] In this investigation, the information found in Ortiz's email account helped demonstrate that he controlled and used that email account. REACT investigators also started tracking him on social media, where he bragged about high priced vacations in Las Vegas, large amounts of money spent at Los Angeles nightclubs, and staying at high-priced Airbnb mansions in Los Angeles. Investigators identified that Ortiz stole more than USD 5 million in cryptocurrency through SIM swaps from more than twenty victims.

When Ortiz mentioned on social media his intent to attend an EDM festival in Europe, the REACT team moved in. They obtained an arrest warrant and arrested Ortiz at the Los Angeles International Airport where he was dressed head to toe in Gucci and on his way out of the country. Ortiz later pleaded guilty, and he was sentenced to ten years in prison for his crimes.

The REACT team did not stop there. Through their investigation of Ortiz, the REACT investigators also identified an accomplice, 19-year-old Xzavyer Narvaez. The investigators discovered that a cell phone used by Ortiz had logged into an email account belonging to Narvaez.[80] With that clue, investigators traced a series of SIM swap crimes to an IMEI number that pinged a cell phone tower in Tracy, California,

---

77. https://www.sanjoseinside.com/2019/04/25/bitcoin-bandit-sentenced-to-a-decade-behind-bars-in-nations-first-sim-swap-conviction/ (accessed 6 Feb. 2020).
78. IMEI is a 15 or 17 digit code that uniquely identifies mobile phone devices, available at: https://whatis.techtarget.com/definition/IMEI-International-Mobile-Equipment-Identity (accessed 6 Feb. 2020). When phones access a network through cell towers, the IMEI number of the device is recorded by the phone company.
79. The U.S. Department of Justice has acknowledged the challenges intrinsic in attributing actions taken using a computer to the individual who took those actions. Prosecutors are advised to rely on circumstantial evidence of identity to overcome questions of attribution, *see* U.S. Department of Justice, *Searching and Seizing Computers and Obtaining Electronic Evidence in Criminal Investigations* 203 (Computer Crime and Intellectual Property Section, Criminal Division 2009).
80. https://krebsonsecurity.com/2018/08/alleged-sim-swapper-arrested-in-california/#more-44746 (accessed 6 Feb. 2020).

within a mile of where Narvaez resided. Further research revealed a California Department of Motor Vehicles report of a traffic stop on Narvaez, in which he had been driving a USD 200,000 McLaren sports car. Investigators contacted the seller of the McLaren, who had sold the car to a buyer other than Narvaez. However, the seller told them that the buyer had paid partially in bitcoin, and partially by trading in an Audi R8 sports car that was registered to Narvaez. When investigators traced the bitcoin used to buy the McLaren, it led back to the digital asset exchange Bittrex. That exchange confirmed that the source of the bitcoins used to pay for the McLaren was an account belonging to Narvaez and that more than 157 bitcoins flowed through that one account between March and June 2018. The REACT team arrested Narvaez in mid-August 2018, approximately one month after Ortiz. Based only on the 157 bitcoins associated with one account at a digital asset exchange, investigators alleged that Narvaez stole more than USD 1 million in cryptocurrency from multiple victims through SIM swaps.

Although these thefts occurred in 2018, and there has been significant publicity about the SIM swap vulnerability, SIM swap driven thefts have continued. In June 2019, more than fifteen individuals prominent in the US digital asset community reported being SIM swapped, many of them T-Mobile and AT&T customers.[81] One of those victims acknowledged having USD 100,000 stolen from his Coinbase digital asset exchange account. The actual amount of losses may be significantly higher, as people prominent in the digital asset community may be reluctant to reveal that they failed to employ adequate information security practices to protect themselves.

In addition to criminal liability, SIM swapping may give victims civil claims they can bring against the perpetrators, and also potentially against the phone companies that swapped their SIM card without permission. In 2018, a California resident, Michael Terpin, was the victim of a SIM swap later alleged to have been committed by Nicholas Truglia.[82] Terpin filed suit against Truglia in California Superior Court alleging that Truglia had stolen millions of dollars in altcoins from him through a SIM swap. After committing this theft, Truglia purportedly bragged to his friends about it, saying that 'today my life changed forever' and offering to hire prostitutes and take his friends to the NFL Super Bowl.[83] Truglia was later arrested. Terpin's complaint against Truglia included an affidavit from one of Truglia's former friends that included allegations of Truglia spending his ill-gotten gains on private jet travel, Rolex luxury watches, and keeping large amounts of money in fiat currency to show his friends.[84] In May 2019, the Superior Court awarded Terpin USD 75.8 million in compensatory and punitive damages against Truglia.

Terpin also filed a civil suit against his mobile phone company, AT&T. In that suit, Terpin alleged that he had been a victim of a prior SIM swap and that the SIM swap

81. https://www.zdnet.com/article/wave-of-sim-swapping-attacks-hit-us-cryptocurrency-users/ (accessed 6 Feb. 2020).
82. https://in.reuters.com/article/us-crypto-currency-lawsuit/u-s-investor-awarded-75-million-in-cryptocurrency-crime-case-idINKCN1SG2CO (accessed 6 Feb. 2020).
83. *See Terpin v. Truglia*, Case No. 18STCV09875, CA Superior Court, County of Los Angeles, Central District (28 Dec. 2018).
84. https://mashable.com/article/sim-swap-cryptocurrency-theft-nicholas-truglia/ (accessed 6 Feb. 2020).

that caused his losses occurred even after AT&T supposedly put him on a 'high-risk and celebrity' security list to prevent future SIM swaps. As part of that extra security, AT&T told Terpin that his SIM card could not be transferred unless he came to a store in person and furnished a special password. However, Truglia was still able to perform a SIM swap and obtain control of Terpin's phone number, and thereby steal millions of dollars in digital assets from Terpin. In July 2019, the court denied AT&T's motion to dismiss the claims based on liability waivers in its customer agreement documents. The litigation has not yet been resolved as of the date of publishing this handbook.

[a] Legal Implications of SIM Swaps

Criminal and civil liability for the perpetrators of SIM swaps is not controversial. The statutes relating to computer crime referenced above in section §2.01[A][3], including the CFAA and CMA, prohibit the unauthorized accessing of electronic data, which is necessary to steal digital assets through a SIM swap. The uncertain, and therefore more interesting, legal question is the potential civil liability for service providers, such as phone companies, when a third party steals cryptocurrency as a result of an unauthorized SIM swap. As it presently stands, that issue likely turns on the facts and circumstances of each specific claim.

There does not appear to be any legislation or judicial precedent that automatically imposes liability on a phone company or access provider simply because a third party gains unauthorized access through a SIM swap. Any liability therefore likely depends on the scope of the phone company's obligations to its customer, its knowledge of the specific risk, and whether the phone company failed to take reasonable steps to prevent the harm. Phone companies also may be able to offer reasonable defences from liability. Phone companies try hard to disavow any such liability as part of their terms of service and customer agreements, which may be upheld by courts as enforceable waivers agreed to by customers. There is also an argument that it is unreasonable to hold phone companies responsible for the conduct of criminals. Phone companies likely will argue that they must have standardized processes to make the transfer of SIM cards fast and inexpensive in order to accommodate their customers' needs, and the vast majority of transfer requests are legitimate. Erecting barriers to the easy transfer of SIM cards from one device to another may protect against SIM swaps, but only by imposing additional burdens on the millions of customers who legitimately need to swap SIM cards to upgrade their phone, replace a legitimately lost or damaged phone, or change phone service while maintaining their current phone number. One alternative to the current model in which relatively low-paid customer service employees in phone banks or retail stores have primary responsibility for transferring SIM cards would be to assign the SIM card transfer function to highly trained cybersecurity or anti-fraud professionals. This would be more expensive than the current system and likely require delays on SIM card transfers.

[b] Policy Implications

There are several alternatives available for policymakers to try to address SIM swaps used to steal cryptocurrency. Legislatures can enact laws to automatically attribute liability to phone companies, or to shield those companies from liability. Either outcome will offer guidance to customers as to who bears primary responsibility for avoiding such thefts. If phone companies are known to be protected, this may encourage customers with risk exposure to find ways to decouple their digital asset access from any connection to their phone numbers, email accounts, or other sites that may be compromised following a SIM swap. Alternatively, this may create a market opportunity for a new telecommunications service provider to step forward, accept responsibility for problems should they arise, and thus attract the business of phone customers who are concerned about this vulnerability. If phone companies are deemed responsible for damages that arise from unauthorized SIM swaps, customers with risk exposure likely will not take significant steps to protect themselves, and the resulting costs from digital asset thefts will be borne by phone companies, and presumably their customers through higher bills to offset the phone companies' increased liability expenses. This would also incentivize phone companies to develop stronger processes to prevent SIM swapping. Since the phone companies participate in every SIM swap, they may be in the best position to prevent unauthorized SIM swaps. Policymakers can also attack the problem through education campaigns to encourage individuals to avoid using their phone numbers as an identifier, password recovery tool, or 2FA device.

[B] Digital Asset Exchanges and Third-Party Services: Different Roles, Different Risks

Perhaps the most popular services that store digital assets for individuals are digital asset exchanges, which offer varying levels of security, accountability and transparency. Exchanges give account holders the ability to buy and sell digital assets for fiat currency. Depending on their nation of domicile, they also offer varying levels of anonymity.[85] In addition to full-spectrum exchanges that hold digital assets and typically allow accountholders to exchange digital assets into multiple different digital assets, there are also entities that promise to issue new digital assets in exchange for investments made using fiat currencies or digital assets.[86] Third parties and entities typically promise to protect the digital assets entrusted to them, but that promise is not always kept.

85. Another third-party storage option that has begun to emerge in the last few years is a custodian, similar to custodians of more traditional financial assets, which charges a fee and offers protections such as insurance and highly developed security protocols.
86. Any discussion in this chapter of digital asset investment products will focus only on the information security issues associated with those arrangements. This chapter by design does not touch on the legal or regulatory implications of digital assets from an investment perspective.

A popular refrain among the digital asset community is 'your keys your bitcoin, not your keys not your bitcoin' or a variation thereof.[87] This reflects the reality for many digital asset owners that if they grant control of their assets to a third party, there may not be a functional mechanism for retrieving those assets when they want them. Possession and ownership are different sets of legal rights. But once an individual gives up possession of his or her digital assets, it may be impracticable to recover them, even if he or she can establish his or her legal right of ownership.

Digital asset exchanges offer a valuable service when operated correctly. But unlike typical digital asset transactions that are recorded on a blockchain for everyone to see, much of what happens within an exchange is invisible to the outside world. Many transactions within digital asset exchanges occur 'off-chain', meaning transactions are settled between internal accounts and recorded only in the exchange's internal records. If a user wants to exchange ETH for bitcoins, the exchange will debit his or her account for the ETH and credit his or her account for the bitcoins, but not process either transaction on a blockchain. Only when an account holder requests a transfer or withdrawal to an address outside of the exchange will the transaction be recorded on a blockchain. This off-chain transaction process can be more efficient for the exchange and its account holders because it does not require the delays and fees associated with blockchain transactions. The potential downside is that the transparency benefits of a public blockchain are removed and account holders often have limited or no information about what is going on within the exchange.

[1] Digital Asset Exchanges: Hacks Happen

In the approximate ten years since the Bitcoin protocol ushered in the modern era of digital assets, digital asset exchanges have become commonplace. One of the earliest and most notable digital asset exchanges was Mt. Gox. Originally founded as an exchange to let people trade 'Magic: The Gathering Online' cards, by 2010 it began trading bitcoin.[88] Shortly thereafter it was sold to a company owned by Mark Karpeles. By 2013, Mt. Gox was the world's largest bitcoin exchange and was estimated to have processed more than 70% of all bitcoin transactions worldwide.[89] Then, on 4 February 2014, CoinDesk reported that a topic thread on Bitcoin Talk discussing problems with delayed withdrawals from Mt. Gox had 3,300 posts.[90] On 7 February 2014, Mt. Gox stopped processing any bitcoin withdrawals, but claimed that the halt was temporary. On 24 February 2014, Mt. Gox went offline and stopped all transactions. Shortly thereafter it filed for bankruptcy protection in Japan, and then in the US.

---

87. https://www.youtube.com/watch?v=dnC5mFaIW3Q (accessed 6 Feb. 2020).
88. Mt. Gox was an acronym for Magic The Gathering Online Exchange (M T G O X). *See* Kaser, R., *How a Card Trading Site Became the Center of a Bitcoin Embezzlement Scandal* (The Next Web Insider, 11 Jul. 2017), available at: https://thenextweb.com/insider/2017/07/11/card-trading-site-became-center-bitcoin-embezzlement-scandal/ (accessed 6 Feb. 2020).
89. Norry, A., *The History of the Mt. Gox Hack: Bitcoin's Biggest Heist* (Blockonomi, 7 Jun. 2019), available at: https://blockonomi.com/mt-gox-hack/ (accessed 6 Feb. 2020).
90. Wong, J.I., *Poll: Are You Having Mt. Gox Withdrawal Issues* (CoinDesk, 4 Feb. 2014), available at: https://www.coindesk.com/poll-mt-gox-withdrawal-issues (accessed 6 Feb. 2020).

Investigations followed and soon thereafter the public learned that there were approximately 850,000 bitcoins missing from Mt. Gox, though 200,000 were later found by Karpeles.[91] Japanese authorities arrested Karpeles in August 2015 for fraud and embezzlement.[92] He was later charged in Japan with embezzlement, breach of trust, and manipulation of data.[93] A variety of groups and entities investigated Mt. Gox following its bankruptcy filing in an effort to understand what had happened. That research indicated that Mt. Gox may have been insolvent for several years prior to its bankruptcy filing.[94] Karpeles also later acknowledged in court to have used an automated trading script, known as Willy Bot, which is alleged to have created new accounts on Mt. Gox and traded bitcoins without using any actual money.[95] Karpeles effectively credited his accounts with money from thin air and then used those accounts to buy bitcoins from account holders looking to sell. The downside to this activity is that following the sale the account holders were told their account balance had been increased by the amount of the sale, but the exchange did not have the money to honour that promise. Some have alleged that Karpeles' bot trading activity was extensive enough to help explain an increase in the price of bitcoin from USD 200 to USD 1,200 over one month in 2013.[96] It was also alleged that Willy Bot helped Karpeles conceal Mt. Gox's insolvency.[97]

Amateur sleuths, and later the U.S. Department of Justice, alleged that Karpeles did not steal the missing bitcoins as some originally thought. The bitcoins were actually stolen from Mt. Gox by a hacker. The vulnerability at Mt. Gox allowed the thief to drain bitcoins as they were deposited. 'It means that you had a hole in the bottom of the well, and someone was just draining the money,' said Michael Gronager, CEO of digital asset analytics firm Chainalysis.[98] The theft of Mt. Gox's bitcoins was later traced to Alexander Vinnik, a Russian who was arrested in Greece in 2017 for his alleged role in operating the Russian-based cryptocurrency exchange and suspected money laundering haven, BTC-e.[99]

It is unclear when Karpeles learned of the losses. He has publicly claimed that so many bitcoins were being deposited at Mt. Gox, and so many new accounts created,

91. Wieczner, J., *Mt. Gox and the Surprising Redemption of Bitcoin's Biggest Villain* (Fortune, 19 Apr. 2018), available at: https://fortune.com/longform/bitcoin-mt-gox-hack-karpeles/ (accessed 6 Feb. 2020).
92. Pollock, D., *The Mess That Was Mt. Gox: Four Years On* (Cointelegraph, 9 Mar. 2018), available at: https://cointelegraph.com/news/the-mess-that-was-mt-gox-four-years-on (accessed 6 Feb. 2020).
93. Rizzo, P., *Mt. Gox CEO Mark Karpeles Arrested in Japan* (CoinDesk, 5 Aug. 2015), available at: https://www.coindesk.com/mt-gox-ceo-mark-karpeles-arrested-in-japan (accessed 6 Feb. 2020).
94. Wieczner, *supra* n. 91.
95. Meyer, D., *Bots Were Responsible for Bitcoin's Stratospheric Ascent, Anonymous Report Claims* (GigaOm, 26 May 2014), available at: https://gigaom.com/2014/05/26/bots-were-responsible-for-bitcoins-stratospheric-ascent-anonymous-report-claims/ (accessed 6 Feb. 2020).
96. *Ibid.*
97. Wieczner, *supra* n. 91.
98. *Ibid.*
99. *Ibid.* BTC-E is alleged to have laundered between USD 4 and USD 9 billion, *see* https://news.bitcoin.com/btc-e-operator-alexander-vinnik-terminates-his-hunger-strike/ (accessed 6 Feb. 2020).

that the losses were not noticed. Others have claimed that Karpeles knew and did not alert his account holders that Mt. Gox was undercapitalized by 600,000 bitcoins or more, allowing new depositors to be victimized.[100]

[a] Legal Implications

In March 2019, Karpeles was convicted in Japan of data manipulation for wrongfully making electronic records related to Mt. Gox, but acquitted on charges of embezzlement and breach of trust.[101] He was given a suspended sentence and has appealed his conviction. Vinnik remains jailed in Greece for his alleged BTC-e-related crimes, amidst an extradition dispute between the US, France, and Russia, although he has not been indicted for his alleged role in the theft of Mt. Gox's bitcoins.

Mt. Gox account holders are still waiting for the return of the bitcoins they had on deposit. After Karpeles found more than 200,000 bitcoins, which have appreciated with the rise in the price of bitcoin, and considering Mt. Gox's other assets, the prospects for account holders to receive a significant recovery looked promising. Unfortunately, according to Japanese bankruptcy laws, the value of each claim was measured in fiat currency and frozen at the time of insolvency in 2014, when a bitcoin was worth approximately USD 480. If this interpretation held, claimants would only receive approximately 6.4% of the current value of their lost bitcoins (per January 2020). The bankruptcy estate's current assets are significantly greater than the value of claims if those claims are valued in fiat currency as of the date of insolvency. As the majority shareholder of Mt. Gox, Karpeles would have received tens of millions of dollars at the conclusion of bankruptcy proceedings, after paying out investor claims at a fraction of their present value.[102] This is a result that even Karpeles acknowledged made little sense and would be unjust. In June 2018, the Tokyo District Court agreed to halt the bankruptcy proceeding and start a civil rehabilitation process, overseen by Tokyo attorney and appointed rehabilitation trustee, Nobuaki Kobayashi.[103] The rehabilitation trust claims process does not include the requirement that claims be valued as of the date of insolvency. The total value of the rehabilitation trust may exceed USD 1 billion, and Mt. Gox depositors may receive significant value for their claims.

100. *Ibid.*
101. Khatri, Y., *Mt. Gox's Mark Karpeles Found Guilty over Data Manipulation in Tokyo Court* (CoinDesk, 15 Mar. 2019), available at: https://www.coindesk.com/mt-goxs-mark-karpeles-found-guilty-given-2-6-year-suspended-sentence (accessed 6 Feb. 2020).
102. Wieczner, *supra* n. 91.
103. Wieczner, J., *$1 Billion Bitcoins Lost in Mt. Gox Hack to Be Returned to Victims* (Fortune, 22 Jun. 2018), available at: https://fortune.com/2018/06/22/bitcoin-price-mt-gox-trustee/ (accessed 6 Feb. 2020); Canellis, D., *Mt. Gox Prepares to Return $1B in Stolen Cryptocurrency to Victims* (The Next Web, 24 Aug. 2018), available at: https://thenextweb.com/hardfork/2018/08/24/mt-gox-cryptocurrency-claims/ (accessed 6 Feb. 2020).

[b] *Policy Implications*

Since Mt. Gox filed for bankruptcy, dozens of digital asset exchanges have announced that they too have been hacked. These hacks have caused billions of dollars in losses, based on today's prices.[104] Individual account holders of these exchanges have suffered very substantial losses. This raises a variety of policy issues.

If governments want to protect their citizens, it may be reasonable to require exchanges to carry insurance sufficient to repay investors in the event of a loss due to hacking. It may also be reasonable to require that exchanges submit to regular financial and information security audits. However, while these may be reasonable policy responses in theory, they may be very difficult to accomplish in practice. There are digital asset exchanges in many countries. Because digital asset commerce exists electronically, it is difficult to impose geographic restrictions on transactions. An exchange does not need to have a physical presence in a country to serve customers in that country. Any individual country may lack the legal authority to effectively impose information security, audit, insurance coverage or other requirements on an entity registered outside its borders. And some policymakers have raised the concern that imposing regulatory burdens on exchanges or other blockchain-based businesses just encourages the businesses to relocate to other countries.[105]

Further, even if policymakers devise a method of ensuring that their citizens only use well-protected domestically regulated exchanges, that may still not be enough to protect them. On 6 February 2014, before Mt. Gox halted withdrawals, bitcoin was trading at over USD 800.[106] On 25 February 2014, after Mt. Gox announced its insolvency, the price of bitcoin fell to USD 420. Even if a country had prevented its citizens from suffering any direct losses at Mt. Gox, the value of those citizens' bitcoins would still have declined more than 45% in a matter of weeks, because an exchange based in another country did not have adequate information security protections. This is admittedly an extreme example, and the market for Bitcoin is both more mature and more decentralized now, such that it is more resilient against exchange failures and negative news. But newer digital assets with less decentralization are still vulnerable to dramatic price swings based on hacks on exchanges. The Mt. Gox price drop highlights the difficulty any country's policymakers may have developing solutions to insulate its citizens from information security risks associated with digital assets.

For any individual citizen, it can be nearly impossible to obtain a clear picture of any exchange's information security measures. There are good reasons from a security standpoint why exchanges will not want to publicize specifics about their information security. To do so would give bad actors vital information about potential vulnerabilities that suggest potential attack vectors. However, without accurate, up-to-date information about steps an exchange has taken to avoid hacking or insider threats,

104. *A Comprehensive List of Cryptocurrency Exchange Hacks* (Selfkey Blog, 19 Oct. 2019), available at: https://selfkey.org/list-of-cryptocurrency-exchange-hacks/ (accessed 6 Feb. 2020).
105. https://www.nytimes.com/2018/06/27/business/dealbook/crypto-industry-regulation.html (accessed 6 Feb. 2020).
106. Historical Bitcoin prices obtained from www.coinmarketcap.com (accessed 6 Feb. 2020).

many would-be depositors are left with an unattractive binary choice of either blindly trusting an exchange to effectively protect their assets or to avoid all exchanges and self-custodian their assets. Given the trustless nature of digital assets, and the practical difficulty of regaining possession of digital assets when lost, even if legal ownership is undisputed, owners that store their digital assets with an exchange are in an inherently vulnerable position.[107]

[2] Reliance on Third Parties: Exit Scams Happen

In December 2018, Gerald Cotten, the Canadian co-founder and CEO of QuadrigaCX, was reported to have died in India at the age of 30 from complications associated with Crohn's disease.[108] Cotten had married Jennifer Robertson in October 2018 and then created a will on 27 November 2018, in which he made his new wife the sole executor of his estate. He travelled with Jennifer to India for a honeymoon and to open an orphanage that bore his and Jennifer's name. Shortly after arriving in India, Cotten was reported dead on 8 December 2018.

Following reports of Cotten's death, Robertson as executor of his estate claimed in court filings that Quadriga possessed CAD 190 million (USD 145 million) of investors' bitcoins and other digital assets, much of which was stored in cold wallets.[109] Quadriga customers also had approximately CAD 70 million in fiat currency deposits at the exchange. At the time, Quadriga had 363,000 registered users, and 92,000 of those had account balances in digital assets or fiat currency. However, Robertson said that Cotten had stored all the relevant digital asset wallet and bank account information on his laptop, which was encrypted and no one other than Cotten could gain access to its contents.

In the days following the announcement of Cotten's death, this story appeared to be a cautionary tale about the vulnerability of private keys. According to Robertson, due to inadequate succession planning, QuadrigaCX suffered a total loss due to a single point of failure – Cotton's death. The story also highlighted the extent to which an individual user of an exchange is vulnerable to hidden risks and information security failures caused by exchange managers or owners.

107. There has recently been a rise in so-called decentralized exchanges. For many of these, a user does not provide his or her digital assets to the exchange. Instead all exchanges are conducted on a peer-to-peer model. This is purportedly safer because users do not give up custody of their assets. However, these exchanges are only as safe as their code provides, and it is difficult for an individual user to identify coding flaws that may lead to losses before they happen.

108. Abraham, R., *A Crypto Millionaire, Loose Ends & a Dead End: A Consignment of Teddy Bears Before Gerald Cotten Died* (The Economic Times, 10 Apr. 2019), available at: https://economictimes.indiatimes.com/magazines/panache/a-crypto-millionaire-loose-ends-a-dead-end-a-consignment-of-teddy-bears-before-gerald-cotten-died/articleshow/68804401.cms (accessed 10. Feb. 2020).

109. *Quadriga Cryptocurrency Exchange Founder Filed Will 12 Days Before He Died* (South China Morning Post, 6 Feb. 2019), available at: https://www.scmp.com/tech/blockchain/article/2185120/quadriga-cryptocurrency-exchange-founder-filed-will-12-days-he-died (accessed 10 Feb. 2020).

Unable to meet its obligations or repay its customers, QuadrigaCX sought protection from its creditors in February 2019 and was assigned to bankruptcy proceedings in April 2019.[110] The Nova Scotia Supreme Court appointed Ernst & Young ('E&Y') as the Monitor to attempt to locate assets for the benefit of the estate and its creditors. More than 76,000 creditors, most of them QuadrigaCX customers, filed claims totalling more than CAD 210 million in fiat and digital assets as of June 2019. As of that date, E&Y had recovered a total of approximately CAD 33 million in digital assets and fiat currency. Cotten had told family members that he had created a 'dead man's switch' that would provide survivors with necessary passwords and information upon his death, but E&Y found no evidence of such a system.

E&Y noted that in spite of QuadrigaCX's claim to be one of the largest digital asset exchanges in Canada, it had little in the way of formal books and records or management structure. It reported that after several months of work, 'the Monitor has been unable to locate any corporate records, to the extent such records exist, other than the limited materials found on (unencrypted) electronic devices controlled by Mr Cotton' and some information provided by QuadrigaCX vendors or counterparties.[111] Further, the Monitor was unable to locate any evidence to suggest that Quadriga maintained any traditional books or accounting records since at least 2016.[112] It appears that the QuadrigaCX platform software tracked, by customer, fiat deposits, digital asset transactions, and the fees charged on those transactions, but did not aggregate that data for analysis or reporting purposes. E&Y was unable to determine whether QuadrigaCX was operating profitably, or whether anyone associated with QuadrigaCX had such information. E&Y could not locate any evidence that QuadrigaCX reconciled pooled funds or digital assets to account for all funds.

The platform did not track or log the activity of those users with full administrative privileges, including Cotten, and it was Cotten who purportedly directed the primary coder of the QuadrigaCX site not to log this activity. The Monitor identified several suspicious accounts that lacked the 'Know Your Customer' information that QuadrigaCX typically collected and stored for such accounts. Those suspicious accounts, in the names of Chris Markay, Aretwo Deetwo, and Seethree Peaohh, were credited with purported deposits of more than CAD 200 million, but the Monitor could not find any record of such deposits.[113] In what appears to be an electronic sleight of hand, those accounts that were credited with hundreds of millions of potentially fictional dollars then 'purchased' bitcoins and Ethereum from other actual QuadrigaCX account holders. In effect, the suspicious accounts received actual digital assets, and the customer accounts were told their accounts were credited with funds, but the funds may not have existed. QuadrigaCX appears to never have had the money to honour those obligations to its account holders. And to make matters worse, the customers'

110. Fifth Report of the Monitor, *In the Matter of Application by Quadriga Fintech Solutions Corp., et al, for Relief Under the Companies' Creditors Arrangement Act* 2, 3 (Supreme Court of Nova Scotia, 19 Jun. 2019).
111. *Ibid.*, at 16. Cotton had several encrypted devices that the Monitor had not been able to meaningfully access.
112. Fifth Report of the Monitor, *supra* n. 110, at 20.
113. *Ibid.*, at 35-36.

digital assets transferred to the suspicious accounts were then sent to other exchanges in accounts that Cotten appears to have controlled. It appears that Cotten bought real assets with pretend money and then moved the real assets out of QuadrigaCX into accounts at other exchanges that only Cotten controlled.

At that point, the story of QuadrigaCX was no longer about succession planning and record-keeping, and instead was about fraud and broken trust. QuadrigaCX supposedly kept only a minimal amount of digital assets in hot wallets. The bulk of QuadrigaCX customer digital assets were purportedly held in cold wallets, which in theory should be safer because they are not connected to the Internet. However, E&Y's research indicates that Quadriga sent a substantial portion of the digital assets from those cold wallets to other exchanges, much of which was then held in accounts in Cotten's name or under his control. In one of those accounts, it appears that Cotten deposited more than 21,500 bitcoins, some of which originated from Quadriga. Then USD 80 million worth of bitcoins in this account were liquidated over the course of three years. It is unclear what happened to the proceeds of those sales, but the money does not appear to have come back to QuadrigaCX. In an account at another exchange, it appears Cotten unprofitably engaged in more than 67,000 transactions in a margin account, and that exchange then liquidated a 'significant portion of the Cryptocurrency in the account to satisfy the margin shortfall'.[114] This looks like Cotten was day trading on margin the digital assets he had taken from his QuadrigaCX customers' accounts, without their knowledge or permission. He did this on another exchange, and did it very badly, suffering huge losses in the process.

In the days following the public announcement of Cotten's death and the unavailability of QuadrigaCX account holder digital assets, a rumour arose that Cotten may have faked his own death to avoid legal responsibility for what he had done or to abscond with account holder assets.[115] That rumour persisted, to the point that on 13 December 2019, a law firm representing users of QuadrigaCX sent the Royal Mounted Canadian Police (RMCP) a letter requesting that the RMCP exhume Cotton's body to confirm his identity and the cause of his death.[116]

[a] Legal Implications

Exchange customers depend on exchange managers to ensure constant access to the digital assets and fiat currency that the exchange holds on behalf of its customers. Initially, the legal issues posed by the QuadrigaCX insolvency appeared to focus on Cotten's inadequate succession planning. Customers typically do not have sufficient information to assess the quality of the exchange's procedures to ensure information

114. *Ibid.*, at 29.
115. Initial drafts of this chapter elected not to address the rumours that Cotton may not have died as claimed, out of respect for Cotton's family. However, because this theory has now led to a widely reported request made of law enforcement on behalf of investors, the author believes this issue should be included in the interest of trying to highlight all the legal issues as they are presently known.
116. https://www.millerthomson.com/wp-content/uploads/2019/12/Cover-Letter-to-RCMP-Final .pdf (accessed 10 Feb. 2020).

security and availability of funds, until it is too late. Absent a method to reverse transactions, a trusted intermediary that will absorb or prevent losses, or insurance to compensate for losses, if an exchange's private keys are lost or cannot be accessed, exchange customers can unexpectedly experience a total and irreversible loss. An injured customer can sue the exchange, but that is typically an expensive process in which success may only result in a legally perfected claim, but not in actual compensation. In the digital asset realm, as in many areas of civil law, a judgment is only as valuable as the ability to enforce it against available, traceable assets.

After E&Y began its analysis of QuadrigaCX, it became clear that the exchange failed due to a very different set of information security failures. QuadrigaCX now appears to be a form of 'exit scam', in which a trusted intermediary breaks faith, and uses the assets entrusted to it for its own purposes or steals them outright. Often an exit scam is confirmed when the counterparty disappears or shuts down a project without returning funds. Here, it appears that Cotten died before his misuse of funds was exposed or he shut down QuadrigaCX. The Monitor's report identified a series of questionable transactions, raised the possibility that QuadrigaCX had long been insolvent, and revealed that the exchange's CEO might have converted customer digital assets for his own benefit. E&Y concluded that 'there is no indication that the Users were aware that Funds were being utilized in this manner'.[117] In transferring digital assets to QuadrigaCX, customers lost the information security protections that blockchain's private key–public key infrastructure typically provides. They also lost the ability to meaningfully trace their digital assets using the blockchain's public ledger. In short, the protections provided by the blockchain that allow for trustless commerce were nullified. Customers instead trusted a counterparty without meaningful insights into that counterparty's activities and suffered losses as a result. The bankruptcy process is providing answers about what happened, but it appears unlikely to be able to return a meaningful percentage of missing assets to QuadrigaCX's customers.

[b] Policy Implications

QuadrigaCX is just one example of a problem that has recurred with some frequency in the digital asset space. There are multiple examples of exchange operators, or operators of digital asset projects or Initial Coin Offerings (ICOs), who absconded with the assets entrusted to them. This occurred with such frequency that the phenomenon popularized the term 'exit scam'. But even if QuadrigaCX's problems were the result of a failure in succession planning, as initially thought, rather than a breach of trust, investors would be left in the same position of having lost the assets they entrusted to a third party.

Most countries have laws to punish the perpetrators of what is essentially a large-scale theft. But it is less clear how best to prevent exit scams. For policymakers, exit scams represent a multilayered threat. The first and most obvious problem exit scams present is that policymakers' citizens have been cheated, with no clear process

117. Fifth Report of the Monitor, *supra* n. 110, at 34.

to recover in part or in whole. Exit scams also threaten the entire digital asset economy by shaking confidence in exchanges and intermediaries. That erosion of confidence is a threat to the successful development of markets and the broad adoption of digital assets.

One possible solution is to regulate exchanges or other entities that take custody of digital assets on behalf of customers. As discussed above in the context of the Mt. Gox failure, policymakers can impose requirements, but if entities feel like regulatory requirements are too great, they may relocate their operations from a jurisdiction with more perceived regulatory oversight to a jurisdiction that imposes fewer regulatory burdens. That prudent regulation may drive away some enterprises that prefer to operate without oversight is not a persuasive argument against regulation. But the fact that digital asset exchanges and related businesses are portable and not tied to geography presents an ongoing policymaking challenge.

Another possible solution is technology driven and relies on smart contracts rather than an intermediary. Some developers have promoted the concept of a decentralized exchange (DEX) as a way to prevent exit scams. In a DEX, individual users do not give up control of their digital assets until they actually exchange them with the ultimate counterparty. The DEX exists to bring together buyers and sellers and provide an infrastructure that offers price discovery. But the DEX never obtains control of a user's digital assets and all transfers occur in a peer-to-peer transaction. Because a DEX never holds its customer's assets, it cannot steal those assets. This may offer some protection against exit scams and information security failures. For policymakers, one downside of a DEX is that it typically does not collect Know Your Customer information or other user data that can be a crucial resource for law enforcement investigations and to prevent money laundering.

[3] Third-Party Exploits: Trust Misplaced

Although the original Bitcoin Whitepaper emphasized the benefits of pure peer-to-peer transactions, in practice, many digital asset owners rely on third parties. That reliance can take many forms, including the use of a custodian, technology provider, or by seeking to increase their digital assets through investment into blockchain developers' projects, such as ICOs. In all of these examples, the security of a user's digital assets is dependent on the effectiveness of his or her technology provider's information security. As described above, users often lack the technical skill or sufficient information to judge for themselves whether a third party's information security is reliable. And relying on the technological bona fides of the developers is not always an adequate predictor for the project's information security.

The example of the Parity multi-signature wallet is instructive. Parity was founded by Gavin Wood, who also served as its Chief Technology Officer. It would be difficult to identify someone with more Ethereum expertise than Wood. He has a Masters in Computer Systems and Software Engineering and a PhD in Computer

Science.[118] He founded Ethereum with Vitalik Buterin, coded the first functional implementation of Ethereum, and invented the Solidity programming language used to code smart contracts on the Ethereum blockchain.[119] Wood then founded Parity with several other early Ethereum developers.

Parity developed a multi-sig wallet[120] for storing ETH, which Parity offered free of charge and on an open-source basis.[121] Specifically, Parity made the wallet available pursuant to a GNU General Public License v.3.0.[122] The Parity wallet was a smart contract that depended for part of its code on a library, which was essentially a separate group of coded functions. The main code referenced the library and ran library code as part of performing functions specified in the main code. On 19 July 2017, an unknown person identified a vulnerability in the library that allowed him or her to unilaterally 'reset the ownership and usage parameters of existing wallets'.[123] This attacker was able to effectively make themselves the owner of three multi-sig wallets. The attacker then used that control to exfiltrate more than 150,000 ETH, then worth USD 30 million, to wallets he controlled.[124] The central purpose of a multi-sig wallet is so that no one person can unilaterally control the assets that the wallet contains. However, the vulnerability in the Parity code allowed the perpetrator to steal the ETH without requiring multiple signatures or consents. The impacted wallets reportedly belonged to projects that had raised money in ICOs,[125] such that the victims of this exploit may have extended beyond the three individual wallets to the investors who had entrusted their money with the impacted projects.

The damage could have been far worse. At around the same time that the exploit occurred, a group of 'white-hat' hackers identified the vulnerability in Parity's code. The group exploited the vulnerability, made themselves the owners of another 593

118. https://en.wikipedia.org/wiki/Gavin_Wood (accessed 10 Feb. 2020).
119. https://gavwood.com (accessed 10 Feb. 2020).
120. A multi-sig wallet, short for multi-signature wallet, requires multiple keys to authorize a transaction. In concept, a multi-sig wallet is more secure than a wallet that relies on one private key, because the wallet owner can distribute private keys across devices or among a group of individuals. Multi-sig wallets often also include M of N capabilities, in which the wallet owner can designate that a certain number of keys (M) out of the total number of keys (N) are required to authorize a transaction. So, for example, in setting up a multi-sig wallet, a user can specify, for example, three of five total private keys are sufficient to authorize a transaction.
121. Choy, W., *When Smart Contracts are Outsmarted: The Parity Wallet 'Freeze' and Software Liability in the Internet of Value* (Proskauer – Blockchain and the Law, 26 Feb. 2018), available at: https://www.jdsupra.com/legalnews/when-smart-contracts-are-outsmarted-the-12326/ (accessed 10 Feb. 2020).
122. https://www.gnu.org/licenses/gpl-3.0.en.html (accessed 10 Feb. 2020).
123. *The Multi-sig Hack: a Postmortem* (Parity Technologies, 20 Jul. 2017), available at: https://www.parity.io/the-multi-sig-hack-a-postmortem/ (accessed 10 Feb. 2020).
124. Zhao, W., *$30 Million: Ether Reported Stolen Due to Parity Wallet Breach* (CoinDesk, 19 Jul. 2017), available at: https://www.coindesk.com/30-million-ether-reported-stolen-parity-wallet-breach (accessed 10 Feb. 2020).
125. Carano, M., *Parity Multisig Wallet Exploit Hits Swarm City Funds: Statement by the Swarm City Core Team* (Medium, 19 Jul. 2017), available at: https://press.swarm.city/parity-multisig-wallet-exploit-hits-swarm-city-funds-statement-by-the-swarm-city-core-team-d1f3929b4e4e (accessed 10 Feb. 2020).

wallets containing more than 377,000 ETH, and then returned control to the true owners after Parity resolved the vulnerability.[126]

Often, after a hack or exploit is publicized, developers will focus on resolving vulnerabilities and making their code more secure. It appears that Parity attempted to do this, but in the process may have created a new and even more dangerous vulnerability. On 20 July 2017, Parity released new code for its multi-sig wallet. In August 2017, a Github user, 3esmit, notified the Parity developers of a potential vulnerability in the library Parity had redeployed following the July 2017 theft. 3esmit indicated that an 'initWallet' function should be called when it was deployed. The Parity developers misinterpreted this as an enhancement suggestion and planned to include it in a future version.[127]

On 6 November 2017, a self-described Ethereum novice, who went by the handle 'devops199', recognized that the Parity multi-sig wallet library smart contract had not been initialized and therefore did not have an owner.[128] He then sent a transaction that made himself the owner of the library smart contract. His control of the library meant that all the Parity multi-sig wallets were also subject to his control. As the owner of the library, devops199 executed a 'self-destruct' command and killed the library. Without that library, many of Parity's multi-sig wallets, which depend on the library, cannot execute any send transactions. In effect, devops199 permanently froze 584 wallets containing more than 500,000 ETH, valued at the time more than USD 240 million. As one commentator described it, 'let's say you physically possessed a safe that held your private key. Well, devops199 disabled the electronic pin pad that would have enabled you to access its contents'.[129]

In 2017, Wood was also developing a project called Polkadot, which raised money by selling tokens. Polkadot had more than 300,000 ETH that it had raised from investors in a Parity multi-sig wallet that was frozen because of the actions of devops199.[130] This suggests that Wood was unaware of the specific vulnerability in the Parity multi-sig wallet, or he would not have trusted it with Polkadot's ETH. It also serves as a stark reminder that a person's development experience and status as an expert does not ensure he or she will take adequate information security measures.

126. Suberg, W., *Parity Hack: White Hat Group Drains $85 Mln as Company Fills Holes* (Cointelegraph, 20 Jul. 2017), available at: https://cointelegraph.com/news/parity-hack-white-hat-group-drains-85-mln-as-company-fills-holes (accessed 10 Feb. 2020).
127. *A Postmortem on the Parity Multi-Sig Library Self-Destruct* (Parity Technologies, 15 Nov. 2017), available at: https://www.parity.io/a-postmortem-on-the-parity-multi-sig-library-self-destruct/ (accessed 10 Feb. 2020).
128. Leung, J., *Legal Issues Surrounding Parity Wallet's 'Kill' Switch* (Medium, 28 Nov. 2017), available at: https://medium.com/blockmatics-blog/legal-issues-surrounding-parity-wallets-kill-switch-c551f02247d3 (accessed 10 Feb. 2020).
129. *Ibid.*
130. Wilmoth, J., *$330 Million: EIP-999 Stokes Debate over ETH Frozen by Parity's Contract Bug* (CCN, 23 Apr. 2018), available at: https://www.ccn.com/330-million-eip-999-stokes-debate-over-eth-frozen-by-paritys-contract-bug/ (accessed 10 Feb. 2020).

[a] Legal Implications

There are a number of legal issues raised by both the theft from the Parity wallets and the freezing of the Parity wallets. Wallet users who suffered losses may be able to bring contract-based claims against Parity, but Parity has significant defences to such claims.[131] Any contractual relationship between a wallet user and Parity is likely governed by Parity's Terms of Website Use and the GNU General Public License. Both those documents include broadly worded liability disclaimers. For example, the Terms of Website Use state: 'We will not be liable to any user for any loss or damage, whether in contract, tort (including negligence), breach of statutory duty, or otherwise, even if foreseeable, arising under or in connection with' the site and its contents. There is a specific provision in the terms of use for business users, which disclaims all liability for damages, lost profits, sales, business interruptions, and loss of business opportunity, among other things. Courts typically enforce terms of use liability limitations, absent some significant ambiguity, or if the liability is the result of intentional conduct, such as fraud.

Parity may have contract-based claims against devops199. The Terms of Website Use are inartfully worded but appear to prohibit using the site to access without authority or damaging items contained in the site or software owned by third parties. However, it is unclear whether there is any actual benefit for Parity in pursuing such a claim. The identity of devops199 remains unknown, and it is unclear whether he has the means to satisfy any judgment that Parity might obtain.

Parity could potentially be liable to its users for tort-based claims, although Parity disclaims liability for negligence in its Terms of Website Use. A court could conclude that Parity violated its duty of care as to the freezing of wallets, in part because Parity received notice of the vulnerability months before devops199 exploited it. A court could also conclude that Parity failed to undertake reasonable steps in the development and deployment of the Parity multi-sig wallet, which include some easy fixes that are obvious in retrospect. But courts typically prefer to focus liability on the party that exploited a vulnerability or hacked a system, rather than the developer who was hacked. In many ways Parity is the victim of the exploits, and courts may be more inclined to impose liability on the unknown thief who conducted the July 2017 thefts and devops199 for the November wallet freezes, rather than Parity.

Injured Parity wallet users in the US may have a claim against devops199 for violating the CFAA, which prohibits intentionally accessing a protected computer without authorization and as a result, causing damage or loss.[132] Here, devops199 intentionally made himself the owner of the library, without authorization. When he then ordered the library to self-destruct, he caused users to suffer damage and loss. But it is not clear if code publicly placed on a blockchain, which is built with a self-destruct function, and is left unlocked for any user to control, is protected by the CFAA. Any victim of a violation of CFAA who suffers at least USD 5,000 in losses may bring a civil

131. https://medium.com/blockmatics-blog/legal-issues-surrounding-parity-wallets-kill-switch-c551f02247d3 (accessed 10 Feb. 2020).
132. 18 U.S.C. § 1030(a)(5).

claim based on that violation. There likely are dozens of Parity wallet users who lost more than USD 5,000 when their wallets were frozen. These users would still need to identify devops199 to successfully bring a claim under the CFAA.

[b] Policy Implications

The Parity exploit is emblematic of a larger challenge that blockchain-based systems presently face. To the extent that policymakers seek to encourage the development and adoption of this technology, it is a challenge that policymakers also must overcome. How can an average user know who to trust, when computer code dictates outcomes, but that code is inscrutable to almost all users. Policymakers can enact legislation to impose obligations on vendors and service providers that may reduce similar vulnerabilities and exploits in the future. Some potential requirements could include that (1) vendors who hold more than a certain value of third-party digital assets must undergo periodic security and code audits, (2) must maintain a certain amount of insurance, or (3) must enact and follow internal security and compliance processes. But the imposition of such requirements is typically most effective as to organizations within that legislature's jurisdiction; many blockchain-based projects move their operations to jurisdictions with the most lax requirements or seek to exist entirely online. Also, while regulatory requirements may reduce the amount of losses from exploits, they likely will also reduce the number and variety of new projects. Open-source and free-to-use software can spur technical developments, but often do not have the funding to meet rigorous oversight and compliance obligations.

Another issue for policymakers to consider is how to help users and owners of digital assets know who they can trust. In a discussion in May 2018, Wood and the Parity co-founder and CEO Steiner described how their lack of trust in intermediaries had led to their work with Ethereum and blockchain.[133] Many users and developers are attracted to blockchain because they do not trust the dominant providers of Internet services, such as Google and Facebook. They may also mistrust the traditional financial system, the failures of which in 2007 and 2008 appear to have partially inspired the Bitcoin Whitepaper. Part of the promise of blockchain is that instead of having to trust intermediaries, with their opaque internal systems, blockchain users or their advisors can directly analyse the code. Wood explained that this makes users safer:

> So, the main thing is that you can, even if you yourself can't check the code, you can find somebody, you can go out, you can put an advert up, you can contact your brother-in-law's mate, but you can find someone that you do trust to some degree, and have them check the code for you, like, someone who's an expert, or you can pay multiple experts, none of whom have aligned interests, and get them all to check the code, in principle, that avenue is open to you, in a system that's open and transparent. It's never open to you in a system that's closed and opaque, like, the traditional corporate Silicon Valley style start-up, where, you know, the operations and the internal workings of the systems are closely guarded.[134]

133. Transcript of Laura Shin interview of Wood and Steiner at Subzero conference, 14 May 2019.
134. *Ibid.*

However, some users lost everything because they trusted experts to ensure the adequacy of the Parity wallet's information security. And Wood's Polkadot investors, among others, also paid the price for trusting the wrong experts. Over the course of several months, the Parity wallet suffered huge losses to a hacker and then much greater losses when the contents of wallets were permanently frozen. Wood has said that the promise of blockchain is that users can trust code more than they can trust the network of intermediaries involved in traditional commerce. But it would be difficult to identify a more trustworthy group to make code secure than the Parity development team that included Wood and other early Ethereum developers. If relying on expert development teams is not enough, what else can digital asset users practically do to protect themselves? If users believe they cannot adequately assess or control the risks associated with interacting with blockchain vendors, services or smart contracts, that will inevitably slow the adoption and development of blockchain technology.

There do not appear to be easy solutions for policymakers to prevent these types of exploits from happening again. Open-source projects like Parity are important to developing new technologies. It is unclear if they could thrive if a legislature or regulator imposed the burdens that are likely to reduce losses, such as requiring insurance, formalized compliance and information security processes, and security audits.

There is a possible solution for the Parity frozen wallets. Ethereum node operators could collectively commit to a hard fork that rewrote the Ethereum blockchain to undo the destruction of the Parity wallet library. But this is purely voluntary; there is no mechanism to require a hard fork by legislation or judicial action. That does not prevent policymakers from advocating for this solution or offering incentives to nodes that agree to adopt a hard fork. A hard fork carries its own risks and complexities. To understand the implications of such a solution, it is instructive to review the only major hard fork of Ethereum, which occurred after a similar exploit of a vulnerable smart contract.

In June 2016, a project called the DAO (Decentralized Autonomous Organization), which had raised more than USD 150 million from investors, suffered a smart contract exploit.[135] In that theft, a DAO user identified a vulnerability that allowed him to withdraw more DAO tokens than he owned. In short order, the attacker stole more than 3.6 million ETH, representing approximately 15% of all ETH that existed at the time.[136] The stolen ETH was then worth more than USD 55 million. After the DAO hack became public, the price of ETH fell from USD 20 to USD 12. In July 2016, perhaps because such a large percentage of the total community had been impacted, a majority of Ethereum nodes agreed to a hard fork that rewrote the blockchain to erase the hacker's thefts from the DAO. Not everyone agreed with this approach, and a group of Ethereum nodes continued mining the pre-fork version of the blockchain, which is now known as Ethereum Classic, and which continues to operate today.

135. Siegel, D., *Understanding the DAO Hack* (CoinDesk, 25 Jun. 2016), available at: https://www.coindesk.com/understanding-dao-hack-journalists (accessed 10 Feb. 2020).
136. *Ibid.*

Wood and the CEO of Parity, Jutta Steiner, advocate that Ethereum should fork again to revive the destroyed Parity wallet library and thereby unfreeze all the impacted Parity wallets. So far, their hard fork proposals have never garnered majority support and the fork has not happened. It is possible that the community has refused in part because Ethereum is much more established now than when it last forked in 2016. Even though the Parity wallet freeze cost users more than USD 240 million, and the DAO investors lost less than USD 55 million, the DAO exploit touched a much larger percentage of the total Ethereum community. The DAO exploit impacted 15% of all ETH at the time, whereas the Parity wallet freeze only impacted approximately 0.5% of all ETH when it occurred.[137] Also, there are now many more smart contracts and ERC-20 tokens. A new hard fork would create much more complexity for projects and developers if they want to support both a newly forked version of Ethereum and the pre-forked version that likely would continue as Ethereum Classic did.

§2.02 TOOLS AND METHODS TO ADDRESS RISKS

As the previous section indicated, there have been some very high-profile information security failures that caused huge amounts of losses for individuals and blockchain markets generally. There are options that digital asset owners can utilize to protect themselves.[138] This section highlights some of those options.

[A] Individual Options for Protecting Digital Assets

[1] Paper Wallets

One way to significantly reduce information security risks for private keys is to ensure they never touch the Internet. By keeping that data offline, private keys are protected against phishing, hacking, and malware attacks, as well as the loss or failure of storage devices. This method of holding digital assets remote from the Internet is known as 'cold storage' or sometimes as a 'cold wallet'. There are a variety of cold storage methods that vary from the simple to the complex.

Perhaps the simplest cold storage method is called a paper wallet. There are several JavaScript-based paper wallet generators available for download. A user can copy one of these tools to a thumb drive and then instal that application on a computer or device that never connects to the Internet. The software generates a public key and private key pair, often including matching QR codes. The user typically then prints out the key pairs, which is why it is called a paper wallet.

Even though the addresses are generated offline, the user can transfer assets to the newly created public key address, and the user can share the public address with others who can transfer digital assets to it. There is no need for the owner of a public

137. These numbers were derived from ETH data, available at: https://etherscan.io/ (accessed 10 Feb. 2020).
138. Nothing in this chapter represents legal or professional advice.

key to ever be online or communicate with the blockchain network in order to receive assets. Only when the owner wants to transfer assets out of the paper wallet do he or she need to use his or her private key on the Internet. To send assets from a paper wallet follows essentially the same steps required to use any kind of private key. The user enters the private key or the corresponding QR code into his or her wallet software to authorize a transfer. At that point, the owner's private key–public key combination is no longer considered to be cold storage because the private key has been used on an Internet-connected device.

If a paper wallet is lost, destroyed, or rendered illegible, it has the same effect as losing a private key. Unless a copy of the private key exists, this will result in a permanent loss of the digital assets stored in the wallet protected by that private key. Many users store their paper wallets in safes or safety deposit banks. It is an interesting irony that one of the preferred ways to protect digital assets is to maintain private keys in perhaps the most analogue way possible.

[2] Hardware Wallets

There are also a variety of commercially available cold storage hardware wallet options. These are devices that generate addresses and store private keys and other data. 'The main principle behind hardware wallets is to provide full isolation between the private keys and your easy-to-hack computer or smartphone.'[139] Many such devices also provide backup capabilities, so if they are lost or damaged, the contents can be restored with a multi-word passphrase. To transfer assets using a hardware wallet usually requires a PIN, biometric data, or another form of authorization to be able to use the device. These protections ensure that losing possession of the hardware device does not make it easy for whoever finds it to access or control the digital assets it secures.

Hardware wallets provide a needed layer of usable security for owners of digital assets. But they do not offer perfect information security and there are still risks associated with using them. There have been reports of counterfeit hardware wallets being sold. There have also been reports of authentic devices being resold after having been altered to give the reseller access to their contents. Hardware wallet manufacturers have identified attacks focused on the firmware used to update the software on the devices. They have also reported fault attacks to disrupt a wallet's functioning. For the most part, these vulnerabilities have not led to the types of high-profile losses outlined in the previous section of this chapter.

139. Larcheveque, E., *Ledger 101 – Part 1: Do You Really Need a Hardware Wallet?* (Medium.com, 24 Sep. 2018), available at: https://medium.com/ledger-on-security-and-blockchain/ledger-101-part-1-do-you-really-need-a-hardware-wallet-7f5abbadd945 (accessed 10 Feb. 2020).

[3] Multi-sig Wallets

As discussed above in the section regarding the Parity wallet failures, multi-sig wallets offer some additional protections because they require more than one private key to authorize a transfer of digital assets. Multi-sig wallets allow users to plan around disruptions based on devices, geography, and personalities. In an M of N arrangement where M is less than N, a single or even multiple information security failures would not imperil control of digital assets.

As discussed in the prior section regarding users suffering losses due to exploits of the Parity wallet, a multi-sig wallet is only as secure as its code. And it is difficult for an average user to identify the type of complex vulnerability that led to the Parity wallet losses. There are a variety of hardware wallets that support multi-sig arrangements, and which have not been reported to have suffered breaches or losses.[140]

Creating a multi-sig environment in which all the related keys are required to authorize a transaction may actually increase the risk of loss. There is some protection because a malicious actor who obtains one of those keys cannot without more steal the user's digital assets. But if any of the keys are lost, or unavailable, the result is a total loss of access to the digital assets.

[B] Outsourcing Security: Custodians

Institutional investors are experienced with custody requirements for traditional assets classes like bonds and securities. The custody requirements they must meet for digital assets are somewhat less settled. A number of service providers have begun offering digital asset custody solutions.[141] The features and prices vary among the various vendors offering these solutions. Most users, including institutional investors, appear to hold their digital assets with exchanges, instead of dedicated custody providers. But considering that there have been more than forty documented breaches of exchanges resulting in more than USD 7 billion in losses,[142] it seems likely that large investors will begin to move away from storage on exchanges in favour of storage with dedicated custodians.

FURTHER READING

The Reports of the Monitor, In the Matter of Application by Quadriga Fintech Solutions Corp., et al, for Relief under the Companies' Creditors Arrangement Act, available

140. This of course does not preclude the possibility of a breach in the future or that a breach occurred which has not yet been discovered. As in many human endeavours, with information security, past performance does not necessarily predict future events.

141. *Emerging Digital Asset Custodians Servicing Institutions* (CAPCO, November 2018), available at: https://www.capco.com/-/media/CapcoMedia/PDFs/Digital-Asset-Custodians-for-Institutions_2page_v7.ashx (accessed 10 Feb. 2020).

142. McCann, C., *Digital Asset Custody: Primer and Landscape* (Medium.com, 19 May 2019), available at: https://medium.com/proofofcapital/digital-asset-custody-primer-and-landscape-a88979e05115 (accessed 10 Feb. 2020).

at: https://documentcentre.eycan.com/Pages/Main.aspx?SID=1445 (accessed 16 March 2020).

Blog by Emin Gun Sirer, available at: https://hackingdistributed.com/ (accessed 16 March 2020).

Introduction to Crypto and Cryptocurrencies, offered by Princeton University through Coursera, taught by Arvind Narayan, Associate Professor, available at: https://www.coursera.org/learn/cryptocurrency#syllabus (accessed 1 June 2020).

The SEC FinHub: available at: https://sec.gov/finhub (accessed 1 June 2020).

Coin Center, a non-profit focused on the policy issues facing digital assets: available at CoinCenter.org (accessed 1 June 2020).

CHAPTER 3
Blockchain Regulation

Thomas Richter

§3.01 DEFINING BLOCKCHAIN FOR REGULATION PURPOSES

[A] Background: The 'Legal Factor'

The increasing interest in the blockchain technology over the past years has only eventually, but then emphatically, drawn the attention to the normative context that this technology is operating in. It goes without saying that blockchains are neither operating above the law nor in a legal vacuum, but are subject to any and all 'applicable laws'. But what are the laws applicable to that nascent technology? There is still little legislation specifically addressing blockchains, and it is often not clear to what extent and in which way existing regulation can be applied accordingly to blockchains with their very particular technological features. Most of the regulations that are applied to blockchains as of this point in time were issued when blockchains were still unknown or at least not a topic which would have particularly been reflected in such regulation, or which even would have been taken into account in the legislative process. This will be referred to in the following chapter as 'existing regulation'. Even further, blockchains and their use cases raise legal questions that may not adequately be covered under existing laws and would by nature require discrete legislation. This will be referred to as 'future regulation'.

For every individual or organization with the intention to acting in a legally compliant way, be it corporates, banks, start-ups, investors or others, it is a prerequisite for the deployment of blockchain technology to have sufficient clarity on the legal questions that are associated with it, and specifically the legality of the very use case. While it could be observed in the past that not all market participants were fully aware of any and all legal and regulatory implications of their usage of blockchains in certain use cases, especially in the area of initial coin offerings and cryptoassets/tokens, which has been described as the 'New Digital Wild West',[1] there is now increasing sensitivity to clear legal questions first and act then. Still, the legal assessment, and the pertinent legal advice, in the context of blockchains in many areas remains 'greenfield work', which may be illustrated with the following quotation: 'After getting as much legal advice as we could, we came to the conclusion this model was also superior to token crowdsales in general. Nothing like this had ever happened before though, and therefore all legal advice was just that, advice.'[2] This example may show how crucial such 'legal factor' is, not only by taking into account – ideally 'by design' – the legal and regulatory implications in the process of developing blockchain models and their legal structuring but also with respect to the actual deployment in a specific way (i.e., 'use case') to ensure the latter is and remains legally compliant.

At the same time, blockchain is also a fairly new phenomenon to lawmakers and regulatory authorities, for which a thorough assessment of the technical features and an understanding of the pertinent regulatory implications as well as a review of the need for new regulation seem to be a particular priority on the agenda in the last few years. One area that thereby stands out is the area of financial services with its particularly high and complex level of regulation, and which is making up for a big part of the blockchain use cases.[3] In advance of more specific legal areas which will follow later in this handbook, the following chapter on 'blockchain regulation' will provide an introduction into the general questions and challenges arising with the regulation of blockchain technology, concepts and approaches to blockchain regulation, the actors who seek to regulate blockchain and the potential addressees of such regulation, as well as certain selected specific regulations as examples to demonstrate various approaches that have been taken so far.

This chapter attempts to take a neutral approach to blockchain beyond any 'hype', in an effort to avoid the appearance of what can be described a 'law lag'[4] in which the law lags behind the developments of a new technology and its impact.[5] Therefore, it does also not foster any specific use case, but tries to examine blockchain as a generic technology open to many applications in the first place. It will, however, also show the limits of such approach from a regulatory point of view in areas where the use case prevails over the generic technology that is used. The chapter is not

---

1. Randolph Robinson II, *The New Digital Wild West: Regulating the Explosion of Initial Coin Offerings*, 85 Tenn. L. Rev. 897 (2018), abstract available at: https://ssrn.com/abstract=3087541 (accessed 11 Mar. 2020).
2. Christoph Jentzsch, *The History of the DAO and Lessons Learned*, slock.it Blog (24 Aug. 2016), available at: https://blog.slock.it/the-history-of-the-dao-and-lessons-learned-d06740f8cfa5 (accessed 11 Mar. 2020).
3. In 2018, it has been held that half of the blockchain use cases were in the financial services industry, Vedat Akgiray, *Blockchain Technology and Corporate Governance*, Report for the Organisation for Economic Co-operation and Development, OECD doc. no. DAF7CA/CG/RD(2018)1/REV1 (6 Jun. 2018) 12, available at: http://www.oecd.org/officialdocuments/publicdisplaydocumentpdf/?cote=DAF/CA/CG/RD(2018)1/REV1&doclanguage=en (accessed 11 Mar. 2020).
4. Carla L. Reyes, *Moving Beyond Bitcoin to an Endogenous Theory of Decentralized Ledger Technology Regulation: An Initial Proposal*, 61 Vill. L. Rev. 202–203 (2016).
5. Such 'lag' may appear not only in the legal context, but also, e.g., in the area of information security, *see* the second paragraph in the introductory section of Chapter 2, *supra*.

intended to cover any kind of blockchain regulation exhaustively, for which a comprehensive case-specific review remains indispensable, but to provide initial guidance on the potential legal and regulatory implications and pitfalls when dealing with blockchains.

[B] The Meaning of 'Blockchain' in the Context of Regulation

[1] The Relevance of a Legal Definition

The first chapter of this handbook provides a technical understanding of blockchain and has described the various forms of blockchains and their technical characteristics, and has also delineated blockchains from the distributed ledger technology in a broader sense.[6] But what does blockchain mean in a legal context and how is it defined? It is probably not unsurprising that there is no generally agreed legal definition of blockchain at this stage, given that this is a nascent technology without a comprehensive legal history. Still, it is remarkable that there is only very little definitional precedence, in particular compared to the attention that the blockchain technology has attracted over the past few years also in the legal community. One of the reasons for this may be that for legal purposes blockchain has rarely been looked at from the perspective of a generic technology, but has mostly been reviewed in a specific use case scenario like cryptoassets/tokens or initial coin offerings. Further to that, the blockchain technology is not very easily accessible as such and also comes in a large variety of different types and forms. Also, given the new and complex nature of blockchain technology, most legal publications start with an introduction that is rather a technical explanation than a legal definition.

However, establishing a legal definition of blockchain goes beyond the question of obtaining an understanding of how that technology works and what its characteristics are. It is about putting blockchain in a legal and regulatory context and finding the right subject matter definition to use it in law. A clear definition is a prerequisite to legally addressing blockchain, for example in statutes or in contracts. For example, the EU Blockchain Observatory and Forum has postulated the need for policymakers 'to clearly define what blockchains and Smart Contracts are under the law'[7] as one of the eight guiding principles.[8] The Government of Liechtenstein, in justification of its recent

6. *See* Chapter 1, section §1.14[A], [B] and [C], *supra*. Most of the issues discussed in this chapter are common to other distributed ledger technology solutions as well and hence can be applied accordingly.
7. Thematic Report of the European Blockchain Observatory and Forum, *Legal and Regulatory Framework of Blockchains and Smart Contracts* 7 (27 Sep. 2019), available at: https://www.eublockchainforum.eu/sites/default/files/reports/report_legal_v1.0.pdf (accessed 11 Mar. 2020). The author has been a member of the Legal Sub-Working Group of the EU Blockchain Observatory and Forum.
8. The other seven are: 'Communicate legal interpretations as broadly as possible', 'Choose the right regulatory approaches for the question at hand', 'Harmonise the law and interpretations of it', 'Help policy makers develop an understanding of the technology', 'Work on high-impact use

'Blockchain Act',[9] has highlighted the importance of a technology-neutral definition of the term 'blockchain' to avoid that the scope of the act may become outdated and too narrow in a few years.[10]

For these purposes, this section starts with a description of the various forms of blockchains as such distinction is relevant for the legal assessment, as well as a description of the relevance of the underlying technological standard. It outlines the specific characteristics that are inherent to the blockchain technology and as such have a shaping influence on the legal assessment. It ends with the attempt to formulate a first definitional summary. Specific legislative definitions of blockchains will be given further down in this chapter.[11]

[2] Various Organizational Forms of Blockchains

'The' blockchain does not exist. The blockchain technology may come in various different forms and shapes and may be best described as a 'class of technology'.[12] While there is no generally agreed typology of the organizational forms of blockchains, they may be mainly distinguished by their organizational set-up and the underlying protocol that is used.

In terms of organizational forms, blockchains are mostly distinguished by the criterion of who can read a blockchain and who can transact on it (i.e., execute and/or validate individual transactions).[13] The following classification takes these factors into account, but draws specific attention to the legal implications that the categorization may have, and therefore looks at the participants, the admission process and the initiators.

The first distinction is between so-called public and private blockchains. This relates to the potential participants that such blockchains target (*who can join a*

---

cases first', 'Closely monitor developments in less mature use cases and encourage self-regulation', and 'Make use of blockchain as a regulatory tool', Thematic Report of the European Blockchain Observatory and Forum, *supra* n. 7, at 7–8.

9. Liechtenstein Token and Trusted Technology Service Provider Act (*Gesetz über Token und VT-Dienstleister*) (3 Oct. 2019), text of the Act available at: https://www.gesetze.li/konso/pdf/2019.301 (accessed 1 Mar. 2020) – in German language only. An English convenience translation is available at: https://www.regierung.li/media/medienarchiv/950_6_08_01_2020.pdf?t=2 (accessed 11 Mar. 2020).
10. *Bericht und Antrag der Regierung an den Landtag des Fürstentums Liechtenstein betreffend die Schaffung eines Gesetzes über Token und VT-Dienstleister (Token- und VT-Dienstleister-Gesetz; TVTG) und die Abänderung weiterer Gesetze, Nr. 54/2019*, 55; available at: https://impuls-liechtenstein.li/wp-content/uploads/2019/12/Bericht-und-Antrag-TVTG.pdf (accessed 11 Mar. 2020) – in German language only.
11. Section §3.06[C], *infra*.
12. Roman Beck & Christoph Müller-Bloch & John Leslie King, *Governance in the Blockchain Economy: A Framework and Research Agenda*, 19(10) J. Assoc. Inform. Sys., Article 1 1021, available at: https://aisel.aisnet.org/jais/vol19/iss10/1 (accessed 11 Mar. 2020).
13. Amanda Anderberg, et al., *Blockchain Now and Tomorrow: Assessing Multidimensional Impacts of Distributed Ledger Technologies*, Susana Figueiredo Do Nascimento & Alexandre Roque Mendes Polvora (eds), EUR 29813 EN, Publications Office of the European Union 14, available at http://publications.jrc.ec.europa.eu/repository/bitstream/JRC117255/blockchain_online.pdf (accessed 11 Mar. 2020).

blockchain). Public blockchains are open to anyone, and the group of addressees is not limited or specified. No specific admission process is applied. It would anyway be impossible to apply any form of discretionary admission requirements, as no control over a public blockchain is retained by the coder(s) and initiator(s) upon its release. It is open source, so anyone who is able to meet the technical requirements may join such a blockchain. Technically more precisely, every participant may download the software and maintain a node, and may then read the ledger and write into the ledger as part of the network, that means append new transactions. In contrast, private blockchains target a specific group of participants. The selection between eligible participants and non-eligible participants in the case of the latter may be effected by a set of predefined criteria built into the blockchain code and vetted automatically, or even by a specific case-by-case decision of admission on a discretionary basis. From the legal perspective, this criterion is noteworthy as it defines if, for example, an offer is made to an unlimited number of counterparties (in the case of a public blockchain) or if it is made to a limited group of counterparties or even specified individuals (in the case of a private blockchain). It also defines who would be eligible to accept such offer. This could be particularly relevant, for example, in the context of the distribution of financial services products, which is strongly regulated, over a blockchain. In summary, this distinction mainly defines the potential 'participants'[14] of a blockchain.

The next distinction is whether a blockchain is 'permissionless' or 'permissioned'. This relates to the question of whether a – public or private – blockchain may freely be joined, without a specific decision of admission (in which case it is permissionless) or if a dedicated admission decision is applied (in which case it is permissioned) (*how a blockchain can be joined*). This distinction is also frequently called 'open' or 'closed'. The 'permissionless/permissioned' distinction seems to overlap with the 'public/private' distinction. This is correct as far as it relates to the application of an admission decision, and as such decision may factually make a blockchain 'private' as such. However, in the 'public/private' distinction, the focus is on the target group, that means who may generally join or not, while the 'permissionless/permissioned' distinction focuses on the question of whether a blockchain may freely be joined without the vetting of any further criteria or whether certain criteria must be met in order for admission to be granted. Hence, the focus for this, both factually and legally, is on the question under which conditions a blockchain may be joined. Blockchains may also be 'public permissioned', in which case the blockchain would be addressed to everyone, and everyone could potentially access and read the ledger, but not create and participate in transactions. This distinction is mainly defined by the role of the 'nodes' as transaction validators, as in a permissioned environment these would have to be preselected by a blockchain administrator.[15] From a legal perspective, a permissioned blockchain not only allows for a vetting (up to a full

14. In this chapter, blockchain 'participants' will be used as a term for the following persons/roles: 'nodes', 'miners', 'users', 'administrators' and 'coders'. The different roles and their distinctive legal qualification is explained below, *see* section §3.04[B], *infra*.
15. Robby Houben & Alexander Snyers, *Cryptocurrencies and Blockchain, Legal Context and Implications for Financial Crime, Money Laundering and Tax Evasion*, Study requested by the

identification) of the participants who want to execute transactions but also provides the framework to imposing conditions for participation on the users, which could, for example, consist in the acceptance of certain terms and conditions for participation as a 'rulebook' between the participants. In fact, a permissioned blockchain reintroduces to a certain extent the concept of a (trusted) third party which may exercise a certain level of control, while public blockchains aim at completely removing any such intermediary.

The last distinction, which is not commonly made from a technical point of view, but which may add value to the legal perspective, relates to the question of who initiates and operates a blockchain (*who is behind the blockchain*). In a public permissionless blockchain, there is no control retained by the coders of a blockchain with no possibility for them to interfere at a later stage, so this criterion may look moot in this case. However, the fact that who has programmed the blockchain may matter for a potential participant from the legal perspective. It may in the first place determine whether a potential participant considers the developer to be trustworthy, and may therefore create a certain 'presumption of legality', if, for example, a public permissionless blockchain would have been set up by a government. In a public permissioned blockchain, the coder has built in a certain admission process for new participants, and participation may be vetted either by automated means or on the basis of a distinct decision by a 'gatekeeper', who then becomes central for the legal regulation perspective as the person factually controlling the blockchain. Such person may be the original coder(s) and initiator(s) of that blockchain, or it may be delegated to another party, or it may be a combination of built-in criteria which are only factually vetted by an 'oracle', i.e. a role that transfers off-chain data as an agent into the blockchain. Finally, in the context of private blockchains, these may also run entirely on private networks as opposed to the public Internet (e.g., intranets) in which case the operators of such blockchain can clearly be identified and held liable for that blockchain's compliance with regulations (so-called enterprise blockchains).

The criteria provided above are by no means exclusive or exhaustive, but they may provide a first orientation on assessing and structuring a blockchain from a legal perspective. Certain legal requirements which may be mandatory prerequisites (e.g., the necessity to know the participants) would have a direct effect on this. Table 3.1 summarizes this categorization for convenience.[16]

TAX3 committee (July 2018), 15, available at: http://www.europarl.europa.eu/cmsdata/150761/TAX3%20Study%20on%20cryptocurrencies%20and%20blockchain.pdf (accessed 11 Mar. 2020).

16. The overview partially follows the scheme suggested by Garrick Hileman & Michael Rauchs, *Global Blockchain Benchmarking Study* (2017) 20, available at: https://www.ey.com/Publication/vwLUAssets/ey-global-blockchain-benchmarking-study-2017/$FILE/ey-global-blockchain-benchmarking-study-2017.pdf (accessed 11 Mar. 2020).

Table 3.1 Main Types of Blockchains and Certain Pertinent Legal Key Considerations

	Admission Model	*Operated by*	*Certain Legal Key Considerations (Non-exhaustive)*
Public	Permissionless	All nodes and miners (no control)	Focus on how legal compliance can be achieved w/o responsible party
	Permissioned	All nodes and miners (no control), permission process (partially) controlled by coder(s)/initiator(s), third party or oracle(s)	Focus on how legal compliance can be ensured through design of the code and the permission process applied; permission process allows to introduce T&Cs between participants, but difficulties in surveillance of adherence to the T&Cs
Private	Permissionless	Specified operator(s) retaining control over writing transactions, but open to anyone for reading transactions	Focus on legal implications of ledger being readable by anyone
	Permissioned (may be in the form of 'consortium' or 'enterprise')	Specified operator(s) retaining control over reading and writing transactions; may be fully or partially on private network	Focus on the T&Cs that are agreed between the participants

[3] Legal Relevance of the Blockchain Protocol

Blockchains may be further distinguished by their underlying protocol. As a blockchain is a decentralized system with many different participants (e.g., users, nodes, miners), and in the absence of a single central authority which is one of the inherent structural and distinct features of that technology, all participants must follow certain rules for the blockchain to form a working network. Those rules are laid down in software protocols which are developed by software coders, called the 'blockchain protocol'. Foremost, the blockchain protocol defines the consensus algorithm which is used to add new blocks of transactions to the blockchain. This may be based on a so-called Proof-of-Work concept, in which new blocks are validated on the basis of miners solving a mathematical problem and being rewarded for this ('mining') or a so-called Proof-of-Stake concept, in which more senior participants with higher stakes (e.g., more crypto coins) validate transactions (assuming their intrinsic interest in the integrity of the network for the sake of their stakes). While all blockchains follow the same general technological principles, protocols vary to a significant degree. There are thousands of different protocols, and within the limits of technical viability, coders are free to design new protocols as they wish. However, certain major blockchain protocols have emerged, the most prominent of which is probably the Bitcoin protocol. Other widely used protocols specifically for enterprise use include Ethereum,[17] Hyperledger,[18] Corda[19] and MultiChain.[20]

The blockchain protocol contains the rules that coders have foreseen and that participants have agreed upon, through either their action of joining a blockchain network that was generally open to new participants in a permissionless blockchain or their request for participation and subsequent admission in a permissioned blockchain. The question is if, and if yes to what extent, the underlying protocol is legally relevant. Typically, as described in the context of the principle of technology neutrality below,[21] legal regulation in the area of technology does not address an individual technology discretely, but rather the specific use of the same. It hence appears to be even less relevant which specific form of the blockchain technology in the form of different underlying protocols is applied. This may be compared to Internet-related regulation. For example, regulations on the usage of cookies on websites would refer to neither the technological solution how such cookies are included in a webpage nor the specific browser that is used for accessing the website or the Internet protocol.[22] Hence, regulation does – at least so far – not distinguish between different blockchain protocols, and any regulatory paradigm that may apply or may be derived for blockchains would not be distinguished accordingly.

However, a blockchain's protocol has two main legal implications. First, the protocol itself needs to be legally compliant, and coders need to take laws and regulations into account when developing code for a specific protocol. For example, a key requirement is the blockchain's compliance with data protection laws, in Europe namely the General Data Protection Regulation (GDPR),[23] which needs to be ensured through the way in which the protocol is developed in the first place. It is evident that coders hence play a key role in a blockchain's legal compliance. Second, the protocol is instrumental in defining the roles and responsibilities of the various blockchain participants, thereby fundamentally creating the blockchain governance. It may contain not only technical but also legal rules. These may consist in certain terms and conditions that the participants need to adhere to, imposed either by purely technical means in a permissionless blockchain or by the requirement of express acceptance in

17. https://ethereum.org (accessed 11 Mar. 2020), for a description of certain Ethereum features and characteristics *see* Chapter 1, sections §1.10–§1.13, *supra*.
18. https://www.hyperledger.org (accessed 11 Mar. 2020).
19. https://www.corda.net (accessed 11 Mar. 2020).
20. https://www.multichain.com (accessed 11 Mar. 2020).
21. *See* section §3.03[A], *infra*.
22. For example, the EU General Data Protection Regulation (GDPR) in describing the nature of 'online identifiers' states broadly: 'Natural persons may be associated with online identifiers provided by their devices, applications, tools and protocols, such as internet protocol addresses, cookie identifiers or other identifiers such as radio frequency identification tags'; Regulation (EU) 2016/679 of the European Parliament and of the Council of 27 Apr. 2016 on the protection of natural persons with regard to the processing of personal data and on the free movement of such data, Recital 30.
23. For more details, *see* Chapter 5, section §5.03[B], *infra*.

a permissioned blockchain upon admittance. In terms of technical rules, it contains the standard on which the blockchain is built and operated, and it ensures that all nodes recognize themselves and thereby 'holds the blockchain together'. From a legal perspective, the entirety of the legal principles in the protocol together with its technical mandatories may be characterized as a blockchain's constitution. And like most constitutions, it may not freely be amended, but parts of it may be unchangeable at all, and others only by a majority vote of all blockchain participants. Hence the protocol has a key influence on the blockchain network and is the place where legal requirements may be localized and build in.

As we have now seen, the protocol is an instrument which defines the mechanisms and governance in a blockchain, and the protocol may be designed in many different ways. However, every blockchain has a number of characteristics which differentiates it from other database technologies, and according to which the protocol's principles are defined to match the definition of being a blockchain. These characteristics and the pertinent legal implications will be discussed now.

[4] Inherent Characteristics of Blockchains and Their Legal Implications

The blockchain technology has a number of fundamental technical characteristics which differentiates it from other database technologies, specifically traditional database models with a central ledger.[24] At the outset of any legal assessment, it is important to acknowledge that these characteristics are inherent to that technology *as such*, and removing them may devaluate the specific benefit that is attributed to them and the blockchain as a technological means for a certain use case in general. In other words, these characteristics are (among others) likely the main reasons why it is given preference to the blockchain technology over another database technology in a specific case. Hence, the legal assessment needs to take them into account as given in principle, which also means that a 'showstopper' from the legal perspective may become an overall showstopper for the use. Hence, it is particularly important to deal with these as early as possible in the process of the legal assessment. Three of these 'constituting' principles will be described here: decentralization, immutability and transparency.[25]

Decentralization: In the form of a public permissionless blockchain, a blockchain is completely decentralized; i.e., it is distributed over a multitude of nodes potentially physically located all over the world. Each participant has the same rights, and the original coders would not withhold any more rights or control than every other participant. Metaphorically speaking, a public permissionless blockchain is 'released by the coder into freedom' and then escapes his control. There are no possibilities of exerting influence, other than through any built-in governance mechanisms by, for example, obtaining or securing more than 50% of the voting rights. In such a public permissionless blockchain, it is claimed that there is no need for a trusted central

24. For database concepts, *see* further Chapter 1, section §1.04, *supra*.
25. *See* also Thomas Richter, *Blockchain – Rechtliche Aspekte aus Sicht der Finanzindustrie*, DGRI Jahrbuch 2017, Robert G. v. Briner & Axel Funk (ed.) 2018, 165–178.

authority since the consensus mechanism described above *as such* creates the trust in the correctness of the blockchain, solely through technological means.

Immutability: Due to the sequential design of the data blocks, and how they are tied together, it is practically impossible to change a transaction once incorporated into the blockchain at any later point in time.[26] For the legal assessment of – at least a public – blockchain, it must hence be assumed that once a transaction has been created, any later need for changes (e.g., on the basis of a respective court order) may simply be impossible from a factual perspective. However, there are technical possibilities to intervene in a blockchain. The so-called forking aims at creating a new 'branch' of the blockchain by sending the proposal of a software update to all participants within the network with the aim of invalidating or at least changing the previous chain or 'splitting off' a transaction branch. Furthermore, the so-called 51-percent attack describes an attack on the blockchain in which the consensus principle is attempted to be overcome by an attacker taking over more than half of the computing power of all participants. Leaving aside the question how possible and feasible this is, it should, however, be noted that in both cases the previous blockchain would be 'invalidated' by such actions but the data would still be existent. It is, however, possible to design a blockchain technically from the outset with the possibility to allow certain participants to make changes to previous transactions. Although this could be seen as an interference with one of the general principles of the blockchain technology, it should be considered as a possible means to achieve legal compliance. A very precise definition of the possible rights of intervention would then be necessary since this design would involve the risk of an oligopoly of these privileged participants and would require to extend the necessary level of trust to those participant(s).

Transparency: Each node in the network has a complete copy of the blockchain. The blockchain mechanism requires that each participant also has reading rights. This means that all transactions are visible to every participant and are therefore (de facto) public. While the data record of the individual transaction itself does not contain any clear data, because there is a separation between the identification and verification level on the one hand and the transaction level on the other, the data record contains at least certain anonymized addresses of the involved parties, which are verified by the system at network level to carry out the transaction. However, it is not technically impossible to decrypt this data and, for example, to establish a personal reference in the meaning of data privacy laws. For legal purposes, it must hence be assumed that such data is not confidential and may be related back to the actual parties by technical means.

[5] Summary

This section has initially outlined the importance of defining blockchain in generic form for legal purposes. It has then introduced the distinction between public and private blockchains on the one hand and permissionless and permissioned blockchains

26. On the technical aspects of immutability *see* Chapter 1, section §1.06[A], *supra*.

on the other hand and has also drawn the attention to the operator(s) of a blockchain. It has further found that the underlying blockchain protocol is as such not a decisive factor for the legal assessment, but may still have important legal implications to consider. It has finally outlined the decentralization, the immutability and the transparency to be inherent features of the blockchain technology that the legal assessment needs to take into account.

These insights allow for a first definitional summary of blockchains, which may in this sense be described as being *a public or private, permissionless or permissioned database network, which may or may not be controlled to a certain extent by (an) operator(s), which is based on certain software code (protocol) and which inherent features are that it is decentralized, immutable and transparent.* This first definitional approach will be further detailed below against specific regulatory examples of actual statutory definitions.[27]

[C] The Meaning of 'Regulation' in the Context of Blockchain

The previous section has elaborated on the question of what 'blockchain' means from the factual perspective for legal purposes. This section will now - vice versa - try to answer the question of what 'regulation' means in a blockchain context. Legal questions in connection with blockchains have very much focused on individual legal topics around specific use cases in the last few years (e.g., on initial coin offerings and cryptoassets) or isolated legal questions (e.g., on a blockchain's compliance with specific data privacy requirements such as the right to be forgotten). In line with the broader approach of this book, the following section will elaborate on blockchain as a generic technology in the legal context to help in particular legal practitioners with the fundamental question: Which regulations are at all relevant for a project adopting blockchain?

[1] Which Kind of Regulation Can Be Relevant for Blockchains?

Starting from a very broad point of view, and withdrawing a comparison to the regulation of the Internet which has certain similar aspects,[28] reference can be made to Lawrence Lessig who in a very famous book has described four factors which regulate behaviour in the cyberspace: Laws, norms, markets and code.[29] He describes all those factors with their specific mode of operation: Laws, which threaten *ex post* sanctions if

27. Section §3.06[C], *infra*.
28. Blockchain technology has been variously described as being the 'internet of value' by virtue of the ability of being able to store, and serve as a means of transaction for, digitally embedded values, *see* e.g., for the 'token economy' Chapter 5, *infra*, and for the 'internet of value' connotation *see* e.g., Roberto Moro Visconti, *Blockchain Valuation: Internet of Value, Digital Networks and Smart Transactions* (2019), on ResearchGate available at: https://www.researchgate.net/publication/329916782_Blockchain_Valuation_Internet_of_Value_digital_networks_and_smart_transactions (accessed 11 Mar. 2020).
29. Lawrence Lessig, *Code Version 2.0* 124-125 (2006), available at: http://codev2.cc/download+remix/Lessig-Codev2.pdf (accessed 11 Mar. 2020).

not adhered to, norms, which if not observed would lead to sanctions imposed by the community, markets, with, for example, charges as being potentially prohibitive for access, and code, as the constraints imposed by the software and hardware.[30] Blockchains are operating in a very similar context, and when applying these factors accordingly, it can be concluded that these go far beyond the pure body of law. This illustrates that it is always important to understand the full context in which a technology is applied, which includes a reasonable understanding of how it works, how it is applied and which implications may result from its use in a specific case, or, in other words, 'do not forget the broader picture'.

In further assessing which specific regulation applies to blockchains, there is a fundamental distinction to draw, which may help understanding better the overall legal context. First, there is the legal relationship between the various blockchain participants (mainly nodes, miners, users, administrators, coders and oracles) on a horizontal level. Their relationship will be mainly covered by private law and depend very strongly on the set-up of the blockchain and what those parties have agreed upon in terms of their governance (in which context the blockchain protocol is again of relevance).[31] This could be characterized as 'regulation *in* the blockchain'. An example for this is general contract law or the law of torts. Second, there is the relationship between the participants and the general (mostly mandatory) laws which apply in a vertical perspective, which are mainly public law subjects (including criminal law), and which all those participants (mandatorily) need to adhere to, and if they do not, could be sanctioned accordingly. This could be characterized as 'regulation *of* the blockchain'. Examples for this are data protection laws, criminal laws and financial services regulations.

For both categories, in the broadest sense, regulation encompasses all applicable laws, statutes, by-laws, subordinate legislation as well as any regulatory requirements from authorities and regulators. However, while in the case of the horizontal relationship between the participants, which is largely based on contractual arrangements, there is generally contractual freedom and most regulation should be dispositive (further depending on the relevant jurisdiction), and hence subject to the parties' specific agreements, the vertical relationship is dominated by mandatory regulation which is not subject to disposition by the parties and which hence always needs to be taken into account as a prerequisite requirement. The blockchain must be designed in a way that it is able to meet such requirements as a basic legal requirement.

Applicable regulations may be further classified as follows: (1) all generally applicable regulation (i.e., those laws that apply to everyone and everything within their scope of applicability), (2) regulation that applies by virtue of the specific use case that a blockchain is deployed for (i.e., for *what* it is used), and (3) regulation that specifically addresses the blockchain as a technology (i.e., which applies by virtue of specifically using blockchain technology in a certain case). Further, the current discussion oscillates between determining how the existing applicable legal framework

30. *Ibid.*
31. Section §3.01[B][3], *supra*.

applies in a blockchain context and the question of how future regulation encompassing blockchain should look like, as the conceptual characteristics of this new technology are inspiring legal scholars, lawmakers and practitioners to think about the latter.

[2] Which Legal Subjects Can Be Relevant for Blockchains?

There is no doubt: Blockchain is a cross-divisional topic touching upon many different areas of law. This is the case for many IT- and digitalization-related topics, but due to the unique structure and the variety of the blockchain use cases, the range of implicated legal subject matters seems to be particularly broad. This handbook examines in more detail some of them which we have considered particularly relevant for legal practice. Broader speaking and in addition to those, the blockchain technology as such, with its characteristics described above, raises legal questions from many different areas of private law (e.g., liability and enforcement questions, contract law questions, IT law questions), criminal law (e.g., in the area of data offences and money laundering) and public and administrative law (e.g., in tax and data protection law). Questions concerning the use of the blockchain in the area of corporate law (e.g., for corporate shareholding matters[32]) and corporate governance[33] are particularly relevant for corporates. This already shows the range of (individual) topics which are currently discussed, and the list is non-exhaustive.

In addition to the general legal requirements, there may be further special requirements depending on who a blockchain uses (regulation that applies to a party as such) and/or the intended specific use case. This is likely to be particularly true for companies in highly regulated industries. For financial institutions, the main requirements are those imposed by supervisory law. These include, for example in Germany, the provisions of the German Banking Act and the Minimum Requirements for Risk Management[34] ('MaRisk'), which must also be complied with when using blockchain technology. Particular emphasis is placed on IT security issues as well. For example, being an IT system, the blockchain must fulfil certain technical and organizational standards to ensure the integrity, availability, authenticity and confidentiality of the data. Anti-money laundering regulations are also important and may contain obligations which may be hard to achieve in a public blockchain environment. Finally, a

32. For a US-law discussion, compare e.g. George S. Geis, *Traceable Shares and Corporate Law*, Virginia Public Law and Legal Theory Research Paper No. 2018-13, 2-50, available at SSRN: https://papers.ssrn.com/sol3/papers.cfm?abstract_id=3129042&download=yes (accessed 11 Mar. 2020).
33. Compare e.g. Wulf A. Kaal, Blockchain-Based Corporate Governance, U. of St. Thomas (Minnesota) Legal Studies Research Paper No. 19-10, 1-43, available at SSRN: https://papers.ssrn.com/sol3/papers.cfm?abstract_id=3441904 (accessed 11 Mar. 2020); Anne Lafarre & Christoph Van der Elst, Blockchain Technology for Corporate Governance and Shareholder Activism, SSRN Electronic Journal (January 2018) 1-26, available at: https://www.researchgate.net/publication/324670400_Blockchain_Technology_for_Corporate_Governance_and_Shareholder_Activism (accessed 11 Mar. 2020).
34. *See* for an English translation https://www.bafin.de/SharedDocs/Downloads/EN/Rundschreiben/dl_rs0917_marisk_Endfassung_2017_pdf_ba_en.html;jsessionid=389C4F6660C68E7702B5C1EA5255BE70.1_cid392?nn=9021442 (accessed 11 Mar. 2020).

blockchain will also need to be able to meet (at least minimum) statutory archiving requirements which exist in certain jurisdictions and for certain types of information (e.g., in Germany for commercial correspondence and accounting documents under tax laws).

On top of that, additional requirements can also result from the specific design of the blockchain solution. Frequently, a blockchain solution is not developed by the party using it, but is built on the basis of standard solutions available on the market ('Blockchain-as-a-Service'). This can in turn result in an additional layer of legal requirements (e.g., if such solutions are offered on the basis of certain standard terms and conditions, not only for the 'purchase' but also for the deployment). If a use case in a financial institute would amount to regulated outsourcing (potentially also including a cloud element), then, for example, in Europe the European Banking Authority's Guidelines on outsourcing arrangements[35] would apply, and the blockchain solution, including the contractual arrangements, would need to meet these requirements.

And finally, in a corporate environment, internal standards and requirements (e.g., corporate policies and guidelines) which implement regulation or supplements it with company-specific standards may apply, which in a stricter sense is not regulation but also needs to be taken into account early on – ideally already in the phase of structuring and designing the blockchain solution.

[3] 'Code Is *Law' and 'Code* As *Law'*

'Code is law' is an expression that was framed in connection with the fundamental importance that software code plays in the shaping of the 'cyberspace', mainly as the underlying and governing structure of the Internet.[36] The idea behind that concept was that if such code constitutes the fundamental structure of the Internet, then building in certain rights and freedoms directly in the code could provide for a 'structural guarantee' of application of those in the cyberspace, structurally in the same way that fundamental rights are built into a constitution.[37] In essence, it expresses the idea that in a digital world 'code has progressively established itself as the predominant way to regulate the behavior of Internet users'.[38] Consequently, those who program the code play an important role for the sake of the power they factually exercise, and it was emphasized that those should incorporate constitutional principles into the code as the code would finally govern the Internet as a whole.[39]

35. EBA Guidelines on outsourcing arrangements (25 Feb. 2019), available at: https://eba.europa.eu/sites/default/documents/files/documents/10180/2551996/38c80601-f5d7-4855-8ba3-702423665479/EBA%20revised%20Guidelines%20on%20outsourcing%20arrangements.pdf (accessed 11 Mar. 2020).
36. *See* Lessig, *supra* n. 29, at 1–8.
37. *Ibid.*, at 4–7.
38. Primavera De Filippi & Sanmer Hassan, Blockchain Technology as a Regulatory Technology: From Code is Law to Law is Code, 12 First Monday 21 (2016) 1, https://arxiv.org/ftp/arxiv/papers/1801/1801.02507.pdf (accessed 11 Mar. 2020).
39. Lessig, *supra* n. 29, at 6.

'Code is law' is now also often used when the regulation of blockchains is discussed. There are mainly two types of software code in a blockchain context. The first type is the code of the blockchain network itself. This layer of code could be described as the 'operating system' of a blockchain. The second type is the code that is used for Smart Contracts,[40] which in a simplified manner can be seen as dedicated software programs which, depending on the specific type of blockchain, are coded separately and which are then executed on the blockchain network. This layer could be described as the 'program' or – more modernistic – the 'app' level. While the former (operating system) layer determines the structure of the whole blockchain, the latter (app) layer would apply between those blockchain users who agree on it – ultimately by virtue of contractual privity as a quite commonly recognized principle of law.

In the first place, both layers (program code and Smart Contract code) are shaped by the purpose which they have to fulfil, which for a use in a legally compliant way includes compliance with applicable regulation. Further to that, it may be shaped by dedicated legal requirements specific to its use. As an example how complex legal rules are applied to code, the International Swaps and Derivatives Association (ISDA) has defined legal guidelines upon which the complex ISDA documentation, which is a comprehensive framework of legal documents that is applied as a financial industry standard for derivatives trading, should be observed when a Smart Contract solution for derivatives trading is implemented.[41] But beyond the 'translation' of such (analogous) requirements into (digital) code, blockchain is also called out to potentially constitute a means for governments and authorities to apply their laws and regulations in an automated and self-executing manner.[42] In the context of derivatives regulation, it could, for example, be used to apply margin requirements that are imposed by the U.S. Dodd-Frank Act in an automated manner if coded into a Smart Contract.[43] This shifts the paradigm from 'code *is* law' to 'code *as* law',[44] from blockchain as a 'regulatable technology' to a 'regulatory technology'.[45]

Finally, 'code *as* law' also ties into the discussion of the emergence of a new form of law, which may be described as 'cryptolaw' or '*lex cryptographica*', the latter of which emphasizes the benefits that the use of blockchains could provide in the application of the law, to governments in terms of efficiency of regulation and the society as a whole.[46] This goes back to the idea of a '*lex informatica*', as a 'set of rules for information flows imposed by technology and communication networks [...] that policymakers must understand, consciously recognize, and encourage'.[47] However, in that discussion, it is important to recall that code is basically a means of transporting

40. For Smart Contracts *see* Chapter 4, *infra*.
41. International Swaps and Derivatives Association, Legal Guidelines for Smart Derivatives Contracts (January 2019), available at: https://www.isda.org/a/MhgME/Legal-Guidelines-for-Smart-Derivatives-Contracts-Introduction.pdf (accessed 11 Mar. 2020).
42. *See* Primavera De Filippi & Aaron Wright, *Blockchain and the Law: The Rule of Code* (2018) 193.
43. *Ibid.*, at 197–198.
44. *Ibid.*, at 199.
45. Michèle Finck, *Blockchain: Regulation and Governance in Europe* 93 (2018).
46. De Filippi and Wright, *supra* n. 42, at 203.
47. Joel R. Reidenberg, *Lex Informatica: The Formulation of Information Policy Rules through Technology*, 76 Tex. L. Rev. 553, 555 (1997–1998).

rules, rather than creating rules. While blockchain can be appreciated as a means to more efficiently enforce the law by automated and reliable means, and as such may contribute to more legal certainty and efficiency, it does not as such create a new form of law, and the aforementioned concepts may, from a practical standpoint, rather be understood as a fragment towards the establishment of a more automated, digital overall regulatory framework. Having said this, various specific use cases of block-chain technology raise a magnitude of (new) legal questions, the answers to which may be described as the emergence of a new subject of law, for example in the area of cryptoassets/tokens.[48] Beyond this, it can be doubted that the mere use of software code to transport legal rules rather than statutory textbooks as such would justify calling out a new form of law. This view does not deny the fact that the emergence of blockchain technology could contribute to eventually transform the law, and to envision 'a world in which law is created first through legislation or regulation written in words and then implemented through cryptographic, smart-contracting computer code'.[49] In practical terms, this means that the code of a blockchain, as well as the blockchain technology as a whole resulting from that code, is subject to the generally applicable laws and regulations in the first place, and may be utilized to apply legal rules (even those that emerge as new subjects of law), but does not as such - as of now - create a new form of law that blockchains would need to adhere and correspond to and that legal practitioners would need to assess in addition to 'traditional' rules. As it has been stated above, a blockchain does not operate in a legal vacuum[50] and consequently it has been held that 'code needs law'[51] to underpin its recognition and enforceability from a legal (not practical or factual) perspective.

[4] Summary

This section has distinguished between the horizontal relationship of blockchain participants ('regulation *in* the blockchain') and regulation that is imposed vertically on blockchain participants ('regulation *of* the blockchain'), in both of which cases regulation has a broad meaning. It has then provided certain examples for the broad variety of legal subject matters that blockchains touch upon and should be considered when assessing blockchains from a legal perspective. It has then elaborated on the notions of 'code *is* law' and 'code *as* law' and has concluded that while blockchain may also be instrumental as a 'regulatory technology', code follows the regulation, and not vice versa.

48. Chapter 5, *infra*.
49. Carla L. Reyes, *Conceptualizing Cryptolaw*, 96 Neb. L. Rev. 384, 400 (2017), full text available at: https://digitalcommons.unl.edu/cgi/viewcontent.cgi?article=3121&context=nlr (accessed 11 Mar. 2020).
50. Section §3.01[A], *supra*.
51. Finck, *supra* n. 45, at 44.

§3.02 REGULATORY CHALLENGES

Blockchain technology, by the very nature of its features, presents some key challenges to its (effective) regulation, some of which will be discussed in the following section.

[A] Decentralization as Key Challenge

To the same extent that decentralization is a constitutive principle of the blockchain technology,[52] it can be a key challenge for the legal aspects. The fact that through the (potential) cross-border decentralization a multitude of different jurisdictions may be affected does create challenges not only for all legal questions where the specific physical place is decisive but also for the questions of effective enforcement of the law. This seems comparable to the situation of the regulation of the Internet. It is, however, important in this context to recognize that a blockchain's decentralization may vary over its life cycle. A public blockchain, as it is the case, for example, for the Bitcoin blockchain, has its origins in one person who develops it and then releases it, and then it spreads (more or less controlled depending on whether it is permissioned or permissionless) as new participants, nodes and miners join. The original developer therefore seems to be the natural first addressee for imposing any regulation on the blockchain, which may be in the form of imposing mandatory requirements that the software code needs to contain or to follow. However, it needs to be considered in this context that as from the point of releasing the public blockchain, the original developer does not retain control over that blockchain, hence imposing legal duties on the developer for any time after such release would be moot from an enforcement perspective.

It is further important to note that decentralization may have a different meaning in the technical context than in the legal context. Decentralization in the technical meaning denotes that a blockchain as a data ledger is spread over a multitude of nodes (which are essentially computers), irrespective from the question of where these nodes are physically located and by whom they are 'owned', for example if many or even a majority of nodes is owned by or under the control of one single party. Decentralization from the legal perspective has a normative meaning, which may however vary depending on the legal subject matter, for example under securities laws[53] or under private international law from the perspective of physical location.

[B] Jurisdiction

The question of jurisdiction in connection with blockchains is manifold. Decentralization is a distinctive and inherent feature of the blockchain technology. It is not the mere fact that blockchains often span across a variety of jurisdictions, which is frequently

52. Section §3.01[B][4], *supra*.
53. *See* Peter van Valkenburgh, *What Could 'decentralization' Mean in the Context of the Law?* (15 Jun. 2018) available at: https://coincenter.org/entry/what-could-decentralization-mean-in-the-context-of-the-law (accessed 11 Mar. 2020).

the case in a globalized world and its cross-border economy and for which private international law provides for the applicable rules, but the fact that blockchains in their purest form as public blockchains may be transnationalized per se, in which scenario traditional jurisdictional anchors and concepts may not be able to answer the questions. In the case of public blockchains, there is no 'root' into any specific country which could be the starting point to determine jurisdiction and applicable law and no 'anchor' which could serve as a regulatory entry point.

It may be useful to draw a distinction again between jurisdiction *in* and *over* blockchains. Jurisdiction *in* a blockchain comprises the question of which laws are applicable to transactions that are carried out by the blockchain users, and in which court a dispute arising from a transaction would be adjudicated. This is mainly a question of the law of contracts and private international law. Jurisdiction *over* a blockchain includes the question of which countries' laws may be applicable to a blockchain, and which authorities could assert jurisdiction over a blockchain and the transactions executed in it. This is mainly a question of public and administrative law.

It is beyond the scope of this chapter to provide answers to all these jurisdictional questions that may arise in the context of blockchains.[54] Nevertheless, for legal structuring purposes, three questions that are particularly important from a practitioner's perspective can be distinguished: (1) what is the law that is applicable between the various blockchain participants and can there be an effective choice; (2) which (state) court may assert jurisdiction over the blockchain, i.e. its participants and potentially a blockchain itself; (3) which countries' financial services regulator may a blockchain be subjected to?

While question 1 is a question of private international law and may be answered, for example for Europe on the basis of the Rome I Regulation, question 2 will (subject to public international law treaties) be answered by the courts by applying their local procedural law, and question 3 finally will be answered by the relevant financial services regulations, which in some jurisdictions may have certain extraterritorial reach.

[C] Anonymity

Anonymity can be another major obstacle for effective regulation. The question here is not so much whether anonymity is absolute in a given context, but whether such anonymity can be overcome by a regulator with the means as such regulator requires, and may be able to reasonably deploy so that this allows for, or at least does not hinder, the effective enforcement of regulation. In many areas where it is particularly important to know the acting party, for example in the context of financial services for the

54. For further reading, *see* e.g. Katherine West, *Where Is Blockchain: Jurisdictional Issues That May Affect Distributed Ledgers*, available at: https://www.lexology.com/library/detail.aspx?g=35f40e2e-38d8-49d7-81ca-9872d8ab9532 (accessed 11 Mar. 2020); Jaak Poldma, *Dragged To Thee U.S: Courts (Part 1): Jurisdiction and the Location of Blockchain Nodes*, available at: https://blogs.orrick.com/blockchain/dragged-to-the-u-s-courts-part-1-jurisdiction-and-the-location-of-blockchain-nodes (accessed 11 Mar. 2020).

prevention of money laundering and terrorist financing, mandatory identification of the parties is imposed by the law. Any solution which is not able to meet those requirements would simply not be permissible. Hence, from a regulatory perspective, the question is not whether the participants of a given blockchain can stay anonymous or not, but whether such anonymity conflicts with existing (or future) identification requirements. It is, for example, hardly imaginable that financial institutions would use public permissionless blockchain solutions in a context in which they are obliged by law to conduct customer checks ('Know-Your-Customer'). Likewise, regulators would now allow the use of any public permissionless blockchain for a use case in which they require the full identification of the participants. It is, however, also argued that there might be a potential dilemma for regulators where there is a strong incentive for the promotion of blockchain solutions that meet the anonymization requirements of data protection laws (namely, the GDPR in the EU), on the one hand, without compromising on the non-facilitation of money laundering and not burdening law enforcement more generally, on the other hand.[55]

There are various options to satisfy identification requirements in the design and set-up of a blockchain solution. For example, in a private permissioned blockchain, a trusted party can be retained to exercise control over the admission of new participants which can include a full identification of new participants. There are technical options which facilitate this being done in a fully digitalized way, for example in a comparable manner than a bank identifies a new customer through online channels for the opening of a bank account online. Should it not be necessary to conduct a full identification, permissioning a blockchain may still allow for sufficiently tracing the identity of a participant when required. From a legal advice perspective, it is of key importance that any identification requirements are identified upfront for the specific use case and that such advice can be taken into account to determine the suitable form of the blockchain to be developed or deployed. It is also worth to mention at this occasion that once a blockchain is up and running, there may be a desire at a later stage to broaden the use case or to add new use cases. This should be anticipated if possible in the legal assessment, as at a later stage the configuration of the blockchain may no longer be changed, so otherwise it may not be possible to meet the requirements and the extended use may not be possible for legal reasons. Finally, identification requirements may also be met through additional parallel off-chain processes.

§3.03 REGULATORY CONCEPTS

There are various conceptual approaches as to how the blockchain technology should be regulated, in terms of both lawmaking and regulatory oversight.[56] The following section describes the predominant approach of 'technology neutrality', by taking into account a use case-focused regulation and the sandbox approach.

55. Finck, *supra* n. 45, at 63–64.
56. Various conceptual approaches are discussed, e.g., by Finck, *supra* n. 45, at 153–165.

[A] The Regulatory Principle of Technology Neutrality

The principle of technology neutrality in regulation may be summarized as 'a policy position that the regulatory perimeter and treatment of financial products and activities is unaffected by the technological medium through which the product is offered or activity takes place'.[57] More broadly beyond financial services regulation, it characterizes a position under which the law is neutral and silent as to any specific technology in its scope and application. It is the predominant position scholars, lawmakers and regulators have taken with respect to new technologies over the last years, 'based on the assumption it promotes statutory longevity and equal treatment of old and new technologies'.[58] This means first of all that, on the one hand, existing regulation applies to the blockchain technology without any restrictions, relaxation or privilege, and a blockchain needs to be designed in a way that it is able to comply with existing regulation. This is in particular relevant for the question if, in a specific case, a public versus a private and a permissionless versus a permissioned blockchain model is chosen, as this has a decisive influence over the ability to meet legal and regulatory requirements. On the other hand, this also means that the use of the generic blockchain technology as such compared to using any other technology does not entail any special additional requirements and would also not subject the blockchain technology to any additional authorization requirements as such.[59] Obviously, this only applies to the extent that the specific features of the blockchain technology would not per se trigger any additional elements of a legal norm.

However, the principle of technology neutrality does not mean that regulation would not be considerate of the specific particularities of blockchains at all. For example, the Swiss Government has recently set out in a report accompanying a new draft bill, concerning the adaptation of Swiss law to the developments of the distributed ledger technology, that Switzerland should continue to pursue a principle-based and technology-neutral legislative and regulatory approach, but where required also to allow for exceptions, in which case the rules should be designed in a competition-neutral way as possible.[60]

---

57. Rory Copeland, *FCA Final Guidance on Cryptoassets: Jettisoning Tech-Neutrality?*, Oxford Business Law Blog (23 Sep. 2019) available at: https://www.law.ox.ac.uk/business-law-blog/blog/2019/09/fca-final-guidance-cryptoassets-jettisoning-tech-neutrality (accessed 11 Mar. 2020).
58. Brad A. Greenberg, *Rethinking Technology Neutrality*, 207 Minn. L. Rev (2016) 1495, available at: https://www.minnesotalawreview.org/wp-content/uploads/2016/04/Greenberg_ONLINE PDF.pdf (accessed 11 Mar. 2020).
59. As formulated by the German Federal Financial Supervisory Authority (BaFin) as an example in the area of financial services regulation: 'The use of blockchain technology is not subject to an authorisation requirement in and of itself because, first and foremost, it is simply a form of technology,' available at: https://www.bafin.de/EN/Aufsicht/FinTech/Blockchain/blockchain_node_en.html (9 Jun. 2017) (accessed 11 Mar. 2020).
60. Botschaft zum Bundesgesetz zur Anpassung des Bundesrecht an Entwicklungen der Technik verteilter elektronischer Register (2019), 7 (1.1.3, III.), available at: https://www.newsd.admin.ch/newsd/message/attachments/59301.pdf (accessed 11 Mar. 2020). Available in German only and translation in the text by the author. The original reads: 'Die Schweiz soll weiterhin einen prinzipienbasierten und technologieneutralen Rechtsetzungs- und Regulierungsansatz

Applying the same approach of eliminating potential hurdles for the blockchain technology in existing laws, the State of Delaware in the United States (US), within the context of the 'Delaware Blockchain Initiative' launched by the then-Governor in May 2016,[61] has amended its corporation laws already back in 2017 by removing prohibitive wording in the Delaware corporate laws to allow for the record-keeping of share issuance and transfer on the basis of the blockchain technology. However, this was done without addressing blockchain, namely in the text, but only in the explanatory synopsis provided with the bill.[62] As a further example from the context of financial services regulation, the Financial Conduct Authority of the United Kingdom (UK) has stated in its 2019 consultation paper on cryptoassets with respect to its regulatory approach:

> The FCA is a technology neutral regulator, and the use of new technology alone does not alter how we consider it fits within the regulatory perimeter. However, while our tech-neutrality means we're agnostic about the type of technology used, the choice of technology may influence the way in which regulation applies. While the use of a certain technology won't usually have an impact on the permissions the firm requires, it might have an impact on the unique risks associated with the carrying on of certain regulated activity.[63]

As an example for a very blockchain-friendly yet technology-neutral overall regulatory and legislative approach, the German Federal Government's Blockchain Strategy may be mentioned. While it underlines 'the goal of using the opportunities in blockchain technology and of mobilising the areas of potential that it offers for the digital transformation',[64] *inter alia* by opening up German law for electronic securities and regulation of the public offering of certain crypto tokens through legislation to follow, a guiding principle for the implementation of the strategy and such new legislation 'is that of technology neutrality. Existing obstacles to the development and application of technologies are being eliminated, provided that doing so is compatible with the existing laws' fundamental objectives',[65] expressly towards the aim of fair

verfolgen, jedoch bei Bedarf auch Ausnahmen zulassen; dabei sind die Regeln möglichst wettbewerbsneutral zu gestalten.' For the Swiss draft bill *see* further Chapter 6, section §6.12, *infra*.

61. *See* https://corpgov.law.harvard.edu/2017/03/16/delaware-blockchain-initiative-transforming-the-foundational-infrastructure-of-corporate-finance (accessed 11 Mar. 2020).
62. Act to Amend Title 8 of the Delaware Code Relating to the General Corporation Law (5.5.2017), Synopsis, section 1, available at: https://legis.delaware.gov/BillDetail/25730 (accessed 11 Mar. 2020).
63. Financial Conduct Authority, *Guidance on Cryptoassets*, Consultation Paper CP19/3* (January 2019) para. 3.14, available at: https://www.fca.org.uk/publication/consultation/cp19-03.pdf (accessed 11 Mar. 2020).
64. Blockchain Strategy of the Federal Government, We Set Out the Course for the Token Economy (18 Sep. 2019) 4, English version available at: https://www.bmwi.de/Redaktion/EN/Publikationen/Digitale-Welt/blockchain-strategy.pdf?__blob=publicationFile&v=3 (accessed 11 Mar. 2020).
65. *Ibid.*

competition. It stipulates very clearly as a 'legal framework condition' that '[c]onsistent with technology neutrality, the legal framework must not favour or disadvantage blockchain technology in relation to other technologies'.[66]

These are only a few examples of many which demonstrate a common way of lawmakers and regulators to approach blockchain regulation under the doctrine of technology neutrality while recognizing the unique and distinctive character of the blockchain technology in the general laws by contemplating appropriate exceptions and eliminating potential hurdles, and by taking the specific features and risks of blockchain into account with respect to exercising regulatory supervision. While there is also a general debate on the utility of the principle of technology neutrality as such,[67] it can be expected that this will remain the predominant approach to regulation over the foreseeable future in terms of blockchain as a generic technology.

However, certain states have taken an approach to distinctively address blockchain by statutory regulation in an effort to foster the technology. Examples for this are the Malta Innovative Technology Arrangements and Services Act 2018[68] and the Liechtenstein Token and Trusted Technology Service Provider Act from 2019.[69]

[B] Regulating the Use Case Versus Regulating the Technology

Against the background of the principle of technology neutrality, most lawmakers and regulators have focused on observing and regulating the specific use cases of the blockchain technology, most prominently those of cryptoassets/tokens and initial coin offerings over the last years. In this connection, it has been a guiding principle that specifically financial services regulators[70] would look at the use case and the underlying business model to assess the applicability of regulation, in what a board member of the European Central Bank has described as the 'golden rule of supervision: same business, same risk, same rules'.[71] This, however, also implies that regulators may use the principle of proportionality, on the basis of applying the same rules, where appropriate to account for any differences that the underlying technology including blockchain may make.

66. *Ibid.*, at 12.
67. *See* e.g. Greenberg, *supra* n. 58, at 1495 et seq. for a critical review of the approach with respect to copyright law.
68. Innovative Technology Arrangements and Services Act (1 Nov. 2018), available at: http://www.justiceservices.gov.mt/DownloadDocument.aspx?app = lom&itemid = 12874&l = 1 (accessed 1 Mar. 2020).
69. Liechtenstein Token and Trusted Technology Service Provider Act, *supra* n. 9.
70. Including, for example, the German Federal Financial Supervisory Authority (BaFin), *see* https://www.bafin.de/SharedDocs/Veroeffentlichungen/EN/Pressemitteilung/2016/pm_160628_FinTechs_en.html (accessed 11 Mar. 2020).
71. Sabine Lautenschlaeger, *A Supervisory Perspective on 2019 and Beyond*, Speech in Dublin, Ireland, 17 Jan. 2019, available at: https://www.ecb.europa.eu/press/key/date/2019/html/ecb.sp190117.en.html (accessed 11 Mar. 2020).

[C] Regulatory Sandboxing

Several countries have adopted a 'sandboxing' approach in connection with the application of regulation to new technologies, specifically in the area of financial services regulation. In computer science, a 'sandbox' is an isolated testing environment in which new software can be tested without any connection to live systems.[72] The intention thereby pursued is to protect the live systems from anything that may go wrong in the course of the testing, hence allowing more flexibility, which ultimately means risk, to the tests. If such testing is successful, then the software may safely be applied in the real world outside of the sandbox.

This concept has been transferred to the application of regulation. In this context, it means that new technologies and pertinent business models are tested with a limited scope in a program that is closely accompanied and controlled by the relevant regulatory authorities. According to the European Banking Authority, '[r]egulatory sandboxes provide financial institutions and non-financial firms with a controlled space in which they can test innovative FinTech solutions with the support of an authority for a limited period of time, allowing them to validate and test their business model in a safe environment'.[73] In turn, regulatory requirements are sometimes lowered in order to avoid that the entry barrier is set too high, thereby especially allowing new and smaller market participants to enter established markets without the need to meet the full regulatory requirements in the early stage of the development. This concept is particularly applied in the context of financial services regulation and financial innovation ('FinTech') for innovative financial services products. The primary aim is the promotion of new and innovative ideas and technologies, often with the goal of creating an innovation-friendly regulatory place and to foster the establishment of research and development activities in this area. It aims to allow financial technology to grow and regulatory authorities to educate themselves in-depth on such new technologies.

However, as much as some countries have promoted this concept in the last years, as much have others been reluctant on changing existing regulatory standards even in a limited context. While the concept, as a potential advantage, aims to promote innovation, and hence economic growth, it is rejected by others as being potentially unfair to other market participants which, if they do not apply technologies that are eligible for the sandboxing, need to adhere to the full set of regulatory requirements which may amount to regulatory arbitrage. As an alternative to still remain innovation-friendly, but neutral from a regulatory perspective,[74] certain countries and their regulatory authorities rely on the principle of proportionality as an appropriate means

72. *See* e.g., https://searchsecurity.techtarget.com/definition/sandbox (accessed 11 Mar. 2020).
73. European Banking Authority, Discussion paper on the EBA's approach to financial technology (FinTech), EBA/DP/2017/02 (4 Aug. 2017) n. 8, available at: https://eba.europa.eu/sites/default/documents/files/documents/10180/1919160/7a1b9cda-10ad-4315-91ce-d798230ebd84/EBA%20Discussion%20Paper%20on%20Fintech%20%28EBA-DP-2017-02%29.pdf?retry=1 (accessed 11 Mar. 2020).
74. Remaining neutral in this context has no negative connotation but merely refers to the regulatory principle of 'technology neutrality' again.

to accommodate the differences between the market participants.[75] It seems well noted within the FinTech community, however, that a regulatory sandbox is not a legal vacuum. The European Fintech Alliance has called upon an EU-wide introduction and harmonization of sandboxes with 'clear and consistent' entry criteria, a 'simple and transparent authorisation' and a 'clear supervision' process as well as public sharing of regulatory learnings and the 'identification of innovation inhibiting EU regulations and their revision as the primary goal'.[76]

Countries which are applying, in various forms, sandbox approaches in the area of financial services are, for example, Denmark, Lithuania, the Netherlands, Poland, the UK, Bermuda, Guernsey and Jersey.[77] Turkey, within the framework of a broader blockchain strategy, has announced to allow for regulatory sandboxing for blockchain projects.[78] This list is non-exhaustive, and it should also be noted that in countries which do not apply a sandbox approach, other forms of experimentation may apply.[79]

§3.04 REGULATORY ACTORS

The previous sections have elaborated on the regulatory context of blockchains. The following section will describe the principal actors, who are relevant for the setting, application and enforcement of regulation, and their roles.

[A] Governments and Law Makers

Many countries have started to review existing regulation regarding the need for amendments or to create new regulation to accommodate the blockchain technology. As the main legislative actors on state level, many governments and lawmakers (parliaments) have not only started to review the blockchain technology and its potential economic benefits but also have started to remove hurdles in their current

75. *See* e.g. the answer of the German Government (*Antwort der Bundesregierung*) to a parliamentary request on regulatory sandboxing, Deutscher Bundestag, Drucksache 19/15103 (13 Nov. 2019) at 3 (in German only), available at: https://www.reguvis.de/fileadmin/Betrifft-Recht/Dokumente/edrucksachen/pdf/1915103.pdf (accessed 11 Mar. 2020).
76. European Fintech Alliance, Regulatory Sandboxes (16 Dec. 2018), available at: https://fintech-alliance.eu/regulatory-sandboxes (accessed 11 Mar. 2020).
77. According to the answer of the German Government (*Antwort der Bundesregierung*) to a parliamentary request on regulatory sandboxing, *infra* n. 75, at 1.
78. https://www.ledgerinsights.com/turkey-blockchain-regulatory-sandbox (accessed 11 Mar. 2020).
79. Experimentation clauses for innovation-driven models are, e.g., not entirely alien to German law. The German Carriage of Passengers Act in section 7(2), e.g., allows for regulatory exemptions with a view, e.g., on autonomous cars: 'In order to allow for the practical testing of new modes or means of transport, the licensing authority may, upon request on a case-by-case basis, authorise exemptions from the provisions of this Act or from provisions adopted on the basis of this Act for a maximum period of four years, insofar as they do not conflict with public transport interests,' translation from the German Federal Ministry for Economic Affairs and Energy, *see* https://www.bmwi.de/Redaktion/EN/Dossier/regulatory-test-beds-testing-environments-for-innovation-and-regulation.html (accessed 11 Mar. 2020).

regulation, and some have also started to develop comprehensive blockchain strategies including the announcement of future regulation on blockchain.

The German Federal Government, for example, as already mentioned above, has issued a comprehensive Blockchain Strategy in September 2019 after a comprehensive online consultation around various stakeholders.[80] The strategy includes the announcement of the short-term publication of draft legislation on the regulation of public offerings of certain crypto tokens[81] and the examination of opportunities to apply the blockchain technology in the area of company law.[82] Liechtenstein has issued its comprehensive 'Blockchain Act' in 2019 as well, to regulate mainly providers in the context of the 'token economy' by statute.[83] These are only two examples, and it can be expected that many other countries will follow.

[B] Regulatory Authorities and Enforcement Agencies

The blockchain technology has received a lot of attention from regulatory authorities worldwide in the last few years. Financial services regulators have particularly been active in issuing warnings to consumers with respect to initial coin offerings, for example, from the German Federal Financial Supervisory Authority (BaFin),[84] the European Securities and Markets Authority[85] and the U.S. Securities and Exchange Commission.[86] There have also been a number of specific enforcement actions against individual coin issuers, for example by the Monetary Authority of Singapore halting a securities token offering for regulatory breach[87] or by the U.S. Securities and Exchange Commission enforcing securities laws against a technology company for an unregistered initial coin offering with imposing a penalty of USD 24 million.[88] It can be observed that while in a first phase regulators have rather been observing the area of blockchain, they then relatively quickly (and often in the absence of specific regulation through statutes as set out above) applied and enforced existing regulatory requirements accordingly and are now issuing more and more dedicated regulatory guidance for blockchain-based models.

[C] Courts

So far, courts have rarely had to decide on cases where blockchain was at the heart of a decision, and hence there is only relatively little precedence as of now (as far as can

80. Blockchain Strategy of the Federal Government, *supra* n. 64.
81. *Ibid.*, at 7.
82. *Ibid.*, at 13.
83. Liechtenstein Token and Trusted Technology Service Provider Act, *supra* n. 9.
84. https://www.bafin.de/SharedDocs/Veroeffentlichungen/EN/Meldung/2017/meldung_171109_ICOs_en.html (accessed 11 Mar. 2020).
85. https://www.esma.europa.eu/press-news/esma-news/esma-highlights-ico-risks-investors-and-firms (accessed 11 Mar. 2020).
86. https://www.sec.gov/news/press-release/2017-131 (accessed 11 Mar. 2020).
87. https://www.mas.gov.sg/news/media-releases/2019/mas-halts-securities-token-offering-for-regulatory-breach (accessed 11 Mar. 2020).
88. https://www.sec.gov/news/press-release/2019-202 (accessed 11 Mar. 2020).

be seen). For the US, a useful blockchain litigation tracker provides some helpful oversight (which is not only focused on court decisions but also includes regulatory enforcement actions).[89] German court decisions include questions around the taxation of gains from crypto-assets sales[90] and a cessation order for Bitcoins,[91] but no decision with specifically the blockchain as (generic) technology in the focus as far as can be seen. It can be expected, however, that the number of blockchain cases tried in court will significantly rise over the next years.

[D] International and European Bodies and National Banks

Global and multinational initiatives play an important role as to the blockchain regulatory strategy beyond national borders and for the harmonization of the same. To only mention a few examples, the European Parliament has formulated certain key policy requests for blockchain regulation in its 2018 Resolution on distributed ledger technologies and blockchains and has held that the EU should not as such regulate blockchain technology, but remove existing barriers, guided by the principles of technology neutrality and business-model neutrality.[92] The EU Commission, as a part of its Capital Market Union and Digital Single Market strategies, has as well included blockchains as a point to focus on in its 2019 FinTech action plan, with the set-up of the EU Blockchain Initiative to specifically foster blockchain research and adaptation.[93] The G20 Summit has first treated the issue of cryptoassets in 2019 on their Osaka meeting, and in the Riyadh 2020 meeting, they confirmed their request to implement certain minimum standards for virtual assets and providers of such assets (Financial Action Task Force standards) and reiterated that 'global stablecoins' need proper evaluation and regulatory addressing before they can start to operate.[94] Stablecoins are 'digital units of value that are not a form of any specific currency (or basket thereof) but rather, by relying on a set of stabilisation tools, try to minimise fluctuations in their

89. https://www.mmlawus.com/newsitem/pdf/Blockchain_Litigation_2019_Year_in_Review_01232020_standard_4777137568842645468.pdf (accessed 11 Mar. 2020).
90. Finanzgericht Berlin-Brandenburg, Beschluss vom 20. Juni 2019 – 13 V 13100/19.
91. Bundesgerichtshof, Beschluss vom 27. Juli 2017 – 1 StR 412/16.
92. European Parliament resolution of 3 Oct. 2018 on distributed ledger technologies and blockchains: building trust with disintermediation (2017/2772(RSP)), nn. 65 and 68, available at: https://www.europarl.europa.eu/doceo/document/TA-8-2018-0373_EN.html?redirect (accessed 11 Mar. 2020).
93. Communication from the Commission, FinTech action plan: For a more competitive and innovative European financial sector, COM(2018)109 final (8 Mar. 2018), available at: https://www.europarl.europa.eu/doceo/document/TA-8-2018-0373_EN.html?redirect (accessed 11 Mar. 2020).
94. *See* the text of the statement: 'We reiterate our statement in October 2019 regarding the so-called "global stablecoins" and other similar arrangements that such risks need to be evaluated and appropriately addressed before they commence operation, and support the FSB's efforts to develop regulatory recommendations with respect to these arrangements,' Communiqué of the G20 Finance Ministers & Central Bank Governors Meeting 22–23 Feb. 2020, Riyadh, Saudi Arabia, at 3, available at: https://g20.org/en/g20/Documents/Communique%CC%81%20Final%2022-23%20February%202020.pdf (accessed 11 Mar. 2020).

price in such currencies'[95] which are based on blockchain systems. They currently seem to be a priority topic for global regulators, and in particular central banks.[96]

§3.05 ADDRESSEES OF REGULATION

One of the most fundamental legal questions in connection with blockchain is to whom any regulation can actually be addressed to. In order for a regulation to be effective, that regulation needs a specific addressee to whom it is directed and to whom it may assign legal rights and obligations. Certain conceptual aspects of the blockchain technology - namely decentralization and anonymity - challenge both the possibility to clearly identify an addressee and the ability to enforce any regulation upon such addressee. However, this strongly depends on the type and form of the specific blockchain. Behind every blockchain, there are ultimately natural or judicial persons. However, once a public blockchain, for example, is 'released', control over such blockchain may be limited or not existent. In a private blockchain, in contrast, this may be possible.

[A] Addressing 'the Blockchain' as Subject of Regulation

Against this background, a discussion has commenced as to whether a blockchain may also be awarded legal personality as such. This discussion may be seen as similar to respective discussions in the context of the 'Internet of things' (IoT) and the potential need to rethink traditional concepts of legal personality in the digital age.

[1] Legal Personality of the Blockchain

Traditionally, legal personality as the capacity to be the subject of legal rights and duties has been granted to a natural person. It has further been extended to organized groups of human beings as 'legal persons', for example by the establishment of corporations which group several natural persons by a commercial purpose predominantly in the context of national commercial and corporation laws and nation states in public international law. Over the last three decades, linked to the progress in computer sciences with the creation of 'intelligent' machines and the rise of Artificial Intelligence (AI), a discussion has started as to whether the concept of legal personality should be extended to certain machines and AI systems (which otherwise, by law, are only recognized as 'things' as regards the hardware and 'rights' as regards the

95. Dirk Bullmann & Jonas Klemm & Andrea Pinna, *In Search for Stability in Crypto-Assets: Are Stablecoins the Solution?*, 230 Occasional Paper Series of the European Central Bank (August 2019), available at: https://www.ecb.europa.eu/pub/pdf/scpops/ecb.op230~d57946be3b.en.pdf (accessed 11 Mar. 2020).

96. *See* e.g. the speech of Governor Lael Brainard from the U.S. Federal Reserve System on '*Update on Digital Currencies, Stablecoins, and the Challenges Ahead*' (18 Dec. 2019), available at: https://www.federalreserve.gov/newsevents/speech/brainard20191218a.htm (accessed 11 Mar. 2020) for a recent summary.

software). One of the main aspects in the discussion of a (limited) legal personality for such systems is their presumed capacity to form 'intelligent', or at least independent, decisions.[97] This is perceived as a 'risk of autonomy', if, for example, these decisions lead to contractual or tortious liability.[98] Against the background of this discussion, and with the purpose of addressing these issues as well as the blockchain-specific challenges discussed above, it has been suggested that blockchains may also be granted their own legal personality.

[2] The Malta Innovative Technology Arrangements and Services Act 2018

Malta has become one of the first countries to attempt a holistic regulation of the blockchain technology, along with other technology arrangements. The Innovative Technology Arrangements and Services Act (ITASA) followed an earlier consultation document issued by the Maltese Government, which held that:

> [w]hilst some Technology Arrangements are owned by a corporate structure, other Technology Arrangements may not have such an ownership structure. This could result in the possibility of transacting on and with the Technology Arrangement without a proper 'legal person' as counterparty. The proposed TAS Bill will try to provide a solution to such a scenario and it is being proposed that certain Technology Arrangements will be able to register with the Registrar for Legal Persons in Malta and acquire legal personality upon satisfaction of a number of requirements.[99]

The idea of granting such (limited) legal personality has been welcomed, with one main argument being the autonomy, for example because 'such autonomous entities may even survive the life of their designers'.[100] However, the ITASA has finally not included such concept and not created a new form of legal persons in that specific way.

[3] Decentralized Autonomous Organizations as a New Corporate Form

One further prominent example which has particularly raised questions over legal personality and corporate form is the *Decentralized Autonomous Organization* (DAO). Essentially, a DAO is a combination of the blockchain technology with Smart Contracts and cryptoassets and may be best characterized as a crowdfunded digital investment vehicle. Today's perception of what a DAO constitutes is largely based on a project

97. For a historically shaped discussion *see* e.g. Evan Joseph Zimmerman, *Machine Minds: Frontier in Legal Personhood* (12 Feb. 2015) 35–41, available at SSRN: https://ssrn.com/abstract=2563965 http://dx.doi.org/10.2139/ssrn.2563965 (accessed 11 Mar. 2020).
98. For an overview on the discussion for autonomous software agents and potential gaps in the liability system *see* e.g. Gunther Teubner, *Digitale Rechtssubjekte? Zum privatrechtlichen Status autonomer Softwareagenten*, 218 AcP 155–205 (2018).
99. Cited after Steve Tendon & Max Ganado, *Legal Personality for Blockchains, DAOs and Smart Contracts*, 1 RTDF (2018) 1-2.
100. *Ibid.*, at 1.

called 'The DAO', which was launched in 2016. The starting point was the coding of a crowdfunding Smart Contract, following which investors would be furnished with tokens, and such token holders would be given far-reaching voting rights over the administration of the project, especially on how the collected funds would be invested. Such voting was effected by digital means, based on funding proposals for products and services that companies could make to the DAO token holders. Likewise, the DAO was a modular concept with its 'core' kept relatively simple, and the idea that the code, and hence the DAO as such, could be updated over time based on coding proposals by its members and pertinent voting. The proposed mechanism of such a DAO was set out in a whitepaper and realized as an open-source code, so that any interested community member could participate and start to create a DAO according to the proposed model. One large community with over five thousand members subsequently created a Smart Contract framework, which was put on the Ethereum blockchain and which then became known as 'The DAO'. The DAO had overwhelming success in the community and collected approximately 12 million Ether, which is the cryptocurrency of the Ethereum blockchain and then worth approximately USD 150 million, in just four weeks. While the DAO received increasing interest, it came under attack as an 'antipattern in solidity' in one of its functions was (mis-)used by an attacker to transfer around USD 50 million into another DAO stream. The DAO community finally managed to undo the transfer through a hard fork of the DAO blockchain and hence to recover the funds.

One of the key characteristics of a DAO is its high degree of autonomy. Once the code of a DAO, or more precisely the conglomerate of Smart Contracts by which it is constituted, has been created and deployed on a blockchain, the coders will not have any advanced control over such DAO, but will rather only have voting rights that attach to any tokens they will 'purchase'. The governance mechanism of a DAO will provide for its automated function, and human intervention would only happen through the members voting and the proposals that may be made in regard to a DAO's organizational structure (through the proposal of an amendment of its code) or the investment decisions (based on the proposals that may be presented to them). Furthermore, the monies (through cryptocurrency) invested by the members would by means of the technical set-up factually be held by the DAO itself, and not by the collectivity of the members any more. It is obvious that this structure raises immediate questions over its legal status, in particular whether such an organization could or should have legal personality and the corporate form.

In light of these characteristics, it is discussed whether a DAO should be equipped with its own legal status, potentially as a new corporate form.[101] Yet, most legal regimes have a 'closed shop' of legal personality forms, and it would hence not exist under current regulation as a separate legal form. However, this does not exclude that DAOs may be seen as fulfilling the conditions of an existing corporate form, for example a partnership. But this will vary based on the relevant jurisdiction. Meanwhile, several countries have revisited, or announced to revisit, their corporation laws

101. *See* for the discussion, for example, Maximilian Mann, Die Decentralized Autonomous Organization – ein neuer Gesellschaftstyp? NZG (2017) 1024 et seq.

with respect to the blockchain technology. However, it is worth noting that most of these initiatives do not aim at creating a new legal form for blockchain-based organizations, but rather at using the blockchain technology for certain corporate housekeeping matters.[102]

[4] Summary

Under existing regulation, blockchains are not legal subjects and do not have their own legal personality as such (unless they fulfil the requirements of a certain corporate form). Hence, the focus in the following sections will be to examine the role of the various blockchain participants as potential subjects of regulation. However, there is a discussion, embedded into the wider question of IoT, on whether blockchains should be granted legal personality by future legislation, which does not seem to be excluded.

[B] Addressing Blockchain Actors as Subjects of Regulation

Against the foregoing, the focus is on the blockchain participants as the focus for any 'legal intervention point'.[103] Such are the nodes, miners, users, coders and oracles in the first place. They may neutrally be called a blockchain 'function'. Behind such function, there may just be a machine (in legal terms, a thing) or a natural or legal person. These functions may also be organized in groups and/or in a specific governance structure. The following section will provide an overview of the extent, and practical feasibility, that they may be used as such 'intervention points' or 'access points'[104] for legal intervention, specifically in using them as addressees for blockchain-related regulation.

[1] Validation Nodes ('Nodes')

Validation nodes, often also just called 'nodes', are computers which are all connected to each other via the Internet on the basis of a predefined, and unchangeable, software protocol. That software protocol may be freely downloadable as open-source software in a public blockchain network, or on a restricted basis in a private blockchain

102. For example the State of Delaware, *see supra* n. 62.
103. Usha R. Rodrigues, *Law and Blockchain*, 104 Iowa L. Rev. 679, 682 (2019), available at: https://ilr.law.uiowa.edu/print/volume-104-issue-2/law-and-the-blockchain (accessed 11 Mar. 2020).
104. Thematic Report of the European Blockchain Observatory and Forum, *supra* n. 7, at 6: 'First will be the evolution of legal and regulatory "tools" to assist authorities with some of the novel aspects of blockchain technology. Many of these already exist. As is the case today with the Internet, authorities have recourse to various "access points" – exchanges for example – to help them monitor and enforce legal and regulatory requirements even in highly decentralised, permissionless environments. The blockchain industry itself has also been developing tools that can assist authorities (and blockchain companies) in enforcing regulatory compliance – for example methods to "pierce the veil" of pseudonymity on blockchains and identify network participants.'

network. Each validation node stores the blockchain file (ledger) and constantly sends and receives updates to the blockchain file as new transactions are added. The sending and receiving of data happens automatically; they are a form of 'autonomous system'.[105] Validation nodes are so-called lightweight nodes, that means they do only download parts of the blockchain file as is necessary to validate the addition of new blocks (which consists of a group of transactions) through a hashing exercise. Validation nodes are hence instrumental for the blockchain's overall integrity.

From the legal perspective, nodes are things (the computer hardware) and rights (the software). As such, they cannot have any legal personality and hence cannot be addressed directly by regulation. However, there are two factors to consider as potential access points. The first is the (natural or legal) person who owns, or controls, the hardware and software which form the validation node. A comparison may be drawn here to cars. A car as such cannot be addressed directly by road traffic regulations, but the owner of the car and the driver who is not the owner (or, in some instances, both). For example, the Federal Communications Commission, the telecommunications regulatory authority in the US, has addressed a notification of harmful interference to a person who operated a bitcoin mining device, in a way negatively interfering with the network operator's broadband network, and ordered that person to stop the use of the device on the basis of telecommunication regulations.[106] A second potential access point is the place where the validation node (the computer hardware and software) is physically located. This could be the access point for any regulation where jurisdiction is established by the place where such things are physically located (*territorial jurisdiction*). However, this would only be possible in jurisdictions which recognize the principle of in rem jurisdiction, such that regulatory jurisdiction could be exercised and enforced against the thing as such, for example by attaching a regulatory notice to the thing and, if not adhered to by the legal persons who owns or controls it, seize it.

It can, however, be difficult, if not impossible in some cases to identify the persons behind the node. But as shown above, a blockchain transaction is not completely anonymous, and it may be possible to trace back the individual person behind a node through the transactional data or the telecommunications data (in which case Internet service providers would play a role as well). But even if the person behind the node could be sufficiently identified to address regulation to him, then the question is whether such person could change anything to the blockchain (and specifically, the transactions) at all. This is not the case for individual nodes in a public blockchain, unless they amount to a group of nodes with a certain computational power in the hands of that person. Hence, in the case of a public blockchain, addressing the person

105. John Salmon & Gordon Myers, *Blockchain and Associated Legal Issues for Emerging Markets*, Emerging Markets Compass Note 63 (January 2019) 4, available at: https://www.ifc.org/wps/wcm/connect/da7da0dd-2068-4728-b846-7cffcd1fd24a/EMCompass-Note-63-Blockchain-and-Legal-Issues-in-Emerging-Markets.pdf?MOD=AJPERES&CVID=mxocw9F (accessed 11 Mar. 2020).

106. Federal Communications Commission, Enforcement Bureau, Case No.: EB-FIELDNER-17-00025658, Letter dated 15 Feb. 2018, available at: https://transition.fcc.gov/Daily_Releases/Daily_Business/2018/db0215/DOC-349258A1.pdf (accessed 11 Mar. 2020).

behind the node would be remote as it would be factually impossible for that person to interfere with the blockchain other than simply deactivating the node, which would normally have no effect on the blockchain due to its decentralized nature. This is different in private blockchains, and wherever individual responsibility of an addressee is a prerequisite (e.g., in financial services regulation) deploying private blockchains would hence be an option to achieve compliance by retaining and addressing control over the nodes.

However, with all these difficulties, it is important to underline that the persons behind the nodes are of course subject to all applicable laws in the capacity of their very person, and 'hiding' behind the node would not relieve them from any of these, as it is the case also for all other functions discussed below as well.

[2] Mining Nodes ('Miners')

Mining nodes, often also just called 'miners', are basically validation nodes which also take part in the process of mining (i.e., trying to solve the 'Proof-of-Work' or 'Proof-of-Stake' exercise). Hence, they are not fundamentally different from the perspective applied here, other than adding any connecting points which may result from the mining. Potential additional entry points may be that miners are often building larger 'mining pools', which are more easily identifiable, and that miners get a reward for the mining exercise (mostly, cryptocurrency) which they may want to eventually convert to fiat money, in which case identifying information may be required. The other way round, as miners are involved as parties in the mining process, they need to be mindful even more than nodes if they would be conducting a regulated activity (e.g., in the case of cryptoassets, a regulated financial services activity which may trigger licensing requirements, and if not adhered to, may lead to sanctions amounting up to a criminal offence).

[3] Blockchain Users

Blockchain users are the parties to a blockchain transaction, for example, in the case of Bitcoin the sender and the receiver of the Bitcoins. The best entry point in imposing regulation on them is in a private blockchain probably the point in time when they join a blockchain (and where legal obligations may then be imposed on them contractually) and in a public blockchain the point of execution of a transaction, as this may be connected to an off-chain activity (e.g., through an exchange platform which applies full identification requirements).

[4] Coders

As it has already been set out above,[107] coders as the programmers of a blockchain's software code are relevant in various instances. First, there are the coders who program the core blockchain software, which is then deployed as the software protocol to connect the nodes. Second, coders program updates which may alter the blockchain at a later stage and may decide on updates as a core group.[108] Coders can be regarded as a key element in the search for a regulatory access point, as they are the developers of the protocol as the 'constitution', and there is probably no better point in time to account for general regulatory compliance than in the beginning of a blockchain's design and software development. Of course, there are not necessarily only coders involved in the design of a blockchain, and, for example, in a corporate environment many functions would be involved. However, the coders are the persons actually implementing any requirements directly into the blockchain through the code; hence they have an instrumental function in this process. It goes without saying again that coders need to act in compliance with all applicable laws both when they program the software and with respect to what the software later does, but this is also the occasion to build in any regulatory requirement by design. This includes the basic question of whether a blockchain should be public or private and permissionless or permissioned.

§3.06 EXAMPLES OF SPECIFIC BLOCKCHAIN REGULATION

The first section above has attempted to provide a first definitional outline of blockchains in a legal context, and the following sections have elaborated on more fundamental questions on the regulation of blockchains by using regulatory examples where appropriate. The following section will look at certain specific pieces of legislation (enacted or proposed) which contain a definition of blockchain (including more broadly the distributed ledger technology) in order to better understand how blockchain as a generic technology is addressed in current regulation, and may be addressed in future regulation, which should also be helpful for dealing with it in a contractual context. The list is non-exhaustive.

[A] United States

While there is no federal US legislation as far as can be seen relative to blockchain so far, US state laws are a fruitful source in terms of specific blockchain definitions.[109]

107. Section §3.01[B][3], *supra*.
108. Finck, *supra* n. 45, at 52.
109. There is already a clear definition in the Code of Laws of the United States of America for the 'Internet' which is defined as follows: 'The term "Internet" means collectively the myriad of computer and telecommunications facilities, including equipment and operating software, which comprise the interconnected worldwide network of networks that employ the Transmission Control Protocol/Internet Protocol, or any predecessor or successor protocol to such protocol, to communicate information of all kinds by wire or radio' (21 U.S.C. § 802 (50)).

Several US states have enacted or proposed legislation that expressly refers to and defines 'blockchain'.

The South Carolina Blockchain Industry Empowerment Act 2019 contains a straightforward definition:

> 'Blockchain' means a digital ledger or database which is chronological, consensus based, decentralized, and mathematically verified in nature.[110]

Similarly, the Bill to amend the Code of Virginia relating to business records electronically registered on a blockchain self-authenticating (in context of business records as evidence) defines blockchain as follows:

> '[B]lockchain' means a mathematically secured, chronological, and decentralized consensus ledger or database, whether maintained via Internet interaction, a peer-to-peer network, or otherwise.[111]

The Utah Blockchain Technology Act 2019 contains a slightly more advanced definition:

> 'Blockchain' or 'blockchain technology' means an electronic method of storing data that is:
>
> (a) maintained by consensus of multiple unaffiliated parties;
> (b) distributed across multiple locations; and
> (c) mathematically verified.[112]

The South Dakota Act to provide a definition of blockchain technology for certain purposes contains the following definition:

> 'Blockchain technology,' technology that uses a distributed, shared, and replicated ledger, either public or private, with or without permission, or driven with or without tokenized crypto economics where the data on the ledger is protected with cryptography and is immutable and auditable.[113]

The Arkansas Act Concerning Blockchain Technology[114] defines 'Blockchain distributed ledger technology' as follows:

110. South Carolina Blockchain Industry Empowerment Act 2019, section 3, available at: https://www.scstatehouse.gov/sess123_2019-2020/bills/4351.htm (accessed 11 Mar. 2020).
111. A bill to amend the Code of Virginia by adding a section numbered 8.01-390.4, relating to business records electronically registered on a blockchain self-authenticating, available at: https://legl.state.va.us/cgi-bin/legp504.exe?191 + ful + HB2415&191 + ful + HB2415 (accessed 11 Mar. 2020).
112. Utah Blockchain Technology Act 2019, section 1, available at: https://le.utah.gov/~2019/bills/static/SB0213.html (accessed 11 Mar. 2020).
113. South Dakota Act to provide a definition of blockchain technology for certain purposes, section 1, available at: https://sdlegislature.gov/docs/legsession/2019/Bills/HB1196ENR.pdf (accessed 11 Mar. 2020).
114. Act Concerning Blockchain Technology, H.B. 1944 section 1 (amends the Arkansas Code), available at: http://www.arkleg.state.ar.us/assembly/2019/2019R/Acts/Act1061.pdf (accessed 11 Mar. 2020).

means technology that uses a distributed, decentralized, shared, and replicated ledger that is:
(A) Either:
  (i) Public; or
  (ii) Private;
(B) Either:
  (i) Permissioned; or
  (ii) Permissionless; and
(C) Contains data that is:
  (i) Securely protected with cryptography;
  (ii) Immutable;
  (iii) Auditable; and
  (iv) Provides an uncensored truth.

The definition of 'Blockchain technology' therein is:

a shared, immutable ledger that facilitates the process of recording one (1) or more transactions and 3 tracking one (1) or more tangible or intangible assets in a business network.

The Arkansas Act has been criticized as being '[a]nother [b]ad [b]lockchain [b]ill' which criticism does, however, more relate to the logic of how its definitions work together.[115]

According to the California Senate Bill No. 373 amending the Health and Safety Act, 'blockchain technology' means 'a mathematically secured, chronological, and decentralized consensus ledger or database'.[116]

The Connecticut Act Requiring the Secretary of the Office of Policy and Management to Develop a Plan to Incorporate Blockchain Technology in the Administration of a State Function defines 'blockchain technology' as:

distributed ledger technology that uses a distributed, decentralized, shared and replicated ledger that may be public or private, permissioned or permissionless and that may include the use of electronic currencies or electronic tokens as a medium of electronic exchange.[117,118]

115. William Denny, Another Bad Blockchain Bill (1 May 2019), available at: https://www.americanbar.org/groups/business_law/publications/committee_newsletters/cyberspace/2019/201905/blockchain (accessed 11 Mar. 2020).
116. California Senate Bill No. 373, Act to add and repeal section 103526.7 of the Health and Safety Code, section 1, available at: http://leginfo.legislature.ca.gov/faces/billNavClient.xhtml?bill_id=201920200SB373 (accessed 11 Mar. 2020).
117. Connecticut Substitute Senate Bill No. 1032, Act Requiring the Secretary of the Office of Policy and Management to Develop a Plan to Incorporate Blockchain Technology in the Administration of a State Function, section 1, available at: https://www.cga.ct.gov/2019/FC/pdf/2019SB-01032-R000384-FC.PDF (accessed 11 Mar. 2020).
118. The same definition is replicated in Connecticut Raised Bill No. 1033, 'Act Concerning Noncompete Agreements in the Blockchain Technology Industry', available at: https://www.cga.ct.gov/2019/TOB/s/pdf/2019SB-01033-R00-SB.PDF (accessed 11 Mar. 2020). The latter Act is in a remarkable context aiming at the prohibition of the use of non-compete clauses in employment contracts in the technology industry, presumably with the aim to foster mobility of blockchain professionals.

and 'distributed ledger' as:

> any database that is consensually shared and synchronized across multiple sites, institutions or geographies allowing for public witnesses to such transactions and may include supporting infrastructure, including blockchain technology.[119]

The Illinois Blockchain Business Development Act defines 'blockchain' as:

> an electronic record created by the use of a decentralized method by multiple parties to verify and store a digital record of transactions which is secured by the use of a cryptographic hash of previous transaction information.[120]

and 'blockchain technology' as:

> computer software or hardware or collections of computer software or hardware, or both, that utilize or enable a blockchain.[121]

The Nevada Act Relating to Electronic Transactions contains a definition of specifically a 'public blockchain':

> means an electronic record of transactions or other data which:
> 1. Is uniformly ordered;
> 2. Is processed using a decentralized method by which two or more unaffiliated computers or machines verify the recorded transactions or other data;
> 3. Is redundantly maintained by two or more unaffiliated computers or machines to guarantee the consistency or nonrepudiation of the recorded transactions or other data;
> 4. Is validated by the use of cryptography; and
> 5. Does not restrict the ability of any computer or machine to:
>   (a) View the network on which the record is maintained; or
>   (b) Maintain or validate the state of the public blockchain.[122]

The State of New York Act to Amend the State Technology Law, in Relation to Blockchain Technology and Smart Contracts gives the following definition for 'blockchain technology' based on the same definition that was previously used by the North Dakota House Bill No. 1045[123] which amended various other codes:

> shall mean distributed ledger technology that uses a distributed, decentralized, shared and replicated ledger, which may be public or private, permissioned or permissionless, or driven by tokenized crypto economics or tokenless. The data on the ledger is protected with cryptography, is immutable and auditable and provides an uncensored truth.[124]

119. *Supra* n. 117, in section 1(2).
120. Illinois House Bill No. 2540, Blockchain Business Development Act, available at: http://www.ilga.gov/legislation/101/HB/PDF/10100HB2540lv.pdf section 5 (accessed 11 Mar. 2020).
121. *Ibid.*
122. Nevada Senate Bill No. 162, Act Relating to Electronic Transactions, section 2, available at: https://www.leg.state.nv.us/App/NELIS/REL/80th2019/Bill/6233/Text (accessed 11 Mar. 2020).
123. North Dakota House Bill No. 1045, available at: https://www.legis.nd.gov/assembly/66-2019/documents/19-0127-06000.pdf (accessed 11 Mar. 2020).
124. State of New York, Bill No. S04142, Act to amend the state technology law, in relation to blockchain technology and smart contracts (1 Mar. 2019), Section 1, available at: https://

Some other state bills and resolutions use the term 'blockchain', but do not separately define it, for example the Ohio bill to allow a governmental entity to utilize distributed ledger technology, including blockchain technology, which simply says:

> A governmental entity may utilize distributed ledger technology, including blockchain technology, in the exercise of its authority.[125]

[B] Outside of the US

There are only very few statutes outside of the US which specifically define blockchain as a legal term. The Malta Innovative Technology Arrangements and Services Act 2018 does not provide a separate definition of blockchains (which are not even mentioned in the text of the Act) and distributed ledger technology, but rather assumes them and puts them in a broader context of 'technology arrangements':

> The following shall be considered to be innovative technology arrangements for the purposes of this Act:
> 1. software and architectures which are used in designing and delivering DLT which ordinarily, but not necessarily:
>   (a) uses a distributed, decentralized, shared and, or replicated ledger;
>   (b) may be public or private or hybrids thereof;
>   (c) is permissioned or permissionless or hybrids thereof;
>   (d) is immutable;
>   (e) is protected with cryptography; and
>   (f) is auditable;
> 2. smart contracts and related applications, including decentralised autonomous organisations, as well as other similar arrangements;
> 3. any other innovative technology arrangement which may be designated by the Minister, on the recommendation of the Authority, by notice from time to time.[126]

The Liechtenstein Token and Trusted Technology Service Provider Act[127] does not refer specifically to the underlying technology of the tokens and does contain a definition neither of blockchain nor of distributed ledger technology, but rather takes a more blockchain-agnostic approach with 'Trustworthy Technology' as a key term which is defined as '[t]echnologies through which the integrity of Tokens, the clear assignment of Tokens to TT Identifiers and the disposal over Tokens is ensured'.[128]

As a final example, the Bermuda Digital Business Act 2018 defines 'distributed ledger technology' as:

---

nyassembly.gov/leg/?default_fld = &leg_video = &bn = S04142&term = 2019&Summary = Y& Text = Y (accessed 11 Mar. 2020).

125. Ohio, A bill to enact section 9.16 of the Revised Code to allow a governmental entity to utilize distributed ledger technology, including blockchain technology, section 1, available at: https://www.legislature.ohio.gov/legislation/legislation-summary?id = GA133-HB-220 (accessed 11 Mar. 2020).
126. Malta Innovative Technology Arrangements and Services Act 2018, *supra* n. 68, in First Schedule.
127. Liechtenstein Token and Trusted Technology Service Provider Act 2019, *supra* n. 9.
128. *Ibid.*, at Art. 2(1)(a).

> a database system in which –
>
> (a) information is recorded and consensually shared and synchronised across network or multiple nodes; and
> (b) all copies of the database are regarded as equally authentic;[129]

[C] Definition and Summary

When comparing the above definitions as to their lowest common denominators, the following elements are the result: 'database', 'decentralized', 'cryptographically verified and secured'. Interestingly, 'immutability' is not commonly used in many of them, and hence seems to be seen as optional.

Read together with the definitional outline that was set out above, in which a blockchain was described 'as being a public or private, permissionless or permissioned database network, which may or may not be controlled to a certain extent by (an) operator(s), which is based on certain software code (protocol) and which inherent features are that it is decentralized, immutable and transparent',[130] and completed by the fact that blockchain technology assumes that the trust is created by the technology itself, a broad and universal definition could, for example, read:

> Blockchain means a decentralized database based on a software protocol, which is cryptographically verified and secured, which may be public or private, may require an admission permission or not, may be controlled by (an) operator(s) or not, may be immutable or not, and in which it is intended that certain trust results from the foregoing principles inherently.

§3.07 OUTLOOK: FINANCIAL SERVICES PRUDENTIAL REGULATION

While so far the regulatory focus in financial services regulation in connection with blockchain specifically for cryptoassets has been on market conduct, there is a raising interest in this topic from a prudential regulation perspective as well which is worth to be briefly mentioned as an outlook. The Basel Committee on Banking Supervision (BCBS) has issued a discussion paper open for comments on the designing of a prudential treatment for cryptoassets on 13 March 2020.[131] The BCBS resumes the rapid growth of cryptoassets in the past few years and outlines the historical total value peak in January 2018 with over USD 800 billion. The BCBS is of the view that despite that the market capitalization of the crypto-asset market remains relatively small

129. Bermuda Digital Business Act 2018, section 2, available at: http://www.bermudalaws.bm/laws/Annual%20Laws/2018/Acts/Digital%20Asset%20Business%20Act%202018.pdf (accessed 11 Mar. 2020).
130. *See* section §3.06[B][5], *supra*.
131. Basel Committee on Banking Supervision, Discussion paper: Designing a prudential treatment for crypto-assets (December 2019), available at: https://www.bis.org/bcbs/publ/d490.pdf (accessed 11 Mar. 2020).

compared to the total size of the global financial system and that the exposure from banks is currently limited, the absolute size is meaningful and has the possibility to raise financial stability concerns.[132] This goes hand in hand with increased regulatory scrutiny of so-called stablecoins[133] which the BCBS also mentions as a subject for further assessment.[134] The paper is aimed for the BCBS to obtain a better understanding of the situation, upon which it would issue a consultation paper should it decide to specify a prudential treatment of cryptoassets.[135] The subject is not entirely new, and other regulators have as well issued respective enquiries in the past.[136]

§3.08 SUMMARY

This chapter has attempted to provide an overview on the implications that legal regulation has on the blockchain technology and has elaborated on definitional aspects, challenges and actors from a broader perspective of the blockchain as a generic technology rather than from a pure use case basis. It is important to note that this chapter is by no means exhaustive, and the legal assessment of a specific blockchain remains subject to a comprehensive review on a case-by-case basis. Also, blockchain is a fast-moving technology, and it can be expected that characteristics may change as well over time – most probably not the constituent ones, but in further details, specifically where it is the question of how blockchain can be made compliant with current and future regulation. Hence, a thorough legal review in each individual case is indispensable.

FURTHER READING

Primavera De Filippi & Aaron Wright, *Blockchain and the Law: The Rule of Code* (2018).

Josias N. Dewey (ed.), *Global Legal Insights Blockchain & Cryptocurrency Regulation* (2nd edition 2020).

Michèle Finck, *Blockchain: Regulation and Governance in Europe* 93 (2018)

Eduard Hofert, *Regulierung der Blockchains* (2018).

Lawrence Lessig, *Code Version 2.0* (2006), available at: http://codev2.cc/download+remix/Lessig-Codev2.pdf (accessed 11 March 2020).

Carla L. Reyes, *Moving Beyond Bitcoin to an Endogenous Theory of Decentralized Ledger Technology Regulation: An Initial Proposal*, 61 Vill. L. Rev. 191–234 (2016).

Thomas Richter, *Blockchain – Rechtliche Aspekte aus Sicht der Finanzindustrie*, at 165–178, DGRI Jahrbuch 2017, Robert G. v. Briner & Axel Funk (eds) 2018.

132. *Ibid.*, at 1.
133. *See supra* nn. 95 and 96.
134. Basel Committee on Banking Supervision, *supra* n. 131, at 1.
135. *Ibid.*, at 2.
136. For example UK Parliament over the effects of blockchain on banking solvency, *see* https://www.coindesk.com/uk-mp-argue-prudential-regulation-needed-for-blockchain-banks (accessed 11 Mar. 2020).

Usha R. Rodrigues, *Law and Blockchain*, 104 Iowa L. Rev. 679, 682 (2019), available at: https://ilr.law.uiowa.edu/print/volume-104-issue-2/law-and-the-blockchain (accessed 11 March 2020).

CHAPTER 4

Blockchain and Smart Contracts*

Philip Trillmich, Matthias Goetz & Chris Ewing

§4.01 TERMINOLOGY AND CHARACTERISTICS: WHAT IS A SMART CONTRACT?

[A] History of the Term 'Smart Contract'

Although many believe that blockchain technology evolved earlier than smart contracts, mentions of smart contracting can be traced back to the 1990s.[1] That is when Nick Szabo developed a theoretical concept of computer programs designed to make all stages of contractual relationships less costly, more secure and more functional.[2] He drew on the real-life example of the vending machine to illustrate the characteristics of a smart contract:

> Within a limited amount of potential loss (the amount in the till should be less than the cost of breaching the mechanism), the machine takes in coins, and via a simple mechanism ... dispense change and product according to the displayed price. The vending machine is a contract with bearer: anybody with coins can participate in an exchange with the vendor. The lockbox and other security mechanisms protect the stored coins and contents from attackers, sufficiently to allow profitable deployment of vending machines in a wide variety of areas.[3]

---

* Special thanks go to Monopoly Christiaan-Rakus, Aleksandra Drabek and Elena Blessing who assisted with this chapter.

1. Szabo, N., *Formalizing and Securing Relationships on Public Networks*, firstmonday, available at: http://firstmonday.org/ojs/index.php/fm/article/view/548/469 (accessed on 24 Feb. 2020); *see* also Wilkens, R. & Falk, R., *Smart Contracts – Grundlagen, Anwendungsfelder und rechtliche Aspekte* 3 (2019); Gyr, E., *Blockchain und Smart Contracts – Die vertragsrechtlichen Implikationen einer neuen Technologie*, available at: https://biblio.unibe.ch/download/eldiss/19gyr_e.pdf (accessed on 24 Feb. 2020).
2. Szabo, N., *supra* n. 1.
3. *Ibid.*

Thus, three features of the original idea of a smart contract deserve attention: (1) its potential to perform a contract with anyone, (2) the automatic performance of the contractual obligations if a specific condition is met, and (3) security mechanisms which make it unattractive to circumvent the agreed processes to obtain the promised goods or services, due to the potential costs of breaches.[4]

Nevertheless, smart contracts remained a theoretical idea for a number of years because of the absence of technology suitable to realize two of the principal features – a more secure performance of contractual promises and a reduction of transaction costs.[5] As such, despite software development being able to automate contractual relationships, no technology could come as close as traditional contracts in guaranteeing the secure performance of contractual obligations.[6] Software programs used by one party in a traditional client-server-environment, for example by automating order processes in a web shop[7], were not transparent enough and could be susceptible to manipulation.

However, it appears this has now changed. The emergence of decentralized blockchain technology is an opportunity to revisit the concept of smart contracts. In practice, we have already seen the first use of smart contracts within the blockchain technology as outlined in §4.02 below. As further described in this chapter, the deployment of smart contracts in blockchain brings with it a number of advantages. These advantages appear to finally fulfil Szabo's idea of smart contracts.

[B] Technical Characteristics of a 'Smart Contract'

Nick Szabo defined smart contracts as 'a set of promises, specified in digital form, including protocols within which the parties perform on these promises'.[8] Max Raskin used a simpler definition to describe the features of a smart contract when indicating that smart contracts are 'agreements wherein execution is automated, usually by computers'.[9] Both of those definitions share similar features. However, no unanimous definition of smart contracts exists. In particular, there is a certain level of disagreement as to the characteristics of smart contracts. The *legal* characteristics will be discussed in more detail in §4.01[C] below. For a detailed description of the technical characteristics and features of a smart contract, see Chapter 1 §1.02 above.

4. Gyr, E., *supra* n. 1.
5. Kaulartz, M. & Heckmann, J., *Smart Contracts – Anwendungen der Blockchain-Technologie* 618 (CR 2016).
6. Wilkens, R. & Falk, R., *supra* n. 1, at 4.
7. Paulus, D. & Matzke, R. *Smart Contracts und das BGB – Viel Lärm um nichts?*, 431, 435 (ZfPW 2018).
8. Szabo, N. *Smart Contracts: Building Blocks for Digital Markets*, available at: http://www.fon.hum.uva.nl/rob/Courses/InformationInSpeech/CDROM/Literature/LOTwinterschool2006/szabo.best.vwh.net/smart_contracts_2.html (accessed on 24 Feb. 2020).
9. Raskin, M., *The Law and Legality of Smart Contracts*, 305, 306 (1 Georgetown Law Technology Review 2017).

[C] Terminology

[1] The Meaning of the Term 'Smart' in Smart Contract

The term 'smart' in 'smart contract' implies that such a contract is, in some sense, intelligent and able to adapt to changing circumstances. However, this view is rather misleading. Smart contracts are not 'smart' in the sense of being intelligent or adaptive. In particular, they are not means of autonomous decision making (for example, and in contrast, smart home concepts such as a device which automatically optimizes room temperature might apply artificial intelligence (AI) to autonomously gather and analyse data and make autonomous decisions[10]).[11] The term 'smart contract' should rather be understood as a 'buzzword' implying that computer programs and codes are involved, which perform in line with their instructions and the way they are programmed to perform.[12]

Usually, modern smart contracts refer to an application of decentralized blockchain technologies, which enable storing and execution of codes in their database. The decentralized blockchain technology enables smart contracts to develop beyond the vending-machine example discussed above, in §4.01[A]. Such a machine is under the control of its owner who can switch it off at any point.[13] This does not apply to a smart contract in a blockchain, which is automatic and autonomously executing.[14] In addition, smart contracts can be programmed in such a way that they can obtain further input from human-controlled processes ('oracle') when certain defined events occur.[15] Therefore, although smart contracts are not 'smart' in an AI sense because they are simply pre-programmed lines of code, it would be fair to say that they have still developed a different kind of 'intelligence'. This is because, due to the use of blockchain technology, they have become more autonomous.

[2] What Does the Term 'Contract' Mean in Smart Contract?

There have been many attempts to assess the extent to which a smart contract actually is a contract in the legal sense. Durovic and Janssen propose that a smart contract is just a 'computer code which is operated by a computer and is self-executing and self-enforcing'.[16] This definition sees smart contracts through the lens of a blockchain,

10. Samsung Newsroom, *A Relaxing Weekend with Samsung's AI-Enabled and Smart Appliances*, available at: https://news.samsung.com/global/a-relaxing-weekend-with-samsungs-ai-enabled-and-smart-appliances (accessed on 24 Feb. 2020).
11. Kaulartz, M. & Heckmann, J., *supra* n. 5, at 618.
12. *Ibid.*
13. Paech, P., *Law and Autonomous Systems Series: What Is a Smart Contract?* (University of Oxford), available at: https://www.law.ox.ac.uk/business-law-blog/blog/2018/07/law-and-autonomous-systems-series-what-smart-contract (accessed on 24 Feb. 2020).
14. *Ibid.*
15. Oracle is an interface that feeds in information about the event, explored in more detail in Chapter 1, §1.11[B], *supra*.
16. Durovic, M. & Janssen, A., *The Formation of Blockchain-Based Smart Contracts in the Light of Contract Law* 753 (26(6) European Review of Private Law, 2018).

indicating that a smart contract is merely a code that can document a contract in the legal sense or automate certain legally relevant processes.[17]

In particular, smart contracts can perform different tasks in the context of contractual relationships, such as: (1) automatically perform certain obligations (unlocking a door to an apartment once payment is made,[18] or remunerating employees[19]), (2) providing access to a person's digital identity stored on blockchain during Know Your Client (KYC) processes,[20] (3) automatically effecting a reaction in case a contractual obligation is not performed (for example, locking a smart lock in the event of a delayed payment or after a contract has ended[21] or using a smart meter to block energy provision as a result of a delayed payment[22]), and (4) recording the effect of contractual relationships (for example, by recording a change in property ownership).[23]

As such, the wide spectrum of uses encouraged a broader understanding of 'smart contracts' and attempts to use them to execute legally binding declarations or perform legally binding acts.[24] Nevertheless, executing legally binding contracts is dependent upon fulfilling legal requirements, rather than the conditions in a code; how far smart contracts are able to fulfil those requirements is discussed in §4.03 below. The issue of 'applicable law vs code in law' is analysed in more detail in §4.03[A] below.

[3] The Attempt to Develop a Definition

As indicated above, there is no universal definition of a 'smart contract'.[25] The recent legal statement on cryptoassets and smart contracts by the UK Jurisdiction Taskforce (UKJT)[26] did not provide a precise definition, pointing out it was 'unlikely to be useful'[27] and instead focused on characteristics and their relevance legally. Indeed, the search for a comprehensive definition is a rather challenging exercise. Like the definition of smart contracts suggested by the Swiss Parliament or the German Federal

17. Paulus, D. & Matzke, R., *supra* n. 7, at 433.
18. Wilkens, R. & Falk, R., *supra* n. 1, at 19.
19. Rampton, J., *Applications for Blockchain in Your Business* 5 (The Economist), available at: https://execed.economist.com/blog/industry-trends/5-applications-blockchain-your-business (accessed on 24 Feb. 2020).
20. Ambisafe *Smart Contracts: 10 Use Cases for Business*, available at: https://ambisafe.com/blog/smart-contracts-10-use-cases-business/ (accessed on 24 Feb. 2020).
21. Paulus, C. & Matzke, R., *supra* n. 7, at 434.
22. Paulus, C. & Matzke, R. *Smart Contracts und Smart Meter – Versorgungsperre für Fernzugriff* 1905, 1906 (NJW 2018).
23. Davies, A., *10 Uses for Smart Contracts*, available at: https://www.devteam.space/blog/10-uses-for-smart-contracts/ (accessed on 24 Feb. 2020).
24. Paulus, C. & Matzke, R., *supra* n. 7, at 433-434.
25. *Ibid.*
26. The UKJT is one of six taskforces under the LawTech Delivery Panel, an industry group which supports the digital transformation of the legal sector. The findings within the legal statement are the result of several rounds of public and private consultations and has the benefit of technical, judicial, legal and academic opinions,
27. UKJT, *Legal Statement on Cryptoassets and Smart Contracts*, The LawTech Delivery Panel (November 2019).

Financial Supervisory Authority,[28] the conception of smart contracts is often limited to blockchain-related use.

However, it is also important to realize that smart contracts are, in principle, technology neutral and can exist outside of the blockchain framework. For example, a computer program on an e-commerce platform that automates the processes of concluding a contract or an application for a car/bike rental which automatically unlocks the vehicle also fulfils the criteria of a smart contract as developed by Szabo and should therefore be classified as a smart contract.[29] The automatic freezing of a credit card in case of fraudulent activities is cited as a further example of a smart contract.[30]

Therefore, not confining their definition to blockchain, Kaulartz and Heckmann define a smart contract as a software program which performs, controls and/or documents legally relevant acts (in particular, the performance of contractual obligations) that are conditional upon digitally verifiable results.[31]

Evidently, and in line with the definition proposed by Kaulartz and Heckmann, smart contracts can be deployed outside of the blockchain. However, there are a number of advantages of a smart contract existing within the blockchain compared to a smart contract existing outside of the blockchain. Some of these advantages are showcased in §4.03[D] below. Based on this and the below, as well as the significant advantages of smart contracts within the blockchain over smart contracts outside of the blockchain, the analysis of smart contracts in this chapter is limited to smart contracts within the blockchain.

[D] Characteristics of 'Smart Contracts' as an Application of a Blockchain

As indicated above, there are many advantages of utilizing smart contracts within the blockchain environment. One of the key benefits is a guarantee of autonomous performance of contractual obligations. This is in contrast to 'offline' contracts, where despite the very best intentions of both parties, breaches such as delayed payment or delayed delivery can occur. As such, the certainty attributed to blockchain can be a significant advantage.

28. The BaFin defined smart contracts as 'programmable contracts, which are defined by the programme code and are automatically executed and enforced in blockchains', *see* Bundesanstalt für Finanzdienstleistungsaufsicht, *Blockchain-Technologie,* available at: https://www.bafin.de/DE/Aufsicht/FinTech/Blockchain/blockchain_node.html (accessed on 24 Feb. 2020); The Swiss parliament in a report gives a similar definition of a smart contract as a computer protocol, which – usually based on a decentralized blockchain system – allows for an automated performance of contractual obligations between two or more parties based on previously coded information, *see* Bundesrat der Schweizerischen Eidgenossenschaft, *Rechtliche Grundlagen für Distributed Ledger – Technologie und Blockchain in der Schweiz – Eine Auslegeordnung mit Fokus auf dem Finanzsektor* 85, available at: https://www.newsd.admin.ch/newsd/message/attachments/55150.pdf (accessed on 24 Feb. 2020).
29. Paulus, C. & Matzke, R., *supra* n. 7, at 435.
30. Moeslein, F., *Smart Contracts im Zivil- und Handelsrecht* 254, 261 (ZHR 2019).
31. Kaulartz, M. & Heckmann, J., *supra* n. 5, at 618; *see* also Wilkens, R. & Falk, R., *supra* n. 1, at 4.

In addition, smart contracts are effectively 'permanently tamperproof',[32] protected from the influence of third parties or institutions as the blockchain is a decentralized system that can only be amended with the consent of all of its members. This makes it a trustworthy way of doing business. In contrast, when smart contracts exist outside of a blockchain, the software is essentially under the control of one party, thereby making it more likely for data or contracts to be manipulated.

Another key advantage of smart contracts within the blockchain is the inherent possibilities and functionalities. It is possible to program complex functionalities,[33] for example, to make the performance of a smart contract conditional upon a digitally verifiable event. For this purpose, an oracle is needed[34] – for a more detailed discussion of oracles, see Chapter 1, §1.11 [B] above. A smart contract in a blockchain environment can also be connected to other smart contracts with different functionalities, enabling further development and building of more complex and sophisticated contracts.[35]

Moreover, other aspects of a blockchain environment provide for effective enforcement mechanisms: (1) a virtual currency is available to perform payment obligations, (2) automatic register entries can be generated to document transfers of property rights, and (3) oracles can also be used to cause a real-world output and thus generate more complex legal effects.[36]

However, there are also disadvantages to using smart contracts within a blockchain environment. For example, whilst the lack of control over blockchain appears to be a significant advantage, there are also difficulties associated with this very feature. Unless the option has been pre-programmed, it is essentially impossible to change the code in a blockchain once it has been programmed to perform (as mentioned above).[37] Because such contracts are automatically executed, this can be a detriment for parties wishing to retain flexibility. To resolve this issue, modifiable smart contracts are making an appearance within the technology world, enabling a smart contract to be, to some extent, reversible in some parts of the program, which are stored within a library.[38] However, a significant drawback of such a modifiable smart contract is the need for a trustworthy relationship with anyone who holds access to the library. This dilutes the above-mentioned advantage of the lack of control over a smart contract in a blockchain environment.

It should also be noted that, as the blockchain allows for the anonymous performance of contractual relationships, with very limited information being available

32. Sultan, K., Ruhi, U., and Lakhani, R., *Conceptualizing Blockchains: Characteristics & Applications*, available at: https://arxiv.org/ftp/arxiv/papers/1806/1806.03693.pdf (accessed on 24 Feb. 2020); Bremann, N.-L., *Smart Contracts im Einsatz* 299, 303-304 (DSRITB 2019); Saive, D., *Rückabwicklung von Blockchain-Transaktionen* 371-372 (DSRITB 2018); Paulus, C. & Matzke, R., *supra* n. 7, at 437-438.
33. Wilkens, R. & Falk, R., *supra* n. 1, at 10; Moeslein, F., *supra* n. 30, at 254, 261.
34. Wilkens, R. & Falk, R., *supra* n. 1, at 14.
35. Heckelmann, M., *Zulässigkeit und Handhabung von Smart Contracts* 504, 505 (NJW 2018).
36. Paulus, C. & Matzke, R., *supra* n. 7, at 433; Moeslein, F., *supra* n. 30, at 254, 261; Paulus, C. & Matzke, R., *supra* n. 22.
37. Paulus, C. & Matzke, R., *supra* n. 7, at 437-438.
38. Wilkens, R. & Falk R., *supra* n. 1, at 12-13.

online (such as a public key, transaction sum and transaction date),[39] this can create difficulties, especially when attempting to trace a person and hold them accountable.

Tied in with this is the fact that enforcement in this area must take different forms; in contrast to traditional contractual disputes, whereby one party seeks to receive compensation for lack of or inadequate performance, smart contracting means guaranteed performance and restitutionary claims. The legal difficulties of smart contracts are analysed in more detail in §4.03 below.

However, as shown above, there are a lot of practical advantages to smart contracts within a blockchain that can be utilized in a number of fields; such fields are further elaborated below.

§4.02 FIELDS OF APPLICATION

[A] Legal Profession

A number of possible use cases for smart contracts are being discussed within the legal industry, such as inheritance or family law. For example, with respect to wills and probate, smart contracts could allow for automatic transactions without intermediaries. This could be as follows: (1) a testator lists the relevant assets in a smart contract will,[40] and (2) the death certificate's registration then automatically triggers distribution of assets and payment of inheritance tax.[41] The significant advantage of such a smart contract is its security over a physical, written will which could be lost or tampered with.[42] In family law, a smart contract could be linked to a marriage certificate which manages the division of accumulated savings during divorce proceedings.[43] Additionally, a smart contract could automatically enforce court orders, such as maintenance payments.[44] This would provide clients with 'greater security, reduced costs and the potential to avoid the need to return to court with an application to enforce the order or an agreement'.[45]

However, blockchain and smart contracts are usually accessible on a public network. Therefore, the lack of privacy could be a possible limitation of using smart contracts for private client or family work.[46] Another problem could arise out of formality requirements. For example, in English law, section 9 of the Wills Act 1837

39. Wilkens, R. & Falk, R., *supra* n. 1, at 14-15. For a more detailed discussion of the blockchain features, please see Chapter 1, §1.02, *supra*.
40. Cheung, A., *Can You Write Your Will onto a Blockchain? Smart Contracts*, available at: https://www.rocketlawyer.com/gb/en/blog/can-you-write-your-will-onto-a-blockchain-smart-contracts/ (accessed on 24 Feb. 2020).
41. DiMatteo, L.-A., Cannarsa, M. and Poncibo, C., *The Cambridge Handbook of Smart Contracts, Blockchain and Technology and Digital Platforms* 47 (2019).
42. Cheung, A., *supra* n. 40.
43. DiMatteo, L.-A. et al., *supra* n. 41.
44. Taylor, K., *How Blockchain Might Transform Family Law*, available at: https://vardags.com/family-law/how-blockchain-might-transform-family-law (accessed on 24 Feb. 2020).
45. *Ibid.*
46. Orcutt, M., *Hate Lawyers? Can't Afford One? Blockchain Smart Contracts Are Here to Help?*, available at: https://www.technologyreview.com/s/612748/hate-lawyers-cant-afford-one-blockchain-smart-contracts-are-here-to-help/, (accessed on 24 Feb. 2020).

provides that a will must be in writing and signed by the testator in the presence of two witnesses.[47] Similarly, German law provides that a will must be handwritten and signed by the testator.[48] For a more detailed discussion of formality requirements, see §4.03[B][2] below.

Another potential use case of smart contracts could be in the field of legal drafting. For example, lawyers could be filling standard forms to generate smart contracts.[49] Such a process could be termed as 'combined drafting'. Equally, the inalterability of blockchain data could assist notaries seeking to prove provenance and authenticity of documentation.[50]

Nevertheless, at this stage, such use cases are merely ideas as there are still issues which prevent the widespread utilization of blockchain within the legal profession; one of which is the particularity of subjective expressions, such as 'fair and reasonable' or 'best efforts'. Such expressions are often used by lawyers when drafting traditional contracts and are not easily translated into computer code. For more details on this issue, see §4.03[F] below.

[B] Insurance Industry

There is a clear opportunity for automation through smart contracts to improve efficiency for consumers in the field of the insurance industry.[51] It could also create considerable savings, especially in light of the 'high cost centres of underwriting, claims management, fraud reduction and reinsurance'.[52] Therefore, there is a likelihood that the use of smart contracts will transform the insurance industry, in particular, because smart contracts can be utilized at multiple stages of the insurance process. At the underwriting stage, various sources, including third-party oracles, could gather information regarding prospective customers and risks. This would shift the onus away from customers to provide such information and could result in more specific and bespoke insurance packages and premiums.[53] An example of such a bespoke insurance package could be a smart flood insurance which would work by providing real-time evidence of water damage through its sensors. Such insurance could also automatically trigger an insurance claim after water levels exceeded a

47. Cheung, A., *supra* n. 40.
48. Paragraph 2247 subs. (1) of the German Civil Code (*Bürgerliches Gesetzbuch*) in the version of 02. Jan. 2002.
49. Vinters, T., *Smart Contracts: A Boom or Bane for the Legal Profession?*, available at: https://www.taylorvinters.com/article/smart-contracts-a-boon-or-bane-for-the-legal-profession (accessed on 24 Feb. 2020).
50. *Ibid.*
51. Queen Mary University of London, Centre for Commercial Law Studies, *Triggering Innovation How Smart Contracts Bring Policies to Life*, available at: https://www.lloyds.com/~/media/files/news-and-insight/risk-insight/2019/triggering-innovation---how-smart-contracts-bring-policies-to-life.pdf (accessed on 24 Feb. 2020).
52. *Ibid.*
53. Gatteschi, V. et al., *Blockchain and Smart Contracts for Insurance: Is the Technology Mature Enough?*, available at: https://www.the-digital-insurer.com/wp-content/uploads/2018/07/1243-futureinternet-10-00020-v2-1.pdf (accessed on 24 Feb. 2020).

certain predefined threshold.[54] In a similar way, crop insurance could be used with sensors monitoring the weather and payment being automated in the event of persistently bad weather.[55]

Another example within the sector could be in relation to customers travelling on significantly delayed flights, who could automatically receive compensation payments without the need to submit a claim.[56] Such automation of claims could enhance transparency and reduce operating costs for the insurance company. The objective nature of claims would provide certainty for customers that payments will be made once the precondition is met and could accordingly reduce disputes.[57]

Nevertheless, the use of blockchain and smart contracts within the insurance industry brings with it a number of concerns. There are fears that the relevant technology would collect sensitive personal data such as race, religion and other discriminatory characteristics, which could subsequently be used to price insurance products. This may result in certain groups of people becoming uninsurable.[58] Similar concerns in relation to data arise regarding the concept of 'pay-per-use' insurance whereby sensors would be used to activate or deactivate polices and blockchain would record the details. Such insurance would rely on the collection of records or data which could engage data protection issues if location or other personal data were collected; see Chapter 5 below. The 'pay-per-use' insurance policy could nevertheless be an attractive option in a number of fields, for example in relation to services with respect to which a policy would only be activated when an individual uses the service.

In addition, there are other concerns which relate to the nature of such smart insurance contracts. One of such concerns is whether these contracts are indeed insurance contracts that are subject to a large volume of regulations or whether they could also just be simple derivative contracts.[59]

There are other significant regulatory and compliance issues arising out of the use of smart contracts, which are explored in detail in Chapter 3 above.

[C] Music Industry/Media industry

The media industry is another area that could benefit from smart contracts. Currently, the music industry suffers from issues regarding ownership and rights.[60] The payment of royalties is often a complex process, with multiple contracts between artists, producers and publishing houses and reliance upon royalty-collection bodies for the

54. Queen Mary University of London, *supra* n. 51.
55. Gatteschi, V. et al., *supra* n. 53.
56. Mlynar, T.-J. and Fettman, R.-M., *Blockchain and Smart Contracts Will Change the Face of Insurance in the U.S.*, available at: https://www.lexology.com/library/detail.aspx?g=b119f47b-764b-464c-9090-89b8e6e58219 (accessed on 24 Feb. 2020).
57. Savelyev, A., *Contract Law 2.0: 'Smart' Contracts as the Beginning of the End of Classic Contract Law*, Information & Communications Technology Law, 116-134 (2017).
58. Mlynar, T.-J. and Fettman, R.-M., *supra* n. 56.
59. *Ibid.*
60. Hu, C., *Are Smart Contracts Smart Enough For the Music Industry?*, available at: https://breakermag.com/are-smart-contracts-smart-enough-for-the-music-industry/ (accessed on 24 Feb. 2020).

distribution of payments. 'Artists regularly sue their labels for withholding payments, and labels often sue streaming services ... for unpaid royalties and copyright infringement.'[61] This is also because royalty-collection bodies gather general airplay statistics which are not directly associated with a rights holder, often resulting in inaccurate payments or unfair compensation, especially in relation to lesser-known artists.[62] It is estimated, that 'in music alone, ageing infrastructure and missing royalties cost rights owners and creators more than $3b every year in lost revenue'.[63]

By using smart contracts, the process of making royalty payments could be simplified, whilst also removing the current uncertainty that exists around the ownership of rights in works. For example, downloading a song could activate a smart contract that would arrange an automatic and real-time payment of royalties, with specific distribution percentages, amongst its contributors.[64] This would remove the need for royalty-collection associations, shifting the power to copyright owners,[65] and reducing the cost of, and time taken to process, royalty transactions. Smart contracts could also assist through automating rights management and remove the need for disputes and the courts' involvement.[66] Further, they 'may [also] play a role in standardizing licensing terms and conditions for copyright works across uses and different jurisdictions, similar to the way in which [Creative Commons] licenses are deployed at a global scale'.[67]

However, 'there remain substantial unresolved issues limiting the applicability of smart contracts' in the media industry.[68] For example, assuming an author posts their work on a blockchain, recording ownership and using smart contracts to automate who has access to the records, difficulties immediately arise in relation to who has access to the works and under what conditions. Further, as a blockchain is not tied to any jurisdiction, there could be issues arising as copyright varies by jurisdiction. For example, Canada and New Zealand offer protection for life of the author and an additional 50 years, whereas the European Union and the United States offer 70 years after the death of the author.[69] Additionally, there are concerns whether smart

---

61. *Ibid.*
62. *Ibid.*
63. Learney, R., *A blockchain music right platform for smooth interactions between musicians and consumers,* available at: *https://www.digicatapult.org.uk/projects/smart-contracts-for-creative-ip-distribution/* (accessed on 24 Feb. 2020).
64. Finck, M. and Mosco, V., *Copyright Law on Blockchain: Between New Forms of Rights Administration and Digital Rights Management 2.0,* available at: https://www.ip.mpg.de/de/publikationen/details/copyright-law-on-blockchains-between-new-forms-of-rights-administration-and-digital-rights-management-20.html?pk_campaign=newsletter1 (accessed on 6 March 2020).
65. Deloitte, *Blockchain @ Media – A new Game Changer for the Media Industry?,* available at: https://www2.deloitte.com/content/dam/Deloitte/tr/Documents/technology-media-telecomm
unications/deloitte-PoV-blockchain-media.pdf (accessed on 24 Feb. 2020).
66. Hu, C., *supra* n. 60.
67. Bodó, Balázs, Gervais, D.† and Quintais, Joao Pedro, *Blockchain and smart contracts: the missing link in copyright licensing?,* available at: https://academic.oup.com/ijlit/article/26/4/311/5106727 (accessed on 24 Feb. 2020).
68. *Ibid.*
69. *Ibid.*

contracts will resolve the issue of payment because 'if you can't accurately identify who owns the music in the first place, you can't even begin the payment process'.[70] Unless there are independent safeguards in place that monitor and verify who can be registered as the owner of rights for certain work, there is also the immediate concern that a person could fraudulently register themselves as the owner of certain rights on the blockchain and incorrectly begin receiving royalty payments.[71]

Another issue arises because smart contracts may not be able to handle the 'sprawling layers of complex, dynamic agreements that pervade the music business today, especially when it comes to digital consumption'.[72] For example, there are complex and subjective clauses in record labels' contracts that are more relational than transactional (such as 'reasonable' and 'good faith'), which 'cannot be encoded in smart-contract form'.[73] More detail on the interpretation of terms in a smart contract is found below in §4.03[F].

As such, due to the complexity of these contracts, it is likely that, in the short term, smart contracts will mainly be used for large volumes of simple contracts, for example licensing music to a TV show[74] that has fewer variables such as the name of a song, name of a TV show, price of a song etc. Regarding copyright licenses, 'for the foreseeable future, this uncertainty surrounding the legal status of smart contracts is likely to limit the emergence of more complex and robust arrangements in the domain of automated copyrights licenses'.[75]

[D] Energy Supply Industry

The energy sector is undergoing significant changes regarding both renewable energy and technology.[76] At a commercial level, smart contracts could affect electricity wholesale trading,[77] particularly in the field of renewable energy production. Currently, wholesale energy markets involve complex third-party intermediaries conducting lengthy activities consolidating and communicating information held by each party. These unnecessary intermediaries naturally inflate the costs of trading and

70. Hu, C., *supra* n. 60.
71. For an interesting example of this in the context of independent verification for artwork and collectibles, see the following blog post https://shkspr.mobi/blog/2018/06/how-i-became-leonardo-da-vinci-on-the-blockchain/ (accessed on 2 Jan. 2020) in which Terence Eden explains how he easily convinced a blockchain-based startup called Verisart that he was the creator of the Mona Lisa.
72. Hu, C., *supra* n. 60.
73. *Ibid.*
74. *Ibid.*
75. Bodó, B. et al., *supra* n. 67.
76. FRS Energy Florence School of Regulation, *Blockchain Meets Energy, Digital Solutions for Decentralized and Decarbonized Sector*, available at: https://fsr.eui.eu/wp-content/uploads/Blockchain_meets_Energy_-_ENG.pdf (accessed on 22 Oct. 2019).
77. Electricity wholesale trading refers to a market, where electricity is traded between generators and suppliers. The energy is obtained at wholesale prices to which a markup is added, resulting in electricity being sold at higher prices to consumers. FRS Energy Florence School of Regulation, *supra* n. 76.

exclude small-scale distributors from the market.[78] Smart contracts could remove these intermediaries, automatically monitoring the demand, delivery and payment of electricity (for example, requesting electricity when prices are below a threshold or when renewable electricity is available).[79] The objective nature, certainty and reduced costs enabled by smart contracts 'would lead to incentives to invest more in these renewable energies and would also make a completely new product possible'.[80]

At the grassroots level, smart contracts have the potential to affect individuals through smart meters and billing. The combination of smart contracts and the Internet of Things (IoT), discussed below, further broadens the influence of smart contracts within the field of energy supply. Additionally, smart contracts could simplify and reduce the time taken to switch energy suppliers, which, in turn, will increase competition in the energy market and reduce tariffs.[81]

[E] Internet of Things

The IoT industry is a computing concept describing 'the idea of everyday physical objects being connected to the internet and being able to identify themselves to other devices'.[82] The industry is growing exponentially, with the number of IoT devices increasing from 8.4 billion to 20 billion from 2017 to 2020 (and estimated to be over 500 billion by 2030).[83]

On a business level, this rapid growth creates a new opportunity to maximize the value of data generated by IoT sensors.[84] 'The IoT will create opportunities for new, exciting applications that will interweave the physical with the cyber world.'[85] Smart contracts would facilitate a novel business model/platform whereby customers can automatically purchase data from IoT sensors (without the need for intermediaries).[86] The smart contract would be entered into between the IoT sensor owner/provider and the customer, whereby payment would automatically provide the customer with a certain quantity of data from IoT sensors. IoT sensors could provide a wide variety of information, and smart contracts would allow the large-scale sharing of that information. Additionally, 'leveraging the trust anchors provided by smart contracts and the underlay blockchain, it should be easier to build open, reliable, and secure distributed

78. *Ibid.*
79. *Ibid.*
80. *Ibid.*
81. *Ibid.*
82. Techopedia Internet of Things, available at: https://www.techopedia.com/definition/28247/internet-of-things-iot (accessed on 6 March 2020).
83. Smatz Platform Blog, *How Blockchain and Smart Contracts Can Impact IoT*, available at: https://medium.com/smartz-blog/how-blockchain-and-smart-contracts-can-impact-iot-f9e77ebe02ab (accessed on 6 March 2020).
84. Papadodimas, G., Palaiokrasas, G., Litke, A. and Vavarigou, T., *Implementation of smart contracts for blockchain based IoT applications*, available at: http://bloomen.io/wp-content/uploads/2018/11/ICCS-nof2018.pdf (accessed on 6 March 2020).
85. Fotiou, N. and Polyzos, G.-C., *Smart contracts for the Internet of Things: opportunities and challenges*, available at: https://arxiv.org/pdf/1901.10582.pdf (accessed on 24 Feb. 2020).
86. Papadodimas, G. et al., *supra* n. 84.

applications, as well as novel security, accountability, and charging mechanisms'.[87] This information sharing could have widespread uses, including marketing and research. However, this would also trigger further data protection concerns, expanded on in Chapter 5, §5.06 below.

Smart contracts could also enhance IoT at an individual level, providing a 'high degree of coordination and authority. Particularly when it comes to managing transactions and interactions, smart contracts ensure proper cohesion'.[88] They could collaborate with IoT sensors in individual homes to take the 'right amount of action at the right time',[89] and they would automatically facilitate transactions once certain pre-set conditions agreed in the smart contract are met. For example, when an existing light bulb burns out, a smart contract could trigger the purchase of a new one, with the program only allowing orders of a certain price and delivery date.[90]

Based on the above, there is a chance for smart contracts to eliminate intermediaries and reduce transaction time and expense.

[F] Sharing Economy

The sharing economy enables groups of individuals to cooperate in providing tangible and intangible assets, with the community subsequently evaluating the asset and paying the provider. The sharing economy has expanded rapidly due to the highly regarded combined review structure from both providers and customers and now encompasses some of the largest and most successful companies.[91] Smart contracts could further enhance and digitize the sharing economy by streamlining and further automating transactions.

The involvement of smart contracts creates the chance to remove the detriment of human error and intermediaries and 'facilitate secure transactions or reduce the fees associated with international currency transfers'.[92] For example, in the context of car hire, as a number of ride-hailing services demonstrate, smart contracts could enable an individual to send payment to a car-hire company, unlock the car and drive – such contracts would automatically come to an end once the car-hire contract expires.[93]

To conclude, the utilization of smart contracts within a sharing economy would result in a reduction or even 'no need for third-party intermediaries who would

87. Fotiou, N. and Polyzos, G.-C., *supra* n. 85.
88. Smatz Platform Blog, *supra* n. 83.
89. *Ibid.*
90. *Ibid.*
91. Miller, D. *The Sharing Economy and How is it Changing Industries,* available at: https://www.thebalancesmb.com/the-sharing-economy-and-how-it-changes-industries-4172234 (accessed on 24 Feb. 2020).
92. Miller, L. *Blockchain and the sharing economy – a match made in heaven? This startup plans to prove it,* available at: https://thenextweb.com/cryptocurrency/2018/04/13/blockchain-and-the-sharing-economy-a-match-made-in-heaven-this-startup-plans-to-prove-it/ (accessed on 24 Feb. 2020).
93. Harrington, L. *Sharing Economy 2.0: Can Blockchain Remove the Need for Single-Asset Ownership?,* available at: https://www.iotforall.com/sharing-economy-can-blockchain-eliminate-single-asset-ownership/ (accessed on 24 Feb. 2020).

normally serve as the trusted platform providing the services',[94] thereby reducing the cost of these services for customers and service providers. The reduced cost for service providers would also inevitably open the market to smaller start-ups, increase competition and revolutionize the sharing economy by opening it up to other areas, beyond accommodation and car hire.

The utilization of smart contracts on a blockchain could bring a number of advantages, such as reducing costs and increasing efficiency. Nevertheless, despite the prospect of revolutionizing the economy and the extraordinary potential of blockchain, smart contracts also create a number of unresolved issues which would need to be dealt with. We have analysed some of these issues in detail in §4.03 below.

§4.03 CONTRACT LAW ISSUES

[A] Applicable Law Versus 'Code in Law'

As has been mentioned above in §4.01[C][2], smart contracts are often viewed as a means to autonomously exercise certain steps in an already established contractual relationship.[95] As such, they perform existing contractual obligations rather than enable the creation of new legally binding obligations through smart contracts. The terms of a contract in its traditional form, setting out the parties' intentions and expectations would be coded onto the blockchain via a smart contract, and the blockchain network would then become, for that contract, a 'governance mechanism ... [that] is enforced by a computer'.[96] In such circumstances, it could be argued that the rules governing such contract are the 'self-executing and self-enforcing'[97] code of the smart contract itself. This would also require that the parties' intended remedies in the event of a breach or dispute are coded into the smart contract so that they can be automatically executed if the necessary conditions are satisfied.

However, even if this view of smart contracts as the means of executing and governing previously established contracts in their traditional form is accepted, there are strong arguments that parties should not anticipate relying solely on smart contracts for governance and execution. As discussed in §4.04[A] below, there is always a risk of parties' previously agreed intentions not being given effect to if, for example, there appears to be an error in code. In such circumstances, the terms contained in the 'traditional' contract (and coded in the smart contract) could be the subject of a dispute, which would need to be heard before, and ultimately enforced by, the relevant court.

How this would work in practice where such a contract is executed by, or in the form of, a smart contract is difficult to predict. Smart contracts cannot be amended or terminated once coded and placed on the blockchain and will self-execute once the

94. *Ibid.*
95. Durovic, M. & Janssen, A., *supra* n. 16.
96. Grinhaus, A., *A Practical Guide to Smart Contracts and Blockchain Law* 157 (Pema Banigan, Matthew Rappard & Zachary Skeith [eds], 2019).
97. Durovic, M. & Janssen, A., *supra* n. 16.

necessary circumstances arise. In a situation where there has been an incorrect transfer of value executed by a smart contract, '[t]he recourse will probably be in the form of an injunction for return of [that value]'[98], but other, more complex uses of a smart contract may not be so simple to resolve once the contract has been self-executed.

Alternatively, if a smart contract is a legally binding contract[99], then what must instead be determined is the law that is applicable not to the underlying, 'traditional' contract (which would in any case likely specify the parties' preferred applicable law), but to the smart contract itself. Given that '[o]ne of the key promises of blockchain technology, and by extension smart contracts, is the development of robust, decentralized and global platforms'[100], it is possible that a large number of people across a number of jurisdictions around the world will be making use of a certain smart contract. Therefore, if the relevant parties do not specify an applicable law when entering into a smart contract, it will presumably be difficult to objectively determine, with certainty, which law should be applicable in interpreting that smart contract in the event of a dispute. It would therefore be advisable for the parties to agree and specify the relevant governing law and jurisdiction, otherwise 'a plaintiff may be relatively unconstrained in choosing where to file a claim or in arguing which substantive law should apply'.[101]

[B] Formation of a Smart Contract

[1] Contracting Parties

In the context of AI, there are some discussions as to which person declarations and actions are attributable. This problem does not arise in the context of smart contracts.[102] As set out in §4.01[B] above, a smart contract is a computer program with a specific if/then logic. It does not generate autonomous actions, but rather performs certain pre-programmed actions. It usually serves as a tool to perform contractual obligations or – under specific circumstances – communicate declarations of the person using it. Thus, even if a smart contract is used in a context in which two software programs interact and exchange transactions, the actions are easily attributable to the person(s) for whom the smart contract performs an action.[103]

98. Grinhaus, A., *supra* n. 96.
99. See below in §4.03 for a further discussion of the formation of a smart contract.
100. Dewey, J.-N., *Blockchain & Cryptocurrency Regulation 2020*, 165 (Global Legal Insights, 1st ed., 2019)
101. *Ibid.*
102. Paulus, D. & Matzke, R., *supra* n. 7, at 446 fn. 111; *see* for a brief discussion of this issue, Paulus, D. & Matzke, R., *supra* n. 7, at 442-445.
103. *See also* Wilkens, R. & Falk, R., *supra* n. 1, at 33; Lupu, R., *Zulässigkeit, Handhabung und rechtliche Grenzen bei der Gestaltung von Smart Contracts* 209, 214 (DSRITB 2019); Paulus, D. & Matzke, R., *supra* n. 7, at 446, noting that this might be different for actions the parties did not want and were caused by faulty programming; in favour of a possible attribution to the programmer, Heckelmann, M., *supra* n. 35, at 506.

However, for contractual agreements that include the use of a smart contract in a blockchain environment, identifying the contracting parties might be more complicated than for traditional contracts. This is because of the use of pseudonyms in a blockchain environment which complicates the identification of the contracting parties. Although the identification of contracting parties could be complicated, in the view of UKJT, it will not be an issue, since there is 'no doubt that a smart legal contract between anonymous or pseudonymous parties is capable of giving rise to binding legal obligations'.[104]

In addition, it is also argued that parties using a smart contract usually have no particular interest or need in knowing the identity of the other party because a smart contract in a blockchain environment guarantees the immediate performance of the contractual obligations.[105] However, in some jurisdictions, the use of pseudonyms can be an issue particularly in business-to-consumer (B2C) contracts. For example, German consumer-protection law stipulates[106] that businesses must disclose their identity and contact details prior to the formation of the contract. Also companies would often want to know about the identity of the party they are contracting with. As a consequence, the concept of smart contracts is likely to be more often deployed for simple, low-value transactions rather than complex contracts. With respect to more complex contracts and transactions, it is advisable to provide contact information to the other party in a suitable way.[107]

[2] Form Requirements

A core principle in contract law which applies in most jurisdictions is the principle of 'freedom of contract'. This means that parties are free to write their bargains in the language and form of their choosing.[108] Generally, this also encompasses smart contracts' computer code. However, contract law across jurisdictions very often still has various formalities that will need to be satisfied.

For example, in Germany, a contract can be null and void if certain formalities are not fulfilled.[109] German law stipulates a number of form requirements for certain types

104. UK Jurisdiction Taskforce, *Legal statement on cryptoassets and smart contracts,* available at: https://35z8e83m1ih83drye280o9d1-wpengine.netdna-ssl.com/wp-content/uploads/2019/11/6.6056_JO_Cryptocurrencies_Statement_FINAL_WEB_111119-1.pdf (accessed on 24 Feb. 2020)
105. Schawe, N., *Blockchain und Smart Contracts in der Kreativwirtschaft – mehr Probleme als Lösungen?* 218, 220 (MMR 2019).
106. S. 312d subs. (1) German Civil Code (*Bürgerliches Gesetzbuch*) in connection with Art. 246a s. 1 subs. (1) sentence 1 lit. 2 Einführungsgesetz zum Bürgerlichen Gesetzbuch (Introductory Law to the German Civil Code) in the version of 21 Sep. 1994 (BGBl. I p. 2494; 1997 I p. 1061), last updated by Art. 2 G. v. 18 Dec. 2018 (BGBl. I p. 2648); *see* also Schawe, N., *supra* n. 105.
107. For details regarding suitable means, *see infra* s. §4.03[D].
108. Durovic, M. & Janssen, A., *supra* n. 16.
109. S. 125 sentence 1 German Civil Code (*Bürgerliches Gesetzbuch*)

of contracts. Common form requirements are text form,[110] written form,[111] official certification[112] and/or notarial recording.[113] It is unclear if and to what extent a smart contract can comply with such form requirements. In any case, a smart contract fulfils the German text form requirement which requires a contract to be readable and submitted on a permanent data carrier.[114] A smart contract in a blockchain is such a permanent medium.[115] In addition, the code of a smart contract is 'readable'.[116] For a contract to be readable, it is irrelevant whether it is only readable with the help of technical means[117] or readable by only a few people, as it can be translated if necessary.[118]

English law usually requires an objectively reached agreement with sufficiently certain terms, an intention to create legal relations and (unless a deed is used), consideration. According to UKJT, there is no reason as to why 'the normal rules should not apply just because a potential contract is a smart contract'.[119] There are further requirements for specific types of contracts, for example, section 2 of the Law of Property (Miscellaneous Provisions) Act 1989 states that contracts for sale, transfer or lease of land must be in writing; similarly, section 90(3) of the Copyright, Design and Patent Act 1977 and section 4 of the Statute of Frauds 1677 have such formalities in relation to assignments or exclusive licenses and guarantees, respectively. As the fundamental nature of a smart contract is the underlying computer code, it is uncertain whether this would satisfy the requirement under English law that such a contract must be 'in writing'. However, upon consideration of the Interpretation Act 1978, which

110. Text form requires a readable declaration that the person making the declaration be named and that it must be made on a durable medium (s. 126b German Civil Code). As an example, text form is required in the context of a lease contract for a request to raise the rent, s. 558a subs. (1) German Civil Code.
111. Written form requires a document with a signature (s. 126 subs. (1) German Civil Code). As an example, written form is required for declaring a personal guarantee, s. 766 German Civil Code or for a temporary lease contract which is longer than one year, s. 550 sentence 1, s. 578 German Civil Code.
112. Official certification requires that a notary certifies the signature of the person declaring (s. 129 German Civil Code). As an example, conditions for a land register entry must be provided to the land registry in officially certified form, s. 29 German Land Registration Code (*Grundbuchordnung*) in the version of 26 May 1994 (BGBl. I p. 1114), last updated by Art. 11 G. v. 12 Dec. 2019 (BGBl. I p. 2602).
113. Notarial recording is the strictest form and requires that a notary records offer and acceptance (s. 128 German Civil Code). As an example, notarial recording is required for sale of real estate (s. 311b subs. 1 German Civil Code) or for the renunciation or sale of an inheritance (s. 2348 and s. 2371 German Civil Code, respectively).
114. Heckelmann, M., *supra* n. 35; Wilkens, R. & Falk, R., *supra* n. 1, at 37; Paulus, D. & Matzke, R., *supra* n. 7, at 457; Gerald Spindler, *Recht der elektronischen Medien* at § 126b para. 1 (Gerald Spindler & Fabian Schuster [eds], 4th ed. 2019).
115. Paulus, D. & Matzke, R., *supra* n. 7, at 457.
116. As required by s. 126(b) German Civil Code.
117. Gyr, E., *supra* n. 1; Einsele, D., *Münchener Kommentar zum Bürgerlichen Gesetzbuch* at § 126b para. 4 (Franz Jürgen Säcker et al. [eds], 8th ed. 2018).
118. Against this: Bertram, U., *Smart Contracts – Praxisrelevante Fragen zu Vertragsabschluss, Leistungsstörungen und Auslegung* 1416, 1418-1419 (MDR 2018), arguing that the information purpose is not fulfilled; arguing that this only applies if the parties can understand code, Gyr, E., *supra* n. 1.
119. UKJT, *supra* n. 27.

serves to interpret common words used in statutes, it becomes clear that such an 'in writing' requirement includes 'modes of reproducing words in a visible form',[120] which arguably encompasses a computer code. As further pointed out by UKJT, the fact that 'the code might not be comprehensible to an … English speaker without an expert translator is irrelevant'.[121]

Furthermore, in relation to the execution of smart contracts, there have been concerns as to whether smart contracts' electronic signatures would satisfy the execution requirement and be regarded as a valid signature under English law. However, under the Communications Act 2000, 'an electronic signature has counted [as] if it is incorporated into, or is associated with, an electronic communication'.[122] This has also been confirmed by the Law Commission which has clarified that 'electronic signatures can be used to sign formal legal contracts under English law'.[123] Also the UKJT is optimistic and points out that private keys are highly likely to meet signature requirements.[124] This is due to the fact that public-key cryptography is a type of electronic signature which generally satisfies statutory signature requirements. The key question is not what the signature looks like, but rather whether a party intended to authenticate the document.[125] As such, electronic signatures should not pose an issue for smart contracts.

Another potential difficulty in relation to form requirements in English law relates to the execution of deeds.[126] A deed has to comply with formalistic requirements by virtue of section 1(3) of the Law of Property (Miscellaneous Provisions) Act 1989 under which an executing party must sign a deed in the presence of a witness. This could be an issue in light of the automatic nature of smart contracts. However, in *R (Software Solutions Partners Ltd)* v. *HM Customs & Excise*,[127] it was held that the 'automatic medium for contract formation can result in valid contracts', and the Law Commission confirmed that 'there is scope … to do even more to make signing formal documents more convenient'.[128] This indicates that the deployment of smart contracts could result in further developments in the legislative sphere, resolving such form requirements and ensuring the validity of such contracts.

---

120. Interpretation Act 1978 section 5.
121. UKJT, *supra* n. 27, at 38.
122. Young, A., *Take note: Emails can be legally binding*, available at: http://www.contractflooringjournal.co.uk/blog/take-note-emails-can-be-legally-binding/ (accessed on 24 Feb. 2020).
123. The Law Commission, *Electronic Signatures are valid say Government's legal experts*, available at: https://www.lawcom.gov.uk/electronic-signatures-are-valid-say-governments-legal-experts/ (accessed on 24 Feb. 2020).
124. UKJT, *supra* n. 27, at 37.
125. *Ibid.*
126. A deed is a written document which is executed with the necessary formality (that is, more than a simple signature), and by which an interest, right or property passes or is confirmed, or an obligation binding on some person is created or confirmed. *See*: Practical Law Glossary.
127. *R (Software Solutions Partners Ltd) v. HM Customs & Excise*, 2007, EWHC 971, para. 67.
128. The Law Commission, *Electronic Signatures are valid say Government's legal experts*, available at: https://www.lawcom.gov.uk/electronic-signatures-are-valid-say-governments-legal-experts/ (accessed on 24 Feb 2020).

[3] *Offer and Acceptance*

If a smart contract is used to form a contractual relationship, specific questions arise concerning the existence and content of offer and acceptance.

A contract is formed by at least two corresponding declarations of will (offer and acceptance), each with the intention to have a legally binding effect and with the purpose of forming a contract.[129] In this context, technology can be used either to communicate a specific declaration of will - for example, via an e-mail - or to automatically generate a declaration of will. For example, with respect to the latter, the German Federal Court of Justice (*Bundesgerichtshof*) has confirmed that an automated declaration of will issued by a software, according to prior programming, can be legally binding.[130] A transaction via a smart contract might be considered an automated declaration of will. In the context of smart contracts, a computer program will initiate a transaction, validating certain conditions, which would trigger a pre-programmed result, acting within the limits of logic set by prior programming. In this way, the automated declarations arguably express the general will of the individual deploying the computer program.[131] The same applies if a contract is formed entirely without human interaction by two corresponding automated declarations of will, for example, a computer programme that detects a fridge is empty and orders certain goods.[132] Usually, in this scenario, the parties would have entered into an underlying contract off-chain (e.g., in the form of a framework contract) before the order is placed via the computer program. In such a situation, the existence and content of contractual obligations must be determined according to the time and circumstances of the previously formed contract and not at the time of the relevant blockchain transaction. If the automated transactions are the first and only communication between the parties, an objective understanding of the specific circumstances could imply that the automated transaction (such as, automatic payment or automated delivery of goods) would form an implicit offer and/or acceptance of the respective parties.[133]

However, the termination of offers could cause some issues. Subject to certain requirements, an offer can be terminated by a lapse of time, withdrawal, rejection by the acceptor, failure of a condition precedent or death of the offeror. Smart contracts could easily include in their terms the time period for which the offer will be valid, or that the offer is only valid so long as certain condition precedents are met. However, an offer within the smart contract cannot be deleted which makes it impossible for that offer to be withdrawn. Furthermore, as the offeror is a 'cryptographic private key representing an individual',[134] it is exceptionally difficult to track whether the offeror has died. Therefore, the withdrawal of offers may need to be reconsidered or carefully drafted within smart contracts.

129. Kaulartz, M. & Heckmann, J., *supra* n. 5, at 621; Wilkens, R. & Falk, R., *supra* n. 1, at 30-31.
130. FCJ, decision of January 25, 2005 - XI ZR 325/03, NJW 976 (2005).
131. Paulus, D. & Matzke, R., *supra* n. 7, at 440-41; Spindler, *supra* n. 114, at. §§ 116 ff. para. 5.
132. For a more detailed discussion on IoT, *see* §4.02[E], *supra*. Wilkens, R. & Falk, R., *supra* n. 1, at 33-34; Paulus, D. & Matzke, R., *supra* n. 7, at 446.
133. Wilkens, R. & Falk, R., *supra* n. 1, at 33-34; Paulus, D. & Matzke, R., *supra* n. 7, at 446.
134. DiMatteo, L.-A. et al., *supra* n. 41.

[C] Regulatory Issues and Smart Contracts

The use of smart contracts may also be subject to certain regulatory requirements. This topic is covered in detail in Chapter 3 above.

[D] Consumer-Protection Laws and Smart Contracts

In certain jurisdictions, consumer-protection laws could pose challenges with respect to B2C smart contracts.

[1] EU Directive 2011/83/EU

In the Member States of the European Union, a number of laws relevant for B2C contracts are based on Directive 2011/83/EU ('Directive' on consumer rights)[135] which has been implemented in the various Member States. For example, in Germany, certain requirements of the Directive are reflected in para 312-312k of the German Civil Code (*Bürgerliches Gesetzbuch*). Subject to certain conditions being met (e.g., the contract being entered into between a business[136] and a consumer[137]), the consumer law provisions apply. Therefore, despite the difficulty of identifying the other party (refer to §4.03[B][1] above for more detail), if such conditions are met, the smart contract itself may be subject to consumer-protection provisions.

Most of the relevant provisions require a distance contract, which means that the contract was negotiated and formed exclusively by means of long-distance communication (e.g., phone, internet, e-mail, or letter) and that the contract was formed under an 'organised distance sales or service-provision scheme'.[138] It therefore seems likely that smart contracts would, in most cases, fulfil a definition of such a distance contract.

When contracting with consumers and prior to forming a contract, the Directive requires the business to disclose its identity and further information, such as the price, delivery conditions, duration of the contract, existence and procedure of a right to cancellation etc.[139] For distance contracts, the business may provide information on a durable or any other medium, provided information is readable and identifies the

---

135. Directive 2011/83/EU of the European Parliament and of the Council of October 25, 2011 on consumer rights, 22 November 2011, OJ EU L 304/64-88.
136. A business, as defined in para. 14 subs. (1) German Civil Code (*Bürgerliches Gesetzbuch*), is a natural or legal person, which when entering into a contract acts in exercise of his or her trade, business or profession.
137. A consumer, as defined in para. 13 German Civil Code (*Bürgerliches Gesetzbuch*) is a natural person, which when entering into a contract acts predominantly outside of his or her trade, business or profession.
138. Para. 312c subs. (1) German Civil Code (*Bürgerliches Gesetzbuch*); Recital 20 of the Directive 2011/83/EU on consumer rights.
139. Para. 312d subs. (1) German Civil Code in connection with Art. 246a subs. (1) and (3) Introductory Law to the German Civil Code. Even if there is no distance contract, most information must be provided nonetheless. This is because of the 'minimum' information obligation in para. 312 subs. (2) sentence 1 German Civil Code in connection with Art. 246 subs. (1) and (3) Introductory Law to the German Civil Code. This is also a requirement of the Directive 2011/83/EU, Article 8.

business.[140] Further, the Directive also necessitates the business to provide information to the customer in plain and intelligible language.[141] With respect to smart contracts, this could be an issue because a computer code is unlikely to be regarded as plain language by most consumers. As such, to get around this, businesses may be required to provide electronic or text forms of the computer code, specifying obligations of the parties.[142]

Furthermore, as discussed above, providing relevant information to consumers is essential. In the absence of the relevant information, the right to cancel applies for 2 years and 14 days from the date of contract formation or delivery.[143]

[2] *Unfair Standard Terms*

Smart contracts in the B2C space will often include a number of standard terms, especially if they enable transactions with a large number of users. Therefore, in certain jurisdictions, certain rules regarding the use and content of such standard terms will often apply.

In Germany, such rules are applicable if: (a) the terms are pre-formulated,[144] (b) one party 'presents' the terms to the other party, and (c) the terms are not individually agreed.[145]

If previously agreed contractual obligations are performed by the smart contract, no smart contract specific problems as to the application of such rules (the provisions on unfair standard terms) arise. If the conditions as to such application are met with respect to the previously agreed contractual terms, the provisions regarding unfair standard terms are applicable.[146] For example, this would be the case where a standard

140. Art. 246a s. (4) subs. (3) Introductory Law to the German Civil Code; however, according to para. 312f subs. (2) German Civil Code, the consumer must receive this information on a durable medium after contract formation. This is also a requirement of Directive 2011/83/EU, Article 7.
141. Directive 2011/83/EU, Article 7.1.
142. Further obligations of the business prior to contract formation include explaining to customers the technical details of how the contract is formed (para. 312i subs. (1) sentence 1 German Civil Code in connection with Art. 246c Introductory Law to the German Civil Code), providing possibilities to correct mistakes and means to access and save the standard terms (para. 312i subs. (1) German Civil Code) and designing the website in a way that makes it clear for customers if they enter into contractual relationship, for example, a payment obligation (para. 312j subs. (3) German Civil Code), otherwise the contract is invalid (para. 312j subs. (4) German Civil Code).
143. Para. 356 subs (3) sentence 2 German Civil Code. According to its sentence 3, this does not apply to contracts for financial services.
144. This is the case if a smart contract is programmed with the intention to use it for several situations. For example, it might be stored in a library. It is irrelevant whether a third party programmed the smart contract, *see* Riehm, Thomas, *Rechtshandbuch Smart Contracts* 104 para. 16 (Braegelmann, T. & Kaulartz, M. [eds], 2019).
145. An individual agreement requires that the negotiation was open-ended. Arguably, there is an individual agreement if parties customize their contract using an automatic generator, *see* Heckelmann, M., *supra* n. 35, at 507.
146. Riehm, T., *supra* n. 144, at 104 para. 15; Berberich, M., *Smart Contracts in der AGB-Kontrolle?* 221, 223 (DSRITB 2019).

insurance contract that includes automated calculation and performance of damage events has been entered into.

If, however, the only communication between the parties is via a blockchain transaction, the identification of contract clauses as being standard terms is likely to be more difficult. Nevertheless, the provisions on unfair standard terms will usually still be applicable if the same smart contract - and thus an identical contractual arrangement - is used for a large number of contracts.[147] There is no reason for such smart contracts to not be subject to the provisions on unfair standard terms.

With respect to the requirements of the application of the provisions on unfair standard terms, it should be noted that a clause in a smart contract will often be pre-formulated. This is the case if a smart contract is programmed with the intention to use it several times. For this purpose, it might be even stored in a library. For the application of these provisions, it is also irrelevant whether the smart contract was programmed by a third party.

In B2C contracts, the party 'presenting' the standard terms must provide reasonable means for the other party to be able to take notice of their content.[148] There are differing opinions as to whether terms in a programme code fulfil such a requirement. It has been argued that contract terms only incorporated in the programme code are not part of the contractual relationship itself. According to this view, it is necessary for the 'presenting' party to provide additional means, such as providing a link or text of the terms to the other party.[149] Others argue that the contract itself is implicit in the program code and therefore contains all relevant contractual provisions.[150]

In any case, where feasible, it appears to be advisable to draft and make available a supplemental document that describes the smart contracts' contractual obligations and standard terms.

[E] Interpretation of Smart Contracts and Their Terms

When interpreting contracts in the event of a dispute, English courts strive to identify the intention of the parties, which should be ascertained objectively. Unless the language is ambiguous, the term will be taken to mean what it actually says.[151] As the

147. Kaulartz, M. & Heckmann, J., *supra* n. 5, at 622; Berberich, M., *supra* n. 146, 225-227 (2019), arguing that this follows from para. 306a German Civil Code (*Bürgerliches Gesetzbuch*), insofar as there is no written document; Schrey, J. & Thalhofer, T., *Rechtliche Aspekte der Blockchain* 1431, 1436 (NJW 2017); Paulus, D. & Matzke, R., *supra* n. 7, at 459-60, arguing that in this case, such clauses will never become part of the contract because they are not incorporated; for this as well, Wilkens, R. & Falk, R., *supra* n. 1, at 39; *see*, however, Heckelmann, M., *supra* n. 35, at 507-08.

148. Para. 305 subs. (2) German Civil Code (*Bürgerliches Gesetzbuch*): Either explicit reference to the standard terms or enabling the other party to reasonably take notice of their content. This provision does not apply B2B, para. 310 subs. (1) sentence 1 German Civil Code.

149. Wilkens, R. & Falk, R., *supra* n. 1, at 38-39; Paulus, D. & Matzke, R., *supra* n. 7, at 459-60; Moeslein, F., *supra* n. 30, at 254, 279 (2019).

150. According to this view, para. 305 subs. (2) German Civil Code (*Bürgerliches Gesetzbuch*) is not applicable, Kaulartz, M. & Heckmann, J., *supra* n. 5, at 622; *see* also FCJ, decision of 27 October 1994 - IX ZR 168/93, 1995 NJW 190 (1995).

151. UKJT, *supra* n. 27, at 34.

computer code would generally be clear and unambiguous, it could be concluded that such contract is an 'extreme example' of a contract from which there is no reason to depart, as the objective meaning is exactly what it says.[152] Some difficulties could nevertheless arise where the meaning would not be easily ascertainable from the computer code; in such circumstances, it would be determined whether the code was intended to be the complete set of obligations or whether it was merely designed to implement such obligations. In both scenarios, extrinsic evidence may be needed.[153]

Further, many contracts contain non-operational clauses and deliberately leave room for ambiguity, using terms such as 'bona fide', 'good faith' or 'reasonable'. Different legal systems will have varying interpretations of the meaning of these terms as well as other terms, such as 'best endeavours' and 'reasonable endeavours'.[154]

Such subjective terms have generated 'a large number of court decisions and corresponding legislation'.[155] Standard contract linguistic freedom, and the ability for a court to interpret theses clauses and solve disputes, allows the flexibility of ambiguous terms and functioning contracts. However, such ambiguous terms do not translate easily, or do not translate at all, into a self-executing smart contract.[156] As such, challenges arise in relation to the lack of flexibility of computer codes, as they are unable to interpret or execute such terms.[157]

Contracting parties often prefer traditional, non-operational clauses due to the flexibility of 'linguistic expansiveness and expressiveness'.[158] Nevertheless, some argue that it would be advantageous for smart contracts to exclude ambiguous terms, as this lack of ambiguous terms could remove the 'associated risk'[159] of interpretation, thereby improving the certainty of contracts. Ambiguous terms are argued to be the last resort of 'lazy lawyer[s]'[160], and it would be advantageous for smart contracts not to have such ambiguity.[161] Smart contracts could solve the ambiguity problem by either: (1) not including any ambiguous terms at all, or (2) including precise and extensive definitions of the various meanings and permutations of ambiguous terms. Whilst it could theoretically be beneficial to remove ambiguity, not only is it not conceivable

152. *Ibid.*, at 35.
153. *Ibid.*, at 36.
154. *Yewbelle Ltd v. London Green Developments Ltd & Anor* [2006] EWHC 3166 (Ch); *IBM United Kingdom Limited v. Rockware Glass Limited CA* [1980] FSR 335; *Overseas Buyers Ltd v. Granadex SA* [1980] 2 Lloyd's Rep 608.
155. Woebbeking, M.-K., *The Impact of Smart Contracts on the Traditional Concepts of Contract Law*, available at: https://www.jipitec.eu/issues/jipitec-10-1-2019/4880 (accessed on 24 Feb. 2020).
156. O'Toole, M., Kelly, C. and Hahn, D., *Smart Contracts Need Smart Corporate Lawyers*, available at: https://www.law360.com/articles/1010335/smart-contracts-need-smart-corporate-lawyers, (accessed on 24 Feb. 2020).
157. ISDA Linklaters, *Whitepaper Smart Contracts and Distributed Ledger – A Legal Perspective*, available at: https://lpscdn.linklaters.com/-media/files/linklaters/pdf/mkt/london/smart_contracts_and_distributed_ledger_a_legal_perspective.ashx?rev=0546d49d-236c-43dd-8944-456f797715ca&extension=pdf&hash=C8AC6A99BA668E447AE0408817EE5843 (accessed on 24 Feb. 2020).
158. O'Toole, M. et al., *supra* n. 156.
159. Woebbeking, M.-K., *supra* n. 155.
160. ISDA Linklaters, *supra* n. 157.
161. *Ibid.*

practically but also ambiguity is a fundamental feature of certain contractual clauses, such as 'reasonableness' or 'good faith'. Further, the adoption of precise and extensive definitions is also not realistic, given it would be impossible to imagine all eventualities and draft language to deal with them. As removing such ambiguous terms may be inadvisable or impossible, it is likely that drafters of smart contracts will have to decipher how to incorporate ambiguous terms within the smart contracts' code and deal with the repercussions.

It has further been suggested that smart contracts could nevertheless incorporate ambiguous terms offline, by creating a 'legal wrapper' which would set out the terms of the contract, incorporating the smart contract code by reference.[162] This would leave 'parts of the agreement outside the blockchain record, as non-smart or modifiable, while other obligations are inserted into the blockchain as self-executory and immutable'.[163] This contract wrapper would also allow terms to be included that permit the smart contract to be terminated and amended in certain circumstances.[164]

Therefore, due to smart contracts' relative novelty and inability to incorporate ambiguous terms in code, 'it becomes clear that smart legal contracts will require, at least for the near future, a blend between code and natural language'.[165]

However, even if non-operational terms, such as 'commercially reasonable' or 'good faith', were somehow incorporated into smart contracts, these could still be subject to dispute. This could add a further layer of complication, as unlike interpreting standard contracts, interpreting a programming language is likely to cause difficulties for the courts.[166] A possible solution to the interpretation of smart contracts could fall on extrajudicial dispute resolution.[167]

[F] Performance and Remedies

As smart contracts are self-enforcing, once agreed, performance is automatic and does not depend on any further approval or action.[168] Generally, the 'performance of a smart contract cannot be stopped neither voluntarily by the parties nor by a central entity, court or any other supervisor'.[169] The advantage of this is that smart contracts eliminate the requirement of trust between parties for performance[170]. There is no 'need to rely on the willingness of the various parties to perform'.[171]

162. DiMatteo, L.-A. et al., *supra* n. 41.
163. *Ibid.*
164. *Ibid.*
165. *Ibid.*
166. Woebbeking, M.-K., *supra* n. 155.
167. *Ibid.*
168. Tulsidas, T.-U., *Smart Contracts from a Legal Perspective* 16, available at: https://rua.ua.es/dspace/bitstream/10045/78007/1/Smart_Contracts_from_a_Legal_Perspective_Utamchandani_Tulsidas_Tanash.pdf (accessed on 6 March 2020).
169. DiMatteo, L.-A. et al., *supra* n. 41.
170. Zou, M., Cheng, G., and Heredia, M.-S., *In Code We Trust? Trustless and Smart Contracts*, available at: https://www.scl.org/articles/10493-in-code-we-trust-trustlessness-and-smart-contracts (accessed on 24 Feb. 2020).
171. DiMatteo, L.-A. et al., *supra* n. 41.

However, smart contracts' automatic nature can cause some issues. One such issue is the automatic performance regardless of real-world external factors. 'Since performance is automatic',[172] smart contracts are unable to adjust their self-performance as events occur, in the sense that a traditional contract can, they cannot respond to parties' changes in circumstances.'[173] Therefore, even if parties change their mind regarding performance, the contract will still be executed as programmed. Additionally, smart contracts 'cannot be revoked or amended, meaning that any recession, rectification, or variation is in principle impossible'.[174]

Further, there are wider public policy concerns. For example, if we allow coders to create financial transactions that are 'unreal' in the sense of not being undertaken by a known entity and not allowing for legal redress, there is a threat to the rule of law,[175] in particular in relation to money-laundering regulations.

One potential solution to smart contracts' automatic self-performance would be to allow the modification of smart contracts. Smart contracts could contain clauses stating that future court decisions are incorporated into the contract through leveraging an oracle. Additionally, smart contracts could be programmed to reflect real-world inputs or predefined events,[176] allowing modification depending on the outcome of these predetermined events.[177] One example of this is the Application Programming Interface (API)[178] that would allow smart contracts to be updated.[179] The API would collect updates to important legal provisions which smart contracts could update accordingly to ensure legality.[180] However, modifying smart contracts may be limited as it would require the parties to: (1) acknowledge their minds may be changed by certain specific future conditions, and (2) prepare the contract on such a basis beforehand.[181] In reality, many contracting parties may not have such foresight or predetermined opinions of how their minds may change. Additionally, it would be difficult to ensure that the API makes changes in the interest of both parties rather than making self-serving changes.

Even if smart contracts are self-enforcing, they must still comply with the fundamental rules of contract law. An unenforceable clause will not be made enforceable by virtue of embedding it into a computer code, and as such, the judicial remedies of adjustment or voidance will continue to be relevant. Furthermore, just because a smart contract is self-executing does not mean that errors will not arise, and accordingly, parties will continue to seek remedies in court. Therefore, traditional contract

172. Zou, M. et al., *supra* n. 170.
173. DiMatteo, L.-A. et al., *supra* n. 41.
174. *Ibid.*
175. Vos, G., *LawTech, Smart Contracts and Artificial Intelligence*, available at: https://www.judiciary.uk/wp-content/uploads/2019/05/CHC-speech-LawTech-Smart-Contracts-and-Artificial-Intelligence.pdf (accessed on 24 Feb. 2020).
176. DiMatteo, L.-A. et al., *supra* n. 41.
177. Tulsidas, T.-U., *supra* n. 168.
178. API is a set of routines, protocols and tools for building software applications. Webopedia, available at: https://www.webopedia.com/TERM/A/API.html (accessed on 24 Feb. 2020).
179. Tulsidas, T.-U., *supra* n. 168, at 33.
180. *Ibid.*
181. DiMatteo, L.-A. et al., *supra* n. 41.

remedies and defences will still be applicable as 'smart contracts cannot transplant contract law',[182] developed further in §4.03[A], above.

The self-enforcing nature of smart contracts does not eliminate the risk of contract breach or nullity triggering the need for remedies[183]. The following example, based on English law, demonstrates the irreplaceability of remedies. A smart contract entered into to transfer an asset from Party A to Party B is invalidated due to fraud, illegality or incapacity. Within the blockchain platform, the asset remains Party B's property;[184] however, in reality, the law recognizes the property as belonging to Party A[185]. In this instance, the court should be able to order a remedy of specific performance requiring Party B to (through the blockchain) transfer ownership of the asset back to Party A[186]. This example highlights the fact that remedies remain necessary, even though smart contracts are self-enforcing. Smart contracts could also be breached or invalidated due to glitches or bugs in the code[187], producing results that are not in the parties' best interests[188], which could give rise to tortious claims of negligence. For example, the divergence between contract as intended by parties and smart contract as created could result in the emergence of torts 'for negligent coding or negligent updating'.[189]

As such, even though smart contracts are automatic and self-enforcing, this does not eliminate the risk of breaches which may still occur through real-life circumstances or bugs. Therefore, either the legislators or the coders need to be creative and respond accordingly to ensure that smart contracts do not exist in a legal vacuum and that breaches are capable of being remedied.

§4.04 OUTLOOK

[A] Benefits, Opportunities and Limitations of Smart Contracts

In light of the above, it can be concluded that the development of smart contracts presents various benefits and opportunities but is also subject to certain limitations.

Smart contracts benefit from an additional level of security compared to traditional contracts. As smart contracts are encrypted and distributed through the blockchain platform, this keeps a permanent record of the contract. Therefore, smart contracts will provide security which traditional contracts are not able to provide. They 'offer a shield against human error, duplicity and malfeasance'[190] as the blockchain is immutable, requiring the consent of all members of the blockchain for any changes to

182. *Ibid.*
183. Sherborne, A., *Blockchain Smart Contracts and Lawyers* (2017).
184. DiMatteo, L.-A. et al., *supra* n. 41.
185. *Ibid.*
186. *Ibid.*
187. Sherborne, A., *supra* n. 183.
188. DiMatteo, L.-A. et al., *supra* n. 41.
189. *Ibid.*
190. Wan, A., *Blockchain Smart Contracts: Weighing the Pros and Cons*, available at: https://blocktribune.com/smart-contracts-weighing-the-pros-and-cons/ (accessed on 24 Feb. 2020).

be made once the smart contract is encoded. Furthermore, traditional contracts may be lost or, if stored electronically, deleted or corrupted. As smart contracts are stored on a decentralized blockchain, they are unable to be deleted as the blockchain will store all of the smart contract's data permanently and the parties 'can retrieve any of the information if there's any data loss'.[191] This security is beneficial for the parties' commercial business relationship.

Additionally, smart contracts are able to be viewed by all members of the blockchain. This transparency is advantageous and also ensures that all members are able to access and see all agreed details at any point, making miscommunications or misunderstandings less likely.[192] In theory, this transparency should enhance contractual relationships, as well as reduce confusion and the amount of time and money spent on litigation of disputed terms.

Smart contracts increase the level of trust between contracting parties for the reasons mentioned above and also because they execute automatically once the necessary conditions are met. This 'remove[s] the need to trust another party's willingness and ability to perform'.[193]

Smart contracts' automatic execution also leads to further advantages, namely greater economy and speed. A traditional contract may require the use of third-party intermediaries to assist with the implementation and execution of that contract, but this introduces an added risk that one of these third-party middlemen may cause a fault or interruption which delays or, in the worst case, prevents the execution of the contract. The use of a smart contract should help to mitigate this risk, however if a smart contract is linked to an 'oracle', the input from which is required for the smart contract to execute, this reintroduces a third-party intermediary, albeit not a human one, which is still at risk of malfunctioning in such a way that it causes a delay in the execution of the smart contract.

Therefore, one must also consider the downsides of smart contracts. The greatest risk when using a smart contract is the effect of errors in the code. As smart contracts require human input for the coding required to 'draft' a smart contract, the inherent risk of human error exists – 'anyone, even the most brilliant engineer, is liable to make a typo here and there.'[194] The effect of an error in software code is often hard to quantify until the program is executed. This may not become apparent in a smart contract until it has been placed on the blockchain network and has begun the process of automatic execution. Whilst the same is true for traditional, written contracts, the effect of a minor error in such a contract is often limited (e.g., a mistake in cross-referencing between clauses), and even in the case of more serious errors the risk is more easily mitigated. A traditional contract can be amended, restated or terminated by the parties via a further written agreement if an error is identified post-signing or, if a dispute arises as a result of an error in the contract, the parties are able to turn to the

191. Anwar, H., *Smart Contracts: The Ultimate Guide for Beginners*, available at: https://101blockchains.com/smart-contracts/#7 (accessed on 24 Feb. 2020).
192. *Ibid.*
193. DiMatteo, L.-A. et al., *supra* n. 41.
194. Wan, A., *supra* n. 190.

courts (or arbitrators) to interpret the contract and the surrounding circumstances in order to give effect to the parties' intentions.

Anyone who has ever attempted to translate a traditional contract from one language to another will understand the technicalities and difficulties that arise when attempting to reflect certain words or phrases. As such, it is conceivable that translating language into a computer code would create even more challenges and perhaps lead to errors. Apart from a human error when translating a code, there is also the risk of glitches between the programming language and the machine code, resulting in smart contracts which do not execute or perform as drafters or coders intended. Arguably, there is also a further risk, that drafters or coders deliberately draft smart contracts to automatically execute the conduct of illegal activities. The root cause of these issues is that, unlike traditional contracts, smart contracts exist on the immutable blockchain network and are not capable of amendment. Smart contracts will therefore permanently retain any errors.

In addition, contracts are often drafted with certain facts or external circumstances in mind, which can easily change. As mentioned above, traditional contracts can be amended or restated should new circumstances arise post-signing. Additionally, 'parties quite often decide not to enforce certain contractual rights to further nurture business relationships'.[195] However, for the reasons given above, this would not be possible once the smart contract is placed on the blockchain network. Therefore, where the parties agree separately that a certain consequence of the contract should not apply in a certain scenario, the smart contract will continue to execute automatically as it has been programmed to do. 'The rigidity of a pre-programmed software code excludes by definition the possibility to adapt an agreement to the mutability of business contracts.'[196]

Although the transparency of smart contracts offers some advantages, some contracts require a certain level of confidentiality, which is not an option if smart contracts are uploaded onto a blockchain network. This lack of confidentiality may not be an issue for simple contracts; however, it will be a limitation to smart contracts' implementation into corporate transactions, such as those relating to insolvency or particularly sensitive acquisitions or divestitures, which require high levels of confidentiality.

As previously discussed in §4.03[F] above, smart contracts are limited by their ability to translate certain contractual obligations into a computer code. Contractual language often has an 'inherent ambiguity'[197] that cannot always be drafted into binary algorithmic software code. This limits the scope of the functions that smart contracts are able to perform and the scenarios to which they can be applied. Furthermore, 'smart contracts do not permit the presence of implied terms and contractual gaps'.[198] It is common for traditional contracts to contain intentional contractual gaps or incorporate implied terms to allow for efficient business relationships in changing

195. DiMatteo, L.-A. et al., *supra* n. 41.
196. *Ibid.*
197. *Ibid.*
198. *Ibid.*

environments. Smart contracts' lack of flexibility, and inability to incorporate any ambiguity, means that the parties must negotiate all clauses upfront to take account of the current situation as well as all possible future situations. In most cases, trying to do this will either be impossible or require a large amount of time which the parties may not have. This limitation will therefore be a major deterrent from using smart contracts. The 'legal world is full of gray areas, and the binary nature of smart contracts as they currently exist makes them maddeningly difficult to adjust in unforeseen circumstances'.[199]

[B] Use of Smart Contracts in the Future

As was discussed above, in §4.01[B] Nick Szabo's original concept of 'smart contracting' highlighted three features of the original idea of a smart contract: (1) its potential to perform a contract with anyone, (2) the automatic performance of the contractual obligations if a specific condition is met, and (3) security mechanisms which make it unattractive to circumvent the agreed processes to get the promised goods or services, due to the potential costs of breaches.[200] Smart contracts on a blockchain, as they have developed since Szabo created his original concept, do fulfil these three features. However, as has been set out in detail throughout this chapter, smart contracts are subject to a number of conceptual and technical limitations. Two important limitations are likely to be driving factors in the slow adoption of smart contracts in the near future.

Legal systems are often slow to adapt to changes and developments in technology and, as we have set out in §4.03 above, it is not yet clear how smart contracts, if we are to view them as legally binding contracts in and of themselves, can satisfy many of the long-standing legal requirements for valid formation of a contract. Whilst this will likely change, such uncertainty will affect the widespread use of smart contracts as a replacement for traditional contracts. Therefore, it has been suggested 'to avoid seeing [smart contracts] as legal contracts that require offer, acceptance and consideration'[201] to make it possible for smart contracts to be more commonly used alongside traditional contracts. However, it seems more likely that the legal framework will develop to ensure smart contracts are able to fit within existing legal principles.[202]

In addition, smart contracts are limited by the nature of computer code as binary and inflexible. Traditional contracts of all types typically contain ambiguous terms or otherwise intentionally contain contractual gaps to which smart contracts will be unable to adapt. Whilst this may not be a concern if a smart contract is being used in a simple scenario, in complex transactions the parties will need to ensure that all potential ambiguous terms, and all possible future scenarios, have been considered, negotiated and agreed before they are coded into the smart contract – this may be an impossible task that drives the continued use of traditional contracts until such technical limitations are overcome.

199. Wan, A., *supra* n. 190.
200. Gyr, E., *supra* n. 1.
201. Grinhaus, A., *supra* n. 96.
202. UKJT, *supra* n. 27, at 36.

FURTHER READING

Mateja Durovic & Andre Janssen, *The Formation of Blockchain-Based Smart Contracts in the Light of Contract Law* 753 – 771 (2018, 26 European Review Private Law, Issue 6)

Max Raskin, *The Law and Legality of Smart Contracts* 305, 306 (1 Georgetown Law Technology Review, 2017)

Philipp Paech *Law and Autonomous Systems Series: What Is a Smart Contract?* University of Oxford, available at: https://www.law.ox.ac.uk/business-law-blog/blog/2018/07/law-and-autonomous-systems-series-what-smart-contract

Savelyev, A., *Contract Law 2.0: 'Smart' Contracts as the Beginning of the End of Classic Contract Law* 116–134 (Information & Communications Technology Law, 2017)

Theodore J. Mlynar and Robert M. Fettman, *Blockchain and Smart Contracts Will Change the Face of Insurance in the U.S.*, available at: https://www.lexology.com/library/detail.aspx?g=b119f47b-764b-464c-9090-89b8e6e58219

Larry A. DiMatteo, Michel Cannarsa and Christina Poncibo, *The Cambridge Handbook of Smart Contracts, Blockchain and Technology and Digital Platforms* (2019)

Maren K. Woebbeking, *The Impact of Smart Contracts on the Traditional Concepts of Contract Law* (10 J. Intell. Prop. Info. Tech. & Elec. Com. L. 105, 2019)

Stuart Levi, Alex Lipton & Cristina Vasile, *Legal Issues Surrounding the Use of Smart Contracts* 155 (Blockchain & Cryptocurrency Regulation, 2020, 2nd ed., Global Legal Insights)

CHAPTER 5

Blockchain and Data Privacy

Matthias Artzt, Lothar Determann & William Long

§5.01 INTRODUCTION AND EXECUTIVE SUMMARY

Blockchain technologies have emerged as a disruptive way of executing business processes in decentralized environments. It was originally created to facilitate cryptocurrency transactions (such as Bitcoin), which are currently facing a downward spiral or 'crypto crisis', with demands for regulation and consumer protection. Blockchain, though, has managed to break free from negative associations and distinguishes itself from cryptocurrencies. Large companies, entrepreneurs and investors have recognized the potential of the underlying technology as a game-changer similar to the Internet. The blockchain technology has been gaining momentum for a big range of industries.

In parallel, the European Union (EU) has introduced the General Data Protection Regulation (GDPR) with the purpose of protecting all EU-citizens' data privacy and empowering them to enforce their rights towards organizations or companies which process personal data. However, it will be shown that some articles of the GDPR clash with the way blockchains work in reality. This is because the GDPR has originally been drafted when the blockchain wasn't such an issue as it is today and, thus, the blockchain technology has not been reflected in the regulation. The mismatch between the GDPR and the blockchain characteristics generates anxiety about the possibility that the regulation might hinder European innovation in blockchain technology. In this Chapter, the data privacy state of play in relation to the blockchain will be analysed from two different angles: the GDPR and the US privacy perspective with a focus on the California Consumer Privacy Act of 2018 (CCPA).

The GDPR differs from US privacy laws significantly: The European regulation restricts and regulates the processing of personal data comprehensively, which adversely affects all information technologies and presents particularly serious obstacles to the adoption of blockchain and distributed ledger technology (DLT), particularly due to restrictions on international transfers of personal data outside the European Economic Area (EEA) and insufficiently limited rights to be forgotten; these and other requirements under the GDPR are discussed in the following sections §5.02 through §5.09, *infra*.

By contrast, US privacy laws do not generally restrict or regulate the processing of personal data and seek to apply only proportionately designed sector-, harm- and situation-specific requirements to safeguard individual privacy against concrete harms. US privacy laws are technology-neutral and do not affect the blockchain technology adversely or specifically. But, the sheer volume of federal and state privacy laws present a challenge for businesses, which must allocate resources to identifying which requirements apply to particular blockchain use cases, as further discussed in section §5.10, *infra*.

This chapter proposes possible ways of achieving GDPR compliance by leveraging state of the art techniques. Further, it provides useful hints to cope with US privacy and CCPA related requirements when dealing with blockchain applications.

§5.02 PERSONAL DATA IN THE CONTEXT OF THE GDPR

[A] Definition of Personal Data in the Context of a Blockchain

When considering the data protection issues in the context of a blockchain, the first concept to address is the definition of personal data and whether it is processed by the blockchain because whether personal data is processed will determine the GDPR's application and is, therefore, central to these discussions in this chapter.

The GDPR applies to personal data, which is defined as 'any information relating to an identified or identifiable natural person (data subject); an identifiable person is one who can be identified, directly or indirectly, in particular by reference to an identifier ...'[1] It follows that, when blockchain technology is processing personal data, the GDPR will apply to that processing. However, defining what constitutes personal data, including in the blockchain context, is not straightforward, particularly given continuing technological developments which allow individuals to be identified based on increasingly tenuous links to data which may not on first review appear to be 'personal', together with the concepts of pseudonymization and anonymization, which are of particular relevance to processing of personal data by blockchain technology. In fact, a fundamental question when applying GDPR principles to the blockchain is: does personal data that has been hashed, pseudonymized or encrypted qualify as personal data and the protections afforded by the GDPR?

A blockchain is likely to contain two main categories of data which may be considered personal: (i) participants' and miners' identifiers (e.g., each participant/miner will have a public key, ensuring identification of the issuer and receiver of a transaction); and (ii) additional data that is contained within a transaction (transactional data). If this additional transactional data includes information about

1. Article 4 section 1 of the GDPR.

another natural person, who can be identified, directly or indirectly, then this data would also be considered personal data for the purposes of the GDPR's application.

[1] Public Keys

In most public blockchains, every published transaction is linked to a public key that represents a user. That key is then encrypted to avoid another individual who views the blockchain being able to directly identify the individual (or a corporate entity[2]). The user then holds a private key (another string of letters and numbers) which allows for the decryption of data which has been encrypted via the public key. The re-use of the public key enables individuals to be singled out by reference to their key, even if the public key does not allow them to be directly identified. This is one of the key purposes of the public key: to ensure that any transactions are attributed to the correct persons.

It is possible that this public key would be considered an 'identifier' as addressed by Recital 30 of the GDPR (i.e., when combined with additional identifiers, the individual can be identified).[3,4] For example, it could be possible to obtain the additional information required to identify the individual because it is held by the service provider or because someone can connect the key to an individual via their Internet Protocol (IP) address.[5] As such, the key would fall within the definition of pseudonymized data per Article 4(5) of the GDPR and Recital 26 of the GDPR which states that the GDPR applies to personal data which have 'undergone pseudonymisation [and] which could be attributed to a natural person by the use of additional information'.[6] This is also the position taken by regulators such as the French Data Protection Authority (DPA) who considers that public keys will likely constitute personal data under the GDPR in the context of blockchain.[7]

2. Note that the public key will only be considered personal data where it relates to a natural person. Public keys used to identify corporate entities will not qualify as personal data that is subject to the GDPR; Bacon, J. et al., *Blockchain Demystified: A Technical and Legal Introduction to Distributed and Centralised Ledgers* 62 (25 Richmond Journal of Law and Technology 1, 2018).
3. For example, the ICO, in its guidance on encryption, confirms that where a public key is used as an encryption technique, both the process of converting the personal data into a public key and subsequent use of the encrypted personal data would constitute processing of personal data for GDPR purposes, available at: https://ico.org.uk/for-organisations/guide-to-data-protection/guide-to-the-general-data-protection-regulation-gdpr/encryption/what-is-encryption/ (accessed 3 Feb. 2020).
4. Other commentators have noted that 'even if personal information only entails reference ID numbers, such identifiers are typically unique to a specific person. While in all such cases additional information may be necessary to attribute information to the data subject, such information would be merely pseudonymised and count as personal information.' Berberich, M. & Steiner, M., *Blockchain Technology and the GDPR: How to Reconcile Privacy and Distributed Ledgers?* (2 European Data Protection Law Review 422, 2016).
5. The *Breyer* case has confirmed that temporary IP addresses assigned to a computing address may constitute personal data even where only a third party (e.g., the internet service provider) has the additional data necessary to identify the individual.
6. Recital 26 of the GDPR.
7. Commission Nationale de l'Informatique et de Libertés (6 Nov. 2018) *Blockchain and the GDPR: Solutions for a responsible use of the blockchain in the context of personal data,* 6 available at: https://www.cnil.fr/en/blockchain-and-gdpr-solutions-responsible-use-blockchain-context-personal-data (accessed 3 Feb. 2020).

A fundamental question when applying GDPR principles to the blockchain is: does personal data that has been hashed, pseudonymized or encrypted qualify as personal data and the protections afforded by the GDPR?

Pseudonymization is defined by the GDPR as the 'processing of personal data in such a manner that the personal data can no longer be attributed to a specific data subject without the use of additional information, provided that such additional information is kept separately and is subject to technical and organisational security measures to ensure that the personal data are not attributed to an identified or identifiable natural person'.[8] It follows that the key criterion for determining whether data is personal data is 'identifiability'. As such, the current view[9] is that pseudonymization should be seen as a security measure, rather than a method of removing the 'personal' element of the data. Unlike anonymized data, pseudonymized data will still be subject to the GDPR.

Under the GDPR, to determine whether a natural person is identifiable, 'account should be taken of all the means reasonably likely to be used, such as singling out, either by the controller or by another person to identify the natural person directly or indirectly'.[10] As such, whether pseudonymized data are personal data, and in turn, subject to the requirements of the GDPR, will depend on whether it is possible to anonymize data to such an extent that natural persons are not identifiable, taking into account all the means reasonably likely to be used.

There are examples in practice which demonstrate that there is the ability to identify individuals from their public keys, either because the data subject has disclosed the information themselves, or where required to comply with other legislations (e.g., wallet exchanges storing parties' real world identities to comply with their Know Your Customer and Anti-Money Laundering duties).[11]

On the other hand, the GDPR does not apply to 'information which does not relate to an identified or identifiable natural person or to data rendered anonymous in such a way that the data subject is no longer identifiable'[12] (i.e., anonymized data). Pseudonymization is not a method of anonymization, and the Article 29 Data Protection Working Party is clear that 'it merely reduces the linkability of a dataset with the original identity of a data subject, and is accordingly a useful security measure'.[13]

The basic principle in determining whether data has been truly anonymized is the reasonable likelihood of identification. The process of anonymization must make it impossible to identify a natural person through any and all of the means 'reasonably likely to be used',[14] and accordingly to the Article 29 Data Protection Working Party,[15]

8. Article 4(5) GDPR.
9. Article 29 Data Protection Working Party, *Opinion 05/2014 on Anonymisation Techniques* 3 (WP 216 Adopted on 10 Apr. 2014).
10. Recital 26 of the GDPR.
11. Bacon et al., *supra* n. 2, at. 61.
12. Recital 26 of the GDPR.
13. Article 29 Data Protection Working Party, *supra* n. 9, at. 3.
14. Recital 26 of the GDPR.
15. It should be noted that this approach was *not* endorsed by the EDPB when it took office in 2018. To view the list of guidance endorsed by the EDPB, available at: https://edpb.europa.eu/node/89 (accessed 3 Feb. 2020).

the process must be irreversible.[16] The Article 29 Data Protection Working Party also acknowledged that it would be very difficult to create a truly anonymous dataset whilst retaining the underlying information as required for the task.[17] However, the view of the UK's Information Commissioner's Office (ICO) is that the relevant criterion is not the possibility of identification but rather the definition of personal data is based on 'the identification or likely identification of the individual'.[18,19]

[2] Transactional Data

Aside from public keys, there will also be other data used on blockchains. This data is categorized as transactional data or additional data. The Commission Nationale de l'Informatique et de Libertés (CNIL) has used the latter term in its blockchain guidance and explains that it denotes data that is contained 'within' a transaction.[20]

In a blockchain, information is encrypted and hashed[21] using specific algorithms and functions before being stored in ledgers. In summary, cryptographic hashing is intended to guarantee the reliability and integrity of blockchains. The process involves running an algorithm to turn a block of data into a fixed-length output (the hash). Each block in the chain will contain a hash (a unique identifier) and in order to link the blocks together, a hash of the previous block, amongst other information. This prevents either block being altered or another block being added in between the two existing blocks and relates to a key blockchain concept of being tamper-evident.

The question of whether hashed personal data should be considered personal data is subject to controversial debates at present. The following assumptions are critical when evaluating such discussions and reaching a conclusion:

> First, it must be taken into account, that not all hashing algorithms are equal and that the most advanced algorithms should always be preferred.[22] Second, the discussions boil down to the question whether hashed personal data may be reconstituted by using brute force decryption. A brute force attack could succeeding reversing the hash if the original data is of a known, and relatively small size. The Blockchain Observatory and Forum recommends to mitigate this risk using

16. Article 29 Data Protection Working Party, *supra* n. 9, at 5.
17. *Ibid.*, at 3.
18. UK ICO; *Anonymisation: managing data protection risk code of practice* 16, available at: https://ico.org.uk/media/1061/anonymisation-code.pdf (accessed 3 Feb. 2020).
19. Note that the ICO's Anonymisation code of practice was drafted under the Data Protection Act 1998.
20. CNIL, *supra* n. 7, at 6.
21. Hashing in a blockchain refers to the process of having an input item of whatever length reflecting an output item of a fixed length. For example, in a cryptocurrency transaction, transactions of varying lengths are run through a hashing algorithm, and all give an output of fixed length, regardless of the input transaction. The output is called a hash. This allows participants to keep track of a transaction much easier, particularly if otherwise, the transaction would involve large volumes of data. Most importantly, the hashing function provides security capabilities to processed transactions, making them immutable.
22. European Data Protection Supervisor and the Agencia espanola proteccion datos, *Introduction to the Hash Function as a Personal Data Pseudonymisation Technique* 21 (October 2019), available at: https://edps.europa.eu/data-protection/our-work/publications/papers/introduction-hash-function-personal-data_en (accessed 3 Feb. 2020).

techniques such as 'salting' or 'peppering' hashes which involve adding extra information to the set of data with the purpose of making the data large enough that a brute force attack would be extremely unlikely to reverse the data.[23] Third, there might be situations where pattern analysis makes it possible to uncover information regarding a particular data subject. This relates to the risk to link encrypted data back to an individual by examining certain patterns of usage or context, or by comparison of other pieces of information.

Commentators seek to achieve a balance between data protection and not restricting the growth of the digital economy by focusing on proven and officially certified encryption technologies. They come to the conclusion that any personal data that was encrypted and vetted by the European Data Protection Board (EDPB) would be considered as not personal for any parties who did not have the encryption key. That would require that the encryption algorithm is well designed and the encryption itself has been properly carried out.[24]

Given that hashing will allow records to be linked, based on the above analysis and the view of the Article 29 Data Protection Working Party and other commentators,[25] it is likely that hashing (of data that is considered personal data without hashing) would be considered a pseudonymization technique,[26] rather than achieving true anonymization. In addition, encrypted data could arguably be traced back to the individual if enough effort is expended.

Overall, it can be concluded, based on the current guidance in relation to pseudonymization and anonymization discussed above, that there is the potential for personal data to be processed by a blockchain, both personal data of the participants themselves and personal data included in the transactional data. This means that privacy rules, including the GDPR, will be applicable to certain data in the blockchain system. The substantive requirements which the GDPR imposes on such processing of personal data applied to blockchains will be discussed further throughout this Chapter.

[B] How Is Personal Data Processed on a Blockchain?

Under the GDPR, the term 'processed' is defined broadly as 'any operation or set of operations which is performed on personal data or sets of personal data',[27] which essentially means that anything done with personal data would constitute processing, including collection, recording, deletion and even simply storing personal data.

23. European Union Blockchain Observatory and Forum, *Blockchain and the GDPR* 22 (16 Oct. 2018) available at: https://www.eublockchainforum.eu/sites/default/files/reports/20181016_report_gdpr.pdf (accessed 3 Feb. 2020).
24. Gresham, J., *Is Encrypted Data Personal Data under the GDPR?* (6 Mar. 2019) available at: https://iapp.org/a/is-encrypted-data-personal-data-under-the-gdpr/?mkt_tok (accessed 3 Feb. 2020).
25. Nisbet, K., *The False Allure of Hashing for Anonymization* (30 Apr. 2018) available at: https://gravitational.com/blog/hashing-for-anonymization/ (accessed 3 Feb. 2020) and Felten, E., *Does Hashing Make Data 'Anonymous'* (22 Apr. 2018) available at: https://www.ftc.gov/news-events/blogs/techftc/2012/04/does-hashing-make-data-anonymous (accessed 3 Feb. 2020).
26. Article 29 Data Protection Working Party, *supra* n. 9, at. 20.
27. Article 4(2) of the GDPR.

It follows that processing personal data in a blockchain network would constitute data processing through automated means, and every flow of personal data in the operation of a blockchain would be included within this definition. For example, the initial addition of personal data to a distributed ledger, the storage of hashes and public keys on a blockchain, the submission or transfer of transactions (where documents may contain personal data) through nodes may all constitute personal data for the purposes of the GDPR.

More generally, a blockchain must be updated regularly among all participants of the network, so that everyone has the most up-to-date version of the complete database. This update across the network may also likely constitute data processing.

[C] Application of the GDPR to the Blockchain

As with any novel form of technology, one of the key questions relates to blockchains regulation, by what legislation and by which governmental or regulatory authorities. If it can be determined that blockchain activity may involve the 'processing' of 'personal data' (*see* sections §5.02[A] and §5.02[B] above), one additional question which will require thought by both government and regulators, as well as controllers of personal data in blockchain networks, relates to the territorial application of the relevant data protection regulations and laws. For the purpose of this paragraph, we will consider the territorial application of the GDPR.

The GDPR has considerably widened the territorial scope of the GDPR beyond its predecessor, the Data Protection Directive 96/46/EC. Article 3 of the GDPR provides that the GDPR will apply to the processing of personal data in a number of circumstances.[28] First, where the processing of personal data occurs 'in the context of the activities of an establishment of a controller or a processor in the Union, regardless of whether the processing takes place in the Union or not'[29] (the establishment criterion).

Importantly, the GDPR will also apply to the processing of personal data of individuals located in the EEA by a controller or processor not deemed established in the EEA where the processing activities relate to: (i) the offering of goods or services (irrespective of whether a payment by the individual is required) to such individuals (the goods and services criterion); or (ii) the monitoring of their behaviour, providing the behaviour takes place within the EEA (e.g., tracking on the Internet for profiling) (the monitoring criterion).[30]

Where a data controller not established in the EEA processes personal data in a blockchain, the GDPR may apply under the goods and services and/or the monitoring

28. On 12 Nov. 2019, nearly a year after the draft guidelines were published and following a public consultation, the EDPB published its final guidelines seeking to clarify the territorial scope of the GDPR (the Territorial Scope Guidelines). The Territorial Scope Guidelines largely reaffirm prior interpretations of the GDPR's territorial application under the establishment criterion and offer further guidance with respect to the goods and services and monitoring criteria.
29. Article 3(1) of the GDPR.
30. Article 3(2) of the GDPR; Artzt, M., *Territorial Scope of the GDPR from the US Perspective* (26 Jun. 2018) available at: https://iapp.org/news/a/territorial-scope-of-the-gdpr-from-a-us-perspective/.

criterion, and the broad reach of the GDPR's territorial scope could result in the application of the GDPR to many blockchain-based transactions which may have a limited nexus to Europe. This is the same issue faced by many global companies in other business activities and is by no means an issue unique to blockchain. However, in the case of blockchain, it may be more complicated than other processing activities to determine the application of the GDPR. Whilst the GDPR is generally considered to have been drafted as independent from technology, it was still conceived with a centralized database in mind. In these scenarios, the entity that is determining the purpose and the means for processing (i.e., the controller) will in many cases also be the entity that has developed the systems to implement the processing.[31] On the other hand, a blockchain can be described as a decentralized network in which transactions or other information are recorded, and the process can involve multiple controllers located around the EEA as well as in 'third countries'[32] internationally. This is likely to be particularly problematic where looking at public, non-permissioned blockchain systems which are often run on nodes located in different countries and everyone who has access to the ledger can process the relevant information (which could include personal data). The creators cannot control the geographical scope of the network,[33] and if it is not possible to fully understand who is involved in the blockchain network, then it will be difficult to determine where certain controllers are based, in turn, whether the GDPR applies and which data protection obligations are applying to the network.

Assuming the identity of the relevant controllers can be determined, then as stated above, the GDPR will apply where the controller is established in the EEA or where a company established outside of the EEA relies on blockchains to process personal data. Equally, where an entity offers goods or services to data subjects in the EEA via blockchain technology, this processing may also be subject to the GDPR. For example, the European Parliamentary Research Service[34] considers that in the case of blockchain; the GDPR may apply where an operator of a blockchain makes available their infrastructure (which they consider could be interpreted as constituting a 'service') to individuals in the EEA.[35] As is the case more generally, the application of the GDPR to processing activities in the context of a blockchain network will need to be analysed on a case-by-case basis.

---

31. European Union Blockchain Observatory and Forum, *supra* n. 23, at. 17.
32. A third country is a country other than the EU Member States and the three additional European Economic Area countries (Norway, Iceland and Liechtenstein) that have adopted a national law implementing the GDPR. Under the GDPR, personal data can only be transferred to such third countries in compliance with Chapter V (Arts 44–50 of the GDPR).
33. Finck, M., *Blockchains and Data Protection in the European Union* 17 (Max Planck Institute for Innovation & Competition Research Paper No. 18-01, 30 Nov. 2017) available at: https://edpl.lexxion.eu/data/article/12327/pdf/edpl_2018_01-007.pdf (accessed 3 Feb. 2020).
34. European Parliamentary Research Service, *Blockchain and the General Data Protection Regulation, 'Can Distributed Ledgers Be Squared with European Data Protection Law?'* 9 (July 2019) available at: https://www.europarl.europa.eu/RegData/etudes/STUD/2019/634445/EPRS_STU(2019)634445_EN.pdf (accessed 3 Feb. 2020).
35. Bacon et al., *supra* n. 2, at 25.

§5.03 IDENTIFYING CONTROLLERS AND PROCESSORS IN A BLOCKCHAIN ENVIRONMENT UNDER THE GDPR

[A] Definition of Controller and Processor

A controller under the GDPR is a natural or legal person, public authority, agency or other body, which, alone or jointly with others, determines the purposes and means of the processing of personal data.[36] It will be shown that a controller under the GDPR bears similarities with 'business' under the CCPA 2018.[37] Some of the obligations of the GDPR also apply to processors which are natural or legal persons, public authorities, agencies or other bodies which process personal data on behalf of the controller based on clear and concise instructions issued by the controller.[38] The GDPR requires a detailed contract or other legal act to be put in place between controllers and processors, laying out the mandate given to processors and other terms of the controller-processor relationship.[39]

In addition, the GDPR provides a model which is the concept of having joint controllers pursuant to its Article 26. Joint Controllers are two or more controllers which jointly determine the purposes and means of processing. When determining the roles of the blockchain participants, this aspect will also come into play.[40]

[B] Legal Status of Participants of a Blockchain Network

[1] Static Number of Roles and Responsibilities

One of the key challenges arising from compliance with the GDPR in a blockchain context is the identification of data controllers (controllers) and data processors (processors). Given the nature of blockchain technology, it is not always easy to determine the legal status of the different participants in blockchain networks such as nodes, miners, oracles, users or developers. Even though developers of blockchain protocols don't process data, they do play an important role in defining how the data is being processed through blockchain protocols.[41] Blockchain and other decentralized technologies don't completely fit into the concept of predefined roles and responsibilities as set out in the GDPR. The regulation only provides a limited number of roles the participants may take over if any. In particular, some blockchain participants do have a role to play, but their legal status in relation to data protection is quite unclear.

It is not up to the blockchain users to allocate roles to single participants arbitrarily if the factual situation does not fit for purpose. This implies, for instance, that the assignment of the role as a controller to one participant is not permissible as

36. Article 4(7) of the GDPR.
37. *See* section §5.10, *infra*.
38. Article 4(8) of the GDPR.
39. Article 28(3) of the GDPR.
40. Artzt, M., *Is Blockchain Compatible with the GDPR?* (18 Jun. 2019) available at: https://platform.dataguidance.com/opinion/eu-blockchain-compatible-gdpr-part-1 (accessed 3 Feb. 2020).
41. Blockchain Bundesverband, *Blockchain, Data protection, and the GDPR* 5 (25.05.2018).

long as this participant does not meet the criteria for acting as a controller defined by the GDPR.[42] Generally speaking, the allocation of roles and responsibilities is not subject to any arrangements of blockchain users. However, only the factual circumstances are driving the determination which role needs to be attributed to each participant. The recommendations of the French DPA, the CNIL, take this into account by pointing out that a group of participants may choose to identify one of them who makes decisions for the group and to designate the said participant as a controller.[43] If the selected natural or legal person is empowered to make decisions, particularly factually determines the purposes and means of the processing of personal data on a blockchain, this person will be acting as a controller.

It is crucial to consider how the notions of the 'means' and 'purposes' ought to be interpreted in relation to the blockchain technology. Regarding the means of personal data processing, the first challenge boils down to identifying the perspective that should be adopted. The parties that exercise influence over the software, hardware and data centres being used to operate a specific blockchain may determine the means of the particular processing activity. Further, the mere use of a blockchain infrastructure made available by others (such as blockchain-as-a-service solutions) may be considered as an implicit determination of the means of processing.[44] Due to the fact that blockchains are distributed databases designed to be operated by many different parties, it is obvious that many actors may have stakes in the determination of the means of processing. In particular, with a view to the public or any type of permissionless blockchains, there is certainly not a single legal or natural person that takes the decision which software, hardware or data centres need to be used. Rather, these decisions are made by a range of different users.[45] For illustration, in proof-of-work systems, miners may make the decision of what hardware and which data centres (for mining purposes) shall be used, whereas software developers decide whether and which software should be updated.[46] If a governance body comprising of a group of blockchain participants has been established, those group members will agree upon what software has to be implemented in order to carry out transactions in a private blockchain context.

The former Article 29 Data Protection Working Party has moreover indicated that emphasis should be placed on the '*effective means*' understood as 'substantial questions' that are 'essential to the core of processing' – the how of processing.[47] This includes what data to process and for how long, which third parties have access to the data, when and how data can be manipulated.[48]

42. Arning, A. & Rothkegel, T., Article 4 DSGVO, in Taeger, J./Gabel, D. (ed.), *DSGVO, BDSG* 143 (3d ed., Deutscher Fachverlag GmbH, 2019); Article 29 Data Protection Working Party, *Opinion 1/2010 on the Concepts of 'Controller' and 'Processor'* 14 (WP 169 Adopted on 16 Feb. 2010).
43. CNIL, *supra* n. 7, at. 2.
44. European Parliamentary Research Service, *supra* n. 34, at 43.
45. *Ibid.*
46. *Ibid.*
47. Article 29 Data Protection Working Party, *supra* n. 42, at 14.
48. *Ibid.*

The criteria for determining the purposes of data processing should be considered as pivotal for assessing the controllership. It is apparent that, particularly in a public blockchain environment, there are many actors which independently define the purpose of data processing whereas a group of blockchain users may form part of a governance body and, therefore, jointly determine the purpose of data processing. Determining the purpose must be interpreted in terms of the particular data processing activity rather than the usage of the blockchain technology in general. The latter criterion points to a macro-perspective which would not be in sync with the interpretation of the means of data processing which should be understood as a granular determination as shown above. The micro level for the purpose determination is related to the individual transaction such as recording a specific transaction onto a blockchain. It is the more appropriate approach given that data protection laws typically deal with specific items of personal data and touch upon specific data processing activities.[49]

It should be noted that not all blockchain users acting as controllers qualify as joint controllers. Particularly, in a public blockchain context, many users independently define the purpose and/or the means of the individual processing operations. They may be considered as co-controllers, albeit the co-controllership is not a legal term under the GDPR. From the practical point of view, the co-controllership is a commonly used model leveraged in those scenarios where the users have a role to play without being processors or joint controllers.

By all means, it is essential to run a case-by-case analysis of the factual circumstances in order to clearly allocate roles and attendant responsibilities, bearing in mind that scenarios may occur in which users have no specific role with regard to the GDPR.

The reason for diligently determining the roles is that data subjects, particularly those whose personal data is being recorded on the blockchain, need to know which natural or legal person they can refer to in order to effectively exercise their rights. Furthermore, data protection authorities must have a contact person who may be held accountable for the processing of personal data and for any data breaches occurred while utilizing the blockchain technology.[50] This contact needs to evidence compliance with its obligations arising from the GDPR.

[2] Miners

According to the National Institute of Standards and Technology (NIST), which belongs to the US Department of Commerce, mining is defined as the act of solving a puzzle within a proof of consensus model.[51] With that, miners do not decide what data is written on a blockchain, beyond analysis for general consensus based on the protocol as defined in the blockchain software. They validate transactions which have previously been submitted by participants. By no means, they are entrusted to make

49. Bacon et al., *supra* n. 2, at. 64.
50. Article 29 Data Protection Working Party, *supra* n. 42, at 14.
51. NIST, *Blockchain Technology Overview* 53 (NISTIR 8202, 2018).

any decisions with regard to any individual processing activity. Since they typically don't determine the specific purposes and means of the processing of personal data sent to the network by a third party, they don't qualify as controllers.[52]

On the other hand, it needs to be acknowledged that miners exercise significant control over the means by choosing which version of the protocol to run. However, the criterion of the means has become subsidiary to the purposes criterion. By no means, miners determine the purpose of a - specific - transaction. Hence, they are not taking over the role of controllers.[53]

Given that miners can't be considered as controllers, the legal questions is whether they may act as processors pursuant to Article 4 section 8 of the GDPR. Following the legal definition set out therein, they need to carry out services or any type of tasks based on the instructions of any other blockchain participants (controller). This usually doesn't happen, particularly in public blockchains, as miners simply have to validate transactions. The validation of transactions doesn't relate to the performing of service on behalf of particular blockchain participants. To add a new block to a blockchain, all miners must come to a consensus over time. With that, the consensus model contradicts the controller-processor relationship where the processor has a subordinate role to play by following instructions issued by a controller.

There is another aspect to be considered: The blockchain protocol may be interpreted as an instruction the miners have to adhere to. The protocol is a software designed by developers (*see* section §5.03[B][6], *infra*). Developers are not regarded as controllers unless special circumstances necessitate another assessment. Irrespective of the above, the blockchain protocol doesn't contain concise instructions as to how to deal with personal data written on a blockchain. The CNIL is of the view that, in some cases, miners can be considered as processors within the meaning of the GDPR stating that they follow the controllers' instructions when checking whether the transaction meets technical criteria (such as format and a certain maximum size) which would facilitate that the transaction can be carried out according to the chain rules.[54] This broadly describes what miners are doing, in general. As a consequence, miners would need to conclude data protection agreements with those participants deemed as controllers in accordance with Article 28 of the GDPR. In public blockchains, this approach in not feasible since it is predominantly not clear who the controllers are who have laid down the related blockchain rules.

The CNIL only exemplifies a controller-processor relationship applicable to private blockchains. For instance, when several insurance companies decide to create a private blockchain for their processing operation following their 'Know Your Customer' obligations, in such a case, according to the CNIL recommendation, the insurance companies may decide that one of them is the controller. The insurance company which validates transactions would be likely to be considered as the processor.[55] This proposal may not resolve the underlying legal problem stemming

52. Blockchain Bundesverband, *supra* n. 41, at 6.
53. European Parliamentary Research Service, *supra* n. 34, at 46.
54. CNIL, *supra* n. 7, at 3.
55. *Ibid.*, at 4.

from the definition of a processor (Article 4 section 8 of the GDPR). Validating a particular transaction doesn't constitute a processing activity within the meaning of Article 4 section 2 of the GDPR (Processing). The processing under the GDPR relates to personal data. The processor needs to act on behalf of a controller responsible for issuing concise instructions as to what kind of personal data is being processed, how and for what purpose the data should be dealt with and safeguarded. The miner's task is limited to checking special technical criteria set out in the protocol and to resolving a mathematic puzzle for validation purposes. The protocol itself doesn't provide any personal data to be processed.

Therefore, miners need to be allocated to the blockchain infrastructure without having particular roles under the GDPR.

[3] Nodes

Nodes are the computers that store a full or partial copy of a blockchain and participate in the validation of new blocks. Once a miner finds a valid hash for a block, the node broadcasts its hash to other nodes, which subsequently run a computation to verify whether the hash is valid (i.e., whether it meets the specifications of the protocol) and where this is the case, they add the new block to their own local copy of the ledger. Nodes verify whether transactions have the correct digital signatures and data format.[56]

Some authors have suggested that each node that triggers a transaction and, hence, distributes information to all other nodes, or that saves a transaction in its own copy of a database should be considered as a controller. They argue that the node pursues its own purpose, especially the participation in the network.[57] The authors are of the view that the node registers, orders and stores data and can freely use the data that is registered on its own computer.[58]

This view can be questioned since a node is simply a computer and may not define any means or purposes of data processing. Further, registering and storing of data is an IT operation which goes automatically and is not linked to a decision-making process of a human being. Irrespective of that, the mere participation in a network is too vague since the determination of the purpose must be interpreted in conjunction with an individual data processing activity rather than the usage of the blockchain technology in general (*see* section §5.03B][1], *infra*).

In addition, qualifying nodes as controller raises considerable complications. The exact number, location and identity of nodes on a chain can't be determined without difficulties given that nodes may be spread over the globe. Furthermore, nodes only see the encrypted or hashed version of the data and, therefore, are not capable of making any changes thereto. Nodes are actually decentralized entities that are not able to comply with the obligations arising from the GDPR.

56. European Union Blockchain Observatory and Forum, *supra* n. 23, at 14.
57. Martini, M and Weinzierl, Q, *Die Blockchain-Technologie und das Recht auf Vergessenwerden*, 1251, 1253 (Neue Zeitschrift für Verwaltungsrecht 2017).
58. *Ibid.*, at 1254.

Irrespective of that, the enforcement of such obligations against nodes is a burdensome exercise. For example, for the Bitcoin blockchain, there were approximately 11,000 nodes around the planet in 2018. From the practical perspective, nodes belong to the blockchain infrastructure and should not be considered as controllers.

[4] Wallets

Wallets are software packages at the application level that allow companies or individual participants to control their own private key and to interact with the blockchain network by sending transactions to miners for validation purposes. The NIST considers wallets as the software used to store and manage asymmetric keys and addresses used for transactions.[59] Even though wallets may pass personal data to miners, it is evident that this happens under the control of the blockchain participants which determine the purpose of the data transfer (creating a new blockchain transaction) as well as the means of such processing (usage of the specific blockchain application). Against this background, wallets have no role to play under the regime of the GDPR; they must be allocated to the blockchain infrastructure as well.

[5] Users of a Blockchain

A blockchain transaction represents an interaction between parties. With cryptocurrencies, for example, a transaction represents a transfer of the cryptocurrency between blockchain network users. Moreover, transactions can be more generally used to transfer all kinds of data. In the case of smart contract systems, transactions can be used to send data, process that data, and store some result on the blockchain. A transaction can also be used to change an attribute of a digitized asset within a blockchain technology-based supply chain system.[60]

From the data privacy point of view, it is critical to determine which user should be deemed as a controller under the GDPR. The question is whether all users who participate in any transactions in a blockchain network can be qualified as controllers provided that those transactions store or process personal data.

The CNIL considers that the user may qualify as a controller when (i) the said participant is a natural person; and (ii) the processing is related to a professional or commercial activity; or when the said participant is a legal person that registers personal data on a blockchain.[61]

This is predominantly in line with the Thematic Report from the Blockchain Observatory and Forum.[62] For private blockchains, the Blockchain Observatory and Forum recommends that a blockchain consortium which needs to be established designates one or more actors that will be responsible for the blockchain and will act as a controller or joint controllers. With respect to public blockchains, the Blockchain

59. NIST, *supra* n. 51, at 54.
60. *Ibid.*, at 10.
61. CNIL, *supra* n. 7, at 3.
62. European Union Blockchain Observatory and Forum, *supra* n. 23, at 18.

Observatory and Forum is of the opinion that it remains quite often a grey area. If network users submit personal data to the blockchain ledger as part of business activity, they are most likely to be considered controllers.[63] If they, however, post their own personal data onto a blockchain for their own personal use, for example, to buy or sell crypto-assets, they are most likely to fall under the household exemption of Article 2(2c) of the GDPR and, therefore, may not be regarded as controllers.

Recital 18 of the GDPR states that the regulation does not apply to the processing of personal data by a natural person in the course of a purely personal or household activity and, thus, with no connection to a professional or commercial activity. Personal or household activities include correspondence and the holding of addresses, or social networking and online activities. The household exemption only applies to those activities which may be linked to the right of privacy of an individual.[64] Criteria for the applicability of the household exemption are neither the size of the data file nor the number of people who might have access to the data being disclosed online.[65]

This parameter is generally ignored by those who differentiate whom the personal data is relating to. They state, that, even if the user's own personal data is being disclosed on a public blockchain and, therefore, on-chain data is made available to an indefinite number of people, the household exemption would not apply.[66] In the case the user puts personal data of other people on-chain, the user would also qualify as a controller.[67]

This rationale shifts the responsibility to the users of the blockchain technology who, particularly with regard to public blockchains, lack the required expertise to make informed decisions regarding the design of the respective technology. The user of a blockchain who, for example, buys or sells Bitcoins, only determines whether a transfer is created and to whom and how many Bitcoins are being transferred.[68] In that scenario, the purpose is predominantly to transfer a special number of Bitcoins to another participant, and this purpose cannot be altered by the user. The user has certainly no influence how long data is stored, which third parties have access and when the data is deleted.[69]

This assumption may not change in the case the data subjects gain control over their own personal data through their private key, which triggers the question of whether the data subjects can qualify as controllers. One may argue that, if an individual hashes his or her own personal information to the blockchain, he or she will be both, the data subject and the controller. That solution looks a bit weird since the GDPR clearly differentiates between the data subject concerned and the controllers whom the data subject rights may be addressed to. In the case both roles are merged,

63. *Ibid.*
64. Schmidt, B., Article 2, in Taeger, J./Gabel, D., *supra* n. 42 at 56.
65. Recital 18 of the GDPR.
66. European Parliamentary Research Service, *supra* n. 34, at 49.
67. *Ibid.*, at 48.
68. Buocz, T. et al., *Bitcoin and the GDPR: Allocating Responsibility in Distributed Networks*, 24 (Computer Law & Security Review, 2019).
69. *Ibid.*

the data subject rights are jeopardized since there is no participant available which can be held liable to respond to them.

In summary, if individuals submit their own personal data to a blockchain, even if they hash their personal information and use a private key and, by doing this, only pursue private purposes, they should not be considered as controllers. Whenever they put their own personal data but also the data of other individuals in a block to be added to a blockchain, they may fall under the household exemption too, provided that this is strictly related to a private activity. In the case they are pursuing commercial purposes, even if this only makes a very small contribution, the GDPR applies, and they should be treated as controllers. It must be taken into account, that the household exemption needs to be interpreted strictly, and the legal classification of blockchain users should follow a case-by-case assessment.

[6] Developer of Smart Contracts

The question arises how developers of smart contracts should be qualified from the data privacy perspective. Smart contracts are pieces of software that can be deployed to a blockchain network and that, once deployed, may be executed independently from their developer (*see* Chapter 3, section §3.01, *supra*). This software is only executed when called by a network user. There are three options which should be factored in when determining which role the developer and the user of such software may have: The software can be seen as being operated by its developer, by the network user or by both.

The CNIL is of the view that, with regards to smart contracts, the software, respectively, the algorithm developer may simply be a solution provider without having a particular data protection role to play. When the developer actively participates in the data processing, he or she may be qualified as a processor or controller depending on the ability to determine the purpose and means of the processing.[70] The CNIL clearly states that the smart contract developer may be deemed as a processor provided he or she processes personal data on behalf of controllers. It specifies this general statement by using the following example: A software developer offers a solution to an airline by virtue of a smart contract that enables passengers to be automatically reimbursed when their flight has been delayed or cancelled.[71]

Following the recommendation of the CNIL, the software developer would be deemed as a processor if he or she intervenes in the data processing, while, in this scenario, the airline would act as a controller. This solution is indeed acceptable in the light of the GDPR. Nevertheless, it needs to be questioned in which scenarios a software developer has an active role to play in conjunction with the processing of personal data. Typically, the software developer doesn't participate in any blockchain transactions. When developing and publishing smart contract algorithms, he or she has nothing to do with any sort of processing activity. Irrespective of this, the software is

70. CNIL, *supra* n. 7, at 2.
71. *Ibid.*, at 3.

not being operated by the developer as he or she only devises a solution to be offered to particular blockchain users who might take advantage of it. They take the decision to operate on the smart contract algorithm by writing personal data to the blockchain. The smart contract developer only delivers a ready-to-go solution to any potential users which will themselves operationalize the smart contract for their own commercial use. Bearing the legal definition of controllers and processors in mind, the software developer neither determines the purpose and means of any particular data processing activity nor follows any instructions issued by a controller. In the usual way of business, the smart contract developer is, at no point of time, involved in any processing activities with regards of personal data since, in the phase of creating an algorithm, there is simply no personal data to be collected or stored.

However, there may be few scenarios where the smart contract developer actively interferes in a particular processing activity. Hence, its role must be vetted in light of the GDPR on a case-by-case basis.[72]

[7] Oracles

An oracle is an agent that allows the transfer of external data to the blockchain for on-chain use in conjunction with the use of smart contracts.[73] Oracles allow users to automate business logic and may be used to process real-world events which occur or occurred externally and have been inputted onto the blockchain. The algorithm contained in the blockchain is digesting the data feed and automatically generates an output of information.

An example is a data set, such as prices, information about flight delays or customer claims. Once entered on the blockchain, the data can be used to automate business processes and services. Without oracles, the blockchain would only operate in its own-closed environment, materially limiting its capabilities.

Oracles are typically operating outside the blockchain network by providing external data feeds to the blockchain. There are indeed similarities with smart contract developers as both groups are acting off-chain. The information from the world outside the blockchain is being processed through an algorithm embedded in the smart contract. By doing this, oracles directly interfere in a data processing activity carried out by the smart contract algorithm. This leads to the question of whether oracles must be deemed as (joint-) controllers.

This assessment could be underlined by various court rulings of the Court of Justice of the European Union (CJEU), which further developed the interpretation of joint controllers in the meaning of Article 26 of the GDPR. The CJEU tends to interpret joint controllership very broadly in order to ensure the effective and complete protection of data subject rights.[74] On 29 July 2019, the CJEU confirmed that a website

72. European Union Blockchain Observatory and Forum, *supra* n. 23, at 18; Chapter 1, section §1.11[B], *supra*.
73. Artzt, M., *supra* n. 40.
74. Case C-210/16 *Wirtschafsakademie Schleswig-Holstein* [2018] C-796/17, para. 16; Case *Fashion ID* [2019] C-40/17.

owner (Fashion ID) that has embedded a third-party social media plug-in (Facebook), such as Facebook's 'Like' button, into its website, may be jointly responsible with that third party for the collection and transmission of personal data relating to visitors. This decision is important because the court considered Facebook and the website owner as joint controllers even though both parties had certainly not reached an upfront determination of the purpose and the means of the data processing as required by the regulation.

With respect to oracles, the said ruling implies that blockchain participants connected by way of smart contracts and oracles may act as joint controllers according to Article 26 of the GDPR even though there has been no legal interaction between them from the outset. The CJEU held that, by inserting a plug-in into its website, Fashion ID also had a strong influence on the collection and transmission of personal data of visitors to Facebook, which would not be the case without the plug-in. These processing operations were carried out in the economic interests of both Fashion ID and Facebook, increasing Fashion ID's visibility, while also providing Facebook with data for its own commercial purposes.

The above aspect distinguishes oracles from smart contract developers. Unlike the typical smart contract developer, who usually creates an algorithm to be offered to potential blockchain participants, an oracle has a strong influence on the particular data processing operation, and its result carried out by the smart contract algorithm.

If an oracle does have a commercial interest in the particular processing activity, in particular the outcome of such activity, he should be considered as a joint controller. This requires both, oracle as well as smart contract participants, to conclude an arrangement pursuant to Article 26 of the GDPR. Both sides need to find an agreement on the purpose and the means of the processing operation in question. By all means, a case-by-case assessment of the underlying circumstances should be taken into consideration.

In the majority of cases, the GDPR doesn't come into play whenever oracles provide data feeds to the blockchain. The reason for this assumption is that oracles usually don't have a commercial interest in the outcome of the single data processing activity, even though they are honoured by virtue of bitcoins.

[8] Governance Bodies and Joint-/Co-controllership

In a private blockchain context, a governance body, comprising of a group of natural or legal persons, can be established to oversee blockchain transactions, particularly by defining the rules for participants beforehand. It is possible that, under certain circumstances, such a governance body may act as a processor in the event it establishes a single point of legal contact within the network. If the governance body has control over personal data by determining the purpose and means of processing, it will most likely be considered as controller depending on the factual circumstances.

Whenever a group of participants decides to carry out processing operations on a blockchain for a common purpose, the CNIL recommends identifying beforehand who of them should be acting as the controller. For example, the participants may create a legal person, or they may choose to designate one participant who makes decisions for the group. In both cases, the appointed legal or natural person will qualify as a controller.[75]

This consideration makes sense since otherwise all participants of the private blockchain could be considered as joint controllers and, hence, would need to jointly agree upon their respective responsibilities to ensure compliance with Article 26 of the GDPR. That arrangement must be concluded in a transparent way due to the fact that data subjects whose data is recorded on the blockchain must be aware of which group member they can approach to effectively exercise their rights under the GDPR, and data protection authorities must have a contact point which can be held accountable for the processing carried out.[76]

Once one or more members of the group have been nominated to act as a (joint-) controller, the other members of the group are either processors or joint controllers depending on whether they are processing personal data. This necessitates that all members of the group must enter into a controller-processor data protection agreement according to Article 28 of the GDPR and/or into a joint controller arrangement according to Article 26 of the GDPR. As a result, it might be the case that two types of contracts need to be in place: On the one hand, a joint controller arrangement and, on the other hand, a controller-processor data protection agreement.

By all means, the joint controllership ought to be assessed and determined on a case-by-case basis given that the EUCJ tends to interpret the legal term of joint controllers very broadly. A use case for a joint controllership would be a consortium of blockchain users established between many actors that are part of the same supply chain. The legal entities created by the consortium would be joint controllers considering that they exercise significant control over the purposes and also the means of personal data processing, e.g., by leveraging smart contract algorithms. The individual companies that have joined the consortium and are subsequently using the infrastructure for their own purposes and, thus, enabling the blockchain technology to process new personal data are more likely co-controllers rather than joint controllers.[77]

[C] Frictions Between Controllership and Obligations under the GDPR

There might be circumstances where single actors qualify as controllers in a blockchain environment. The related blockchain users identified as controllers have very limited influence over the respective means of data processing. This may result in a situation where controllers may be unable to meet the GDPR obligations due to the fact that they have no or insufficient control over the data being processed. For example, a blockchain user may not be capable of complying with a data subject's request for access under Article 15 of the GDPR as the relevant data is fully encrypted. Same applies to a request for the erasure of personal data since the blockchain user will have no control over the data which is subject to such request. As a result, acting as a controller in a

75. CNIL, *supra* n. 7, at 2.
76. *Ibid.*
77. European Parliamentary Research Service, *supra* n. 34, at 45: joint controllership.

blockchain network may conflict with the capability to perform any obligations under the GDPR.

The issue is how that mismatch can be resolved. Commentators are of the view that, whenever a controller is not able to service any kind of data subject right request, he should make sure that other participants which may act as (joint-) controllers shall respond to those requests accordingly.[78] In other words, actors who have taken the decision to use blockchain technology to process personal data must ascertain that there are appropriate governance arrangements with other blockchain users in place that enable the effective exercise of any data subject rights.[79]

This approach, however, requires the existence of an agreement between particular blockchain participants aiming to comply with requests raised by data subjects irrespective of whether the users are deemed as co- or joint controllers. From the operational standpoint, this is hardly feasible even though it may be contractually viable to re-allocate responsibilities from one controller to another one. Practically speaking, operating a governance structure is only possible in private blockchains,[80] whereas this doesn't work in a public blockchain network.

§5.04 LEGAL BASIS AND CONSENT UNDER THE GDPR

In order to process personal data in accordance with the first principle in Article 5 of the GDPR, personal data must be processed lawfully, fairly, and in a transparent manner. Taking the first element of these three requirements as our focus: in order to process personal data lawfully, the processing must be based on one or more conditions specified in Article 6 of the GDPR, known as a lawful (or legal) basis. Whilst the choice of legal basis is an important consideration in and of itself, it is also worth noting that the choice of lawful basis is closely tied to data subject rights[81] given certain lawful bases provide exemptions to the availability of certain data subject rights. Although not all processing activities will be able to avail themselves of every lawful basis, this is a factor worth bearing in mind from the outset when designing any processing activities. The Article 6 conditions can be summarized as: (i) the data subject having unambiguously given his consent to the processing of his personal data for one or more specific purpose; (ii) the processing is necessary for the performance of a contract to which the data subject is a party or in order to take steps at the request of the data subject prior to entering into a contract; (iii) the processing is necessary for compliance with a legal obligation to which the controller is subject (whether pursuant to EU or national Member State law); (iv) the processing is necessary to protect the vital interests of the data subject or of another natural person; (v) the processing is necessary for the performance of a task carried out in the public interest; or (vi) the processing is

78. European Parliamentary Research Service, *supra* n. 34, at 53.
79. *Ibid.*, at 72.
80. A good example is a company which offers *Blockchain as a Service* (BaaS) acting as a processor on behalf of one or more controllers.
81. For further discussion around data subject rights in the context of the blockchain, please *see* section §5.06, *infra*.

necessary for the purposes of the legitimate interests pursued by the controller or by a third party to whom the data is disclosed, except where the processing is unwarranted in any particular case by reason of prejudice to the rights and freedoms or legitimate interests of the data subject, in particular, where the data subject is a child.[82]

In addition, where a controller is processing special categories of personal data (e.g., health data, data revealing racial or ethnic origin, political opinions, etc.),[83] or data related to criminal convictions or offences, an additional legal ground (as well as an Article 6 ground) to reflect a higher level of protection for those categories of personal data, will need to be relied upon. The Article 9 conditions are: (i) the data subject has given his explicit consent; (ii) the processing is necessary for the purposes of carrying out the obligations and specific rights of the controller in the field of employment law, social security law, or social protection law in so far as it is authorized by national law providing for appropriate safeguards; (iii) the processing is necessary to protect the vital interests of the data subject or of another person where the data subject is physically or legally incapable of giving consent; (iv) the processing is carried out by a not-for-profit body with a specific aim and does not involve the disclosure of data to a third party without the data subject's consent; (v) the data subject has deliberately made the information public; (vi) the processing is necessary for establishing, exercising, or defending legal claims; (vii) the processing is necessary for reasons of substantial public interest on the basis of EU or national Member State law; (viii) the processing (by a person subject to the obligation of professional secrecy) is necessary for the purposes of preventative or occupational medicine, the assessment of the working capacity of the employee, medical diagnosis, the provision or management of health or social care systems, and services pursuant to a contract with a healthcare professional; (ix) the processing is necessary for reasons of public interest in the area of public health, such as protecting against serious cross-border threats to health or ensuring high standards of healthcare, medicinal products, or medical devices; or (x) the processing is necessary for archiving purposes in the public interest, for scientific or historical research purposes, or statistical purposes.[84]

On a similar note, in the case of data relating to criminal convictions and offences, controllers must have both a lawful basis under Article 6 of the GDPR and either legal authority or official authority for the processing under Article 10 of the GDPR. The EU Member State implementing legislation sets out specific conditions providing lawful authority to process these types of personal data. For example, the UK Data Protection Act 2018 treats criminal conviction and offences data in a similar way to a special category of personal data.

82. Article 6 of the GDPR.
83. Special categories of personal data are defined by Art. 9(1) of the GDPR as personal data revealing racial or ethnic origin, political opinions, religious or philosophical beliefs, or trade union membership, and the processing of genetic data, biometric data for the purpose of uniquely identifying a natural person, data concerning health or data concerning a natural person's sex life or sexual orientation.
84. Article 9(2) of the GDPR.

Therefore, those deemed controllers in a blockchain that are processing personal data[85] will be required to identify and document the lawful basis under which they are processing personal data. As is the case for many of the GDPR requirements (which we will discuss in more detail throughout this chapter), given the decentralized nature of the blockchain network, it is not always straightforward to determine on what legal basis personal data in the blockchain is being processed in reliance on. It is considered by some commentators that the 'most likely and hopeful legal grounds for processing are that there is a contract or consent in play'.[86] We discuss these grounds in further detail below, as well as the potential ability to rely upon the controller's legitimate interests and the consent of the data subject.

[A] Contractual Necessity

Article 6(1)(b) of the GDPR provides for the lawful processing of personal data where it 'is necessary for the performance of a contract to which the data subject is party or in order to take steps at the request of the data subject prior to entering into a contract.'[87] Although the GDPR does not provide guidance as to when this ground may be appropriate to rely upon, the EDPB has adopted a strict interpretation of this legal ground in the context of the provision of online services to data subjects.[88] The EDPB takes the view that where a service requested by the data subject can be provided without the specific processing taking place, it is not necessary for the performance of a contract, and it may be more appropriate to rely on another legal ground. The EDPB also introduces an objective assessment of what is considered 'necessary' for the performance of a contract. According to the EDPB, where there are realistic, less intrusive alternatives to achieve the same objective, the processing is not necessary, and an alternative legal ground will be more appropriate. As such, reliance in a blockchain scenario on this ground may be limited, although it may still have some relevance in the context of concluding smart contracts using blockchain technology.

[B] Consent

Personal data can also be processed where the data subject has given clear consent to the processing of their personal data for a specific purpose.[89] The GDPR standard of consent is high, and consent is defined by the GDPR as: 'any freely given, specific, informed and unambiguous indication of the data subject's wishes by which he or she, by a statement or by clear affirmative action, signifies agreement to the processing of

85. Please *see* discussion on processing personal data in the context of a blockchain in section §5.02[B], *supra*.
86. Ibáñez, L-D., O'Hara, K. & Simperl, E., *On Blockchains and the General Data Protection Regulation*, 3 available at: https://eprints.soton.ac.uk/422879/1/BLockchains_GDPR_4.pdf (accessed 3 Feb. 2020).
87. Article 6(1)(b) of the GDPR.
88. EDPB draft guidelines 2/2019 on the processing of personal data under Art. 6(1)(b) of the GDPR, adopted on 9 Apr. 2019.
89. Article 6(1)(a) of the GDPR.

personal data relating to him or her.'[90] In order for consent to be freely given, the data subject must have a genuine choice as to whether to consent or not. Controllers must also comply with their transparency obligations in ensuring individuals are appropriately informed about details of the processing, including the identity of the controller, the type of data processed and the specific purposes for which consent is being sought. Where consent is used as the legal ground for processing special categories of personal data (e.g., health data), then the consent will also need to be explicit.

A fundamental issue in the blockchain context is that under the GDPR consent can be withdrawn by a data subject at any time.[91] Although the withdrawal of consent does not impact the lawfulness of the processing prior to such consent being withdrawn, if a controller cannot demonstrate reliance on an alternative legal ground following the withdrawal, the processing has to be stopped. This approach is problematic in itself, given guidance from the ICO is clear that reliance on consent should not be used if an alternative legal basis can be relied upon.[92] Further, withdrawal of consent where there is no alternative legal ground to rely upon may be difficult, given the immutable nature of the blockchain: once personal data is included in one of the blockchains' blocks, it may continue to be processed for as long as the ledger exists.

Another key question when looking at the reliance on consent as a legal basis in the context of blockchain is 'who does a user give consent to?' This is important, for one because under the GDPR a controller must be able to demonstrate that consent was given (and the extent to which the consent was given),[93] which in turn will require that accurate records are kept. As discussed further in section §5.03, *supra*, one of the key challenges arising from compliance with the GDPR in a blockchain context, is the identification of the relevant controllers and processors. There may, in some instances, exist a grey area where it is not possible to identify a controller, for some (but not all) blockchain networks, particularly those in the public sphere. For private blockchains, it will be possible to identify an entity who acts as an intermediary between the user and the blockchain and so this issue may be easier to resolve. This demonstrates another issue which reinforces the position taken by the CNIL[94] and others: that public blockchains generate the most concerns from a data protection perspective and private (permissioned) blockchains may be the way forward from a privacy perspective.

On this note, in a public blockchain, the use of consent will be particularly problematic. It is unlikely that an individual will be able to identify which nodes, and to which recipients, their data will be transferred, and it cannot be known which participants may be involved in the network. The process, at least from the perspective of a public blockchain, seems at odds, at least with some elements of GDPR-standard consent; that the consent must be specific and informed.

90. Article 4(11) of the GDPR.
91. Article 7(3) of the GDPR.
92. UK ICO, Guide to the General Data Protection Regulation, Lawful basis for processing, available at: https://ico.org.uk/for-organisations/guide-to-data-protection/guide-to-the-general-data-protection-regulation-gdpr/lawful-basis-for-processing/ (accessed 3 Feb. 2020).
93. Recital 42 of the GDPR.
94. CNIL, *supra* n. 7, at 5.

Overall, it is important to remember that, in most cases, given the inherent difficulties with obtaining valid GDPR-standard consent across the board, which will also apply to processing in the blockchain context, the GDPR has marked a movement away from reliance on consent and controllers are tending to rely on an alternative legal ground for most processing activities to avoid the issues it creates, including those discussed above. It follows that the same reasoning should likely apply where the processing of personal data occurs in the blockchain. In many cases, the GDPR-standard will be difficult to achieve, and organizations should proceed with caution where looking to rely on the legal ground of consent.

[C] Legitimate Interest

Article 6(1)(f) of the GDPR provides that processing of personal data is lawful where the 'processing is necessary for the purposes of the legitimate interests pursued by the controller or by a third party, except where such interests are overridden by the interests or fundamental rights and freedoms of the data subject which require protection of personal data, in particular where the data subject is a child …'.[95]

This is perhaps the most flexible of the GDPR's legal grounds and so the legal basis which could be relied upon most frequently in the processing of personal data in a blockchain context. Legitimate interests are not centred around a particular purpose (e.g., the performance of a contract) nor have the data subjects agreed to the processing (e.g., via consent). In short, a controller must be able to demonstrate that its interests are not outweighed by the interests of the data subject. As such, in order to determine whether the legitimate interest as the legal ground can be relied upon, controllers are required to carry out a balancing test (or complex assessment as it is described by the Article 29 Data Protection Working Party[96]) to consider and address the competing interests of the relevant parties. This test can be split roughly into three elements:[97]

(1) *Purpose:* To fulfil the first element, the 'purpose' test, it should be considered whether the parties are pursuing a legitimate interest. In the case of blockchain, it should be considered what the blockchain is trying to achieve, including the potential benefits to the public and the relative importance of those benefits.
(2) *Necessity:* Next, is the processing 'necessary' for the purposes of that legitimate interest. Does the blockchain advance the interest identified in the 'purpose test'? Would there be less invasive ways of fulfilling the same interest?

95. Article 6(1)(f) of the GDPR.
96. Article 29 Data Protection Working Party, *Opinion 06/2014 on the notion of legitimate interests of the data controller under Article 7 of the Directive 95/46/EC* 33 ff. (WP 217, adopted on 14 Nov. 2014).
97. This 'three-part test' is advocated by the UK ICO in its Guide to the General Data Protection Regulation, *supra* n. 92.

(3) *Balancing Test:* Lastly, the 'balancing test' requires controllers to consider whether the data subject's interest overrides the controller's purported legitimate interest. In this assessment, various factors should be considered, including: (i) what is the relationship between the controller to the data subjects in question; (ii) what type of personal data is being processed; (iii) what does the data subject expect to be done with their personal data; and (iv) what is the potential impact on the data subject?

The GDPR does not provide an exhaustive list of what processing activities may constitute a legitimate interest, but it does list fraud prevention,[98] ensuring network and information security[99] or indicating possible criminal acts[100] as constituting legitimate interests. As with any processing activity where the controller seeks to rely on legitimate interests as the legal ground, this assessment should be documented by way of legitimate interest assessment (LIA).[101]

In relation to the 'Balancing Test', the European Parliamentary Research Service has considered whether this could be satisfied in the blockchain context. For example, it is arguable that an individual who purchases a crypto asset would 'reasonably expect' that it would involve the processing of certain personal data (e.g., the public key). In reality, the European Parliamentary Research Service considers it is 'unlikely that most users in fact realize that the public keys are personal data and the transaction may reveal information about the data subject'.[102]

[D] Compliance with a Legal Obligation

Recital 45 of the GDPR states that 'where processing is carried out in accordance with a legal obligation to which the controller is subject ... the processing should have a basis in [EU] or Member State law'. In other words, the obligation must be imposed by law as opposed to a contractual obligation, and it must be based on the laws of the EU or of an EU Member State (i.e., not the laws of a third country). However, Recital 41 of the GDPR makes it clear that it does not have to be an explicit statutory obligation, as long as the application of the law is foreseeable to those individuals subject to it. As such, reliance on this lawful basis could include processing to affect compliance with common law obligations. Examples of processing that can rely on this legal ground will include processing for Anti-Money Laundering and Know Your Customer requirements, which are imposed by EU law.[103]

98. Recital 47 of the GDPR.
99. Recital 49 of the GDPR.
100. Recital 50 of the GDPR.
101. Note that the term LIA or 'legitimate interest assessment' is not explicitly referenced in the GDPR.
102. European Parliamentary Research Service, *supra* n. 34, at 64.
103. Directive (EU) 2018/843 of the European Parliament and the Council of 30 May 2018 amending Directive (EU) 2015/849 on the prevention and use of the financial system for the purposes of money laundering or terrorist financing, and amending Directives 2001/138/EC and 2013/36/EU.

[E] Special Categories of Personal Data

It should also be noted that where participants in a blockchain are processing special categories of personal data, there will be additional considerations, for example, obtaining explicit consent from the data subject or relying on the processing being necessary for the purposes of carrying out the obligations and specific rights of the controller in the field of employment law, social security law, or social protection law[104] (e.g., an employer processing employee health data to comply with its employment law obligations). The requirement for an additional legal ground will make the processing of special categories of personal data (e.g., using blockchain in the healthcare sector where large volumes of health data are processed) more challenging.

§5.05 SECURITY OF DATA PROCESSING ON A BLOCKCHAIN IN THE CONTEXT OF THE GDPR

[A] Personal Data Versus Anonymous Data

The GDPR only applies to the processing of personal data unless it has been anonymized. Therefore, the GDPR does not apply to anonymized data. The bar for what qualifies as anonymized is very high. By all means, the anonymization technique must make it impossible to identify a natural person through any and all of the means which may reasonably likely to be used. The process of anonymization must also be irreversible. This implies that it is not possible to reconstitute the original data from the anonymized form.[105] Any techniques that do not comply with this standard are not sufficient for getting the data anonymized, and such data remains pseudonymous. Pseudonymized data remains personal and is, therefore, subject to GDPR obligations.

Given the immutability of data in blockchain networks, the storage of personal data in a clear and readable format on a shared ledger, be it on public, be it on private blockchains, is not in line with the GDPR obligations under Article 32 section 1 of the GDPR. Both the controller and the processor must safeguard the data being processed by implementing appropriate technical and organizational measures.

[B] Particular Security Techniques

There are many techniques to meet the requirement set out in Article 32 section 1 of the GDPR, for example, data obfuscation, encryption, hashing or data aggregation, all of them aiming to de-identify personal data in a way that makes it impossible to link such data to an individual.

---

104. Article 9(2)(b) of the GDPR.
105. Article 29 Data Protection Working Party, *supra* n. 9, at 8.

[1] *Encryption*

Where data is encrypted, the holder of the encryption key can still re-identify each data subject through decryption of the dataset because the personal data is still contained therein, albeit in an encryption form. Assuming that a state-of-the-art encryption scheme was applied, decryption is only possible with the knowledge of the key.[106]

As a result, encrypted data remains personal data,[107] at least for the holder of the key. This is confirmed by the former Article 29 Data Protection Working Party in its Opinion on Cloud Computing which pointed out that encryption does not render personal data irreversibly anonymous although encryption may significantly contribute to the confidentiality of personal data if implemented correctly.[108]

There are debates as to whether a state-of-the-art encryption may turn personal data into anonymous data as long as the cloud service provider has no access to the key. That view is not in line with Article 32 section 1(a) of the GDPR, which describes encryption as one technical measure for safeguarding personal data. This implies that encryption may adequately secure personal data but will not switch its legal nature into the status of anonymous data. Another technical aspect comes into play: Even if strong encryption is employed on personal data, the result is pseudonymous, not anonymous data. This is for the simple reason that, as long as the encryption key exists somewhere, the data can always be decrypted. It is possible to reverse the process and reconstitute the original data.[109]

[2] *Hashing*

Hashing is at the heart of many of the most important properties of blockchains, providing much of the magic of decentralization.[110] Hashing is a method of calculating a unique output (called a hash digest) for the input of nearly any size of data by applying a cryptographic hash function to the input data. Theoretically, the input data could be stored outside the blockchain because the data's integrity could be verified by re-running the hash function (for further details *see* Chapter 1, section §1.06[B][4], *supra*).

As outlined above, hashing as an encryption technique typically generates pseudonymous, but not anonymous data, given that the data subject can indirectly be identified.[111] This is also in line with the former Article 29 Data Protection Working Party, which has made clear that the hash function is a useful security measure but not a method of anonymization.[112] Nevertheless, the former Article 29 Data Protection

106. *Ibid.*, at 20.
107. Section §5.02[A][2], *infra*.
108. Article 29 Data Protection Working Party, *Opinion 05/2012 on Cloud Computing* 15 (WP 196 Adopted on 1 Jul. 2012).
109. European Union Blockchain Observatory and Forum, *supra* n. 23, at 21.
110. *Ibid.*
111. Section §5.02[A][2], *supra*; Finck, M., *Blockchain: Regulation and Governance in Europe* 93 (Cambridge University Press, December 2018).
112. Article 29 Data Protection Working Party, *supra* n. 9, at 20.

Working Party considered that the use of deterministic encryption or keyed-hash functions with deletion of the key might reduce the reasonable likelihood of re-identification and decryption of the hash function.[113] That solution may constitute a state-of-the-art security technique at present.

[3] Multi-layered Blockchains

To the extent that personal data must be stored and processed on a blockchain, it is essential that the related blockchain where the data is being stored is controlled as tightly as possible. In this context, personal data should be restricted to a private blockchain with a small number of nodes governed by a consortium whose members need to agree on contractual terms that, *inter alia*, define precisely the privacy policy towards the users as well as the process for amending the data where required.[114]

With that in mind, one additional safeguard is a multi-layered blockchain design which typically involves two interoperable blockchains: A private blockchain in the form of a consortium, operated by only a limited number of nodes, where the actual real-time processing of personal data or the exchange of crypto-assets takes place. This network is fast but not very decentralized, and it is not interoperable with other networks worldwide.[115] The second layer is a base, public blockchain, operated by a multiple (thousands) of nodes. That network is very decentralized and difficult for anyone to take control of, but, on the other hand, not very fast. This base blockchain can be used to store crypto-assets or personal data over long periods of time, particularly when that information is not required any more or shall not be subject to further processing.

In such a design, the base, public blockchain makes it possible for the private network to interoperate with other networks worldwide. One of the downsides of this model is that personal data which is exchanged back and forth between the two layers may be compromised. Moreover, it remains unclear who will be responsible for such data leakage. However, this can showcase a robust technique that allows personal data to be removed from the private blockchain and transferred to the public blockchain when it is no longer needed.

[4] Storing Personal Data Off-Chain

Whenever it becomes obvious that it is not necessary to keep storing personal data which form part of a particular transaction or processing activity on the blockchain, those data can be stored in another, off-chain database and linked to the distributed ledger through a hash pointer. This implies that only a hash of the data remains on the blockchain; the hash is linked to a particular transaction. On-chain hashes of off-chain

113. *Ibid.*, at 21.
114. European Union Blockchain Observatory and Forum, *supra* n. 23, at 30.
115. *Ibid.*

data would qualify as personal data. Personal data can be recorded in a referenced, encrypted and modifiable database and not on the blockchain itself.[116]

The off-chain personal data is kept in a separate database, e.g., in a pdf file. From that point of time where the data is being stored outside the blockchain, it is non-transactional data that is either too large to be stored on the blockchain efficiently, or, requires the ability to be changed or deleted. Taking out bulk data outside blockchain may also resolve the scalability problem because more transactions can be processed on the blockchain when data which is not used any more is set aside, namely outside the blockchain.

[C] Principles of Purpose Limitation and Data Minimization

Given that the above described security techniques under sections §5.05[B][3] and §5.05[B][4] do not alter the nature of personal data and, hence, the GDPR applies, the legal issue is whether they are in line with the key data privacy principles alike purpose limitation and data minimization.

[1] Purpose Limitation

Article 5 section 1(b) of the GDPR states that personal data shall be collected for specific, explicit and legitimate purposes and not further processed in a manner that is incompatible with those purposes. Any further processing shall not be permitted unless the data subject has consented to the new purpose. The reason for establishing this principle is to prevent the use of the personal data of individuals in a way or for further purposes that they might find unexpected, inappropriate, or otherwise objectionable.[117]

Purpose limitation is described by the former Article 29 Data Protection Working Party as being the 'cornerstone of data protection' and provides that the principle is designed to offer a balanced approach: 'an approach that aims to reconcile the need for predictability and legal certainty regarding the purposes of the processing on the one hand and the pragmatic need for some flexibility on the other'.[118]

However, there are exceptions to this purpose limitation principle. For example, if the further processing is for archiving purposes in the public interest, scientific or historical research purposes or statistical purposes, then in accordance with Article 89(1) – the further processing will not be considered '*incompatible*'. Recital 50 provides further clarity in determining whether the purpose of further processing is compatible with the initial purpose. It states that the data controller should consider: (i) any link between the purposes; (ii) the context in which the personal data is collected; and (iii) the reasonable expectations of the data subject based on the relationship between the

116. Finck, *supra* n. 111, at 94.
117. Article 29 Data Protection Working Party, *Opinion 03/2013 on purpose limitation* 11 (WP 203 Adopted on 2 Apr. 2013).
118. *Ibid.*

parties; (iv) the nature of the personal data; (v) the consequences of the further processing; and (vi) the existence of appropriate safeguards.

Article 5(1)(c) of the GDPR also requires that personal data must be *adequate, relevant* and *limited* to what is necessary in relation to the purposes for which they are processed. It should be noted that this is not an obligation to limit data processing to an absolute minimum but rather an obligation to minimize data collection to an adequate level with regard to the purposes of the processing.

Blockchain, by nature, continuously processes data once it is on the ledger. It is possible that in certain cases, post-transaction 'processing' of personal data on the grounds that such data is now part of an immutable chain of blocks could violate the purpose limitation principle. The question arises whether the further processing of personal data after the execution of a transaction for which it has been initially added to the ledger can be qualified as compliant with the purpose limitation principle. It may be argued that those data are not needed any more since the transaction has been completed. Given the append-only nature of the DLT, data will permanently continue to be stored on the ledger, even in such a case where, for example, a crypto-asset transaction has been successfully executed, and the pertaining transactional data was turned into legacy data. Same applies to the data stored on a public key. Such storage and processing of personal data can be considered as non-compliant with the principle of purpose limitation.

On the other hand, this view may be challenged by arguing that the storage of such data in subsequent transactions forms part of the original purpose of processing and, therefore, meets the purpose limitation principle. With other words, if the purpose includes not only the initial transaction but also the subsequent data storage, then arguably the replicated nature of these distributed databases and the continuous storage of data could be considered to be in sync with the purpose limitation principle.

This is indeed questionable since the purpose of the collection must be clearly and specifically identified; it must be detailed enough to determine what kind of processing activity is or is not included within the specified purpose, and, to allow compliance with the law, can be assessed and data protection safeguards applied.[119] A broad and vague purpose description does violate that principle.[120]

This leads to the following legal question as to whether any lack of specification may be cured by a clear communication towards the data subjects that the controller is using the blockchain technology and that the processing of the related personal data is not limited to the original transaction, but the data will continue to be stored after the particular transaction has taken place. It goes without saying that those who act as controllers in a blockchain environment must clearly communicate to the related data

119. *Ibid.*, at 15.

120. The CNIL imposed a fine on Google LLC amounting to about EUR 50 million on 21 January 2019 for compliance violations under the GDPR. Amongst others, the CNIL found that Google did not provide users with information relating to the purpose of data processing. Google users had to give their consent in general, for all processing activities and purposes. That does not meet the requirement to gather specific consents in relation to particular processing activities. The purpose description needs to be specific in order to obtain valid consents of the users.

subjects, at the time of collecting their personal data, how their data will be used, including how it may be processed in the future as new blocks are added.

However, such information does not necessarily give rise to adhering to the purpose limitation principle.[121] As a result, storing personal data on the blockchain post execution of the initial transaction doesn't stand up to scrutiny and infringes the principle of purpose limitation. Transmitting the personal data which is not needed any more outside the blockchain is the only measure which complies with that principle.

[2] Data Minimization

The principle of data minimization essentially means that only those data which is necessary to meet the purpose determined by the controller must be collected and processed. It partly overlaps with the principle of purpose limitation. The data minimization principle requires, in particular, to ensure that the period for which the personal information is being stored is limited to a strict minimum.[122] Two artefacts of a blockchain are clashing with the data minimization principle: First, the ever-growing nature of such databases as data can only be removed in extraordinary circumstances. Second, the data is replicated in a distributed network, where each node stores a full copy of the database. Strictly speaking, personal data is being replicated indefinitely, and the information transmitted through the blockchain is visible to every node, which could be argued to conflict with the principle of data minimization.

Recording transaction data off-chain while minimizing the data would help in this respect. However, it would be more challenging for public keys to comply with the GDPR as they cannot be stored off-chain.

[3] Evaluation in the Light of the Principles of Purpose Limitation and Data Minimization: Multi-layered Blockchains Versus Off-Chain Storage

Generally, it is legally possible to keep data on the blockchain indefinitely as long the data has been completely anonymized. Those data don't fall in the applicability of the GDPR. Vice versa, the personal data which is not needed any more has to be segregated in order to meet both, the data minimization principle as well as the purpose limitation principle.

The UK ICO has recognized that erasing data from digital systems is not always a straightforward matter. It has, therefore, proposed that putting personal data beyond use may be an alternative to achieve data minimization.[123] If there is no intention of the controller to access or use the data, then this may be held to be compliant.[124] Moreover,

121. European Parliamentary Research Service, *supra* n. 34, at 66.
122. Recital 39 of the GDPR.
123. Information Commissioner's Office, *Deleting Personal Data* 4 (26 Feb. 2014), available at: https://ico.org.uk/media/fororganisations/documents/1475/deleting_personal_data.pdf (accessed 3 Feb. 2020).
124. *Ibid.*

the ICO's statement clearly underlines what kind of security techniques should be taken into account when dealing with legacy personal data.

Whenever personal data is not needed any more, because, for example, the particular transaction has been completed or a certain matter (compensation request raised by a data subject) has been closed, such data will turn into legacy data. In the normal way of business, those data are archived in other files or systems. In a blockchain environment, the related data must be segregated, aiming to achieve GDPR-compliance.

One technique which may be leveraged to reach GDPR-compliance is the usage of multi-layered blockchains. That measure differs from the other instrument, namely putting personal data off-chain. The multi-layered blockchain technique boils down to removing data from a private blockchain and transferring it to a public blockchain. Both blockchains are intertwined and the public blockchain links in the private one.

Even though this mechanism facilitates the interoperability of blockchain technology, the problem remains unsolved in terms of the given principles. Even if the legacy data is being put on the public blockchain, it is fully replicated in the distributed network, and, albeit not in use any more, it is still visible. With that, the usage of multi-layered blockchains is a good instrument for safeguarding personal data, but it doesn't entail compliance with the above described principles.

In contrast, storing the legacy personal data in an off-chain database and hashing it, may be deemed as a measure to comply with the principles in question. The rationale is that such legacy data is actually removed from the blockchain and kept anywhere else. Following aspects should be considered.

First, the hash of the related data remains on the blockchain. The hash constitutes the key for the original, transactional and personal data which has previously been transferred off-chain. Hashing is generally considered as an encryption technique which generates pseudonymous, but not anonymous data. From the practical perspective, if a request to be forgotten has been raised, one only needs to erase any off-chain data that could be used to identify the subject if linked to the on-chain hash. That approach meets the erasure request sufficiently.

Second, hashing-out results in storing personal data in a database under the control of an identifiable controller. For that reason, compliance with the GDPR principles is much easier. However, and that is the downside, commentators have raised concerns because this might be considered a betrayal to the decentralization concept of blockchains as a certain degree of control on data remains in the hands of a single centralized party.[125]

In summary, the hashing mechanism is, from a legal point of view and for the time being, the best option for approaching the compliance status with respect to the principles of data minimization and purpose limitation. Besides, taking data off-chain is described as a pruning technique which, once employed, meets the GDPR erasure

125. Ibáñez, et al., *supra* n. 86, at 8.

requirements.[126] Consequently, hashing-out is deemed as an alternative for implementing the right for erasure.[127] Further details on this will be covered under section §5.06 [D][2].

[D] Recommendation for Security Measures in a Blockchain Environment

In the context of private blockchains, the CNIL recommends to:

- determine a minimum number of miners to avoid a coalition that could control over 50% of powers over the blockchain;
- implement organizational and technical measures to mitigate the impact of an algorithm failure on the security of the transactions. This should include a contingency plan to modify algorithms where vulnerability is detected;
- document the governance of changes to the software used to create transactions and to mine; technical and organizational procedures should be set out to ensure alignment between planned permissions and practical application; and
- ensure the confidentiality of the blockchain by implementing appropriate measures.[128]

With respect to public blockchains, there are no recommendations of data protection authorities in place to date. However, it is clear that data protection authorities tend to take a broad view that any encryption technology that uses keys can fundamentally be decrypted if those keys can be obtained.

Furthermore, the so called linking risk should be factored in when implementing security measures on a blockchain. Pseudonymized data may, with enough research and diligence, be linked to a specific individual and decrypted in that way. It is, therefore, essential that any business which stores personal data outside the blockchain environment has sufficient control and security measures in place to block any kind of linking approaches.

[E] Implications in the Case of Security Breaches

Article 33 section 1 of the GDPR states that 'in the case of a personal data breach, the controller shall without undue delay and, where feasible, not later than 72 hours after having become aware of it, notify the personal data breach to the supervisory authority (...)'.

From the practical point of view, the legal issue is whether all controllers are facing this obligation given that there are many of them, in particular in the context of public blockchains. In a private blockchain, as outlined under section §5.03[B][8], the participants usually appoint a legal or natural person who makes decisions for the

126. *Ibid.*; European Union Blockchain Observatory and Forum, *supra* n. 23, at 31.
127. *Ibid.*
128. CNIL, *supra* n. 7, at 10.

group. That person is acting as a controller and, hence, has to comply with the notification obligation according to Article 33 section 1 of the GDPR. In a public blockchain context, it remains unclear, whether all controllers or co-controllers are facing that obligation and, if so, how they can accomplish GDRP-compliance.

It is the view of the European Parliamentary Research Service that, whenever a controller is not able to service any kind of data subject right requests, the controller should make sure that other participants acting as controllers shall respond to those requests accordingly.[129] Consequently, each joint or co-controller would need to ascertain that there are appropriate governance arrangements with other controllers in place which trigger the notification of the competent supervisory authority whenever a data breach occurs. Such incidents may be the result of any attacks described under Chapter 2, section §2.01, *supra*.

As outlined above, the governance model necessitates the existence of an agreement or, at least, a consensus between particular blockchain participants which is practically not viable in a public blockchain network. The problem is aggravated since each controller who fails to implement the required security measures (Article 32 of the GDPR) and to meet the seventy-two hours timeline (Article 33 of the GDPR) may be subject to draconic administrative fines up to EUR 10,000,000 or up to 2% of the total worldwide annual turnover of the preceding financial year, whichever is higher (Article 83 section 4 of the GDPR). For the time being, there is no guidance of any data protection authorities in place covering that legal issue.

§5.06 DATA SUBJECT RIGHTS UNDER THE GDPR

[A] How Do Data Subject Rights Apply to the Blockchain?

Articles 15–22 of the GDPR set out a huge variety of specific rights for data subjects impacted by the processing of their personal data. Once a block contains data of individuals and the particular block is added to the blockchain as described in Chapter 1,section §1.06, *supra*, the GDPR comes into play. The storage of personal data in a blockchain environment is considered as a processing activity within the meaning of Article 4 section 2 of the GDPR. The question arises how such rights may be exercised against the controller. The controller is obliged to comply with the rights provided to the data subjects. In theory, it looks very simple: For example, an individual has submitted his or her own personal data to a blockchain and requests information on the purpose of the data processing pursuant to Article 15 section 1a of the GDPR. Such request needs to be addressed vis-à-vis the controller. As outlined under section §5.03[B], it is not crystal clear which actor actually qualifies as a controller and, as soon as one or, most likely, more controllers have been identified, whether they may be capable of facilitating the exercise of the data subject rights (Article 12 section 2 of the GDPR).

129. European Parliamentary Research Service, *supra* n. 34, at 53.

In a private blockchain environment, it is more likely for the data subject concerned to find the right controller whom the data subject right may be addressed with. In this context, the data subject typically has to deal with the governance body, which has been established to oversee the private (permissioned) network. The governance body may act as processor contracting with controllers who have collected personal data from individuals and serve a single point of contact with the network. Further, that body can either be a single controller or a joint or co-controller provided it has influence over the purpose and means of the data processing.[130]

Unlike private blockchains, it is much more difficult to identify a controller in a public blockchain who may be able to carry out the obligations imposed on controllers according to Articles 15–22 of the GDPR. The regulatory bodies, for example, the data protection authorities, are confronted with the same issue whenever they envisage driving enforcement actions against particular blockchain actors considered as controllers.

The problem is aggravated since some data subject rights under the GDPR appear to conflict with a fundamental attribute of the blockchain: namely, that once a transaction has been recorded, it is not technically possible to alter or delete entries on a blockchain. These rights which most likely clash with the core blockchain features are the rights to access personal data, to rectify personal data respectively to have any errors amended and, in certain circumstances, to delete it from the system. Other data subject rights do not essentially raise any specific problems in the context of blockchain technology. Indeed, one of the most discussed issues concerns the right to get personal data deleted. The potential need to identify and contact all the necessary nodes with a request to delete or even rectify personal data gives rise to substantial concerns. Further, any changes in a tamper-resistant database may erode the participants' trust in the blockchain technology itself.

[B] Right to Access Personal Data

The right to access of personal data is a basic right in the European data protection law since it enables and is often a prerequisite for, the exercise of any of the other rights of the data subjects. Accessing personal data facilitates to better understand which data is being processed and for what purpose. It is necessarily the first step before executing other rights, such as the right of rectification or deletion.

The access right is set out in Article 15 of the GDPR which states that the data subject shall have the right to obtain from the controller confirmation as to whether or not personal data concerning him or her is being processed, and, where that is the case, to access the personal data in question.

The right to access personal data can be met easily in a private blockchain context where one or more controllers have been established and tasked with performing the obligations under the GDPR. In the case of a joint-controllership, any requests for

130. Blockchain Bundesverband, *supra* n. 41, at 7.

access can be addressed to any of the joint controllers according to Article 26 section 3 of the GDPR.

In a public blockchain, however, the hurdles of the blockchain technology become obvious: The controllers, once identified, are factually unable to access data on a blockchain as they typically see encrypted or hashed data where data has been modified when put on the blockchain. Hence, those actors can't even determine whether the related data is personal or not.

The European Parliamentary Research Service fosters the concept of establishing appropriate governance arrangements between blockchain users/controllers with the purpose of enabling the effective exercise of data subject rights.[131] The GDPR, however, doesn't allow this approach explicitly nor gives room for interpretation in this regard. Irrespective of any legal justifications, such governance arrangements are not viable from the practical point of view. Consequently, the execution of the right of access is most likely in vain whenever personal data is registered on a public blockchain.

[C] Right to Rectification

The data subject shall have the right to request rectification of inaccurate personal data concerning him or her. Moreover, the data subject shall have the right to have incomplete personal data completed, taking into account the purposes of the processing (Article 16 of the GDPR).

The impossibility to modify any kind of data once submitted to the blockchain may also conflict with the right of rectification under Article 16 of the GDPR. It has to be taken into consideration that blockchains are append-only ledgers which are intentionally created to make it impossible or, at least, extremely burdensome to modify or supplement the data being added to the blockchain. Such immutability is the backbone of the blockchain technology which aims to secure data integrity and trust in the network. By contrast, one of the fundamental principles of the GDPR is that personal data must be mutable in order to, upon request, get them changed or rectified.

The above described tension between the right of rectification and the key feature of blockchains makes it difficult or impossible for controllers to comply with requests to rectify personal data. Two aspects exacerbate that tension.

First, the personal data of the requestor, the data subject concerned, is being stored in a distributed network of multiple nodes or computers that keeps track of data transactions. The blockchain is accessible to all participants or to a predefined set of participants depending on the way the blockchain has been set-up (public or private). In a public blockchain, everyone with an internet connection to the network has the same rights to access and/or update the ledger according to the pre-defined consensus mechanism. Therefore, all transactions are transparent and visible.[132] This implies that transparent data in a public blockchain will evoke a legal problem when such data need

131. European Parliamentary Research Service, *supra* n. 34, at 72.
132. European Commission, *Blockchain Now and Tomorrow*, 17 (July 2019).

to be altered due to errors, inaccuracies or other problems in data entry. That is currently one of the most disputed issues – a still unsolved trade-off between transparency and privacy in public blockchains.[133]

Second, in theory, after having received the request of rectification submitted by the data subject, the controller may copy and paste the personal data in a new block and rectify it therein. That action may be considered as appropriate remediation, but will not entirely meet the rectification request due to the fact that the preceding blocks still contain the personal data which remains unchanged. Creating a new block may lead to a secondary chain resulting in a change of the official blockchain. As outlined, the node will start selecting new candidate blocks from the memory pool to proceed from that new longest blockchain onwards which can effectively entail further problems as demonstrated in Chapter 1, section §1.08[B], *supra*.

The European Commission considers the storage of confidential, sensitive or personal data off-chain or in other databases as a possible solution.[134] The rectified data being stored outside the blockchain would be linked to the blockchain through a hash reference, keeping access to the original unchanged data.

[D] Right to Erasure

[1] What Does Erasure Mean?

The right to the erasure of personal data is better known as the right to be forgotten. Essentially, the data subject may demand the erasure of his or her personal data under certain circumstances as set out in Article 17 of the GDPR. This right provides the data subject with a tool to exercise full control over the personal data provided that one of the grounds listed in Article 17 section 1 of the GDPR applies. The right to the erasure of personal data is multi-faceted and was subject to judicial review.

The CJEU held that the operator of a search engine (Google) has a responsibility for ensuring the individual's right to privacy. Accordingly, the GDPR obligation would apply to search engine operators after a request has been made by the relevant individual to remove the link in the search results to the page containing sensitive personal information.[135] This implies that the search engine is effectively conducting a data processing activity, which is subject to special restrictions and obligations. With that, the operator has to assess whether the individual has a right to request that the information in question be no longer associated with his or her name in the search results. With this in mind, there is a tendency in the jurisdiction of the CJEU to foster the right to the erasure of individuals in the social media environment.

It should be noted that erasure is a term which gives room for diverging interpretations. While the former Article 29 Data Protection Working Party stated that the destruction of hardware could arguably qualify as erasure in the meaning of Article

133. Finck, *supra* n. 33, at 29.
134. European Commission, *supra* n. 132, at 17.
135. CJEU 24.09.2019, C-507/17 and C-136/17.

17 of the GDPR,[136] some data protection authorities, similar to the ICO in the UK, argued that instances, where data is put beyond use, can also be an appropriate method for erasure.[137] It is clear that erasure doesn't automatically mean to expunge or delete personal data, including the corresponding back-up systems. The former Article 29 Data Protection Working Party has ruled that other methods may be considered as equivalent for getting the data erased safely, e.g., overwriting of data.[138]

Article 35 section 1 of the German data protection act (Bundesdatenschutzgesetz as of 30 June 2017, BGBl. I S. 2097) assumes that the data may not be deleted in instances of non-automated data processing when the specific mode of the data storage makes the erasure impossible. This implies that any alternative solutions, namely the restriction of the processing, is acceptable and legally tolerated. The German legal framework clearly demonstrates that the GDPR opens the door to adopt the right to erasure to the features and possibilities of the blockchain technology and to accept alternative solutions when the erasure is not viable.

By all means, whether a particular technique factually equals with the erasure of data needs to be considered on a case-by-case basis.

[2] The Techniques to Erase Data

A couple of alternative techniques are debated in the data protection community. One technique is the destruction of the private key. The CNIL fosters that solution stating that, where the private key is deleted together with information from other systems, erasure may be obtained.[139] It observes that the use of cryptographic solutions like hash functions does allow data subjects to get closer to an effective exercise of their right of erasure.

Indeed, the controller can make the personal data practically inaccessible by deleting the keyed hash function's secret (private) key. Proving or verifying which information has been hashed would no longer be possible. In practice, the hash would no longer pose a confidentiality risk. According to the CNIL, it is necessary that the information also needs to be deleted in other systems where it has been stored for processing such as other blockchains or even off-chain databases.

Strictly speaking, this solution doesn't result in an erasure of the data, insofar as the data would still exist in a hashed format, albeit inaccessible. The above mentioned technique actually provides a state-of-the-art solution and gets the data subject closer to an effective exercise of the right of erasure.[140]

A similar solution focuses on the treatment of off-chain, external databases containing source data which correspond to encrypted or hashed data on the

136. Article 29 Data Protection Working Party, *supra* n. 108, at 12.
137. UK ICO, *supra* n. 123, at 4.
138. Article 29 Data Protection Working Party, *supra* n. 108, at 12; the Austrian data protection authority (DPA 5.12.2018, DSB-D123.270/009-DPO/2018) ruled that erasure doesn't necessarily require the final destruction of the data and a possible measure of erasure could also be the removal of the personal reference, i.e., anonymization.
139. CNIL, *supra* n. 7, at 8.
140. *Ibid.*, at 9.

blockchain. One view is that, if the corresponding data on those external databases is being deleted, then this may be sufficient to comply with the right of erasure. The rationale is that, even though the corresponding encrypted data or the hash will remain on the blockchain, since it has nothing to relate to, then it will become a random string with no meaning. Whenever hashed data remains available on a blockchain, but the underlying unhashed data is deleted and not even reconstructable, there is the view that this would meet the right to erasure if the hashed data is not reasonably likely to be tied to an individual.

As outlined in section §5.05[C][3], *supra* and in accordance with the Blockchain Observatory and Forum, enterprises which envisage establishing blockchain platform for operating their businesses are well advised to put personal data off-chain for erasure upon request of the data subject concerned.[141] Once successfully employed, this mechanism constitutes the basis for meeting the GDPR erasure requirements.

As long as the personal data is stored on-chain, it must be factored in that, from a legal point of view, effective compliance with Article 17 of the GDPR can only be ascertained where the personal data in question is erased from all the nodes that participate in the network.[142] This implies that where a data subject addresses a request for erasure vis-à-vis a controller, that controller must not only remove the personal data in question from its own server but also initiate erasure from other controllers and processors that also process personal data. It may be argued that pursuant to Article 17 section 2 of the GDPR, the controller is obliged to incentive other controllers to undertake erasure of personal data. The backbone of that approach is a governance model which describes the ideal world but is, practically speaking, not feasible given the multiple nodes in a public blockchain environment which are typically spread over the whole globe.

Moreover, deletion of on-chain personal data can be achieved by installing a system in which encrypted databases are replicated in nodes, which a hash of each entry stored on a blockchain that can verify the accuracy and creation date for each entry. There could be a process through which the use of corresponding private keys or authorization codes could delete a database entry in every node that hosts the database. To the extent this is all code driven, it may be argued it is computationally feasible, even though the nodes may be geographically dispersed. The only way a node could elect not to honour a deletion code or 'kill command' would be to stop participating in the underlying blockchain protocol. Unlike the governance model described above, this scenario, albeit, in theory, illustrates what may be accomplished going forward, aiming to reach the compliance status.

Given the uncertainties around the appropriate deletion mechanisms under the regime of Article 17 of the GDPR, any guidance from the data protection authorities, in particular from the EDPB, is required which should shed light on the question whether

141. European Union Blockchain Observatory and Forum, *supra* n. 23, at 31; Timmons, J. & Hickman, T., *Blockchain and the GDPR: Co-existing in Contradiction* 211 (Blockchain & Cryptocurrency Regulation, Global Legal Insights, 2020).
142. European Parliamentary Research Service, *supra* n. 34, at 77.

and to what extent a particular technique may be considered as a deletion measure in the meaning of Article 17 of the GDPR.

[3] *Public Keys/Identifiers of Blockchain Users*

Irrespective of any personal data being stored on a blockchain in clear text or as hashed data, there is another aspect which is worthwhile to be taken into account when talking about the erasure of personal data in a blockchain context. That issue may be better illustrated by using the Bitcoin example: In the Bitcoin system, users are represented by individual addresses, the so-called identifiers. An address can be regarded as being similar to a bank account number.

Addresses are created by using public key cryptography.[143] The identifier comprises of a series of alphanumeric characters which constitute the public key to the participant´s account. This public key is linked to a private key, known only by the related participant.[144] Only the public key is visible in the blockchain, whereas the private key is never disclosed there. Both public and private keys are tied up via cryptographic means. Public keys can't qualify as anonymous data as a matter of EU law.[145] For data to qualify as being anonymous, identification must be irreversibly prevented.[146] Practice, however, reveals that this can't be the case in relation to public keys. They are considered as pseudonymous and, hence, personal data. As a result, public keys are subject to the erasure requirement under the GDPR.

For example, with Bitcoin, Ethereum and some of their derivative digital assets, blockchain analytics companies can accurately attribute many public keys to entities such as exchanges, dark web markets or gambling sites. The greater the number of transactions and the larger the number of counterparties, the more likely it is that a blockchain analyst may be able to link a pseudonymous public key with a person's real identity. Every form of extensive activity is potentially subject to re-identification. Researchers and law enforcement agencies have already been able to re-identify bitcoin activity through the application of transactional graph analysis to identify bitcoin merchants and customers. In fact, they have applied similar methodologies to smart contract operations as well.

The most broadly adopted blockchains have identifiers that are always visible since it is essential for the proper functioning of the related blockchains. Nevertheless, there are other initiates going on, e.g., privacy coins, which purport to obscure the sender and recipient public keys in a transaction. However, for those blockchains that rely on public keys, this set of data can never be deleted as it is contained in each block, which can't be changed. Therefore, the identifier can't be effectively erased from the blockchain.[147] Unlike transactional data, public keys can't be moved off-chain to be

143. European Commission, *supra* n. 132, at 20.
144. Section §5.02[A][1], *supra*.
145. Finck, *supra* n. 111, at 96.
146. Section §5.02[A][1], *supra*.
147. CNIL, *supra* n. 7, at 6 stating that the identifiers are always visible and cannot be further minimized as they are essential for its proper functioning.

subject to any erasure or modification activities. GDPR-compliant solutions that enable the required manipulations of data are, accordingly, more difficult to identify.[148]

The issue of erasure is certainly the most controversial topic discussed in the blockchain community and should be evaluated by the EDPB. The CNIL made a proposal even though it remains unclear how commercially viable this approach might be, but it does provide a clue as to how the regulators attempt to reconcile this issue.

§5.07 ACCOUNTABILITY PRINCIPLES UNDER THE GDPR

Organizations are subject to enhanced accountability principles under the GDPR, including requirements such as: (i) conduct data protection impact assessments; (ii) implement data protection by design and by default; (iii) maintain a detailed record of their processing activities; and (iv) appoint a Data Protection Officer (DPO), where required. The specific requirements imposed by the GDPR will depend on whether an organization is defined as a controller or a processor in the carrying out of its data processing activities. Processors now have specific statutory obligations under the GDPR, such as notifying controllers without undue delay after becoming aware of a personal data breach. The GDPR further includes joint and several liability for controllers and processors to compensate affected individuals.

Article 24 of the GDPR broadly addresses the concept of accountability in its requirement for controllers to 'implement appropriate technical and organizational measures to ensure and to be able to demonstrate that processing is performed in accordance with [the GDPR].'[149]

The concept of accountability is at the core of the GDPR and should, according to the former Article 29 Data Protection Working Party, 'contribute to moving data protection from "theory to practice" as well as helping [DPAs] in their supervision and enforcement tasks.'[150]

The European Data Protection Supervisor further defined the principle of accountability in a keynote as the requirement for controllers to 'put in place internal mechanisms and control systems that ensure compliance and provide evidence – including internal policies and audit reports – to demonstrate compliance to external stakeholders, including supervisory authorities.'[151]

Essentially, the GDPR requires the integration of data protection into the business. In other words, under the GDPR, controllers and processors should concentrate on implementing practical measures as opposed to adopting a tick-box approach to data privacy compliance.

148. Finck, *supra* n. 111, at 97.
149. Article 24 of the GDPR.
150. Article 29 Data Protection Working Party, *Opinion 03/2010 on the principle of accountability* 2 (WP 173 00062/10/EN, adopted on 13 Jul. 2010).
151. European Data Protection Supervisor, Giovanni Buttarelli, Value of the EU Data Protection Reform against the Big Data challenges, Keynote address, Berlin, 4 May 2015, available at: https://secure.edps.europa.eu/EDPSWEB/webdav/site/mySite/shared/Documents/EDPS/Publications/Speeches/2015/15_05_04_Speech_EDPD_Berlin_EN.pdf (accessed 3 Feb. 2020).

Current blockchain protocols involve continuous duplications of a full copy of the ledger at each validating node, which may make it difficult to comply with some of the data protection principles laid out in Article 5 of the GDPR. Therefore, any organization using blockchain should make sure they fully understand the requirements under the GDPR and the Article 5 principles described below in order to ensure they are in compliance.

[A] Lawfulness, Fairness and Transparency

Article 5(1)(a) of the GDPR requires that personal data is processed lawfully, fairly, and in a transparent manner. Although neither 'fairly' nor 'lawfully' are defined in the GDPR, in practice both terms have a broad application.

The standard of fairness is an objective standard, so due regard should be given to how individuals, in general, might reasonably expect their data to be obtained and subsequently processed, and whether individuals would consider the systems and processes that are used as fair and appropriate. Recital 39 of the GDPR does, however, provide guidance in relation to the concept of 'transparency' and states that 'any information and communication relating to the processing of ... personal data be easily accessible and easy to understand, and that clear and plain language be used.'[152] It should be noted that there is no requirement to inform data subjects of the specific technology (e.g., blockchain) used to process personal data.

In addition to transparency, there should be legitimate grounds for the collection and use of personal data. The method used to obtain and process personal data will determine whether the processing is fair and lawful. Individuals should not be misled or deceived when providing personal data, nor should the data be used in ways that might have unjustified adverse effects on the individuals concerned.

In particular, in order to process personal data lawfully, the processing must be based on one or more conditions laid down in Articles 6 and 9 of the GDPR (*see* section §5.04, *supra*).[153]

---

152. Recital 39 of the GDPR.
153. The Art. 6 conditions include: (i) the data subject having unambiguously given his consent to the processing of his personal data for one or more specific purpose; (ii) the processing is necessary for the performance of a contract to which the data subject is a party or in order to take steps at the request of the data subject prior to entering into a contract; (iii) the processing is necessary for compliance with a legal obligation to which the controller is subject; (iv) the processing is necessary to protect the vital interests of the data subject or of another natural person; (v) the processing is necessary for the performance of a task carried out in the public interest; or (vi) the processing is necessary for the purposes of the legitimate interests pursued by the controller or by a third party to whom the data is disclosed, except where the processing is unwarranted in any particular case by reason of prejudice to the rights and freedoms or legitimate interests of the data subject, in particular where the data subject is a child.

    The Art. 9 conditions include: (i) the data subject having given explicit consent; (ii) the processing being necessary for the purposes of carrying out the obligations and specific rights of the controller in the field of employment law in so far as it is authorized by national law providing for adequate safeguards; (iii) the processing being necessary to protect the vital interests of the data subject or of another person where the data subject is physically or legally

In practice, a controller should assess the legal ground for processing various types of personal data and regularly update all its data protection notices, consents, and policies.

The concept of transparency can be quite challenging to comply with in blockchain. The European Parliamentary Research Service notes that in certain blockchain uses (e.g., private blockchain), enabling such transparency will be achievable.[154] However, it goes on to state that where there are no channels of communication between the controller or data subjects, the requisite transparency requirements may be hard to achieve.[155]

Generally speaking, the handling of personal data through a blockchain-based system is not an end in itself, but rather a means of achieving a particular purpose. Organizations must be able to identify the purposes for which personal data are processed in a blockchain system in order to comply with the fair and lawful processing obligations under Article 5 (1)(a) and (b) of the GDPR.

[B] Purpose Limitation, Data Minimization and Storage Limitation

The principles of purpose limitation and data minimization and their implications on processing personal data on a blockchain have been analysed in section §5.05[C], *supra* in greater detail.

Another principle of the GDPR is the storage limitation principle set out in Article 5(1)(e) of the GDPR which provides that personal data must be kept in a form that permits identification of data subjects for no longer than is necessary for the purposes for which it was processed. Recital 39 of the GDPR requires that the storage of personal data be 'limited to a strict minimum.'[156] It further provides that the controller should establish time limits for erasure or for periodic review of the personal data.

As with the principle of data minimization, complying with storage limitation principle of the GDPR may be more challenging in blockchain setting since it is virtually impossible to remove information from the blockchain. Also, the fact that blockchain users may not necessarily know if and what type of personal data is available on the blockchain may be an issue when complying with the principle of storage limitation.

incapable of giving consent; (iv) the processing being carried out by a non-profit-seeking body with a specific aim and does not involve the disclosure of data to a third party without the data subject's consent; (v) the data subject having deliberately made the information public; (vi) the processing being necessary for establishing, exercising, or defending legal claims; (vii) the processing being necessary for reasons of substantial public interest on the basis of EU or national Member State law; (viii) the processing (by a person subject to the obligation of professional secrecy) being necessary for the purposes of preventative or occupational medicine, for the assessment of the working capacity of the employee, medical diagnosis, the provision or management of health or social care systems. and services pursuant to a contract with a healthcare professional; (ix) the processing being necessary for reasons of public interest; or (x) the processing being necessary for archiving purposes in the public interest or for scientific or historical research purposes, or statistical purposes.

154. European Parliamentary Research Service, *supra* n. 34, at 65.
155. *Ibid.*
156. Recital 39 of the GDPR.

However, as with the principle of purpose limitation, there is an exception that permits organizations to store data for longer periods where the processing is for archiving purposes in the public interest, scientific and historical research purposes, or statistical purposes.[157] Overall, putting personal data off-chain will provide a proper remediation measure for being compliant with the storage limitation principle.

As there is little guidance on what is meant by the concept 'for no longer than is necessary', a reasonable approach should be taken with consideration being given to other local law requirements.

[C] Use of Data Privacy Impact Assessment

Article 35(1) of the GDPR sets out the requirement for a data controller to carry out a data protection impact assessment in advance of the processing where the processing uses new technologies and is likely to result in a high risk for data subjects. Article 35(3) of the GDPR provides that a data protection impact assessment must be required in the case of:

- Where there is a systematic, extensive evaluation of personal aspects, including profiling.
- Large-scale processing of sensitive personal data.
- Systematic monitoring of a publicly accessible area on a large scale (such as CCTV and other public monitoring).

In addition, organizations must carry out a Data Privacy Impact Assessment (DPIA) when:

- using new technologies; and
- the processing is likely to result in a high risk to the rights and freedoms of data subjects.

A DPIA involves balancing the interests of the data controller against those of the data subject. Article 35(7) of the GDPR states that such an impact assessment should contain as a minimum:

- a description of the processing operations and the purposes, including, where applicable, the legitimate interests pursued by the controller;
- an assessment of the necessity and proportionality of the processing in relation to the purpose;
- an assessment of the risks to data subjects; and
- the measures in place to address risk, including security and to demonstrate that organizations comply.

The objective of the processing of data is relevant, namely if it could lead to a high risk to data subjects' rights. Though whether a DPIA is needed will depend on the

157. Article 5(1)(e) of the GDPR.

project on a case-by-case basis, it is important to note that each controller must fulfil his obligations with regard to a DPIA.

In a blockchain setting, a DPIA is likely to be required in the case of a specialized blockchain designed to process personal data. In this type of blockchain where processing personal data is the purpose of the system, privacy protections must be built into the system to ensure the system does not pose a risk to the rights of data subjects.

It should also be noted that the use of a new technology may be considered as giving rise to high risk. For example, in the UK, the ICO states in its GDPR guidance that a DPIA must be carried out whenever a new technology is used.[158] Whether or not blockchain should be considered a 'new technology' is not clearly defined, and thus, users of blockchain should assess the risk on a case-by-case basis.

The use of blockchain technology can have a significant impact on the rights of individuals regarding the processing of their personal data. Whenever transactional personal data is stored on a blockchain, albeit encrypted or hashed, a DPIA should be carried out due to the inherent potential for harm to the rights and freedoms of affected data subjects. This applies to all events where the blockchain technology has been implemented to process personal data even if the data is stored off-chain and merely linked to the blockchain through a hash pointer. As outlined, on-chain hashes of off-chain personal data would still qualify as personal data. Even if a DPIA is legally not strictly required, i.e., because there is no likelihood to result in a high risk to the rights and freedoms of natural persons, organizations are well-advised to conduct an assessment so as to identify and minimize any kind of data privacy risk. The rationale of carrying out a DPIA is not to eliminate all data privacy risks. It has been designed to assist organizations in identifying and minimizing such risks, and in determining whether or not that level of risk identified is acceptable bearing in mind the benefits of what the organization is striving to achieve. By all means, controllers should document their assessments diligently in order to demonstrate compliance with Article 35(1) of the GDPR.

[D] Data Protection by Design and Default

The GDPR requires controllers to establish appropriate technical and organizational measures to implement data protection principles and safeguard individual rights. This concept is often referred to as 'privacy by design' and is based on Article 25 of the GDPR. Controllers must give prior thoughts to the appropriateness of the chosen technology to implement its processing and choose a format of that technology with the least impact on an individual's rights and freedoms. Recital 78 of the GDPR states:

> When developing, designing, selecting and using applications, services and products that are based on the processing of personal data or process personal data to fulfil their task, producers of the products, services and applications should be encouraged to take into account the right to data protection (...) and, with regard

158. https://ico.org.uk/for-organisations/guide-to-the-general-data-protection-regulation-gdpr/accountability-and-governance/data-protection-impact-assessments/ (accessed 3 Feb. 2020).

to the state of the art, to make sure that controllers and processors are able to fulfil their data protection obligations.

In November 2019, the European Data Protection Supervisor issued a set of guidelines for public consultation on privacy by design and default pursuant to the GDPR.[159]

Given the requirement of privacy by design, the challenge is to ensure that blockchain is a suitable technology to be used. An important aspect to be considered and to feature in any privacy impact assessment will, therefore, be to weight the advantages of using the blockchain, against the risks of doing so. The key question in that regard is whether privacy consideration has been factored in from the outset.

Accordingly, the controller has to implement measures which can include, *inter alia*, the minimization of data to be processed, pseudonymization of data as soon as possible and the improvement of security features.[160] This includes the consideration of whether personal data should be submitted to the blockchain rather than storing it off-chain or anywhere else. Controllers are well advised to spend thoughts as to whether it is inevitable to register personal data on the blockchain. By all means, it is the preferable solution to keep personal data outside the blockchain. In this context, the CNIL recommends that, whenever it is mandatory to store personal data on a blockchain, the controller should register the data in the form of a hash generated using a hash function with a key, or, at least, in the form of encryption ensuring a high level of confidentiality.[161]

However, there are multiple use cases which necessitate the storage of personal data on a blockchain. For instance, in the health sector, doctors, patients, hospitals and other healthcare providers could store electronic health records in blockchain-based decentralized management systems in which they can encrypt personal data and/or sensitive information and grant access to records only to authorized parties via appropriate credentials.[162] The capacity to record and authenticate medical data and customize its use for other parties can leverage the information and economic value of such data. It could stimulate new business models in the health sector, i.e., personalized medicine; data sharing for drug, treatment and public health research; or selling and buying medical data for any number of stakeholders. Further, smart contracts can be used for clinical-trial phase control, whereby patients need to consent explicitly for data analysis purposes. Patients could implement dynamic consents through smart contracts, by defining data access rights stating, for example, the type of data to be disclosed, intended uses, authorized third parties or storage limits. Under these conditions, they could easily share their sensitive records and, among others, ask different doctors for second opinions, etc. Even in the medical sector, data privacy and security are major concerns, so any blockchain-driven solutions must put in place

159. EDPB Plenary Meeting November 2019, *Guidelines 4/2019 on Article 25 Data Protection by Design and by Default* (Adopted on 13 Nov. 2019).
160. Recital 78 of the GDPR.
161. CNIL, *supra* n. 7, at 6.
162. Ekblaw, A. et al., *A Case Study for Blockchain in Healthcare: 'MedRec' Prototype for Electronic Health Records and Medical Research Data* (IEEE Technology and Society Magazine, 2016).

strong privacy mechanisms in compliance with the GDPR,[163] particularly from the privacy by design and default perspective. Any security measures to be put in place must be state-of-the-art[164] and must encompass encryption techniques. Some blockchain developers have tried adding additional layers of privacy to design around the availability of participant and transaction information on the blockchain via 'privacy coins'. For example, Zcash uses a 'zero-knowledge proof algorithm' to verify the transaction without the need to disclose the identity of blockchain participants or the amount of each transaction. Monero is another example of a blockchain-based network that obfuscates digital currency data, including transaction sources and amounts by using advanced cryptography, transaction-specific, one-time addresses, and obfuscated signatures. While these approaches can help prevent re-identification, masking network participants makes it more difficult for legitimate businesses to perform Anti Money Laundering measures to identify illegal transactions where required.

In the case, it is not possible to put personal data off-chain, and when justified by the purpose of the processing and a privacy impact assessment has proven that the residual risks are acceptable, personal data can be stored on a blockchain. This necessitates that all appropriate security measures need to be built in whereby it should be taken into account that, as a rule of thumb, a public blockchain has a higher risk exposure in terms of the privacy rights of data subjects concerned than a private blockchain. Nevertheless, when implementing technical and organizational measures, blockchain developers must account for the data protection by design and default (DPDD) principle from the outset, irrespective of which kind of blockchain is being used.[165] This comprises, in particular, minimizing the processing of personal data and pseudonymizing personal data in the earliest phase. Article 25 section 2 of the GDPR requires that, by default, only personal data which is necessary for each specific purpose of the processing is processed. This obligation applies to the amount of personal data that is collected, the extent of its processing as well as the period of storage and accessibility.[166] Given that each full node holds a complete copy of each blockchain, that provision runs contrary to the data minimization principle enshrined in the GDPR and is a stumbling block for blockchain developers who strive to get the blockchain GDPR-compliant (section §5.05 [C][2] *supra*).

It is apparent that the GDPR was framed for centralized models of data collection, storage and processing. The blockchain technology creates tension with regards to some fundamental privacy rights. It should be noted that some national governments have been scrutinizing the blockchain technology against national and/or European law.[167]

---

163. European Commission, *supra* n. 132, at 83.
164. EDPB Plenary Meeting November 2019, *supra* n. 159, at 7, 8.
165. German Government, *Blockchain-Strategie der Bundesregierung* 13 (2019), available at: https://www.bmwi.de/Redaktion/DE/Publikationen/Digitale-Welt/blockchain-strategie.pdf?__blob=publicationFile&v=10 (accessed 3 Feb. 2020).
166. Article 25(2) of the GDPR.
167. For example, the government in Netherlands has been weighting the pros and cons of the blockchain technology, available at: https://www.lexology.com/library/detail.aspx?g=a8cd5d22-c729-4a5d-a393 (accessed 3 Feb. 2020).

[E] Record of Processing Activities

The GDPR requires data controllers and data processors (together with their representatives) to maintain records of their processing activities to help demonstrate compliance with the GDPR. These records must include as per Article 30(1) of the GDPR (amongst others):

- the name and contact details of the data controller;
- the purposes of the processing; and
- a description of the categories of data subjects and of categories of personal data.

The GDPR requires that records be in writing which include electronic forms and that they be made available on request.[168] The obligation to keep records of processing activities does not apply to organizations with fewer than 250 employees unless:

- the processing is likely to result in a risk of the rights and freedoms of data subjects;
- the processing is not occasional; and
- the processing includes special categories of data referred to in Article 9(1) GDPR or criminal convictions data in Article 10.

With blockchain, categorizing data subjects and personal data can be challenging since the controller may not know with certainty what sort of data will be stored on the blockchain.

[F] Appointment of a DPO

Another key concept of accountability is the appointment of DPOs. Article 37 of the GDPR requires that data controllers and data processors (where their respective data processing activities fall within specific criteria set out below) appoint a DPO for their organization. It also sets out what that role entails, and creates employment protection for actions taken as a result of a DPO exercising his/her function. Article 38 (1) of the GDPR requires that the DPO be 'involved, properly and in a timely manner, in all issues which relate to the protection of personal data'.

A DPO, whether or not they are an employee of the respective legal entity, must be able to perform their duties in an independent manner.

The DPO's role would include understanding and upholding data subjects' rights, implementing data protection by design and by default, maintaining and updating records of processing activities, understanding and championing security of the processing of personal data and notification, management and communication of security breaches to the supervisory authority.

168. Article 30(3) and (4) of the GDPR.

Article 37 (1) of the GDPR states that a data controller or a data processor shall be required to appoint a DPO in any case where:

- they are a public authority;
- the core activities of the controller or the processor consist of processing operations which, by virtue of their nature, their scope and their purposes, require regular and systemic monitoring of data subjects on a large scale; or
- the core activities of the controller or processor consist of a large scale of special categories of data (*i.e.*, sensitive personal data) and personal data relating to criminal convictions and offences (emphasis added).

The above requirement applies to blockchain the same way it does to other businesses, regardless of the type of technology implemented.

§5.08 INTERNATIONAL DATA TRANSFERS ON A BLOCKCHAIN UNDER THE GDPR

Under the GDPR, there is a general prohibition against transferring personal data of data subjects to countries outside of the EEA (otherwise known as third countries) that are not considered by the European Commission to offer an 'adequate protection' of personal data unless appropriate safeguards have been adopted in order to legitimize the transfer of personal data to third countries.

The GDPR provides that an international transfer may take place where the European Commission has decided that the third country in question ensures an adequate level of protection. A finding of adequacy can also be made under GDPR in respect of a territory or processing sector within a third country or an international organization (e.g., the financial sector). Countries currently deemed adequate by the Commission are: Andorra, Argentina, Canada (commercial organizations), Faroe Islands, Guernsey, Israel, Isle of Man, Japan, Jersey, New Zealand, Switzerland and Uruguay.[169] Following Brexit, the UK will be deemed a third country unless and until an adequacy finding is made by the European Commission in relation to the UK.

The main safeguards include:

(1) *Consent* - International transfers from the EEA are technically allowed with the consent of the data subject concerned. However, it may be difficult for companies to obtain valid consent (because the requirements for valid consent are onerous as discussed in section §5.04[B]) and where, for example, the personal data are received from a third party and not directly from the data subject. Therefore, other exemptions should be considered for systematic international transfers of personal data.

169. European Commission, Adequacy of the protection of personal data in non-EU countries, available at: https://ec.europa.eu/info/law/law-topic/data-protection/data-transfers-outside-eu/adequacy-protection-personal-data-non-eu-countries_en (accessed 3 Feb. 2020).

(2) *Model Contracts* – otherwise known as Standard Contractual Clauses (SCC), model contracts are effectively a European standard form of data transfer agreements and were an existing transfer mechanism under the Directive and remain available under GDPR. Model Contracts allow for data exports from the EEA because the data importer and data exporter agree in the Model Contract to be bound by rigorous contractual obligations and EU data protection laws to protect the exported Personal Data. There are two forms of Model Contracts available (i.e., that allow for transfers between):
   (i) two Controllers (so-called Controller-to-Controller Model Contracts); and
   (ii) a data exporter who is a Controller, on the one hand, and a data importer who is a Processor, on the other hand (so-called Controller-to-Processor Model Contracts).

(3) *EU-US Privacy Shield* (Privacy Shield) – the Privacy Shield permits entities in the EU to transfer Persona Data to certifying US organizations. In order for a US organization to certify to the Privacy Shield, it must be regulated by either the Department of Transport or the Federal Trade Commission (FTC) and must comply with the Privacy Shield Principles, a set of seven privacy principles that generally align with data protection standards reflected in privacy laws in many jurisdictions.

(4) *Binding Corporate Rules* (BCRs) – BCRs are given statutory recognition by the GDPR as an appropriate safeguard for transfers of personal data for the EEA. BCRs are effectively a global code of practice and program based on European data protection standards that, once approved by the European Data Protection Authorities, allow an international organization to transfer personal data to its other group companies in third countries, such as parents, subsidiaries and affiliates under common control.

The international data transfer restrictions in the GDPR apply the same way to the blockchain as they do to any other business, but is particularly important for blockchain technology since nodes will likely be located in jurisdictions outside the EU, and, in the case of public blockchains, it is virtually impossible to control the node location. The French DPA, CNIL, warns in its blockchain guidance that using blockchain for cross-border data transfers 'can be particularly problematic, especially in the case of public blockchains.'[170]

One potential solution to resolve this complication would be for blockchain network users to create and agree to a contractually binding governance framework incorporating SCC at the time such blockchain network is created. By including SCC in the governance framework, such clauses become part of a multilateral agreement between the members of the blockchain. This approach was endorsed by the former

170. CNIL, *supra* n. 7, at 2.

Article 29 Data Protection Working Party as a valid means of complying with restrictions on international data transfers.[171]

§5.09 OUTLOOK

It will be interesting to see the position of other DPAs and the EDPB as the potential of blockchain technology evolves. One of the most pressing questions is how the lack of control over personal data stored on a blockchain can be reconciled with the GDPR and its core principles. In the absence of more detailed guidance issued by the European DPAs, it is advisable to adhere to the rule-of-thumb principles which have been published by the Blockchain Observatory and Forum.[172] In essence, those principles are, in the order showcased on the below:

- Start with the big picture: How is user value created and how is data used and do you really need blockchain.
- Store personal data off-chain or, if the blockchain can't be avoided, prefer the private blockchain networks.
- Make full use of data hashing, obfuscation, encryption and aggregation techniques in order to anonymize or, at least, pseudonymyze data.
- Consider personal data carefully when connecting private blockchain with public ones.

In addition, it is key to stick to the basic security requirements which have been fleshed out in the CNIL recommendations, particularly with regard to technical and organizational measures to limit the impact of potential algorithm failure on the security of transactions. More importantly, the European DPAs and particularly the EDPB need to develop a list of proven encryption technologies. Any personal data that is encrypted with those technologies assessed by these regulatory bodies could be considered as not personal for those parties which do not have the encryption key.

Finally, with private blockchains, it is possible that some of the data protection issues can be satisfactorily addressed, e.g., by suitable contractual arrangements or through the presence of a 'blockchain gatekeeper' which may, under certain circumstances, be classified as the single data controller.

§5.10 BLOCKCHAIN AND US PRIVACY LAW

While EU data protection laws restrict and regulate all processing of personal data (as discussed in the immediately preceding sections §5.02–§5.09, *supra*, US data privacy laws seek to apply only proportionately designed sector-, harm- and situation-specific requirements to safeguard individual privacy against concrete harms. US privacy laws are technology-neutral and do not affect blockchain or DLT adversely or specifically.

171. Article 29 Working Party, Letter to ESMA (14 Jun. 2017), available at: http://ec.europa.eu/newsroom/document.cfm?doc_id=45447 (accessed 3 Feb. 2020).
172. European Union Blockchain Observatory and Forum, *supra* n. 23, at 28–30.

Companies have to consider hundreds of federal and state privacy laws to determine which requirements apply to particular blockchain use cases. This section §5.10, *infra* provides [A] an overview regarding US privacy law with a comparative perspective in reference to EU data protection regulation, [B] an introduction to federal versus state privacy laws, [C] guidance regarding terminology, [D] a summary assessment of the effects of general and specific privacy laws on blockchain and distributed ledger use cases, and (E) a deeper dive into the effects of the CCPA of 2018 on blockchain deployment.

[A] US Privacy Law Versus EU Data Protection Regulation

The terms 'data privacy' and 'data protection' are often used interchangeably, in particular in the context of comparisons of Anglo-Saxon data privacy laws and continental European data protection laws. Actually, the two terms and legislative concepts have quite different origins and purposes.[173]

EU data protection regulations are about protecting individuals (the data subjects) from the effects of automated data processing with a default prohibition. Companies are generally prohibited from processing personal data unless they obtain consent from the data subjects or they find an applicable statutory exemption.[174] Companies have to justify the processing of personal data in a blockchain by identifying and disclosing in the privacy notices a 'legal basis.'[175] If companies cannot find a compelling legal basis, they must not process personal data in blockchains. This approach affects the deployment of any information technology adversely, including blockchain and distributed ledgers.

The United States and many other countries outside of Europe, by contrast, generally allow data processing. Data privacy laws are primarily intended to protect individuals from intrusion into seclusion and interception of confidential communications. Given this focus, individuals are usually not protected under US privacy laws, unless they have a reasonable expectation of privacy in a particular situation or a policy objective justifies restrictions on individual freedom.[176] Companies can – and frequently do – vitiate expectations of privacy by notifying individuals of the companies'

173. Determann, L., Determann's Field Guide to Data Privacy Law: International Corporate Compliance Chapter 0.14 et seq. (4th ed., Edward Elgar Publishing Ltd., 2020).

174. Governments are also subject to restrictions on data processing under national European data protection laws, but details vary from country to country. In 2014, people in Europe reacted with outrage to revelations about large-scale surveillance regarding electronic communications by the United States National Security Agency (NSA) and European intelligence services. Yet, current drafts of the EU Data Protection Regulation continue to largely exempt data processing for national security purposes, due to different views in the 28 EU Member States on this topic. *See* Determann, L. & zu Guttenberg, K.-T., On War and Peace in Cyberspace: Security, Privacy, Jurisdiction 875 et seq. (41 Hastings Constitutional Law Quarterly, 1, 13, 2014).

175. *See* Arts 6(1) and 12–14 GDPR and sections §5.02 through §5.09, *supra*.

176. *See*, e.g., *Moreno v. Hanford Sentinel, Inc.*, 172 Cal. App. 4th 1125, 1129 (Cal. Ct. App. 2009) ([T]o prevail on an invasion of privacy claim, the plaintiff must have conducted himself or herself in a manner consistent with an actual expectation of privacy.); Cal. Pen. Code, § 632. On the concept of 'reasonable expectations of privacy,' *see* Freiwald, S., First Principles of Communications Privacy (2007 Stanford Technology Law Review 3); Determann, L. &

data collection and processing activities (e.g., in employee handbooks, website privacy statements and in-store warnings about security cameras).[177] Individuals receive relatively more privacy protection in the sanctity of their homes, for example, but communications and activities outside receive little or no protection (e.g., the information in public records, records shared with third parties, photos taken in public, audible phone conversations in public, postings on the internet or via social networking platforms).[178]

When Hessen and then other German states and European countries started enacting data protection laws in the 1970s, the United States also considered this option but decided against comprehensive regulation of data processing. Congress felt it was too early to appropriately identify and address potential privacy harms and balance privacy interests with freedom of information, innovation, and economic freedoms.[179] Therefore, the United States resolved to pass sector-, situation-, and harm-specific privacy laws as the need arises, at the state and federal level. This allowed information technology companies in Silicon Valley to grow and become industry leaders in semiconductor technologies, software, e-commerce, cloud computing, social media, big data, and other data-intensive products and services.[180] But, the reactive approach with narrowly crafted, specific laws resulted in hundreds of diverging and constantly evolving privacy laws across the United States. Companies and government agencies find it increasingly difficult to navigate the maze of US privacy laws. Businesses are particularly concerned about the CCPA of 2018, which adds extensive new disclosure requirements and individual rights to existing laws in order to reign in perceived risks emanating from data selling.[181]

In addition to data privacy laws, the United States have also enacted data security laws. These laws aim to protect individuals from specific harms resulting from unauthorized access to personal information, in particular, identity theft (e.g., criminals using someone's personal data to acquire or charge credit cards). Examples include data security breach notification laws (California passed the first law in 2002, with most US states and many countries following suit thereafter, the EU effective 2018

Sprague, R., Intrusive Monitoring: Employee Privacy Expectations Are Reasonable in Europe, Destroyed in the United States 979 (26 Berkeley Technology Law Journal 2011).

177. *See*, e.g., In re Yahoo Mail Litig., 7 F. Supp. 3d 1016, 1028–1032 (N.D. Cal. Aug. 12, 2014) (holding that by agreeing to terms of service, email service provider's users had explicitly consented to provider's practice of scanning and analysing emails, therefore, barring their claim under the federal Wiretap Act).

178. *See*, e.g., *Evens v. Superior Court*, 77 Cal. App. 4th 320, 324 (Cal. Ct. App. 1999) (holding that teacher had no reasonable expectation of privacy in her communications made in the classroom); *United States v. Standefer*, No. 06-CR-2674-H, 2007 WL 2301760, at *3 (S.D. Cal. Aug. 8, 2007) (There is no reasonable expectation of privacy in financial records such as checks, deposit slips, and financial statements maintained by third party institutions, such as banks because a depositor takes the risk, in revealing his affairs to another, that the information will be conveyed by that person to the Government).

179. Schwartz, P.M., Preemption and Privacy 902, 910–916 (118 Yale Law Journal 902, 910–916, 2009).

180. Chander, A., *How Law Made Silicon Valley* 63 (Emory Law Journal 639, 2014), available at: https://ssrn.com/abstract=2340197 (accessed 3 Feb. 2020).

181. Determann, L., *California Privacy Law, Practical Guide and Commentary: U.S. Federal and California Law, CCPA Supplement* Chapter 2-26a (3rd ed., IAPP, 2018).

with Articles 33 and 34 GDPR), detailed prescriptions regarding technical and organizational measures to protect health information in the Health Insurance Portability and Accountability Act (HIPAA) and US state laws in California, Massachusetts, Nevada and New York requiring the encryption of certain data in certain circumstances.

Outside the scope of data protection, data privacy and data security are data residency, data retention and property laws. According to data residency and data retention laws, companies have to retain data in a certain location and for certain minimum time periods to be available in case of government audits; such laws are anti-privacy laws in nature.[182] The United States has not enacted general data retention or residency laws, and companies in the US are generally free to transfer personal data internationally.

Like EU data protection laws, US data privacy laws are not concerned with property rights. No one owns personal data.[183]

In summary, US privacy law consists of hundreds of sector-, situation- and harm-specific privacy laws that impose numerous obligations and prohibitions to protect reasonable data privacy expectations of individuals.[184] Companies can satisfy most obligations and overcome most prohibitions by providing notice or seeking consent from data subjects. Without a reasonable expectation of privacy, data subjects do not tend to have many rights under California or US federal privacy laws.[185] Companies can set, qualify and negate privacy expectations by way of notice. Only very few US privacy laws do not recognize notice or consent as an exception to prohibitions.[186] Therefore, privacy notices play a key role in US privacy laws.

Data subjects can enforce most laws by way of individual or class-action lawsuits. The FTC, the California attorney general and other regulators can also bring lawsuits or impose fines and other sanctions, but private lawsuits under data privacy laws are much more prevalent in the United States than in other jurisdictions. US

182. Determann, L., *Data Residency Rules Cutting into Clouds: Impact and Options for Global Businesses and IT Architectures* (Bloomberg BNA Data Privacy & Security Law Report, 16 PVLR 496 - 04/03/2017); Determann, L. & Weigl, M., *Data Residency Requirements Creeping into German Law* (Bloomberg BNA Privacy & Security Law Report, 15 PVLR 529 - 3/14/2016); Bekeschenko, E., et al., *Keep Russian Data in Russia and Out of Clouds?* 32 (6 Computer & Internet Lawyer 1, 2015).

183. Determann, L., *No One Owns Data* (70 Hastings Law Journal 1, 2018).

184. Solove, D. & Schwartz, P., *Information Privacy Law* (6th ed., Aspen Publishing Co., 2018) and *Privacy Law Fundamentals* (IAPP, 2019).

185. *See*, for example, *Safari Club Int'l v. Rudolph*, 845 F.3d 1250 (9th Cir. 2017); *USA v. Michael Marr et. al.*, Case No. 14-cr-00580-PJH, Pretrial Order No. 3 (N.D. California 2016); Todd, R., *Courthouse Steps Listening Devices Not Illegal, Hamilton Says* (The Recorder, 25 Jul. 2016) and On the concept of 'reasonable expectations of privacy', *see* Freiwald, S., First Principles of Communications Privacy (2007 Stanford Technology Law Review 3); Determann & Sprague *supra* n. 176, at. 979.

186. Exceptions include the Song-Beverly Credit Card Act (Cal. Civ. Code §§1747 et seq.), which prohibits merchants from collecting personal information from credit card users regardless of their consent, except as necessary to process credit card payments, Cal. Lab. Code § 435, which prohibits employers from placing security cameras in toilets and locker rooms.

privacy laws have been enforced and complied with more effectively for much of their existence, compared to EU data protection laws.[187]

For an overview regarding US privacy laws with the perspective of EU data protection laws, it is also helpful to consider what US privacy law is *not*:

- *No one omnibus statute:* Unlike many European, Latin American and Asian countries, neither the United States nor California have enacted one comprehensive data privacy statute.
- *No default prohibition of data processing:* In the United States, companies are generally allowed to process personal data. Unless a particular restriction or prohibition applies, data processing is permitted.
- *No data minimization requirements:* Unlike European laws, California and the United States do not require companies to avoid or minimize the processing of personal data. Companies can collect and process as much data as they want, so long as they comply with applicable consent, notice and security requirements. 'Big data' is generally allowed.
- *No data protection authorities:* Neither California nor the United States federal government has established European-style data protection authorities. In California, the attorney general enforces privacy laws and created a Privacy Enforcement and Protection Unit in 2012.[188] At the federal level, the FTC has protected consumer privacy quite effectively based on its powers to enforce general unfair competition laws and some specific privacy laws, including the CAN SPAM Act and the Children Online Privacy Protection Act (COPPA).[189]
- *No data protection registries or filings:* The United States has not established any database registries or filing requirements under privacy laws.
- *No data protection officers:* Under federal healthcare sector privacy law (HIPAA), covered entities have to appoint a data privacy official and a data security official.[190] Other US privacy laws do not require such appointments. Many US companies have voluntarily appointed data privacy and security officers.
- *No specific restrictions on international data transfers:* California and the United States have traditionally stood for free trade and free information flows. International data transfers are not specifically restricted, unlike under the laws in Europe and an increasing number of other countries.

187. Determann, L., Social Media Privacy: 12 Myths and Facts (7 Stanford Technology Law Review 4, 2012); Schwartz, P., Preemption and Privacy 902, 910 et seq. (118 Yale Law Journal 2009).
188. http://oag.ca.gov/news/press-releases/attorney-general-kamala-d-harris-announces-privacy-enforcement-and-protection (accessed 3 Feb. 2020).
189. Serwin, A., The Federal Trade Commission and Privacy: Defining Enforcement and Encouraging Adoption of Best Practices 809 (48 San Diego Law Review 2011).
190. 45 C.F.R. § 164.308(1)(1)(ii)(D)(2): covered entities and business associates have to appoint security official; 45 C.F.R. § 164.530(a)(1): covered entity has to appoint privacy official.

- *No general translation requirements:* English is the official language of California.[191] Under California and federal privacy laws, companies are not explicitly required to provide translations of privacy notices, privacy policies or other privacy-related documentation. But, § 999.305(a)(2)(c) of the draft regulations of the California Attorney General pertaining to the CCPA requires that companies issue privacy notices required under the CCPA 'in the languages in which the business in its ordinary course provides contracts, disclaimers, sale announcements, and other information to consumers'. Separately, companies in California have to provide translations of certain types of consumer contracts if they negotiate such contracts primarily in the Spanish, Chinese, Tagalog, Vietnamese or Korean language; this requirement could also extend to privacy-related documentation if it is part of such a contract.[192] Also, government agencies and employers can be required to provide translations under certain circumstances.[193]

The fact that US privacy law is conceptually so different from EU data protection laws makes it difficult to compare them and assess their effectiveness fairly. 'Adequacy decisions' by the European Commission look at the similarity of statutory wording and fail to measure or consider enforcement, actual compliance levels, or effectiveness for individual privacy in the United States versus the EEA and other 'third countries,'[194] leave alone the flaws in EU and national data protection laws.[195] Globally, data privacy legislation is at crossroads and in need of serious reconsideration.[196]

191. California Constitution, Art. 3, section 6.(b): 'English is the official language of the State of California.' The USA have not prescribed an official language by law, but some states have, available at: http://en.wikipedia.org/wiki/Languages_of_the_United_States (accessed 3 Feb. 2020).
192. Cal. Civ. Code §1632. *See* Shikai, Y.M., *Applying the California Translation Act to Consumer Agreements* 11–15 (Los Angeles Lawyer, September 2012).
193. For example, long-term health care facilities, must provide translations of the Patients' Bill of Rights (which could include privacy policies) into any language that is used by at least 1% of the facility's population, Cal. Health & Saf. Code § 1599.61. State and local authorities are required to provide written materials in languages other than English, for example, under Cal. Gov. Code §§ 7290 et seq. (state agencies in general); Cal. Lab. Code, § 105 (Dept. of Labor Stds. Enforcement); Cal. Unemp. Ins. Code § 316 (unemployment compensation); Cal. Welf. & Inst. Code § 19013.5 (Dept. of Rehabilitation) and § 10607 (Dept. of Social Services). In *Samaniego v. Empire Today LLC*, 205 Cal. App. 4th 1138 (Cal App. 1st Dist. 2012), the court found an employment contract to be unconscionable where an employer did not provide a Spanish translation of a contract that contained a number of one-sided provisions.
194. Determann, L., *Adequacy of Data Protection in the USA: Myths and Facts* (International Data Privacy Law, 2016); Determann, L., *US-Datenschutzrecht – Dichtung und Wahrheit* 561 (Neue Zeitschrift für Verwaltungsrecht, 2016).
195. Veil, W., *The Emperor's New Clothes: On the Structural Shortcomings of Both the Old and the New Data Protection Law* 686–696 (Neue Zeitschrift für Verwaltungsrecht, 2018).
196. Determann, L., *Healthy Data Protection* (26 Michigan Technology Law Review 229, 2020); Determann, L., *Privacy and Data Protection**КОНФИДЕНЦИАЛЬНОСТЬ И ЗАЩИТА ПЕРСОНАЛЬНЫХ ДАННЫХ*** 18–26 (Moscow Journal of International Law 2019 No. 1).

[B] Federal and State Law

The United States Congress enacts US federal laws, as contemplated by the US Constitution, which allocates specific subject matter areas to federal legislative jurisdiction. To the extent the US Constitution does not provide for federal legislative jurisdiction, the states are generally empowered to make laws.[197]

In California, for example, the California Legislature makes new law in statutes and also codifies court-made law, including, for example, the privacy torts. In the California Civil Code, the California legislature clarifies that it does not mean to ossify the common law through codification and California courts shall remain in charge of further developing common law.[198]

[C] Diverse Terminology

US privacy laws do not typically or uniformly use terms found in the GDPR and addressed in previous Chapters of this book,[199] such as 'personal data', 'controller', 'processor', 'processing' or 'data subject'. Ever since Congress decided to react to privacy issues with narrowly crafted, specific legislation, lawmakers at the federal and state level crafted terms and distinctions for every new privacy law. As a result, terminology and definitions in US privacy laws are varied and disparate.

For example, a number of California statutes use the term 'personally identifiable information' but define it differently.[200] In the California Civil Code, you can find different definitions of similarly sounding terms like 'personal identification information',[201] 'personal information'[202] and 'personally identifiable information',[203] each defined differently.

197. US Constitution, Art. I, § 8 and Amendment X.
198. *See* Cal. Civ. Code §5.
199. Sections §5.02–§5.09.
200. Cf. Cal. Bus. & Prof. Code § 22577(a); Cal. Str. & H. Code § 31499(o).
201. Cal. Civ. Code §1747.08. The Song-Beverly Credit Card Act uses the term 'personal identification information', which courts have interpreted to cover any information relating to a person, even a zip code, *see Pineda v. Williams-Sonoma Stores Inc.*, 51 Cal. 4th 524, 530 (2001). The statutory definition in Cal. Civ. Code §1747.08(3)(b) states: 'For purposes of this section, "personal identification information" means information concerning the cardholder, other than information set forth on the credit card, and including, but not limited to, the cardholder's address and telephone number'.
202. Cal. Civ. Code §1798.83(e)(7). The California Shine the Light Law defines the term 'personal information' with an enumerative list of data categories. Cal. Civ. Code §1798.80 (e) contains a much broader definition: 'Personal information means any information that identifies, relates to, describes, or is capable of being associated with, a particular individual, including, but not limited to, his or her name, signature, social security number, physical characteristics or description, address, telephone number, passport number, driver's license or state identification card number, insurance policy number, education, employment, employment history, bank account number, credit card number, debit card number, or any other financial information, medical information, or health insurance information. Personal information does not include publicly available information that is lawfully made available to the general public from federal, state, or local government records.' Only a couple of sections further, in Cal. Civ. Code §1798.81.5(d)(1), on data security breach notifications, the term 'personal information' is defined with a enumerated list of data categories.

Even within one statute, you can find different definitions for different subsections. For example, the CCPA of 2018, which is only one of the dozens of privacy laws within the California Civil Code, uses two different definitions of 'personal information', a relatively narrow definition in the context of security breach liability[204] and an extremely broad definition for all other subsections.[205] Consequently, for purposes of applying US privacy laws to blockchain applications, one has to consider the scope, definitions and terminology of every applicable statute separately and on its own terms.

[D] General and Specific US Privacy Laws applied to Blockchain

Blockchain or DLT, as such, is not regulated under US privacy laws. US privacy laws tend to be technology-neutral and focus either on individual privacy (with general privacy laws) or a particular industry sector (such as financial, healthcare), situation (e.g., online privacy, credit card payments, video rental history), data subjects (e.g., children), or harm (e.g., identity theft).

With respect to blockchain deployment, companies and individuals have to comply with [1] general privacy laws, including the California constitutional guarantee of privacy as well as common law, torts, consumer protection and unfair competition laws, and [2] sector-, harm- and situation-specific privacy laws.

[1] General US Privacy Laws

Companies are compelled to provide clear privacy notices by a number of general privacy and consumer protection laws in the United States, including the California

203. Cal. Civ. Code §1798.81.5[d][1] not only uses and defines the term 'personal information' but also uses 'personally identifiable information' in subsection [f], without separate definition: 'Any person or business that is required to issue a security breach notification pursuant to this section to more than 500 California residents as a result of a single breach of the security system shall electronically submit a single sample copy of that security breach notification, excluding any personally identifiable information, to the Attorney General'.
204. According to Cal. Civ. Code §1798.150(a)(1) and § 1798.81.5(d)(1)(A), 'Personal information' means either of the following: '(...) An individual's first name or first initial and the individual's last name in combination with any one or more of the following data elements, when either the name or the data elements are not encrypted or redacted: (i) Social security number. (ii) Driver's license number, California identification card number, tax identification number, passport number, military identification number, or other unique identification number issued on a government document commonly used to verify the identity of a specific individual. (iii) Account number or credit or debit card number, in combination with any required security code, access code, or password that would permit access to an individual's financial account. (iv) Medical information. (v) Health insurance information. (vi) Unique biometric data generated from measurements or technical analysis of human body characteristics, such as a fingerprint, retina, or iris image, used to authenticate a specific individual. Unique biometric data does not include a physical or digital photograph, unless used or stored for facial recognition purposes'.
205. According to Cal. Civ. Code §1798.140(o)(1) 'Personal information means information that identifies, relates to, describes, is reasonably capable of being associated with, or could reasonably be linked, directly or indirectly, with a particular consumer or household'.

Constitution, which contains an explicit guarantee of the right to privacy that also applies between private individuals and companies (whereas the US federal constitution only applies to state actors).[206] Also, under tort and unfair competition laws, companies have to avoid infringing reasonable privacy expectations such as by intrusion upon seclusion, public disclosure of private facts, false light, and misappropriation of name or likeness.[207] Blockchain and distributed ledger technologies do not raise any particular issues pertaining to such general laws. But, like other information technologies, blockchain and distributed ledger technologies involve the processing of personal information, which can result in infringements of privacy expectations.

Companies and individuals should take steps to ensure that they are not violating anyone's reasonable privacy expectations when they use blockchain or DLT. This requires an analysis of potential privacy expectations of persons involved, expected use cases, and potential risks of misuse and harm. With respect to any new technology, a key risk is that users misunderstand functionalities, rules or consequences, or misjudge the impact on their privacy or other interests. Most privacy violations on social media platforms are committed by the victims themselves, or their friends and family, often inadvertently, due to insufficient understanding of functionalities;[208] nevertheless, the social media platform operators are publicly blamed and often sued or politically held responsible.[209] Therefore, it is in the best interest of technology companies to educate users of potential privacy harms, to reduce the risk of violations and protect themselves against blame and liability.

The most effective way to qualify privacy expectations and reduce the risk of being held liable for intruding on privacy or engaging in unfair or misleading business practices is for companies to issue clear and simple user manuals and privacy notices, ideally with hands-on technology training, real-time tips and on-the-spot privacy warnings. With respect to crypto-currencies, individuals should be advised of limits to transaction privacy, the publicity of public key information, and what personal information will end up in a particular blockchain (e.g., depending on the use case, health information or education history and credentials).

To achieve this goal, companies have to craft short, situation-specific notices that use plain language. Additional disclosures that companies have to issue under CCPA, GDPR and other regimes may have to be provided separately in the form of supplemental notices (which must track all statutory disclosure requirements and will be referred to by regulators, plaintiffs, journalists, etc., but which cannot be expected to be read or understood by consumers).

206. Article 1, section 1 of the California Constitution states: 'All people are by nature free and independent and have inalienable rights. Among these are enjoying and defending life and liberty, acquiring, possessing, and protecting property, and pursuing and obtaining safety, happiness, and privacy.' The people of California added this explicit right of privacy to the California Constitution by a ballot measure in November 1972, *American Acad. of Pediatrics v. Lungren* (1997) 16 Cal. 4th 307, 326.
207. Prosser, W., Privacy (48 California Law Review 383, 1960).
208. Determann, L., *Social Media @ Work 2014* (BNA/Bloomberg Social Media Law & Policy Report, 2 SMLR 49, 12/17/2013).
209. Determann, L., *Social Media Privacy: A Dozen Myths and Facts* (2012 Stanford Technology Law Review 7, 2012).

When companies issue privacy notices to qualify individual privacy expectations, they have to be careful to avoid misleading consumers or misrepresenting any facts. The FTC, State Attorneys General, City Attorneys and private plaintiffs can pursue claims against companies for unlawful, unfair, or fraudulent business conduct.[210] Particularly, companies should avoid marketing fluff and declarations of good intentions in privacy notices, such as 'We take privacy seriously', 'Your privacy is important to us' or 'We deploy state-of-the-art data security measures.' Such statements do not provide the data subject with meaningful information and merely provide additional ammunition to plaintiffs' attorneys and regulators who believe the company did not, in fact, sufficiently respect privacy interests or comply with laws.[211]

Also, companies should avoid cramming disclosures required for multiple jurisdictions into one global privacy notice, as this will inevitably expand the volume of the notice to an unreasonable length, address topics that do not absolutely have to be addressed in each jurisdiction, and add complexity and unfamiliar terminology. For example, a company that is required under Article 13(1)(f) GDPR to state in a privacy notice to blockchain users in Europe that it 'intends to transfer personal data to a third country or international organisation and the existence or absence of an adequacy decision by the Commission, or (...) the appropriate or suitable safeguards and the means by which to obtain a copy of them or where they have been made available' should not include such verbiage in a privacy notice addressed to blockchain users in the US as this would be confusing and detracting from relevant or required disclosures. Conversely, the very detailed lists of personal information categories and counterintuitive terminology that companies have to adhere to under the CCPA of 2018 would render privacy notices for European residents unreasonably long, arguably in violation of Article 12(1) GDPR, which requires that privacy notices be framed in 'concise, transparent, intelligible and easily accessible form, using clear and plain language'.

Thus, most companies are better off with one core privacy statement targeted at the company's home jurisdiction or key market plus supplemental privacy notices to address technicalities for other jurisdictions.[212]

[2] Specific US Privacy Laws

Congress and state legislatures have not enacted privacy laws particularly focused on the blockchain or DLT. But, many sector-, harm- and situation-specific laws may apply

210. Cal. Bus. & Prof. Code §§ 17200–17210. More generally *see* Federal Trade Commission, available at: www.ftc.gov/about-ftc (accessed 3 Feb. 2020); Statutes Enforced or Administered by the Federal Trade Commission, available at: www.ftc.gov/enforcement/statutes (accessed 3 Feb. 2020).
211. For example, in In re iPhone Application Litig., 844 F. Supp. 2d 1040, 1072 (N.D. Cal. 2012), the court dismissed most claims under specific privacy statutes but declined to dismiss claims under California unfair competition law because 'Apple makes affirmative representations regarding its protection of user's personal information'.
212. For more detail on this topic and drafting recommendations for privacy notices, please *see* Determann, *supra* n. 173, at 3.18 et seq.

to blockchain applications depending on the businesses, data subjects, and data categories involved.

For example, financial institutions may have to comply with the federal the Gramm-Leach-Bliley Act,[213] the Fair Credit Reporting Act,[214] the Fair Debt Collection Practices Act (FDCPA),[215] and the Right to Financial Privacy Act[216] as well as numerous state laws including, for example, California's Financial Information Privacy Act, the California Consumer Credit Reporting Agencies Act,[217] California's Rosenthal Fair Debt Collection Practices Act of 1977 (Rosenthal Act),[218] California's Right to Financial Privacy Act in 1976,[219] the Song-Beverly Credit Card Act of 1971,[220] the Areias Credit Card Full Disclosure Act of 1986[221] and various other laws and industry standards, including the Payment Card Industry Standards for credit card data.[222] Fintech companies may be able to avoid becoming entangled with some or all of the US privacy laws that apply to financial institutions if they follow the motto 'more tech than fin', e.g., by focusing on technology supply and leaving regulated activities to licensed institutions.[223]

If healthcare providers want to use blockchain technology to promote standardized electronic medical records for patients, healthcare providers, and health insurance providers, they may have to comply with the privacy and security rules under the federal Health Insurance Portability and Accountability Act of 1996 (HIPAA).[224] HIPAA

213. *See* 15 U.S.C. § 6809. With regard to the Financial Privacy Requirements of the Gramm-Leach-Bliley Act see Federal Trade Commission, available at: https://www.ftc.gov/tips-advice/business-center/guidance/brief-financial-privacy-requirements-gramm-leach-bliley-act (accessed 3 Feb. 2020).
214. 15 U.S.C. §§ 1681 through 1681x. On the history of credit bureaus and regulation, *see* Rowena Olegario, Credit-Reporting Agencies: Their Historical Roots, Current Status, and Role in Market Development, available at: http://siteresources.worldbank.org/INTWDRS/Resources/477365-1257315064764/2429_olegario.pdf (accessed 3 Feb.2020).
215. *See* 15 U.S.C. §§ 1692 et seq. When it passed the FDCPA, Congress was faced with 'abundant evidence of the use of abusive, deceptive, and unfair debt collection practices by many debt collectors', 15 U.S.C. § 1692(a).
216. 12 U.S.C. §§ 3402 et seq.
217. *See* Cal. Civ. Code §§1785.1–1785.36. The law became effective in California in 1975 and has been subject to several amendments, *see* for example: www.leginfo.ca.gov/pub/09-10/bill/sen/sb_0901-0950/sb_909_cfa_20100621_110753_asm_comm.html (accessed 3 Feb. 2020).
218. Cal. Civ. Code §§1788–1788.33. For a history of both the federal and California laws, see for example: http://www.leginfo.ca.gov/pub/13-14/bill/sen/sb_0201-0250/sb_233_cfa_20130621_120929_asm_comm.html (accessed 3 Feb. 2020).
219. Cal. Gov. Code §§ 7460 et seq.
220. Cal. Civ. Code §1747.08. *See* generally Song, Alfred H., Oral History Interview (California State Archives State Government Oral History Program), available at: http://archives.cdn.sos.ca.gov/oral-history/pdf/song.pdf (accessed 3 Feb. 2020) (discussing the history of the Song-Beverly Credit Card Act: State Senator Albert H. Song [Democrat, Monterey Park] drafted the original bill and introduced it with State Senator Robert G. Beverly [Republican, South Bay] and Governor Ronald Reagan signed the bill into law).
221. Cal. Civ. Code §§1748.10 through 1748.14.
222. www.pcisecuritystandards.org/ (accessed 3 Feb. 2020).
223. Determann, L. & Lorenz, M., *FinTech: Ground Rules and Checklist for Starting Up and Going Global* (BNA's Banking Report, 27 Nov. 2017); Determann, L. & Lorenz, M., *Fintechs im Dschungel der Regulierungen* 13 (Börsenzeitung, 1 Apr. 2017).
224. *See* Pub. L. 104–191, 110 Stat. 1936, enacted 21 Aug. 1996; 45 C.F.R. §§ 160–164; 78 Fed. Reg. 5566 (final omnibus rule), available at: http://www.gpo.gov/fdsys/pkg/FR-2013-01-25/pdf/2

prescribes disclosure and consent requirements, data subject access rights, contract terms for business associates, security measures, and various other requirements. Software and hardware providers that target patients directly may be subject to the California Confidentiality of Medical Information Act (CMIA),[225] which prescribes requirements similar to HIPAA plus additional obligations and details, including a duty for companies to obtain written consent in certain situations that must be handwritten by the person who signs it or in a typeface no smaller than 14-point type; clearly separate from any other language present on the same page; executed by a signature that serves no other purpose than to execute the authorization; signed and dated.[226]

Any company that targets children online with a blockchain use case has to comply with the Children Online Privacy Protection Act (COPPA),[227] which requires parental consent before companies may collect personal information from children under 13 years.

Companies that process video purchase or rental history information have to comply with the Video Privacy Protection Act,[228] which contains specific written consent requirements for disclosures and since 2012 permits companies to obtain customer consent through electronic means using the internet, provided that the consent is in a form that is 'distinct and separate from any form setting forth other legal or financial obligations of the consumer'[229] and video tape service providers give customers a choice between consenting to disclosure: (1) in advance for a set period of time up to two years or until consent is withdrawn by the consumer; or (2) each time disclosure is sought.

Thus, every business has to determine for itself which specific US privacy laws it has to comply with pertaining to a particular blockchain or DLT deployment. For an overview regarding sectoral US privacy laws, *see Privacy Law Fundamentals*.[230] For a detailed commentary and guidance on US Federal and California privacy laws, *see California Privacy Law, Practical Guide and Commentary*, which addresses the scope of applicability, compliance requirements and sanctions for every federal and California state privacy law.[231] For a list and summaries of other states' laws, *see Information Security and Privacy: A Guide to Federal and State Law Compliance*.[232]

013-01073.pdf (accessed 3 Feb. 2020); Hirsch, R. & Deixler, H., Final HIPAA Omnibus Rule Brings Sweeping Changes to the Health Care Privacy Law: HIPAA Privacy and Security Obligations Extended to Business Associates and Subcontractors (BNA Privacy and Security Law Report 12 PVLR 168, 2013).

225. Cal. Civ. Code §§56–59.
226. Cal. Civ. Code §56.11.
227. 16 C.F.R. §§ 312.1–312.13 (implementing 15 U.S.C. §§ 6501 et seq.); For children's Privacy, see Federal Trade Commission, available at: http://www.business.ftc.gov/privacy-and-security/childrens-privacy (accessed 3 Feb. 2020).
228. 18 U.S.C. § 2710.
229. 18 U.S.C. § 2710(b)(2)(B).
230. Solove, D. & Schwartz, P., *Privacy Law Fundamentals*, *supra* n. 184.
231. Determann, *supra* n. 181, Chapter 2.
232. D, A.B., *Information Security and Privacy: A Guide to Federal and State Law and Compliance 2019-2020 ed.* (Thomson Reuters, 2019).

[E] Blockchain and CCPA

Many companies around the world are currently struggling to meet compliance requirements under the CCPA of 2018, a law that is much broader and more restrictive than most other US privacy laws and frequently compared with the GDPR.[233] Unlike the GDPR, the CCPA is not an omnibus privacy law, but one of the hundreds of laws intended to protect individual privacy. Like other US privacy laws, the CCPA is focused on a particular activity that is considered to be harmful to consumer privacy, namely the selling of personal information. But, unlike other US privacy laws, the CCPA comes with an excessively broad scope due to counterintuitive definitions including 'consumer' (defined to mean any California resident), 'personal information' (defined to mean any information that is related to an individual or household) and 'selling' (defined to mean any sharing of information for any valuable information, thus covering most forms of information exchanges and sharing that one would not normally associate with 'selling'). CCPA applies to companies around the world, Business-to-Business and Business-to-Consumer and in all sectors, except to the extent its exemptions apply.

Jerry Brown, the Governor of California, signed the CCPA into law on 28 June 2018.[234] The legislative process was unusually rushed. The California Legislature debated only six days and passed the bill on the condition that a ballot initiative with a similar focus be withdrawn. For more than 100 years, Californians have voted at general elections not only on candidates for public office but regularly also on various constitutional and legislative ballot initiatives. In fact, in 1972, California added a right to privacy to Article 1 section 1 of the California Constitution by way of a ballot initiative. Such initiatives are often sponsored by special interest groups, businesses and wealthy individuals.[235] In 2017, a real estate millionaire had teamed up with a Central Intelligence Agency analyst and a financial services industry professional to propose measure No. 17-0039 regarding the Consumer Right to Privacy Act of 2018 (the Initiative), seemingly wording and organizing the draft bill in a way to appeal to general voters.[236] By June 2018, it was clear that the proponents of the Initiative had gathered more than the required number of signatures and the Governor would have had to certify the Initiative if not withdrawn by 28 June 2018. As a result, Californians would have voted on the Initiative at the general election on 6 November 2018; had the

233. Determann, L. & Gupta, C., *Indian Personal Data Protection Act of 2018: Draft Bill and Its History, Compared to GDPR and California Privacy Law* 37 (Berkeley Journal of International Law 481, 2019).
234. Determann, L., *Broad Data and Business Regulation, Applicable Worldwide* (IAPP Advisor, 02/07/2018); Determann, Lothar, *Datenschutz auf Kalifornisch* (FAZ v. 11/07/2018).
235. Boyd, T.M., *How a Rich Californian Hijacked the Legislature: Threatened with a Ballot Initiative, Lawmakers Pass a Ruinous Data-Privacy Law* (The Wall Street Journal, 04/07/ 2018), available at: www.wsj.com/articles/how-a-rich-californian-hijacked-the-legislature-1530723133 (accessed 3 Feb. 2020).
236. www.caprivacy.org/about (accessed 3 Feb. 2020). Myers, J. & Ulloa, J., *California Lawmakers Agree to New Consumer Privacy Rules That Would Avert Showdown on the November Ballot* (Los Angeles Times, 21/06/2018), available at: www.latimes.com/politics/la-pol-ca-privacy-initiative-legislature-agreement-20180621-story.html (accessed 3 Feb. 2020).

Initiative passed, it could not have been amended, modified or repealed afterwards, except by another ballot initiative or by a 70% majority in the California Legislature, but then only to further the objectives of the Initiative. To prevent the risk of a largely unchangeable law, the California Legislature hashed out compromise legislation with the proponents of the Initiative. After the Legislature passed and the Governor signed the CCPA, the proponents withdrew their Initiative, and the legislative bill became the law. Since its enactment in June 2018, the California Legislature amended the CCPA twice, once in September 2018 and once in October 2019, but without postponing its 1 January 2020 effective date. Since then, the proponents of the 2018 Initiative reported on May 4, 2020 that they have collected more than the required number of signatures to add a new initiative for a California Privacy Rights Act (CPRA) to the 2020 election ballot, which would expand CCPA and create a California Privacy Protection Agency.[237] On June 2, 2020, the California Attorney General submitted final proposed regulations under the CCPA to the California Office of Administrative Law.

[1] Scope of CCPA

Principally, all California residents are protected under the CCPA with respect to any information that relates to them. Californians are not just protected in their roles as consumers, but also as employees, patients, tenants, students, parents, children, etc., because the term 'consumer' is defined to mean any 'natural person who is a California resident'.[238] Unlike other sections of the California Civil Code and most other US privacy laws, Cal. Civ. Code §1798.140(o)(1) defines the term 'personal information' broadly as 'any information that ... relates to ... a particular consumer or household'. Data can be protected even if it does not relate to a single individual (since 'households' are covered) and if it does not contain a name. For example, annual water or energy consumption of a household, a particular employee's job description, an IP address, web browsing history and 'purchasing tendencies' will be regulated as personal information, even if no names are associated. Thus, public and private keys, as well as any information relating to transactions between or involving individuals on a blockchain or sidechain, can qualify as personal information under CCPA.

Excluded from the protection of personal information is '*publicly available information*', but the term is narrowly defined to mean information from government records made publicly available in accordance with the purpose for which the government record was created,[239] which will not apply to most blockchain or DLT

237. Determann, L, *California Privacy Rights Ballot Initiative: Businesses, Watch This Space* (The Recorder 22/05/2020).
238. Cal. Civ. Code §1798.140(g) refers to 'Section 17014 of Title 18 of the California Code of Regulations, as that section read on September 1, 2017, however identified, including by any unique identifier.' According to these regulations, a 'resident' includes (i) every individual who is in the State for other than a temporary or transitory purpose, and (ii) every individual who is domiciled in the State who is outside the State for a temporary or transitory purpose, subject to a number of clarifications and specifications set forth in section 17014 of Title 18 of the California Code of Regulations.
239. Cal. Civ. Code §1798.140(o)(2).

applications. Also excluded is information collected from Californians when they are outside the state, and the related 'commercial conduct takes place wholly outside of California',[240] but whether this set of facts applies will not normally be known to blockchain participants. CCPA also excludes 'aggregate' and 'de-identified' information from the definition of 'personal information'. Aggregate information means statistical information that does not relate to individuals. De-identification standards under CCPA are met only by 'information that cannot reasonably identify, relate to, describe, be capable of being associated with, or be linked, directly or indirectly, to a particular consumer'. By irreversibly encrypting and destroying the personal information related to a public and private key, it may be possible to de-identify information included in a blockchain.

[2] Which Blockchain Participants Must Comply with CCPA?

Businesses around the world have to comply with the CCPA if they receive personal information from California residents and if they exceed one of three thresholds: (1) annual gross revenues of USD 25 million; (2) personal information of 50,000 or more California residents, households, or devices annually; or (3) 50% or more annual revenue from selling California residents' personal information.[241] This applies to sole proprietorships, partnerships, limited liability companies, corporations, associations or other legal entities organized or operated for profit or financial benefit. Parent companies and subsidiaries controlling, or controlled by, a covered business and using the same branding fall into the definition of 'business', even if they themselves do not exceed the applicable thresholds.[242]

Non-profit institutes and individuals who are acting for altruistic reasons may be excluded on the basis that they do not operate for profit. Also, many individuals may not meet the revenue thresholds established by CCPA, for example, individual bitcoin miners, even if they operate serious mining equipment for profit and thus arguably qualify as a 'sole proprietorship'.

Whether the USD 25 million revenue threshold counts only California revenue or global sales is not clear. While Cal. Civ. Code §1714.43(a)(1) defines the scope of the California Transparency in Supply Chains Act expressly in reference to 'annual worldwide gross receipts', the new Cal. Civ. Code §1798.140(c)(1)(A) merely refers to 'annual gross revenues' without an expanding reference to 'worldwide'. Yet, a limiting reference to California is also missing, as for example contained in section 17942(a)(2) of the California Revenue and Taxation Code, which refers to 'total income from all sources derived from or attributable to this state'.

Companies may pass the '50,000 consumers annually' threshold more quickly than one would think because the definition of personal information is so broad. For example, most companies operate websites and inevitably capture IP addresses.

240. Cal. Civ. Code §1798.145(a)(6).
241. Cal. Civ. Code §1798.140(c)(1).
242. Cal. Civ. Code §1798.140(c)(2).

Notably, companies need to comply regardless of whether the website targets businesses or individual customers in California, given that the term 'consumer' is defined to mean any 'resident'. Even individual bloggers and relatively small businesses outside California may find it difficult to ensure that they do not receive personal information of more than 50,000 California resident visitors to their website annually, simply from having it be passively accessible from there. 137 visitors a day will add up to 50,000 in a year. Within California, most retailers, fitness studios, music venues and other businesses will meet this threshold,[243] and many blockchain users may become subject to CCPA on this basis, too.

A company without a physical presence or affiliate in California may be able to avoid complying with the statute, however, if it can ensure that its 'commercial conduct takes place wholly outside of California' for purposes of Cal. Civ. Code §1798.145(a)(6) and that it is not doing 'business in the State of California' for purposes of Cal. Civ. Code §1798.140(c)(1). Most US companies will find it difficult to determine that they are not doing business in the State of California because the term 'doing business' is generally understood very broadly. According to California Revenue and Taxation Code (R&TC) section 23101(a), an out-of-state company is 'doing business in California if it actively engages in any transaction for the purpose of financial or pecuniary gain or profit in California'. Furthermore, according to California Corporations Code sections 191(a), 15901.02(ai) and 17708.03(a), companies outside of California and qualified to do business in California may be subject to the law if they enter 'into repeated and successive transactions' in California, which could occur remotely and online. Blockchain users cannot determine easily – leave alone control – whether other users or participants have nexus to California.

[3] CCPA Compliance Obligations

The harshest CCPA obligations apply to businesses that 'sell personal information'. According to CCPA, 'selling' means any 'selling, renting, releasing, disclosing, disseminating, making available, transferring, or otherwise communicating orally, in writing, or by electronic or other means, a consumer's personal information ... to another business or a third party for monetary or other valuable consideration'.[244] Wherever companies share data in the context of a contractual relationship, they receive some form of consideration. Consideration is a basic condition to valid contract formation under the US law.[245] Regarding relationships where a company pays a service provider to host data, manage payroll, operate a website or perform other services, the parties do not normally view data sharing as 'selling' of information, but rather as making data available for the limited purpose of enabling the service provider to perform the work.

243. Eric Goldman, available at: https://blog.ericgoldman.org/archives/2018/06/a-privacy-bomb-is-about-to-be-dropped-on-the-california-economy-and-the-global-internet.htm (accessed 3 Feb. 2020).
244. Cal. Civ. Code §1798.140(t)(1).
245. Legal Information Institute, available at: www.law.cornell.edu/wex/consideration (accessed 3 Feb. 2020).

Yet, given the counterintuitive definition of 'selling' as any 'transferring for any valuable consideration', the services themselves are part of every bargain and potentially to be considered as 'consideration'. Also, some service providers price their services differently – or offer services free of charge – based on the value of data they process as part of the arrangement. California Civil Code §1798.140(t)(2)(C) contemplates very narrow and qualified exceptions for data sharing with service providers, which could be understood to imply that service provider arrangements are not generally exempt from rules on 'selling'. In light of these facts and the broad definition of 'personal information', companies have to prepare for the possibility that more information sharing activities could potentially be covered by the new law than arrangements that would commonly be characterized as a sale.

As a counter measure, companies can expressly clarify with their business partners in written contracts that certain unintentional or incidental information-sharing (e.g., public keys or optional personal data that a block chain participant added to a block) is not intended to be for consideration. Terms to this effect could be included in smart contracts or blockchain whitepapers, which could clarify, for example, that blockchain or sidechain participants pay for crypto-currency, not for any personal information exchanged as part of transactions.

Also, companies can try to claim one of the complex definitional exceptions in the CCPA, according to which a business is not deemed to sell personal information if:

(1) Consumer's Deliberate Intent:
A consumer uses or directs the business to intentionally disclose personal information or uses the business to intentionally interact with a third party, provided the third party does not also sell the personal information unless that disclosure would be consistent with the provisions of the CCPA. An intentional interaction occurs when the consumer intends to interact with the third party, via one or more deliberate interactions. Hovering over, muting, pausing, or closing a given piece of content does not constitute a consumer's intent to interact with a third party.

(2) Use of Identifiers to Comply with Opt Out Requests:
The business uses or shares an identifier for a consumer who has opted out of the sale of the consumer's personal information for the purposes of alerting third parties that the consumer has opted out of the sale of the consumer's personal information.

(3) Necessary for Business Purposes with Service Provider:
The business uses or shares with a service provider personal information of a consumer that is necessary to perform a business purpose if the following conditions are met: data is necessary for services that the service provider performs on the business' behalf, the service provider also does not sell the personal information, the business has provided notice that information being used or shared in its terms and conditions, and the service provider does not further collect, sell, or use the personal information of the consumer except as necessary to perform the business purpose.

(4) Data Transfers in M&A and Other Transactions:

> The business transfers to a third party the personal information of a consumer as an asset that is part of a merger, acquisition, bankruptcy, or other transaction in which the third party assumes control of all or part of the business and provides that information is used or shared consistently with the CCPA.

Yet, claiming any of these exceptions will require additional efforts and likely revisions to existing contracts, disclosures, internal processes and business practices. Each of the exceptions refers to additional terms that are defined in the statute in counterintuitive and very prescriptive ways.

Many companies will find it difficult to get comfortable that they are not somewhere somehow sharing personal information in a manner that qualifies as 'selling' under the broad and counterintuitive definition in the CCPA. They are obligated to obtain prior opt-in consent from minors under 16 years of age (and parental consent from minors under 13 years) before they share their information in a manner that qualifies as 'selling'.[246] And, companies must provide a clear and conspicuous hyperlink with the words 'Do Not Sell My Personal Information' that direct users to a web page enabling them, or someone they authorize, to opt out of the sale of the resident's personal information.[247] If a California resident opts out, the company must not approach the person with a request to consider opting in again before at least twelve months have passed since the opt-out.[248]

An opt-out could pose difficulties in a blockchain context, as the personal information in existing blocks would normally be transferred to additional users. Therefore, blockchain operators should ensure that blockchains are not used to sell personal information and clarify (smart-) contractually that any consideration paid is for services or items other than personal information. Where this is not practical, operators on blockchains should consider data deletion techniques or de-identification measures as also proposed for erasure requests.[249]

Companies must update their privacy policies with the newly required information, whether or not they engage in 'selling of personal information', and include a description of California residents' new data subject rights, including access, erasure and portability[250] as well as channels to exercise such rights, including, at a minimum, a toll-free telephone number.[251]

If a California resident exercises any of the new rights, including access, erasure of information, portability or prohibitions on data 'selling', companies must not discriminate against such resident by denying goods or services, charging different

246. Cal. Civ. Code §1798.120(d). Companies can try to obtain parental consent by providing a consent form to be signed by the parent and returned via US mail, fax, or electronic scan, available at: www.ftc.gov/tips-advice/business-center/guidance/complying-coppa-frequently-asked-questions#Verifiable%20Parental (accessed 3 Feb. 2020).
247. Cal. Civ. Code §1798.135(a)(1).
248. Cal. Civ. Code §1798.135(a)(5).
249. Section §5.06[D][2], *supra*.
250. Cal. Civ. Code §1798.135(a)(2).
251. Cal. Civ. Code §1798.130(a).

prices, providing a different level or quality of goods or services, or otherwise.[252] Companies may apply a different price, rate or quality only if that difference is reasonably related to the value of the consumer's data.[253]

Many companies that have been offering online services free of charge and relied for funding on data monetization may now have to introduce user fees, given that consumers are free to opt out of data sharing or request erasure of information and companies cannot penalize consumers for the exercise of their rights. Companies will also have to consider alternative business models and web/mobile presences, including California-only sites and offerings.[254]

[4] Data Access and Deletion Rights

As noted with respect to GDPR, data access and deletion rights can pose particular challenges with respect to blockchain and distributed ledger technologies.[255]

If a California resident demands access to data held by a business that is subject to the CCPA, then such business would have to provide information about the personal information it holds, including data in a blockchain or distributed ledger, and make a copy available. If part of the data is encrypted and the business is unable to decrypt the data, then it may have to make the encrypted information available or refer the data subject to publicly accessible copies of the data. Data access requests may result in additional costs and burdens on resources, but do not ultimately have to be prohibitive in most situations.

With respect to deletion rights, CCPA offers several exceptions that should shield blockchain participants from insurmountable obstacles. 'A business or a service provider shall not be required to comply with a consumer's request to delete the consumer's personal information if it is necessary for the business or service provider to maintain the consumer's personal information in order to: (1) Complete the transaction for which the personal information was collected … . provide a good or service requested by the consumer, or reasonably anticipated within the context of a business' ongoing business relationship with the consumer, or otherwise perform a contract between the business and the consumer. (2) Detect security incidents, protect against malicious, deceptive, fraudulent, or illegal activity; or prosecute those responsible for that activity. (3) Debug to identify and repair errors that impair existing intended functionality. (4) Exercise free speech, ensure the right of another consumer to exercise that consumer's right of free speech, or exercise another right provided for by law. (…) (6) Engage in public or peer-reviewed scientific, historical, or statistical research in the public interest that adheres to all other applicable ethics and privacy laws, when the business' deletion of the information is likely to render impossible or seriously impair the achievement of such research, if the consumer has provided informed consent. (7) To enable solely internal uses that are reasonably aligned with

252. Cal. Civ. Code §1798.125. (a)(1).
253. Cal. Civ. Code §1798.125. (a)(2).
254. Cal. Civ. Code §1798.135(b).
255. *See* this book, section §5.06[D], *supra*.

the expectations of the consumer based on the consumer's relationship with the business. (8) Comply with a legal obligation. (9) Otherwise use the consumer's personal information, internally, in a lawful manner that is compatible with the context in which the consumer provided the information.'[256]

This last-mentioned exception under #9 (other internal use), should be sufficient to permit companies to continue using personal information in blockchains in company-internal applications. For public blockchains, exceptions #1 (complete transaction) and #8 (legal obligation) could serve as justifications to continue using personal information after a deletion request where the contractual commitments and transactions underlying the blockchain arrangement require continued use of the information.

[5] Sanctions and Remedies

According to the new Cal. Civ. Code §1798.155, companies can be ordered in a civil action brought by the California Attorney General to pay penalties of up to USD 7,500 per intentional violation of any provision of the CCPA, or, for unintentional violations, if the company fails to cure the unintentional violation within thirty days of notice, USD 2,500 per violation under section 17206 of the California Business and Professions Code. Such penalties collected by the State of California shall be allocated to a new 'Consumer Privacy Fund' to fund and encourage enforcement.

According to a somewhat separate section within the new CCPA,[257] companies that become victims of data theft or other data security breaches can be ordered in civil class action lawsuits to pay statutory damages between USD 100–USD 750 per California resident and incident, or actual damages, whichever is greater, and any other relief a court deems proper, subject to an option of the California Attorney General to prosecute the company instead of allowing civil suits to be brought against it.

With respect to statutory damages for data security breaches only, the new Cal. Civ. Code §1798.150(a) refers to the definition of 'personal information' in the existing Cal. Civ. Code §1798.81.5(d)(1)(A), which covers: 'An individual's first name or first initial and his or her last name in combination with any one or more of the following data elements, when either the name or the data elements are not encrypted or redacted:

- Social security number.
- Driver's license number or California identification card number.
- Account number, credit or debit card number, in combination with any required security code, access code, or password that would permit access to an individual's financial account.
- Medical information.
- Health insurance information'.

256. Cal. Civ. Code §1798.105(d).
257. Cal. Civ. Code §1798.150.

This definition of 'personal information' is much narrower than the broad new definition that applies to the remainder of the CCPA (which covers any information relating to a California resident or household), and it is also narrower than the definition of 'personal information' in the existing California data security breach notification laws, which list similar information plus 'information ... collected through ... an automated license plate recognition system'.[258]

'Encrypted 'means rendered unusable, unreadable, or indecipherable to an unauthorized person through a security technology or methodology generally accepted in the field of information security.[259] Courts may also refer to this definition to determine the meaning of 'unencrypted and unredacted' in the new law.

But the new law does not extend to two situations covered under the existing breach notification laws, namely where individuals are protected with respect to encrypted information if the security of the encryption has been compromised,[260] and where a user name or email address, if used in combination with a password or security question and answer, would permit access to an online account.[261] Moreover, the new law does not refer to the existing definition of a data security breach, but creates a new concept by referring to 'unauthorized access and exfiltration, theft, or disclosure'.[262]

Companies around the world are already required to notify California residents of data security breaches under California's existing breach notification law, which California enacted in 2002 and has updated several times since then.[263] But the potential liability resulting from breaches was somewhat contained by the fact that the original 2002 version of the California breach notification law only prescribed notification obligations; there were no penalties or other remedies for the actual breach – only for failures to notify.

Based on existing law, plaintiffs are able to refer to various general causes of action, including torts, consumer protection and unfair competition laws, but often find it difficult to show 'an invasion of a legally protected interest' that is 'concrete and particularized' and 'actual or imminent, not conjectural or hypothetical', as required for standing under federal law according to *Spokeo, Inc. v. Robins*.[264] Particularly in the context of class action lawsuits, plaintiffs' lawyers prefer to assert general harms potentially associated with security breaches as opposed to concrete, individual injuries, which could prevent class action certification.[265]

Since 1 January 2016, operators and users of automated license plate recognition (ALPR) systems were subjected to specific data security requirements and notification obligations in case of a data security breach under Cal. Civ. Code §§1798.90.5, 1798.29 and 1798.82; individuals harmed by a violation of the California ALPR law were also

258. Cal. Civ. Code §1798.82(h); Cal. Civ. Code §1798.29(g).
259. Cal. Civ. Code §1798.82(i)(4) and Cal. Civ. Code §1798.29(h)(4).
260. Cal. Civ. Code § 1798.82(a).
261. Cal. Civ. Code § 1798.82(h)(2).
262. Cal. Civ. Code §1798.150(a)(1).
263. Determann, L., *New California Data Security and Breach Notification Requirements* (Bloomberg BNA Privacy & Security Law Report, 15 PVLR 219, 2 Jan. 2016).
264. 136 S. Ct. 1540 (2016).
265. Determann, *supra* n. 181, at Chapter 2-15:1 and 6-2:2.

entitled to bring a civil action against persons who knowingly caused the harm – including harm by data security breaches – and claim actual damages, liquidated damages in the amount of USD 2,500, punitive damages (upon proof of wilful or reckless disregard of the law), reasonable attorney's fees and other litigation costs, and preliminary and equitable relief.[266]

Now, based on the new cause of action in Cal. Civ. Code §1798.150 for statutory damages, plaintiffs generally do not have to show concrete, individual harm associated with certain data security breaches captured by the new statute, at least not in California courts, where no particular standing requirements apply. Therefore, companies have to prepare themselves for significantly increased liability exposure in cases of data security breaches. For example, if a hospital falls victim to a cyberattack or plain old burglary and theft of an appointment calendar with 10,000 patient names for doctor visits (without any sensitive medical history), the hospital could be exposed to damages claims between USD 1 million and USD 7.5 million plus the cost of litigation, even if not one patient suffers any concrete harm of any kind.

FURTHER READING

Dan Solove and Paul Schwartz, *Information Privacy Law* (Aspen Publishing Co., 6th ed., 2018).

Dan Solove and Paul Schwartz, *Privacy Law Fundamentals* (IAPP, 2019).

Primavera De Filippi and Aaron Wright, *Blockchain and the Law, the Rule of Code* (2019).

Lothar Determann, *Determann's Field Guide to Data Privacy Law: International Corporate Compliance* (Edward Elgar Publishing Ltd., 4th ed., 2020).

Lothar Determann, *California Privacy Law, Practical Guide and Commentary* (IAPP, 3rd ed., 2018).

Ibáñez, L-D., O'Hara, K. and Simperl, E., *On Blockchains and the General Data Protection Regulation*, available at: https://eprints.soton.ac.uk/422879/1/BLockchains_GDPR_4.pdf.

NIST, *Blockchain Technology Overview* (NISTIR 8202, 2018).

Andrew B. Serwin, *Information Security and Privacy: A Guide to Federal and State Law and Compliance* (2019-2020 ed.).

Timmons, J. & Hickman, T., *Blockchain and the GDPR: Co-existing in Contradiction* (Blockchain & Cryptocurrency Regulation, Global Legal Insights, 2nd ed., 2020).

266. *Ibid.*, at Chapter 2-5:5, 2-15.1.54 and 2-19:6.9.

CHAPTER 6
Capital Markets

Michael Juenemann

§6.01 CAPITAL MARKETS AND BLOCKCHAIN

Michael Juenemann

[A] What Makes a Token a Security?

Issuing coins or token(s)[1] by using blockchain or distributed ledger technology (DLT) is achieved through linking rights and value to data packages similar to signing a (share bond or other) certificate. The process of an Initial Coin Offering (ICO), Initial Token Sale (ITS) or Security Token Offering (STO) or any other participation in an offer, sale, or distribution of a digital value (so-called *crypto assets*) is both technically and legally challenging. The global discussion around Tokens that emerged since 2018 generally distinguishes three types of Tokens: Utility Tokens, Currency Tokens and Security Tokens. A Token can carry various rights and obligations, even accumulate characteristics of more than one of those categories, eventually becoming a 'hybrid' Token. As different types of Tokens carry different rights and obligations, they also fall under different areas of law. The regulation of Tokens depends largely on the answer to the key legal question of whether the Token as a digital asset is a 'security' under applicable national laws.[2] One consequence of a Token being classified as a security

1. Hereinafter: 'Token(s)'.
2. Blockchain Bundesverband, *Statement on Token Regulation with a focus on token sales*, https://bundesblock.de/wp-content/uploads/2019/01/180209_Statement-Token-Regulation_blockchain-bundesverband.pdf (accessed 11 March 2020); US Securities and Exchange Commission, *Framework for 'Investment Contract' Analysis of Digital Assets*, https://www.sec.gov/corpfin/framework-investment-contract-analysis-digital-assets (accessed 11 March 2020).

can necessitate issuing a prospectus to be approved by the competent supervisory authority. Essential for the classification of a Token as a security is its nature.

Utility Token is a kind of digital voucher which can be redeemed against a promised service of the issuer. They do not grant membership rights or a similar financial relationship and do not substantiate monetary claims.[3] Utility Tokens are only accepted by the issuer but not by third parties, and only the issuer can carry out the promised service. This specified exchange value of Utility Tokens typically disqualifies them as e-money.[4] Utility Tokens can be exempted from capital market regulation in some jurisdictions. It is true that for some - or perhaps for most purchasers - Utility Tokens have an investment component as purchasers hope to profitably trade them on the secondary market.[5] Mere labelling of a Token as 'Utility Token' does not result in a corresponding qualification. At the same time a Token is not turned into a security by a profit expectation of the purchaser alone. It is important to keep in mind that some regulators seem to take this view contrary to the fact that the purchaser's expectation is beyond the issuer's control. The negotiability of Utility Tokens on the capital market is also not sufficiently given. But even if Utility Tokens remain outside of classical banking and capital markets regulation, this does not mean that they are subject to no regulation at all. In this respect, an issuer should be cautious when emphasizing the utility characteristics of the proposed Token and claiming that it is not a security and therefore 'unregulated'. Depending on the applicable law, Utility Tokens can be subject to (national) contractual, consumer protection, trade and tax laws.

Currency Tokens (e.g., Ether) seek to be (ideally) universally accepted and come with a money-replacement character.[6] Functioning as a unit of account, they may or may not be backed by reserve, thus may or may not fluctuate in their nominal value against one or more fiat currencies (the so-called stable coins do not fluctuate). Depending on the applicable law, Currency Tokens could be considered money, things, copyrighted software, a personal intellectual creation, or other rights. Therefore, Currency Tokens are typically subject to civil law. With regard to financial regulations, Currency Tokens could, for example, be classified as financial instruments, e-money, capital investments, units in an investment fund, securities or some other instrument regulated under national law.

By issuing Security Tokens, the issuer promises some sort of return. Depending on the design, Security Tokens can constitute securities. The question of what makes a Token a security is naturally linked to the definition of a security under the applicable national law. This means different standards apply in the European Union than, for example, in the United States (US) or Singapore.

3. Paul P. Momtaz, Kathrin Rennertseder & Henning Schröder, *Token Offerings: A Revolution in Corporate Finance?* 49 The Capco Institute Journal of Financial Transformation, 32, 37 (2019).
4. Michael Juenemann & Johannes Wirtz, *ICO: Legal Classification of Tokens: Part 4 – Utility Token*, https://www.twobirds.com/en/news/articles/2019/global/ico-legal-classification-of-tokens-utility-token (accessed 11 March 2020).
5. Juenemann & Wirtz, *supra* n. 4 (accessed 11 March 2020).
6. Michael Juenemann & Johannes Wirtz, *ICO: Legal Classification of Tokens: part 3 – Currency Token*, https://www.twobirds.com/en/news/articles/2019/global/ico-legal-classification-of-tokens-3 (accessed 11 March 2020).

In contrast to Utility Tokens, Tokens regarded as securities are subject to capital markets law in all major economies. Capital markets law is typically intended to mitigate the structural and systemic weaknesses of the capital markets. Capital markets are not only characterized by diverging interests between the various market participants (issuers, investors, shareholders, capital seekers and management) but also a strong potential for information asymmetry between them, in particular investors and issuers. At times, abusive behaviour is tempting for certain participants, considering the monopoly position of the stock exchange. Capital markets law therefore aims to ensure the proper functioning of the markets and protect investors. Investor protection means both the protection of the individual investor, which is basically a special form of consumer protection, and the protection of the institutional investor. The latter aims at the protection of the investor community as a whole, i.e., the functioning of the capital market. These principles apply equally on a national, European and global level.

The European concept of securities refers to their fungibility which is consequentially the central principle used to compare Tokens to other well-established securities. In order to satisfy the concept of a security, a Token must be standardized, negotiable and transferable in (capital) markets. European law does not have a 'catch-all' definition of securities, such as US American law that has in the form of 'investment contracts'.[7] The securities concept of European law originates from Markets in Financial Instruments Directive II (MiFID II), which aims to counter the weaknesses of the European financial markets that were revealed during the financial crisis. The European Securities and Markets Authority (ESMA) has already clarified that Tokens can be securities within the meaning of the Prospectus Directive. This also applies to the Prospectus Regulation which has (gradually) replaced the Prospectus Directive. Securities are those 'classes of securities which are negotiable on the capital market',[8] with the exception of 'instruments of payment'[9] and, for prospectus law, 'money market instruments ... having a maturity of less than 12 months'.[10]

Alongside with Europe, the US is the other most vibrant region for Token offerings.[11] According to the US Securities and Exchange Commission (SEC), 'depending on the nature of the digital asset, including what rights it purports to convey and how it is offered and sold, it may fall within the definition of a security under the US federal securities laws'.[12] The term 'security' includes an 'investment contract', as well as 'other instruments such as stocks, bonds, and transferable shares'.[13] The US Supreme Court decided in *SEC v. W. J. Howey Co.* (328 U.S. 293 (1946) – also known

7. US Securities and Exchange Commission, *supra* n. 2 (accessed 11 March 2020).
8. Article 4(1) no. 44 directive 2014/65/EU, (2014).
9. *Ibid.*
10. Article 2. a) Regulation EU 2017/1129 (2017).
11. Philipp Maume & Mathias Fromberger, *Regulation of Initial Coin Offerings: Reconciling U.S. and E.U. Securities Laws*, 19(2) Chicago Journal of International Law, 548, 548 (2019).
12. Bill Hinman, *Statement on 'Framework for "Investment Contract" Analysis of Digital Assets'*, https://www.sec.gov/news/public-statement/statement-framework-investment-contract-analysis-digital-assets (accessed 11 March 2020).
13. US Securities and Exchange Commission, *supra* n. 2.

as the 'Howey Case') that an 'investment contract' exists where there is found 'the investment of money in a common enterprise with a reasonable expectation of profits to be derived from the efforts of others'.[14] Both the SEC and the US federal courts use the so-called investment contract analysis to determine whether a Token is a security subject to US federal securities laws.[15]

However, many questions with regard to the regulation of Tokens are still unanswered. Time will tell whether there will be a regulatory patchwork or a similar framework under US law, European law, the national laws of the Member States of the European Union and the other jurisdictions with large capital markets. The following country reports will answer the question 'What makes a Token a security?' for many individual jurisdictions.

[B] Blockchain Finality

The technical structure of a Token is flexible similar to the rights related to it. A general assumption is that any transfer of a Token is irreversible, thus technologically final.[16] The decentralized design is believed to be completely tamper-proof.[17] These 'facts' suggest a finality which can also be found in securities trading. However, analysing the historical developments of DLTs reveals many cases that negate such finality.[18] And so far, finality has always been a legal fiction designed to promote the frictionless functioning of capital markets.

In case of a 'hard fork',[19] the 'original' chain and the new chain become incompatible. When the underlying right is a security which exists as an individual entity and is, thus, traded and negotiated, the law needs to address what happens in the case of two strings of the chain operating the exact same security. Furthermore, '51% attacks'[20] cause all following transactions to rely on falsified information that is subsequently verified as the leading block.[21] However unlikely these events may or may not be, they do exist.[22] In the event of technical malfunction, the question arises

14. *Ibid.*
15. Hinman, *supra* n. 12 (accessed 11 March 2020).
16. A Report by UK Government Chief Scientist Adviser: *Distributed Ledger Technology, beyond blockchain* https://assets.publishing.service.gov.uk/government/uploads/system/uploads/attachment_data/file/492972/gs-16-1-distributed-ledger-technology.pdf (accessed 11 March 2020).
17. Marcella Atzori, *Blockchain Technology and Decentralized Governance: Is the State Still Necessary?*, https://papers.ssrn.com/sol3/papers.cfm?abstract_id=2709713 (accessed 11 March 2020). *See* Chapter 1, §1.06 [A], *supra*.
18. Vitalik Buterin, *On Settlement Finality*, https://blog.ethereum.org/2016/05/09/on-settlement-finality (accessed 11 March 2020).
19. Crypto forks, *What are forks in cryptocurrency? Risks, Opportunities and Calendar for all 2018 forks*, https://www.fxstreet.com/cryptocurrencies/resources/what-are-cryptocurrency-forks (accessed 11 March 2020).
20. *See* Chapter 1, §1.08 [G], *supra*.
21. Sarwar Sayeed & Hector Marco-Gisbert, *Assessing Blockchain Consensus and Security Mechanisms Against the 51% Attack*, https://doi.org/10.3390/app9091788 (accessed 11 March 2020).
22. *See* Chapter 1, §1.08 [G], *supra*.

whether legal finality needs to be addressed by the applicable law or should influence the classification of a Token as a security.

There is no general rule that transactions have to be legally final. For example, in the event of multiple assignments in a chronologically extended sequence to different assignees (assignment chain), each of the assignees successively acquires the sole legal title to the claim. However, if one of the assignments is void, the following assignments are void as well. Since the title to the claim is not linked to any external evidence, e.g., possession or entry in a public register, typically the assignee cannot rely on a bona fide acquisition rule or concept under applicable law.

Legal finality produces legal certainty as required for the frictionless functioning of trading on capital markets. The legal certainty of bookings and transactions is a particular prerequisite for the success of DLT systems in Europe.[23] Most countries have principles to establish legal finality. One of them is the aforementioned bona fide acquisition rule originating from Roman law.[24] The bona fide acquisition rule protects good faith purchasers who acquire property without notice of misconduct, representing a compromise between the interests of transaction efficiency and the protection of ownership.[25] Bona fide purchasers acquire title to the property free from the risk that the property may be claimed by the 'rightful' owner resulting in the loss of ownership or title for the 'rightful' owner.[26] Therefore, the 'rightful' owner's remedy is limited to actions against the 'thief'[27] or otherwise unauthorized person that sold the property to the good faith acquirer. The bona fide acquisition rule is based on the concept that possession is strong evidence of ownership.

It is argued that the possibility of bona fide acquisition is the only way to ensure orderly processing and trading on the financial market. MiFID II lays down the conditions of fungibility and tradability on the financial market but does not state a requirement for bona fide rights protection.[28] In respect of trading on the financial markets, an elaborate chain of title due diligence is not possible. Unlimited negotiability on the market requires that transactions can be processed securely and easily and that there can be no objections from third parties. Therefore, the classic understanding of capital market negotiability is based on the possibility of bona fide acquisition.

However, in transactions involving the purchase of Tokens, there is more than one possible approach to establish legal finality. One approach is to treat all transactions recorded on the blockchain as valid. This is on the basis that blockchains permanently record all transactions and therefore allow users to trace transactions. In this way, blockchain technology could provide a substitute for a bona fide purchase. The cryptographic rendition of the chain of ownership allows for each transaction to be

23. Statement of the FinTech Council concerning the blockchain strategy of the German government in the context of public consultations, https://www.bundesfinanzministerium.de/Content/EN/Standardartikel/Topics/Financial_markets/Articles/2019-04-15-two-years-fintech-council.html (accessed 11 March 2020).
24. Andrew Balthazor, *The Bona Fide Acquisition Rule Applied to Cryptocurrency*, no. 3 Georgetown Law Technology Review 402, 408 (2019).
25. Balthazor, *supra* n. 24, at, 408, 409 (2019).
26. *Ibid.*, at 405, 409 (2019).
27. *Ibid.*, at 409 (2019).
28. Hagen Weiß, *Tokenisation*, https://www.bafin.de/dok/12477346 (accessed 11 March 2020).

transparent in a way that the ownership of the underlying right is inseparably linked to the Token. This could provide sufficient protection against ineffective Token transfers for capital market trading. Accordingly, the data written on the blockchain would be considered similar to a public register thus subject to public credence. However, difficulties are encountered in cases such as a 'fork', where two strings of the blockchain operating with the exact same underlying right would exist. If this scenario arose in a title-transfer transaction, it would be impossible to determine the true holder of the title. Other problems arise with Token theft, where the unauthorized use of access data may result in dispositions by non-entitled individuals, or in a case where the transfer agreement for the Token may be void due to incapacity to contract, e.g., because of a pathological mental disturbance.[29]

Furthermore, if a private key is not kept confidential, an unauthorized person can use the key for further disposure of a Token.[30] Whereas a certificate can only ever be in the possession of one person, data can be copied without an original being detectable. The Token would have to be retransferred[31] as the right on which it is based, and its valid transfer must be considered. It could also not be argued that a purchase process could not be reversed due to anonymity and that this resulted in functional equivalence with a bona fide purchase. It would be very much against well-established legal principles to accept a Token transaction, which is based, for example, on a computer crime, as final because of factual difficulties.

The use of permissioned blockchains could solve most of these problems. Although blockchains differ greatly in their technical and governance set-up,[32] common references to 'blockchain' usually mean public and permissionless blockchains. 'Public' means that the reading of blockchain data and the submission of transactions are not restricted, whereas 'permissionless' means that all users are eligible transaction processors.[33] Therefore, such blockchains are – leaving aside the technical and economic restrictions around mining and software governance – characterized by the fact that anyone, who downloads the open source software, can join the ledger, read the chain, make legitimate changes or download the ledger without a permission by the gatekeeper.[34] A well-known example of a public and permissionless blockchain is the Ethereum Blockchain.

However, there are also private and permissioned blockchains where access and performance of transaction processing require permission by the single party or consortium acting as a gatekeeper.[35] Under this model, only previously selected

29. Paul Varul, Anu Avi & Triin Kivisild, *Restrictions on Active Legal Capacity*, Juridica International IX, 99,106, https://www.juridicainternational.eu/public/pdf/ji_2004_1_99.pdf (accessed 11 March 2020).
30. Michael Juenemann & Johannes Wirtz, *ICO: Legal Classification of Tokens: part 2 – security token*, https://www.twobirds.com/en/news/articles/2019/global/ico-legal-classification-of-tokens-2 (accessed 11 March 2020).
31. Juenemann & Wirtz *supra* n. 30 (accessed 11 March 2020).
32. Michèle Finck & Valentina Moscon, *Copyright Law on Blockchains: Between New Forms of Rights Administration and Digital Rights Management 2.0*, ILC 50, 77, 90 (2019).
33. *See* Chapter 1, §1.14 [A] and [B], *supra*.
34. Finck & Moscon *supra* n. 32 at, 77, 90.
35. *Ibid*; Michèle Finck, *Blockchain Regulation and Governance in Europe* 15-15 (2018).

participants (nodes) are authorized to access the blockchain. Examples of this are R3 Corda and Hyperledger Fabric. Permissioned blockchains are particularly preferred by investors in order to mitigate the risk of public and permissionless blockchains. That, in particular, makes them suitable for a Security Token. The risk of tampering with permissioned blockchains is expected to be much lower than with public and permissionless blockchains due to the restrictions on access and transaction processing. A licensed state actor could additionally be appointed as gatekeeper. The competent national supervisory authority could, together with a national institute, regularly review the technology used to mitigate the risks related to general information technology (IT) security, tampering and malfunctioning software. Were such a system to be put in place, legal finality could be established by the confidence that all records on the private and permissioned blockchain are valid.

Whether the bona fide acquisition rule can be applied to blockchain transactions and other means of establishing legal finality will be addressed in the country reports. However, the bona fide purchase of Tokens does not depend on the blockchain technology itself but on the underlying right. For example, if this right (an interest claim or profit sharing) is transferred by assignment or by the assumption of contract, a bona fide purchase may be excluded (depending on applicable laws).[36]

If a bona fide purchase is not possible and no substitutes exist (due to determination), the legal consequence is obvious: if the Token has been transferred by a person who is not entitled to the underlying right, the actual holder of the claim can also demand 'reversal'; i.e., the underlying right has never been validly transferred, but the data packages must be returned by anyone who controls such data. There may be factual difficulties to enforce such claims, but that does not question its existence as long as the applicable law does not stipulate finality.

[C] Special Requirements for Prospectuses

The issuance of securities is typically subject to the requirements of prospectus regulations. When issuing a Security Token, this is no exception. Any public offering of securities requires the prior publication of a prospectus unless the public offering falls under exemptions of the applicable regulation. Both the product and the issuer must meet the regulatory standards of the respective jurisdiction where the Token is being offered. Generally speaking, the prospectus has to contain all the information necessary to enable the investor to make an appropriate assessment of the securities offered and of their issuer. If an investor lacks the relevant information, their financial interests are at risk as they are incapable of making an informed decision. Which information needs to be included in a prospectus for Tokens and blockchain technology? There is currently no definitive answer to this question. In general, the prospectus should point out the essential risks resulting from the nature of blockchain technology and Tokens since without knowing these specific risks, the investor will be unable to make an informed decision. For example, the prospectus requires special attention to risks

36. Juenemann & Wirtz *supra* n. 30.

associated with the technical design of the Token, the finality of transactions on the blockchain or any incompatible wallet.

Since the blockchain on which Tokens are issued can change, the issuer will generally not take any responsibility for the finality of the transfer of Tokens.[37] In particular, blocks may be reset by 'hard forks', which can create considerable risks for the investors. There is also the risk of hacking attacks on the blockchain (e.g., mining attacks) or the smart contracts. After all, smart contracts and other applications used in an STO are, like any other code, prone to errors and malfunctioning software may cause security gaps. As a result, the risk of hacking attacks leading to unauthorized transactions or 'forks' increases. In case of a 'fork', Tokens would be available on both forks of a chain. In this case, all nodes have to either upgrade the software if they want to use the new Token, maintain the existing protocol to run the old Token, or run two separate versions of the software.[38]

The risk of malfunction may lead to a Token being allocated late or falsely in connection with the investments which has been made.[39] A further risk is that not only the issuer of the Token but also the operator in the form of a crypto-exchange can be attacked. The issuer has no control over this event and is dependent on the security procedure of the crypto-exchange operator.[40] Technical hazards like, for example, DDoS attacks may decelerate the STO or pause it.[41]

While the risk of software malfunction is a risk that is not blockchain specific, it is particularly high due to the requirements of blockchain technology, where an issuer may be dependent on key personnel such as programming experts for smart contracts. The loss of key personnel can have a material adverse effect on the issuer's business and the technological function of its business concept.

Risks may also arise in connection with amendments to the protocol and technical advancements. If the issuer uses smart contracts based on a protocol (like the Ethereum Protocol) that plans to change from a proof of work to a proof-of-stake algorithm, Tokens could be lost or stolen.[42] Any change of the technology underlying or related to the smart contracts or applications used for the STO may adversely affect the value of the Tokens. Therefore, the investors could lose all or part of their investment. Their liability is limited to the value of their investment.[43] Tokens could also be lost due to the aforementioned technical advances, such as the development of quantum computing.

Moreover, there is a risk that the code does not represent the conditions specified in the prospectus. The code itself is not accessible to the investor, and even if it was, very few investors are sophisticated enough to determine whether the code of the smart

37. Prospectus for the issue/public offer of up to 190,000,000 Crowdlitokens ISIN LI0432942626 https://crowdlitoken.com/wp-content/uploads/doc/prspct/CRT-Prospectus_EN_digital.pdf (accessed 11 March 2020).
38. *See* Chapter 1, §1.09, *supra*.
39. Crowdlitokens *supra* n. 37.
40. *Ibid.*
41. *Ibid.*
42. *Ibid.*
43. *Ibid.*

contract reflects the conditions set out in the white paper.[44] The investor has to rely on a portal to read the code, and it is still unclear how the investor can have the capacity to evaluate the coded rights and obligations. One option is the mandatory verification of the code by a trustworthy third party and the requirement for the prospectus to clearly display such verification.[45]

Tokens are digital, meaning that they do not need physical storage. However, the private key that gives the owner access to the Tokens needs to be stored securely. If an investor loses or forgets the private key, access to the Tokens or carrying out any transactions via the blockchain becomes impossible. The same may be the case due to a malfunctioning or incompatibility of a digital wallet. Tokens also become inaccessible if the Token holder dies without giving his successor access to the private key. 'Lost' Tokens are paused indefinitely.[46] Token thieves may acquire private keys not only by malware and hacking but also by social engineering or coercion because private keys can be stored digitally online, offline or even be encoded in devices or simply written down on paper.[47]

In this context, it is important to ask who is responsible for the prospectus. Both the IT specialists who wrote the code and the initiators of the respective Token project could be regarded as 'issuers'. However, the contribution of the IT specialists does not go beyond coding. Therefore, only the initiators of the Token project should qualify as 'issuers' under applicable law. Furthermore, in many jurisdictions, the prospectus has to be approved by the appropriate authority which has not always proved to be a swift process in all jurisdictions.

[D] Regulatory Specifics for Organized Trade

The usual path a security takes from the issuer to the investor is by way of an intermediary. This intermediary is a regulated financial service provider, usually a bourse, a multilateral trading facility (MTF), a broker, etc. Such intermediary is often the subject of regulatory requirements to ensure investor protection. These may include licenses, specific limitations on targeted investor groups or reporting to the national financial supervisory authority. A blockchain-based Security Token offers the issuer the chance of direct access to investors through the issued Token (if it is not an anonymous product). This may economically be very attractive to the issuer because the regulated intermediary is forced out of the process. Notwithstanding regulation designed to target the product and the issuer, the regulatory requirements targeting the intermediary could, in this course, either be passed on to the issuer, the wallet provider or become inapplicable. This is particularly true if former clients of financial service providers become direct market participants or contractual counterparties, rendering obsolete the financial service previously provided by intermediaries. Going forward,

44. Gerald Spindler, *Initial Coin Offerings und Prospektpflicht und -haftung*, WM 2109, 2110 (2018).
45. Spindler, *supra* n. 44 at 2115 (2018).
46. Crowdlitokens *supra* n. 37.
47. Max I. Raskin, *Realm of the Coin: Bitcoin and Civil Procedure,* 20(4) Fordham Journal of Corporate and Financial Law 969, 977, 989 (2015); Balthazor, *supra* n. 24, at 407 (2019).

national regulation might shift to targeting the investor or the issuer who would need to meet certain requirements before entering the crypto market.

Whether the trading of a Token is regulated or not depends on the criteria set out in the respective legal system or supervisory authority. While regulation usually applies to the trade of securities-like Tokens, this may not be the case for Utility Tokens: the (organized) trade of any Token is not necessarily subject to regulation. Considering the character of (pure) Utility Tokens as digital vouchers and Currency Tokens, capital markets regulation may not apply. If the assessment of the Token shows it is a financial instrument, regulation will be the usual approach.

Accessing clients directly through the product may ultimately render certain regulations designed for organized trade obsolete. Notwithstanding the regulation of the issuer or the product itself, regulation of the Token placement could be inapplicable. The basic idea derives from the so-called issuer's privilege. This privilege, possibly varying in each jurisdiction, exempts an issuer from further licence requirements and regulation when placing its own securities products on the market. A broker or other intermediaries usually require an individual licence as they operate with several different securities products and function as the point of contact for the investors requiring protection. Theoretically, an issuer organizing the trade of its own blockchain-based Tokens and acting as its own intermediary could enjoy issuer's privilege and be exempt from licensing requirements.

Another new phenomenon comes into play if the infrastructure to facilitate the organization of the trade is provided through a decentralized exchange (DEX) (examples for more of less-DEXs are: IDEX, Etherdelta, Newdex, OpenLedger or CryptoBridge). Any ideal DEX is a trading platform without a single point of failure that is characterized by peer-to-peer interactions. There is no authentication process to be carried out in order to buy and sell on the DEX. The DEX neither acts as a trustee nor stores information about the users, but it is a protocol run by each user individually. Buyers and sellers interact directly on the platform. The exchange is therefore 'decentralized', meaning that the funds remain with the exchanging parties at all times. This is a central feature of a DEX. If the Token is stored by the platform, it is no longer a DEX. In this case, there is a central point of attack (honey pot). Certain regulations could be linked to such storage. DEXs like Bitsquare achieve decentralization through the use of 'The Onion Router Network' (TOR). The exchanging parties are the only ones being able to access each other's information because the communication is end-to-end encrypted. As a result of the decentralized structure, a DEX offers hardly any room for attacks. Unlike centralized exchanges (CEX) that have difficulty adequately defending themselves against hacker attacks, particularly as they grow, DEX are unattractive targets as buyers and sellers hold their own money.

The DEX itself could be subject to regulation. However, this would require justification as to why the DEX is acting not simply as an infrastructure but as a new type of intermediary. Whether regulation is being triggered is linked to the presence of a central element as a touchstone of regulation. The degree of (de-)centralization of the exchange depends in particular on the following factors: custody of Tokens or fiat, the way of settlement, the (non-)existence of an order book, the price negotiation and the trading partner. For example, if an order book is available on the platform, there is a central element. Furthermore, if the execution of the transaction by fulfilling the payment obligations and transaction duties is up to the platform, a central intermediary is required to facilitate the transaction. The latter will then also be responsible. This is the touchstone for regulation.

The same is true in cases of on-chain price negotiations with regard to inter-blockchain trades. Whereas in the event of off-chain price negotiations the calculation is under control of users that determine privately at which price they want to trade, there is a central element (the smart contract) in on-chain negotiations. Furthermore, the trading partner is usually the other user, but if the platform operated an order-matching system, there would again be a central element because an interim purchase would take place on the platform. Each of those central elements could trigger regulation because, under the applicable law, each of these activities could constitute a (financial) service to the other market participants. Whether these activities are regulated depends on national law. An exchange is only unregulated in the absence of any regulated activity.

§6.02 CAPITAL MARKETS AND BLOCKCHAIN: COUNTRY REPORT – AUSTRIA

Johannes Frank & Philipp Kinsky[48]

Austrian capital markets law relevant for security Tokens includes *inter alia* the capital markets act (KMG 2019), the stock exchange act (BörseG 2018), the custodian act (DepotG), the investment fund act (InvestmentfondsG 2011) and the banking act (BWG). Austria does not provide for certain laws focusing exclusively on Security Tokens and/or crypto assets. However, as of December 2019, there is one law, which partly provides explicit provisions in respect of crypto assets: the financial markets anti-money laundering act (FM-GWG). The FM-GWG stipulates a registration obligation with the Austrian financial market authority (FMA) in respect of virtual currency service providers.[49] Such service providers are required to obtain the aforementioned registration before starting their respective services in Austria. The FMA may refuse to register such service providers in case of indications that they may not be able to comply with the FM-GWG. Further, the FMA may refuse registration in case of any doubt concerning the personal reliability of the significant shareholders and/or managers or other persons actually providing the respective services of such service providers. This may enable the FMA to examine the business model of such service providers to a certain extent and to mitigate any negative impacts on the capital market in advance.

48. Co-Founder of the Legal Tech Hub Vienna (LTH) and partner at Herbst Kinsky Vienna, Dr Philipp Kinsky underlines his intricacies of the legal frameworks around start-ups. More than ten years of Banking and Finance, insurance and capital market law expertise enables him to focus on the understanding of the client's needs in today's fast-changing business. Associate at Herbst Kinsky Johannes Frank advises in start-up companies, capital markets, crypto-assets, alternative investment funds, as well as securities and payment services.
49. §32a FM-GWG.

[A] What Makes a Token a Security?

The Austrian prospectus regime distinguishes between security (*Wertpapiere*) and non-security investments (*Veranlagungen*) and, therefore, provides a security and a non-security prospectus regime.[50]

Austrian laws provide for two different definitions of securities. On the one hand, according to the definition of Austrian securities law, a deed (*Urkunde*) is considered to be a security if the enforcement of any rights contained in such security requires its proper holding.[51] On the other hand, securities within the meaning of the Austrian capital markets law (e.g., the Prospectus Regulation), are defined as all kinds of securities, which are negotiable on the capital market, with the exception of instruments of payment, in particular, but not limited to shares and other shares in companies, partnerships or other securities, equity certificates, debentures or other securitized debt securities etc.

The Austrian civil law's and the Austrian capital markets law's definition of securities differ *inter alia* in a certain aspect relevant for Security Tokens. According to the Austrian FMA and part of literature, a security shall not necessarily be securitized by way of a physical 'paper'; however, a registration within a certain register should suffice.[52] This opens up the possibility to qualify Tokens as a security in case the other prerequisites are met, which is feasible under the current Austrian law regime.

Non-security investments (*Veranlagungen*) are defined as an economic right (*Vermögensrecht*) which is not securitized (as defined above), derived from the direct or indirect investment of capital of several investors on their common account and common risk or common account and common risk with the issuer unless the investors are managing the capital invested on their own.

According to this definition, non-security investments may be offered by way of offering of limited partnership shares, shares in a limited liability company or in a real estate investment fund. However, a Token may also be structured in such a way that it qualifies as a non-security investment.

The main differences between a security and a non-security investment prospectus may be outlined as follows. The relevant FMA is not in charge to approve a non-security prospectus. In contrary to that, a prospectus auditor (as denominated by the FMA) shall evaluate such prospectus. On the one hand, the structure of such non-security investment prospectus differs (slightly) from the security prospectus as a security prospectus follows the general European guidelines and the non-security investment prospectus is governed by the KMG 2019 providing for Austrian law

50. As the Regulation (EU) 2017/1129 of the European Parliament and of the Council of 14 June 2017 on the prospectus to be published when securities are offered to the public or admitted to trading on a regulated market, and repealing Directive 2003/71/EC provides for the securities regime, the Austrian capital markets act has been amended and provides for the non-securities investments regime only.
51. Cf. Susanne Kalss & Martin Oppitz & Johannes Zollner, *Kapitalmarktrecht*^{2} §11 n. 15 (2015).
52. Cf. Stefan Paulmayer et al., *Die kapitalmarktrechtliche Einordnung von Token* in Sabine Kirchmayr-Schliesselberger et. al. (ed.), *Kryptowährungen* 324 (2019); Kalss, Oppitz & Zollner, supra n. 51, at 11 n. 15; Oliver Völkel, *Initial Coin Offerings aus kapitalmarktrechtlicher Sicht*, 3 ZTR 013 (2017).

specifics. On the other hand, as a significant difference, a non-security investment prospectus is not able to be notified to other countries according to a European scheme and, thus, cannot be offered in other countries of the European Union by way of notification; in case of an envisaged publication of a non-security investment prospectus in several European countries, a respective prospectus has to be set up in every such country, observing the relevant respective regulatory prerequisites of each country.

[B] Blockchain Finality

The Blockchain technology provides a variety of possibilities to store and/or transfer Tokens. These transactions are saved in the protocol of the blockchain (i.e., the respective blocks). Now, it seems to be the common understanding that these transactions may not be deleted or reversed and, thus, are technically final. In terms of blockchain security, however, it may occur that transactions may be 'reversed' by means of certain attacks or changes of the protocol. The possibility of such attacks or changes is typically derived from the (technical) rules of the Blockchain.

Recent history and experience have shown that the following attacks and/or protocol changes are the most important threats to Blockchain finality: forks (hard and soft forks), majority attacks (i.e., double spending), Sybil attacks and 'timejacking'.

Where during a fork a new copy of the blockchain is created and - in order to be valid for users - must be accepted by such users, the success of a majority attack is based on the rules of the Blockchain itself. Usually, a Blockchain provides for the rule that the users follow the longest (heaviest) version of the (block) chain. This means that the version of the Blockchain with the most blocks and with the most difficulty is detected and followed by the clients. If a person acquires more hash power than all other (mining) clients in the network combined, such person may be able to create the longest (heaviest) version of the (block) chain and, thus, force all other clients to accept his copy of the (block) chain (containing, as the case may be, some malicious code as, i.e., double spending transactions).

In case of a Sybil attack, the attacker may achieve a similar result, by introducing nodes in the network which are controlled by the attacker. In case a user connects to such a node, the attacker may - among other - be able to cause the user to refuse relying on other blocks than such blocks created by the attacker. In effect, this could cause the user to connect to a new copy of the (block) chain and, thus, he would be threatened to double-spending attacks.

Further, the Blockchain network typically would only accept blocks showing a time stamp, which differs not more than a certain amount of minutes from the network time. In the course of a 'timejacking' attack, an attacker aims basically to utilize this rule of the network by slowing down the target node clock and accelerating the clock of the majority of the mining resources. Further, by sending a block with an adjusted time stamp, the attacker would, thus, cause the target node to reject such block due to the slowed-down clock of the node and to continue using the previous version of the Blockchain. In contrary to that, the miners, having an accelerated clock time, would accept such block. This would isolate the target node from the network processing and enable the attacker to send transaction confirmations to the target node. Such confirmed transactions would cease to be valid in case the attack stops as the target node (again) uses the (block) chain version used by all the other participants in the network. In such a way, the attacker would be able to double spent Tokens.

However, Austrian capital laws do not particularly address these topics and may be subject to general penal or civil law (proceedings).

[C] Special Requirements for Prospectuses

The Austrian FMA is in charge of approving any security prospectus, evaluating the coherence, completeness and comprehensibility of the provisions of the prospectus.[53] The issuer itself shall *inter alia* be responsible for the correctness of the content.

However, tokenized securities – due to lack of specific laws – may according to current practice require *inter alia* to draw specific attention to the following issues and topics in respect of the prospectus.

There should be included general and specific risk factors of the relevant Security Token relating to the Token offered. Such factors may differ in case of permissionless or permissioned Blockchains, different types of storage, Masternode implications or the respective proof of work/stake mechanisms. Depending on the exact mechanisms of the issuance of the Tokens, specific risks may be associated with the storage of Tokens and a subsequent airdrop and/or other transfer of Tokens in the course of the respective issuance. Further, any investor should be informed about the tradability of any Tokens and/or about any potential (significant) weaknesses of the network in respect of certain scenarios.

The draft of the prospectus shall provide for a detailed description of the technical structure of the offering, the way of potential transfers of Tokens, respectively, of the underlying technology of the Tokens and/or the company as well as of the business side of the company.

Further, the prospectus shall include information on the taxation treatment of the securities, where the proposed investment attracts a tax regime, specific to that jurisdiction where a public offer shall take place.

[D] Regulatory Specifics for Organized Trade

This section will, on the one hand, briefly describe which major requirements an issuer and/or wallet service provider shall comply with in case of a direct issuing of Security Tokens to investors. On the other hand, it shall provide an overview of potential regulatory implications for centralized, organized trade of Security Tokens.

An issuer of Security Tokens typically acts in its own name and on its own account selling its own products (i.e., Tokens). Banking and/or security supervisory laws typically postulate that a third party provides a service, which shall be regulated

53. Article 20 Prospectus Regulation.

by certain regulatory laws. Thus, such laws would typically not apply to the issuer in case of an issue of Security Tokens if the issuer acts in its own name and on its own behalf. Nevertheless, as stated above, prospectus regime shall be complied with, as the case may be.

The aim of the Regulation (EU) no. 1286/2014 (packaged retail and insurance-based investment products - PRIIPs) is to foster EU markets to be more efficient by helping investors to better understand and compare the key features, risk, rewards and costs of certain investment products, by means of access to a key-information document. Regulation (EU) no. 1286/2014 (PRIIPs) may apply *inter alia* in case the crypto asset may qualify as 'packaged retail investment product'. Such a product qualifies as PRIIP in case the crypto asset qualifies as an investment, regardless of its legal form, where the amount repayable to the retail investor is subject to fluctuations due to exposure to reference values or to the performance of one or more assets which are not directly purchased by the retail investor.[54]

In case crypto assets qualify as a security and shall be traded on a trading platform (*Handelsplatz*) and/or are admitted on a regulated stock exchange, the anti-market abuse laws could apply.[55]

In case Security Tokens are traded automatically on an organized exchange, several further regulatory implications may be triggered.

Such an exchange could be qualified as a 'stock' exchange, an MTF or an organized trading facility (OTF). In such cases, the operation of an exchange may require a license as 'stock' exchange company according to the Austrian stock exchange act (BörseG 2018) or as an investment firm (IF) under the Austrian securities supervision act (WAG 2018). In most cases, a license as an IF under the WAG 2018 could suffice, when such systems trade Tokens in the course of a centralized orderbook or compare trades in respect to other trading models.[56]

In respect of a potential trade on a stock exchange in Austria, the Austrian stock exchange act states that a listing of securities which are not securitized in a (global) certificate and deposited with a central depository agency (and, thus, linked to a respective clearing system) or which are registered with a central depository agency shall not be traded on a regulated market (*amtlicher Handel*).[57]

As a physical securitization of any Token is technically not feasible, the registration of such security with the central depository agency could be a potentially possible solution to comply with the aforementioned provision of the BörseG 2018. However, such registration service for Tokens is not (yet) available with the Austrian central depository agency.[58]

54. Article 4 lit. 1 Regulation (EU) No. 1286/2014.
55. Cf. *inter alia* Regulation (EU) No. 596/2014 (MAR), Directive 2014/57/EU (MAD) and Directive 2013/50/EU (Transparency Directive).
56. Cf. Florian Pekler & Ralph Rirsch, *Ausgewählte kapitalmarktrechtliche Aspekte bei der Emission von Crypto-Assets* in Kirchmayr-Schliesselberger, supra n. 52 *at* 391.
57. Section 38(5) BörseG 2018.
58. Information according to factual knowledge due to personal encounters with the Austrian central depository agency as of December 2019.

Further, the operators of MTFs and OTFs shall provide for deposition of any and all financial instruments (which securities are a part of) with a central depository agency to be traded within their MTF and/or OTF systems.[59]

Thus, Tokens may only be traded outside MTF and/or OTF or a regulated market.[60] However, several (private) initiatives aim to change the respective requirement of physical securitization in order to enable a non-physical securitization of securities to foster a more efficient operation of deposition and storage of securities and Tokens.

§6.03 CAPITAL MARKETS AND BLOCKCHAIN: COUNTRY REPORT – BELARUS

Klim Stashevsky & Mikhail Khodosevich[61]

[A] What Makes a Token a Security?

Belarusian regulations[62] specifically outline that legal rules on securities and securitization, alongside with the security market activity license requirements, shall not be applied to operations with Tokens in Belarus. Therefore, from the viewpoint of Belarusian regulatory authorities, a Token cannot be considered a security.

Instead of this, the Belarusian lawmakers decided to create a separate legal framework specifically for operations with Tokens, making such operations valid if they comply with strict requirements and take place within the special regime of the High Technologies Park.

On 21 December 2017, the President of Belarus signed Decree no. 8 'On Development of Digital Economy' that elaborated initial provisions on the legal status of Tokens which put it in a totally new division of objects of civil rights.

This Decree gives a definition of a Token (or a 'digital sign', as it is also qualified) as a record in a transaction block ledger (blockchain) or another distributed information system. Legislation provides two possible qualifying attributes of Tokens:

- it verifies that its owner has a right to certain objects of civil law (for instance, corporate or exclusive rights);

59. Section 75(2) no. 3 BörseG 2018 in connection with Art. 3(2) Regulation (EU) No. 909/2014 (CSDR).
60. According to the situation as of December 2019, as described above.
61. Head of Arzinger's IT & Media sector group Klim Stashevsky advises his clients with a focus on innovative technologies in data protection and IP having been ranked by Chambers and Legal 500 as a rising star. Working with Arzinger since 2016, Associate Mikhail focuses on the needs of IT companies performing business activities in Belarus. He understands the frameworks around high technologies and his client's admission to the High Tech Park as residents. Both Klim and Mikhail developed and tested legal algorithms of administrative procedures of the Republic of Belarus to be included in the electronic registry establishing an e-government.
62. Decree no. 8 of the President of the Republic dated 21 December 2017 *On Development of Digital Economy*, http://law.by/document/?guid = 3871&p0 = Pd1700008e (accessed 11 March 2020).

- it is a cryptocurrency. In its turn, a cryptocurrency is defined as a bitcoin, another digital sign (Token) used in international circulation as a universal means of exchange.

In contrast to some modern legal systems, this definition characterizes Tokens as neither securities nor derivative financial instruments. In the Belarusian legal system, securities are determined as documents or a set of records certifying - per a defined form - proprietary and non-proprietary rights. Each security shall possess obligatory details and requisites, which Tokens cannot have due to their unique legal and technical nature.

Moreover, the Belarusian legislation directly excludes Tokens from the regulation of these legal instruments and categories: securities, securitization, and licensed exchange activities in securities. Therefore, the legislation that regulates these categories is not applied to relations connected to blockchain and Tokens. Legal effect of the currency legislation is excluded as well which means that Tokens do not have a status of currency values (besides securities, currency values include a national currency, foreign currencies and payment instruments). Tokens do not relate to the term 'funds' within the meaning of the legislation on countering laundering of criminal assets, financing terrorism and proliferation of weapons of mass destruction and have a special regulation in this sphere.

At the same time, from an accounting perspective, Tokens are treated as assets. The Ministry of Finances of the Republic of Belarus adopted a special regulation on proper accounting of Tokens.[63] According to this document, business entities may account Tokens as 'long term or short term financial investments', 'current incomes' or 'goods'. This variety of legal features of Tokens shows an exclusive position of Tokens in the Belarusian legal field.

[B] Blockchain Finality

The finality of blockchain transactions has not received sufficient legal regulation status in Belarus yet. From this perspective, Tokens have a quite similar status with tangible property: transfer of a Token from one entity to another entails a complete and permanent transfer of rights certified with this Token. Transfer of a Token shall be deemed performed at the moment of reflection of a relevant approved transaction in a transaction block ledger (blockchain) or another distributed information system according to its rules and protocols.

The said principle is not applied to transfer of rights which additionally require a state registration (for instance, rights of ownership to a real estate or exclusive rights to a trademark).

63. Resolution no. 16 of the Ministry of Finances of the Republic of Belarus dated 6 March 2018, *On Approval of the National Standard of Accounting and Reporting 'Digital Signs (Tokens)' and Amendments and Alterations to Some Resolutions of the Ministry of Finances of the Republic of Belarus*.

For a documentary reflection of a blockchain transaction, each party (business entity) shall draft a primary accounting document. Unlike a majority of other business transactions when entities are obliged to draft bilateral or multilateral primary accounting documents (such as acts of acceptance), parties to blockchain transactions may draft unilateral acts based on information on blockchain transactions. A business entity shall attach a documentary evidence (for instance, a printout of blockchain transactions) to this primary accounting document.

[C] Special Requirements for Prospectus

A prospectus or a 'White paper' declaration is a document with information on the investment project in the form of a Token offering and participants of this process.[64] Per the Belarusian legislation, this is an obligatory document for any ICO. Ways to amend the white paper after the start of a Token offering is very limited.

There is a certain variability regarding an entity which shall draft a white paper. It can be a customer – an entity particularly interested in a Token offering (hereinafter referred to as the 'Customer') or an ICO organizer – a professional participant of a Token services market arranging and conducting the process of ICO for a Customer and drafting a white paper based on information provided by this Customer.

An entity may also perform an ICO of its own Tokens, including drafting a white paper, without the participation of an ICO organizer. However, such entity shall have the status of the resident of the High Technologies Park of Belarus and its business plan shall cover activities in the sphere of Tokens as described below in section 4.

Legislation provides an exhaustive list of requirements to a white paper. As a general rule, each white paper shall contain:

(1) information on the Customer, including a title, a legal address, a tax ID number and an e-mail address;
(2) information on the ICO organizer and an entity that has created Tokens (if it is an entity other than the ICO organizer) and a general description of contractual relations between the Customer, the ICO organizer and the entity that has created Tokens. If there are any interdependence or affiliation relations between the participants of the ICO or an immediate interest of the ICO organizer (its shareholders, affiliated entities) in the Token offering, the white paper shall reflect this information as well;
(3) general description of contractual relations between the Customer and/or the ICO organizer and an 'anchor' investor, as well as their interdependence or affiliation relations, if any. An 'anchor' investor is considered as a renowned investor having a positive business reputation. Purchase of Tokens by an 'anchor' investor can usually be regarded by other potential investors as an indicator of the reliability of Tokens as investments;

64. *Rules on Rendering Services Connected to Creation and Placement of Digital Signs (Tokens) and Related Transactions*, http://www.park.by/content/docs/Regulations-on-Crypto/ICO.pdf (accessed 11 March 2020).

(4) information of financial indicators of the Customer, including its balance sheet, an income statement, a statement of changes in equity, a statement of cash flows, notes to the balance sheet and an audit report for the preceding year. These documents shall be attached to the white paper as its annexes;
(5) description of main risks of the ICO and major competitors of the Customer;
(6) disclosure of information on the Customer: its CEO, shareholders, a chief accountant and an officer responsible for ICO – at least their names (titles) and states of their residence (incorporation);
(7) information on any court proceedings of the Customer and their outcomes for three preceding years;
(8) facts of administration liability of the Customer for three preceding years and any current administration proceedings;
(9) description of rights of Token holders, a Token circulation period and a possibility of the early performance of rights of Token holders;
(10) description of main conditions of purchase of Tokens by the Customer. White paper may also stipulate that the Customer may not purchase Tokens till the full performance of obligations certified with these Tokens;
(11) description of the essence of the Token investment project, including a reasoned assessment of financial expenses for each stage of this project and expected financial results upon its implementation. Information on the investment project shall also describe its technical part and terms of implementation of its separate stages;
(12) restriction of transfer of Tokens from their first holders to other holders and consequences of violation of this restriction;
(13) information on the applied blockchain or another distributed information system, an opinion on its reliability (potential resistance against technical failures and unlawful interference), a date and results of the last technical audit, if any;
(14) means of securing obligations certified with the Tokens, if any;
(15) information on any breaches related to Tokens committed within three preceding years by the Customer (its shareholders, CEO or the officers responsible for ICO);
(16) description of how Token holders can receive information on the current state of the Token investment project;
(17) other information that may help potential Token holders maximize their risk assessment.

A single white paper may relate to an ICO of Tokens of a single or of several types. The general assumption is that Customers may not use objects of civil rights attracted with ICO for purchase of other Tokens or for other purposes which are not mentioned in the white paper. However, a relevant white paper may provide otherwise.

The Customer shall have a white paper on its website at least until the full performance of all obligations certified with the Tokens.

[D] Regulatory Specifics for Organized Trade

Legal regulation of Tokens in Belarus is expressed in two key characteristics. First, the legal regime of using Tokens for private persons and business entities substantially differs. The second specific feature is that Token activities are closely bound up with a special legal regime – the High Technologies Park of Belarus and Belarus-based entities enjoying its preferences.

Private persons in Belarus are free to perform mining, purchase and hold Tokens in virtual wallets, exchange Tokens, sell them for national or foreign currency and electronic money, gift and bequeath Tokens. Private persons are not required to declare Tokens and pay an income tax for them until the end of 2022. Token-related activities of private persons are not qualified as their professional business activities (therefore, no business registration is needed).

Professional Token activities in Belarus is mostly concentrated in the High Technologies Park, a special IT cluster for doing business in the sphere of modern technologies. This cluster is open for IT companies and startups; however, preliminary approval of their business plans with the perspectives of development and assessment of a team and resources of the company by the Supervisory Board of the High Technologies Park is required. Residents of the Park receive significant tax and other legal benefits, but they shall do business exclusively in the sphere that is specified in their business plan. Arranging and performing an ICO, creating special platforms for trade in Tokens and their exchange in Belarus are available only for residents of the High Technologies Park with respective business plans. Legislation provides three main types of professional participants of the Tokens market:

(i) cryptographic platform operators holding and managing platforms designed for trade in Tokens;
(ii) cryptocurrency exchange operators conducting the processes of exchange of Tokens;
(iii) professional entities working in other Token-related spheres. This category includes ICO organizers, companies which perform ICO of their own Tokens and companies rendering information and consulting services.

Other Belarus-based business entities may trade Tokens, exchange them and perform ICO of their Tokens exclusively via residents of the High Technologies Park.

Cryptocurrency exchange operators and cryptographic platform operators shall meet stricter criteria to be admitted to the High Technologies Park than other IT companies: cryptocurrency exchange operators shall keep in Belarusian banks not less than BYN 200,000 to ensure their obligations to their clients, and for cryptographic platform operators the threshold is higher – BYN 1,000,000.

Additionally, the High Technologies Park has elaborated detailed regulation on anti-money laundering (AML) and know your customer (KYC) polices for Token activities. Business entities shall approve rules of internal control, identify and verify all their clients, use only a certified software, report to financial controlling state bodies regarding suspicious financial transactions, block these transactions and freeze the funds. Each such company shall appoint a compliance officer or officers whose rank is no lower than a deputy director.[65]

The process of trade in Tokens at a cryptographic platform also has a comprehensive legal regulation. For admission to a platform, a cryptographic platform operator (hereinafter referred to as the 'Operator') shall conclude contracts with potential clients - both private persons and legal entities without reference to a state of their residence/registration.[66] Regarding private persons, an Operator shall collect information on their contact details, full names, date of birth and state of residence, regarding legal entities - their title, legal address and Tax ID number. Operators are prohibited from establishing relations with underage persons and persons involved in terrorist activities. In relation to foreign citizens and entities, Operators are also obliged to check that trade at a cryptographic platform is not prohibited for these potential clients under the legislation of the state of their residence/registration. After the conclusion of a contract, a client receives an account in the cryptographic platform system. The Client may not have more than one account.

Private persons - citizens of Belarus - have an additional stage of verification for admission to a bidding process. An Operator shall preliminary check their competence and knowledge in the sphere of the trade in Tokens by filling in the questionnaire. For other categories of clients (legal entities and foreign citizens), an Operator may establish its own requirements to their financial state and business reputation.

The Operator shall provide its clients with comprehensive information on contract provisions, terms and conditions of the work of the cryptographic platform and risks they take by participating in the trade in Tokens. The Operator may not advise clients on any aspects which may induce them to buy or sell particular Tokens.

The Operator is entitled to choose software and technical means in order to provide the clients with the access to the bidding system and give them the right to observe the bidding process for its maximum transparency. The Operator shall prevent bidders from manipulating with Token prices and unfair usage of any insider information that they may have. The Operator shall not admit to the bidding the Tokens that anyhow violate legislation requirements, or which are based on the principle of full anonymity of transactions.

Generally, the process of trade in Tokens contains the following steps. The bidder shall credit money, electronic money or Tokens to a respective account of an Operator. These funds are reflected in the account of the bidder on the trading platform. The Operator shall ensure a separate accounting of funds of all its clients and its own funds. The Operator shall collect information on all cash flows and transactions of the client, prepare daily reports with this data and keep it for five years.

For making a deal, the bidder places an order for purchase, sale or exchange of Tokens. Specific requirements to these orders and to the procedure of their placement

65. *Regulations on the Requirements for the Internal Control Rules of Residents of the High Technologies Park,* http://www.park.by/content/docs/Regulations-on-Crypto/AML.pdf (accessed 11 March 2020).
66. *Requirements to Cryptoplatform Operators*, http://www.park.by/content/docs/Regulations-on-Crypto/CryptoExchange.pdf (accessed 11 March 2020).

are specified in internal regulations of Operators. After the trading system detects an offsetting order of another bidder with suitable conditions, the Operator shall immediately execute it and transfer funds from the account of one bidder to another. The principle of 'last look' when the execution of orders can be postponed is not applicable.

The Operator may provide bidders with Tokens for participation in bidding subject to the payment of interest by these bidders. For each transaction that these bidders enter, a proportion between borrowed Tokens and their own Tokens shall not be more than 5 to 1.

Upon a client's consent, an Operator may use client's Tokens for entering into transactions on its behalf and for its own benefit if all the following conditions are met:

- the transactions are aimed at increasing liquidity of the Operator;
- counterparties of the Operator under these deals are legal entities having a special license for Token trade business under the legislation of its registration;
- these deals do not involve more than 50% of all funds of the respective client;
- the Operator has a reasonable belief that these deals will not lead to the Operator's failure to transfer all funds which are due to be paid by the Operator under the contract to the client.

As seen from above, the sphere of trade in Tokens and a blockchain technology in the Republic of Belarus has only started its development path, and some provisions stay in the theoretical field. Taking into consideration that relevant legislation has been adopted only recently, we believe that depending on the results and first practical conclusions in the coming years, blockchain legislation may become more progressive and develop further.

§6.04 CAPITAL MARKETS AND BLOCKCHAIN: COUNTRY REPORT – ESTONIA

Kirsti Pent[67]

[A] What Makes a Token a Security?

Estonian law does not include any comprehensive regulation regarding Tokens. Tokens are either qualified as certain financial instruments regulated under European Union law and respective national laws (e.g., a security) or as a 'virtual currency'. The latter is a term introduced by Estonian law. Virtual currency is a value represented in digital form, which is digitally transferable, preservable or tradable and which natural or legal persons accept as a payment instrument, but which is not the legal payment instrument of any country or funds for the purposes of Article 4(25) of the Payment

67. Partner at FORT Legal, Kirsti Pent integrates knowledge of financial institutions in regulatory issues. Kirsti is noted by Legal 500 (2017) as a financial lawyer, who adopts 'a straight-to-the-point approach' and advises, in addition to financial law, in energy law.

Services Directive 2 (PSD2)[68] or a payment transaction for the purposes of points (k) and (l) of Article 3 of PSD2.[69]

Although the definition of a virtual currency only excludes payment instruments, it also does not apply if a Token meets the criteria of any other regulated financial instrument, e.g., a share, a fund unit, a derivative instrument, any other type of a security or even a deposit. Therefore, in order to determine the legal classification of a particular Token, the analysis should always start from establishing whether the Token may constitute another regulated financial instrument.

While there is no established case law in Estonia to clearly distinguish between virtual currencies and other regulated financial instruments, the Estonian Financial Supervisory Authority (EFSA) has issued an opinion on the classification of Tokens reaffirming that substance should be considered over form.[70]

Most significantly, Tokens may be securities. The definition of securities is set forth in the Securities Market Act as well as in the Law of Obligations Act. The Securities Market Act defines securities in terms of capital markets. Each of the following proprietary rights, obligations or contracts, if transferable on the basis of at least a unilateral expression of will, constitutes a security, even without a document being issued therefor:

- a share or another similar tradable right;
- a bond, convertible security or another tradable debt;
- a subscription right or another tradable right granting the right to acquire securities specified above;
- an investment fund unit or share;
- a money-market instrument;
- a derivative security or a derivative contract;
- a tradable depositary receipt;
- a greenhouse gas emission allowance.[71]

Other than the above, Estonian national law does not provide further guidance for determining what constitutes a security. Rather, MiFID II and the opinions of the ESMA and the Committee of European Securities Regulators (CESR) are used to furnish the definition. Thereby, securities are proprietary rights or obligations which are standardized, negotiable and freely transferrable on (capital) markets. As a result, one practical way to preclude the application of the securities' regulation is to impose

68. Directive (EU) 2015/2366 of the European Parliament and of the Council on payment services in the internal market, amending Directives 2002/65/EC, 2009/110/EC and 2013/36/EU and Regulation (EU) no. 1093/2010, and repealing Directive 2007/64/EC (OJ L 337, 23.12.2015, pp. 35–127).
69. Money Laundering and Terrorist Financing Prevention Act, Art. 3(9) (26 October 2017), RT I, 17.11.2017, 2, https://www.riigiteataja.ee/en/eli/525032019005/consolide (accessed 11 March 2020).
70. EFSA, *The Legal Framework of Initial Coin Offering in Estonia*, https://www.fi.ee/en/investment/aktuaalsed-teemad-investeerimises/virtuaalraha-ico/legal-framework-initial-coin-offering-estonia (accessed 11 March 2020).
71. Securities Market Act, Art. 2(1) (17 October 2001), RT I 2001, 89, 532, https://www.riigiteataja.ee/en/eli/522032019007/consolide (accessed 11 March 2020).

restrictions of the transferability of the Token, e.g., rights of pre-emption or other limitations as to who can acquire the Tokens.

The EFSA has explained that if Tokens are transferable and give the investors certain rights in respect to the issuer or if the value of the Tokens is tied to the future profits or success of the issuer, then the Tokens are likely to be considered securities.[72] For example, Tokens classify as securities if they provide voting rights of the issuer or give the investor an expectation of a return on their investment (e.g., a right to a part of the issuer's profit, regular cash flows, or any other promise about future profit), regardless of whether the funds raised are repayable by maturity date or no maturity date exists (e.g., a perpetual bond).[73]

If the aim of issuing Tokens is to further invest the funds raised in common interests, the Tokens may constitute a specific type of securities - investment fund units. An investment fund is a legal entity or pool of assets which raises capital from a number of investors with the view of investing it in accordance with a defined investment policy for the mutual benefit of the investors.[74] Thus, Tokens may qualify as fund units depending on the structure and objective of the Token issued - the guidelines issued by the ESMA are used to make the determination.[75] As a general rule, an investment fund must have a fund manager, i.e., a company whose main and permanent activity is the management of one or several funds.[76] Depending first on whether the funds are offered publicly and the volume of assets under management, the fund manager must be either licensed by or registered with the EFSA.

In principle, a Token may also be a derivative instrument: a derivative security or a derivative contract. A derivative security is a tradable security (expressing a right or obligation to acquire, exchange or transfer) the underlying assets of which are other securities or the price of which depends directly or indirectly, for example, on the exchange or market price of a security or a commodity, interest rate, or another financial index or financial indicator.[77] As a general rule, a Token is not a derivative instrument, because it is not intended to hedge risks and it has none of the specific underlying assets set forth in the law.[78] Most often, Tokens give their holders the right to use the services of the issuer, but not to acquire the specific commodities the same way as commodity futures contracts do.

Assuming that a Token is not a derivative instrument, it may constitute a money-market instrument: an unsecured, transferable and marketable (liquid) debt

72. EFSA, *supra* n. 70.
73. EFSA, *Information for Entities Engaging with virtual Currencies and ICOs*, https://www.fi.ee/en/investment/aktuaalsed-teemad-investeerimises/virtuaalraha-ico/information-entities-engaging-virtual-currencies-and-icos (accessed 11 March 2020).
74. Investment Funds Act, Art. 2(1) (14 December 2016), RT I 31.12.2016, 3, https://www.riigiteataja.ee/en/eli/527032019004/consolide (accessed 11 March 2020).
75. European Securities and Markets Authority, Guidelines on the key concepts of the AIFMD, https://www.esma.europa.eu/sites/default/files/library/2015/11/2013-611_guidelines_on_key_concepts_of_the_aifmd_-_en.pdf (accessed 11 March 2020).
76. *Ibid.*, Art. 2(3) and Art. 3(1).
77. Securities Market Act, Art. 2(3), *supra* n. 71.
78. Kadi Saluste, *Token'ite kvalifitseerimine Eesti õiguse alusel ning kehtiva õiguse sobivus ICO-de reguleerimiseks*, 6 Juridica, 390, 394 (2018).

obligation which is normally traded on the money market, including a treasury bond, commercial paper, certificate of deposit, bill of exchange secured by a credit institution and other securities which comply with the conditions provided for in Article 11 of Commission Delegated Regulation (EU) 2017/565.[79] However, it is doubtful if a Token meets the liquidity criterion. A Token may be regarded as a money-market instrument if it can easily be exchanged into fiat currency, but in practice, such an exchange is often complicated and may be restricted by the issuers.[80]

If a Token is deemed to be any of the following securities, it has to be registered with the Estonian register of securities:

- debt obligation issued by a legal person registered in Estonia, the public offer prospectus of which is registered with the EFSA pursuant to the Securities Market Act;
- the shares of public limited companies registered in Estonia;
- the units and shares of investment funds registered in Estonia, which are admitted for trading on a regulated securities market or in a MTF;
- subscription rights for shares and securities subject to entry in the register which are publicly issued or publicly offered.[81]

In addition to securities, Tokens may also be qualified as repayable funds if the main business activity of the issuer is to provide loans in its own name and account – such activity is financed through funds received from the public in the form of a Token issue and the Tokens grant their holders the right to get their investment back.[82] Such a business model may be deemed as that of a bank which requires authorization from the EFSA.

If a Token does not give its holder any right to expect a return on the investment (i.e., the Token is not a security or a repayable fund), the Token would be classified as one of the following:

- a virtual currency as defined at the beginning of this chapter. For example, the Supreme Court has ruled that bitcoin is a virtual currency.[83] The courts have explained that bitcoins are virtual currencies since bitcoins' value in fiat is determinable at any time, it is possible to buy and sell bitcoin for fiat and a number of merchants accept bitcoins as means of payment.[84] Specific legislation applies in respect to service providers who offer wallets or operate exchanges for trading in virtual currencies – these are discussed in the subchapter 'Regulatory specifics for organized trade';

---

79. Securities Market Act, Art. 2(2), *supra* n. 71.
80. Saluste, *supra* n. 78, at 390, 394 (2018).
81. Securities Register Maintenance Act, Art. 2(1) (14 June 2000), RT I, 26.06.2017, 1, https://www.riigiteataja.ee/en/eli/527032019007/consolide (accessed 11 March 2020).
82. EFSA, *supra* n. 70.
83. Case no. 3-3-1-75-15 of the Supreme Court of Estonia, https://www.riigikohus.ee/et/lahendid?asjaNr=3-3-1-75-15 (accessed 11 March 2020).
84. Kadri Siibak, *Mõningad virtuaalrahaga seotud õiguslikud probleemid*, V Juridica 326, 330 (2015).

- a donation;
- a Utility Token in case it provides its holder access to a platform, the right to use the services or acquire the products of the issuer. In such cases, contract law applies to the Tokens, including provisions regarding prepayments;
- once the Crowdfunding Regulation of the European Union is adopted and enters into force, a Token may also be an instrument within its scope.

Contract law (including provisions on concluding agreements online), consumer protection regulations, advertising requirements and tax laws must be complied with when issuing or trading in any Tokens; however, the exact requirements under these laws depend on the classification of Tokens. It is also possible that the tax treatment of a Token does not correspond to its classification for regulatory purposes.

[B] Blockchain Finality

The finality of Token transactions depends on the classification of the Token. Generally, Tokens represent rights.[85] Claim rights are assignable irrespective of the debtor's (e.g., the issuer of the Token) consent.[86] Even if the parties have agreed that the claim right may not be assigned, such agreement has no effect in respect to the acquirer and the assignment is valid regardless.[87] If the creditor (the holder of the Token) assigns the one and the same Token more than once, the earliest assignment is deemed to be valid.[88]

As a general rule, the bona fide acquisition rule does not apply to claim rights, such as Tokens. First, bona fide acquisition is possible in case of physical objects and rights entered into public registers if the law prescribes that an entry in a specific register carries such protection for the acquirer. National laws do not specifically provide for such legal protection in respect to Token purchases made by relying on the blockchain (even if it is a public blockchain). Therefore, purely from a legal standpoint, the legitimate holder of the Token has the right to demand the reversal of an unauthorized Token transfer.

In case a Token would constitute a certain type of a security (e.g., a publicly offered debt obligation issued by a legal person registered in Estonia), it would have to be registered in the Estonian register of securities. In case of entry in the register, bona fide acquisition of the security would be possible. According to the Securities Register Maintenance Act Article 9(2), if a person acquires a security or a right to a security in good faith relying on the register, the register is deemed correct.[89] The registrar shall

85. Estonian Ministry of Finance, *Analysis for Developing a Policy for the Possible Recognition and Use of Virtual Currencies*, https://www.rahandusministeerium.ee/et/system/files_force/document_files/2016-vv_virtuaalvaaringute_analuus-22-07.pdf?download=1 (accessed 11 March 2020).
86. Law of Obligations Act, Art. 164(1) (26 September 2001), RT I 2001, 81, 487, https://www.riigiteataja.ee/en/eli/507032019001/consolide (accessed 11 March 2020).
87. *Ibid.*, Art. 166(2).
88. *Ibid.*, Art. 164(3).
89. Securities Register Maintenance Act, Art. 9(2) (14 June 2000), RT I 2000, 57, 373, https://www.riigiteataja.ee/en/eli/ee/524072017013/consolide (accessed 11 March 2020).

have tested whether blockchain technology could be used for voting online at shareholder meetings and also looked into using blockchain for security transactions, but does not currently enable registration of Tokens.[90]

[C] Special Requirements for Prospectus

A prospectus must be prepared, registered with the EFSA and published in case Security Tokens are offered publicly in Estonia and the volume of the offer is more than EUR 2,500,000 per all European Economic Area (EEA) states in total calculated per a one-year period.[91] An offer of securities to the public means communication in any form and by any means, presenting sufficient information on the terms of the offer and the securities to enable an investor to decide on the purchase or subscription.[92] A prospectus is not required in case any of the exceptions set forth in the Securities Market Act or the Prospectus Regulation apply, for example, if the offer is made solely to qualified investors or the denomination of the securities per unit amounts to at least EUR 100,000.

In the case of an offer of securities in the amount of up to EUR 8,000,000 in Estonia (calculated over a period of one year), the issuer may choose whether to prepare the prospectus in accordance with the Prospectus Regulation or a regulation to be adopted by the Minister of Finance.[93] The requirements of the latter are to be somewhat more lenient compared to the Prospectus Regulation. However, such a prospectus is not valid for the public offer of securities across borders. In the case of a public offer exceeding EUR 8,000,000, the prospectus must be prepared in accordance with the Prospectus Regulation.

The content and the level of detail of the prospectus depends on the type of the securities offered; for example, the requirements somewhat differ for shares and bonds. Estonian law does not currently provide for exceptions or any special provisions regulating the public offer of Tokens.[94] However, the Prospectus Regulation grants some exceptions for startup companies when preparing a prospectus (i.e., companies established less than three years ago).

Any prospectus must include information on the risks associated with the issuer, any guarantor, and the securities offered. Thus, the risks posed by the utilization of the blockchain technology should also be described in the prospectus. However, as already noted, certain publicly offered securities must be registered in the Estonian register of securities. In such cases, the technological risks related to blockchain are probably irrelevant, since the safekeeping, transfer and other aspects of such securities are prescribed by the law.

90. Estonian Ministry of Finance, *supra* n. 85.
91. Securities Market Act, Art. 15, *supra* n. 71.
92. *Ibid.*, Art. 12 and Regulation (EU) 2017/1129 of the European Parliament and of the Council of 14 June 2017 on the prospectus to be published when securities are offered to the public or admitted to trading on a regulated market, and repealing Directive 2003/71/EC, Art. 2(d) (the '*Prospectus Regulation*')
93. Securities Market Act, Art. 15(6), *supra* n. 71.
94. EFSA, *supra* n. 70.

If the prospectus includes false or inaccurate information or is incomplete and this affects the valuation of the securities, the issuer or any other responsible person set forth in the prospectus must compensate the damages caused by the difference between reality and the information included in the prospectus to the owners of the securities, provided the responsible person should have been aware of the shortcoming and the owner of the security was not aware of it. Such liability arises also if the summary of the prospectus or its translation is misleading, inaccurate or in conflict with the other parts of the prospectus.[95] Instead of compensating damages, the responsible person may also acquire the security from its owner for the same price as paid by the owner.[96]

[D] Regulatory Specifics for Organized Trade

Services related to Security Tokens generally require an authorization from the EFSA to operate as an IF. Among other, the following services involving securities constitute regulated financial services: receipt and transmission of transaction orders, execution of orders, portfolio management, organizing an offer or issue of securities, operation of an MTF or OTF.[97] The main characteristic of both trading facilities is that they bring together interests of different parties for acquisition and transfer of securities under non-discretionary conditions in a way that results in a contract; i.e., they use automated matching of buy and sell orders. This service should be distinguished from, for example, bulletin boards which only provide information on buy and sell offers, but do not match them.

Whereas the legislation applicable to Security Tokens derives from MiFID II, Estonia has also adopted a specific regulation applicable to exchanges and wallets for virtual currencies. Such service providers must obtain a license from the Estonian Financial Intelligence Unit. Exchanges must obtain the license in case they exchange virtual currencies against fiat currencies, vice versa, or one virtual currency for another. The main requirements for obtaining the license is applying AML/KYC procedures to the clients, proving that the management and owners are reputable (including submission of criminal records), minimal share capital of EUR 12,000, physical location in Estonia and an account opened with a bank or a payment institution established in the EEA and authorized to provide services in Estonia. Most of these requirements were introduced recently to enhance supervision over the service providers. In the past, it was quite easy to obtain the license which made it very popular with foreign service providers, even though the license is not automatically passportable for operations in other jurisdictions.

95. Securities Market Act, Art. 25, *supra* n. 71.
96. *Ibid.*, Art. 26.
97. *Ibid.*, Art. 43(1).

§6.05 CAPITAL MARKETS AND BLOCKCHAIN: COUNTRY REPORT – FINLAND

Mika Puurunen[98]

The Finnish market has recently seen first regulatory steps related to issuance and exchange of digital value on a blockchain or DLT, as the Finnish Act on Virtual Currency Providers (572/2019, as amended, the VCP Act) entered into force on 1 May 2019.[99] The VCP Act is applicable to business operations of virtual currency providers, and it stipulates that any natural or legal person issuing virtual currency (e.g., Tokens used as currency/instruments of payment), providing virtual currency exchange services, maintaining a virtual currency marketplace or offering virtual currency wallets has to register with the Finnish Financial Supervisory Authority (FIN-FSA).[100] Following such registration, service providers have to comply with certain requirements on safekeeping of client assets, customer due diligence (KYC rules) and marketing. However, as the VCP Act is more or less constructed to regulate the virtual currency service provider, but not to legally categorize the underlying digital asset, the support for the legal construction of Tokens in the context of Finnish securities laws remains very limited. The VCP Act includes a reference to the Finnish Securities Markets Act (746/2012, as amended, the SMA) and sets out that if a virtual currency constitutes a financial instrument as referred to in the SMA, the SMA is applicable. The reference is purely clarifying in nature and does not draw any conclusions on the relevant application criteria for Tokens.

For the time being no such laws have been enacted in Finland that would regulate either the position of Tokens as digital assets under Finnish securities markets or the applicability of Finnish provisions on securities offerings to any issuance or sale of Tokens. The same conclusion applies to any official guidance or regulation by Finnish public authorities. Thus, any analysis on the applicability of Finnish securities law requirements to Tokens and/or any sale or issuance thereof has to be made on a case-by-case basis.

Given the above introduction, the applicability of specific securities law constructions on Token offerings (such as general good conduct principles, transaction finality, prospectus disclosure and market abuse regime) needs to be analysed based on general premises of Finnish civil law and the applicable EU legislation – in the following, there will be a concise overview of such aspects. Prospectus regime will be discussed only from the perspective of public security offerings and not admissions to trading, as the former can currently be seen more relevant in the context of Tokens.

98. Having joined Bird & Bird in 2019, Counsel Mika Puurunen focuses on assignments related to capital markets, M&A and corporate law. In addition, Mika has deep sector knowledge on regulatory frameworks around different types of investment funds and is known for rendering business-minded and solution-oriented advice for his clients.
99. The related transition period has ended and all virtual currency providers have been fully subject to the VCP Act as from 1 November 2019.
100. The FIN-FSA supervises that procedures for customer due diligence and risk management comply with statutory requirements. In case of non-compliance, the supervised entity may be subject to administrative sanctions.

The Finnish securities laws are nowadays highly harmonized with the applicable EU legislation. For example, due to the new EU Prospectus Regulation[101] that became fully effective on 21 July 2019, basically all national Finnish provisions on prospectuses were repealed. The same applies to the national provisions concerning the disclosure of inside information, which have been replaced by the EU Market Abuse Regulation (MAR).[102] Accordingly, the definitions of a security and a financial instrument are very much derived from the EU legislative framework and implemented in the Finnish legislation basically as such. The following section will contemplate the position of Tokens as securities under Finnish law, blockchain finality, the disclosure requirements related to Token offerings in Finland, and finally, the applicability of the market abuse regime to Tokens subject to public trading. The definitions of a 'security' and 'financial instrument' are used in parallel, and it is appropriate to note that where all securities are financial instruments, all financial instruments are not necessarily securities.

[A] What Makes a Token a Security?

There are no exemptions in the Finnish capital markets law for any specific Token type or categorization. Any analysis made is very much case specific and needs to be done through examining the Token qualifications in question. Could digital assets (e.g., Utility Tokens, Currency Tokens or Security Tokens) be construed as securities under Finnish law? Intuitively, it seems apparent that the answer to such question is yes. However, analysing the circumstances where this might happen requires a systematic approach both to the definition of a security and the characteristics of the specific digital asset in question.

Pursuant to the SMA, a security is negotiable and issued (or meant to be issued) to the public together with several other securities with similar rights (requirement of fungibility[103]). Finnish civil law deems securities as bearer-bond documents, and the requirement of negotiability has been construed to mean that a transferee of the bearer bond is protected against any subsequent third-party claims. Holding a security on a book-entry securities account in dematerialized form has traditionally been considered to produce the same protection against third-party claims as to the possession of a physical bearer-bond document.[104] This analogy might be extended to Tokens held on

101. Regulation (EU) 2017/1129 of the European Parliament and of the Council of 14 June 2017 on the prospectus to be published when securities are offered to the public or admitted to trading on a regulated market, and repealing Directive 2003/71/EC (the *Prospectus Regulation*).
102. Regulation (EU) no. 596/2014 of the European Parliament and of the Council of 16 April 2014 on market abuse (market abuse regulation) and repealing Directive 2003/6/EC of the European Parliament and of the Council and Commission Directives 2003/124/EC, 2003/125/EC and 2004/72/EC (MAR).
103. The fungibility requirement means, in practice, that no distinction can be made between the issued securities based on the attached rights, i.e., from investor's perspective it does not matter which security he or she owns.
104. There is an established view in the Finnish jurisprudence that the SMA may be applied where a person has the possibility to obtain proof for his or her ownership right, e.g., by requesting an extract from a custody system where such ownership right has been recorded.

a blockchain database. Thus it may be possible to meet the requirement of transferability also in relation to instruments issued in dematerialized form on a blockchain platform (*see* section §6.05[B] on Blockchain Finality). However, the negotiability (transferability) of the Token cannot be restricted, for example, in the issuer's Articles of Association – otherwise, the Tokens will not qualify as securities.

Pursuant to the SMA, a security may be:

(i) a share in a limited liability company or a corresponding share of another entity as well as a depositary receipt in respect of such right;
(ii) a bond or other securitized debt as well as a depositary receipt in respect of such right;
(iii) any other security giving the right to acquire or sell a security referred to in items (i) and (ii);
(iv) a security giving rise to a cash settlement determined by reference to a security, currency, interest rate or yield, commodity or other index or measure; or
(v) a unit in a common fund, or a unit issued by a collective investment undertaking comparable thereto.

Rights to possess a specific apartment, other premises or real estate have been carved out from the definition of a security. Also money-market instruments are out of scope.[105]

As the issuance of Tokens through blockchain or DLT means to assign digital value, the characterization of such Tokens under applicable securities laws needs to be done by examining the nature of the digital value in question, i.e., the rights and obligations attached to the Token. As we can see from the definition of a security, the underlying value of a security can be a number of things. Whether the underlying value of a Token to be issued is made of rights attached to shares or bonds or any other security establishing rights to acquire or sell such rights; it seems clear that such Token can be categorized as a security provided that the Token is negotiable on a securities market (e.g., on a blockchain platform). Where a transferable Token carries profit-sharing rights and/or voting power, it is likely that we are dealing with securities (Security Tokens).

In the case of Utility Tokens, the classification as securities is harder to construe, but it cannot be excluded that Utility Tokens could be securities as well. This is very much a question of the characteristics of a specific Utility Token, and first, its negotiability and settlement mechanisms. If a Utility Token can be settled in cash, for example, based on a reference to a commodity price, such a Token could be construed as a security.[106] In respect of Currency Tokens, ESMA has taken the view that pure

105. The definition of a 'security' in the SMA is based on the definition of a 'transferable security' in item (44) of Art. 4(1) of the Directive 2014/65/EU of the European Parliament and of the Council of 15 May 2014 on Markets in Financial Instruments and amending Directive 2002/92/EC and Directive 2011/61/EU (MiFID II).

106. The preparatory works of the SMA specifically note that also such instruments where the settlement is determined by a reference to commodity products can be securities under the SMA.

payment-type crypto assets are unlikely to qualify as financial instruments under MiFID II.[107] The FIN-FSA is likely to follow such guidance.

[B] Blockchain Finality

Where transactions on securities recorded on the book-entry system maintained by the Finnish Central Securities Depository benefit from statutory legal finality rules, Finnish law does not include any legal finality rules for transactions conducted on blockchain platforms. The question of blockchain finality and the related protection mechanisms against third-party claims should thus be construed under general principles of Finnish civil law.

As security ownership data recorded on a blockchain ledger does not carry public credence (i.e., bona fide third party does not benefit from statutory legal protection in relation to a transaction conducted on the basis of ownership data recorded on the blockchain ledger), the buyer of a Token carries a risk of third-party claims in case there would be a parallel transaction on the same identified ownership right.[108] In such collision of rights, the main principle to be applied would be the time priority rule, i.e., the party whose right of ownership has been established prior to the other party's will gain legal ownership to the Token in question. Evidencing such right could mean, in practice, that the first buyer (*primus*) of the Token would need to obtain an extract of the conducted transaction validated by several blockchain mining nodes and compare it to the secondary buyer's (*secondus)* corresponding data.

It is possible to deviate from the above-mentioned time-priority rule by affording an extinction right to secondus. However, usually, such right is based on the requirement that the secondus was bona fide at the time of the transaction and has since taken active steps to validate his/her ownership right (e.g., by registering such right on a public register). However, as transactions conducted on (public) blockchain platforms are all registered automatically by definition of the technology itself, seeking such registration may not offer any additional protection towards primus whose transaction has also been recorded on the blockchain ledger.

As long as there is no legal blockchain finality, the general transaction time-priority rule seems to offer the most efficient ultra partes protection for Token transaction participants. Public credence is a difficult concept in the context of decentralized ledger technology, where there is no centralized party who would carry the responsibility of proper functionality of the blockchain protocol. If protection is afforded based on public credence of incorrect-ownership data, there would be no one single party to claim damages from for recording such incorrect data or the malfunction of blockchain protocol causing such entry. After all, could you really establish legal

107. ESMA, *Advice on Initial Coin Offerings and Crypto-Assets*, https://www.esma.europa.eu/sites/default/files/library/esma50-157-1391_crypto_advice.pdf (accessed 11 March 2020).

108. In normal circumstances within the blockchain network, this should not be technically possible, but in case there is a malfunction or change in the blockchain protocol, parallel transaction could happen.

finality without a party who takes on the related obligations meant to guarantee the finality-creation process?

[C] Special Requirements for Prospectus

Assuming we would be offering Tokens categorized as securities under Finnish law – in such an offering we would need to comply with the applicable disclosure requirements related to the offering of transferable securities, i.e., prospectus regime and existing good conduct principles of the Finnish securities market. What would be the right prospectus disclosure rules to comply with? There are no specific schedules for Tokens in the Prospectus Regulation or the delegated acts of the Commission, and the FIN-FSA has not issued any guidance on selecting applicable disclosure criteria for public Token offerings. Thus, the appropriate disclosure criteria should be determined based on the underlying value of the Tokens to be offered, i.e., the rights and obligations the Tokens provide for their holders. If the Token provides rights and obligations that of a shareholder (represents a share/equity portion in the issuer), then the prospectus disclosure to be followed would be one for equity securities. If the Token provides rights and obligations, for example, of a bondholder (represents a bond/debt instrument of the issuer), the prospectus disclosure to be followed would be one for non-equity securities. These two types of STOs are most likely the most common ones to be seen in the Finnish market in the first place, if and when the relevant market picks up.

Offering Tokens under a prospectus would, in practice, mean preparing a summary, registration document and a securities note based on the selected disclosure criteria (e.g., criteria for equity securities or non-equity securities). Such disclosure criteria include several prospectus content requirements related to the securities offered. For example, the prospectus should include:

(1) a description of the material risks specific to the securities being offered;
(2) a description of the type and class of the securities offered;
(3) an indication whether the securities are in registered form or bearer form and whether the securities are in certificated form or book-entry form;
(4) a description of the rights attached to the securities, any limitations thereof and procedure for the exercise of those rights;
(5) method and time limits for payment and delivery.

The above items are examples of such prospectus content requirements, where the special digital nature of Tokens as instruments held and kept in custody by means of a blockchain technology has special significance. In terms of item (1), risks related to the blockchain technology used to hold and transact with the offered Tokens would be elaborated pursuant to this requirement in the risk-factors section of the prospectus. This would mean evaluating the materiality of the recognized risks on the securities offered based on the probability of their occurrence and the expected magnitude of their negative impact. Conducting this assessment, in practice, can be very challenging and requires a deep understanding of the blockchain technology used. Risk of several blockchain strings operating with the same underlying right (fork), losing one's private key to dispose of Tokens at a given address, risk of being hacked or risk of failure in the Token custody and transaction verification ecosystem are examples of issues that would need to be described in the prospectus.

Pursuant to item (2), one would describe the underlying value of the offered Tokens, i.e., the rights and obligations produced for the holder of the Token. In terms of item (3), the starting point would be to assume that the offered Tokens are in bearer form. However, it appears to be a somewhat problematic question whether the offered Tokens should be categorized as certificated securities or book-entry form securities. Certificated form would imply issuing a physical certificate on the underlying right (e.g., a share certificate). This would not work in relation to transfers of title in the blockchain ecosystem, as the physical certificate would have to follow the purchaser (this is why there is a requirement to cancel all certificates before issuing any securities relating to such certificates in the book-entry system maintained by the Finnish Central Securities Depository). Then again it seems that Tokens cannot be in book-entry form, as book-entry form securities have been specifically defined in Finnish law to refer to securities that have been registered on a book-entry system maintained by a licensed central securities depositary (CDS). Thus, having book-entry form Tokens would imply that the blockchain infrastructure service provider would need to be a licensed central securities depository. Accordingly, tokenization of financial assets on a blockchain infrastructure seems to fall somewhere in between the said categories. In any case, it seems that the requirement as per item (3) would need to be adjusted to meet the specifications of the offered Tokens in question (*see* section §6.05[B] on Blockchain Finality).

In terms of item (4), the prospectus would need to include a description of the mechanisms through which the rights attached to the offered Tokens are exercised, i.e., there would need to be a description of the actual process for using voting power and/or financial rights attached to the Token. Pursuant to item (5), one would describe the actual technical process of payment and delivery in the blockchain environment to be utilized and the blockchain protocol to be used for transaction validation. The descriptions could end up being very technical in nature and thus hard to grasp for an individual investor. As the technology used can vary from one offering to another, it might be difficult for investors to understand the process or compare specifications of different platforms in a meaningful manner.

When contemplating an STO, the issuer should always analyse whether (i) a prospectus exemption is available and whether (ii) the Token offering exceeds the national prospectus threshold of EUR 8 million.[109] Where the total offer consideration is between EUR 1 and EUR 8 million, the offering may be made by making available a concise basic information document (no FIN-FSA approval needed). If the total consideration is below EUR 1 million, no mandatory disclosure document is needed,

109. Finland has decided to exempt public security offerings from the obligation to publish a prospectus, where the total consideration of public offers in the EU is less than EUR 8 million calculated over a period of twelve months.

but the offer is governed under general good conduct principles of the Finnish securities market (elaborated further below). In respect of the prospectus exemptions, the most commonly used are offers to qualified investors, offers to less than 150 non-qualified investors and offers with a total consideration of at least EUR 100,000 per investor. By default, these exemptions should be normally available for STO as well.

It should be noted that regardless of the applicability of prospectus exemptions or the fact that the national prospectus threshold is not exceeded in relation to an individual offering, the general good conduct principles of the SMA have to be always complied with. This means, in practice, that regardless of the size of the offering, the issuer of Tokens shall not provide false or misleading information on the offering, the offered Tokens or the issuer itself. Further, pursuant to the good conduct principles, the issuer has an obligation to correct and/or supplement without undue delay in an adequate manner any information which is revealed to be untruthful or misleading in nature and which may be of material significance to an investor. The issuer has also a general obligation to keep sufficient information on factors that may have a material effect on the value of the offered security equally available to all investors. In offerings executed without a prospectus or other official offering document, such general information obligation is usually met with information memorandums and/or company presentations.

[D] Regulatory Specifics for Organized Trade

The FIN-FSA has not issued any official guidance or regulation that would contemplate whether a Token that is subject to public trading should be legally construed based on the fundamental principles of the existing market abuse regime. Such an interpretation would mean that information relating to Tokens or issuers of such could constitute inside information as referred to in MAR and further that provisions concerning, e.g., insider trading, unlawful disclosure of inside information and market manipulation would become applicable. Applicability criteria of MAR are twofold: (i) there needs to be a financial instrument that (ii) has been admitted to trading (or for which a request for admission to trading has been made) on a trading venue referred to in MiFID II. As discussed in section §6.05[A], Tokens may well be categorized as securities under Finnish law depending on their characteristics. In terms of MAR applicability, the key question seems to be the admission to a trading venue.

The European Securities Market Authority has taken the view that where Tokens qualify as financial instruments, any platform trading such Tokens with a central order book (or matching orders under other trading models) are likely to qualify as multilateral systems.[110] Pursuant to MiFID II, such platforms should operate as regulated markets, multilateral trading facilities or organized trading facilities (i.e., trading venues under MiFID II). Trading Tokens qualifying as financial instruments on such trading venues trigger the applicability of MAR. This would mean that the issuer

110. ESMA *supra* n. 107.

of the Token would have an ongoing obligation to disclose all inside information relating to such issuer to the public.

[E] Conclusion

In Finland, Tokens are a new digital asset class and the market is very much in its infancy. In terms of regulation, the part of the Finnish securities laws that have not been already repealed are very much aligned with the EU capital markets law. The existing Finnish securities laws have not been drafted with digital assets or blockchain technology in mind. Thus it seems clear that there are areas of national law where the categorization of Tokens as securities in the context of capital markets regulation creates a need for a certain level of interpretation to allow a meaningful application of provisions. Also such scenarios might arise where there are no relevant provisions available at all. The FIN-FSA is likely to follow closely the guidance and advice of ESMA and will most likely adopt best practices from more experienced markets once available. New EU regulation to be adopted will most likely be implemented on a national level without any significant gold-plating.

§6.06 CAPITAL MARKETS AND BLOCKCHAIN: COUNTRY REPORT – FRANCE

Bertrand Levy[111]

[A] What Makes a Token a Security?

France has been very active over the past years in order to create a legal environment which would be favourable to the development of digital technology. In particular, France enacted in 2019 the so-called PACTE (Plan d'Action pour la Croissance et la Transformation de l'Entreprise)[112] law governing ICOs and creating a regulatory framework for digital asset service providers, thus setting-up the definition of digital assets which can be divided into two main categories: cryptocurrencies and Tokens.

The French financial and monetary Code[113] provides a definition of Token: 'a token is constituted by any intangible asset representing under digital format one or several rights which can be issued, registered, stored or transferred by means of a shared electronic registration system which enables to identify, directly or indirectly, the owner of such property.' A natural tendency might be to assimilate Tokens to financial instruments, which would in the end have the merits of simplicity in terms of legal treatment but would create a rather stringent legal framework. This is not the path that was chosen by the French legislator because French law privileges substance over

111. Bertrand Lévy is a corporate partner at Bird & Bird based in Paris. Bertrand has extensive expertise in M&A and LBO transactions with a strong focus on Fintech matters.
112. Law no. 2019-486 dated 22 May 2019.
113. Article L. 552-2 of the French financial and monetary Code.

form. In other words, if a Token falls within the definition of financial instruments, it will follow the legal regime applicable to financial instruments. For instance, if a Token is qualified as a financial instrument as per French law, the relevant provisions regarding prospectus will be applicable in case of public offers. The consequence of this principle is that the terms and conditions of each Token should be reviewed in order to determine whether it can be qualified as a financial instrument.

What is a Security Token under French law? In order to answer this question, we first need to know what a security is under French law. Rather than providing for a theoretical definition of security, the French Financial and Monetary Code[114] provides a list: financial securities are (i) share capital securities issued by stock companies, (ii) debt securities, and (iii) shares of collective investment schemes (CISs). If a Token has characteristics which fall within these categories, it can be qualified as a Security Token.

As an example, a Security Token can be constituted by a share of capital which is registered on a shared electronic registration system instead of being registered in a traditional book-entry form as is usually the case in practice. We will see below that French law recognizes such a Security Token with corresponding legal consequences. Some might also name certain Tokens which are not securities that have been digitalized but represent the underlying securities as 'Security Tokens'. This type of Tokens is more construed as a new type of securitization instrument rather than a pure Security Token. We will base our analysis below on Security Tokens that can actually qualify as securities under French law.

[B] Blockchain Finality

The notion of shared electronic registration system has been introduced in France by two ordinances dated 28 April 2016[115] and 8 December 2017[116] relating respectively to: (i) savings bonds (so-called minibonds) and (ii) financial instruments which were implemented by a Decree dated 24 December 2018.[117]

The 'minibonds' constitute a new category of savings bonds which are intermediated by crowdfunding platforms and can be issued by limited liability companies under certain conditions for an amount not exceeding EUR 2,500,000 per year. Such bonds are nominative and non-negotiable. The provisions of the French financial and monetary Code[118] provide that the issuance and transfer of such bonds can be implemented through a shared electronic registration system. In addition, French law implicitly recognizes the validity of the 'smart contract' which is constituted by the transfer of the 'minibonds' in the shared electronic registration system.[119]

114. Article L. 211-1 II of the French financial and monetary Code.
115. Ord. 2016-520 dated 28 April 2016.
116. Ord. 2017-1674 dated 8 December 2017.
117. Decree no. 2018-1226 dated 24 December 2018.
118. Article L. 223-12 of the French financial and monetary Code.
119. Article L. 223-13 of the French financial and monetary Code.

More importantly in terms of legal impact, the Ordinance dated 24 December 2018 enables to register, transfer and pledge securities as defined by French law on a shared electronic registration system.[120] However, listed securities are not included in the type of securities which can benefit from these provisions. Nevertheless, this constitutes a significant breakthrough in terms of recognition of shared electronic registration systems for purposes of Security Token issuance. French law thus provides in theory for equal legal strength, hence protection, for securities which are registered in a traditional book-entry form (the 'old fashion' way) or in a shared electronic registration system. The holders of Security Tokens therefore benefit from the same rights as the holders of a security which is not tokenized.

In particular, the provisions of the French financial and monetary Code specifically provide that the bona fide acquisition rule apply to transfer of securities carried out through a DLT.[121] French law recognizes that digital assets can constitute financial securities, which is the natural step after dematerialization which occurred quite a long time ago and perhaps the first step towards full digitalization of financial securities. However, we will see below that the will of the legislator to grant the same legal effects for securities registered under a shared electronic registration system and under book-entry form will require a few further legal adaptations.

It should be noted that French law is theoretically neutral from a technical standpoint and does not refer to a specific underlying technology or type of shared electronic registration system (public, private or consortium). However, specific legal requirements might impose the recourse to a private- or consortium-shared electronic registration system on which to register Security Tokens so that certain legal provisions can be enforceable. In particular, French law now provides that it is the responsibility of the issuer, or an agent appointed by the issuer, to keep the register in a book-entry form or in a shared electronic registration system.[122] For instance, French law provides that a seller and a purchaser of shares can freely determine the effective date of transfer for their shares. If there is no account manager, this flexibility can be difficult to achieve, in practice, on a blockchain. Another example is the enforcement of pledges. French law provides that a pledge has to be enforced against the custodian of the securities, which might prove difficult, in practice, against public blockchains.[123] There is also a legal difference in terms of rules regarding the pledge of securities. The legal regime applicable to the pledge of securities is constructed so that it is the account itself which is the subject of the pledge, not the securities, which creates theoretical and practical questions as to how these legal provisions can apply for securities registered in a shared electronic registration system since there is no account anymore.

---

120. Article L. 221-20, VII of the French financial and monetary Code.
121. Article L. 211-16 of the French financial and monetary Code.
122. Article R. 228 of the French Commercial code, Art. R. 211-2 and R. 211-3 of the French financial and monetary code.
123. Vincent Malassigné, *Blockchain et droit des sociétés*, the principle of equivalence of book-entry registration and registration in a shared electronic recording device.

There is clearly a will from the legislator to grant the same legal effect to the registration of securities in a shared electronic registration system and in the book-entry form, but there is still some fine tuning to reach full equivalence, but most importantly, confidence from security holders on this new technology must be gained.

[C] Special Requirements for Prospectus

France is of course subject to EU prospectus regulations, and the issuance of Security Tokens should therefore be specifically reviewed in this respect as well as local French requirements. Any public offering of securities requires the prior publication of a prospectus unless the public offering falls under exemptions of the applicable regulation.

If there is no exemption, the prospectus will have to provide the relevant information required by law, with a specific focus on risk factors related to the shared electronic registration system. In particular, the prospectus will have to describe the specificities of the Security Tokens. For instance, how the revenue streams are generated from the underlying asset (dividends, interest, etc.) and distributed to the Token holder. If the Token issued is actually a share, the prospectus will have to describe the type of shares represented by the Token and the various rights attached to the shares such as dividends (preferred or not), information rights or any other type of rights provided by law or by contract. It could be envisaged that specific shareholders' rights which are usually set forth in a separate shareholders' agreement be included in the Token code in the form of a smart contract (lock-up periods, waivers of preferred subscription rights, right of first offer, audit rights, etc.). Voting rights could also be exercised via the shared electronic registration system.

French law provides an exception to the prospectus requirement which might be of interest in the context of STOs for small- or medium-size companies.

The general regulations of the French FMA provide in Article 211-2 that public offerings below EUR 8,000,000 do not constitute public offers subject to prospectus. The total amount of the offer is calculated on a twelve-month period following the first offer. In this specific case, the issuer benefits from a simplified procedure which consists in providing to the subscriber a simplified information document which includes basic information detailed in Article 212-44 of the general regulations issued by the French FMA:

(1) presentation of the issuer and a description of its activity, project and use of proceeds, together with the latest financial statements available, financial forecast, fundraisings, financings and cash position, as well as an org chart of the management and shareholding;
(2) information on the level of commitment of the management in the proposed offer;
(3) comprehensive information on all rights attached to the securities to be issued (voting rights, financial rights and information rights);

(4) comprehensive information on all rights (voting rights, financial rights and information rights) attached to securities not offered to the public as well as the beneficiaries of such securities;
(5) description of the provisions mentioned in the by-laws or shareholders' agreement governing the liquidity of the securities;
(6) the conditions under which copies of the registration of the ownership of the investors in the issuer can be obtained;
(7) description of the risks implied by the activity of the issuer and the contemplated project;
(8) if available, a copy of the reports prepared to the attention of the general assembly of the last financial year and the current financial year as well as the reports prepared by the statutory auditors if any;
(9) the date of the simplified information document.

Such information document and the communications relating thereto, whatever their format or communication method, have to be provided to the French FMA which can require specific disclaimer to be included. It should, however, be noted that securities listed (or to be listed) on a regulated market or MTF cannot benefit from this exemption.

The new regulations recognizing the registration and transfer of securities in a shared electronic registration system combined with the prospectus exemption referred to above create a favourable legal framework for the development of securities Token offerings in France for transactions below EUR 8,000,000, but such offerings remain for the moment confidential. The legal framework relating to STOs on the primary market will not be in a position to develop if there is no secondary market which actually enables to exchange the Tokens once they are issued.

Several transactions qualifying as STOs were identified on the French market in 2019. The French FMA identified seven STOs in 2018 and 2019, most of which took place in the form of private placements open to qualified investors and were exempted from prospectus requirements.[124] For instance, the STO of Authenticao carried out in October 2019 with the objective of raising EUR 7.9 million was open to qualified investors and not subject to prospectus requirements.[125]

Another example is the Société Générale which took place in France on 18 April 2019. Covered bonds were issued for an amount of EUR 100,000,000 in the form of Security Tokens registered on Ethereum.[126]

124. FMA, *Review and analysis of the application of financial regulations to security tokens*, https://www.amf-france.org/sites/default/files/2020-03/legal-analysis-security-tokens-amf-en_1.pdf (accessed on 27 May 2020).
125. https://www.globenewswire.com/news-release/2019/04/02/1794894/0/en/Chaineum-acts-as-STO-Advisor-for-Carthagea.html (accessed 11 March 2020).
126. Press release issued by Société Générale on 23 April 2019.

[D] Regulatory Specifics for Organized Trade

As mentioned above, the scope of the Decree dated 24 December 2018 only concerns non-listed securities, which means in other words that the securities thus issued by securities Token offering cannot be admitted to operations by a CDS nor settled in a securities settlement system (SSS). This also means that such Tokens can be exchanged through a platform provided that no CDS or SSS is involved. The regulation of exchange platform becomes thus crucial for the development of STOS.

The French so-called PACTE – law referred to above aims to provide a legal framework for exchange platforms by organizing a legal regime for digital asset service providers. In particular, the PACTE – law enables digital asset service providers to operate a trading platform of digital assets. The purpose of this regulation is to provide a legal framework to transfer digital assets. When setting up digital asset exchange platforms, the important question is therefore about the differentiation between an MTF or a regulated market as defined by MiFID II (which requires formal clearance by local regulators to operate as such) and the trading platform of digital assets created by the PACTE law for which clearance is optional.

ESMA's preliminary view[127] is that 'where crypto-assets qualify as financial instruments, platforms trading crypto-assets with a central order book and/or matching orders under other trading models are likely to qualify as multilateral systems and should therefore either operate under Title III of MiFID II as Regulated Markets or under Title II of MiFID II as MTFs or OTFs '. In other words, if an exchange platform of digital assets uses a central order book or matching orders, it is very likely to be regulated by MiFID II and will require clearance by local regulators to operate. This means that digital asset exchange platforms will have to operate in a decentralized manner, which has a significant impact in terms of fluidity of the exchanges if they want to benefit from the advantages of the legal regime set by the PACTE law.¶

The French FMA issued a position on 6 March 2020 regarding the notion of trading venue applicable to financial instruments registered in a distributed ledger.[128] The French FMA considers that systems organized as bulletin boards used only for advertising buying and selling interests do not constitute regulated markets or multilateral trading facilities and therefore does not require an authorization for the operation of a trading venue as per MiFID II. It is, however, crucial that the said platform does not directly provide communication means between buyer and purchaser and that the transaction be carried out bilaterally outside the platform.

French law has been with other jurisdictions at the forefront of regulating digital assets with a specific legal regime for ICOs, the recognition of shared electronic registration systems for the transfer of securities and specific legal regime applicable to digital asset service providers. However, these efforts have been made on a local basis,

127. *Advice on Initial Coin Offerings and Crypto Assets* dated 9 January 2019.
128. AMF, *AMF Position -DOC 2020-02, Clarification Regarding the Notion of Trading Venue. Applicable in Particular to Financial Instruments Registered in a Distributed Ledger*, https://doctrine.amf-france.org/en_US/Reglementation/Doctrine/Doctrine-list/Doctrine?docId = workspace%3A%2F%2FSpacesStore%2F5218f99f-b4c3-4369-888f-8614ab2c01b2&category = V + - + Market + infrastructure&docVersion = 1.0&langSwitch = true (accessed on 27 May 2020).

and the challenge will now be to create legislation at EU level and perhaps to enable the issuance and transfer of listed Security Tokens, with all underlying impacts in terms of market infrastructure and technological challenge.

§6.07 CAPITAL MARKETS AND BLOCKCHAIN: COUNTRY REPORT – GERMANY

Michael Juenemann[129]

[A] What Makes a Token a Security?

The answer to the key question of what makes a Token a security determines which and to what extent European capital markets and, in particular, securities regulation law will apply to it.[130] There is no specific regulation of crypto assets in Germany, and as a result, the Federal Financial Supervisory Authority (BaFin) classifies Tokens on a case-by-case basis depending on the design of the Token and the existing supervisory laws (none of which were formulated with crypto assets specifically in mind). Depending on its legal structure, a Token could be classified as security and thus be subject to regulation according to the German Securities Trading Act (Wertpapierhandelsgesetz – WpHG) and Regulation (EU) 2017/1129 (EU Prospectus Regulation). The classification of a Token as a security triggers certain obligations such as the requirement to publish a securities prospectus in the absence of applicable exemptions.

Pursuant to the German Securities Prospectus Act (Wertpapierprospektgesetz – WpPG), 'securities' has the meaning of securities within Article 2(a) EU Prospectus Regulation. Article 2(a) of the EU Prospectus Regulation defines securities as 'transferable securities' pursuant to point (44) of Article 4(1) of Directive 2014/65/EU ('MiFID II') with the exception of money-market instruments having a maturity of less than twelve months. Pursuant to MiFID II, 'transferable securities' are those classes of securities which are negotiable on the capital market, with the exception of instruments of payment, e.g., shares in companies. Within WpHG (the German implementation of MiFID II), the meaning of securities includes all categories of transferable securities, whether or not represented by a certificate, with the exception of instruments of payment which are by their nature negotiable on the financial markets.

In summary, a Token can only be classified as a security under German law if it has certain essential characteristics: negotiability, transferability on (capital) markets and incorporation of rights comparable to securities.[131] Negotiability requires that the security is sufficiently standardized: each Token that is issued must contain the same

129. Head of international Finance and Financial Regulation Group at Bird & Bird, Dr Michael Juenemann understands the intricacies of the legal frameworks around FinTech and is one of the few to integrate knowledge of technology with capital markets law.
130. Rüdiger Veil, *Token-Emissionen im europäischen Kapitalmarktrecht*, 183 ZHR, 346, 354, (2019).
131. BaFin, *Prospektpflicht – Rechtslage seit dem 21.07.2019*, https://www.bafin.de/DE/Aufsicht/Prospekte/Wertpapiere/Prospektpflicht/prospektpflicht_node.html (accessed 11 March 2020).

characteristics so that a sufficient degree of certainty can be achieved simply by indicating the number of the Token.[132] The Token must be *fungible*.[133] This is not the case if the issuer of the Token offers individual adjustments according to the wishes of the purchaser in deviation from the usual model, e.g., adjustments to the maturity, the face value or the basic price of the Token.[134]

The Token must be tradable on financial markets but not actually traded.[135] Furthermore, the Token must be transferable in order to be negotiable in capital markets.[136] This is the case if the Token can be transferred to a transferee technically and legally unaltered.[137] Since BaFin follows the 'substance over form' approach of the ESMA, securitization in a certificate is not a mandatory requirement of a security.[138] However, the question is whether the conceptual similarity of Security Tokens with traditional securities is sufficient to establish tradability on capital markets, or if an extra requirement of legal finality is necessary to make a Security Token a security under German law (legal finality is discussed further in the section §6.07[B] below).

Neither the formal name of the Token nor any advertisement with regard to the Token is determinative of its status.[139] Essential to a Token's classification as a security is the (corporate) membership or financial rights associated with it. The concept of securities is therefore notably fulfilled by Tokens that are functionally similar to 'classic' securities such as stocks, bonds or certificates – unless such classic securities have formality requirements which cannot be met by blockchain-based Tokens: for example, with equity Tokens that represent shares of a German limited liability company (GmbH), the security classification does not apply due to the formality requirement of notarization.[140]

In contrast to Security Tokens, 'pure' Utility Tokens or Currency Tokens are not regarded as securities.[141] Utility Tokens are Crypto Tokens that allow access to certain services or products, similar to a voucher.[142] Currency Tokens are intended to be used

132. Michael Juenemann & Johannes Wirtz, *ICO: Rechtliche Einordnung von Token – Teil I*, Zeitschrift für das gesamte Kreditwesen 27, 28 (2018).
133. Christoph Kumpan, *Kapitalmarktrechts-Kommentar* s. 1 § 2 marginal no. 7 WpHG, Eberhard Schwark & Daniel Zimmer ed. (4th ed. 2010).
134. Peter Zickgraf, *Initial Coin Offerings – Ein Fall für das Kapitalmarktrecht?*, Die Aktiengesellschaft 293, 299, 300 (2018).
135. BaFin, supra n. 131.
136. Deutscher Bundestag, *Gesetzesentwurf der Bundesregierung, Finanzmarkt-Richtlinie-Umsetzungsgesetz*, Deutscher Bundestag Drucksache 16/4028 53 (2007).
137. BaFin, supra n. 131.
138. BaFin, *Initial Coin Offerings: Hinweisschreiben zur Einordnung als Finanzinstrumente*, WA 11-QB 4100-2017/0010 (2018).
139. Hagen Weiß, *Tokenisation*, https://www.bafin.de/SharedDocs/Veroeffentlichungen/EN/Fachartikel/2019/fa_bj_1904_Tokenisierung_en.html (accessed 11 March 2020).
140. Andreas Fuchs, *Wertpapierhandelsgesetz* s. 2 marginal no. 15 (2nd ed. 2016).
141. BaFin, supra n. 131.
142. BaFin, *Zweites Hinweisschreiben zu Prospekt- und Erlaubnispflichten im Zusammenhang mit der Ausgabe sogenannter Krypto-Token*, https://www.bafin.de/SharedDocs/Downloads/DE/Merkblatt/WA/dl_wa_merkblatt_ICOs.html (accessed 11 March 2020).

as an alternative means of payment.[143] With regard to Hybrid Tokens, the functions that the Token focus on and the circumstances of the individual case are decisive.[144]

Concepts for the definition of security known from other jurisdictions, such as (1) vouchers issued in relation to goods or services not yet available, (2) profit expectations of the Token purchasers or (3) a profit coming from the efforts of a promoter or a third party are not relevant under German law.

[B] Blockchain Finality

There is a general consensus that finality and immutability are characteristics of blockchain transactions.[145] However, contrary to popular belief, transactions on the blockchain are not technically 'final' but only 'probably final', since forks and software errors are possible at any time. Solutions to this uncertainty, such as the definition of a certain period of time after which a transaction is considered 'final', are discussed.

That transactions on the blockchain are not technically final raises the question of how legal finality of blockchain transactions can be established under German law. Considering the speed at which individual transactions take place - even outside of high-frequency trading - it is obvious that legal finality is an indispensable prerequisite for trading on the capital market. Therefore, the classic understanding of capital market negotiability is based on the possibility of bona fide acquisition.[146] The functionality of the market requires that titles can be traded without restrictions and transactions can be processed securely and easily without objections from third parties. Otherwise, buyers of securities would be exposed to incalculable risks because they would not know if they had acquired securities from a person who is entitled to transfer them.[147] This is where concepts such as the bona fide acquisition rules come into play.

If the data written on the blockchain was a sufficient substitute for a bona fide acquisition, there would be no need to apply this concept to Tokens. Blockchain could be considered as a (decentralized) register similar to a public register (such as the land registry which is administrated by a neutral and independent government body).[148] Thus, the blockchain could be subject to public credence. Therefore, the blockchain would have to provide complete information on the legal relationships with regard to the relevant Token. Due to the cryptographic rendition of the chain of ownership, the transmissions of Tokens are recorded on the blockchain. It is therefore argued that the ownership of the underlying right is inseparably linked to the Tokens by the illustration of the specific right on the blockchain (*tokenization*). However, the German legislator

---

143. BaFin, supra n. 131.
144. *Ibid.*
145. Tobias Zepf, Blockchain, *Technologie, Innovationen und Anwendungen – oder eine Kette, die Ketten sprengt* 9-9 (2016).
146. 17 A Ralf Wehowsky, *Becksche Kurz Kommentar Erbs/ KohlhaasStrafrechtliche Nebengesetze vol 1* D. 30 marginal no. 2 Peter Häberle ed. (226th ed. 2019).
147. Wehowsky, *supra* n. 146, *at* marginal no. 2; Kumpan, *supra* n. 133, at marginal no. 9.
148. Harald Wilsch, *The German 'Grundbuchordnung': History, Principles and Future about Land Registry in Germany*, Zeitschrift für Geodäsie, Geoinformation und Landmanagement 224, 225 (2012).

determines what is subject to public credence, and since it has not made any provision in this regard, the blockchain is, *lege lata*, not subject to public credence.

In addition, a bona fide acquisition of Tokens is ruled out as there are no proprietary rights to data under German law. However, the underlying right of the Token has to be taken into account. If this right is transferred by assignment within the meaning of section 398 German Civil Code (Bürgerliches Gesetzbuch - BGB) or by an assumption of contract, a bona fide acquisition is excluded. There is no statutory provision that makes the right embodied in a Token comparable to certificated bonds negotiable on the capital market (which can be subject to a bona fide acquisition even if the certificate has been stolen or lost).[149] It would require a legislative act to grant Tokens the status of a '*digital certificate*'.[150] In March 2019, the Federal Ministry of Finance and the Federal Ministry of Justice and Consumer Protection announced that the blockchain strategy of the German government aims to promote electronic securities - while safeguarding investor-protection requirements - and to create the necessary legal certainty and application security in both civil and supervisory law.[151] In order to adapt German law for electronic securities, the requirement for a security to be embodied in a certificate will no longer apply without restrictions.[152] The plan is to enable the creation of electronic securities by registration according to the model of the German Federal Government Debt Management Act (Bundesschuldenwesengesetz - BSchuWG). The documentation function of the securities certificate for electronic securities will be replaced by the recording of the corresponding rights in an electronic securities register. Such registration will guarantee the core elements of electronic securities: legitimation function, liberation effect and transfer function. Since there is a risk of manipulation, the respective issuer will not be allowed to keep the securities register to himself, but the register will have to be kept by a central government agency or an agency under government supervision unless the use of blockchain technology prevents unauthorized alterations of the register entries. In this case, the issuer or a third party will be allowed to act as the keeper of the register.[153]

However, if a bona fide acquisition of Tokens is not possible, the holder of a claim can demand to have the transfer reversed if the person who transferred the Tokens was not entitled to the underlying right. In this event, the underlying right has never been transferred. Thus, the data packages must be returned, or else the data on the

149. 6A Mathias Habersack, *Münchener Kommentar zum Bürgerlichen Gesetzbuch*, s. 793 BGB, marginal. no. 27, Franz Jürgen Säcker, Roland Rixecker, Hartmut Oetker & Bettina Limperg ed. (7th ed. 2017).
150. Robert Oppenheim & Eric Romba, *Initial Coin Offering (ICO) aus rechtlicher Sicht: Der Token als digitale Urkunde?*, https://www.it-finanzmagazin.de/initial-coin-offering-ico-rechtliche-sicht-token-digitale-urkunde-65569 (accessed 11 March 2020).
151. BMF & BMJV, *Eckpunkte für die regulatorische Behandlung von elektronischen Wertpapieren und Krypto-Token*, https://www.bundesfinanzministerium.de/Content/DE/Gesetzestexte/Gesetze_Gesetzesvorhaben/Abteilungen/Abteilung_VII/19_Legislaturperiode/2019-03-07-Eckpunktepapier-Wertpapiere-Krypto-Token/2019-03-07-Eckpunktepapier-regulatorische-Behandlung-elektronische-Wertpapiere-Krypto-Token.pdf;jsessionid=D5779523DB71FD407E8FE439C0A5C0D3?__blob=publicationFile&v=7 (accessed 11 March 2020).
152. BMF & BMJV, *supra* n. 151.
153. *Ibid.*

blockchain will not correspond to the legal ownership status of the Tokens under German civil law.

For that reason, a common approach under German law is to peg the digital Token to its underlying rights in the terms and conditions of the Token issuer. Such terms and conditions oblige the holder of a Token not to transfer the Token without transferring the underlying rights embodied in such Token and vice versa. However, such legal technique has effect only between the parties and is lacking the *inter omnes* effect of good faith acquisitions and the legal finality created by it. Consequently, any envisaged transferee of a Security Token should conduct a proper title due diligence regarding the transferor's ownership of the Token before any payment is made – a precaution which is rather difficult to reconcile with the idea of faster and efficient capital markets. For this reason, the logic of BaFin's approach to qualifying financial instruments as securities once they are put on the blockchain must be questioned. This does not mean that the so-called Security Tokens are unregulated. Under the German law, they are in any event regulated as capital investments requiring a prospectus, but the consequence of this is that there is no access to the European passports for security prospectuses.

[C] Special Requirements for Prospectus

Provided that Tokens are classified as securities under German law, their issuance is subject to the requirements of the EU Prospectus Regulation. This regulation serves as the basis for the approval and validity of securities prospectuses and is complemented by Regulations (EU) 2019/979 and (EU) 2019/980 which specify the content and presentation of such prospectuses. The WpPG contains provisions for exemptions to the prospectus requirement, on prospectus liability, on the securities information sheet, as well as provisions relating to the authority of BaFin and the punishment for offences. According to Article 3(1) of the EU Prospectus Regulation, securities shall only be offered to the public after the prior publication of a prospectus in accordance with the regulation. Thus, in Germany, securities may not be offered to the public without a prospectus approved by BaFin. This prospectus must contain all information related to the relevant issuer and the securities being offered. The rationale is to provide information to enable an investor to obtain an accurate understanding of the offer and to make an informed investment decision. According to the EU Prospectus Regulation, the prospectus shall in particular contain all information on the assets, liabilities, profits, losses, the financial situation of the issuer and of any guarantor, the rights attached to the securities, the reasons for the issue and the impact on the issuer.[154]

The term 'offer of securities to the public' is defined in Article 2(d) of the EU Prospectus Regulation as 'a communication to persons in any form and by any means, presenting sufficient information on the terms of the offer and the securities to be offered, so as to enable an investor to decide to purchase or subscribe for those

154. BaFin, supra n. 131; Rüdiger Koch, *Neue Regeln für Wertpapierprospekte*, https://www.bafin.de/SharedDocs/Veroeffentlichungen/DE/Fachartikel/2019/fa_bj_1906_Wertpapierprospekte.html (accessed 11 March 2020).

securities'. There is a domestic reference if investors resident in Germany are targeted by the offer. According to BaFin, this is the case if the offer is accessible from Germany.[155] BaFin derives from circumstantial evidence in each individual case whether there is a public offer to the domestic market. In doing so, BaFin evaluates the facts of the respective case as a whole.[156] If a public offer is made on the internet without restriction of access or to the audience addressed, the worldwide public is deemed to be addressed.[157] According to BaFin, the obligation to publish a prospectus in Germany will apply in this case unless certain exemptions (such as private placements) apply.[158] BaFin has pointed out that even if there is no domestic reference, a prospectus requirement may exist if foreign laws provide for it.[159]

The whitepapers published in the context of ICOs often do not meet the requirements that supervisory law imposes on securities prospectuses since they lack comparable informative value and structure.[160] Although the first Token securities prospectuses have been approved by BaFin since January 2019, there remain unanswered questions with regard to the special requirements for prospectuses in relation to Security Tokens. German regulator BaFin has not yet stated which information a Token securities prospectus has to contain - over and above the requirements for a traditional securities offering - but has only made a general statement about the main risks of Crypto Tokens (market liquidity and volatility risks, counterparty and project risks as well as technical and operational risks (e.g., cyber security risks)).[161] However, according to Article 16 of the EU Prospectus Regulation, the risk factors featured in a prospectus shall be limited to risks which are specific to the issuer and/or to the securities and which are material for taking an informed investment decision. ESMA has stated that the prospectus should include detailed information on the features and rights attached to the Tokens, the issuer's venture, the expected timetable of the offer, the use of the proceeds of the offer, the terms and conditions and the specific risks related to the underlying (blockchain) technology.[162]

The kind of special or additional information that has to be contained in Token securities prospectuses according to BaFin can be derived from the Token securities prospectuses already approved by the German regulator: These contain information on the central risks associated with blockchain technology, such as investors losing their private keys, Token theft or wallet hacking, vulnerability of the underlying blockchain protocol and infrastructure (e.g., the Ethereum Network) to hacking that could result in a loss of Tokens, software errors or bugs, exchange or exchange rate losses if an investor has to exchange fiat money or other cryptocurrencies and the possibility that a payout in cryptocurrencies (e.g., Ether) won't be possible for technical reasons

155. BaFin, *supra* n. 142.
156. *Ibid.*
157. *Ibid.*
158. *Ibid.*
159. *Ibid.*
160. BaFin, *BaFinPerspektiven*, 1 BaFinPerspektiven 1 63 (2018).
161. BaFin *supra* n. 142 at 65, 66 (2018).
162. ESMA, *Advice Initial Coin Offerings and Crypto-Assets*, https://www.esma.europa.eu/sites/default/files/library/esma50-157-1391_crypto_advice.pdf (accessed 11 March 2020).

because the network (e.g., the Ethereum Network) is no longer operated and in case of token-based bonds, where applicable, the limited fungibility of the token-based bonds.[163] In accordance with the requirements of the German Capital Investment Act (Vermögensanlagengesetz – VermAnlG), a prospectus must also be prepared for investment products which are not regarded as securities within the meaning of the EU Prospectus Regulation. Where a public offer of Tokens is made without a required prospectus, BaFin can prohibit the public offer and initiate an administrative offence proceeding.

[D] Regulatory Specifics for Organized Trade

Security Tokens may amount to financial instruments within the meaning of the German Banking Act, as investments according to the German Capital Investment Act or as investment funds within the meaning of the German Capital Investment Code (Kapitalanlagegesetzbuch – KAGB).[164] Trading of Security Tokens often takes place on crypto-exchanges. The German regulator BaFin regards crypto-exchanges as 'capital markets' or 'financial markets' if Security Tokens are traded on those markets.[165] Currently, Security Tokens are not traded on 'traditional' capital markets, which includes the organized market (section 2 paragraph 11 of the WpHG) as well as off-market trading (non-organized market), i.e., trading via multilateral trading systems (section 2 paragraph 21 of the WpHG)) or on the OTC (over the counter) market.[166]

Trading of Tokens may be subject to approval under the German Banking Act if they represent financial instruments. Although the German Banking Act (Kreditwesengesetz – KWG) does not (yet) specifically refer to Tokens, Tokens fall within its scope. According to BaFin, Tokens which carry rights to dividend-like payments or rights under the law of obligations with regard to property rights against the issuer, which are interchangeable and negotiable, qualify as debt instruments (*Schuldtitel*) and are therefore financial instruments according to KWG.[167] From 2020 onwards, cryptocurrencies, Security Tokens and Investment Tokens will also be classified as 'crypto values' (*Kryptowerte*) within the meaning of the KWG-E.[168] The trading of Security Tokens on the secondary market can qualify as principal brokering service (*Finanzkommissionsgeschäft*), as underwriting business (*Emissionsgeschäft*), investment brokering (*Anlagevermittlung*), investment advice (*Anlageberatung*), operation of an MTF

163. FUND Real Estate, https://fnd.group/de (accessed 11 March 2020).
164. BaFin, supra n. 142.
165. BaFin, *Initial Coin Offerings: Hinweisschreiben zur Einordnung als Finanzinstrumente*, WA 11-QB 4100-2017/0010, https://www.bafin.de/SharedDocs/Downloads/DE/Merkblatt/WA/dl_hinweisschreiben_einordnung_ICOs. (accessed 11 March 2020).
166. Fuchs, *supra* n. 140, at s. 2 WpHG, marginal no. 16 (2016).
167. BaFin, supra n. 142.
168. Bundesregierung, *Regierungsentwurf eines Gesetzes zur Umsetzung der Änderungsrichtlinie zur Vierten EU-Geldwäscherichtlinie RL (EU) 2018/843*, https://www.bundesfinanzministerium.de/Content/DE/Gesetzestexte/Gesetze_Gesetzesvorhaben/Abteilungen/Abteilung_VII/19_Legislaturperiode/2019-05-24-Gesetz-4-EU-Geldwaescherichtlinie/0-Gesetz.html (accessed 4 December 2019).

(*Betrieb eines multilateralen Handelssystems*), placement business (*Platzierungsgeschäft*), operation of an OTF(*Betrieb eines organisierten Handelssystems*)), contract brokering (*Abschlussvermittlung*), portfolio management (*Finanzportfolioverwaltung*), proprietary trading (*Eigenhandel*) or asset management (*Anlageverwaltung*).[169]

However, the issuer is privileged under German law: The initial offer of Security Tokens by the issuer does not constitute a financial service within the meaning of the German Banking Act. If the issuer carries out the issuance of Tokens without the involvement of third parties, a license by BaFin is not required even if the Tokens qualify as financial instruments.[170] It is possible for the issuer to buy back the issued Tokens and sell them again, e.g., on his own trading facility. In this case, the aforementioned privilege could also apply. However, the buying and selling of the Tokens could also constitute the financial service of proprietary trading (*Eigenhandel*), section 1 paragraph 1a no. 4 KWG. Proprietary trading is, e.g., the purchase and sale of financial instruments for one's own account as a service for others. The purchase of financial instruments means in particular the conclusion of purchase contracts for financial instruments, and the sale of financial instruments is the conclusion of contracts relating to the sale of financial instruments. For one's 'own account' means that the provider of the service bears the entire price and performance risk.[171] Still, the proprietary trade is 'a service for others'. To be a service, the trader must have a special relationship with the customer that requires an imbalance between the trader and the customer: The trader has to have better access to the market than the customer, for example, because the trader provides the customer with access to it.[172] This criterion could be fulfilled if the issuer buys and sells Tokens on his own trading facility. Thus, the buying and selling of Tokens by the issuer could qualify as proprietary trading (*Eigenhandel*).

The above-mentioned criteria that trigger regulation are not met through simply operating decentralized software on a number of computers. Thus, if the infrastructure for the trading is provided through a DEX, the question arises if it is still subject to regulation according to German supervisory law. Centralized trading venues such as stock exchanges offer buyers and sellers certain functionalities (such as an order book or price-fixing mechanisms). Those functionalities (central elements) are typically subject to regulation. However, many of the so called DEXs are not 'pure' DEX but contain central elements. For example, Boerse Stuttgart Digital Exchange (BSDEX), where tokenized securities will be traded from 2020 onwards, is operated as an MTF within the meaning of section 2 paragraph 12 KWG.

The administrator of a DEX operates an MTF within the meaning of the KWG and the WpHG if he brings the interests of a large number of persons in buying and selling

169. BaFin, supra n. 142.
170. BaFin, supra n. 142; 1 A, Sernetz Schäfer, *Kommentar zu Kreditwesengesetz, VO (EU) Nr. 575/2013 (CRR) und Ausführungsvorschriften* marginal no. 113 Karl-Heinz Boos, Reinfrid Fischer & Hermann Schulte-Mattler ed. (5th ed. 2016).
171. BaFin, *Merkblatt – Hinweise zu den Tatbeständen des Eigenhandels und des Eigengeschäfts*, https://www.bafin.de/SharedDocs/Veroeffentlichungen/DE/Merkblatt/mb_110322_eigenhandel_eigengeschaeft_neu.html (accessed 11 March 2020).
172. BaFin, *supra* n. 171, at no. 1.c) cc).

of financial instruments within the system and in accordance with established rules in a manner together which results in a contract for the purchase of such financial instruments. Furthermore, if Tokens are stored on the platform, this qualifies as safekeeping and management of securities for others within the meaning of the KWG and might classify as a cryptographic safekeeping business pursuant to the KWG-E respectively.[173] Furthermore, if the platform operates an order-matching system and an interim acquisition by the platform takes place, the activity of the platform might qualify as a central counterparty in accordance with the KWG.

In order to avoid regulation, a 'pure' DEX must not involve any regulated activity. The only task of such a DEX could be to distribute software on different servers or different computers of exchange participants. However, without order matching, the potential contractual partners could perhaps still find each other but would have to conclude bilateral contracts. In the absence of pricing mechanisms, they would have to negotiate an individual price which would at best come close to the best price available at the time (that the parties would never know).

Whether the German legislator will introduce regulation also for 'pure' DEXs remains to be seen. A possible trigger for regulation could be programming: The person who puts software into circulation in a targeted manner in order to establish a DEX, or the person who participates in this, could be regulated.

§6.08 CAPITAL MARKETS AND BLOCKCHAIN: COUNTRY REPORT – ITALY

Stefano Febbi[174]

[A] What Makes a Token a Security?

The word *Token* is not precisely defined under Italian law, and it is a term generally capable of designating tangible and intangible objects, representing something, typically value or information.

Based on their prevailing function/nature, a Token is often distinguished in payment Tokens (means of payment for the purchase of goods or services); Investment or Security Tokens (which attribute the owner either with property or administrative right in the issuer of the Tokens in the same way as equity or non-equity financial instruments, or a promise of financial return, as in financial products); Utility Tokens

173. Bundesregierung, *supra* n. 168.

174. Stefano Febbi is a Partner at Bird & Bird's Finance & Financial Regulation Group and co-head in the Financial Services Group based in Milan. Specialized in financial services legislation, Stefano advises major clients on topics such as measures to comply MiFI as well as the Insurance Distribution Directive (IDD) and AML Directives. An expert in drafting essential operational agreements for financial institutions and insurance companies, Stefano was appointed by Top Legal Industry Award (2017) as the Lawyer of the Year in the practice area of Insurance.

(which give the owner the right to use/receive a good or service) and Hybrid Tokens (which envisage a combination of the aforementioned types).[175]

With respect to the capital markets, the main problem is concentrated on the Initial Token Offering (ITO). ITO evokes a consolidated practice in the financial markets (Initial Public Offering – IPO) typically aimed at raising funds to finance a company or a business.

In more common ITOs, Tokens are alphanumeric codes (which are thus digital) representing (not values or information but rather) 'rights or claims', often correlated to a project/business. Digital Tokens that are offered to the public, normally without any intermediation, as consideration for the contribution of legal currencies (or even cryptocurrencies).

The most delicate aspect in ITOs from a legal and regulatory perspective is the protection of customers and public savings. In other words, the most critical issue is to determine if and to which extent protections required under the national financial market act (FMA)[176] should apply also to ITOs.

In the absence of specific laws or regulations, the application of FMA's provisions assumes that the digital Token can be classified either as a financial product (*prodotto finanziario*), a financial instrument (*strumento finanziario*) and/or a transferable security (*valore mobiliare*).

According to Italian law:

- '*transferable securities*' are securities that can be traded in capital markets;[177]
- '*financial instruments*' are the instruments listed in section C of Annex I of MiFID II directive,[178] including transferable securities;
- '*financial products*' are financial instruments and every other form of investment of a financial nature.¶

The main consequence of the classification of Tokens as financial products would be the application of FMA's provisions requesting the preparation and publication of a prospectus[179] and regulating the 'remote offering' (*offerta a distanza*) of financial products,[180] while the classification as financial instruments (or transferable securities) would imply the full application of rules transposing in Italy the MiFID II directive and regulating the performance of investment services.

175. Edoardo Rulli, *Incorporazione senza res e dematerializzazione senza accentratore: appunti sui* token, 1 Rivista Orizzonti del diritto commerciale, 1 ff (2019).
176. Legislative Decree no. 58 of 24 February 1998.
177. For example: (*a*) company shares and other titles equivalent to company shares, of partnership or of other parties and share deposit receipts; (*b*) bonds and other debt titles, including the deposit receipts relative to said shares; (*c*) any other transferable security that permits buying or selling transferable securities indicated in letters (*a*) and (*b*) or that involve spot settlement determined with reference to transferable securities, foreign exchange, interest rates or rates of return, commodities or other indices or measurements.
178. That is, the Directive (EU) 2014/65/EU (The markets in financial instruments Directive II).
179. According to Art. 94 of the FMA, any offering of investment products requires the prior publication (and delivery to investors) of a prospectus.
180. Pursuant to Art. 32 of the FMA and relevant implementing regulation issued by Consob, only banks and investment firms authorized in accordance with MiFID II rules may carry out the activity of '*remote offering of financial products*'.

However, currently, the offering of Tokens that do not fall within the definition of financial instruments or products would be substantially unregulated.

In the recent past, the Italian Supervisory Authority (Consob) has intervened on numerous occasions by classifying the offered Tokens as 'financial products'.[181] This has led to the suspension of the offerings due to the absence of a prospectus and exposes the offerors to criminal and administrative sanctions.

[B] Blockchain Finality

The use of blockchain technology allows the circulation of rights and claims through alphanumeric codes (Tokens) that legitimize the exercise of right or claim of those with the availability of that code. This circulation is not specifically regulated by Italian law and is based on the expression of consent of the parties. Therefore: (a) the contractual rules are applicable and, in details, the relationship between the parties involved is subject to the principle of good faith; and (b) Italian law has recently addressed the issue of the written form of the circulation of rights and claims by blockchain technology only in relation to the smart contracts. Article 8 *ter* of Legislative Decree no. 135/2018, on the one hand, defines the smart contract as 'a computer program functioning with technologies based on distributed ledgers and whose execution automatically binds two or more parties on the basis of effects predefined by them', and on the other hand, specifies that, in regard to the form, 'smart contracts satisfy the requirement of written form through identification of the interested parties by means of IT, through a process meeting the prerequisites set by the agency for digital Italy, with guidelines to be implemented within ninety days after the law converting this decree law enters into force'.

Neither of these statutes can be applied in fact since: (1) no rules follow the definition if not specific definition of the form; and, nevertheless, (2) the rules of written form require an indication of additional rules (the guidelines for establishing the requirements of the identification process), which are presently missing.

[C] Special Requirements for Prospectuses

If the Tokens can be specifically included in the financial products and are offered to the public, to be intended as:

> every communication to persons in any form and by any means, presenting sufficient information on the terms of the offer and the financial products to be offered, so as to enable an investor to decide to purchase or subscribe for those securities, including the placing through financial intermediaries.[182]

As anticipated, the rules set out in Articles 94 et seq. of the FMA, concerning public offerings of financial products (requiring the publication of a prospectus), shall

181. Consob Resolution no. 20660 of 31 October 2018; Resolution no. 20740 and Resolution no. 20741 of 12 December 2018.
182. Article 1, lit. t, of the FMA.

be applied as well as the rules provided for by the Regulation implementing FMA concerning the discipline of issuers of financial products (*Regulation no. 11971/1999*).

Due to the lack of a specific model, the contents of the prospectus shall comply with the model set out in the Annex 1A of Regulation no. 11971/1999. In any case: (*a*) on the basis of Article 94, §2°, of the FMA, the prospectus shall contain (1) '*the information that, depending on the characteristics of the financial products and the issuer, is necessary for investors to make an informed assessment of the issuer's assets and liabilities, profits and losses, financial position and prospects and of the financial products and related rights*' and (2) '*a securities note which briefly gives key information, in non-technical jargon, in the language in which the prospectus was originally drafted*', the format and content of which '*give adequate information on the fundamental features of the financial products in order to aid the investors to decide whether or not to invest in such products*'; (*b*) for the offer of financial products other than transferable securities, (1) '*the issuer or the offerer may request Consob to establish the content of the prospectus, where this has not been defined in general*'[183] and (2) '*if Consob believes, on reasonable grounds, that additional information is necessary, it shall inform the issuer or the bidder*'.[184]

Even if, vice versa, the Tokens are deemed to be transferable securities,[185] and are offered to the public, the rules on the prospectus provided for by the FMA and by Regulation no. 11971/1999 are completed by those set out in the Regulation (EU) 2017/1129. The information set out in the prospectus, then, pursuant to Article 6, §1 of the Regulation (EU) 2017/1129, may '*vary depending on any of the following: (a) the nature of the issuer; (b) the type of* [transferable] *securities; (c) the circumstances of the issuer; (d) where relevant, whether or not the non-equity securities have a denomination per unit of at least EUR 100,000 or are to be traded only on a regulated market, or a specific segment thereof, to which only qualified investors can have access for the purposes of trading in the transferable securities*'. Furthermore, on the basis of the type of interest or claim connected to the Tokens (as transferable security) the format and the content of the prospectus set out in the Annexes of the Commission delegated Regulation (EU) 2019/980 will be applied, completed with the provision provided for by the Commission delegated Regulation (EU) 2019/980.

However, the exemptions from the obligation to publish the prospectus set out in FMA, as detailed in both Regulation no. 11971/1999 and Regulation (EU) 2017/1129, are applicable.[186]

183. Article 5 of the Regulation no. 11971/1999.
184. Article 8, §4, of the Regulation no. 11971/1999.
185. As defined '*in point (44) of Article 4(1) of MiFID II le 2 (D), with the exception of money market instruments as defined in point (17) of Article 4(1) of Directive 2014/65/EU, having a maturity of less than 12 months*': Article 2, lit. a, Regulation (EU) 2017/1129.
186. Basically, prospectuses are expected for the public offerings concerning transferable securities whose total consideration of each offer in the European Union, calculated over a period of 12 months, is between EUR 1,000,000 and EUR 8,000,000 [Art. 34 *ter*, § 01, of the Regulation no. 11971/1999 and Art. 1, §4, of the Regulation (EU) 2017/1129]. In general, the rules set out in the FMA (concerning the appeal to public savings and, in details, the public offering of European Union financial instruments and financial products other than open-end undertaking for the collective investment in units or shares) shall not apply (at least) to the public offerings:

[D] Regulatory Specifics for Organized Trade

With respect to the trade, there are no specific rules. In particular, the rules on mandatory centralized management of financial instrument do not seem to apply, since they are linked to the circumstance that securities are traded on a trading venue[187] (i.e., on a regulated market, a trading system or an OTF[188]). Nevertheless, to the extent that the Token can be classified as a financial instrument, the application of the voluntary centralized management system provided for in the third paragraph of Article 83 *bis* of the FMA[189] cannot be excluded. In such a case, the Tokens circulate by accounts that are kept and managed by qualified intermediaries.[190]

In addition, if the Token can qualify as a 'financial instrument' within the meaning of Article 2, let. h, of the Regulation on the collection of risk capital via online portals (*Regulation no. 18592/2013*),[191] the rules on the collection of the capital of small- and medium-sized enterprises provided for by Article 50 *bis* and Article 100 *ter* of the FMA as well as by Regulation no. 18592/2013 shall apply.

More, in general, and with regards to the Italian corporate law, it should be noted that the Token: (*i*) may be assumed by a joint-stock company as a 'technique of legitimization and circulation' of the shares based on a specific provision of the by-laws;[192] and (*ii*) may represent the quotas of a private liability company (s.r.l.) at least[193] where the relevant standardization is allowed.[194] Consequently, in such cases, an adaptation of the rules on the circulation of the shares/quotas and on the

(*a*) addressing fewer than 150 persons, other than the qualified investors; (*b*) addressing qualified investors; (*c*) whose consideration for each offer in the European Union, calculated over a period of 12 months, is below EUR 8,000,000; (*d*) for a total consideration of at least EUR 100,000 per investor and per each separate offer; (*e*) of a *minimum* unit nominal value of at least EUR 100,000 (Art. 100 of the FMA and Art. 34 *ter* Regulation no. 11971/1999).

187. Article 83 *bis*, §1, FMA.
188. Article 1, §5 *octies*, lit. c, of the FMA.
189. *See* also Art. 15, §3, of the Rules governing central depositories, settlement services, guarantee systems and related management companies adopted by the Bank of Italy and Consob with provision of 22 February 2008 (*Regulation of 2008*).
190. V. Art. 83 *bis* ff. of the FMA and Regulation of 2008. Please also note the possibility that the application of the rules on centralized management is imposed to the issuer pursuant to Art. 83 *bis*, §2, of the FMA and Art. 15, §2, let. b and c, of the Regulation of 2008 in case of Tokens deemed as: (*i*) 'transferable securities that represent risk capital, bonds and other debt securities or other financial instrument that allows for the purchase of other financial instruments and relative indices, where the issuer has other financial instruments listed on the Italian regulated markets, or is to be considered disclosed' by Consob; or (*ii*) 'bonds and other debt securities where the amount of the issue exceeds € 150 million'. Should the absence of a document relate to the Token, Art. 85 of the MFA is not applicable.
191. By which financial instruments are 'the shares or units representing the share capital or the Undertaking for Collective Investment in units which are offered to the public through the portals'.
192. Article 2346, §1, of the Italian Civil Code.
193. On the contrary, the representation by Tokens of no-standardized quotas of private limited companies (s.r.l.) appears more complicated.
194. In the case of small- and medium-sized private limited companies (s.r.l.): *see* Art. 100 *ter*, §1 *bis*, of the FMA and Art. 26, §2, of the Law Decree no. 179/2012, converted with Law no. 221/2012. In this sense, some Italian authors deem the quotas of small- and medium-size private limited companies (s.r.l.) as transferable securities: first, Emanuele Cusa, *Le quote di s.r.l. possono essere valori mobiliari*, in *Riv. Soc.*, 675 ff (2019).

legitimization to the exercise of the social rights is required and shall be reconstrued on a case-by-case basis.

Furthermore, ITO have also been recently examined by Consob in a draft paper submitted to public consultation on 19 March 2019 (hereinafter, the 'Consultation Paper') which contains some innovative proposals and questions to the market, thus not mandatory but indicative of possible leanings of the Supervisory Authority.[195]

A preliminary and important statement reiterated by Consob is that new rules applicable to ITOs should apply where Tokens offered to the public do not classify as financial instruments and/or PRIIPs (including insurance-based investment products), in which case FMA's provisions regarding the prospectus and those transposing MiFID II (and IDD[196]) shall (continue to) apply.

However, also in the consultation paper Consob does not provide any guidelines to determine when a Token should be classified as a proper financial instrument. The classification as financial instrument shall therefore follow the same criteria and principles set forth for any instrument in MiFID II framework.

In fact, the definition of Tokens proposed by the authority in the consultation paper includes digital instruments that do not qualify as financial instruments, 'but which may feature elements of a financial product, consisting in digital ledger entries representing rights connected with investments in business projects, created and transferable in encrypted form through a shared and distributed electronic ledger (blockchain or Distributed Ledger Technology), to be used in trading or traded on token exchange systems'.[197]

In other words, Tokens subject to a new regulation would be digital assets that may (or may not) be a financial product and which may be traded in ad hoc trading venues.

The regulatory approach proposed by Consob in the consultation paper is based on the voluntary adoption (according to an opt in model) of specific procedures for initial offerings (i.e., the 'primary market'), which would entail the recourse to duly authorized online platforms, managed by managers of already existing crowdfund portals[198] or by new players subject to light authorization requirements. A sort of *Token crowdfunding* regulation that would leverage on a 'reputational and affordability incentive'.

After initial offerings, Tokens may be exchanged on 'secondary' markets, consisting of trading venues/markets that shall be entered in a register kept by Consob and

195. Consob, *Le offerte iniziali e gli scambi di cripto-attività*, http://www.consob.it/documents/46180/46181/ICOs_rapp_fin_20200102.pdf/70466207-edb2-4b0f-ac35-dd8449a4baf1 (accessed 27 May 2020).

196. That is, the Directive (EU) 2016/97 (Insurance Distribution Directive) regulating the way insurance products are designed and sold both by insurance intermediaries and directly by insurance undertakings.

197. Consob, *Le offerte iniziali e gli scambi di cripto-attività* Paragraph 2, http://www.consob.it/documents/46180/46181/doc_disc_20190319.pdf/64251cef-d363-4442-9685-e9ff665323cf (accessed 27 May 2020).

198. On 26 June 2013, Consob issued Resolution no. 18592, by means of which a regulation on the raising of venture capital by innovative startups through online portals was introduced.

could be managed by the same operators who manage the primary-market platforms or by others meeting the requirements established by Consob.

First commentaries to Consob's consultation paper highlighted that the draft document published by the authority does not address a number of issues:

- the definition of Tokens should be clarified, as it remains difficult to clearly fix which features would allow distinguishing a Token from a financial instrument;
- in the current legal framework, Consob does not seem to have the authority to regulate certain types of Tokens (e.g., pure Utility Tokens);
- for Tokens that could also be classified as *titoli di credito* (negotiable instruments) under Italian law, blockchain technology is not yet recognized as a valid way to transfer legal ownership.[199]

In conclusion, the current application of financial market rules concerning, in particular, the prospectus, remote offering of investment products, and investment services[200] (still) depends on the assessment of the characteristics, to be made on each occasion, of the actual Token and, thereby, the possibility of subsuming it in the different regulatory 'notions' that underpin that application, and first, in the 'notions' of financial products, financial instruments, and securities,[201] but even, possibly, in the 'notions' of insurance products and pre-assembled products. If and when the new draft regulation proposed by Consob becomes effective, Tokens (which are not financial instruments or PRIIPs) would become a brand new 'object' for the purposes of financial regulation and be subject to a voluntary regime, similar to the model already adopted by the Italian regulator for crowdfunding platforms.

For the sake of completeness, if the Token is used as *quid* aimed at the social-economic function of circulation of wealth,[202] the qualification of the Token as a negotiable instrument (*titolo di credito*) cannot be excluded: in this case, the discipline of circulation will be subject to the Articles 1992 et seq. of the Italian Civil Code, through which a higher level of security in the circulation of rights and claims is ensured with respect both of the position of the debtor (whose duty, under certain conditions, is considered to be fulfilled even if this is carried out with reference to a legitimate party who does not hold the right or the claim[203]) and of the position of the creditor (limiting the exceptions that can be opposed by the debtor[204] and acquiring, under certain conditions, the ownership of the right or of claim incorporated in the negotiable instrument through the '*a non domino*' way[205]). This qualification,

199. But *see* below.
200. In particular, provided for by Art. 21 and following of the FMA.
201. Maurizio Onza & Luigi Salamone, *Prodotti, strumenti finanziari, valori mobiliari,* in *Commentario del codice civile,* directed by E. Gabrielli, *Delle promesse unilaterali. Dei titoli di credito,* 539, 569 (2015).
202. *See* Paolo Spada, *Introduzione al diritto dei titoli di credito. Documenti circolanti, circolazione intermediato e* password, Torino, passim.
203. Article 1992 of the Italian Civil Code.
204. Article 1993 of the Italian Civil Code.
205. Article 1994 of the Italian Civil Code.

however, requires a brand new perspective of the reconstruction of the legal notion of a negotiable instrument that excludes the necessity of the document in respect of which there is still no certainty at the moment.[206] Nevertheless, one cannot exclude the possibility to apply the rules provided for the negotiable instruments through an agreement, binding only the relevant adherents as parties of the 'system' and using accounts. In this perspective, the blockchain technology does not appear, to date, capable of ensuring a circulation of the rights and claims with regard to third parties, presupposing an adhesion to the 'system'. In any case, due to Regulation (EU) no. 909/2014, providing and maintaining (security) accounts is revered if it is carried out in a centralized manner.

§6.09 CAPITAL MARKETS AND BLOCKCHAIN: COUNTRY REPORT – LIECHTENSTEIN

Johannes Dür[207]

Liechtenstein is one of the first countries worldwide which has introduced a legal framework for all applications of the so-called token economy, particularly in order to ensure legal certainty. For that purpose, the Liechtenstein Parliament has adopted on 3 October 2019 the Law on Tokens and TT Service Providers (Tokens and TT Service Provider Act, also known as 'Blockchain Act', hereinafter: TVTG),[208] which has entered into force on 1 January 2020. This country report for Liechtenstein particularly deals with and is based on the legal framework of the TVTG.

The TVTG constitutes a comprehensive legal framework for transaction systems based on so-called trustworthy technologies, which mainly addresses Blockchain or other Distributed Ledger Technologies (TT); TT are the core connecting factor for the applicability of the TVTG. The definition of TT is agnostic and technology-neutral and shall ensure applicability of the TVTG also for subsequent technology generations; it suggests that TT must ensure that the correctness and integrity of Tokens cannot be manipulated or at least only with disproportionate efforts.[209]

With the TVTG, the Token as a new legal object is introduced into Liechtenstein law to enable the representation of the 'real' world on TT Systems in a legally secure manner. Under the TVTG, 'Tokens' are understood as a kind of 'container' and are

206. Indeed the application of Art. 1992, 1993 and 1994 of the Italian Civil Code without a document is allowed only pursuant to a specific provision of the law (*see*, with respect to the dematerialization of the financial instruments, Art. 83 *quinquies*, §§ 1 and 2, and 83 *septies* of the MFA).

207. Johannes Dür, co-founder and partner at advocatio Attorneys at Law, understands that legal questions make up only one aspect of a business problem. He holds double diploma in Management, and uses his learning to consider economic aspects and impacts in his legal analysis and advice. Johannes is specialized in litigation and advisory in corporate, commercial and banking matters.

208. German: *Gesetz über Token und VT-Dienstleister* (*Token- und VT-Dienstleister-Gesetz; TVTG*).

209. Government of Liechtenstein, *Bericht und Antrag der Regierung an den Landtag des Fürstentums Liechtenstein betreffend die Schaffung eines Gesetzes über Token und VT-Dienstleister (Token- und VT-Dienstleistergesetz; TVTG) und die Abänderung weiterer Gesetze*, Report and Application no. 54/2019, 135, https://impuls-liechtenstein.li/wp-content/uploads/2019/06/bua_054_2019_tvtg.pdf (accessed 11 March 2020).

characterized as digital representations of analogous rights, which cannot be transferred or enforced without the Token itself.[210] Tokens can represent claims or rights of membership against a person, rights to property, other absolute or relative rights or even nothing.[211] The TT System shall ensure 'the secure transfer and storage of Tokens and the rendering of services based on this by means of trustworthy technology' (TT System).[212]

Due to its abstract formulation, the TVTG shall apply for all applications of the token economy, irrespective of the kind of Tokens involved; it regulates mainly the essential aspects of the token economy, such as generating and storing of Tokens, change and exchange platforms, the public sale of Tokens as well as the transfer of rights represented by a Token. However, it is not a regulation of activities related to the financial market and reaches far beyond financial services.

Financial market regulation is in general technology-neutral and thus also applicable for regulated activities involving TT Systems. The application of financial market regulation laws often depends on terms like 'legal currency', 'security' or 'financial instrument'. Thus, Tokens representing legal currencies, securities or financial instruments are also to be classified as such in accordance with financial market regulation.[213]

The TVTG includes a civil law chapter and a regulatory chapter. The civil law part governs the qualification of Tokens and the disposal over Tokens and its underlying rights under civil law. It follows widely the concept of classic securities law and adapts other pre-existing laws to the token economy. The civil law provisions play an important role to achieve legal finality and legal certainty of transactions on TT Systems (*see* below).

The regulatory approach of the TVTG is not aimed at a regulation of the technology itself. Instead, it defines several types of professional service providers of the token economy (TT Service Provider), who are obliged to apply for prior registration in a public register and are subject to (non-prudential) supervision by the Liechtenstein FMA. The requirements for such a registration include amongst others: personal reliability, technical suitability, a headquarter or place of residence in Liechtenstein, a suitable organizational structure and a procedure to deal with conflicts of interest, appropriate written internal proceedings and control mechanisms. In the course of the registration process, the FMA examines also possible obligations to obtain a licence according to financial markets legislation.[214] Precisely, the TVTG identifies and regulates the following TT Service Providers: *Token Issuer* (person who publicly

210. Government of Liechtenstein, supra n. 209, at 59 et seq. and 166.
211. Article 2 (1) c) TVTG.
212. Article 2 (1) b) TVTG.
213. Government of Liechtenstein, *supra* n. 209, at 44; Liechtenstein FMA, *Faktenblatt 'Initial Coin Offering'*, 2, https://www.fma-li.li/files/fma/fma-faktenblatt-ico.pdf (accessed 11 March 2020).
214. Government of Liechtenstein, *Stellungnahme der Regierung an den Landtag des Fürstentums Liechtenstein zu den anlässlich der ersten Lesung betreffend die Schaffung eines Gesetzes über Token und VT-Dienstleister (Token- und VT-Dienstleistergesetz; TVTG) und die Abänderung weiterer Gesetze aufgeworfenen Fragen*, Report and Application no. 93/2019, 21, https://www.llv.li/files/srk/bua_093_2019_stellungnahme-tvtg.pdf (accessed 11 March 2020).

offers tokens in its own name or in the name of a client), *Token Generator, TT Key Depositary, TT Token Depositary, TT Protector* (person who holds and disposes over Tokens on TT Systems in its own name on the account for a third party), *Physical Validator* (person who ensures the enforcement of rights represented in Tokens in terms of property law), *TT Exchange Service Provider* (person who exchanges legal currencies against Tokens and vice versa and Tokens for Tokens), *TT Verifying Authority* (person who verifies the legal capacity and requirements for disposal over a Token), *TT Price Service Provider* and *TT Identity Service Provider* (person who identifies the person in possession of the right of disposal related to a Token and records it in a directory).

[A] What Makes a Token a Security?

Ever since, Liechtenstein security law has been strongly influenced by the notion of the connection of a right with a physical carrier (certificate).[215] The securitization of rights in a physical document, however, has been long outdated. Therefore, the concept of genuine book-entry security is introduced into Liechtenstein law[216] together with the adoption of the TVTG. Such uncertificated or book-entry securities (German: *Wertrechte*) have – if properly created – all the functions of a classic security of public faith (bearer or order paper), namely: transport function, legitimation function and liberation function, transaction protection and objection restriction.[217]

Book-entry securities are to be recorded by the debtor in an (electronic) register; they come into legal existence with, and have the legal effects pursuant to, the entry in the register (constitutive effect). The register has to be organized in such a manner that unauthorized intervention of the debtor in the rights of creditors is prevented. It may also be kept using trustworthy technologies according to the TVTG, such as Blockchain. Hence, with the introduction of genuine book-entry securities into Liechtenstein law, a new interface between the TVTG and securities law is created.[218]

Depending on the specific characteristics of a Token, it may be treated as security or financial instrument under the Liechtenstein financial market legislation (substance over form). As Liechtenstein is a member of the EEA, in principle, the regulatory framework for financial and capital markets of the EU is applicable also in Liechtenstein.

Hence, the question, whether under Liechtenstein financial market laws, a Token is treated as security or not is determined by the respective definition of the European

215. Section 73(1) Final Part of the Persons and Companies Law (PGR); nevertheless, immobilized and dematerialized uncertificated securities have not been completely unknown to the Liechtenstein legal system; cf. Government of Liechtenstein, *supra* n. 209, at 108.
216. Section 81a Final Part of the (amended) Persons and Companies Law (PGR).
217. Government of Liechtenstein, *supra* n. 209, at 110.
218. *Ibid.*, at 108 et seq.

concept of securities, namely in MiFID II.[219,220] Therefore, standardization, transferability and negotiability are the crucial elements for the classification of Tokens as securities also under Liechtenstein law, and the Liechtenstein practice widely conforms to the practice in other EU Member States, such as Germany.[221] Due to the substance over form approach, neither certification[222] nor tradability on (traditional) capital markets[223] are necessary for the treatment of Tokens as securities.

According to the current practice of the Liechtenstein FMA, Utility Tokens and cryptocurrencies are in Liechtenstein basically treated as commodities;[224] therefore, the production and use of cryptocurrencies and Utility Tokens usually do not require a specific license of the FMA.[225] However, such a license may be necessary for certain business models related to any kind of Tokens, depending on the characteristics of the business model and the specification of the involved Tokens.

[B] Special Requirements for a Prospectus

For the public offering of Tokens, which are regarded as transferable securities according to MiFID II, the prior publication of an approved prospectus is required, and the provisions of the Prospectus Regulation[226] are fully applicable. If such a public offer shall not be notified to other EU/EEA Member States and, if its total consideration does not exceed the amount of EUR 8 million over a period of twelve months, it is exempted from the obligation to publish a prospectus in Liechtenstein.[227]

Due to the applicability of the respective legislative provisions of the EU, reference is made, particularly with regard to the contents of the prospectus, to the respective statements in the country report for Germany, which, in principle, also apply to Liechtenstein.[228]

219. Directive 2014/65/EU of the European Parliament and of the Council of 15 May 2014 on markets in financial instruments and amending Directive 2002/92/EC and Directive 2011/61/EU.
220. Liechtenstein FMA, *FMA-Mitteilung 2019/2 – Pflichten für Emittenten von Wertpapieren und Security Token*, https://www.fma-li.li/files/list/fma-mittteilung-2019-2-emittenten-wp-st.pdf (accessed 11 March 2020).
221. Cf. the legal practice in Germany (Michael Juenemann), §6.07 [A], *supra*.
222. Liechtenstein FMA, supra n. 220, at 4 et seq.
223. For example, the so-called book-entry securities are transferred by entry in the respective register and not on traditional capital markets.
224. Depending on its specific design, a utility token may nevertheless fulfil the requirements of MiFID regarding securities and/or financial instruments and are thus treated as such, which is assessed by the FMA on a case-by-case basis.
225. Patrick Bont, Liechtenstein FMA, speech 'Kryptowährungen – und was machen die Regulatoren?', handout sheet no. 13, https://www.fma-li.li/files/fma/fma-digital-banking-liechtenstein.pdf (accessed 11 March 2020); Thomas Nägele & Josef Bergt, Kryptowährungen und Blockchain-Technologie im liechtensteinischen Aufsichtsrecht, 2 Liechtensteinische Juristenzeitung, 65 (2018); Government of Liechtenstein, supra n. 209, at 44.
226. Regulation (EU) 2017/1129 of the European Parliament and of the Council of 14 June 2017 on the prospectus to be published when securities are offered to the public or admitted to trading on a regulated market.
227. Article 3 EEA Securities Prospectus Implementation Act (EWR-WPPDG).
228. Cf. Michael Juenemann, §6.07 [C], *supra*.

In view of the strict statutory prospectus liability, it is in any event recommended to describe in the prospectus all the legal, regulatory and technical uncertainties and risks specifically related to the STO, Security Tokens and the underlying Blockchain technology in detail. The Liechtenstein FMA has to date approved four prospectuses for Security Tokens;[229] these four prospectuses contain specific remarks and warnings regarding legal and technical risks in connection with the STO and the underlying Blockchain technology which mainly concern the following issues: restriction of tradability risk and risk of illiquid markets (lack of admission of trading on a regulated or unregulated market), other market risks (such as price manipulation, hacking of the crypto-exchange, systemic risks and correlations within markets for digital assets), risk of invalidity of the transfer of Tokens and finality risks, risk of malfunction, bugs and technical errors of applications and/or smart contracts (including changes of the underlying Blockchain technology), risks due to legal uncertainties with regard to Tokens and due to (future) legal and regulatory developments, wallet and private key risks (e.g., risk of loss or inaccessibility of the private key, risk of wrong wallet address, risk of incompatibility of a wallet), risk of loss of key personnel as well as the risk of hacking and data theft and specific technical risks regarding the execution of the STO.[230]

If there is no obligation to publish a prospectus, the issuer of a Token is at least obliged to compile and publish basic information, including information about the Token and the associated rights, the purpose and nature of the legal transaction of the Token issuance, the purchase and transfer conditions and the risks associated with the purchasing of the Tokens.[231]

[C] Blockchain Finality

The civil law provisions in the TVTG aiming to achieve legal certainty are only applicable: (1) if Tokens are generated or issued by a registered Liechtenstein TT Service Provider, or (2) if the parties declare applicability of its provisions in a legal transaction. In case of such applicability, the Token is considered to be an asset located in Liechtenstein with the effect that the courts of Liechtenstein have jurisdiction in related civil law disputes.[232]

229. Liechtenstein FMA, *Liste gebilligte Prospekte bis 20. Juli 2019*, and *Liste gebilligte Prospekte ab 21. Juli 2019*, http://register.fma-li.li/index.php?id=277 (accessed 11 March 2020); these four prospectuses were approved before the TVTG has come into force.
230. Crowdlitoken AG, *Prospectus for the Issue/Public Offer of Up to 190,000,000 Crowdlitokens*, 12 April 2019, https://crowdlitoken.com/das-produkt/#rechtliche-dokumente (accessed 11 March 2020); Invao Trading AG, *Security Prospectus to Issue 52,500,000 IVO Tokens*, 19 November 2019, https://invao.org/ivo-bond/#downloads_block_5d88da8aa7ab0 (accessed 11 March 2020); Enercom AG, *EEA Growth Prospectus for the Public Offering of 200,000 Enercom Tokens*, 21 November 2019, https://www.enercom.ag/prospectus-approved-by-fma/ (accessed 11 March 2020); Curio AG, *Wertpapierprospekt für die Emmission von CT1 Token*, https://curioinvest.com/templates/assets/docs/CurioProspekt.pdf (accessed 11 March 2020).
231. Articles 30 et seq. TVTG; (minor) offerings are exempted from this obligation under certain circumstances.
232. Article 3(2) and 4 TVTG; Government of Liechtenstein, supra n. 209, at 183.

In view of legal certainty of transactions executed on a TT System, the relationship and coordination between the digital representation of rights in a Token and the underlying 'analogous' rights are essential. The aim is that the disposal over the Token shall also effectuate a valid and effective transfer of the rights represented by the Token. This is achieved in the TVTG, on the one hand, by the provision that the 'disposal over the Token results in the disposal over the right represented in the Token'. This programmatic legal order works particularly with Security Tokens respectively book-entry securities registered in TT Systems and governed by Liechtenstein law.[233]

On the other hand, in cases where such a synchronization of digital and analogous disposal cannot be achieved by law (e.g., in case the Token represents movable or immovable property or if the represented underlying right is governed by foreign law), the person obliged under the disposal over the Token must ensure the following: (1) that the disposal over the Token directly or indirectly procures the effective transfer of the represented right, and (2) that a competing disposal over the represented right is excluded. The obligated person has to take appropriate organizational, structural and/or legal measures to achieve this, e.g., deposition of a physical object with a Physical Validator or other custodians, or – with regard to claims – stipulation of provisions in the underlying contract or in terms of issue of a financial instrument, according to which the transfer of the claim is only possible in accordance with the rules of the TT System.[234]

In this context, the TVTG determines the requirements for a valid disposal over Tokens (the term 'disposal' also includes the creation of limited rights in rem, namely the establishment of securities or of rights of usufruct to a Token): following the principle of title and mode of the Liechtenstein property law, lawful disposal requires a valid contractual agreement between the parties and a transfer of the Token in line with the regulations of the TT System as well as the prerequisite that the transferring party is in possession of the right of disposal over the Token.[235] The right of disposal comes close to the right of ownership of a physical object and may be granted/delegated to a third party (agency).[236]

On TT Systems, such as Blockchain, the TT key (i.e., private key) is required to dispose over a Token; thus, the holder of the private key has de facto the power to dispose over the Token, but he is not necessarily legally entitled to do so; for example, in case of theft of the private key, the thief is not entitled to dispose over the Token, or in case of bankruptcy proceedings regarding the holder of the private key, the right of disposal is withdrawn.[237] For practicability reasons, there is the rebuttable statutory presumption that the holder of the TT key also has the right of disposal over a Token. This means, that in case of unlawful appropriation of the private key, the aggrieved

233. Article 7(1) TVTG; Government of Liechtenstein, *supra* n. 209, at 168 et seq.
234. Article 7(2) TVTG; Government of Liechtenstein, *supra* n. 209, at 170 et seq.
235. Article 6 TVTG; Government of Liechtenstein, *supra* n. 209, at 190 et seq.
236. Government of Liechtenstein, *supra* n. 209, at 67 et seq.
237. Article 16(1) Bankruptcy Act.

party has to initiate respective court proceedings and prove its legitimate right of disposal.[238]

Under the TVTG it is assumed that, due to the underlying technology (e.g., Blockchain), transactions on TT Systems are largely final (at least in technical terms).[239] Problems arise when the nominal legal situation does not correspond to the factual situation as validated on the TT System. Such a situation is given if a Token is disposed over without a valid legal ground (e.g., unlawful agreement) or if the legal ground subsequently ceased to exist (e.g., in case of bankruptcy proceedings).[240] Due to the inalterability of transactions on TT Systems, the TVTG adopts the principle of abstraction for dispositions of Tokens (as opposed to the principle of causality, according to which dispositions without an underlying legitimate cause are basically void). This, however, does not mean that the unlawful disposition as validated on the TT System is absolutely final. Instead, the transaction has to be reversed according to the law of enrichment: the unduly enriched person has to – by way of a new transaction – transfer back the Tokens to the person unduly deprived of the Tokens. The unduly enriched person may be forced to do so by a court judgment.[241]

However, the TVTG stipulates a bona fide rule which protects those who have in good faith and for valuable consideration acquired a Token or obtained a restricted right in rem, even if the transferring party was not entitled to dispose of the Token. Thus, the disposal over the Token is final and effective. The aggrieved party can only hold liable the party which unlawfully transferred the Token. The bona fide rule is generally applicable in case of a lack of the right to dispose over the Token and not in case this entitlement ceased to exist.[242]

Furthermore, the TVTG clarifies that in general the obliged party regarding the right represented by a Token may pay or perform his duties with debt-discharging effect to the authorized person regarding the Token as identified in the TT System. This rule largely corresponds to the legitimation and liberation function in securities law.[243]

Another means of protection for Token 'owners' is the cancellation of Tokens in case of loss of the private key or inoperativeness of a Token (e.g., because of bugs). For that purpose, the person entitled to dispose over the Token has to file an application with the court and may, in case of success, execute the represented rights without the Token or demand production of a new Token on own costs.[244]

The TVTG does not explicitly deal with forks, material technical malfunctions or hacks; it rather seems that the responsible TT Service Provider has the duty to appropriately deal with such constellations[245] and may be held liable for breach of his

238. Article 5 TVTG; Government of Liechtenstein, *supra* n. 209, at 184 et seq.
239. Government of Liechtenstein, *supra* n. 209, at 126 et seq. and 135.
240. *Ibid.*, at 68 et seq.
241. Article 6(3) TVTG; Government of Liechtenstein no. 54/2019, *supra* n. 209, at 191 et seq.
242. Article 9 TVTG; Government of Liechtenstein, *supra* n. 209, at 208 et seq.
243. Article 8 TVTG; Government of Liechtenstein, supra n. 209, at 206 et seq.
244. Article 10 TVTG.
245. Government of Liechtenstein, *supra* n. 209, at 84.

duties. One opportunity for TT Service Providers to cope with such risks might be the use of a private/permissioned Blockchain.[246]

The TVTG opens a range of possibilities for Token 'owners' to reduce their risks, particularly the risk of loss or theft. For example, the TT key (i.e., private key) may be securely deposited with a TT Key Depositary; or the Token is held by a TT Token Depositary in the name and on behalf of the Token 'owner' or alternatively by a TT Protector on its own name but on account for the principal ('beneficial Token owner').[247] Another option is the engagement of a TT Identity Service Provider who identifies and registers the person entitled to dispose over a Token.[248] All these TT Service Providers must comply with minimum standards, are subject to registration and publication duties, are supervised by the FMA and usually have contractual obligations with liabilities in case of breach. Furthermore, Tokens or TT keys deposited with or held by such a TT Service Provider constitute a separate asset in case of bankruptcy or foreclosure proceedings and are therefore protected against creditors of the TT Service Provider.[249]

[D] Regulatory Specifics for Organized Trade

Emanating from the applicability of the regulatory framework of the EU for financial markets, the EU provisions for trading are also applicable in Liechtenstein. Thus, trading of Tokens may be subject to the approval of FMA if these are classified as financial instruments according to the definition in MiFID II.[250] Furthermore, the provisions of the MiFID framework regarding the operation of a regulated market or MTF or OTF are also applicable in Liechtenstein.[251]

But even if Tokens do not constitute a security or financial instrument, the trading of Tokens or the provision of related services may be subject to registration requirements under the TVTG: Any person or entity who professionally exchanges (fungible) Tokens against Tokens or legal currencies or vice versa has to apply for registration as TT Exchange Service Provider with the FMA.[252] According to the legislative materials, all service providers who exchange Tokens in the above sense on their own account and who neither hold Tokens nor TT keys of their clients are classified as TT Exchange Service Provider. If the service provider holds Tokens or TT keys of their clients, they are to be registered as TT Token Depositary or TT Key Depositary.[253] Furthermore, the professional provision of aggregated price information on the basis of purchase and sale offers or completed transactions falls under the

246. *See*: the legal practice in Germany (Michael Juenemann), §6.01[B] Blockchain finality, pp. 8 et seq.
247. Government of Liechtenstein, *supra* n. 209, at 153 et seq.
248. *Ibid.*, at 163 and 209.
249. Article 25 TVTG.
250. Article 3 Bankengesetz (Banking Act, hereinafter: 'BankG').1
251. Cf. the respective statements in the country report for Germany (Michael Juenemann) §6.07 [D], *supra*.
252. Article 2 (1) q) TVTG; Government of Liechtenstein, *supra* n. 214, at 9 et seq.
253. Government of Liechtenstein, *supra* n. 209, at 102 et seq. and 160 et seq.

definition of the TT Price Service Provider.[254] Therefore, the classification of crypto-exchanges (centralized as well as decentralized platforms, with or without matching function) under the TVTG strongly depends on the concrete business model and may trigger registration duties with the FMA either as TT Exchange Service Provider, TT Token Depositary, TT Key Depositary or TT Price Service Provider.

§6.10 CAPITAL MARKETS AND BLOCKCHAIN: COUNTRY REPORT – POLAND

Aleksandra Widziewicz[255]

[A] What Makes a Token a Security?

In Poland, at the moment of preparing this paper, there is no comprehensive legal regulation creating or facilitating the operation of the digital economy and the development of blockchain technology. However, it can be noticed that the Polish legislator is taking an increasing interest in blockchain technology and DLT.

In April 2018, Poland signed a declaration on participating in the European Blockchain Partnership. The Partnership is designed to be a tool for cooperation between the Member States on exchanging expertise in the technical and regulatory areas and for preparing to launch EU blockchain applications. This will facilitate a more dynamic development and implementation of blockchain applications in Europe and parallelly in Poland.

In spite of the lack of any regulation that would fully and comprehensively regulate issues related to blockchain and DLT, some government legislation drafts do address the issue in certain provisions. One example is Article 300 (1-134) of the Commercial Companies Code, which introduces a simple joint-stock company. Article 300 (31) §3 of the Commercial Companies Code states that records regarding such companies may be kept in a dispersed and decentralized database that ensures the security of the data contained therein and the proper performance of the duties of the entity keeping the records. This is a signal that the Polish legislator is beginning to see the possibilities offered by blockchain and DLT.

The blockchain technology used to register a simple joint-stock company is associated with the latest Polish law concepts of understanding a 'document'. The idea of this concept is information authorization. Significant importance is placed on the ability to reproduce information, not the form in which the information is provided.

254. Article 2 (1) s) TVTG; Government of Liechtenstein, *supra* n. 209, at 162.

255. Aleksandra Widziewicz is Head of Compliances Committee at ICC (International Chamber of Commerce) Poland and Head of Compliance Academy at Lazarski University in Warsaw; Aleksandra Widziewicz is Of-Counsel at Bird & Bird's Finance & Financial Regulation Group and Compliance Task Force Leader at Bird & Bird Warsaw; Aleksandra Widziewicz widely advises on the legal and regulatory compliance, including implementation of integrated compliance functions, MiFID, FATCA/CRS, anti-money laundering and corporate governance functions; she is an experienced FinTech lawyer.

The Polish definition of a document, arising from Article 77(3) of the Civil Code[256] and the definition from the eIDAS Regulation of Article 3 point 35,[257] places emphasis on the medium. The medium is not associated with the traditional physical approach. In 2010, provisions on the interoperability of IT systems were adopted in Poland.[258] In simple words, interoperability is to enable various entities, their systems and registers to share information and knowledge, implemented through data exchange. The purpose indicated in the above-mentioned Act, i.e., interoperability, is implemented fully in a dispersed register.

The above-described change in understanding the form of the document brings us to the development of smart contracts. The most important element of contract law is the declaration of will. Article 60 of the Civil Code introduces its legal definition, according to which the behaviour of a person who performs a legal act reveals his will in a sufficient manner, such behaviour aiming at creating, changing or terminating the legal relationship. An entity's act is qualified as a declaration of will if the effects are actually realized by the person submitting the statement. The above-mentioned concept of a declaration of will also applies to declarations of will made in electronic form (even in an automated manner).

Polish law provides that the conclusion of a contract requires a mutual expression of intent of the parties. The expression of intent may be explicit or implied. Civil Code provides that the declaration of a will shall be expressed by any behaviour. As a result, it is possible to conclude a smart contract, which is inseparable from Tokens and blockchain technology.

In order to establish a legally binding smart contract, all the essential elements of the proposed contract must be clearly provided in the computing program. It should be sufficiently precise, clear and understandable to be validly accepted by all parties.[259] Some contracts are required by law to be concluded in a certain form, e.g., in writing. Such contracts would not be valid if they were registered using blockchain technology. In this scope, the change in Polish law is required.

Blockchain technology is connected with Tokens. In Poland, digital Tokens still raise many controversies. This is due to the lack of legal regulation in this respect and the inability to recognize a Token as a 'security' and in general as a 'financial instrument'.[260] The legal framework for their offering in the ICO process is also particularly interesting.

A Token is recognized as a property right within the meaning of the Civil Code. Thus, they can be the subject of civil law relations/relationships. The key question to be asked regarding the application of existing regulations in Poland to Tokens and ICO

256. The document is an information carrier enabling familiarization with its content.
257. An electronic document is any content stored in electronic form, in particular text or sound, visual or audio-visual recording.
258. Amendment to the Act on Computerization dated 12 February 2010 on the amendment to the Act on the Computerization of Entities Performing Public Tasks and certain other Acts.
259. Kaprzyk Karolina. *The Concept of Smart Contracts from the Legal Perspective.* 3 Review of European and Comparative Law, 101-118 (2018).
260. Jakub J. Szczerbowski, *Lex Cryptographia. Znaczenie prawne umów i jednostek rozliczeniowych opartych na technologii Blockchain*, 92–93 (2018).

is whether a Token has the features of a financial instrument in accordance with the applicable legal definition.

To answer the above question, it is necessary to assess whether a Token is a security. In accordance with Article 921(6) of the Civil Code, a security has the following basic features:

- has the form of a document,
- results from the obligation of the debtor concerned,
- its possession is necessary to effectively demand that the debtor fulfils the obligation.

Due to the changes in the Civil Code discussed above regarding the definition of the document, it can be stated that the Token will meet the first of the criteria. Moreover, if the Token is a source of the obligation between different entities, it will also meet the second criterion. If the possession of the Token is required to meet the commitment, the third criterion will also be met.

However, the regulations do not allow to definitively state that each Token is a financial instrument. A specific analysis should be carried out each time for a specific type of Token. Depending on the results of such analysis, the ICO process will be covered or not covered by the supervision of the Polish Financial Supervision Authority (PFSA).

[B] Blockchain Finality

The finality of blockchain transactions has not yet received any sufficient legal regulation in Poland. The finality of Blockchain is a situation: 'after the transaction is confirmed. Finality is the state of the blockchain, under which the transaction cannot be cancelled, reversed or changed by any of the participants in this network under any circumstances. In other words, no one can do anything to the transaction and everything that happened within this transaction remains on the blockchain supposedly forever'.[261]

From this perspective, Tokens as property rights have a quite similar status with tangible property. According to Article 155 §1 of the Polish Civil Code, a contract of sale, exchange, donation, of property transfer or other contract obliging to transfer ownership of the object specified as to its identity shall transfer the ownership to the acquiring party unless a specific provision provides otherwise or the parties decide otherwise. Additionally, under Article 555 of the Polish Civil Code, the provisions on the sale of objects shall apply accordingly to the sale of property rights.

However, as mentioned below, if Tokens are classified as financial instruments (securities), their ownership transfer is regulated in the separate legal provisions.

261. Blockchain Finality. http://alevtina.io/blockchain-finality-explained-what-and-why (accessed 11 March 2020).

[C] Special Requirements for Prospectus

According to the provisions of the Polish Public Offering Act (Public Offering Act) and Regulation (EU) 2017/1129 of the European Parliament and of the Council on the prospectus to be published when securities are offered to the public or admitted to trading on a regulated market (EU Prospectus regulation), the ICO can be considered as a public offer (on the basis of Article 2 point d of EU Prospectus Regulation) in the situation when the issued Tokens can be classified as securities.

Confirmation of the above conclusions can be found in the position of the PFSA, which in its communication of 22 November 2017 indicated: 'Depending on the structure, ICOs may operate outside the scope of the regulations applicable to the financial market or be offered without the required authorisation, and in connection with this, buyers may be deprived of special legal protection related to this market.'[262]

The PFSA did not indicate whether in its opinion the ICO process should be qualified as a public offer within the meaning of Polish and European regulations. The PFSA also did not specify what criterion it would use to assess whether the ICO process should be qualified as a public offer within the meaning of Polish regulations.

As there are no specific legal regulations regarding the collection of funds through ICO, one should think about the possible use of legal instruments belonging to different areas of law. According to the PFSA's position, ICO and the sale of Tokens can be discussed in the context of legal regulations regarding the offering and trading of financial instruments. Appropriate application of the provisions on investment funds is also possible.

Issuers of Tokens under ICOs, if they are covered by the Public Offering Act and EU Prospectus Regulation, would be obliged, *inter alia*, to draw up an issue prospectus or an information memorandum. Imposing stringent requirements related to the public offering on the entities organizing ICO and drawing up a prospectus or information memorandum may lead to the decline of the attractiveness of ICOs (especially after taking into consideration relatively low own capitals and limited HR of such entities).

[D] Regulatory Specifics for Organized Trade

As long as there are no complex legal regulations on a blockchain, some initiatives connected with this technology are taken by different market participants (not only from the private sector but also from the public sector).

Since the beginning of 2018, the PFSA has established a new fintech department whose tasks include supporting the development of innovations on the financial markets, including managing the sustainable development thereof through integrated activities in the area of financial, regulatory and supervisory technologies.[263] The PFSA has also launched a programme called Innovation Hub, which is designed to support innovative fintech and blockchain initiatives. The Innovation Hub programme is a tool

262. The PFSA's statement on Initial Token Offerings – ITOs and Initial Coin Offerings – ICOs.
263. https://www.knf.gov.pl/?articleId=61228&p_id=18 (accessed 11 March 2020).

by means of which the authority conducts a dialogue with FinTech sector entities, providing them with appropriate explanations to queries and supporting the development of modern technologies on the financial market while maintaining security and protecting clients adequately.[264]

Also worthy of mention is an initiative by the Ministry of Digitization that supports the development of distributed register technology as part of 'Blockchain/DLT Stream and Digital Currencies'.[265] The main objectives of the project are: to create conditions for the development of Polish-related projects of cryptocurrency trading, to ensure the government's adequate supervision over blockchain projects, and to ensure the use of blockchain technology for the needs of processes in the fields of business and administration.

In January 2018, the Polish Banks Association (*Związek Banków Polskich*) came up with an initiative to use blockchain, in cooperation with the National Clearing House (*Krajowa Izba Rozliczeniowa*) and the Credit Information Bureau (*Biuro Informacji Kredytowej*). These organizations prepared a joint report on the industry solution relating to a durable medium, in which two of the three solutions suggested for banks are to be based on blockchain technology.

Another key initiative in the area of applications of blockchain technology in public space is an agreement on cooperation between the Ministry of Digitization and the Warsaw Stock Exchange.[266] The purpose of the agreement is to increase the use of blockchain technology in capital markets and then implement similar solutions where this can improve the efficiency, effectiveness and productivity of processes in the economy and administration. The cooperation is being undertaken in order to form the basis for developing projects in blockchain technology and promoting increased confidence in the business sector and public administration for such solutions. The most important priorities of the Minister of Digitization and the Warsaw Stock Exchange are the development of security standards in business trading and public administration, the creation of a test environment (also known as the Sandbox) for the evaluation of new solutions for business and public administration, as well as the development of requirements for DLT solutions, including tokenization of documents.

The Central Securities Repository of Poland (*Krajowy Depozyt Papierów Wartościowych* – KDWP) has implemented a Blockchain Platform for the Capital Market.[267] According to the public information about the platform, it should be an open, fully secure infrastructure for the capital market that supports post-transaction services. One of its most important applications is to be an eVoting application providing support for general meetings. According to KDPW, the application 'will provide capital market participants – such as KDPW, public companies, as well as banks and brokerage

264. https://www.knf.gov.pl/dla_rynku/fin_tech/Innovation_Hub?articleId = 60603&p_id = 18 (accessed 11 March 2020).
265. https://www.gov.pl/web/cyfryzacja/strumien-blockchain-dlt-i-waluty-cyfrowe (accessed 11 March 2020).
266. https://www.gpw.pl/aktualnosc?cmn_id = 107748&title = Porozumienie + Ministerstwa + Cyfryzacji + i + GPW + w + sprawie + wykorzystania + technologii + blockchain (accessed 11 March 2020).
267. https://blockchain.kdpw.pl/en/ (accessed 11 March 2020).

houses – with joint access to data on exercising voting rights in almost real time, as well as access to reliable results of electronic (remote) voting. Blockchain technology will provide a common, decentralised register, storing the history of events related to a given shareholders' meeting, a list of resolutions subject to voting, the number of registered participants and votes, and data on voting results. This will result in greater accessibility, responsibility and transparency for all system participants'.[268]

The Warsaw Stock Exchange is also working on a Private Market platform based on blockchain, which is to connect investors with non-public (unlisted) companies seeking capital. Therefore, it is supposed to be a de facto crowdfunding (social investing) platform, but for companies at every stage of development.[269] The construction of this platform is one of the main points of the Warsaw Stock Exchange strategy.

Despite the multitude of public initiatives described above, the vast majority of blockchain-related initiatives are identified in Poland in the area of banking and finance.

The use of blockchain technology results in a change of processes and workflows. It affects business structures and the corresponding regulatory and compliance requirements. Polish banks and financial institutions have recognized the potential of blockchain technology. However, the development of blockchain in Poland has been hindered by a lack of comprehensive legal regulations covering all aspects of this technology, including consumer protection, cyber security (not only ***General Data Protection Regulation***), business integrity and other compliance-related issues.

§6.11 CAPITAL MARKETS AND BLOCKCHAIN: COUNTRY REPORT – SPAIN

Jose Luis Lorente Howell[270]

[A] What Makes a Token a Security?

To date, there is no specific harmonized law governing ICOs in Spain, and no cryptocurrency issuing has been registered, authorized or verified by an official regulator or supervisory agency in Spain.

Following the trend started by the UK regulator in 2016, in July 2018 the Spanish Ministry of Economy and Business published the preliminary draft bill for the Law of

268. https://www.obserwatorfinansowy.pl/forma/rotator/rok-2019-moze-byc-czasem-innowacji-na-gieldach/ (accessed 11 March 2020).
269. https://www.stockwatch.pl/wiadomosci/gpw-zastosuje-blockchain-oraz-chce-byc-dostawca-infrastruktury-dla-crowdfundingu,akcje,240997 (accessed 11 March 2020).
270. Recognized by Legal 500 and Best Lawyers in Spain (2020) in the practice areas of Banking and Finance and Insolvency and Reorganization law, Jose Luis Lorente is head of the Finance & Financial Regulation Group at Bird & Bird Madrid. Jose widely advises on financial regulatory, payment services regulation, electronic banking and virtual financial services, compliance standards and procedures, including the Spanish Central Bank, the Spanish Securities and Exchange Commission (CNMV) and the General Directorate of Insurance and Pensions (DGS).

'digital transformation of the financial system' which shall provide for a Sandbox and which is expected to go into operation during 2020.[271]

Spanish market participants are engaging in the implementation of blockchain technology at different levels. Spanish banking, energy and telecommunications companies are participating in an initiative known as *Alastria*, a non-profit consortium - with Banco Sabadell as founding partner - created in order to establish a semi-public blockchain infrastructure. Additionally, many Spanish entities are developing their own innovation laboratories where they are testing DLT.

The Spanish Stock Market Commission (Comisión Nacional del Mercado de Valores - CNMV) is aware of the worldwide proliferation of this phenomenon and, accordingly, has taken an active approach on the implications of blockchain-based cryptocurrencies - and more generically, '*crypto assets*' - when issued and/or commercialized in Spain. In this sense, the CNMV launched in 2016 a Fintech & Innovation portal in its website,[272] through which companies can engage to enquire about different aspects of securities market legislation surrounding the FinTech environment, including the need to obtain an authorization or license prior to startup certain activities.[273] The CNMV publishes periodically a summary of the questions received through this portal, highlighting the position of the CNMV in relation to specific questions and issues. Such summary of Q&As has become a valuable legal resource for lawyers and entrepreneurs.[274]

On 8 February 2018, the CNMV and the Central Bank of Spain published a joint press statement on '*Cryptocurrencies and Initial Coin Offerings*'.[275] This statement clarified that the concept of *ICO* involves, in the eyes of Spanish securities market regulator, not only the issuance of 'pure' cryptocurrencies (such as Bitcoins or Ether) but also the issuance of other assets commonly referred to as 'tokens'. The statement of the CNMV describes two categories of 'tokens':

(1) 'Security Tokens' which are defined as those that generally provide a share in the future revenues or increased value of the issuing venture or business; and
(2) 'Utility tokens' are defined as those granting access to a service or a product, despite that mention is commonly made at the time of offering to the

271. Ministerio de Economía y Empresa, *Proyecto de Ley de medidas para la transformación digital del sistema financiero*, http://www.mineco.gob.es/portal/site/mineco/menuitem.32ac44f94b634f76faf2b910026041a0/?vgnextoid=968f662b79d83610VgnVCM1000001d04140aRCRD (accessed 11 March 2020).
272. https://www.cnmv.es/portal/Fintech/Innovacion.aspx?lang=es (accessed 11 March 2020).
273. According to the disclaimer that appears in the CNMV portal: 'This document is not regulatory. Its purpose is to transmit to the sector and, in particular, to entities wishing to operate in the FinTech field, interpretation criteria for the proper implementation of the securities market rules that may apply to them.'
274. As of January 2019, from a total of 258 requests of consultation, 63 were related to crypto assets and blockchain.
275. Banco de España & Comisión Nacional del Mercado de Valores (CNMV), *Joint Press Statement by CNMV and Banco de España on 'Cryptocurrencies' and 'Initial Coin Offerings' (ICOs)*, http://www.cnmv.es/Portal/verDoc.axd?t={6f310cc7-6b39-4405-a8f7-70d2b1e682d1} (accessed 11 March 2020).

appreciation and liquidity expectation or to the possibility of trading them on specific markets.

Simultaneously to the joint press statement with the Central Bank of Spain, the CNMV published in February 2018 a separate document under the title *'CNMV considerations on cryptocurrencies and ICOs addressed to market professionals'*.[276] In this document, the CNMV states that a good number of operations structured as *ICOs* should be legally treated as public offerings of transferable securities and thus be subject to the regulatory requirements under the Spanish Securities Market Act (*Ley del Mercado de Valores* – LMV)[277] due to the broad definition of *'transferable security'* set forth in Article 2 of the LMV; that is, 'any particular right, regardless of its name, which, because of its own legal configuration and system of transfer, is capable of being traded in a generalized and impersonal way on a financial market.'

It would appear, from the initial criteria of the CNMV, that both types of Tokens are not necessarily mutually exclusive, and therefore Utility Tokens can also be considered by the CNMV as a speculative investment asset provided that it is offered referring explicitly or implicitly to the expectation that the investor will obtain a profit as a result of its rise in value or of some remuneration associated with the instrument, its liquidity or tradability.

On 20 September 2018, the CNMV published through the Fintech & Innovation portal an update on *'Criteria in relation to ICOs'*[278] according to which the CNMV confirmed its inclination for excluding from the category of *'transferable securities'* on a case-by-case basis those models in which it is not reasonable to establish a correlation between the revaluation or profitability expectations of the Token and the evolution of the underlying business or project.

Should an ICO be considered as a public offering of transferable securities, the issuance of the relevant Tokens would, in principle, require an authorization of the issuer by the CNMV, approval of a prospectus and full compliance with detailed regulation pertaining to public offerings, including a duty to register with the CNMV the issuer's financial statements duly audited and requirements relating to the admission to trading of the securities in regulated markets contained in the LMV. Furthermore, in theory, it would trigger the duty to submit a declaration of responsibility of Directors, relevant information and market-abuse monitoring, own-shares regime (Article 126 LMV), and periodic information duties compromising both annual and half-year reports (Articles 118-123 LMV) with an indication of significant events and their impact on the financial position of the issuer.

However, it must be noted that the LMV reflects a degree of flexibility and proportionality when setting the above-mentioned regulatory duties based on available

276. Comisión Nacional del Mercado de Valores (CNMV), *CNMV considerations on cryptocurrencies and ICOs addressed to market professionals*, http://www.cnmv.es/Portal/verDoc.axd?t={62395018-40eb-49bb-a71c-4afb5c966374} (accessed 11 March 2020).

277. Real Decreto Legislativo 4/2015, de 23 de octubre, por el que se aprueba el texto refundido de la Ley del Mercado de Valores.

278. Comisión Nacional del Mercado de Valores (CNMV), *Criteria in relation to ICO*, http://cnmv.es/DocPortal/Fintech/CriteriosICOsEN.pdf (accessed 11 March 2020).

adaptations or exceptions which may be upheld depending on specific categories of securities, markets or issuers, a principle which is expected to become relevant for new projects when clarifying on a case-by-case basis with the regulator the specific applicable duties out of the full catalogue contained in the LMV arguing, for instance, the conceptual and operational differences between traditional securities and distributed ledger technology or DLT-based Tokens.

[B] Blockchain Finality

From a civil law perspective, there have been attempts to consider Blockchain as a (decentralized) register similar to a public register, such as the land registry which is administrated by a neutral and independent government body, and therefore that, in theory, could be subject to public credence and legal presumption of correctness and integrity (*Principio de la Fe Publica Registral*). However, in Spain, the legislator determines what is subject to public credence, and since it has not made any provision in this regard, the blockchain is, *lege lata*, not subject to public credence and therefore, at least for now, incapable of creating bona fide acquirers protected under Spanish law. As a result, any envisaged transferee of a Security Token should conduct a proper title due diligence regarding the transferor's ownership of the Token before any payment is made - similarly to any acquirer of shares in a non-listed liability company or *Sociedad Limitada*.

[C] Special Requirements for Prospectus

There are cases under which an ICO may not be considered a public offering of securities under Spanish law, depending on the volume and the addressees, cases in which in turn the prospectus will not be required. According to Article 35(2) of the LMV, an ICO will not be considered a public offering:

(1) If it is exclusively addressed to qualified investors.
(2) If it is addressed to less than 150 natural or legal persons per EU Member State, without including qualified investors.
(3) If it is addressed to investors who acquire securities for a total consideration of at least EUR 100,000 each.
(4) The unit nominal value amounts to at least EUR 100,000.
(5) It is issued for a total amount of less than EUR 5 million in the European Union, which limit shall be calculated over a period of twelve months.

However, irrespective of whether or not the ICO qualifies as a public offering, if the Tokens themselves can be considered as tradable securities, the applicable regulation will be that of the investment services. Particularly, if the placement and commercialization comprise tradable securities generally addressed to the public and is carried out using any form of media communication or advertising, a financial institution authorized to provide investment services (placement and/or underwriting, as the case may be) must intervene for the purposes of marketing.[279]

Also it should be pointed out that, irrespective of the place of issuance of the Tokens, if they qualify as a transferable security, its active marketing in Spain (for instance, the availability of websites in Spanish language offering the Tokens) would also be subject to the rule of intervention by an authorized financial institution.

When preparing a prospectus for an ICO, difficulties may be encountered due to the absence of a harmonized model at European level, which, in turn, may lead to dysfunctions with other European authorities. However, when a prospectus is necessary due to the characteristics of the transaction, as already mentioned, the CNMV has made public its intention to take a flexible approach bearing in mind the principle of proportionality (especially when it is foreseeable that the transactions will not be large) in order to reduce the complexity and length of the document to the extent possible.

[D] Special Requirements for Organized Trade

According to the criteria of the CNMV as published through the FinTech & Innovation portal,[280] securities market trading regulations should apply to platforms that carry out trading activities of financial products. Accordingly, should the relevant crypto asset be considered a financial instrument, in theory, the platform should request an authorization, including where appropriate, authorization as a trading venue (such as a regulated market, an MTF or OTF). Furthermore, the management of the trading venue should be carried out by an IF or a market operator and would be subject in general to market regulations and CNMV's supervisory scope.

However, the expectations of the CNMV towards platforms where cryptocurrencies or other crypto assets are traded go beyond the trading of regulated financial products. In this sense, CNMV has clarified that in its view these trading platforms should be subject to rules related to custody, registration, management of conflicts of interest between clients and transparency on fees, as well as anti-money-laundering requirements.[281]

The applicability of the standard securities market regulation has been challenged by certain Spanish scholars arguing that most of the Token-based projects which have been launched recently do not comply with the key feature required under Article 5 of the LMV for tradable securities, that is, the requirement of being represented by either book entries or certificates, neither of which apply to Tokens precisely because crypto assets are essentially decentralized data structures.

279. Article 35(3) LMV *(Real Decreto Legislativo 4/2015, de 23 de octubre, por el que se aprueba el texto refundido de la Ley del Mercado de Valores)*, https://www.boe.es/buscar/act.php?id=BOE-A-2015-11435 (accessed 11 March 2020).
280. Comisión Nacional del Mercado de Valores (CNMV), *supra* n. 278.
281. Comisión Nacional del Mercado de Valores (CNMV), *Questions and Answers Intended for FinTech Companies on Activities and Services That May Be Related to the CNMV*, section 6.4, https://www.cnmv.es/docportal/Legislacion/FAQ/QAsFinTech_EN.pdf (accessed 11 March 2020).

Also Tokens – as opposed to tradable securities – do not necessarily incorporate autonomous credit rights that allow trading independently from the underlying smart contract. Moreover, it is also argued that as long as the Token solely confers a right to access a digital usage, platform or service, it should not be considered a security. However, according to the updated criteria of the CNMV published in September 2018,[282] Article 6 of the LMV allows the interpretation that certain securities may be represented by neither book-entry form nor titles since the permissible verb 'may' is used by the LMV in Article 6 rather than 'should' or 'must'. Therefore, the possibility of registering rights that may be considered transferable securities through DLT or blockchain cannot be legally excluded in the opinion of the CNMV.

Despite such possibility, the CNMV does not consider feasible, at least for now, to trade Tokens on Spanish regulated markets, MTF or OTF since Article 6 of the LMV would require in such case for Tokens to be represented by book-entry form, and Article 8(3) of the LMV would require that the records be kept by a central securities depository.

According to the CNMV, if the Tokens are to be traded on markets other than Spanish markets, CNMV is not competent to require that they be represented by book entries, and it will be the law (and the competent authority) of the country in which the market on which the Tokens are to be traded the one that determines to what extent a specific form of representation of the securities is required for trading on an organized market and, where appropriate, the need for a central securities depository to keep the records.

It does not seem possible either, in the view of the CNMV, to generate an internal market on an unregulated platform in Spain, or for Tokens to be traded on an exchange platform located in Spain since in the case of Tokens considered transferable securities, these platforms should have the necessary authorizations to carry out their activity, including those applicable to a trading venue (as a regulated market, MTF or OTF) or as an IF or credit institution operating as a systematic internalizer. Therefore, the trading venue should have to be managed by an IF or a market-governing body and would generally be subject to market regulations and CNMV's supervisory scope. Furthermore, the same objection already raised would also apply in respect of the need for representation by book-entry form and participation of a central securities depository.

Spanish Law does not provide a formal definition of what must be understood by '*financial market where securities are traded in a generalized and impersonal way*' while Spanish case law tend to define the concept from an instrumental perspective and, far from setting up requirements of size, number of participants or volume traded in order to fit the legal definition -- which may be argued to exempt from it restricted entry networks, permissioned or private platforms –, Spanish legal doctrine defines '*financial market*' as the mere physical scenario or place where 'financial instruments' are traded, which takes us back again to the concept of tradable securities under Spanish Law.

282. Comisión Nacional del Mercado de Valores (CNMV), *supra* n. 278.

Overall, it becomes essential to undertake a close analysis of the features and rights embedded in each project where Tokens are issued in order to assess whether or not beyond acting as a digital voucher of a future product or service, it also entails the right to benefit from a potential revaluation of the market price of the Token.

Therefore, our recommendation based on experience would be to, prior to any attempt of implementation of a Token-based project in Spain, engage in educational lobbying efforts with key officials of the CNMV in order to explain the business model behind and clarify the regulatory applicable framework in Spain. Also this dialogue would give the opportunity to test arguments used in other jurisdictions and benefit from any endorsements received from other European authorities.

§6.12 CAPITAL MARKETS AND BLOCKCHAIN: COUNTRY REPORT – SWITZERLAND

Olivier Favre & Fabio Elsener[283]

Switzerland can be considered as an early adopter and pioneer of the blockchain technology and is home to an active community of enterprises working in the blockchain space. This development was possible thanks to a favourable regulation and a pragmatic approach of the Swiss Financial Market Supervisory Authority (FINMA). FINMA applies the general regulatory framework for financial market activities on the basis of a 'same risks, same rules' approach. At the same time, FINMA takes a technology-neutral approach when applying existing regulations to new technologies.

However, for Tokens to become a new type of capital markets instruments, the current Swiss legal framework would have to be stretched too much. With the aim to facilitate such development, Switzerland is in the process of amending certain points in its current laws to overcome obstacles that have so far stood in the way of the development of a functioning secondary market for Tokens that are a digital representation of capital markets instruments. A new bill[284] (hereinafter: DLT Bill) is proposed to that effect, which shall introduce: (i) 'DLT Rights' as a new category of assets that may be created with a registration on a distributed ledger and would be available for securities issued on a blockchain,[285] and (ii) a new license category for trading venues where such 'DLT Rights' can be traded.[286] The DLT Bill has yet to be discussed in the Swiss Parliament and, although a timely implementation is envisaged, the implementation date is still unknown. However, the DLT Bill has been approved by the

283. Olivier Favre is a Banking & Finance Partner at Schellenberg Wittmer. He advises clients on financing and capital markets transactions and regulatory matters. He co-heads the Blockchain Technologies and FinTech group at the firm. Fabio is a Senior Associate in the Banking & Finance Group at Schellenberg Wittmer and specializes in advice on Blockchain Technology.

284. Federal Council, *draft regarding amendments to Swiss federal law in connection with the developments with the distributed ledger technology (Bundesgesetz zur Anpassung des Bundesrechts an Entwicklungen der Technik verteilter elektronischer Register) of 27 November 2019.*

285. *See* §6.12 [B] [3], *supra*.

286. *See* §6.06 [C] [3], *supra*.

responsible parliamentary commission of the Swiss National Council, and it is to be expected that the DLT Bill will have the relevant support to be approved by the Swiss Parliament.

[A] What Makes a Token a Security?

According to its guidelines of February 2018 (hereinafter: ICO Guidelines),[287] FINMA classifies Tokens from a regulatory perspective into the following three categories:[288]

(1) Payment Tokens or cryptocurrencies: Means of payment that do not confer any claims against the issuer or third parties. Payment Tokens may be used as private means of Payment if agreed between the parties to a transaction. The issuance and exchange of Payment Tokens are subject to the Swiss AML regulation.
(2) Utility Tokens: Tokens that provide rights to access or use a digital application or service, provided that such application or service is already operational at the time of the Token sale. Such Tokens must not have an investment purpose.[289] The issuance and exchange of Utility Tokens are usually subject to the Swiss AML regulation.[290]
(3) Asset tokens: Tokens which are the digital representation of an asset, for instance a debt or equity claim against the issuer or a third party, or a right regarding an underlying asset.¶

This regulatory classification is in place since February 2018 and is not meant to change with the adoption of the proposed DLT Bill.

FINMA clarified that Tokens may take a hybrid form, including elements of more than one of these categories. Such Hybrid Tokens must comply cumulatively with the regulatory requirements applicable to each relevant Token category. FINMA also acknowledges that the classification of a Token may change over time.

In addition to the ICO Guidelines, FINMA also provided its views on the regulatory classification of stable coins. These are Tokens backed by an underlying asset, e.g., a pool of fiat currency or other assets. They are not a separate type of Token category in Swiss regulation.[291] Depending on the rights that investors have according to the terms of the stable coins, these would be usually classified as Asset Tokens or as

287. FINMA, *Guidelines regarding the regulatory framework for ICOs published 16 February 2018.*
288. Note that the classification largely corresponds with the distinction between different Token categories as defined in (1) above.
289. If such an investment purpose exists, such Tokens usually fall under the Asset Tokens category.
290. An exemption from the scope of the Swiss anti-money laundering regulation is available if any payment function of a utility Token is considered to be only of ancillary nature (exception applied restrictively by FINMA).
291. FINMA, *Supplement to the guidelines for enquiries regarding the regulatory framework for initial coin offerings (ICOs)* (11 September 2019).

a hybrid between cryptocurrencies and Asset Tokens. With this approach, a case-by-case analysis of stable coins is needed to assess their regulatory implications under Swiss law.

Asset Tokens would be classified as securities (*Effekten*) under Swiss law if they: (1) confer an enforceable right against the issuer or a third party; (2) are issued as uncertificated security, derivative or book-entry security; and (3) are offered with identical terms to more than twenty investors. A classification of the Tokens as securities must, for instance, be taken into account when issuing Tokens on behalf of third parties[292] and for secondary market trading activities.

The classification of Tokens as securities under Swiss law does not depend on the legal finality of a transfer of Tokens. However, such legal finality of the transfer of Tokens is of importance for the valid transfer of the legal title in Tokens.[293]

[B] Blockchain Finality

As regards the civil law classification of Tokens, it is decisive whether a Token confers enforceable rights to the Token holder or not.

[1] Payment Tokens and Utility Tokens Without Claims

The majority of the Swiss legal scholars as well as the Swiss Federal Council qualify Payment Tokens and Utility Tokens that do not digitally represent an enforceable claim against an issuer or a third person as factual immaterial assets (*immaterielle Vermögenswerte*).[294] Since such Tokens are not the digital representation of any enforceable rights or claims, they are not subject to any particular Swiss law requirements regarding entitlement and transfer. As a consequence, the title in, and transfer of, such Tokens result solely from the rules applicable to the blockchain concerned.

[2] Asset Tokens and Utility Tokens Conferring Claims

Asset Tokens and Utility Tokens that are a digital representation of enforceable rights against an issuer or a third party require under the law as applicable to date, in addition to a valid transfer on the relevant distributed ledger, that the rights represented in such Tokens are validly created and transferred to the transferee. As a result, the legal finality of a transfer depends on the validity of the transfer of the underlying asset. It

292. However, the issuance of own Asset Tokens is not subject to a license requirement in Switzerland, except for the issuance of Asset Tokens qualifying as derivatives.
293. *See* §6.12 [B], *supra*.
294. Federal Council, *Rechtliche Grundlagen für Distributed Ledger-Technologie und Blockchain in der Schweiz*, 54, 67, https://www.newsd.admin.ch/newsd/message/attachments/55150.pdf (accessed 11 March 2020); for a detailed analysis of the legal qualification of bitcoins, *see* Samuel Zogg, *Bitcoin als Rechtsobjekt – eine zivilrechtliche Einordnung*, 2 recht, 95 et seq. (2019).

would not be sufficient to consider the transfer as final only on the basis of the relevant blockchain.

For instance, to the extent that the rights digitally represented in an Asset Token or Utility Token qualify as uncertificated securities[295] or contractual claims, a valid transfer of such assets requires under Swiss law a declaration of assignment by the transferor as the assignor. Such declaration must comply with the written-form requirement, i.e., the parties must either provide a wet-ink signature, which can be delivered through a scan or a certified electronic signature according to Article 14(2bis) CO. We are not aware of any distributed ledger that would currently support such certified electronic signatures; therefore, a written-form requirement can, to date, not be substituted by a transaction of Tokens on a distributed ledger.

A work-around to solve this issue is the use of terms and conditions of the Tokens specifying that the transfer of such Tokens to a new Token holder shall be construed as a transfer of the contractual relationship. With such a structure, the new Token holder assumes the entire contractual position from the previous Token holder. Such transfers may be made in the form of a tripartite agreement between the issuer, the old and the new Token holders. For the purpose of this transfer, it could be argued that all participants of a distributed ledger, including the old and new Token holders and the issuer, implicitly agree by participating in the distributed ledger to such a method of transferring Tokens. However, it would be prudent to provide, at least, that the issuer must keep a record of the current Token holders and acknowledge any transfer to a transferee before any transferee may exercise any rights resulting from the Tokens.

To date, this written-form requirement could only be avoided if the Asset Tokens and Utility Tokens representing enforceable rights were structured as intermediated securities pursuant to the Federal Intermediated Securities Act (hereinafter: the FISA). This would require, however, that the Tokens be registered with a financial institution acting as securities custodian. Once created, such intermediated securities could be transferred by way of book entry between the custodians involved in the transaction. However, it is unclear if and how a blockchain could be used as a basis for such book entries.[296]

[3] Developments: DLT Rights

The Federal Council proposed in the DLT Bill the introduction of a new type of asset for Tokens representing enforceable rights against the issuer or a third party (hereinafter: DLT Rights). The DLT Bill provides that DLT Rights would be issued by entering into an agreement between the issuer and the first holder regarding the registration of rights on a blockchain (e.g., in an Asset Token) and the registration of such DLT Rights on the relevant blockchain. As a result of such registration, the DLT Rights may only be transferred and exercised on such blockchain. For these purposes, the distributed ledger must meet the following requirements: (a) it must create a link between the DLT

295. Article 973c Swiss Code of Obligations; *see* Federal Council, *supra* n. 294, at 56 et seq.
296. Federal Council, *supra* n. 294, at 62.

Rights and the distributed ledger in the sense that the holders of the DLT Rights (but not the debtor) must have the power to dispose of the DLT Rights; (b) it must protect the integrity of the DLT Rights by appropriate technical and organizational measures against unauthorized access and changes;[297] (c) its terms of operation, the terms of the DLT Rights and the terms governing the registration must be recorded on, or be accessible through, the distributed ledger; and (d) the creditors of the DLT Rights must be able to consult independently the integrity of the entries relating to the DLT Rights in the distributed ledger.[298] Once created, DLT Rights follow the principle of blockchain finality and can only be transferred by a transfer of the relevant Tokens on the relevant blockchain. Thereby, legal finality could be achieved. Moreover, the DLT Bill proposes that holders of the DLT Rights on the relevant blockchain benefit from bona fide protection rights similar to the protection of the owner of a paper-form security certificate.[299]

Furthermore, it is proposed in the DLT Bill to amend the FISA to allow the creation of book-entry securities with DLT Rights as the underlying assets. To hold DLT Rights in the form of book-entry securities under the amended FISA, the DLT Rights would have to be transferred to an eligible financial institution acting as securities custodian, and such custodian has to credit the entitlements of the relevant DLT Rights to a securities account.[300] Once created, DLT Rights held as book-entry securities may only be transferred as book-entry securities under the rules of the FISA and no transfer of the DLT Rights on the distributed ledger is possible.

[C] Regulatory Specifics for Organized Trade

[1] Payment Tokens and Utility Tokens

Organized trading services for payment and Utility Tokens which operate in or from Switzerland are subject to the Swiss AML regulation as such activities usually qualify as payment services. Swiss AML regulation requires *inter alia* the affiliation with an authorized self-regulatory organization (SRO) as well as KYC and reporting obligations in connection with suspicious transactions and client relationships. Furthermore, to the extent that the trading facility provides for routing of such payment and Utility Tokens to third parties, the identity of such third party must be verified.[301]

297. Such measures include cryptographic validation procedures for the access to, and transfer of, DLT Rights. However, the DLT Bill will not require a minimum number of participants in the ledger (i.e., a permissioned distributed ledger may meet this requirement even with only few participants), and it will not provide rules as to the consensus mechanism (e.g., proof-of-work, proof-of-stake etc.).
298. DLT Bill, Art. 973d Code of Obligations.
299. Cf. DLT Bill, Art. 973e Code of Obligations; DLT Bill, Federal Council, report on DLT Bill (*Botschaft zum Bundesgesetz zur Anpassung des Bundesrechts an Entwicklungen der Technik verteilter elektronischer Register*) of 27 November 2019 (hereafter: 'Federal Council, DLT Bill Report') 52.
300. DLT Bill, Art. 6 FISA.
301. FINMA, *Guidance 02/2019, Payments on the blockchain.*

As regards decentralized trading facilities, the Swiss AML regulation only applies to the extent that the trading facility can dispose of the traded Tokens. Thus, the mere intermediation of buyers and sellers without involvement in the transaction is not subject to the Swiss AML regulation.[302] Yet, FINMA has adopted a restrictive practice, and it should be clarified on a case-by-case basis whether a decentralized trading application falls under the Swiss AML regulation.

[2] Asset Tokens

Organized trading services for Asset Tokens which usually qualify as securities under Swiss regulation require, depending on the offered trading structure, either a license as a stock exchange or as an MTF or OTF.

Offering multilateral trading services in relation to Asset Tokens according to non-discretionary rules, i.e., matching of trades according to rules of the facility without discretion of the operator, triggers a license requirement either as an MTF or, if the securities are formally listed, as a stock exchange. However, the license of an MTF or a stock exchange would usually not be practicable for the trading of Asset Tokens, since the eligible participants are limited to prudentially supervised persons (no retail participants). Furthermore, the involvement of separate central counterparties and central securities depositories for the purpose of clearing and settlement of transactions is mandatory. This would not allow post-trading activities, which are integrated into the trading platform, as it is usual with the trading of Tokens. At present, there are no MTF or stock exchanges in Switzerland that are licensed for the trading of Asset Tokens.

An OTF is a trading facility providing either for multilateral trading of securities according to discretionary rules or of other financial instruments[303] according to discretionary or non-discretionary rules, or for bilateral trading between the participants and the operator of the OTF.[304] OTFs can only be operated by supervised banks, securities dealers, stock exchanges or MTFs that are authorized by FINMA to operate an OTF. Therefore, in relation to Tokens which qualify as securities, an OTF is only suitable if the trading between participants is executed according to discretionary rules, i.e., the trading facility must have discretion regarding the matching of a trade.[305] Subject to this limitation, banks, securities dealers, stock exchanges or MTFs may at present offer organized trading services in relation to Asset Tokens that qualify as securities.

302. *See* Federal Council, *supra* n. 294, at 146 et seq.

303. Financial instruments will be defined as of 1 January 2020 in Art. 3 lit. a of the Financial Services Act and comprise, in particular, debt and equity securities, derivatives, structured products and index or exchange-linked deposits which do not qualify as securities (*see* §6.12[A]) and the definition is in in particular relevant for derivatives.

304. Article 42 Financial Market Infrastructure Act (hereinafter: FMIA).

305. Article 23 Financial Market Infrastructure Ordinance.

The above license requirements apply, in principle, also to decentralized trading facilities, provided that such decentralized structures qualify as a trading facility. Please note that FINMA specified that systems not providing for the execution of trades, e.g., bulletin boards or order-routing systems, do not constitute a trading facility.[306] However, the Federal Council emphasized that such decentralized trading facility facilitates the transfer of assets and, therefore, should fall under the AML regulation.[307]

[3] Developments: Introduction of DLT Trading Facility

Due to current difficulties for establishing an MTF for Tokens that qualify as securities, the Federal Council proposed in the DLT Bill the creation of a new license category for the offering of multilateral trading services according to non-discretionary rules in relation to DLT Rights and similar Tokens represented on a blockchain (hereinafter: DLT Trading Facility).[308] Such DLT Trading Facility must provide one of the following: (i) trading is allowed by unregulated participants, (ii) the operator of the trading system centrally deposits the eligible Tokens on the basis of uniform rules, or (iii) the operator of the trading system performs the post-trading activities in relation to the eligible Tokens on the basis of uniform rules and procedures.[309]

With this proposal, the Federal Council departs from the technology-neutral approach and introduces a specific license for MTFs for DLT Rights qualifying as securities which eliminates the hurdles currently existing with MTFs regarding the mandatory use of separate financial infrastructures for post-trading activities and the limitation of eligible participants. However, the regulation is aimed at centralized exchanges and is not designed for decentralized trading facilities.[310] Also, please note that the DLT Bill at present does not provide for authorization requirements for foreign DLT Trading Facilities that will admit Swiss direct participants. In this respect, the proposed regulation is more liberal than the regulation of MTFs, as foreign MTFs do require a FINMA authorization before admitting Swiss direct participants.

306. FINMA *circular 2018/1, organized trading facilities*, no. 10.
307. Federal Council, Explanatory Report on the consultation draft regarding amendments to Swiss federal law in connection with the developments with the distributed ledger technology (*Erläuternder Bericht zur Vernehmlassungsvorlage des Bundesgesetzes zur Anpassung des Bundesrechts an Entwicklungen der Technik verteilter elektronischer Register*) of 22 March 2019, 24 et seq.
308. Federal Council, DLT Bill Report, 40 et seq.
309. Cf. DLT Bill, Art. 73a FMIA.
310. Federal Council, DLT Bill Report, 41.

§6.13 CAPITAL MARKETS AND BLOCKCHAIN: COUNTRY REPORT – SINGAPORE

Kim Kit Ow[311]

[A] What Makes a Token a Security?

As a global financial hub, Singapore has also been a frontrunner in the Fintech scene, and it has certainly been making headlines in Asia for being a staunch promoter of innovation while embracing a balanced and calibrated regulatory approach towards the application of blockchain in capital markets. This can be evidently seen in the Singapore government's attitude towards the regulation of blockchain-based digital Tokens, such as virtual currencies. The use of blockchain technology in itself is not new and has been commonly used in smart contracts and decentralized operations to facilitate trade and transfer of digital assets. Virtual currency or cryptocurrency is one of the many uses of blockchain technology.

The focus on the use of blockchain technology in capital markets in Singapore has been on the offering or issuance of digital Tokens. Unlike some other jurisdictions, Singapore has not classified nor regulated digital Tokens on a standalone basis, deciding instead to regulate them based on their characteristics and the activities which they are used for. Therefore, depending on its characteristics and what it is used for, a digital Token could be considered a security, a commodity or a utility.

In 2017, the Monetary Authority of Singapore (MAS) clarified that if a digital Token (e.g., blockchain-based) constitutes a product under Singapore's securities laws, then the offer or issuance of such digital Token shall comply with the relevant securities laws under the Securities & Futures Act of Singapore (Chapter 289)[312] (SFA). The MAS is the integrated regulator and supervisor of financial institutions in Singapore in the banking, capital markets, insurance and payments sectors. This clarification was seen as necessary against the backdrop of a slew of ICOs, heightened concerns over AML and countering the financing of terrorism (CFT) and the potential risks that such activities may negatively impact consumers. In developing a more targeted regulatory approach, the MAS issued a 'Guide to Digital Token Offerings' on 14 November 2017, which has since had two revisions, with its latest version dated 5 April 2019 (the DTO Guide).

Where capital markets are concerned, it is important to consider the situation when a digital Token falls under the definition of 'capital markets product' under the SFA and its regulatory treatment. As stated clearly by the MAS in the DTO Guide, an offer or issuance of digital Tokens may be regulated by the MAS if the digital Tokens are

311. Leading Singapore's Bird & Bird Finance & Financial Regulation Group Partner Kim Kit Ow specializes in financial services, FinTech, corporate and banking transactions. In 2009, she was announced as the Asian regional director for the International Chamber of Commerce (ICC) and in 2018 appointed onto the ICC Commission on Arbitration and ADR.

312. Media release 'MAS clarifies regulatory position on the offer of digital tokens in Singapore' (Monetary Authority of Singapore 1 August 2017).

'capital markets products'.[313] Capital markets products may include securities, derivatives contracts as well as units in a CIS (e.g., an investment fund). The MAS in a non-exhaustive manner set out some instances in the DTO Guide when a digital Token may constitute a 'capital markets product'. The following are three examples listed therein:[314]

(1) a share,[315] where it confers or represents an ownership interest in a corporation, represents liability of the Token holder in the corporation, and represents mutual covenants with other Token holders in the corporation *inter se*;
(2) a securities[316] -based derivatives contract, which includes any derivatives contract of which the underlying thing is a share, debenture or unit in a business trust; or
(3) a unit in a CIS, where it represents a right or interest in a CIS, or an option to acquire a right or interest in a CIS.

MAS further stated in the DTO Guide that it will 'examine the structure and characteristics of, including the rights attached to, a digital Token in determining if the digital Token is a type of capital markets products under the SFA'.[317] We would observe that such an approach is indeed very measured, looks beyond mere labels and does not seek to over-regulate. Given that Singapore already has extensive laws and regulations in the SFA, its subsidiary legislation and MAS-issued notices and guidance, to the extent that a digital Token has characteristics and risks that are associated with a capital markets product or such regulated activity (e.g., dealing in capital markets products) in connection thereto, then it will accordingly be regulated under current laws.

[B] Blockchain Finality

There are no specific statutory provisions governing the legal status of blockchain transactions in Singapore at the moment. This is unlike traditional capital market products such as listed shares, which transfers have for many years now had both legal and technical finality. A transfer of listed shares now would typically take the form of

313. *See* Guide to Digital Token Offerings at para. 2.1. Also *see* section 2(1) of the SFA which defines 'capital markets products' to include any securities (which includes shares, debentures and units in a business trust), units in a CIS, derivatives contracts (which includes derivatives of shares, debentures and units in a business trust), spot foreign exchange contracts for the purposes of leveraged foreign exchange trading, and such other products as MAS may prescribe as capital markets products.
314. *See* Guide to Digital Token Offerings at para. 2.3 where examples are provided by the MAS on how digital Tokens may be considered as 'capital markets products'.
315. *See* section 2(1) of the SFA, read with section 4(1) of the Companies Act (Cap. 50). The term 'share' means 'a share in the share capital of a corporation and includes stock except where a distinction between stocks and share is expressed or implied'.
316. Includes shares, debentures and units in a business trust. *See* section 2(1) of the SFA for the definition of 'securities' under the SFA.
317. *See* Guide to Digital Token Offerings at para. 2.2.

book entries which are lodged, registered and finally recorded in an electronic central ledger, held at The Central Depository (Pte) Limited (CDP), which is a wholly owned subsidiary of SGX which provides integrated clearing, settlement and depository services for many products in the Singapore securities market.

In terms of the common law, the only specific guidance provided by the courts so far is that cryptocurrencies may be treated as property that may be held on trust.[318] It is not yet clear how the courts will apply existing case law to the potentially different context of blockchain transactions.

In the absence of any specific legal authorities, blockchain records have no particular legal significance in Singapore. Entries in the blockchain record do not confer or amend legal rights in themselves. Ultimately, one will have to look at the underlying legal transactions to determine if the blockchain record is an accurate reflection of legal status. There is no reason to doubt that the legal doctrines of mistake and rectification will apply in the same way to this context, such that a court may give a remedy to 'correct' an 'inaccurate' entry on the blockchain record.

The *nemo dat* rule is likely to be applicable in this context, such that assignments of legal rights reflected in the blockchain record will only be valid insofar as the assignors actually had the requisite legal rights to assign, regardless of what may be reflected in the blockchain record.

If the decision of the High Court in *B2C2 v. Quoine* that cryptocurrencies are property is correct, there is the possibility that certain parties who rely on the blockchain records may be afforded some measure of protection in practice. A bona fide purchaser for value in a blockchain transaction may have relied on the blockchain records and be entitled to keep the property in this case. It is worth noting that it is not the entry in the blockchain record itself that confers this limited extent of finality, but the bona fides of the purchaser, which may be established through reliance on the record.

The difficulty with this view is that it is unclear whether the court's classification in *B2C2 v. Quoine* of cryptocurrencies may be extended to other legal rights recorded in the blockchain records. Further, there is an argument that this finding in the case was, strictly speaking, *obiter*.[319] Also, there is at least one academic view that even if cryptocurrencies can be held on trust, that in itself is not determinative of whether they are property.[320] Thus, it is questionable whether the court's finding that cryptocurrencies are property is legally binding.

In summary, blockchain records are not currently a recognized registry, and for now, no legal rights arise from entries into the blockchain records in themselves.

318. *B2C2 Ltd v. Quoine Pte Ltd* [2019] 4 SLR 17 (SGHC). Appealed to and heard by the Singapore Court of Appeal, with judgment expected to be delivered early next year.
319. *See B2C2 Ltd v. Quoine Pte Ltd* [2019] 4 SLR 17 (SGHC), [142].
320. Low and Mik, https://www.law.ox.ac.uk/business-law-blog/blog/2019/11/unpicking-finetech-mess-can-old-doctrines-cope-21st-century (accessed 11 March 2020).

[C] Special Requirements for Prospectus

In the examples set out above under §6.13[A], offers or issuance of digital Tokens which constitute securities, securities-based derivatives contracts or units in a CIS will be subject to the same regulatory regime and treatment under Part XIII of the SFA, as offers of securities, securities-based derivatives contracts or units in a CIS. To this end, there are several aspects that one has to be concerned with, including how an 'offer' is made and its accompanying prospectus requirements.

An offer of digital Tokens which constitute securities, securities-based derivatives contracts or units in a CIS can only be made if it complies with the requirements under Part XIII of the SFA.[321] The offer must also be made in or accompanied by a prospectus that is prepared in accordance with the SFA and is registered with MAS (*Prospectus Requirements*) unless specifically exempted. Where an offer is made in relation to units in a CIS to retail investors, the CIS is further subject to authorization or recognition requirements[322] prescribed by the MAS. An authorized CIS or a recognized CIS under the SFA must comply with various conditions and restrictions set out under the Code on CISs, published by the MAS.

Under Part XIII of the SFA, an offer as described above may be exempt from the Prospectus Requirements,[323] where, amongst others:

(1) the offer is a small (personal) offer that does not exceed SGD 5 million (or its equivalent in a foreign currency) within any twelve-month period, subject to certain conditions;
(2) the offer is a private placement offer made to no more than fifty persons within any twelve-month period, subject to certain conditions;
(3) the offer is made to institutional investors only; or
(4) the offer is made to accredited investors, subject to certain conditions.[324]

There are no exceptions made insofar as a digital Token is concerned in this regard. To the extent that a digital Token constitutes a security and its offer is required to be made in or accompanied by a prospectus that is prepared in accordance with the SFA and is registered with MAS, it will have to comply with all the relevant guidelines. As a matter of practical observation, given that the underlying specifics to a digital Token is not as common as traditional capital markets product (e.g., listed shares), it is even more important for those specifics, especially the risks associated with the product to be fully disclosed.

Another aspect that a person who offers digital Tokens that constitute securities, securities-based derivatives contracts or units in a CIS needs to be concerned with is if the said digital Token is also traded on the market (e.g., on an exchange). This is

321. *See* sections 240 and 296 of the SFA.
322. *See* sections 286 and 287 of the SFA, read with Part II of the Securities and Futures (Offers of Investments) (Collective Investment Schemes) Regulations 2005.
323. In the case of units in a CIS, exempt from the authorization and recognition requirements.
324. *See* Guide to Digital Token Offerings at para. 2.7.

because a person who establishes or operates a trading platform in Singapore in relation to digital Tokens which constitute securities, derivatives contracts or units in a CIS may be considered to be establishing or operating an organized market.[325] A person who establishes or operates an organized market, or holds himself out as operating such a market, must be approved by MAS as an approved exchange or recognized by MAS as a recognized market operator under the SFA unless otherwise exempted.[326]

In the DTO Guide, MAS sets out eleven case studies wherein it assesses how (if at all) the current legislation and regulations in respect of financial markets may apply to the offers of digital Tokens and the activities related thereto. While MAS makes it clear that these case studies are merely for illustrative purposes,[327] it does provide some guidance on MAS's regulatory approach on how it would deal with similar situations – to assess each underlying digital Token to see if it may fall within the definition of 'capital markets products', and if so, then apply the relevant legislation and regulations applicable traditionally to such products to the said digital Token.

When intermediating digital Tokens (i.e., dealing, buying and selling or broking), it is also important to note that even if a digital Token is not be considered a 'capital markets product', it may still be caught as a 'Digital Payment Token' under the Payment Services Act 2019[328] (PS Act). Under the PS Act, 'digital payment token' is broadly defined as:

> 'digital payment token' means any digital representation of value (other than an excluded digital representation of value) that –
>
> (a) is expressed as a unit;
> (b) is not denominated in any currency, and is not pegged by its issuer to any currency;
> (c) is, or is intended to be, a medium of exchange accepted by the public, or a section of the public, as payment for goods or services or for the discharge of debt;
> (d) can be transferred, stored or traded electronically; and
> (e) satisfies such other characteristics as the authority may prescribe.

Therefore, to the extent that a person facilitates the exchange of digital payment Tokens, that person will need to be regulated under the PS Act.[329] This has been part of the wider policy considerations that MAS dealt with in the earlier consultation periods for the PS Act wherein MAS considered the AML/CFT risks associated with

325. *Ibid.*, at para. 2.11 and also *see* Part I of the First Schedule to the SFA for the definition of an 'organized market'.
326. Also *see* Guidelines on the Regulation of Markets (Guideline no. SFA02-G01 https://www.mas.gov.sg/-/media/MAS/resource/legislation_guidelines/securities_futures/sub_legislation/Guidelines_Regulation_of_Markets.pdf, accessed 11 March 2020) for guidance.
327. *See* Guide to Digital Token Offerings at para. 4.1.
328. The Payment Services Act 2019 has been passed into law but has not come into effect as of 2019. It is anticipated that it will come into effect in January 2020 (*see* FAQs on the Payment Services Act dated 4 October 2019 published by the MAS).
329. *See* section 5 of the PS Act read with First Schedule Parts 1 and 3.

digital payment Tokens/virtual currency and accordingly the appropriateness of regulating these intermediaries.[330] This is elaborated below.

[D] Regulatory Specifics for Organized Trade

When a security is issued, investors would go through an intermediary to access the investment. In Singapore, this intermediary has to be a regulated entity, such as a broker or similar. Such an intermediary shall be subject to regulatory requirements that aims to ensure investor safeguards. These would include licences, specific limitations on specific investor groups and reporting to the MAS etc. Similarly, where a blockchain-based Security Token is offered through such intermediaries, the same regulatory expectations would apply. To the extent that the underlying product that is offered for investment is a 'capital markets product' (e.g., a security), then an intermediary which is dealing in such products shall be required to hold a Capital Markets Services licence under the SFA.

The heightened concerns surrounding the use of blockchain in digital Tokens in recent times have centred on money-laundering and terrorism-financing risks. Singapore has on all fronts been very vigilant and has also been very particular in complying with the recommendations and standards of the Financial Action Task Force in this regard.[331]

MAS has through the DTO Guide emphasized that all persons who are deemed to be an intermediary conducting regulated activities shall be bound to comply with the relevant MAS Notices on Prevention of Money Laundering and CFT which are applicable to them.[332] This is also now bolstered by the AML/CFT requirements that will also apply to digital payment Tokens intermediaries which will be regulated under the PS Act, where their Tokens are not regulated as 'capital markets products' under the SFA. Digital payment Token intermediaries are *'the points of intersection that provide gateways to the regulated financial system and nodes through which value may be moved'*. Given the ML/TF risks they pose, MAS views the regulation of such digital payment Token intermediaries for AML/CFT as appropriate. Should public use of digital payment Tokens become significant enough at a later stage to warrant more user protection, MAS would consider further measures.[333]

These are the collective efforts by the MAS to ensure that most of the money-laundering and terrorism-financing risks associated with digital payment Tokens/virtual currency may be addressed based on whether the Tokens are 'capital markets products' or not. This approach is in line with other general obligations imposed under Singapore law to combat money laundering and terrorism financing, including:

330. *See* 'Response to Feedback Received on the Proposed Payment Services Bill' published by MAS dated 19 November 2018 at para. 3.19.
331. http://www.fatf-gafi.org/publications/fatfrecommendations/?hf = 10&b = 0&s = desc(fatf_releasedate) (accessed 11 March 2020).
332. *See* Guide to Digital Token Offerings at para. 3.1.
333. *See* para. 3.19 of the Response to Feedback Received on the Proposed Payment Services Bill dated 19 November 2018.

- an obligation pursuant to section 39 of the Corruption, Drug Trafficking and Other Serious Crimes (Confiscation of Benefits) Act, to report suspicious transactions to the Commercial Affairs Department; and
- prohibitions from dealing with or providing financial services to designated individuals and entities pursuant to the Terrorism (Suppression of Financing) Act and various regulations that give effect to the United Nations Security Council Resolutions.[334]

[E] Conclusion

The fast-paced developments and evolution of blockchain technology must be seen to be both a boon and bane to our financial world. While innovation should not be stymied, it cannot be allowed a free reign without any regulations and control. The approach that Singapore has adopted in relation to accommodating blockchain in its capital markets has been a calibrated one, ensuring that our laws keep pace with innovation and that Singapore continues to be at the forefront without compromising any global regulatory standards.

§6.14 CAPITAL MARKETS AND BLOCKCHAIN: COUNTRY REPORT – CANADA

Daniel Fuke & Mike Stephens[335]

Until 2017, the use of blockchain technology and crypto assets in fundraising transactions was almost unheard of in Canada. Since then, however, Canadian founders have increasingly used blockchain technology and crypto assets both for fundraising, such as through ICOs, and for related business lines, such as cryptocurrency exchanges, investment funds invested in crypto assets, and advisory services relating to such businesses. But as cryptocurrency prices corrected throughout 2018 and securities regulatory scrutiny on the industry increased, many of those businesses proved untenable, and some ultimately failed.

Today, Canada is at a crossroads with respect to how its capital markets will incorporate blockchain technology and crypto assets, and how the industry will be regulated. Canada's stable democracy, promotion of technological innovation, and

334. *See* Guide to Digital Token Offerings at paras 3.3.1 and 3.3.2.

335. Recognized leader in the British Columbia technology ecosystem, Mike Stephens works as a Partner at Fasken. He advises start-ups, executives and company boards on corporate and business issues, with particular focus on early-stage entrepreneurs in understanding the potential of Blockchain & Distributed Ledger Technology to transform into businesses. Daniel Fuke is Partner at Fasken in Securities and M&A group and is related to investment funds and Blockchain technologies. He holds Fasken Seminars on 'Blockchain and the Gold Industry – A Digital Certificate at the end of the Rainbow?' combined with publications on 'Regulatory Net Tightening on the "Wild West" of the Blockchain and Cryptocurrency Industry' which underlines his expertise in share and asset purchase transactions, investment fund formations and ICOs.

secure infrastructure have led to its emergence as a world-renowned technology hub and have positioned Canada as a potential leader in the blockchain and crypto asset industry.

However, the blockchain and crypto asset industry must overcome certain obstacles to do so, including reputational issues from its close connection to cryptocurrency and a conservative approach from local securities regulators. As a result, the incorporation of blockchain technology and crypto assets into Canadian capital markets could be a very rewarding, but slow, process.

[A] What Makes a Token a Security

According to a PricewaterhouseCoopers report, Canadian companies closed ten ICOs, raising approximately USD 163 million in gross proceeds during 2017.[336] We expect, however, that the real numbers are much higher, and that PricewaterhouseCoopers ran into difficulty in getting industry participants to provide detailed information. As discussed below, 2017 was a time of regulatory uncertainty, and accordingly, industry participants may not have wanted to publicize their deals.

Related business lines also flourished during this time, including cryptocurrency exchanges and brokerages and ICO advisory firms. Coinsquare, a leading Canadian cryptocurrency exchange launched in 2014, took massive strides in 2017, resulting in its recognition from LinkedIn as the second fastest-growing startup from July 2017 to July 2018, accumulating an employee base growth of 92%.[337] In addition to its large growth in staff to accommodate increasing users, Coinsquare also raised CAD 30 million in 2017, which signalled the market's acceptance of its growth potential.[338]

Throughout the first half of 2017, Canadian securities regulators were silent as to the application of securities laws on ICOs and cryptocurrencies. The key regulatory question in Canada during this period was whether cryptocurrencies and other crypto assets should be considered securities and regulated accordingly. Applying securities laws to the blockchain and crypto asset industry would have imposed significant time and cost obligations on participants, such as requiring ICO issuers to prepare prospectuses, requiring cryptocurrency exchanges to be regulated as 'marketplaces',[339] and

336. According to PricewaterhouseCoopers, 10 Canadian ICOs closed in 2017, raising an aggregate of approximately USD 163 million.

337. https://www.newswire.ca/news-releases/coinsquare-ranks-2nd-on-linkedins-2018-list-of-canadas-top-startups-692686911.html (accessed 11 March 2020).

338. https://www.ivey.uwo.ca/scotiabank-digital-banking-lab/canada-fintech/blockchain-crypto/coinsquare (accessed 11 March 2020).

339. Per section 1(1) of *Securities Act*, RSO 1990, c-S.5, 'Marketplace' means any of the following, but does not include an inter-dealer bond broker:

1. An exchange.
2. A quotation and trade reporting system.
3. A person or company not included in paragraph 1 or 2 that,
   i. constitutes, maintains or provides a market or facility for bringing together buyers and sellers of securities or derivatives,
   ii. brings together the orders for securities or derivatives of multiple buyers and sellers, and

requiring advisory firms to be registered with Canadian Securities Administrators (CSA) as 'dealers'[340] or 'advisers'.[341]

Notwithstanding the cost and scrutiny that would come with being subject to securities regulation, many industry participants would have welcomed regulation as a means to legitimize the developing industry and keep out bad actors. Others, however, took the position that silence from securities regulators meant their activities were entirely unregulated. For some, these decisions came with harsh consequences, as described below under 'Enforcement'.

In North America, securities regulatory action first came from the SEC, who published in July 2017 an investigative report on the ICO of the Decentralized Autonomous Organization (DAO Report) which concluded that the DAO's USD 150 million ICO in May 2016 was a non-compliant securities offering that was not registered under US securities laws.[342]

The CSA, an umbrella organization of Canada's provincial and territorial securities regulators, issued CSA Staff Notice 46-307 – *Cryptocurrency Offerings* (*Staff Notice 46-307*) on 24 August 2017, shortly after the publication of the DAO Report. In it, the CSA concluded that, 'in many cases' cryptocurrency coins and Tokens 'should properly be considered securities',[343] a position that was consistent with the SEC's analysis in the DAO Report.

Canadian securities legislation defines a 'security' to include, among more commonly used categories like shares and bonds, 'any investment contract'. The test in Canada for when a particular instrument is an investment contract, and therefore a security, comes from the 1978 Supreme Court of Canada case *Pacific Coast Coin Exchange of Canada v. Ontario (Securities Commission)* (Pacific Coast Coin). The test states that 'an investment contract will be found where there is: (a) an investment of money; (b) with an intention of expectation of profit; (c) in a common enterprise, in which the fortunes of the investor are interwoven with and dependent upon the efforts and success of those seeking the investment or of third parties; and (d) that the efforts made by those other than the investor are the undeniably significant ones, those essential managerial efforts which affect the failure or success of the enterprise'.[344]

iii. uses established non-discretionary methods under which the orders interact with each other, and the buyers and sellers entering the orders agree to the terms of a trade.

4. With respect to securities, a dealer who executes a trade of an exchange-traded security outside a marketplace described in paragraph 1, 2 or 3; ('marché').

340. 'Dealer' means, except for the purposes described in subsection (1.2) of the *Securities Act*, a person or company engaging in or holding himself, herself or itself out as engaging in the business of trading in securities as principal or agent; ('courtier').
341. 'Adviser' means a person or company engaging in or holding himself, herself, or itself out as engaging in the business of advising others as to the investing in or the buying or selling of securities.
342. https://www.sec.gov/litigation/investreport/34-81207.pdf (accessed 11 March 2020).
343. https://www.osc.gov.on.ca/documents/en/Securities-Category4/csa_20170824_cryptocurrency-offerings.pdf (accessed 11 March 2020).
344. *Pacific Coast Coin Exchange v. Ontario (Securities Commission)*, 1977 CanLII 37 (SCC), [1978] 2 SCR 112 at 128.

While Staff Notice 46-307 was encouraging because it meant that Canadian regulators were alive to the securities law issues presented by cryptocurrencies, it was also disappointingly vague. Cryptocurrencies and other crypto assets are inherently different from the traditional investment structures discussed in Pacific Coast Coin and other case law, yet Staff Notice 46-307 made no such distinction, forcing industry participants and their advisors to apply a 39-year-old test to revolutionary technology.

Some industry participants chose to accept the notion that crypto assets are securities and applied to CSA for exemptions from or specialized categorization within securities laws in order to proceed with their businesses. The decisions in Token Funder[345] and Impak[346] both resulted in the applicable company obtaining exemptions in order to conduct ICOs, and investment fund managers (IFMs) First Block Capital[347] and Majestic Asset Management[348] expanded their securities registrations in order to allow them to launch investment funds exposed to cryptocurrencies.

Others, however, took the position that the crypto assets with which they were dealing were not captured by Pacific Coast Coin because the crypto assets in question had utility (*Utility Tokens*) within an online ecosystem and were therefore inherently distinguishable from securities.

While the global ICO frenzy continued throughout 2017, by late that year, Canadian regulators had put the industry on notice, and several industry participants had legitimized CSA's position by submitting to its jurisdiction.

[B] Crypto Winter

The bull market for cryptocurrencies and the momentum behind ICOs came to an abrupt halt in 2018. After reaching its all-time high of approximately USD 20,000 per coin in December 2017, the price of bitcoin fell by 67% in the two months of 2018 to approximately USD 7,000 and continued a steep slide over the year.[349] By the end of 2018, bitcoin's market capitalization had shrunk by 80%.[350]

The actions of Canadian regulators in early 2018 may also have contributed to the slowdown in the blockchain and crypto asset industry. On 11 June 2018, CSA published Staff Notice 46-308 – *Securities Law Implications for Offerings of Tokens*[351] (*Staff Notice 46-308*), in which it took the position that most, if not all, offerings of

345. https://www.osc.gov.on.ca/en/SecuritiesLaw_ord_20171023_token.htm (accessed 11 March 2020).
346. https://www.osc.gov.on.ca/documents/en/Securities-OSCB/20170824_oscb_4034_toc.pdf at 18 (accessed 11 March 2020).
347. https://www.theglobeandmail.com/investing/globe-wealth/article-high-net-worth-investors-now-able-to-hold-bitcoin-in-registered (accessed 11 March 2020).
348. https://news.coinsquare.com/investing/csa-authorizes-three-digital-currency-investment-funds (accessed 11 March 2020).
349. https://www.theguardian.com/technology/2018/nov/20/bitcoin-price-plunges-2018-low-cryptocurrency-value (accessed 11 March 2020).
350. https://coinmarketcap.com/currencies/bitcoin/historical-data/?start=20130428&end=20191031 (accessed 11 March 2020).
351. https://www.osc.gov.on.ca/documents/en/Securities-Category4/csa_20180611_46-308_implications-for-offerings-of-tokens.pdf (accessed 11 March 2020).

crypto assets would be an issuance of securities. Staff Notice 46-308 took a purposive look at crypto assets and took the position that the economic reality on an offering must be considered, regardless of how the instrument was characterized and regardless of an asset being a Utility Token.

This meant that, in CSA's view, virtually all business dealing with crypto assets, whether they be ICO issuers, cryptocurrency exchanges, or advisory firms, would be subject to securities laws, even if they had been operating their businesses prior to Staff Notice 46-308.

The blockchain and crypto asset industry was in a difficult place at the end of 2018. Not only were cryptocurrency markets down considerably, but tightened regulatory scrutiny forced industry participants to reconsider how to approach their businesses. Crypto asset issuers in particular faced two principal alternatives: (i) redesign their crypto asset to avoid securities regulatory application which, based on Staff Notice 46-308, would be difficult, or (ii) pivot to an STO.

[C] Special Requirements for Prospectus

As mentioned above, some industry participants valued regulatory certainty so much that they embraced the idea that their crypto assets were securities and actively complied with securities regulations. A good example of this is issuers who, rather than undertaking an ICO, undertook an STO.

As the name suggests, Security Tokens are securities by nature, representing ownership of a company, debt obligation, value of underlying assets, or an investment contract. Security Tokens share almost all of the same characteristics as traditional securities, except that they are distributed digitally rather than in certificate or book-entry form.

STOs take advantage of many of blockchain technology's benefits, including ease of communication between management and security holders, greater transparency, ease of transfer among security holders, and lowering transaction costs by eliminating intermediaries.

Although they exist on the blockchain, Security Tokens are subject to all Canadian securities laws. Token issuers have the same obligation when distributing to prepare a prospectus or rely on an exemption from the prospectus requirement, such as those available in respect of accredited investors and where an offering memorandum is prepared. Security Tokens distributed in Canada pursuant to a prospectus exemption are subject to resale restrictions prescribed by National Instrument 45-102 - *Resale of Securities*, including that the first sale of which requires a prospectus or a further exemption in respect of the secondary seller.

[D] Regulatory Specifics for Organized Trade

[1] Registration Request and Oversight

Canadian securities laws also impose registration requirements on certain industry participants. Businesses that are in the business of trading in securities, including receiving a commission for arranging for Security Token purchasers, are required to be registered as a dealer. In addition, an entity that is managing an investment fund invested in cryptocurrencies is required to register as an IFM. Exchanges that facilitate secondary trading of Security Tokens are required to be recognized as marketplaces by CSA and are subject to the oversight of the Financial Transactions and Reports Analysis Centre of Canada (FinTRAC).[352]

[2] Regulatory Gaps

Given the speed with which the blockchain and crypto asset industry has developed, it is not surprising that comprehensive regulation dealing with all aspects of the industry has not yet been implemented.

One area where the gap between existing securities regulation and the nature of blockchain technology is the biggest relates to exchanges. The decentralized nature of blockchain technology allows cryptocurrencies to be traded between users with great efficiency, but any exchange that lists crypto assets that are securities would be subject to the same regulation as major stock exchanges such as the Toronto Stock Exchange. This has slowed down the development of secondary markets in Security Tokens, which has in turn reduced the number of STOs. Recently, however, the Ontario Securities Commission (OSC) approved a pilot project by TokenGX[353] in Toronto to test secondary market Security Token trading.

Another area with a regulatory gap relates to investment dealers (i.e., brokers). Because Security Tokens are issued on a blockchain rather than in paper form, investment dealers and clearing agencies are not able to follow their standard transaction confirmation procedures and very few are willing to be involved in STOs. This has slowed down primary issuances of Security Tokens.

[3] Enforcement

Canadian securities regulators play an important role in protecting investors and preserving the integrity of capital markets and must walk a fine line between that mandate and promoting efficient capital markets. To this point, Canadian securities regulators have understandably taken a conservative approach to this new industry.

352. http://www.gazette.gc.ca/rp-pr/p2/2019/2019-07-10/html/sor-dors240-eng.html (accessed 11 March 2020).
353. https://www.osc.gov.on.ca/en/SecuritiesLaw_ord_20191023_tokengx.htm (accessed 11 March 2020).

While CSA and other Canadian enforcement agencies have put the entire crypto asset industry on notice that securities laws apply to most crypto assets, their enforcement actions have generally been limited to seeking out instances of fraudulent ICOs[354] and advisors who promoted ICOs while not registered as an investment dealer. The OSC has issued hundreds of letters to organizations that have led to various orders, rulings and decisions for issues based on their regulatory disclosure documents or business activities in 2019 alone.[355]

One such example is the recent July 2019 OSC settlement with CoinLaunch Corp., a provider of various ICO-related services to ICO issuers. Following an investigation by the OSC, it was determined that CoinLaunch engaged in and held itself out as engaging in the business of trading in securities without registration under securities law as they advertised and marketed promotional services to two ICO issuers. The services CoinLaunch provided to the issuers included creating and preparing promotional materials for the issuers' Token offerings, directly introducing the issuers to potential investors, and taking the offerings on roadshows to help solicit investors. CoinLaunch and the OSC settled, and CoinLaunch agreed to cease their cryptocurrency business and pay over CAD 50,000 in penalties.

Another interesting story from the industry, while not originating from an enforcement action, involved the now-defunct cryptocurrency exchange Quadriga CX. This unregulated exchange (because it ostensibly did not list for trading any crypto assets that are securities) was once one of Canada's largest cryptocurrency exchanges, but after the sudden death of its CEO, it was found that he had moved roughly CAD 180 million of client assets into personal accounts only he could access.[356]

The OSC ultimately began looking into the matter in February 2019 as there was harm to Ontario investors and their investigation exposed the regulatory vacuum in the crypto assets industry over who would be held accountable if an unregulated cryptocurrency exchange suddenly prevented its customers from accessing their assets.

Perhaps to address this vacuum, on 14 March 2019, CSA and the Investment Industry Regulatory Organization of Canada (a SRO of investment dealers) published the Joint Securities Administrations/Investment Industry Regulatory Organization of Canada's Consultation Paper and Proposed Framework for Crypto Asset Trading Platforms,[357] which sought input from the industry regarding how best to regulate cryptocurrency and Security Token exchanges.

A final example of securities regulatory approach in Canada can be seen from the 3iQ case. 3iQ Corp. (3IQ) is an IFM that sought to launch The Bitcoin Fund, a bitcoin-only fund, to retail investors in Canada by way of a prospectus, thereby requiring review by CSA. CSA Staff refused to let the offering proceed based on

354. https://www.coindesk.com/police-freeze-bank-accounts-seize-luxury-cars-in-probe-of-22-million-ico-promoter-vanbex (accessed 11 March 2020).
355. https://www.osc.gov.on.ca/en/5610.htm?query=registration&x=16&y=17 (accessed 11 March 2020).
356. https://www.reuters.com/article/us-quadrigacx-crypto-canada/ontario-securities-regulator-looking-into-digital-platform-quadriga-idUSKCN1PX26G (accessed 11 March 2020).
357. https://www.osc.gov.on.ca/en/SecuritiesLaw_csa_20190314_21-402_crypto-asset-trading-platforms.htm (accessed 11 March 2020).

concerns relating to the liquidity of bitcoin, the ability to accurately value bitcoin, the custody of the fund's assets and whether an audit could be completed on the fund. However, 3iQ challenged Staff's decision and the OSC Commissioner mandated that the offering be allowed to proceed.[358]

[E] Conclusion

The use of blockchain technology and crypto assets in Canadian capital markets experienced a rapid rise in 2017 and a similarly rapid descent in 2018 to today, but one should not expect this is the end. Those who were attracted to the industry seeking an unregulated 'wild west' in which to get rich quickly are largely gone, leaving industry participants who believe that blockchain technology and digital assets have a crucial role to play in making Canada's capital markets more efficient.

Canadian securities regulators have come a long way, from standing on the sidelines in 2017 to positioning crypto assets as a securities law jurisdiction, to the decisions in TokenGX and 3iQ, where they embraced novel concepts and found ways for those to work within existing regulatory frameworks.

While it may be several years before blockchain technology and digital assets are used in mainstream Canadian capital markets transactions, they have the ability to improve the efficiency and transparency of such markets, and as a result, should continue to be pursued by industry participants and regulators alike.

§6.15 CAPITAL MARKETS AND BLOCKCHAIN: COUNTRY REPORT – USA

James Gatto[359]

[A] What Makes a Token a Security?

In the US, there are both federal and state laws and regulations that apply to digital assets (including cryptocurrencies and Tokens). At the federal level, there are no new laws that have been passed. Rather, the relevant agencies have issued guidance on how the existing law and legal principles apply to digital assets, and they have engaged in various enforcement actions. Some states have passed new laws that apply to digital

358. https://business.financialpost.com/pmn/press-releases-pmn/business-wire-news-releases-pmn/3iqs-the-bitcoin-fund-receives-favourable-ruling-from-ontario-securities-commission-panel (accessed 11 March 2020).

359. Leading the Blockchain Technology and Digital Assets Team and Social Media and Games Team Partner at Sheppard Mullin, James G. Gatto leverages his unique combination of over thirty years of IP and technology law experience, business insights and attention to technology trends. James's leadership on Blockchain & Cryptocurrencies has been selected for a National Law Review Go-To Thought Leadership Award by acknowledging his insightful, helpful and timely insight for NLR readers in these complicated areas of law, as well as the digital media industry and technology trends.

assets. This report will primarily cover federal issues but will highlight some of the state law issues.

Various federal agencies have exerted jurisdiction over digital assets. Their jurisdiction seems to be overlapping, at least for now. In part, this is due to the fact that these different agencies have classified various digital assets, and cryptocurrency in particular, in conflicting ways. This table shows a high-level summary of these classifications:

Agency	*Classification*
SEC	Security
CFTC	Commodity
FinCEN	Money
IRS	Property

A more detailed explanation of the legal issues that these agencies address is set forth below.

[1] US SEC

The SEC has been one of the most active agencies in this area. The SEC regulates securities and securities exchanges. The mission of the SEC is to protect investors; maintain fair, orderly, and efficient markets; and facilitate capital formation. The SEC strives to promote a market environment that is worthy of the public's trust.

The SEC has been primarily focused on whether digital assets are securities. The term 'securities' is defined to include a number of things (including stocks, bonds and transferable shares).[360] None of these traditional types of securities seem to cover most cryptocurrencies and Tokens. However, the definition of security further includes the term 'investment contracts'. When analysing whether cryptocurrencies and Tokens are securities, the SEC has focused most of its analysis on this category of security.

The primary test that the SEC uses to determine if a Token is an investment contract (and thus a security) is the *Howey* test.[361] This test defines an offering as an investment contract if there is: (i) an investment of money; (ii) in a common enterprise; (iii) with a reasonable expectation of profit; (iv) derived solely from the efforts of others.[362]

360. The term 'security' is defined in section 2(a)(1) of the Securities Act of 1933 (the 'Securities Act'), section 3(a)(10) of the Securities Exchange Act of 1934, section 2(a)(36) of the Investment Company Act of 1940, and section 202(a)(18) of the Investment Advisers Act of 1940.

361. *SEC v. W.J. Howey Co.*, 328 U.S. 293.

362. The *Howey* case limited the fourth prong of the test to profits derived 'solely' from the efforts of others. Over time, the courts relaxed this requirement. Thus, according to the SEC, it is not necessary that the profit comes solely from the efforts of others.

According to the SEC, the focus of the *Howey* analysis is not only on the form and terms of the instrument itself (in this case, the digital asset) but also on the circumstances surrounding the digital asset and the manner in which it is offered, sold, or resold (which includes secondary market sales). It has indicated that labels do not matter, but the totality of the facts and circumstances do. For example, calling a Token a 'Utility Token' will not exclude it from being a security. The SEC has stated that most Token offerings that it has seen, in particular ICOs, are securities, but bitcoin and ether are not.

The federal securities laws require all offers and sales of securities, including those involving a digital asset, to either be registered under its provisions or to qualify for an exemption from registration. The registration provisions require persons to disclose certain information to investors, and that information must be complete and not materially misleading. This requirement for disclosure furthers the federal securities laws' goal of providing investors with the information necessary to make informed investment decisions.

The SEC has issued various guidance to help assess whether a digital asset is a security. The most recent is its *Framework for 'Investment Contract' Analysis of Digital Assets*, April 2019.

[2] The Commodities Futures Trading Commission

The mission of the Commodities Futures Trading Commission (CFTC) is to foster open, transparent, competitive, and financially sound markets. By working to avoid systemic risk, the Commission aims to protect market users and their funds, consumers, and the public from fraud, manipulation, and abusive practices related to derivatives and other products that are subject to the Commodity Exchange Act (CEA). The CFTC has asserted jurisdiction over various types of digital assets based on its view that they are commodities. According to the CFTC, the definition of 'commodity' in the CEA is broad and includes 'all services, rights, and interests … in which contracts for future delivery are presently or in the future dealt in'. This nebulous language allegedly covers most cryptocurrencies.

The CFTC's jurisdiction is implicated when a virtual currency is used in a derivatives contract, or if there is fraud or manipulation involving a virtual currency traded in interstate commerce. Beyond instances of fraud or manipulation, the CFTC generally does not oversee 'spot' or cash-market exchanges and transactions involving virtual currencies that do not utilize margin, leverage, or financing.

According to the CFTC, a smart contract, depending on its structure, operation, and relevant facts and circumstances, could be a Commodity, Forward Contract, Futures Contract, Option on Futures Contract or a Swap.

The CFTC has issued various guidance documents, including *A CFTC Primer on Virtual Currencies* and *A Primer on Smart Contracts*.

[3] The Financial Crimes Enforcement Network

Financial Crimes Enforcement Network (FinCEN's) mission is to safeguard the financial system from illicit use, combat money laundering, and promote national security through the strategic use of financial authorities and the collection, analysis, and dissemination of financial intelligence. FinCEN is responsible for administering regulations relating to the Bank Secrecy Act (BSA) and its amendments. The BSA is focused on AML and CFT.

FinCEN was quite forward-looking and issued initial guidance in 2013 '*Application of FinCEN's Regulations to Persons Administering, Exchanging, or Using Virtual Currencies*', and various updates to that guidance, including on 9 May 2019 '*Application of FinCEN's Regulations to Certain Business Models Involving Convertible Virtual Currencies*'.

According to its guidance, FinCEN 'In contrast to real currency, "virtual" currency is a medium of exchange that operates like a currency in some environments, but does not have all the attributes of real currency.' Its guidance addresses 'Convertible' Virtual Currency (CVC). This type of virtual currency either has an equivalent value in real currency or acts as a substitute for real currency.

This guidance refers to the participants in generic virtual currency arrangements, using the terms 'user' 'exchanger' and 'administrator'. A user is a person who obtains virtual currency to purchase goods or services.[363] An exchanger is a person engaged as a business in the exchange of virtual currency for real currency, funds, or other virtual currency. An administrator is a person engaged as a business in issuing (putting into circulation) a virtual currency, and who has the authority to redeem (to withdraw from circulation) such virtual currency.

A user who obtains CVC and uses it to purchase real or virtual goods or services is not a Money Services Business (MSB) under FinCEN's regulations. An administrator or exchanger that (1) accepts and transmits a CVC or (2) buys or sells CVC for any reason is a money transmitter under FinCEN's regulations unless a limitation to or exemption from the definition applies to the person.[364] FinCEN interprets these exemptions strictly. Therefore, a person may not take advantage of a particular exemption if the activity he or she engages in does not conform fully to an exemption.

FinCEN's regulations define the term 'money transmitter' as a person that provides money transmission services, or any other person engaged in the transfer of funds. The term 'money transmission services' means 'the acceptance of currency,

363. FinCEN notes that how a person engages in 'obtaining' a virtual currency may be described using any number of other terms, such as 'earning', 'harvesting', 'mining', 'creating', 'autogenerating', 'manufacturing', or 'purchasing', depending on the details of the specific virtual currency model involved.

364. FinCEN's regulations provide that whether a person is a money transmitter is a matter of facts and circumstances. The regulations identify six circumstances under which a person is not a money transmitter, despite accepting and transmitting currency, funds, or value that substitutes for currency. 31 CFR section 1010.100(ff)(5)(ii)(A)-(F).

funds, or other value that substitutes for currency from one person and the transmission of currency, funds, or other value that substitutes for currency to another location or person by any means.'[365]

The label applied to any particular type of CVC (such as 'digital currency', 'cryptocurrency', 'crypto asset', 'digital asset' etc.) is not dispositive of its regulatory treatment under the BSA. Additionally, transactions denominated in CVC will be subject to FinCEN regulations regardless of whether the CVC is represented by a physical or digital Token, whether the type of ledger used to record the transactions is centralized or distributed, or the type of technology utilized for the transmission of value.

According to FinCEN, a person still qualifies as a money transmitter if that person's activities include receiving one form of value (currency, funds, prepaid value, value that substitutes for currency - such as CVC, etc.) from one person and transmitting either the same or a different form of value to another person or location, by any means. Similarly, a money transmitter may accept and transmit value in either order. That is, a person is still a money transmitter under FinCEN regulations if the person transmits value first, and only later accepts the corresponding value for this transfer.

FinCEN has made it clear that, in its view, persons accepting and transmitting value that substitutes for currency, such as virtual currency, are money transmitters. Persons accepting and transmitting CVC are required (like any money transmitter) to register with FinCEN as an MSB and comply with AML programme, record-keeping, monitoring, and reporting requirements, including the filing of suspicious activity reports (SARs) and Currency Transaction Reports (CTRs). These requirements apply equally to domestic and foreign-located CVC money transmitters doing business in whole or in substantial part within the US, even if the foreign-located entity has no physical presence in the US.

Most recently, the leaders of the CFTC, FinCEN and the SEC issued a joint statement to remind persons engaged in activities involving digital assets of their AML and CFT (AML/CFT) obligations under the BSA. This joint statement provides further clarity on some of the many laws potentially applicable to cryptocurrency and other digital assets and highlights the need for anyone operating in the space to obtain legal advice to understand their legal compliance obligations. According to the statement, AML/CFT obligations apply to entities that the BSA defines as 'financial institutions', such as futures commission merchants and introducing brokers obligated to register with the CFTC, MSBs as defined by FinCEN, and broker-dealers and mutual funds obligated to register with the SEC. Among those AML/CFT obligations are the requirement to establish and implement an effective AML Program and record-keeping and reporting requirements, including SAR requirements.

365. 31 CFR section 1010.100(ff)(5)(i)(A).

[4] FINRA

FINRA is a government-authorized not-for-profit organization that oversees US broker-dealers. It issued a report *'Distributed Ledger Technology: Implications of Blockchain for the Securities Industry'* in January 2017. The report notes that DLT has the potential to affect various aspects of the securities market, including market efficiency, transparency, post-trade processes and operational risk. The report highlights many of the potential implications of DLT on broker-dealers. The report is not intended to express any legal position, and it does not create any new legal requirements or suggest any change in any existing regulatory obligations. Nor does it provide relief from any regulatory obligations. Rather, the report highlights certain operational and regulatory areas that broker-dealers may wish to consider as they explore adopting DLT.

[5] The IRS

The Internal Revenue Service (IRS) issued initial guidance in 2014 and updated guidance in 2019. The guidance addresses how existing general tax principles apply to transactions using virtual currency. According to the IRS, for federal tax purposes, virtual currency is treated as property. General tax principles applicable to property transactions apply to transactions using virtual currency. It is not treated as a currency that could generate foreign currency gain or loss for US federal tax purposes. One of the ramifications of this is that, according to the IRS, a taxpayer who receives virtual currency as payment for goods or services must, in computing gross income, include the fair market value of the virtual currency, measured in US dollars, as of the date that the virtual currency was received. If the fair market value of property received in exchange for virtual currency exceeds (is less than) the taxpayer's adjusted basis of the virtual currency, the taxpayer has taxable gain (loss).

A taxpayer generally realizes capital gain or loss on the sale or exchange of virtual currency that is a capital asset in the hands of the taxpayer. For example, stocks, bonds, and other investment property are generally capital assets. Arguably, this applies to cryptocurrencies that are deemed securities or other investment property. A taxpayer generally realizes ordinary gain or loss on the sale or exchange of virtual currency that is not a capital asset in the hands of the taxpayer. Inventory and other property held mainly for sale to customers in a trade or business are examples of property that is not a capital asset.

Few people have reported taxable gains on the disposition of cryptocurrencies. The IRS has announced an enforcement campaign to educate taxpayers and compel compliance.

[6] State Laws

Most states have money transmitter laws that require companies to obtain a license in that state if they engage in money transmission services. Some states, such as New York, impose a separate requirement to obtain a 'BitLicense.' Subject to certain exceptions, anyone engaging in any of the following activities may be required to obtain a BitLicense in New York: (i) virtual currency transmission; (ii) storing, holding, or maintaining custody or control of virtual currency on behalf of others; (iii) buying and selling virtual currency as a customer business; (iv) performing exchange services as a customer business; (v) or controlling, administering, or issuing a virtual currency.

Delaware is the most popular state for incorporation in the US. Recent changes to the Delaware General Corporate Law expressly permit the keeping of corporate records in the form of electronic networks and databases. These changes permit a corporation to maintain the required stock ledger using DLT/blockchain technology.

Space constraints limit the ability to address in this report much more about the many state laws that have been passed that relate to digital assets. The National Conference of State Legislatures maintains a very helpful collection of blockchain-related state laws.

FURTHER READING

Bala, Sebastian Kopyściański, Tomasz Srokosz, Witold, Kryptowaluty jako elektroniczne instrumenty płatnicze bez emitenta. Aspekty informatyczne, ekonomiczne i prawne (2016).

Berndsen, Ron Wandhöfer, Ruth, Proof-of-Work Blockchains and Settlement Finality: A Functional Interpretation, Journal of Financial Market Infrastructures, (2012) https://www.risk.net/journal-of-financial-market-infrastructures/6813151/proof-of-work-blockchains-and-settlement-finality-a-functional-interpretation (accessed 15 November 2019).

Bird & Bird LLP, Blockchains Uncut: Risks, Rewards & Regulation (2019).

Blemus, Stéphane Pion, Claire, Blockchain minibons et titres financiers, des règles ad hoc pour les chaînes de blocs, Revue de Droit bancaire et financier n°1, janvier 2019, étude 2.

Bonneau, Thierry Verbiest, Thibault, Fintech et droit, RB édition (2017).

Buterin, Vitalik, On Settlement Finality (2016). https://blog.ethereum.org/2016/05/09/on-settlement-finality (accessed 4 December 2019).

Cremers, Thiebald, La Blockchain et les titres nominatifs, Revue de Droit bancaire et financier n°1, janvier 2019, étude 4.

Ciupa, Katarzyna Maria, Blockchain technology and its impact on the development of capital market infrastructure, Capital Market – regulations and foundations, scientific editor Teresa Czerwińska, Alojzy Z. Nowak (2018).

Dauvergne, Géraldine, Société Générale mise sur la blockchain publique, Revue Banque (2019).

De Vauplane, Hubert, Charpiat, Victor, Réglementation des cryptoactifs, la France pionnière, Agefi Hebdo (14 June 2019).

De Vauplane, Hbert, Après les ICO, le temps des STO ? Revue Banque (28 February 2019).

Finnish Financial Supervisory Authority, Regulations and Guidelines 4/2019 – Virtual Currency Providers, 14 June 2019 | FIVA 12/01.00/2019 (2019).

Granier, Thierry, Verbiest, Thibault, Marchés financiers et technologie blockchain, Banque & Droit n°187 September - October 2019.

Legeais, Dominique, L'utilisation de la blockchain pour les titres de sociétés non cotées, Droit des sociétés n°2, Février 2019, étude 2.

Legeais, Dominique, Blockchain et actifs numériques, LexisNexis (2019).

Le Quintrec, Florent, Les STOs démocratisent les levées via la blockchain, L'Agefi Hebdo (18 to 24 April 2019).

Michna, Marcin, Bitcoin jako przedmiot stosunków cywilnoprawnych (2018).

Piotrowska, Anna Iwona, Bitcoin. Płatnicze i inwestycyjne zastosowania kryptowaluty (2018).

Rogowski, Wojciech, Regulacje finansowe. FinTech - nowe instrumenty finansowe - resolution (2017).

Szostek, Dariusz, Blockchain a prawo (2018).
Szpringer, Włodzimierz, Blockchain jako innowacja systemow. Od internetu informacji do internetu wartości. Wyzwania dla sektora finansowego (2019).
Vamparys, Xavier, La blockchain au service de la finance, RB édition (2018).

CHAPTER 7
Blockchain and Intellectual Property

Andreas Holzwarth-Rochford

§7.01 INTRODUCTION

Blockchain and Distributed Ledger Technology (DLT) have a lot of different aspects and are becoming more and more relevant for ample applications and use cases. Beside financial applications like cryptocurrencies, these technologies are usable in a huge variety of fields to increase the cryptography and record keeping. Some are smart contracts, supply chain management, data sharing, digital voting, and food safety.

On the other hand, the legal area of Intellectual Property (IP) also provides a lot of different aspects and ample possibilities on how to protect non-tangible assets.

In the following chapter, it is tried to show how and in which way these two areas match with each other. The aim is to clear out different prejudices often experienced in industry sectors not customarily being in contact with the field of IP rights, also called the green field.

Companies are sometimes giving up the possibility to delimit themselves from competitors and to hinder competitors from entering the same market based on a monopoly right. Often, this happens only due to unknowingness of what is protectable in which way.

In the following subchapters, an overview of the protective right that might be of relevance for the different aspects of blockchain and DLT technologies and use cases are summarized. Probably surprisingly for the one or the other – there are a number of registered IP rights that can be used to protect products and services in these technologies in addition to copyrights that can be used to protect creations like texts, software and three-dimensional objects.

Such registered IP rights are (a) trademarks – used to signal the origin of products, (b) designs – used to protect how a product looks, and (c) patents/utility models – used to protect the abstract technical teaching of inventions in all fields of technology, for example, Information Technology (IT).

A first overview of how the registration/creation of the different registered IP rights is taking place can be found on the webpage of the European Union Intellectual Property Office (EUIPO).[1]

The focus of the following subchapters will, however, be the protection by patents and utility models and its prerequisites and impacts.

IP rights are territorial restricted, and thus the regulations on how to reach protection, the scope of protection and the enforcement are different from country to country, but general rules exist. These rules are specially defined in a plurality of regional and multilateral agreements. Examples for such agreements are the Paris Convention for the Protection of Industrial Property, the Trade-Related Aspects of Intellectual Property Rights (TRIPS) agreement, the Patent Cooperation Treaty (PCT), and the European Patent Convention (EPC).

In this chapter, such general rules will be summarized, however, from a European/German perspective. Furthermore, for some aspects, particularities in respective other jurisdictions will be outlined.

Furthermore, multinational organizations executing and administrating such international and multilateral agreements are existing in the IP area. These organizations provide the infrastructure to implement these agreements.

To be mentioned especially is the World Intellectual Property Organization (WIPO) (www.wipo.org) hosting (a) the Madrid System for registering and managing trademarks in up to 122 countries (https://www.wipo.int/madrid/en/) being based on the Madrid Agreement, (b) the Hague System for International Registration of International Designs in 73 contracting parties covering ninety countries (https://www.wipo.int/hague/en/) being based on the Hague Agreement, and (c) the PCT system assisting applicants in seeking patent protection internationally for their inventions in up to 153 contracting states.[2] Furthermore, regional organizations like the European Patent Office (EPO) (www.epo.org) for granting patents being valid in countries of the European Union (EU) as well as in a variety of further European and non-European countries, the already before mentioned EUIPO (www.euipo.europa.eu/) for the registration of EU wide designs and trademarks are existing and non-European regional organizations like the Eurasian Patent Organization (EAPO) (https://www.eapo.org/en/) for providing legal protection for inventions in the Contracting States on the basis of the single Eurasian patent.

1. European Union Intellectual Property Office, *The Intellectual Property Metro,* available at: https://euipo.europa.eu/tunnel-web/secure/webdav/guest/document_library/contentImages/rcd_design_definition/intellectual-property-metro.zip (accessed on 21 Dec. 2019).
2. All numbers of parties/countries as of 21 Dec. 2019.

§7.02 TRADEMARK

[A] Definition

The WIPO generally defines a trademark as 'a sign capable of distinguishing the goods or services of one enterprise from those of other enterprises'.[3] A registered trademark thus comprises a reproduction of the sign together with a list of goods and services for which the sign is protected.

[B] Duration

In comparison to other registered rights discussed later, a trademark has the advantage of a generally unrestricted protection duration. Generally, the trademark is registered for an initial duration of five years or ten years, depending on the jurisdiction. This term can be extended by payment of renewal fees. Most jurisdictions do not provide a limit for the number of such renewal fees.

[C] Territory

As all IP rights, trademarks also are territorial protective rights, i.e., providing protection only in a restricted territory.

Beside national trademarks also regional trademarks, especially the European Community trademark, are existing. Such regional trademarks have the advantage to allow to reach protection for the entire territory/region by one single registration. However, also the trademark can be invalidated for the complete region in a central revocation procedure being advantageous for third parties aiming to revoke the trademark but increasing the risk for the trademark holder.

The EU Member States allow, however, parallel protection of the identical sign by a national trademark and European Community Trademark. This is in contrast to the protection of a patent in some countries, for example, in Germany. As long as the Agreement on a Unified Patent Court (UPC) will not be ratified by the German government, parallel protection by a national patent granted by the German Patent and Trademark Office and a patent granted by the EPO is not allowed according to Article II §8 IntPatÜbkG.[4]

Furthermore, the WIPO offers the Madrid System for International registration in up to 122 countries by a single application.[5] Although the registration leads to

3. WIPO, *Trademarks*, available at: https://www.wipo.int/trademarks/en/ (accessed on 21 Dec. 2019).
4. Gesetz zu dem Übereinkommen vom 27. November 1963 zur Vereinheitlichung gewisser Begriffe des materiellen Rechts der Erfindungspatente, dem Vertrag vom 19. Juni 1970 über die internationale Zusammenarbeit auf dem Gebiet des Patentwesens und dem Übereinkommen vom 5. Oktober 1973 über die Erteilung europäischer Patente.
5. WIPO, *Madrid System*, available at: https://www.wipo.int/madrid/en/ (accessed on 21 Dec. 2019).

independent national registrations, it significantly eases the registration, renewal and amendment procedure for the respective national registrations.

[D] Goods and Services

A sign can be protected as a trademark for specific types of goods and services. These types of goods and services have to be defined in most jurisdictions with the filing of the trademark application. The goods and service have been standardized in the so-called Nice Classificasstion.[6]

For products and services being based on blockchain and DLT technologies due to a variety of possible use cases, a plurality of classes might also be possible. Noteworthy are especially:

- (good) class 9 that 'includes mainly apparatus and instruments for (...) information technology equipment ...'[7] with regard to hardware and software used in blockchain and DLT applications, for example, security tokens being encryption devices;
- (service) class 36 that 'includes mainly services rendered in financial and monetary affairs and services rendered in relation to insurance contracts of all kinds'[8] with regard to cryptocurrencies and issuance of tokens of value;
- (service) class 38 that 'includes mainly services that allow at least one party to communicate with another, as well as services for the broadcasting and transmission of data' with regard to the transmission of tokens, for example, relating to cryptocurrencies or distribution chains,[9] and
- (service) class 42 that 'includes mainly services provided by persons in relation to the theoretical and practical aspects of complex fields of activities, for example ... computer programming ...'[10] with regards to data encryption services.

[E] Types of Trademarks

As signals to identify the origin of a product can be directed in various ways to the different human senses also different trademark types exist. According to the EUIPO,[11] trademarks can especially have the following forms:

6. WIPO, *Nice Classification*, available at: https://www.wipo.int/classifications/nice/en/ (accessed on 21 Dec. 2019).
7. Explanatory note for Class 9 published by WIPO.
8. Explanatory note for Class 36 published by WIPO.
9. Explanatory note for Class 38 published by WIPO.
10. Explanatory note for Class 42 published by WIPO.
11. EUIPO, *Trade mark definition*, available at: https://euipo.europa.eu/ohimportal/en/trade-mark-definition (accessed on 21 Dec. 2019).

- wordmark (comprising solely words or letters, numerals, other standard typographic characters or a combination thereof) – protects the word in any outer appearance like font, colour or size;
- figurative trademark (comprising only figurative elements and/or non-standard characters, stylization or layout, a graphic feature or a colour);
- shape mark (a sign that relates to a three-dimensional shape of, for example, a product itself, containers, package);
- position mark (the special manner in which a sign is located or attached to a product);
- colour mark (using exclusively a single colour or a combination of colours as an indication of origin);
- pattern mark (a plurality of elements arranged in a regular manner);
- motion mark (sign is represented by a movement or a change of a position of an element of the sign);
- multimedia mark (a sign that is formed by a combination of visual and audible elements), and
- hologram mark (sign having holographic properties).

Depending on the respective national regulations and jurisdictions in some countries, only a part of the above-listed trademark forms is accepted. The representation of the trademark is often seen differently in the respective jurisdiction.

[F] Registration Process

In the following, the registration process of a Trademark is outlined exemplarily based on the registration process of the EUIPO.

Once the trademark application has been filed,[12] the trademark will run through an examination period and opposition period before the trademark will be registered.

In the examination period, the respective patent office, here the EUIPO, will check the trademark application for formal requirements and the trademark for so-called absolute grounds. In this step, it is checked whether the general public has an interest in using the sign. This could be, for example, that the sign is describing the goods and services it is filed for, at least is similar to such descriptions and/or similar products. Such concerns against the registration of the trademark might also be brought forward by third parties in the form of a so-called third-party observation.

For example, an absolute ground should be given to register the trademark 'Distributed Ledger' for IT services, especially in the area of banking and finance. The general public has an interest in being able to use this wording without restrictions.

In this regard, it is important to note that the descriptiveness obviously depends on the mother tongue of the person assessing the descriptiveness. For example, 'gedistribueerd grootboek' would not necessarily be understood as descriptive for an

12. EUIPO, *Registration process*, available at: https://euipo.europa.eu/ohimportal/en/registration-process (accessed on 21 Dec. 2019).

English language speaking person although it has the same meaning as a distributed ledger, however in Dutch.

In case of absolute grounds, the trademark application is (partly) refused. Partly refused means that the trademark is refused only for a part of the goods and services for which protection was applied for. In such a case, the applicant has to at least partly remove the respective goods and services from the list of goods and services.

In the opposition period as well as later nullification proceedings, third parties can raise concerns against the registration of the trademark for so-called relative grounds. Such relative grounds are especially the risk of confusion with existing trademarks registered for the same or similar goods and services. For example, a trademark might be identical to a trademark already registered before, and the goods and services might be similar to each other. Also, in case the goods and services are identical, and the signs are tonal, visual written similar such a relative ground might be given. Also, the opposition proceedings might lead to a revocation of the trademark as whole or partly for respective services and goods.

[G] Post Registration

For a legal validity, it is furthermore necessary to use the trademark for the registered goods and services. In most jurisdictions, any third party might request the revocation for the goods and services not used for a respective duration after the registration, for example, the past five years for European Community trademarks.

Thus, after the registration of the trademark, it should be continuously checked, on the one hand, whether the trademark is used for registered goods and services. In case the trademark is planned to be used for further services and goods, a further trademark also covering these additional goods should be applied for. On the other hand, it should be checked on a regular basis whether the trademark is used for all the registered services and goods. Well before the respective time limit, the use should be extended to the services and goods for which is what not used before to reduce the risk of a (partly) cancellation of the trademark for these goods.

[H] Enforcement

The trademark gives its holder the exclusive right to use the trademark sign for the registered goods and services. However, depending on the strength and popularity of the trademark, so-called distinctiveness, this protection can also extend to similar signs and/or similar goods and services.

Signs may be seen as similar, for example, based on a phonetic similarity, visual similarity and/or similarity of the content of meaning. For the similarity of goods and services, it is *inter alia* assessed whether the consumers for the registered and the used goods and services are at least overlapping and whether the goods and services are usually produced/provided by the same companies.

The similarity is in most jurisdictions decided by a judge assessing whether the judge is of the opinion that for the informed consumer there is a risk of confusion between the registered and the used trademark for the respective (similar) goods and services. In case the confusion is seen as given, the trademark holder can be asked for a cease and desist, for damages and for providing the accounting.

[I] Examples and Practical Hints

Also, market actors in the area of blockchain and DLT are similar to traditional technical and industrial sectors active in the area of registration of trademarks for the offered products and services. A plurality of trademarks has already been registered for a variety of goods and services.

For example, the wordmark 'CORDA'[13] of the open-source blockchain platform is registered in the (goods) class 9, *inter alia* for computer programs. The wordmark 'TETHER'[14] of the Tether Operations Limited issuing the stablecoin Tether is registered for (service) class 36, *inter alia* for issuance and redemption of digital/virtual currency for currency as well as tokens of value, and (service) class 38, *inter alia* providing access to an online peer-to-peer (digital/virtual) currency or valuable token financing platform. A further example is the trademark 'Libra' registered by the Libra Association in the (good) class 9 *inter alia* for '... software for sending, receiving, accepting, buying, selling, storing, transmitting, trading and exchanging digital currency, virtual currency, cryptocurrency, digital and blockchain assets, digitized assets, digital tokens, crypto tokens and utility tokens ...' as well as the (service) classes 35 ('... networking services for investors to conduct business, namely, financial trades and exchange of digital currency, virtual currency, cryptocurrency, digital and blockchain assets, digitized assets, digital tokens, crypto tokens and utility tokens ...'), 36 ('... digital currency, virtual currency, cryptocurrency, digital and blockchain asset, digitized asset, digital token, crypto token and utility token trading services ...'), 41 ('... News reporting services in the field of financial news ...') and 42 ('... providing software enabling users to invest in digital currency, virtual currency, cryptocurrency, digital and blockchain assets, digitized assets, digital tokens, crypto tokens and utility tokens ...').[15]

These few examples show that before a new product or service is put on the market, surveillance of existing trademarks in the specific area should be carried out before deciding on the sign for the product/service. A search can be carried out, for example, with the help of the database TMview[16] allowing access to the trademark registers of sixty-nine states via a single webpage.

Once an appropriate sign is found for the products/services, it should be protected in the relevant markets by national and/or regional trademarks. In this

13. EUIPO, *eSearch*, available at: https://euipo.europa.eu/eSearch/#details/trademarks/W01302565 (accessed on 21 Dec. 2019).
14. EUIPO, *eSearch*, available at: https://euipo.europa.eu/eSearch/#details/trademarks/017053307 (accessed on 21 Dec. 2019).
15. EUIPO, *eSearch*, available at: https://euipo.europa.eu/eSearch/#details/trademarks/018083389 (accessed on 21 Dec. 2019).
16. EUIPO, *TMView*, available at: https://www.tmdn.org/tmview/welcome (accessed on 21 Dec. 2019).

process, all available types of trademarks should be taken into consideration, especially also colour marks, motion marks and multimedia marks due to the nature of the offered goods and services in the area of blockchain and DLT technology.

One strategy could be that first, a trademark application is filed for the most relevant market. According to Article 4 of the Paris Convention, such a first trademark application allows the applicant or the successor in title to claim the priority of this first filing for further filings in one of the Member States of the Paris Convention within a six-month time period. When claiming the priority, the further filing 'cannot be invalidated by reason of any acts accomplished in the interval, in particular, another filing, ... the use of the mark, and such acts cannot give rise to any third-party right or any right of personal possession'.[17]

Furthermore, a trademark watch should be installed to timely recognize trademark applications that might give reasons to be attacked based on relative grounds in an opposition procedure to keep the area of the own trademark free of similar trademarks. Such trademarks should be attacked in an opposition.

§7.03 DESIGNS

[A] Definition

According to the definition of the WIPO, 'in the legal sense, an industrial design constitutes the ornamental or aesthetic aspect of an article. An industrial design may consist of three-dimensional features, such as the shape of an article, or two-dimensional features, such as patterns, lines or colour.'[18]

For example, Article 3(a) of the Design Regulation for European community designs[19] defines a design to be 'the appearance of the whole or a part of a product resulting from the features of, in particular, the lines, contours, colours, shape, texture and/or materials of the product itself and/or its ornamentation.'

[B] Duration/Territory

In comparison to trademarks, the maximum protection duration of designs is limited.

The duration is different from country to country. For example, for design applications filed with the US Patent and Trademark Office (USPTO), designs for which a design application has been filed on or after 13 May 2015 have a term of fifteen years from grant, according to 35 U.S.C. §173. According to the Manual of Patent Examining

17. Paris Convention for the Protection of Industrial Property, Art. 4(B).
18. WIPO, *Industrial Designs*, available at: https://www.wipo.int/designs/en/ (accessed on 21 Dec. 2019).
19. Council Regulation (EC) No. 6/2002, of 12 Dec. 2001, on Community designs (OJ EC No L 3 of 5.1.2002, p. 1) amended by Council Regulation No 1891/2006 of 18 Dec. 2006 (OJ EC No L 386 of 29.12.2006, p. 14).

Procedure (MPEP) at the USPTO, 'however, patents issued from design applications filed before 13 May 2015 have a fourteen year term from the date of grant'.[20]

In Europe, national laws also provide for national design protection. In addition, the EUIPO provides a system to protect industrial designs within the EU Member States by one single design right. This protection can be reached by a registration with the EUIPO in the form of a so-called Registered Community Design (RCD) but also in the way of an unregistered Community Design (CD). The maximum duration of a CD is, according to Article 11 of the Design Regulation,[21] three years whereas the maximum duration of an RCD is, according to Article 12 of the Design Regulation, up to a total term of 25 years as by the payment of renewal fees every five years.

Thus, it can be applied for design protection as national designs, regional designs, like the RCD.[22] Furthermore, the WIPO offers in a central procedure under the so-called Hague System,[23] the possibility to file a design application that can include up to 100 designs[24] covering 90 countries. Following a positive check for formal requirements of the international application, the design is registered in the International Register of the WIPO and represents a bundle of national/regional applications that are independent of each other, especially regarding examination, revocation and renewal. However, a central renewal procedure is possible. The term of protection is five years counted from the date of the international registration, but the international registration can be renewed 'for one or more additional terms of five years, in respect of each designated Contracting Party, up to the expiry of the total term of protection allowed by those Contracting Parties' respective laws'.[25] The maximum duration varies between ten and twenty-five years.[26]

Also, for designs, the Paris Convention provides under Article 4 for a first design application for an applicant or the successor in title to claim the priority of this first filing for further filings in one of the Member States of the Paris Convention within a six-month time period. When claiming the priority, the further filing 'cannot be invalidated by reason of any acts accomplished in the interval, in particular, another filing, (...) the putting on sale of copies of the design (...) cannot give rise to any third-party right or any right of personal possession'.[27]

Thus, an appropriate filing strategy might be to, first, file a design an application in the core jurisdiction and use the following six months to decide where to apply for further foreign designs.

20. MPEP at the USPTO, Ninth Edition, Revision 08.2017, Last Revised January 2018, Chapter 1500, section 1505.
21. Council Regulation (EC), *supra* n. 19.
22. EUIPO, *Designs in the European Union*, available at: https://euipo.europa.eu/ohimportal/en/designs-in-the-european-union (accessed on 21 Dec. 2019).
23. WIPO, *Hague – The International Design System*, available at: https://www.wipo.int/hague/en/ (accessed on 21 Dec. 2019).
24. WIPO, *Frequently Asked Questions: Hague System*, available at: https://www.wipo.int/hague/en/faqs.html (accessed on 21 Dec. 2019).
25. *Ibid.*
26. Declarations Made by Contracting Parties under the 1999 Act and the Common Regulations under the 1999 Act and the 1960 Act (last updated on 13 Dec. 2019), available at: https://www.wipo.int/hague/en/declarations/declarations.html.
27. Paris Convention for the Protection of Industrial Property, Art. 4(B).

[C] Registration/Invalidity Procedures/Protection Requirements

In the following, the most important aspects of the protection requirements, as well as the registration process for an RCD at the EUIPO, will be outlined. The registration process in the respective other countries and jurisdictions varies, however, in the members' states of the EU, the national design laws have been harmonized by the Directive 98/71/EC[28] to the regulations for the RCD given in the Design Regulation.

For the registration of an RCD to allow the EUIPO to carry out an examination whether the application is directed to a subject matter being a design in accordance with the above definition (a not for example a living plant) and to define the scope of protection, an applicant has to file a reproduction of the design. In most cases, it comprises a plurality of views onto the design and a description of the product representing the design including, similar to trademarks, an indication of a product class. In comparison to, for example, European Community Trademarks which are categorized in the Nice classification system, Community Designs are categorized in the so-called Locarno Classification. The Locarno Classification is the international classification system for industrial designs and is administered by the World Intellectual Property Organization (WIPO).[29]

Once the formal requirements, as well as the substantive requirements (is the application directed to design and does the design contain an element that goes against public policy and morality[30]), have been positively examined, the design is registered.

As already mentioned before, the Design Regulation also provides protection by an unregistered Community Design (CD). Such a CD is generated by the first publication of the design within the EU.

Until this point of the registration procedure of the RCD and the generation of the CD respectively, the further protection requirements are not examined. For the RCD and CD to be legally valid, it has, *inter alia*, to be novel and has to have individual character according to Article 4(1) of the Design Regulation.

To be novel, the design has not been made available to the public, wherein designs shall be deemed to be identical if their features differ only in immaterial details (Article 5 of the Design Regulation). The Design Regulation, however, also provides for a so-called grace period. That means that a disclosure 'shall not be taken into consideration (...) if a design for which protection is claimed under a registered Community design has been made available to the public by the designer, his successor in title, or a third person as a result of information provided or action taken by the designer or his successor in title (...) during the 12-month period preceding the date of filing of the application or, if a priority is claimed, the date of priority'.[31]

28. Directive 98/71/EC of the European Parliament and of the Council of 13 Oct. 1998 on the legal protection of designs, Official Journal of the European Communities, L 289/28.
29. WIPO, *Locarno Classification*, available at: https://www.wipo.int/classifications/locarno/en/ (accessed on 21 Dec. 2019).
30. For further details it is referred to EUIPO, *Registration process*, available at: https://euipo.europa.eu/ohimportal/en/rcd-registration-process (accessed on 21 Dec. 2019).
31. Directive 98/71/EC, Art. 7(2).

Regarding the second requirement of individual character, it is important to notice that this does not mean that respective creativity or artistic height has to be given. According to Article 6 of the Design Regulation, 'a design shall be considered to have individual character if the overall impression it produces on the informed user differs from the overall impression produced on such a user by any design which has been made available to the public before'.

Whether the registered design fulfils these protection requirements is not checked by the EUIPO of its own motion. The EUIPO describes disputes on the legal validity as follows: 'unlike trademarks, where disputes can arise before registration of the trade mark, designs can only be challenged once registered. This challenge is called – in legal jargon – an application for a declaration of invalidity.'[32] Such an attack against the legal validity of the design can be brought forward not only in national courts, especially during infringement procedures, but also in a central procedure at the EUIPO.

In case that neither the design owner surrenders the Community design nor the invalidity applicant withdraws the application, for example, based on a settlement, the EUIPO issues a decision that concludes the proceedings. This decision might be (partly) the rejection of the design or the rejection of the invalidity application. In case the Community design is declared invalid, it will be deemed never to have existed.

The decision on the invalidity is open for an appeal to the Boards of Appeal for the party being negatively influenced by the first instance decision. Decisions of the boards of appeal are, in turn, under specific circumstances appealable to the Court of Justice of the European Union.

[D] Enforcement

A design right, especially the RCD and CD, gives according to the summary of the WIPO the holder 'right to prevent third parties from making, selling or importing articles bearing or embodying a design which is a copy, or substantially a copy, of the protected design when such acts are undertaken for commercial purposes'.[33]

For the RCD and CD, this is further defined in Article 19(1) of the Design Regulation that 'the (...) use shall cover, in particular, the making, offering, putting on the market, importing, exporting or using of a product in which the design is incorporated or to which it is applied, or stocking such a product for those purposes'.

For the CD, the contested use is restricted in Article 19(2) of the Design Regulation to a use that results from copying the protected design. In this regard, 'the contested use shall not be deemed to result from copying the protected design if it results from an independent work of creation by a designer who may be reasonably thought not to be familiar with the design made available to the public by the holder'. Thus, the CD does not only differ from that RCD by way of its creation and duration but also by the given scope of protection.

32. EUIPO, *Disputes*, available at: https://euipo.europa.eu/ohimportal/en/disputes (accessed on 21 Dec. 2019).
33. WIPO, *supra* n. 18.

The rights of the design holder can be enforced in court actions at the respective civil courts of the EU Member States.

[E] Examples and Practical Hints

The definition of industrial designs on the first view does not really allow to detect a link to blockchain technology and DLT technology services, as these are usually not embodied in tangible elements.

However, it is well accepted that this definition also covers virtual elements, like the design of characters and font sets as well as pictograms, graphical user interfaces (GUI) and the like. As such elements are often part of products or services using blockchain technology or DLT, the protection of these elements should be taken into consideration before launching or publishing the details of the service that might be protectable as a design.

In this regard, it is important to recall that for the legal validity of the design, it has to be novel. Although a grace period is provided in some jurisdictions that design application should be filed as soon as possible. It is not uncommon that identical or similar designs are generated by designers independently. In this case, the grace period does not take effect, as only publications by the designer, his successor in title, or a third person as a result of information provided or action taken by the designer or his successor in title are not taken into consideration. The design that has been filed after the other independently developed design has been published will not be novel anymore.

Thus, the rule should be to first file before publishing the design.

As most jurisdictions allow the filing of multiple applications combining a plurality of different designs within the same class providing cost benefits in comparison to single applications, a plurality of designs differing to such an extent that the overall impression they produce on the informed user differs should be filed. In this way, the protection of a core design could be extended to reach broad protection.

On the other side, before developing a design, it should be checked whether similar designs are already existing that might be infringed by the planned design. A search can be carried out, for example, with the help of the database Design View[34] allowing access and search to the design registers of sixty-six states via a single webpage.

For the user of the design, it is furthermore important that the rights in the design are transferred to the user by the designer. As generally, the designer is the initial holder of the rights, and respective agreements with the designer have to be made to transfer the rights to the user. For example, respective regulations with an employee should be made by the employer to ensure that the rights are transferred. This can be reached in most jurisdictions by respective clauses in the employment agreement.

34. EUIPO, *DesignView,* available at: https://www.tmdn.org/tmdsview-web/welcome (accessed on 21 Dec. 2019).

In case the design is designed by an external designer as commission work, respective agreements should be made with the designer or the employer of the designer that the rights in the design are transferred to the user.

§7.04 COPYRIGHT

[A] Definition

As described under §1.05 of Chapter 1, blockchain protocols and blockchain frameworks can be used as a basis for the new blockchain developments, especially to be adapted to the respective application.

As a software tool, the blockchain protocols are generally falling under copyright law.

The WIPO defines a Copyright (or author's right) to be '(...) a legal term used to describe the rights that creators have over their literary and artistic works. Works covered by copyright range from books, music, paintings, sculpture, and films, to computer programs, databases, advertisements, maps, and technical drawings'.[35]

For example, the German copyright law (Urheberrechtsgesetz, UrhG)[36] defines under §2(1) *inter alia* that by the UrhG 'literary works, such as [...] computer programs' are protected. This means that the author of the work enjoys a certain right. In §2(2) UrhG, it is further specified that 'only the author's own intellectual creations' are protected.

[B] Rights Given by Copyright, Duration and Practical Hints

In most jurisdictions, especially being the Member States of the Bern Convention,[37] like most of the EU states, especially Germany, the United Kingdom, France, as well as the US, Japan, and China, copyright protection is obtained automatically without special formal requirements like a registration or the like. Anyhow, some countries provide a voluntary system for copyright registration, for example, the USA.[38] Such an official system is, for example, not available in Germany, so that it is important to document the date of creation and publication to have evidence in later disputes on the creation or ownership situation of the copyright.

The protection under the copyright gives the author so-called moral rights, *inter alia* the right to decide whether and how his work shall be published, communicate or

35. WIPO, *Copyright*, available at: https://www.wipo.int/copyright/en/ (accessed on 21 Dec. 2019).
36. https://www.gesetze-im-internet.de/englisch_urhg/englisch_urhg.html#p0018 (accessed on 21 Dec. 2019).
37. Berne Convention for the Protection of Literary and Artistic Works of 9 Sep. 1886, completed at PARIS on 4 May 1896, revised at BERLIN on 13 Nov. 1908, completed at BERNE on 20 Mar. 1914, revised at ROME on 2 Jun. 1928, at BRUSSELS on 26 Jun. 1948, at STOCKHOLM on 14 Jul. 1967, and at PARIS on 24 Jul. 1971, and amended on 28 Sep. 1979.
38. The United States Copyright Office, available at: https://www.copyright.gov/recordation/ (accessed on 21 Dec. 2019).

describe the content of his work to the public and be identified as the author of the work. Also, the author might oppose changes to a work that could harm the creator's reputation.

Furthermore, the author is granted with the exclusive right of reproduction, of distribution and of an exhibition of the work. This means that the author can agree upon the owner of a copy of his work, how and to which extent the acts of reproduction and distribution can be realized.

As summarized by the WIPO, 'economic rights have a time limit, which can vary according to national law. In those countries which are members of the Berne Convention, the time limit should be equal to or longer than 50 years after the creator's death. Longer periods of protection may however be provided at the national level.'[39]

Regarding the blockchain technology and DLT technology relevant fields of software, such rights are usually regulated in software licence agreements between the author or the successor in the title, on the one hand, and the user of the software, on the other hand.

However, it should be kept in mind that also other works might be of relevance for applications of blockchain technology and DLT technology. For example, a manual or Financial Product Prospectus in most cases will also fall under copyright law. It is further discussed whether and under which circumstances database structures, data collections and data models might be protectable under copyright law.

Similar to design rights, it is important that the party that wants to exploit the work becomes the successor in title for the work. Thus respective agreements with employees and external service providers should be made to ensure that the respective rights in work are transferred. This is, for example, important for private blockchains. For these, often external software developers are engaged, and the contracting authority should ensure that are rights on the work result are transferred.

§7.05 OPEN SOURCE

As being software, the blockchain Protocols and also developed based on these Protocols are generally falling under the copyright law, *see* section §7.04 above, and the use and exploitation rights are generally ruled by licence agreements. Like 'usual' software also, open-source software is provided under the so-called open-source software licences.

Publicly available blockchain protocols like 'Ethereum', 'Hyperledger Fabrics' or 'R3 Corda' are widely applied as being suitable as a basis for the development of a Blockchain-based software solution. Under these protocols, software solutions can be developed and tested quickly and easily. However, also, the use of these protocols is restricted by open source licences.

As being an open-source, the protocols can be supplemented, improved or edited or used in any other way by developers – without a licence fee being charged. In this regard, opens source software has to be distinguished from copyright-free software.

39. WIPO, *supra* n. 35.

Such non-copyrighted software 'allows people to share the program and their improvements ... but it also allows ... to convert the program into proprietary software'.[40] As this proprietary application software being developed based on the copyright-free software is then not any more freely distributable due to the own developments although being based on the non-copyrighted software the idea of making the initial software available to the general public is not be reached anymore.

Thus, open-source software is subject to copyright obligations being defined in the open-source software licence. Such open-source software licenses often include restrictions and obligations that might heavily influence how the software which has been developed based on the open-source software can be used and exploited.

Some open-source licenses might include a so-called copyleft obligation. This obligation might heavily influence the use of the own developed software up to questioning the complete business model being based on the own developed software.

By the copyleft obligation, the user of the open-source software is forced to make available any edits like changes, further developments or adaptations of the open-source software created by the development of the application software. This publication of the edits has to be conducted under the same open-source licence as the basic software in the form of the protocol.

In the open source software licences, it is furthermore defined what 'editing' means. Depending on the respective licence, 'editing' might cover the entire self-developed software. This might, for example, be the case when the newly developed software does not include code of the open source software but only provides an interface to the open source software.

Thus, the developer of the application software being based on or using the open-source software being subject to strict copyleft regulations is forced to make the own developed software available as an open-source.

By this obligation, commercial use of the application software would not be possible anymore, and thus, the complete business model might be questioned.

Thus, it is essential that before the developing of software is initiated the licence agreements of the basic software is checked. For open source software, it has especially to be checked whether the open source software is subject of a licence agreement, including strict obligations like copyleft obligations. Such an obligation can be contrary to a planned business model. The copyleft obligation can, for example, hinder the fee-based marketing of the developed software.

There is, however, open source software being provided under a so-called Apache 2.0 license.[41] The Apache 2.0 license is described as 'Permissive Licence'.[42] This means that it does not contain a copyleft, i.e., no obligation on the part of the licensee to publishing software created using the licensed software under the Apache

40. GNU project, *What is Copyleft*, available at: https://www.gnu.org/licenses/copyleft.en.html (accessed on 21 Dec. 2019).
41. Apache Software Foundation, *Apache License, Version 2.0*, available at: https://www.apache.org/licenses/LICENSE-2.0 (accessed on 21 Dec. 2019).
42. Wikipedia, *Permissive software license*, available at: https://en.wikipedia.org/wiki/Permissive_software_license (accessed on 21 Dec. 2019).

2.0 license. The Apache 2.0 license, therefore, does not prevent the use of these blockchain protocols to create proprietary applications in view of copyleft obligations.

Examples for such open-source software under Apache 2.0 license are Hyperledger Fabrics[43] and the Corda open-source platform.[44]

On the other hand, for Ethereum, one of the most commonly used protocols, it is unclear which open source licence is used. The various components of Ethereum were published under different open source licences, including the so-called GPLv3. This licence is also a free, copyleft licence.[45] Thus, the developing of proprietary software code for commercial use might not be possible depending on the specific components used in the application software.

Therefore, both when selecting a blockchain protocol for a proprietary development and when investing in a blockchain-related business, it must be very carefully examined which licensing regulations apply to the software used and to what extent this can 'infect' the proprietary software code.

Another problem with the use of open-source platforms could be that there are isolated open source offers that are only sufficient for the creation of test applications. Once the test application has been further developed to go live into regular operation, the problem might arise that a chargeable 'Enterprise Version' of the open-source platform has to be used to implement essential functions, for example, with regard to IT security, which is missing in the test version. These 'Enterprise Versions' are often made available under stricter licence fee and further licence conditions.

This results in a dependency on the provider of the open source software since a change to a different blockchain protocol might not be easily possible. Most of the protocols lack compatibility of the different blockchain protocols so that the application software might have to be newly developed to be usable with other blockchain protocols.

The same principles apply as for any software that is required for essential business functions irrespective of the use of blockchain technology or DLT. The long-term availability of the software with sufficient cost control must be ensured.

Thus, a check regarding open source compliance should be carried out before the proprietary application software is planned and developed to avoid to be bound to one-sided licence agreements or agreements including the obligation to not use the developed software as proprietary software.

43. Hyperledger Foundation, *FAQ*, available at: https://wiki.hyperledger.org/display/HYP/FAQ (accessed on 21 Dec. 2019).
44. Corda, *Open Source*, available at: https://www.corda.net/ (accessed on 21 Dec. 2019).
45. GNU Operating System, *GNU General Public License*, available at: https://www.gnu.org/licenses/gpl-3.0.en.html (accessed on 21 Dec. 2019).

§7.06 PATENTS/UTILITY MODELS

[A] Definition/Content of Patent Application

According to the summary of the WIPO, 'a patent is an exclusive right granted for an invention, which is a product or a process that provides, in general, a new way of doing something, or offers a new technical solution to a problem'.[46]

To get a patent, technical information about the invention must be disclosed to the public in a patent application. To fulfil this purpose, a European patent application and a patent, respectively, comprise the following obligatory elements:[47]

(1) a description in which:
  - the technical field to which the patent application/patent is relating;
  - the state of the art existing before;
  - the technical problems existing in the state of the art;
  - the proposed solution of these problems; and
  - examples of how this solution can be realized are described
(2) patent claims, in which the subject matter for which protection is requested (patent application) or granted (granted patent) is defined;
(3) in case it is referred to drawing in the description and/or the claims, these drawings; and
(4) an abstract describing in a limited number of words for what protection is requested/granted – the abstract does only fulfil informative purposes for evaluating if it is worth considering the whole content of the application[48] and does not have any limiting effect, in fact, does (not even) form a part of the disclosure of the patent application.

[B] Rights Provided by a Patent

A patent gives its holder the exclusive right to prevent or stop others from commercially exploiting the patented invention as defined in the claims. In other words, 'patent protection means that the invention cannot be commercially made, used, distributed, imported or sold by others without the patent owner's consent'.[49]

Thus, it is important to note that a patent does not give a positive right to use but only a negative right to prohibit the use of the claimed invention by other parties.

To show consequences of this difference, the following example gives a bit more flavour: A patent might have been granted on a car with a brake (assuming that this

46. WIPO, *Patents*, available at: https://www.wipo.int/patents/en (accessed on 22 Dec. 2019).
47. EPO, *Art 78 EPC of 5 October 1973 as revised by the Act revising Article 63 EPC of 17 December 1991 and the Act revising the EPC of 29 November 2000*, available at: https://www.epo.org/law-practice/legal-texts/html/epc/2016/e/ar78.html (accessed on 22 Dec. 2019).
48. EPO, Guidelines, F-II-2.1, available at: https://www.epo.org/law-practice/legal-texts/html/guidelines/e/f_ii_2_1.htm (accessed on 22 Dec. 2019).
49. WIPO, *supra* n. 46.

was not known before and thus is seen as (i) novel, and furthermore (ii) inventive, *see* below) for a party I. A party II further develops the brake of the car in an inventive way. A patent on a car with a brake, including the further development, is awarded to party II. Now the situation arises that party I can prohibit party II to use a car with a brake including the further development as party II will inevitably use a car with a brake. Thus party II, although having been awarded a patent does not have the positive right to use the claimed subject matter of the own patent.

This situation is called dependent patents.

On the other hand, party I is probably interested in using the further development of party II. However, party II can prohibit party I from using further development. The situation is usually solved by a cross licence. That means party I gives party II a licence to use a car with a brake whereas party II gives party I the right to use further development.

[C] Territory

The patent protection can be applied for by filing national, regional or international patent applications.

A national patent application is examined by a respective national patent office wherein the examination procedure ends with a refusal of the application or a grant of a patent given the before described negative prohibition right.

Regional patent applications can be filed with the following regional patent offices:[50]

- European Patent Organisation;[51]
- African Intellectual Property Organization (OAPI);[52]
- African Regional Intellectual Property Organization (ARIPO);[53]
- Eurasian Patent Organization (EAPO);[54] and
- Patent Office of the Cooperation Council for the Arab States of the Gulf (GCC Patent office).[55]

The above offices provide a centralized search and examination procedure. The result of the examination, however, differs.

50. WIPO, *Examination by a Regional Patent Office*, available at: https://www.wipo.int/patents/en/topics/worksharing/regional-patentoffices.html (accessed on 22 Dec. 2019).
51. European Patent Office (EPO), available at: https://www.epo.org/index.html (accessed on 22 Dec. 2019).
52. African Intellectual Property Organization (OAPI), available at: http://www.oapi.int/index.php/en/ (accessed on 22 Dec. 2019).
53. African Regional Intellectual Property Organization (ARIPO), available at: https://www.aripo.org/ (accessed on 22 Dec. 2019).
54. Eurasian Patent Organization (EAPO), available at: https://www.eapo.org/en/ (accessed on 22 Dec. 2019).
55. Patent Office of the Cooperation Council for the Arab States of the Gulf (GCC Patent office), available at: https://www.gccpo.org/DefaultEn.aspx (accessed on 22 Dec. 2019).

[1] European Patents/Planned European Unitary Patent

An examination at the EPO leads to a grant of a so-called European Patent. A European patent is granted based on the European Patent Convention (EPC).[56] All (as of November 2019) twenty-eight Member States of the EU are Member States of the EPC. In addition, the group of EPC Member States also comprise non-EU states, namely Albania, Switzerland, Island, Liechtenstein, Monaco, North Macedonia, Norway, Serbia, San Marino, and Turkey.[57]

However, this does not mean that the patent has effect for all Member States of the EU and EPC. A grant of a European patent does not lead to automatic protection in all EPC Member States. The Member States have agreed upon to accept the decision of the EPO to grant a patent and also grant a national patent. Thus, after the grant of a European Patent, and probably its confirmation in an opposition procedure, the national patent offices will accept the legal validity of the patent. After the patent grant by the EPO, the national patent offices also register a national patent upon a further step of the applicant/patent holder, the so-called validation. For such validations in some Member States, translations of the claims or the complete patent have to be filed and/or in some Member States a national representative has to be appointed.

Beside the EPC Member States, the European Patent might also take effect in additional states, so-called extension states[58] and validation states,[59] respectively. To reach an effect in these states during the examination procedure, respective validation and extension fees have to be paid, and after the grant, respective validation and extension steps have to be taken.

Due to this validation and extension steps, it is said that a European Patent becomes a bundle of national (independent) patents.

Thus, the designation as the regional patent is misleading for the European Patent. Such European patents can only be enforced and revoked in national legal procedures being directed to the validated national parts of the European Patent without any direct effect for the other parallel national parts arising from the same European Patent. Also for each of the states, separate national annuity fees have to be paid on a yearly basis to extend the duration of the patent to a maximum of up to twenty years.

Since the beginning of the establishment of the European Patent Organization, it was its aim to provide a procedure to reach a grant of a patent having a unitary character in all EU Member States. All the initiatives failed, however, due to the discussions on the languages. Especially Italy and Spain did not accept that its national languages would not have become additional official languages at the EPO besides

56. EPO, *The European Patent Convention*, available at: https://www.epo.org/law-practice/legal-texts/epc.html (accessed on 22 Dec. 2019).
57. EPO, *Member states of the European Patent Organisation*, available at: https://www.epo.org/about-us/foundation/member-states.html (accessed on 22 Dec. 2019).
58. EPO, *Extension states*, available at: https://www.epo.org/about-us/foundation/extension-states.html (accessed on 22 Dec. 2019).
59. EPO, *Validation states*, available at: https://www.epo.org/about-us/foundation/validation-states.html (accessed on 22 Dec. 2019).

German, French and English. They did not want to accept that a patent in one of these three languages will have effect without obligatory translations into Italian and Spanish, respectively.

A solution was found when the EU decided that irrespective of a unanimity at least nine EU Member States can agree upon enhanced cooperation in respective legal areas. The enhanced cooperation was, for example, used to find a common regulation in a part of the Member States regarding divorce right in 2008.

In 2011, the tool of enhanced cooperation was then used to bring the Unitary Patent (UP), formally called European patent with unitary character,[60] on its way. The cooperation entered into force in 2013 for twenty-five EU Member States (except Italy and Spain). In 2015, Italy also joined the cooperation so that up-to-date (as of November 2019) all EU Member States, besides Spain and the later joining Croatia, are participating in the UP.

The UP will, however, only apply to the participating Member States once the respective state, also the related Agreement on a UPC,[61] will enter into force. The UPC, once being established, will handle as international court all questions regarding patentability and infringement for UPs as well as European bundle patents for the participating twenty-five Member States. This group comprises all states participating in the UP except for Poland. The UPC will enter into force once that German government will ratify the agreement on the UPC. As a complaint against the agreement at the German constitutional court was successful,[62] the ratification process has to be redone in Germany. Thus, the expectations that in 2021 the UPC might be established[63] has not been fulfilled.

Once the UPC is established and the rules on the UP are applied, a patent applicant will have the option after the grant of a European Patent to select for the countries not participating in the enhanced cooperation, especially the non-EU states for validation and/or extension in the usual way. For the states participating in the UP, the applicant can then select whether for these countries a UP should be granted or for all or a part of these states bundle patent should be granted. As for the UP, only one further translation will have to be filed, and the annuity fees will be in the height of annuity fees of about three national parts of a European patent the costs will be significantly lower for protection in a plurality of states compared to today. However, for the UP, it will be possible to be revoked in a central procedure for all states.

This will most likely open, for example, in Germany the possibility to have protection for an invention based on a national German patent that is litigated in front of national German courts and in parallel by a UP litigated in front of the UPC. The

60. EPO, *Unified Patent Court,* available at: https://www.epo.org/law-practice/unitary/unitary-patent.html (accessed on 22 Dec. 2019).
61. *Ibid.*
62. Bundesverfassungsgericht, *Act of Approval to the Agreement on a Unified Patent Court is void,* Press Release No. 20/2020 of 20 March 2020, https://www.bundesverfassungsgericht.de/SharedDocs/Pressemitteilungen/EN/2020/bvg20-020.html (accessed on May 31, 2020)
63. Kluwer Patent Blog, *If German complaint is dismissed, Unified Patent Court could be operation early 2021* (28 Nov. 2019), available at: http://patentblog.kluweriplaw.com/2019/11/28/if-german-complaint-is-dismissed-unified-patent-court-could-be-operation-early-2021/ (accessed on 22 Dec. 2019).

German government plans according to a draft law[64] to allow such a coexistence of national patents, on the one hand, and UP as well as national German parts of EP patents being litigated in front of the UPC, on the other hand.

[2] Further Regional Patents European Patents/Planned European Unitary Patent

Today's system of the EPO that a granted patent leads to a bundle of national patents in specifically designated countries is also applied for patents granted by the ARIPO. Thus, an applicant has to designate the countries of the total of eighteen Member States in which protection is intended.[65]

Also, the grant system of the EAPO is comparable to the EPO system. In a central examination procedure, a patent is granted for all nine Member States being a former Member State of the Soviet Union. However, the grant does not lead to a patent with unitary character. It is possible to uphold the patent in only a part of the Member States, and invalidation is also possible for single states by national courts.[66]

In contrast to the EPO, ARIPO and EAPO, a grant of a patent of the OAPI leads to UP protection being extended to all seventeen mostly Francophobe Member States.[67] Also, a patent granted by the GCC Patent office leads to a UP being valid in all six Arabic Member States.[68]

[D] Protection Requirements EPO

[1] Novelty/Grace Period

As explained later, for a patent to be legally valid, the claimed subject matter has to be *inter alia* novel and inventive. Novelty means that there has been no publication before the filing of the application disclosing all of the claimed features to persons not being bound by confidentiality. In most countries, the absolute novelty has to be given, i.e., any publication, so-called disclosure, is taken into consideration, especially written

64. Federal Ministry of Justice and Consumer Protection, *Draft law on the adaptation of patent law provisions due to the European patent reform,* available at: https://www.bmjv.de/SharedDocs/Gesetzgebungsverfahren/DE/Anpassung_patentrechtlicher_Vorschriften_nach_euopaeischer_Patentreform.html (accessed on 22 Dec. 2019).
65. ARIPO, *Patents,* available at: https://www.aripo.org/ip-services/patents/ (accessed on 22 Dec. 2019).
66. EAPO, *Procedures,* available at: https://www.eapo.org/en/feature.html (accessed on 22 Dec. 2019).
67. WIPO, *African Intellectual Property Organization (OAPI),* available at: https://www.wipo.int/export/sites/www/patent_register_portal/en/docs/oapi.pdf (accessed on 22 Dec. 2019).
68. WIPO Magazine, *Gulf Cooperation Council Patent Office offers fast-track patent grant procedures,* available at: https://www.wipo.int/wipo_magazine/en/2018/06/article_0008.html (accessed on 22 Dec. 2019).

disclosure, oral disclosure, disclosure by use or in any other way, as, for example, codified in Article 54(2) EPC.[69]

However, the date until when disclosures are taken into consideration differs from jurisdiction to jurisdiction. For a European Patent and most of the national European patents, any disclosure also by the applicant until the filing date of the application is taken into consideration as long as it is not based on abuse in relation to the applicant or has occurred on specific exhibitions like world exhibitions.

In other countries, for example, the US, Russia and Japan, a so-called grace period is granted. That means that specific disclosures by the applicant or the successor in title are not taken into consideration as long as they have been taken place a specific time before the filing date of the application, in some countries six months and other countries twelve months.[70]

Although the grace period might be granted in respective jurisdictions, it is always advisable to file the patent application before the invention is disclosed to third parties, especially published. This has mainly two reasons. First, it is quite often that developments are made independently of each other in parallel by different inventors to solve a technical problem. In case one inventor publishes the invention, another inventor cannot rely upon the grace period for the same invention as the publication is not based on an own publication. More importantly, the first country might grant a grace period, but in other countries, a parallel foreign national patent application may not provide such a grace period. For these applications, the own publication of the applicant forms novelty destroying state of the art.

[2] Priority

To comply with the novelty requirement, an applicant would generally be forced to apply for a patent simultaneously in all countries in which protection is intended. So save a filing date that is as early as possible to avoid that disclosure of the claimed subject matter takes away novelty from the claimed subject matter. This would especially mean that a plurality of patents would have to be filed in parallel without having certainty on the patentability.

This procedure is unsatisfying and for the applicant expensive. To avoid the necessity of initially filing a plurality of parallel applications as of November 2019, a total of 177 states signed the Paris Patent Convention.[71] One of the central regulations of this convention is the right of priority:

69. EPO, *Art 54 EPC of 5 October 1973 as revised by the Act revising Article 63 EPC of 17 December 1991 and the Act revising the EPC of 29 November 2000*, available at: https://www.epo.org/law-practice/legal-texts/html/epc/2016/e/ar54.html (accessed on 22 Dec. 2019).
70. WIPO, *Certain aspects of national/regional patent Laws, (4) Grace period* (status as of October 2019), available at: https://www.wipo.int/export/sites/www/scp/en/national_laws/grace_period.pdf (accessed on 22 Dec. 2019).
71. WIPO, *Paris Convention for the Protection of Industrial Property*, available at: https://www.wipo.int/treaties/en/ip/paris/ (accessed on 22 Dec. 2019).

> The Convention provides for the right of priority in the case of patents (and utility models where they exist), marks and industrial designs. This right means that, on the basis of a regular first application filed in one of the Contracting States, the applicant may, within a certain period of time (12 months for patents and utility models; 6 months for industrial designs and marks), apply for protection in any of the other Contracting States. These subsequent applications will be regarded as if they had been filed on the same day as the first application. In other words, they will have priority (hence the expression 'right of priority') over applications filed by others during the said period of time for the same invention, utility model, mark or industrial design.[72]

Thus, an applicant can first file a national patent application in one of the contracting states of the Paris Convention and can await the first examination report for the first application giving a first indication for the patentability before spending costs on filings in other countries and jurisdictions. Within the priority year, the applicant can make a decision on whether and in which foreign countries or regions patent protection should be aimed for.

[3] International Patent Applications

Under some circumstances, however, also this twelve-month time limit is too short for making a final decision on the election of the countries.

This is one of the reasons why the PCT system[73] was established by the WIPO. This system allows filing so-called international patent applications. The description 'international' is, however, also misleading as by such applications only, a centralized search and examination procedure is carried out not leading to a patent grant. The international patent application can be seen as a place holder for national/regional patent applications in the 153 (as of November 2019) Member States of the PCT.[74]

The international examination procedure allows the applicant to have the claimed subject matter examined by a further patent office to get a second independent opinion on the patentability of the claimed subject matter in the form of an International Preliminary Report on Patentability (IPRP) being, however, not binding for the PCT Member States. It means that in the IPRP, the patentability might be admitted, but the national patent office does not have to grant a patent but might raise further arguments against the patentability.

Within a time limit of thirty months, for some Member States up to thirty-four months,[75] after the filing date and if the priority of an earlier application is claimed, after the priority date, the applicant has to then convert the international patent application into national/regional patent applications. This process is called the entry

72. WIPO, *Summary of the Paris Convention for the Protection of Industrial Property*, available at: https://www.wipo.int/treaties/en/ip/paris/summary_paris.html (accessed on 22 Dec. 2019).
73. WIPO, *PCT – The International Patent System*, available at: https://www.wipo.int/pct/en/ (accessed on 22 Dec. 2019).
74. WIPO, *The PCT now has 153 Contracting States*, available at: https://www.wipo.int/pct/en/pct_contracting_states.html (accessed on 22 Dec. 2019).
75. WIPO, *Time Limits for Entering National/Regional Phase under PCT Chapters I and II*, available at: https://www.wipo.int/pct/en/texts/time_limits.html (accessed on 22 Dec. 2019).

into the national/regional phases, often making the translation of the international patent application into the national language necessary.

As the costs for the following national/regional examination/grant procedures are mainly the same as for direct filings in the respective countries/regions, it is often said that the PCT system allows buying time for the final, cost-intensive decision in which jurisdictions the national patent applications are to be filed.

[4] Exclusion from Patentability

As mentioned before, patents are granted on subject matter that has to fulfil respective requirements. For example, European patents are granted according to Article 52(1) EPC for inventions 'provided that they are new, involve an inventive step and are susceptible of industrial application'.[76]

However, there is an important restriction to this Rule in the EPC that is also existing in other national European patent laws. According to Article 54(2) EPC, there is a list of subject matter that is not regarded as an invention. This list especially covers:

(...)

a) discoveries, scientific theories and mathematical methods;
b) aesthetic creations;
c) schemes, rules and methods for performing mental acts, playing games or doing business, and programs for computers;
d) presentations of information.

The basis for this restriction is that there is a general interest of the public that specific things do not become the subject matter of a monopoly right and that for some of the specific things, other protective rights exist, namely design rights and copyright.

Especially, the exclusions (a) and (c) are of special interest for blockchain-related inventions. These blockchain inventions are mainly based on mathematical methods and are mostly realized by programs for computers.

Thus, on the first view, patent applications directed to the use of blockchain technologies as being at least partly realized as computer programs do not seem to be patentable by themselves. This is also often the received opinion that software is not patentable.

This is, however, incorrect.

Article 52(2) EPC is restricted by Article 52(3) EPC clarifying that Article 52(2) EPC 'shall exclude the patentability of the subject-matter or activities referred to therein only to the extent to which a European patent application or European patent relates to such subject-matter or activities as such'. It is, however, well accepted in the jurisdiction that the wording 'as such' has to be interpreted strictly.

Thus, it is well accepted that subject matter that goes beyond the program as such, for example, the source code is generally not excluded from the patentability. As

76. EPO, *Art. 52 EPC*, available at: https://www.epo.org/law-practice/legal-texts/html/epc/2016/e/ar52.html (accessed on 22 Dec. 2019).

outlined in the Guidelines for examination at the European Patent Office[77] under G-II-3.6,[78] 'the exclusion does not apply to computer programs having a technical character'. In other words, an abstract technical idea forming the basis for the invention might be patentable although being implemented in the computer. Such inventions are called computer-implemented inventions (CII).

To have technical character, a computer program must produce a 'further technical effect' when running on a computer. That is a technical effect which goes beyond the 'normal' physical interactions between the program (software) and the computer (hardware) on which it is run. The normal physical effects of the execution of a program, e.g., the circulation of electrical currents in the computer, are not in themselves sufficient to confer technical character to a computer program.[79]

The principles developed for programs for the computer and CII are thus essential to assess the patentability of blockchain-related inventions as outlined in the Guidelines for Examination at the EPO F-IV-3.9.3.[80]

[5] Assessing Patentability of CII: Examples of Blockchain-Related EP Patents

To take these general principles of technical character and technical effect into account, the EPO has developed a two-step testing scheme for CII.

The first step is to check whether the claimed item is software in itself. In principle, this examination already leads to a positive result meaning that no exclusion is given if the technical system 'computer' is included in the patent claim. For this purpose, the patent claim is directed, for example, to a method executed by a computer, a data processing apparatus having means arranged to execute such a method, or a computer program (product) comprising instructions which, when the program is executed by a computer, causes the computer to execute the steps of the method. Examples for specific formulations are given in the Guidelines under F-IV-3.9–3.9.3.[81]

Like all other inventions, the claimed CII, in particular, blockchain application, must also be new and inventive.

A claimed object is new if there was no prior publication anywhere in the world showing all the features of the claimed object. Novelty, therefore, exists if the claimed application deviates from previously known applications by at least one peculiarity.

77. EPO, *Guidelines for Examination in the European Patent Office* (November 2019), available at: https://www.epo.org/law-practice/legal-texts/html/guidelines/e/index.htm (accessed on 22 Dec. 2019).
78. EPO, Guidelines, G-II-3.6, available at: https://www.epo.org/law-practice/legal-texts/html/guidelines/e/g_ii_3_6.htm (accessed on 22 Dec. 2019).
79. *Ibid.*
80. EPO, Guidelines, F-IV-3.9.3, available at: https://www.epo.org/law-practice/legal-texts/html/guidelines/e/f_iv_3_9_3.htm (accessed on 22 Dec. 2019).
81. EPO, Guidelines, F-IV-3.9 to 3.9.3., available at: https://www.epo.org/law-practice/legal-texts/html/guidelines/e/f_iv_3_9.htm (accessed on 22 Dec. 2019).

If this is the case, it must then be examined whether the application is inventive, i.e., whether it was not suggested to the skilled person on the basis of the previously known technical information.

The second step, including the assessment of the technical character of the testing scheme developed for CII, now takes effect in this test.

In Part G, Chapter II, 3.6., the Guidelines for Examination in the European Patent Office cite, 'for example, the control of a technical process or the control of the internal functioning of the computer itself or its interfaces as further technical effects'.[82]

Practical examples of inventive and non-inventive CII are also given in Part G, Chapter VII, 5.4.2.[83] For example, for a method of facilitating shopping on a mobile device, it has been decided that besides the feature of using a distributed system comprising a mobile device connected to a server computer which has cache memory and is connected to a database, further features providing technical character are existing.

The claimed method also comprised the feature, that an optimal shopping tour is determined by the server by accessing the cache memory in which optimal shopping tours determined for previous requests are stored, which has been novel in view of the state of the art known before. In view of the EPO, this feature was seen to make a technical contribution going beyond a business concept underlying the method since it does not only define the producing of an ordered list of shops to visit which sell respective products. The technical contribution of this feature was seen in the technical implementation of the producing of a list having the technical effect of enabling rapid determination of the optimal shopping tour by accessing previous requests which are stored in the cache memory.

A further example of a technical contribution has been seen by the EPO in increasing the user-friendliness in a method of rearranging icons on a GUI.

The EPO's view of the future importance of blockchain applications and the relevance of patenting them is illustrated by the fact that the EPO devotes a full-day conference[84] exclusively to this topic. This attention has so far only been given to the field of artificial intelligence and machine learning.

In the recent past, the EPO has already granted patents related to Blockchain applications. For example, the following applications were considered patentable, i.e., in particular, new and inventive:

- The granted European Patent EP 3 257 191 B1[85] is directed to a procedure for controlling the visibility and/or performance of a contract. In the claimed method using of an unspent output (UTXO) linked to the location of a repository where the contract is stored, it was considered inventive to use that

82. EPO, *supra* n. 77.
83. EPO, Guidelines, G-VII, 5.4.2., available at: https://www.epo.org/law-practice/legal-texts/html/guidelines/e/g_vii_5_4_2.htm (accessed on 22 Dec. 2019).
84. EPO, *EPO holds first major conference on blockchain*, available at: https://www.epo.org/news-issues/news/2018/20181205.html (accessed on 22 Dec. 2019).
85. https://data.epo.org/publication-server/pdf-document?pn = 3257191&ki = B1&cc = EP&pd = 20180411 (accessed on 22 Dec. 2019).

UTXO to interpret whether the contract should be considered open or valid. The inventive step was justified by the fact that this step leads to a further technical effect: For the first time, it is possible to automatically check the conditions in the contract by means of a technical system and automatically trigger the contractual consequences of the fulfilment of the conditions.[86]

- For computer-implemented methods of verifying ownership of computer software for installation and after installation, respectively, and before running the computer software the following, as claimed in EP 3 295 362 B1,[87] was considered inventive: The circumstance that in a license enforcement a special use of a second public user key (PU2), a second public key (P2), a distributed hash table, and a peer-to-peer distributed ledger is provided in combination with the comparison of the keys using a transaction record stored in the ledger. From the EPO's point of view, the procedures using blockchain principles should increase the security of the technical process of installing and starting the software as a further technical effect.[88]
- Inventive to a computer-implemented method for verifying the integrity of computer software, as claimed in EP 3 295 349 B1,[89] was considered to be the use of a third hash value, a fourth hash value, and metadata associated with a transaction record stored on a peer-to-peer distributed ledger. The third hash value is determined on the basis of the computer software, and the fourth hash value is determined from an entry in a distributed hash table. The verification of the integrity of the computer software is based on the comparison of the third hash value (H3) and the fourth hash value (H4). This is intended to improve the technical process of verifying the integrity of the software.[90]

These examples show that the EPA is open to the protection of applications of blockchain principles in technical areas where these principles have not previously been used.

However, it remains to be seen whether and how the granted patents will withstand attacks against the legal validity through cancellation proceedings.

For the three before mentioned examples, no opposition proceedings have been initiated before the EPO according to the register at the EPO.

86. https://register.epo.org/application?documentId = E0B6BTDK1654DSU&number = EP17708587&lng = en&npl = false (accessed on 22 Dec. 2019).
87. https://data.epo.org/publication-server/pdf-document?pn = 3295362&ki = B1&cc = EP&pd = 20180711 (accessed on 22 Dec. 2019).
88. https://register.epo.org/application?documentId = E0P1F1V73736DSU&number = EP17724454&lng = en&npl = false (accessed on 22 Dec. 2019).
89. https://data.epo.org/publication-server/pdf-document?pn = 3295349&ki = B1&cc = EP&pd = 20180711 (accessed on 22 Dec. 2019).
90. https://register.epo.org/application?documentId = E0P1FZPX9589DSU&number = EP17724453&lng = en&npl = false (accessed on 22 Dec. 2019).

[6] Opposition Procedure

Such opposition proceedings can be initiated according to Article 99 EPC[91] by any third party within nine months after the decision to grant a European patent is published. In this procedure, the legal validity of the patent can be challenged in front of an opposition division at the EPO. The advantage of this procedure for the third party is that in a central procedure, all validated national parts of the European patent can be attacked. The opposition can be based on the grounds given in Article 100 EPC,[92] namely that:

- the subject matter of the patent is not patentable as being excluded from patentability, being not novel, being not inventive or being not susceptible of industrial application;
- the European patent does not disclose the invention in a manner sufficiently clear and complete for it to be carried out by a person skilled in the art (so-called lack of sufficient disclosure/lack of enablement); and/or
- the subject matter of the European patent extends beyond the content of the application as filed (so-called inadmissible extension of disclosure).

The opposition procedure allows the general public to question the legal validity to avoid that obvious not legally valid patents are upheld. Especially it allows the general public to provide the EPO with state of the art information the EPO cannot be aware of. This especially relates to prior public uses, publications of the claimed subject matter on fairs or by the oral description which cannot be researched by the EPO.

The decision of the opposition division to uphold the granted patent in amended form or to revoke the patent is according to Article 106 EPC[93] appealable to the Board of Appeal of the EPO. Such an appeal has to be filed within a time limit of two months after the written decision of the opposition board has been forwarded according to Article 108 EPC.[94] Once the opposition procedure, including a possible appeal, has led to a confirmation of the EP at least in amended form, the national parts of the EP can only be attacked in national revocation procedures independent of each other.

91. EPO, *Art. 99 EPC*, https://www.epo.org/law-practice/legal-texts/html/epc/2016/e/ar99.html (accessed on 22 Dec. 2019).
92. EPO, *Art. 100 EPC*, available at: https://www.epo.org/law-practice/legal-texts/html/epc/2016/e/ar100.html (accessed 22 Dec. 2019).
93. EPO, *Art. 106 EPC*, available at: https://www.epo.org/law-practice/legal-texts/html/epc/2016/e/ar106.html (accessed on 22 Dec. 2019).
94. EPO, *Art. 108 EPC*, available at: https://www.epo.org/law-practice/legal-texts/html/epc/2016/e/ar108.html (accessed on 22 Dec. 2019).

[7] Enablement

The before mentioned ground of revocation of a sufficient disclosure/enablement is based on the requirement of Article 83 EPC[95] that 'the European patent application shall disclose the invention in a manner sufficiently clear and complete for it to be carried out by a person skilled in the art'.

To fulfil this requirement, it is necessary to provide a detailed description of at least one way of carrying out the invention according to the Guidelines.[96] In the jurisdiction of the EPO,[97] this requirement was further specified such that 'the application must contain, in addition to the examples, sufficient information to allow the person skilled in the art, using his common general knowledge, to perform the invention over the whole area claimed without undue burden and without needing inventive skill'.[98] In this regard, the interpretation of the features in the claim has to be carried out such that 'the skilled person, when considering a claim, should rule out interpretations which are illogical or which do not make technical sense. He should try, with a synthetic propensity, i.e. building up rather than tearing down, to arrive at an interpretation of the claim which is technically sensible and takes into account the whole disclosure of the patent. The patent must be construed by a mind willing to understand, not a mind desirous of misunderstanding.'[99,100]

To fulfil these requirements is often problematic in the field of blockchain applications. It is necessary to avoid the description of black boxes for which it is only described – what is the input in the box and what is the output of the box. It is necessary to describe explicitly how the input is processed and in what way to arrive at the described output.

This might cause problems, on the one hand, with regard to the possibility to describe in a general technical description of the internal processes without unnecessarily restricting the claimed subject matter to specific embodiments. For CII, it is necessary to describe the elements used in the application not only in terms of structure but also in terms of function.

Describing such functions, however, has to be done such that the features in the claim lead to a scope of protection that is as broad as possible but, on the other hand, still allows the person skilled in the art to carry out the invention over the complete claimed range.

A further limiting aspect is that the patent application is published at a predefined time after the application or priority date. In general, a patent is an agreement between

95. EPO, *Art. 83 EPC*, available at: https://www.epo.org/law-practice/legal-texts/html/epc/2016/e/ar83.html (accessed on 22 Dec. 2019).
96. EPO, Guidelines, F-III-1, available at: https://www.epo.org/law-practice/legal-texts/html/guidelines/e/f_iii_1.htm (accessed on 22 Dec. 2019).
97. T727/95, available at: https://www.epo.org/law-practice/case-law-appeals/recent/t950727ex1.html (accessed on 22 Dec. 2019).
98. EPO, *supra* n. 95.
99. EPO, Case Law of the Boards of Appeal, II. A. 6.1., available at: https://www.epo.org/law-practice/legal-texts/html/caselaw/2016/e/clr_ii_a_6_1.htm (accessed on 22 Dec. 2019).
100. T190/99, available at: https://www.epo.org/law-practice/case-law-appeals/recent/t990190eu1.html (accessed on 22 Dec. 2019).

the general public and the inventor. The general public is interested in getting information on the invention to further develop the existing technology. On the other hand, the inventor is interested in getting a monopoly right to use the invention. Both these interests are outweighed such that the inventor gets a monopoly right in case it turns out that the invention is patentable, i.e., novel, inventive and susceptible of industrial application. On the other hand, the invention will be published after a predefined time, in most jurisdictions after eighteen months. This allows the general public to get knowledge of the invention and to use it as a basis for four further developments and inventions. The delay in the publication is based on the idea to give the inventor a timely advantage in comparison to the general public for further developments.

For some cases, it might be more advantageous for the inventor to not file the application and thus publish the invention to such an extent that it can be easily reproduced by third parties. Thus, it might be worthwhile to not file a patent application but to handle the invention and the internal functionality as a trade secret, *see* section §7.09 below.

A trade secret should especially be taken into consideration in case the invention:

- cannot be reversed engineered, i.e., it is not possible to easily extract from the marketed product/service the invention;
- is characterized by rapid development, i.e., the invention will be obsolete when the grant of the patent takes place;
- is such that the independent development is highly challenging; and/or
- cannot be described without extreme efforts.

A strategy might be to try to only include limited information in the application to fulfil the enablement requirement and to handle core features as trade secrets, to not give up a technical advantage compared to competitors.

[E] Protection Requirements USPTO: Examples of Blockchain-Related US Patents

The general principles explained before for the patentability at the EPO are also applicable to other jurisdictions, however, with respective differences in procedural and substantive aspects.

In the following, the handling of blockchain-related inventions at the USPTO will be summarized shortly.

General differences between the European and US grant procedures are, for example, summarized in Annexe 8 of 'Das US-Patent'.[101] Since the implementation of the America Invents Act in 2011, also the US patent system knows a revocation procedure in the form of the Post Grant Review procedure having similarities to the European Opposition procedure. This procedure is now handled by the Patent Trial and

101. Mayer, R., Butler, J., Molnia, D., *Das US-Patent: Erwirkung und Durchsetzung unter besonderer Berücksichtigung der Rechtsprechung*, Annex 8 (5th ed. 2017).

Appeal Board (PTAB) of the USPTO. The PTAB also handles an invalidation procedure similar to the German comparable to the German nullification procedure and the planned nullification procedure at the UPC. This procedure is called Inter Partes Review procedure.

Under the US law (35 U.S.C. 101),[102] generally, 'whoever invents or discovers any new and useful process, machine, manufacture, or composition of matter, or any new and useful improvement thereof may obtain a patent therefor …'.

Similar to the EPC, the US law provides exceptions from the patentability.

In the MPEP,[103] these so-called judicial exceptions are summarized as being:

- abstract ideas;
- laws of nature; and
- natural phenomena (including products of nature).

These general terms have been specified by the USPTO in view of the recent case law and summarized as follows:[104,105]

Like the EPO the USPTO applies a two-step test. In the first step (step 1: statutory categories), it is analysed whether the claim is directed to a machine, manufacture, or composition of matter. In case this is given, it is continued to step 2 in which it is assessed in a first part step (step 2A) whether the claim is directed to a judicial exception. If this is not the case, the eligibility test is finalized with a positive result so that the further patentability requirements are checked.

In case the step 2A leads to the result that the claim is directed to a judicial exception, especially an abstract idea, in a step 2B whether the claim recites additional elements that amount to significantly more than a judicial exception.

In 2019, it had been clarified that the step 2A had to be divided into two subsections. The first subsection still comprised the assessment whether the claim recited an abstract idea, a law of nature or a natural phenomenon. In the added second subsection, it was assessed whether the judicial exception was integrated into a practical application. In case such a practical application can be identified in the claims and the specification, the claim is not directed to such a judicial exception per se.

Abstract ideas are seen in mathematical concepts (mathematical relationships, mathematical formulas or equations and mathematical calculations), mental processes (concepts performed in the human mind (including an observation, evaluation, judgment, opinion) and certain methods of organizing human activity (like fundamental economic principles or practices (including hedging, insurance, mitigating risk),

102. USPTO, *35 U.S.C. 101*, available at: https://www.uspto.gov/web/offices/pac/mpep/mpep-9015-appx-l.html#d0e302376 (accessed on 22 Dec. 2019).
103. USPTO, *Manual of Patent Examining Procedure (MPEP)* (9th ed., revision August 2017, last revised January 2018), https://www.uspto.gov/web/offices/pac/mpep/index.html (accessed on 22 December 2019).
104. Federal Register, *2019 Revised Patent Subject Matter Eligibility Guidance* (vol. 84, No. 4, 7 Jan. 2019), available at: https://www.govinfo.gov/content/pkg/FR-2019-01-07/pdf/2018-28282.pdf (accessed on 22 Dec. 2019).
105. USPTO, *2019 Revised Patent Subject Matter Eligibility Guidance – Advanced Module* (January 2019), available at: https://www.uspto.gov/sites/default/files/documents/2019peg_advanced_module_05mar2019.pptx (accessed on 22 Dec. 2019).

commercial or legal interactions (including agreements in the form of contracts; legal obligations; advertising, marketing or sales activities or behaviours; business relations) or managing personal behaviour or relationships or interactions between people (including social activities, teaching, and following rules or instructions)). Further details on these specific abstract ideas have been issued by the USPTO in the October 2019 Patent Eligibility Guidance Update.[106]

In the October 2019 Guidance update, it is outlined how to assess the integration into a practical application by improving the functioning of a computer:

> In short, first the specification should be evaluated to determine if the disclosure provides sufficient details such that one of ordinary skill in the art would recognize the claimed invention as providing an improvement. The specification need not explicitly set forth the improvement, but it must describe the invention such that the improvement would be apparent to one of ordinary skill in the art. ... Second, if the specification sets forth an improvement in technology, the claim must be evaluated to ensure that the claim itself reflects the disclosed improvement. That is, the claim includes the components or steps of the invention that provide the improvement described in the specification. The claim itself does not need to explicitly recite the improvement described in the specification ... [T]he 'improvements' analysis in Step 2A determines whether the claim pertains to an improvement to the functioning of a computer ... without reference to what is well understood, routine, conventional activity. That is, the claimed invention may integrate the judicial exception into a practical application by demonstrating that it improves the relevant existing technology although it may not be an improvement over well understood, routine, conventional activity.

Especially in the area of autonomous vehicles, a plurality of use cases for blockchain applications other than financial applications and documentation applications like distribution chains are existing.

An example of a practical application for the use of a blockchain for privatizing data to be used in the control of autonomous vehicles is US 10249194 B2. It claims a method, apparatus, and computer program product for assessing one or more features of drivers within a threshold distance of a self-driving vehicle which has sensors to monitor driving conditions on a travel route within the threshold distance, predicting the behaviour of one or more vehicles within the threshold distance based on the assessment of those features, and utilizing the predicted behaviour for the self-driving vehicle to drive on the travel route. It is proposed that the information regarding other drivers are stored, privatized and utilized using a blockchain system.

Other applications for which patent protection is applied are, for instance, automatically distributed electric power systems and computation systems for controlling such power systems. For example, in US 2018299852 A1, it is proposed to use blockchain technology in the to peer-to-peer settlement for participation in energy and for energy consumption in distributed networks.

106. USPTO, *October 2019 Update: Subject Matter Eligibility*, available at: https://www.uspto.gov/sites/default/files/documents/peg_oct_2019_update.pdf (accessed on 22 Dec. 2019).

[F] Practical Hints Protection by Patents

[1] Strategic Considerations

In summary, patentability offers opportunities for innovative companies developing new applications for blockchain technologies to have another tool to distinguish from competitors. Thus, not only the protection of the special implementation of the application in the form of software is available to these companies. Rather, the abstract ideas on which these applications are based can also be protected with a much larger scope of protection.

That can strengthen the market position. Patents can especially be used to prohibit third parties to copy the claimed subject matter. But patents might fulfil further functions.

An (additional) patent that does not cover the specific solution the applicant/patent proprietor is using, but the patent covers that alternative solutions of the used technology might be filed and granted. Although the claimed subject matter of such a blocking patent is not used by the patent proprietor, it might on the first view be seen as 'dead capital'. But the blocking patent hinders competitors from using alternative solutions of the solution used by the applicant. Thus, neighbouring technological fields of the used solution are also blocked so that all these fields are reserved for the patent proprietor.

Especially such blocking patent can be used to, last but not least, generate licensing revenues by licensing the technology. In such license agreements, it can then also be defined that further developments have to be filed together, allowing the licensor to also participate in such further developments.

For the drafting of patent applications, it is, however, important to make the link from the abstract blockchain-based algorithm or mathematical method to the technical applications to overcome the eligibility checks and inventiveness checks, respectively, especially at the USPTO and the EPO. It is important to show what effect the application of the algorithm to a technical system to fulfil a technical purpose and to solve a technical problem. All these effects and advantages are preferably already included in the originally filed application documents to be used during the examination procedure to support the arguments for eligibility and inventiveness. However, this detailed description will also disclose significant know-how that will then become available for competitors.

So far, already a number of basic applications have already been registered or even protected, especially in Europe and the USA.

[2] Observation/Surveillance of Third-Party Rights

On the other hand, the area should also be closely monitored for patents applied for, patents expected to be granted and patents granted in order to minimize own risks by the infringement of protective rights of third parties. In Germany, for example, every businessman has an obligation to observe the market in this regard to determine whether the IP rights of third parties are infringed by his own activities. The excuse 'I knew nothing about this patent' doesn't count.

So, market players have to prepare themselves for not stepping into mines on the future blockchain battlefield, which some observers will see coming.[107] In such patent disputes, it has already proved to be very helpful in the past to be able to offer one's own IP rights as a bargaining chip, for example, for cross-licensing.

For example, the US-based JPMorgan Chase & Co. has been sued by Lighthouse Consulting Group, LLC at the Texas Eastern District Court for infringing of the patent FinTec patents US 8,590,940 and US 7,950,698[108] being directed to Image Capture Systems for Checks. The Lighthouse Consulting Group, LLC is described as a so-called NPE (non-practising entity).[109]

The business model of such NPEs, also referred to as patent trolls, is to generate income by forcing third parties to license own, often only for this purpose acquired, patents necessary for the third party to continue its business.

Often the license agreements are enforced by threat of legal actions or by actually enforcing the patents against the third party. NPEs mostly do not manufacture products or supply services based upon the patents in question. In comparison to patent-holding companies that license their patented technologies on reasonable terms in advance, NPEs attempt to enforce patent rights against accused infringers far beyond the patent's actual value when the actual infringer is allegedly using the patented technology already since a long time.[110]

Furthermore, the monitoring of patent documents offers the possibility to use the preparatory work of others. As mentioned before, patent applications are published after a certain time after their filing, in most jurisdictions eighteen months. This means that existing developments do not have to be carried out again, and it is easier to carry out further developments and improvements based on existing developments as described in such patent application publications.

[3] Transfer of Rights

Furthermore, it is very important that the employer ensures that all rights on the invention are transferred/assigned to the employer from the inventors.

Generally, only the inventors are entitled to file a patent application. For the employer to be entitled to file a patent application in the own name and to hold the

107. O'Neal, S., *Is Blockchain about to Become a Patent War Battleground?* (Cointelegraph, July 2018), available at: https://cointelegraph.com/news/is-blockchain-about-to-become-a-patent-war-battleground (accessed on 22 Dec. 2019).
108. Case 2:19-cv-00283 – *Lighthouse Consulting Group, LLC et al. v. J.P. Morgan Chase & CO. et al.* (represented by Jones Day, Chicago); Texas Eastern District Court.
109. https://www.unifiedpatents.com/insights/2019/12/16/lighthouse-check-depositing-patent-challenged-as-likely-invalid (accessed on 23 Mar. 2020).
110. Patentlyo, *Chief Judge Rader: Improving Patent Litigation* (27 Sep. 2011), available at: https://patentlyo.com/patent/2011/09/rader-patent-litigation.html (accessed on 23 Mar. 2020).

rights on the invention, it is necessary that an agreement with the inventors is found. Such an agreement is important for external inventors but also for employee inventors.

In this regard, national regulations heavily differ from each other. In some countries, the employee inventor is obliged to transfer all rights to the employer for no or only marginal remuneration.

Such a transfer can be agreed upon in some jurisdictions already in the employment agreement in advance. In other jurisdictions, very strict rules apply. For each invention, a separate agreement between the employee inventor and the employer has to be found.

[a] German Act on Employee Inventions

An example of comparable strict and formalistic regulations to handle the transfer of rights from employee inventors to employers is the German Act on employee inventions (Gesetz über Arbeitnehmererfindungen, ArbnErfG).[111]

This Act prescribes a defined way of how the transfer of rights has to be accomplished and defines a remuneration to be paid to the employee inventor in addition to the usual salary.

The Act codifies that the employee inventor is obliged to disclose the further development that might be protectable under patent or utility model law to the employer without delay (§2, §5 ArbnErfG). This covers any potential invention that is made by the employee during the duration of the employment (service invention, §4(2) ArbnErfG), irrespective whether the development is made during the work time, free time or holidays. Furthermore, also developments that are not connected to the work of the employee (free invention, §4(3) ArbnErfG) in view of the employee has to be reported to the employer so that the employer can assess whether the development is unrelated to work. The employee is obliged to hold the development secret as long as it does not become free (§24(2) ArbnErfG).

Once the development has been disclosed to the employer, and the disclosure does include the necessary information, the employer has a four-month time limit to decide whether the invention is claimed or is given free to the employee (§6 ArbnErfG). In the last case, the employer might reserve a right to use the invention for an adequate royalty fee.

In case the invention is claimed, all rights are transferred to the employer, but the employer also has different duties, especially:

- a patent/utility model application has to be filed in case the invention will not be handled as a trade secret (*see* below) (§13(1) ArbnErfG);
- a remuneration in addition to the salary has to be paid (§9 ArbnErfG);

111. Federal German Ministry of Justice and Consumer Protection, Gesetz über Arbeitnehmererfindungen in der im Bundesgesetzblatt Teil III, Gliederungsnummer 422-1, veröffentlichten bereinigten Fassung, das zuletzt durch Artikel 7 des Gesetzes vom 31. Juli 2009 (BGBl. I S. 2521) geändert worden ist available at: https://www.gesetze-im-internet.de/arbnerfg/ArbnErfG.pdf (accessed on 5 Feb. 2020).

- in case the employer does not want to extend the application to foreign countries, such foreign filings have to be timely offered to the employee inventor (§14 ArbnErfG);
- in case the employer does not want to prosecute further the application or does not want to uphold a granted patent/registered utility model, it has to be offered to the employee (§16 ArbnErfG).

As the impacts of not fulfilling these obligations and in case one of the employer or employee does not comply with these obligations, the other party can claim damages, it is important to build up a disclosure system for employee inventions/developments within a company. For example, the publication of the development by the employee before it becomes free can hinder the protection of the development by a patent or utility model. Due to the missing monopoly right, the employer might face a severe economic disadvantage. Vice versa, the employee inventor might have marketed the development in other foreign countries in which the employer is not interested in and might have generated extensive licence revenues.

It is possible for the employer to pay the employee inventor a lump sum to 'buy' the before described obligations, and it is highly recommended to do so to avoid claims.

Furthermore, the remuneration might be paid in the form of lump sum payments instead of payments based on a licence analogy, as suggested in the guidelines for the remuneration of employee inventions.[112] Such licence analogy payments lead to a high administrative effort, and furthermore, the books have to be opened for the employee to enable him to check the correctness of the payments.

All these payments and agreements have to be made separately for each invention. A pre-arrangement of a transfer of the rights or the pre-determination of a remuneration amount in an employment agreement in advance is not allowed under the Act (§22 ArbnErfG).

Also, trade secrets as discussed later fall under the Act so that its regulations have to be considered and followed to ensure that all rights are transferred to the employer and to avoid later claims of the inventor for a transfer of a patent or patent application as a right holder and to avoid later claims for remuneration by an employee.

[G] Utility Models

[1] Background

As the blockchain technology field is and will most likely for quite a time be a fast-developing field, in some cases, protection by patents might take too long to be effectively usable against competitors.

112. Richtlinien für die Vergütung von Arbeitnehmererfindungen im privaten Dienst vom 20. Juli 1959, Beilage zum Bundesanzeiger Nr. 156 vom 18. August 1959, geändert durch die Richtlinie vom 1. September 1983 (Bundesanzeiger Nr. 169, S. 9994), available at: https://www.dpma.de/docs/dpma/richtlinienfuerdieverguetungvonarbeitnehmererfindungen.pdf (accessed on 22 Dec. 2019).

According to the 'EPO Quality report 2018',[113] it took the EPO, for example, in 2018 in the middle 4.4 months to establish a search report (*see* page 27 of the report) and another 22.3 months to finalize the examination procedure (*see* page 34 of the report). Due to the timelines given to the applicant to request the examination (six months after the publication of the search report, that is in most cases taking place with the publication of the application eighteen months after the filing of the application) and the timelines for responding to an intention to grant of the EPO by the applicant of four months and the time it takes until the grant of the patent is published (around four–six weeks), it might take three–four years from the filing date until the publication of the grant of the patent being necessary to enforce the patent.

According to the 'Data Visualization Center of the USPTO',[114] the timelines at the USPTO are about twenty-six months from the filing of the application until the issue or (first) abandonment as of December 2019. This time does not include, however, often necessary requests for continued examinations (RCE) after the USPTO issues a final office action. By the RCE procedure, the grant is delayed for an additional period so that also at the USPTO the grant often takes place about three years after filing the application.

To provide a way to arrive at an enforceable protective right being directed to technical aspects of new development in some jurisdictions, the protection of abstract technical ideas is possible by way of a so-called utility model. A list of countries providing this protective right is available at the webpage of the WIPO.[115]

[2] Registration Procedure: Branching Off

The regulations on these utility models have not been harmonized between the countries so far. For example, the grant procedure, the maximum duration and also the protectable subject matter differs from country to country to name only some differences.

That means in some countries utility models are registered after passing only a formal examination, i.e., without an examination for novelty and inventiveness, for example, in Germany, whereas in other countries an examination for patentability is carried out, for example, in China. The omission of the examination of a substance makes the registration process cheaper and also faster. For example, it is possible to reach a registration of a utility model within less than two weeks.[116]

113. EPO, *EPO Quality Report 2018*, available at: http://documents.epo.org/projects/babylon/eponet.nsf/0/79B3608B5B4D3F71C125842D0040675A/$FILE/quality_report_2018_en.pdf (accessed on 22 Dec. 2019).
114. USPTO, *Data Visualisation Center*, available at: https://www.uspto.gov/corda/dashboards/patents/main.dashxml?CTNAVID = 1004 (accessed on 22 Dec. 2019).
115. WIPO, *Where can Utility Models be Acquired?*, available at: https://www.wipo.int/sme/en/ip_business/utility_models/where.htm (accessed on 22 Dec. 2019).
116. https://register.dpma.de/DPMAregister/pat/register?AKZ = 2020170071444&CURSOR = 1 (accessed on 22 Dec. 2019).

This makes the utility model to a very useful instrument to go against infringers on fairs or the like or to protect intermediate development steps in fast-moving technical areas.

Especially some jurisdictions allow to branch off utility models from pending patent applications. These have not been necessarily national patent applications for this country but could also be regional or international patent applications potentially having effect for the respective country.

The German law on utility models (Gebrauchsmustergesetz GebrMG) requires, according to §5 GebrMG,[117] only an application having effect for Germany, i.e., a European patent application designating Germany or an international patent application designating Germany directly or via a European patent application.

Such a branch off might be helpful, for example, in case a patent office has already affirmed the patentability of a subject matter during the examination procedure of a patent application, but due to different reasons, a decision to grant has not been issued yet and will take a longer time to be issued, a parallel utility model can be registered in a short term and can then be enforced against infringers that use the technology claimed in the patent application.

[3] Protection Requirements/Duration

Also, the requirements for the legal validity of utility models differ. In all countries, the novelty of the claimed subject matter of the utility model has to be given; however, often in comparison to utility patents, a grace period is given. This means that a publication that has been made by the applicant within a specific time, for example, six months in Germany, before the filing/priority date of the utility model is not taken into consideration when assessing the novelty and inventiveness. Also, in some jurisdictions, the state of the art does not comprise all ways of publication; for example, prior public uses might not be taken into consideration under specific circumstances. Further, in some jurisdictions, the requirements to be met to be inventive are lower for a utility model than for a patent.

Also, the 'maximum duration differs from country to country usually six to fifteen years'.[118] For example, the maximum duration is ten years in Germany according to §23(1) GebrMG,[119] have been six years in France (for a so-called Utility certificate) but has been extended in France since 11 January 2020 to also ten years and is seven years for a Greek utility model certificate.[120]

117. Article 5 GebrMG; Gebrauchsmustergesetz published on 28 Aug. 1986 (BGBl. I S. 1455), amended by Art. 10 on 17 Jul. 2017 (BGBl. I S. 2541), available at: https://www.gesetze-im-internet.de/gebrmg/5.html (accessed on 22 Dec. 2019).

118. WIPO, *Utility models*, available at: https://www.wipo.int/patents/en/topics/utility_models.html (accessed on 22 Dec. 2019).

119. Article 23 GebrMG, available at: https://www.gesetze-im-internet.de/gebrmg/23.html (accessed on 22 Dec. 2019).

120. The Hellenic Industrial Property Organisation, *Patents and Utility Models*, available at: https://www.obi.gr/OBI/Default.aspx?tabid=266 (accessed on 5 Feb. 2020).

[4] *Protectable Subject Matter*

In Germany, a utility model can only be registered for devices as according to § 2 No. 3 GebrMG[121] methods are excluded from the protection, but a coexistence between patents and utility models for the same claimed subject matter is possible, whereas, for example, in France also methods are protectable by a utility model; however, a coexistence between patents and utility models is not possible.[122] Also, in some countries, the protection as a utility model is restricted to specific technical fields, or respective technical fields are excluded from the protection by a utility model.

[5] *Summary of Pros and Cons of Utility Models*

Thus generally utility models provide the advantages of:

- being less expensive than patents;
- being registered/granted and thus enforceable in most jurisdictions faster and in a less complex procedure;
- protection parallel to patents in some jurisdictions, especially during the examination procedure of a parallel patent application; and
- protection requirements that are less stringent in some countries.

On the other hand, utility models provide:

- less legal certainty in case of not being examined;
- shorter term of duration compared to patents;
- in some jurisdictions, protection only for restricted subject matter, like only devices, or only for specific technical fields.

However, the disadvantage for the applicant of legal uncertainty might, in turn, be an advantage against competitors. Especially in case of not yet published parallel patent applications, the competitors cannot rely upon search and examination results of this patent application in comparison to the applicant of the utility model. Also, in case no (parallel) search has been carried out for the subject matter of the utility model, the third party has to invest time and efforts in the analysis of the legal validity of the utility model before having certainty on its (partial) legal invalidity before being sure to be allowed to use the claimed subject matter.

Thus, for each new development, it might be worthwhile to check for protection of the new development, especially in parallel to a patent application, by a utility model. This applies especially for blockchain use cases being related to fast-changing technical areas to take advantage of a fast registered protective right. Especially a

121. Article 2 GebrMG, available at: https://www.gesetze-im-internet.de/gebrmg/__2.html (accessed on 22 Dec. 2019).
122. Jones Day Commentary, January 2020, *French PACTE Act: Provisional Patent Application and the Evolution of the Utility Certificate*, available at: https://www.jonesday.com/en/insights/2020/01/french-pacte-act-provisions-enter-into-force (accessed on 31 May 2020).

competitor copying the protectable new development could be directly attacked, and a cease and desist order could be requested. In contrast, in case of a published but not yet granted patent application, only an adequate compensation could be reached retroactively, but the competitor can only be stopped by a cease and desist order after the grant of the patent.

A German utility model allows filing a utility model application with simultaneously requesting a search for a relevant state of the art. Then within six–eight months, the search report will provide more certainty on which aspects of the new development might be protectable or in other words, which parts of the utility model might be legally valid. At this point of time, the utility might be already registered so that the legally valid parts might be enforced straight away. In comparison to a patent application, it would not be necessary to carry out the time-consuming patent grant procedure before enforcement becomes possible.

The registration of the utility model will also publish the new development. In some cases, this might not be wanted before the marketing and put in practice, i.e., publication, of the new development as giving up a time advantage with regard to competitors. For these cases, the German utility model law allows requesting a cost-free deferment of the registration by up to eighteen months after the filing of the utility model. Thus, the registration of the utility model might be coordinated with the publication of the new development and would offer the possibility to enforce the utility model from the time of the marketing of the new development.

§7.07 TRADE SECRET

[A] General Background

Under special circumstances, the protection of a new development by a patent or utility model might not be the best choice to secure its own rights.

As mentioned, patent applications are published after a defined time period, in most jurisdictions after eighteen months. Thus, at this point in time, the competitors are informed about the new development and can use it for further developments and the like. The situation becomes problematic in case it turns out that the new development is not eligible for patent protection. For example, it might be problematic to disclose the invention in such a sufficient way that a person skilled in the art can carry it out. Also, it might turn out that the new invention is not seen as inventive, especially the patent office might not be of the opinion that it has technical character in case of the EPO or might be of the opinion that the judicial exception has not been integrated into a practical application. In such a case, the applicant would not be awarded a monopoly right but would have disclosed the new development to the public by the automatic publication of the patent application eighteen months after the filing of the patent application.

For example, a respective algorithm used in a blockchain application cannot be reverse-engineered from the blockchain application of the product as put on the market. That means a third party might not be able to gather all features of the algorithm from the marketed product, for example, by decoding the software of by analysing the behaviour of the software depending on different inputs and comparing it to the respective outputs. Assuming the algorithm might, however, give the developer or the user of the algorithm a significant, economic relevant advantage the developer does not want to disclose the details of the algorithm to the public.

For example, in such cases, it might be worthwhile to handle the new development as a trade secret.

[B] Legal Basis: Definition

A trade secret has been defined in the TRIPS Agreement. The TRIPS Agreement is an agreement between all Member States of the World Trade Organization (WTO). The WIPO describes[123] that this agreement 'establishes minimum standards of protection that each government has to give to the Intellectual Property of (...) WTO members (...)'.

In Article 39 TRIPS,[124] it is defined that:

> natural and legal persons shall have the possibility of preventing information lawfully within their control from being disclosed to, acquired by, or used by others without their consent in a manner contrary to honest commercial practices so long as such information (a) is secret in the sense that it is not, as a body or in the precise configuration and assembly of its components, generally known among or readily accessible to persons within the circles that normally deal with the kind of information in question; (b) has commercial value because it is secret; and (c) has been subject to reasonable steps under the circumstances, by the person lawfully in control of the information, to keep it secret.

These regulations had been transposed into law in different ways, also within the EU in the past.

For example, in Germany trade secrets had been protected by special provisions in different laws, especially the law on unfair competition. In other European countries and also in the US, the TRIPS regulations have been implemented by special laws.

In June 2016, the European Parliament and European Counsel issued the directive 2016/943[125] on the protection of undisclosed know-how and business information (trade secrets) against their unlawful acquisition, use and disclosure. By the directive, the national European laws on trade secret protection have been harmonized in Europe.

123. WIPO, *Advice on Flexibilities under the TRIPS Agreement*, available at: https://www.wipo.int/ip-development/en/policy_legislative_assistance/advice_trips.html (accessed on 23 Dec. 2019).

124. World Trade Organization (WTO), *Annex 1C of the Marrakesh Agreement Establishing the World Trade Organization* Art. 39 (signed in Marrakesh, Morocco on 15 Apr. 1994), available at: https://www.wto.org/english/docs_e/legal_e/27-trips_04d_e.htm (accessed on 23 Dec. 2019).

125. European Union, *Directive (EU) 2016/943 of 8 June 2016 on the protection of undisclosed know-how and business information (trade secrets) against their unlawful acquisition, use and disclosure*, available at: https://eur-lex.europa.eu/legal-content/EN/TXT/?uri=CELEX%3A32016L0943 (accessed on 23 Dec. 2019).

For example in Germany, although the Directive had to be implemented into national law until 9 June 2018, it took until April 2019 that the Directive was implemented in national German law by way of a special law in the form of the 'law for the protection of trade secrets' (GeschGehG).[126] In this law, the definition of a trade secret of TRIPS has been adopted in Article 2.[127]

Inter alias the GeschGehG also codifies in Article 7[128] in line with Article 10 of the Directive 2016/943 that the owner of the trade secret has a claim against an infringer for a recall of the infringing product, permanent removal of infringing products from the distribution channels, destruction of the infringing products or withdrawal of the infringing products from the market if the protection of the trade secret is not affected by this. The trade secret owner has furthermore a claim for information against the infringer, a claim for damages that have to be enforced at civil chambers of local district courts. In case the trade secret exists, the trade secret is held confidential during and after the court procedures, especially the participating parties abound to confidentiality.

Thus, by the Directive and the respective national laws, the holder of trade secrets have effective ways to secure and enforce the trade secret.

Also, in the US, the protection of a trade secret has been enforced. 'The Defend Trade Secrets Act of 2016'[129] came into force. The USPTO summarizes the core aspects of protection as a trade secret under the US Act as follows:[130]

> Courts can protect trade secrets by enjoining misappropriation, ordering parties that have misappropriated a trade secret to take steps to maintain its secrecy, as well as ordering payment of a royalty to the owner. Courts can also award damages, court costs, and reasonable attorneys' fees.

[C] Practical Aspects

This protection is, however, very limited because a trade secret holder is only protected from unauthorized disclosure and use, which is referred to as misappropriation. If a trade secret holder fails to maintain secrecy or if the information is independently discovered, becomes released or otherwise becomes generally known, protection as a trade secret is lost.

On the other hand, if the holder can ensure that the Trade Secret remains secret, the Trade secret does not expire, so protection continues until discovery or loss.

126. Gesetz zum Schutz von Geschäftsgeheimnissen vom 18. April 2019 (BGBl. I S. 466), available at: https://www.gesetze-im-internet.de/geschgehg/ (accessed on 23 Dec. 2019).
127. Article 2 GeschGhG, available at: https://www.gesetze-im-internet.de/geschgehg/2.html (accessed on 23 Dec. 2019).
128. Article 7 GeschGhG, available at: https://www.gesetze-im-internet.de/geschgehg/7.html (accessed on 23 Dec. 2019).
129. Defend Trade Secrets Act of 2016, Public Law 114–153, 11 May 2016, available at: https://www.congress.gov/114/plaws/publ153/PLAW-114publ153.pdf (accessed on 23 Dec. 2019).
130. USPTO, *Trade Secret Policy*, available at: https://www.uspto.gov/ip-policy/trade-secret-policy (accessed on 23 Dec. 2019).

Such a discovery might, however, take place by independent development of the subject matter by third parties. Such third parties might also reach a grant/registration of a protective right for the subject matter by, for example, a patent or utility model. As the subject matter of the trade secret would not have been made public by the owner, it would not form the state of the art and could not be used to challenge the legal validity. In case the trade secret could be against the assessment of the owner also reversed engineered in end products the owner of the IP right might raise claims against the owner of the then not any more secret subject matter. The owner might then defend himself with a right of prior use that however is subject to restrictions.

For example, a blockchain relevant algorithm has been developed and handled as a trade secret. The algorithm has been used in products/applications that have solely been marketed in a specific country/region. Region/country means in this context, the country /region in which a patent would have an effect. The right of prior use would then only cover this specific country region. Furthermore, the right of prior use would only cover the specific products/applications in which the algorithm would be used and would not cover further future developments of the algorithm or the use of the algorithm in other blockchain products.

Further, the right of prior use would only cover the specific legal person using the algorithm. So the right of prior use of the subsidiary generally does not give a right of prior use to the mother company or sister companies.

Thus, a trade secret might be used for the subject matter, giving an advantage relative to competitors when being kept secret. However, especially in view of the fluctuation of employees and secret holder, it might be problematic whether it is possible to maintain it under reasonable safeguards to protect its secrecy. Every disclosure will defeat the trade secret.

For planning the strategy with regard to protecting a new development, the following questions should thus be taken into consideration:

(i) Is the new development a patentable subject matter?
(ii) Is it possible and if yes with what effort is it possible to reverse engineer the subject matter or to independently detect and/or develop the claimed subject matter?
(iii) Is there a risk that a third party with file a patent application directed to the subject matter?
(iv) What is the expected duration for the subject matter to be valuable?
(v) How likely is it that the subject matter can be maintained secret?

In case questions (i)–(iii) can be answered with yes, a clear indication is there that the subject matter should be protected by a registered protective right like a patent or utility model.

Depending on the answer to question (iv), the protection by a patent should be taken into consideration. Is the answer to (iv) more than five years a patent application should be taken into consideration, especially accompanied by a parallel utility model application being registered already during the examination of the patent application in case patentability is likely.

In case all questions (i)–(iii) are answered with no, the protection as a trade secret should be taken into consideration, especially in case questions (iv) is answered with a duration of more than five years. Prerequisite is, however, that also questions (v) can be answered with a predominant likelihood.

Also, a combination of both a registered/granted IP right in combination with a trade secret should be taken into consideration. For example, it might be worthwhile to protect the core, preferably long-term valuable subject matter by a patent and to keep results of the further research and data sets secret in the form of a Trade Secret.

In any way, respective measures should be taken before the filing of the IP right application that the subject matter is held secret if necessary by non-disclosure agreements (NDAs), and internal measures for securing those fluctuations of the persons being involved in the development of the subject matter does not lead to a disclosure of the subject matter.

The confidentiality should furthermore be upheld as long as possible after the filing of the application, especially as long as the application is not published by the respective patent office.

First, in this way, the forming of state of the art that might be taken into consideration for assessing any further developments for which additional patent protection will be aimed for later is avoided. In case the subject matter of the first application is disclosed before the publication of the patent application, the disclosure could be taken into consideration for assessing the inventiveness, whereas the content of the application itself in most jurisdictions can only be taken into consideration for assessing the novelty.

That means any further feature of the further development not disclosed in the non-published application is sufficient to render the non-published application not relevant for assessing the patentability of further development. An important exception of this rule is, however, the US.

Under the US patent act[131] also, non-pre-published applications form the full state of the art and are taken into consideration for assessing the inventiveness.

Second, when not publishing the subject matter of a not yet published patent application, competitors are not taught with the content of the application otherwise allowing the competitor to further develop it and file own applications on such further developments.

With regard to NDAs, it is furthermore important to note that a violation of the NDA does not necessarily mean that the publication violating the NDA is not forming state of the art and is not taken into consideration for assessing the patentability of a subject matter claimed with a patent application filed after the violation of the NDA. Thus, the patent applicant might not be awarded a patent grant due to a publication of the claimed subject matter by a third party representing a violation of the NDA. In this case, the applicant, in most cases, does only have claims against the party violating the NDA based on a breach of a contract in the form of the NDA. In such a situation, it is

131. 35 U.S.C. 102 (a) (2).

likely that the claims will be less than the profit the applicant might have taken advantage of in case a patent would have been granted.

For the claim, the applicant would have to specify the suffered damages. This is however only possible for a hypothetical situation if the applicant would have been awarded a patent, would have the ability to hinder competitors from using the claimed subject matter and would have reached an increased a higher market share. As these circumstances are uncertain and also dependent on other factors, it is most likely that the awarded damages are below the actual damages.

Thus the rule should be 'first file the invention then talk about it', better 'first wait for the publication of the application, then talk about it.'

FURTHER READING

Monika Huppertz, Helge B. Cohausz, *Das Patentsekretariat: Die Bürofachkraft im gewerblichen Rechtsschutz* (4th ed., 1 November 2013).

James A. Cox, Mark W. Rasmussen, *Blockchain for Business Lawyers* (American Bar Association, 1st ed., 7 August 2019).

Helge B. Cohausz, *Gewerblicher Rechtsschutz und angrenzende Gebiete* (3rd ed., 1 September 2018).

Claudia Schwarz, Sabine Kruspig, *Computerimplementierte Erfindungen – Patentschutz von Software?* (2nd ed., 1 October 2017).

European Patent Office, available at: https://www.epo.org/learning-events/materials/inventors-handbook.html.

Adam Jolly, *Winning with IP – Managing Intellectual Property Today* (2019).

Daniel Closa, et al., *Patent Law for Computer Scientists: Steps to Protect Computer-Implemented Inventions* (2010).

Adam Jolly, *The Handbook of European Intellectual Property Management* (3rd ed., 2012).

CHAPTER 8

Blockchain and Antitrust

Jay Modrall

§8.01 INTRODUCTION

Introduction of new technologies with the potential to disrupt competition across many markets inevitably raises questions about those technologies' antitrust implications. Indeed, blockchain technologies have attracted considerable interest from antitrust authorities and commentators for several years. In June 2018, the Organisation for Economic Co-operation and Development (OECD) held a roundtable on 'Blockchain and competition policy'.[1] One commentator asked, 'Is Blockchain the Death of Antitrust Law?'[2] For better or worse, rumours of antitrust's death by blockchain are greatly exaggerated.

The application of blockchain technologies can indeed raise antitrust issues, but these issues are not different in kind from those raised by other business conduct. That said, companies implementing blockchain solutions must carefully consider their antitrust implications and take precautions to avoid inadvertently breaching antitrust law. In parallel, antitrust authorities are scrambling to understand blockchain and other new technologies and considering how their traditional approaches need to be updated. While most of the debate in antitrust circles has focused on the antitrust implications of the growth of large online platforms and their collection and use of 'big data', the growing application of blockchain (and smart contract solutions) also raise interesting antitrust issues.

1. https://www.oecd.org/competition/blockchain-and-competition-policy.htm (accessed on 21 Feb. 2020).
2. Schrepel, T., *Is Blockchain the Death of Antitrust Law?* (The Blockchain Antitrust Paradox), available at: https://papers.ssrn.com/sol3/papers.cfm?abstract_id=3193576 (accessed on 21 Feb. 2020).

In this chapter, blockchain issues in three general contexts are discussed: (i) application of blockchain technologies by two or more undertakings in potentially anticompetitive agreements, decisions and concerted practices; (ii) application of blockchain technologies by a single undertaking holding a 'dominant position'; and (iii) implications of the use of blockchain for the review of mergers and acquisitions involving companies using these technologies to store large volumes of data. In each section, the relevant antitrust concepts are introduced, and antitrust issues are covered that blockchain applications may be expected to raise.

This discussion is based primarily on European Union (EU) antitrust law. However, similar principles apply in many jurisdictions, and antitrust authorities around the globe can be expected to consider issues similar to the European Commission (EC). The issues raised in any particular business context are highly fact-specific, and this discussion will necessarily be general and not cover all business contexts in which blockchain will be used.

§8.02 ANTICOMPETITIVE AGREEMENTS, DECISIONS AND CONCERTED PRACTICES

[A] Introduction to Concepts

Article 101(1) of the Treaty on the Functioning of the European Union (TFEU) prohibits:

> all agreements between undertakings, decisions by associations of undertakings and concerted practices which may affect trade between Member States and which have as their object or effect the prevention, restriction or distortion of competition within the internal market, and in particular those which:
>
> (a) directly or indirectly fix purchase or selling prices or any other trading conditions;
> (b) limit or control production, markets, technical development, or investment;
> (c) share markets or sources of supply;
> (d) apply dissimilar conditions to equivalent transactions with other trading parties, thereby placing them at a competitive disadvantage;
> (e) make the conclusion of contracts subject to acceptance by the other parties of supplementary obligations which, by their nature or according to commercial usage, have no connection with the subject of such contracts.[3]
>
> Agreements, decisions and concerted practices (collectively, agreements) that are caught by Article 101(1) TFEU are automatically void under Article 101(2) TFEU unless they yield competitive benefits recognized in Article 101(3) TFEU:
>
> [agreements which contribute] to improving the production or distribution of goods or to promoting technical or economic progress, while allowing consumers a fair share of the resulting benefit, and which [do] not:
>
> (a) impose on the undertakings concerned restrictions which are not indispensable to the attainment of these objectives;

3. OJ 115, 9/5/2008, pp. 88–89, available at https://eur-lex.europa.eu/legal-content/EN/TXT/HTML/?uri=CELEX:12008E101&from=EN (accessed on 21 Feb 2020).

(b) afford such undertakings the possibility of eliminating competition in respect of a substantial part of the products in question.

Thus, Article 101(1) TFEU applies only where there is (i) an 'agreement', 'decision' or 'concerted practice' involving (ii) multiple 'undertakings' or associations of undertakings and having (iii) an anticompetitive 'object or effect' within the EU.

Each of these elements has been the subject of extensive discussion and enforcement action. For present purposes, it suffices to note that the terms agreement, decision and concerted practice (collectively, agreements) are interpreted broadly to include both formal and informal agreements. However, so-called tacit collusion, where competitors' behaviour is influenced by one another's expectations as to how they will behave, without any actual communication, is not caught by Article 101(1) TFEU. The line between parallel but independent actions and coordinated actions can be difficult to draw. In the coming years, the proliferation of smart contracts entered into by independent companies using the same or similar algorithms can be expected to test the boundaries between legal tacit collusion and illegal coordination.

The criterion of effect on competition in the EU's internal market may be met by any but the most localized conduct. If a blockchain solution otherwise raises antitrust issues, it is likely to meet this criterion except in the case of highly localized blockchain applications.

The term 'undertaking' includes a wide variety of business organizations and even individuals, but for the sake of convenience I use the more common terms 'company' or 'joint venture' instead of 'undertaking.' The distinction between violations 'by object' and 'by effect' relates to the standard of proof an antitrust authority must meet to show that a violation has occurred.

Another fundamental distinction is made between so-called horizontal agreements among head-to-head competitors and so-called vertical agreements among companies at different levels of a supply chain. As a general rule, horizontal agreements are viewed more negatively from an antitrust perspective, while vertical agreements are considered less likely to raise antitrust concerns. However, the application of blockchain technologies can raise antitrust issues in both horizontal and vertical agreements.

As mentioned, the EC has adopted so-called block exemption regulations exempting certain horizontal agreements among competitors (certain research and development agreements[4] and 'specialization agreements', such as joint production agreements[5]) and vertical agreements among suppliers and customers[6] from the scope of EU competition law. In parallel, the EC published guidelines on the EU approach to

4. EC, Commission Regulation No 1217/2010 on the application of Article 101(3) of the TFEU to certain categories of research and development agreements, OJ L335, 18/12/2010, pp. 36–42.
5. EC, Commission Regulation No 1218/2010 on the application of Article 101(3) of the TFEU to certain categories of specialisation agreements, OJ L335, 18/12/2010, pp. 43–47.
6. EC, Commission Regulation No 330/2010 on the application of Article 101(3) of the Treaty on the Functioning of the European Union to categories of vertical agreements and concerted practices, OJ L102, 23/4/2010, pp. 1–7 (the 'VBER').

assessing the legality of horizontal cooperation agreements[7] and vertical cooperation agreements.[8]

Although some blockchain-related agreements could be covered by the EC's block exemption regulations, the conditions set out in these regulations are quite technical and are unlikely to apply in most cases. Thus, there is no need to discuss them in this chapter in greater detail.

On the other hand, in the discussion below, emphasis has been put on the EC's Horizontal and Vertical Guidelines, which are the most comprehensive and authoritative analysis of the EU antitrust treatment of such agreements. It should be noted that these block exemptions and guidelines are currently under review. They are likely to be amended in the coming years, notably to take account of technological and market evolution. Proposed revisions will likely be published in late 2020 or 2021.

[B] Horizontal Agreements and Blockchain

Anticompetitive horizontal agreements include the most well-known examples of antitrust violations, price-fixing and market sharing cartels. Such hardcore violations will not be discussed in this chapter, except to note that the use of blockchain or smart contract technology to implement such illegal agreements will not protect the parties from a finding of infringement and the imposition of significant fines and (in some jurisdictions) criminal penalties.[9]

Article 101(1) can also capture many cooperative agreements involving competitors that are not hardcore antitrust violations, including cooperative agreements involving blockchain.

As the EC notes in paragraphs 2–3 of the Horizontal Guidelines:[10]

> Horizontal cooperation agreements can lead to substantial economic benefits, in particular if they combine complementary activities, skills or assets. Horizontal cooperation can be a means to share risk, save costs, increase investments, pool know-how, enhance product quality and variety, and launch innovation faster.
>
> On the other hand, horizontal cooperation agreements may lead to competition problems. This is, for example, the case if the parties agree to fix prices or output or to share markets, or if the cooperation enables the parties to maintain, gain or increase market power and thereby is likely to give rise to negative market effects with respect to prices, output, product quality, product variety or innovation.

7. EC, Communication from the Commission – Guidelines on the applicability of Article 101 of the Treaty on the Functioning of the European Union to horizontal co-operation agreements, OJ 54, 14/1/2011, pp. 1–70 (the 'Horizontal Guidelines').
8. EC, Commission Notice – Guidelines on Vertical Restraints, SEC(2010) 411, available at: https://ec.europa.eu/competition/antitrust/legislation/guidelines_vertical_en.pdf (the 'Vertical Guidelines') (accessed on 21 Feb. 2020).
9. Cf. Decision of the UK Competition and Markets Authority, Online sales of posters and frames, Case 50223 of 12 August 2016, available at: https://assets.publishing.service.gov.uk/media/57ee7c2740f0b606dc000018/case-50223-final-non-confidential-infringement-decision.pdf (accessed on 21 Feb. 2020).
10. *Supra* n. 7.

Blockchain technology can be used in a wide variety of horizontal cooperative agreements discussed in the Horizontal Guidelines, including research and development agreements, joint production agreements, purchasing agreements, and commercialization agreements. A discussion of all horizontal cooperative agreements in which blockchain may be used would be well outside the scope of this chapter if one were even possible. Instead, it is worthwhile to discuss two antitrust issues on the below that may be raised by blockchain applications in many types of agreement: information exchange and Standardization.

[1] Information Exchange

At their heart, blockchains are a means of recording and sharing information. The EC recognizes that '[i]nformation exchange is a common feature of many competitive markets and may generate various types of efficiency gains[, including solving] . . . problems of information asymmetries[, improving] . . . internal efficiency through benchmarking[, saving] . . .costs by reducing . . . inventories, enabling quicker delivery of perishable products to consumers, or dealing with unstable demand etc. Furthermore, information exchanges may directly benefit consumers by reducing their search costs and improving choice'.[11]

On the other hand, 'the exchange of market information may also lead to restrictions of competition in particular in situations where it is liable to enable undertakings to be aware of market strategies of their competitors'.[12] '[I]nformation exchange can constitute a concerted practice if it reduces strategic uncertainty in the market thereby facilitating collusion, that is to say, if the data exchanged is strategic. Consequently, sharing of strategic data between competitors amounts to concertation, because it reduces the independence of competitors' conduct on the market and diminishes their incentives to compete.'[13,14]

The extent to which blockchain applications raise information-sharing concerns is a function of the sensitivity of the information stored on the blockchain and the rules governing who can access that information. At one extreme, a company setting up a private blockchain to store information that will be accessible only within the corporate group will not raise any antitrust concerns, regardless of the sensitivity of the information stored on the blockchain.

At the other extreme, setting up a public blockchain on which public or otherwise non-competitively sensitive information will be accessible to all interested parties will also normally raise no antitrust issues. The Horizontal Guidelines note, however, that 'the possibility cannot be entirely excluded that even genuinely public exchanges of information may facilitate a collusive outcome in the market.'[15]

---

11. *Ibid.*, para. 57.
12. *Ibid.*, para. 58.
13. Information exchange may also constitute, or facilitate the implementation of, a cartel, but as noted this chapter does not cover such hardcore violations.
14. *Supra* n. 7, para. 61.
15. *Ibid.*, para. 94.

Antitrust issues are most likely to arise in situations between these two extremes, where a private blockchain is created by competitors to store proprietary information that will be accessible only to certain market participants. In these situations, stakeholders must take care of both in the design and operation of the blockchain to avoid infringing antitrust rules.

As with any cooperation among competitors, the first step in the design of a private blockchain intended to store competitively sensitive information of competitors should be to determine whether there is a procompetitive rationale for the cooperation and whether the efficiencies to be generated by it outweigh the potential for competitive harm. This may be the case, for example, where a single operator is able to realize cost savings and offer capacity to competitors in a market as a sort of industry utility. In such a case, however, it will be important to ensure that the permissions built into the blockchain operating rules ensure that participants have access only to their own competitively sensitive information, and not to that of competitors. Such 'compliance by design' is critical to ensure that the creation of the blockchain does not infringe antitrust law.

Even assuming that a private blockchain storing competitively sensitive information for competitors has a procompetitive rationale and does not infringe antitrust law, care must be taken to ensure that antitrust laws are not infringed in the blockchain's day-to-day operation. For example, if the blockchain is structured as a joint venture in which competitors are equity holders, the joint venture's reports to equity holders and their representatives on the joint venture's board or other managing organs may not include competitively sensitive information. The joint venture and its personnel should adopt antitrust compliance policies and training procedures to mitigate the risk of inadvertent sharing of competitively sensitive information. Special procedures may be required if equity holder personnel are seconded to the joint venture.

What information is competitively sensitive must be determined on a case-by-case basis. The Horizontal Guidelines explain that exchanges of strategic data are more likely to be caught by Article 101(1) TFEU because competitors' access to such information of other competitors reduces their uncertainty and decreases their incentives to compete. 'Strategic information can be related to prices (e.g., actual prices, discounts, increases, reductions or rebates), customer lists, production costs, quantities, turnovers, sales, capacities, qualities, marketing plans, risks, investments, technologies and R&D programmes and their results. Generally, information related to prices and quantities is the most strategic, followed by information about costs and demand. However, if companies compete with regard to R&D, it is the technology data that may be the most strategic for competition. The strategic usefulness of data also depends on its aggregation and age, as well as the market context and frequency of the exchange.'[16]

As reflected in the detailed discussion of information-sharing issues in the 2011 Horizontal Guidelines, the information-sharing issues raised by blockchain applications are not new. These issues are familiar from a number of business contexts, such

16. *Ibid.*, para. 86.

as trade associations and joint ventures. The permissioning arrangements to ensure that competitively sensitive information of one blockchain participants is not accessible to its competitors are analogous to the firewalls traditionally employed to avoid the sharing of competitively sensitive information among participants in a joint venture.

[2] Standardization

The creation of a blockchain on which competitors may store information for procompetitive purposes may require a level of Standardization, for instance, as to the type and format of information to be stored. The Horizontal Guidelines address so-called standardization agreements, defined as agreements that 'have as their primary objective the definition of technical or quality requirements with which current or future products, production processes, services or methods may comply.'[17]

The guidelines recognize that 'Standardization agreements usually produce significant positive economic effects, for example by promoting economic interpenetration on the internal market and encouraging the development of new and improved products or markets and improved supply conditions. Standards thus normally increase competition and lower output and sales costs, benefiting economies as a whole. Standards may maintain and enhance quality, provide information and ensure interoperability and compatibility (thus increasing value for consumers).'[18]

On the other hand, 'Standard-setting can ... also give rise to restrictive effects on competition ... through three main channels, namely reduction in price competition, foreclosure of innovative technologies and exclusion of, or discrimination against, certain companies by prevention of effective access to the standard.'[19] Thus, in developing standards for information to be included in a blockchain, competitors must avoid 'anticompetitive discussions [that] could reduce or eliminate price competition in the markets concerned, thereby facilitating a collusive outcome on the market'.[20]

Second, to the extent that design of a blockchain may involve a choice of alternative standards for information to be included, competitors must consider whether the approach adopted could create barriers to entry for other competitors and potentially exclude them from a market or otherwise limit innovation. According to the Horizontal Guidelines, 'The risk of limitation of innovation is increased if one or more companies are unjustifiably excluded from the standard-setting process.'[21]

For example, if competitors representing a significant proportion of a relevant market agree on certain types and formats for information to be stored on a blockchain and that approach is expected to become an actual or de facto standard for customers in the market, a competitor following a different approach who was excluded from the process could suffer competitive harm. The Horizontal Guidelines recognize that

17. *Ibid.*, para. 257.
18. *Ibid.*, para. 263.
19. *Ibid.*, para. 264.
20. *Ibid.*, para. 265.
21. *Ibid.*, para. 266.

standardization agreements 'may lead to anticompetitive results by preventing certain companies from obtaining effective access to the results of the standard-setting process'.[22]

Special considerations apply where the design of a blockchain among competitors involves intellectual property rights (IPRs), in particular, if those rights include so-called standard-essential patents.

[C] Vertical Agreements and Blockchain

As mentioned, so-called vertical agreements between companies active in different levels of a supply chain are less likely than horizontal agreements to raise antitrust issues. The EC has adopted a block exemption regulation exempting certain vertical supply and distribution agreements (the VBER)[23] and published guidelines on vertical restraints (the Vertical Guidelines).[24] The VBER and Vertical Guidelines provide a framework for analysing any restrictions on competition contained in vertical blockchain-related agreements, such as blockchain-related supply chain management platforms.

The VBER defines 'vertical agreements' as agreements between two or more companies operating for this purpose 'at a different level of the production or distribution chain, and relating to the conditions under which the parties may purchase, sell or resell certain goods or services'. The VBER does not generally apply to agreements between competing companies.[25] The VBER also does not apply to agreements between companies with market shares over 30% of the relevant upstream or downstream markets, or to agreements containing so-called hardcore restrictions, namely restrictions on the buyer's ability to determine its sales price (known as 'resale price maintenance', or RPM); restrictions on the territory into which, or of the customers to whom, the buyer may sell the contract goods or services (with exceptions for exclusive distribution networks, agreements with wholesalers, selective distribution agreements and component sales); restrictions on active or passive sales to end users by members of a selective distribution system (subject to exceptions); restrictions on cross-supplies between distributors within a selective distribution system; and restrictions on buyers of components that use the components to manufacture finished goods from reselling the components as spare parts.

Even if the VBER applies to a particular agreement, it does not exempt certain so-called excluded restrictions that may be contained in otherwise-exempted agreements. These are non-compete obligations with duration over five years (unless the

22. *Ibid.*, para. 268.
23. EC, Commission Regulation No. 330/2010 on the application of Article 101(3) of the TFEU to certain categories of vertical agreements and concerted practices, OJ L102, 23/4/2010, pp. 1-7.
24. EC, Commission Notice, *supra* n. 8.
25. With the exemption of non-reciprocal vertical agreements where (a) the supplier is a manufacturer and a distributor of goods, while the buyer is a distributor and not a competing undertaking at the manufacturing level; or (b) the supplier is a provider of services at several levels of trade, while the buyer provides its goods or services at the retail level and is not a competing undertaking at the level of trade where it purchases the contract services.

buyer operates from premises owned or leased by the supplier); restrictions on the buyer's right to manufacture, purchase, sell or resell goods or services after the termination of the agreement (unless these are limited to one year, and other conditions are met); and restrictions on the ability of members of a selective distribution agreement to sell the brands of particular competing suppliers.

The Vertical Guidelines discuss the application of the VBER and the analysis under Article 101(1) TFEU of certain common categories of vertical agreements: single branding, exclusive distribution, exclusive customer allocation, selective distribution, franchising, exclusive supply, upfront access payments, category management agreements, tying and resale price restrictions. The Vertical Guidelines also explain that certain categories of vertical agreements - de minimis agreements; agency agreements and subcontracting agreements - will not normally infringe Article 101(1) TFEU whether or not the VBER would otherwise apply.

Blockchains are used increasingly for supply chain management in a wide variety of vertical agreements between suppliers and buyers. Many of these agreements are covered by the VBER, including in common categories of the agreement, such as single branding, exclusive distribution, exclusive customer allocation, selective distribution, franchising and category management agreements. Importantly, the use of blockchains in such agreements does not impact the application (or not) of the VBER.

Given the variety of contexts in which blockchains may be used, a discussion of each such category is outside the scope of this chapter. For companies considering the use of blockchain in a vertical agreement or network of agreements, however, the VBER's list of 'hardcore' and 'excluded' restrictions provides a useful checklist of areas where companies need to be especially careful. Antitrust advice should be sought in particular if companies' proposed blockchain (or smart contract) structures could involve:

- RPM;
- restrictions on cross-border sales of goods or services except in limited situations;
- restrictions on sales to end-users or cross-supplies by members of a selective distribution system;
- non-compete obligations with duration over five years;
- restrictions on a buyer's right to manufacture, purchase, sell or resell goods or services after the termination of the agreement; and
- restrictions on the ability of members of a selective distribution agreement to sell the brands of competing suppliers.

It should be noted, that where a group of buyers or suppliers competing with one another at the upstream or downstream level set up a blockchain-based platform to manage the supply chains of multiple companies, the VBER will not apply. In such cases, the considerations above relating to horizontal agreements will apply.

[D] Appropriate Safeguards

Given the enormous variety of relationships, both horizontal and vertical, in which blockchain and smart contracts can be used, each situation must be assessed on a case-by-case basis. It goes without saying that hardcore antitrust violations, such as price-fixing and market partitioning, are illegal and subject to very significant sanctions, whether or not they involve blockchain or smart contracts.

Apart from avoiding such hardcore violations, particular care from an antitrust perspective is required whenever a blockchain application is developed in cooperation among competitors. In many cases, such cooperation will be procompetitive, allowing multiple stakeholders in a market to benefit from the efficiencies offered by blockchain. But in structuring such cooperation, the potential procompetitive effects must be balanced against any potential harms to competition. Where such potential harms are identified, possibilities to mitigate such harms should be considered. Even where proposed cooperation is considered procompetitive, care must be taken to ensure that competitors do not share competitively sensitive information without appropriate safeguards, both in the structuring and negotiation of the cooperation arrangements and through the blockchain application itself once operational.

Blockchain applications involving purely vertical relationships, such as supply chain management platforms, will normally raise fewer antitrust issues than applications involving cooperation among competitors. Indeed, many such arrangements will be exempted from EU competition law under the VBER. Nonetheless, proposed vertical blockchain applications must also be carefully reviewed from an antitrust perspective, in particular, if they are likely to involve potentially problematic features mentioned above.

§8.03 ABUSE OF DOMINANCE

[A] Introduction of Concepts

Article 102 TFEU provides that:

> Any abuse by one or more undertakings of a dominant position within the internal market or in a substantial part of it shall be prohibited as incompatible with the internal market in so far as it may affect trade between Member States.
>
> Such abuse may, in particular, consist in:
>
> (a) directly or indirectly imposing unfair purchase or selling prices or other unfair trading conditions;
> (b) limiting production, markets or technical development to the prejudice of consumers;
> (c) applying dissimilar conditions to equivalent transactions with other trading parties, thereby placing them at a competitive disadvantage;
> (d) making the conclusion of contracts subject to acceptance by the other parties of supplementary obligations which, by their nature or according to commercial usage, have no connection with the subject of such contracts.

Thus, Article 102 TFEU applies only where there is (i) an 'abuse', of (ii) a 'dominant position' in the EU or a substantial part of it by (iii) an 'undertaking', and (iv) that abuse affects trade between the Member States. As with Article 101(1) TFEU, each of these elements has been the subject of extensive discussion and enforcement. The definition of 'undertaking' is discussed above. As with Article 101(1) TFEU, any but the most localized blockchain applications in the EU are likely to affect more than one Member State. Thus, the critical elements of an Article 102 TFEU infringement for present purposes are the existence of a 'dominant position' and the 'abuse' by the dominant company.

To assess whether a company holds a dominant position, the EC defines the product market and the geographic market and then assesses the company's market power in that market. How a relevant market is defined for antitrust purposes is often critical to the EC's analysis of whether, and if so which, parties may have a dominant position. The EC's approach to the market definition is outlined in its 1997 notice on the definition of the relevant market for the purposes of Community competition law.[26] As this notice explains, 'Basically, the exercise of market definition consists in identifying the effective alternative sources of supply for the customers of the undertakings involved, in terms both of products/ services and of geographic location of suppliers.'[27] In 2020, the EC is expected to conduct a consultation on updates to its 1997 notice and to publish an updated version possibly in 2021, but the basic framework will likely remain the same.

Once a relevant antitrust market is defined, the next step in the analysis is normally to estimate stakeholders' shares in that market. The EC considers market shares as a useful first indication of the importance of each firm on the market in comparison to the others. The higher the market share, and the longer the period of time over which it is held, the more likely it is to be a preliminary indication of dominance. If a company has a market share of less than 40%, it is unlikely to be dominant. The EC also takes other factors into account in its assessment of dominance, including the ease with which other companies can enter the market – whether there are any barriers to this; the existence of countervailing buyer power; the overall size and strength of the company and its resources; and the extent to which it is present at several levels of the supply chain (vertical integration).[28]

Under EU law, holding a dominant position is not in itself illegal; dominant companies are entitled to compete on the merits like any other company. However, a dominant company may be found to abuse that position based on a number of different commercial behaviours. Examples of behaviour that may amount to abuse include: requiring that buyers purchase all units of a particular product only from the dominant company (exclusive purchasing); setting prices at a loss-making level (predation); refusing to supply inputs indispensable for competition in an ancillary market;

26. OJ C372, 9/12/1997, pp. 5–13.
27. *Ibid.*, at para. 13.
28. *See generally*, https://ec.europa.eu/competition/antitrust/procedures_102_en.html (accessed on 21 Feb. 2020).

charging excessive prices.[29] The EC has published guidance on its enforcement priorities in relation to certain of these abusive behaviours, known as 'exclusionary' abuses,[30] but in general, less guidance is available in relation to Article 102 TFEU than in relation to Article 101 TFEU.

As with anticompetitive agreements, the variety of markets in which blockchains and smart contracts may be used precludes a detailed discussion of EU precedents on individual types of conduct that may be found abusive. Given that blockchains can be used to store significant quantities of data and may be used by platforms accessible to multiple stakeholders, however, I briefly discuss two areas in which abuse of dominance issues may arise for companies using blockchain applications in their businesses: big data and online platforms.

Big data and online platforms have come under intense scrutiny in the EU and elsewhere, largely as a result of the growth of major business-to-consumer (B2C) platforms. However, the potential for enhanced enforcement is not limited to the B2C context. The discussion below draws to a significant extent on the 2019 report of three special advisors to the EC on 'Competition Policy for the Digital Era' (the Digital Era Report or Report),[31] but a large number of official studies have been published in recent years. Other important studies include the 2019 'Furman Report' in the UK[32] and the joint Franco-German 2016 study on competition law and data (the Franco-German Study).[33] EU and other law in this area can be expected to evolve in significant respects in the coming years.

[B] Big Data

Much of the debate around big data and its potential relevance for abuse of dominance cases revolves around two questions: (i) whether, and if so how, the accumulation of big data can contribute to the creation of a dominant position within the meaning of Article 102 TFEU and (ii) under what conditions can dominant companies be required to share such data to remedy an abuse of a dominant position under Article 102 TFEU. Such debates tend to assume that these questions are linked, in the sense that where the accumulation of big data gives rise to a dominant position, Article 102 TFEU may require the dominant company to give competitors access to that data.

29. *Ibid.*
30. EC, Communication from the Commission – Guidance on the Commission's enforcement priorities in applying Article 82 of the EC Treaty to abusive exclusionary conduct by dominant undertakings, OJ C45, 24/2/2012, pp. 7–20.
31. Crémer, J., de Montjoye, Y.-A. and Schweitzer, H., *Competition Policy for the Digital Era*, available at: https://ec.europa.eu/competition/publications/reports/kd0419345enn.pdf (accessed on 25 Feb. 2020).
32. Unlocking Digital Competition – Report of the Digital Competition Expert Panel, available at: https://assets.publishing.service.gov.uk/government/uploads/system/uploads/attachment_data/file/785547/unlocking_digital_competition_furman_review_web.pdf (accessed on 25 Feb. 2020).
33. Autorité de la Concurrence and Bundeskartellamt, *Competition Law and Data*, available at: https://www.bundeskartellamt.de/SharedDocs/Publikation/DE/Berichte/Big%20Data%20Papier.pdf?__blob=publicationFile&v=2 (accessed on 25 Feb. 2020).

In fact, the issues of dominance and remedy are independent. As noted above, the first step in an abuse of dominance case is to define the relevant antitrust market. Where data are themselves a product offered by a potentially dominant company, the accumulation of a large share of the relevant type of data may indeed be an indication of a dominant position. This has arguably been the situation in a number of Article 102 TFEU cases unrelated to blockchain.[34] Notably, the remedy sought in these cases has not typically been accessed to the underlying data, but rather remedies to facilitate competitors marketing their own data-related services.

Much of the recent debate about big data, and the big data-related proposals in the Report, revolves around the alleged need for companies to gain direct access to competitors' data. The Report notes: 'The significance of data and data access for competition will ... depend on an analysis of the specificities of a given market, the type of data, and data usage in a given case.' In relation to proposals to require dominant companies to grant competitors access to data under Article 102 TFEU, the Report stressed the need for care. 'It is necessary to distinguish between different forms of data, levels of data access, and data uses.'

Much of the Report's big data discussion focuses on conditions in which antitrust law can be used as a tool to require companies to give competitors access to their data, but the Report also discusses new issues raised by companies voluntarily sharing and pooling data. Without discussing the issue in detail, the Report also notes the need for a new legal regime governing rights in data. The Report's approach to big data in these contexts is summarized below.

[1] Mandating Data Access

In a long and detailed analysis, the Report examines arguments for and against mandating data access in different contexts, depending on how the data are obtained (whether they are volunteered, observed, or inferred) and how data are used (use of non-anonymous individual-level data, anonymous individual-level data, aggregated data, or contextual data).

The Report notes that the 'debate is mostly framed as a debate on whether the criteria of the so-called essential facilities doctrine (EFD) are met'. In the data access context, however, the Report argues against the application of the EFD and for the application of a broader interest-balancing test. In particular, the Report argues against application of the requirement that a claimant under the EFD show that it requires

34. *See*, e.g., Case COMP D3/38.044 - NDC Health/IMS Health: Interim measures, OJ L59, 28/2/2002, pp. 18-49 (IMS considered dominant in a market for German regional pharmaceutical data. The EC proposed to adopt interim measures requiring IMS to license its '1 860 brick structure', which it considered to be a de facto industry standard for structuring such data. Although the European courts determined that the criteria for interim measures were not satisfied, IMS remains a seminal 'big data' case); and CASE AT.39654 - Reuters Instrument Codes, available at: https://ec.europa.eu/competition/antitrust/cases/dec_docs/39654/39654_2861_16.pdf (accessed on 25 Feb. 2020). Thomson Reuters found dominant in the worldwide market for consolidated real-time data feeds and to have abused that position by restricting the use of Reuters Instrument Codes in relation to data feeds of other providers; Thomson Reuters offered commitments to resolve the EC's concerns.

access to the essential facility to develop a 'new product.' The goal of the 'new product rule' is to preserve a dominant firm's investment incentives by ensuring a sufficient degree of appropriability of profits for the firm. But the Report argues that in some 'access to data' cases, the danger that the firm will lose the incentive to invest in data collection and innovation is lower. Thus, rather than a formal 'new product rule', authorities applying Article 102 TFEU to 'access to data' cases should verify that an access mandate will not eliminate the appropriability of benefits resulting from successful investments. According to the Report, this consideration may be especially important outside the platform context.

As under the 'standard' EFD, a precondition for data access remedies under Article 102 TFEU should be indispensability. To determine whether data access is indispensable for Article 102 TFEU purposes, it is important to distinguish access to a data set from access to the data in close to real-time where no substitutes exist. The non-substitutability of data may result from the richness ('number of columns') and size ('number of rows') of the dataset, in particular, where machine-learning algorithms play a role. The frequency of data generation also needs to be taken into account when discussing data access, both for providing a service to the person who generated the data and for aggregated applications.

The balancing of interests needs to take account both of the need to protect the dominant firm's investment incentives and the need to ensure that strongly entrenched positions of market power, protected by high barriers of entry, remain contestable. In some settings, such interest-balancing can result in a duty to grant access to data in a form that allows competitors to compete effectively in neighbouring markets, which may include a duty to ensure data interoperability.

The Report outlines several data access 'scenarios' to identify situations in which data access mandates would be more or less likely to be appropriate. Access mandates would more likely be appropriate where the data controller holds a gatekeeper position (i.e., access to its data is essential for competing on one or more neighbouring markets) or data access requests are somewhat standardized. Access mandates would be less appropriate where a firm requests data for the purpose of training algorithms for uses unrelated to the fields of activity of the data controller, although even in such case an access mandate could be imposed 'where the dominant firm is a large player in data markets and has an infrastructure for data access requests in place'.

In the balancing of interest context, the Report discusses whether the threshold for granting access to data should be lowered as compared to cases involving access to infrastructure or IPRs, at least where data is produced as a by-product of another activity and incentives to generate such data will persist irrespective of a possible access mandate, for instance, in relation to machine-generated sensor data in the Internet of Things context. While the value of data to a dominant data controller may be taken into account at the original price (and therefore, needs to be protected under competition law), competition law should not protect an aftermarket monopoly.

Indeed, the Report supports a more interventionist approach to data access – and possibly data interoperability – for use in complementary markets or aftermarkets, which are part of the broader 'ecosystem' served by the data controller. The EC and EU courts have frequently had occasion to address the relevance of secondary markets and aftermarkets in the Article 102 TFEU context. But the Report argues that 'some of the specificities of data could imply that the competition policy treatment of access to data should be different from that of standard aftermarkets. . . but there is very little economic analysis of these issues, so [their] conclusions should be considered as very preliminary'.

In the specific case of individual-level data, the Report discusses the implications of the data portability right under the EU's General Data Protection Regulation (GDPR)[35] but notes that data portability in the GDPR does not provide a right to continuous data access or interoperability, but simply a right to receive a copy of some accumulated past data. Thus, it may facilitate a data subject's switching between services but not facilitate multi-homing or the offering of complementary services, which frequently requires continuous and potentially real-time data access. Accordingly, 'more demanding' data access regimes than the GDPR could be mandated under Article 102 TFEU for dominant firms, or through sector-specific regulation, in particular, to open up secondary markets. Tension with the GDPR may also arise where an access mandate involves personal data. The Report notes that the UK and French competition authorities have resolved this tension in past cases by ordering data access on an opt-out basis or permitted access to data only for specified purposes and specified acts of processing.

In summary, the Report concludes that Article 102 TFEU may be used in appropriate cases to give competitors access to data, but only from dominant firms and after a thorough analysis of whether such access is truly indispensable and after weighing the legitimate interests of both parties. Access to individual-level data to serve a user should only be granted if that user consents, irrespective of whether personal or non-personal data is at issue. Where the user can switch his/her service provider with sufficient ease without access to data, no mandated access is required. Where access to bundled individual-level data or aggregate data is requested, the indispensability criterion may be met if the data holder is a dominant platform whose dominance is strongly entrenched and exclusive data control may reinforce and extend such power.

[2] Policing Data Sharing and Pooling

Although much of its discussion focuses on the potential imposition of data-sharing requirements, the Report also discusses the antitrust treatment of voluntary data sharing and pooling. Data sharing and data pooling arrangements will frequently be procompetitive, enabling firms to develop new or better products or services or to train algorithms on a broader, more meaningful basis. Such arrangements can be anticompetitive, however, for example where some competitors are denied access or granted access only on less favourable terms; data sharing amounts to an anticompetitive

35. Regulation (EU) 2016/679 of the European Parliament and of the Council of 27 April 2016 on the protection of natural persons with regard to the processing of personal data and on the free movement of such data, and repealing Directive 95/46/EC (General Data Protection Regulation), OJ L119, 4/5/2016, pp. 1–88.

information exchange including competitively sensitive information; data sharing or pooling discourages competitors from differentiating and improving their own data collection and analytics pipelines; or where the granting of access to data on terms that are not 'fair, reasonable and non-discriminatory' (FRAND) results in an exploitative abuse. Where a dominant, vertically integrated platform provides privileged data access to its own subsidiaries, this can constitute a form of self-preferencing (see above). Where a data pool has market power and gives its members a significant advantage, the pool may be under a duty to give access to others, perhaps on FRAND or similar terms.

The Report references the treatment of data access issues under Article 102 TFEU and merger control, as well as established rules on R&D agreements and patent pools, but notes that it may be more difficult to establish market power of a data pool based on market shares due to the multi-purpose use of data. Thus, an access regime may need to differ depending on the type of use, and the duty to give access should be proportional to the pool's market power. For example, a group of smaller players pooling their data to gain a competitive advantage should not be forced to give their pooled data to a much larger player. Where there is a FRAND or similar duty to provide data access, and the pool's data format standard is proprietary, the standard owner should not be able to raise its fees over time as the pool becomes more important in the market (by analogy to 'patent ambushes'), and such duties should apply to both access to the data pool and the use of the data format standard.

The Report notes that the competition law treatment of data sharing and pooling arrangements is relatively new and under-researched, and recommends that the EC use guidance letters and 'no infringement' decisions, as well as the next version of the EC's Guidelines on horizontal cooperation. Indeed, a separate a block exemption regulation on data sharing and pooling may be called for.

[C] Online Platforms

As with big data, antitrust enforcement against online platforms is a major focus of the Digital Era Report and the EC's thinking about antitrust policy in the digital sphere. Depending on how a blockchain is structured, the evolving policy on online platforms may result in enhanced antitrust scrutiny. Indeed, the Report takes a relatively broad view of the definition of an online platform, rejecting arguments for limiting the discussion to two- or multi-sided platforms. The Report's definition of platforms includes networks and goes beyond online intermediation to include desktop, mobile operating systems and browsers, 'offline' software, and app stores.

The Report notes that, especially in view of network effects, there might be room for only a limited number of 'platforms', especially in the absence of multi-homing, protocol and data interoperability, or differentiation. The Report discusses ways to protect competition both 'for the market' and 'in the market', arguing that platforms play a form of regulatory role as they determine the rules according to which their users interact, and, when they are dominant, have a responsibility to ensure that competition on their platforms is fair, unbiased, and pro-user. More specifically, the Report argues that dominant platforms have a responsibility to ensure that their rules ensure a level playing field. While non-dominant platforms also play a regulatory role, the Report argues, no far-reaching general rules would be needed for such platforms to the extent that they are disciplined by competition.

[1] Most Favoured Nations

The Digital Era Report discusses several specific issues in the online platform context, including the so-called most favoured nation (MFN) clauses, multi-homing, interoperability, transparency, leveraging and 'self-preferencing'.

The Report acknowledges the possible procompetitive benefits of MFNs but argues for strict scrutiny of such clauses because of their potential to protect platforms' incumbency advantages. In markets where there is a sufficiently vigorous competition between platforms, 'wide MFNs' that prevent sellers on a platform from price differentiating between platforms should be prohibited, while 'narrow MFNs' preventing sellers from offering lower prices on their own websites should be allowed. Where competition between platforms is weak, however, the Report argues that both forms of MFN should be prohibited.

[2] Multi-homing

The Digital Era Report also takes a nuanced approach to multi-homing. In general, the Report argues that any measure by which a dominant firm restricts multi-homing, including technical means and commercial practices such as fidelity rebates and bundling, should be suspect and such firms should bear the burden of providing a solid efficiency defence. On the other hand, the effects of multi-homing can be different when the competition is 'in the market' rather than 'for the market', and multi-homing between large platforms could actually limit competition.

[3] Interoperability

The Digital Era Report distinguishes between three types of interoperability: protocol interoperability, data interoperability, and full protocol interoperability. Protocol interoperability, which allows for the development of complementary services and competition on the merits, may require the development of standards, but such standards could hinder innovation if defined too strictly or too early. Data interoperability allows for complementary services to be developed in a larger range of cases than protocol interoperability. On the other hand, data interoperability can also limit incentives for new forms of data collection. Full protocol interoperability would involve the imposition of interoperability requirements to give direct competitors access to positive network effects stemming from the large user base of one platform extend to other platforms, but the need for strong Standardization with full protocol interoperability could significantly dampen platforms' ability to innovate. The Report argues for imposing duties to grant protocol interoperability and (with the concerned users' consent) data interoperability upon dominant platforms but urges great caution in imposing a duty to grant full protocol interoperability.

[4] Transparency

The Report argues that transparency can be a competition policy issue because a lack of transparency presumably distorts competition. Platforms' actions to prevent research, from technical measures purposely designed to prevent transparency to legal measures such as making studies contractually inadmissible, should be viewed with great suspicion. The Report concludes that the impact of platforms on society requires more transparency vis-à-vis civil society and that public authorities should find ways to ensure a sufficient understanding of how platforms work, potentially including full access to data and algorithms in the context of competition law cases.

[5] Leveraging

The Report argues that large platforms possess strong competitive advantages over new entrants, because of, *inter alia*, network externalities and privileged access to data, that translate into advantages in related services. If bundling is efficient thanks to the shared use of data, data interoperability can help to level the playing field. Enforcement should be especially strict where dominant platforms try to use consumers' data to bundle services and products.

[6] Self-Preferencing

According to case law, Article 102 TFEU may prohibit self-preferencing by the owner of an 'essential facility', and even below this threshold where it is not justified by a procompetitive rationale and is likely to result in a leveraging of market power. In other words: self-preferencing is not abusive per se but should be subject to an effects test. In markets with particularly high barriers to entry and where the platform serves as an intermediation infrastructure of particular relevance, the Report proposes that platforms should bear the burden of proving that self-preferencing has no long-run exclusionary effects on product markets. Full platform unbundling should not be the general remedy to a finding of abusive self-preferencing; however, less restrictive ways to preclude self-preferencing may exist.

[D] Article 102 TFEU and Blockchain

Given the growing use of blockchain to store large volumes of data on platforms accessible to select groups of industry participants and antitrust authorities' growing focus on big data and online platforms, companies adopting blockchain applications may need to consider potential abuse of dominance risks. The potential for blockchain applications to contribute to the EC or other authority finding that a blockchain operator has a dominant position or that particular blockchain-related conduct may be found to abuse a dominant position must clearly be considered on a case-by-case basis. Given the wide range of blockchain applications, a complete review of ways in which abuse of dominance issues may arise is beyond the scope of this chapter. Instead, this section discusses aspects of blockchain applications that may give rise to particular concern from this perspective and steps that participants can take to address them.

In blockchain applications, abuse of dominance issues may arise, in particular, where the format for information stored on the blockchain or the blockchain itself can be expected to become a de jure or de facto industry standard and/or where access to information stored on the blockchain may be considered essential to industry participants' ability to compete.

Where the blockchain format may become an industry standard, competitors may seek access to intellectual property (IP) needed to permit interoperability, such as an application programme interface (API), rather than to the data stored on the blockchain as such. The Report suggests a number of changes to existing EU legal tests that would make it easier for the EC to find an abuse in such a situation and to order remedies to encourage interoperability.

Where the data stored on a blockchain are themselves critical to stakeholders' competitiveness, those stakeholders may seek access to the underlying data on the ground that a refusal to provide access may amount to an abuse of a dominant position under Article 102 TFEU. The legal tests for such a remedy are, and will likely remain, very strict, and such cases can be expected to be rare. On the other hand, the Report supports changes to the existing EFD criteria to facilitate access to data remedies, not necessarily to direct competitors of the blockchain owners but more likely to would-be competitors in related or downstream markets.

'Online platform' related concerns may arise, in particular, in applications where a blockchain is operated by a company or group of companies that grant access to the blockchain to third parties for whom such access becomes important to their competitiveness. Although each situation will be highly fact-specific, issues may most likely arise where blockchain owner/operators adopt practices that have been singled out as potentially problematic, such as imposing MFNs on blockchain users; limiting third parties' freedom to use multiple blockchains; restricting interoperability to limit third parties' use of alternative blockchains; limiting transparency on the blockchain's operations, for instance as regards the blockchain's data access rules and algorithms; leveraging the competitive significance of the blockchain by bundling other products or services with blockchain access; and introducing a measure to give preference to goods and services offered by the blockchain owner/operator over those offered by third parties.

[E] Appropriate Safeguards

As with horizontal and vertical agreements, the enormous variety of situations in which blockchain and smart contracts can be used means that the potential for blockchain applications to raise abuse of dominance concerns must be assessed on a case-by-case basis. Such concerns arise, in principle, only where a party holds a dominant position in a relevant antitrust market, which would normally be the antitrust market in which the blockchain is proposed to be used. Care should also be taken where a blockchain will be, or has the potential to become, an industry-standard or otherwise become essential for competitors.

§8.04 MERGER CONTROL

[A] Introduction to Concepts

A variety of corporate transactions, including acquisitions of companies and joint ventures, may trigger merger filing requirements if relevant thresholds are met. The types of transaction that may be caught, as well as the applicable thresholds, vary considerably from jurisdiction to jurisdiction. At the EU level, the applicable requirements are set out in the EU Merger Regulation (EUMR),[36] but national measures at the Member State level may apply where a transaction is not caught by the EUMR.

Subject to exceptions, the EUMR applies to 'concentrations', defined as 'a change of control on a lasting basis [that] results from: (a) the merger of two or more previously independent undertakings or parts of undertakings, or (b) the acquisition, by one or more persons already controlling at least one undertaking, or by one or more undertakings, whether by purchase of securities or assets, by contract or by any other means, of direct or indirect control of the whole or parts of one or more other undertakings'.

'Control' is in turn defined 'the possibility of exercising decisive influence on an undertaking, in particular by: (a) ownership or the right to use all or part of the assets of an undertaking; (b) rights or contracts which confer decisive influence on the composition, voting or decisions of the organs of an undertaking'. The EC's Consolidated Jurisdictional Notice (the CJN) under the EUMR[37] clarifies that the concept of 'control' includes not only the positive power to determine a company's competitive policy, for instance through ownership of a majority of the company's shares but also the power to block certain actions, for example through veto rights of minority shareholders under a company's articles of incorporation or similar documents or applicable joint venture or shareholder agreements.

Creation of a joint venture qualifies as a 'concentration' where the joint venture performs 'on a lasting basis all the functions of an autonomous economic entity'; i.e., 'full-function' joint ventures.

Concentrations must be notified to the EC and approved prior to implementation if they meet the following thresholds: '(a) the combined aggregate worldwide turnover of all the undertakings concerned is more than EUR 2 500 million; (b) in each of at least

36. Council Regulation (EC) No 139/2004 of 20 January 2004 on the control of concentrations between undertakings, OJ L24, 29/1/2004, pp. 1-22.
37. Commission Consolidated Jurisdictional Notice under Council Regulation (EC) No 139/2004 on the control of concentrations between undertakings, OJ C95, 16/4/2008, pp. 1-48.

three Member States, the combined aggregate turnover of all the undertakings concerned is more than EUR 100 million; (c) in each of at least three Member States included for the purpose of point (b), the aggregate turnover of each of at least two of the undertakings concerned is more than EUR 25 million; and (d) the aggregate Community-wide turnover of each of at least two of the undertakings concerned is more than EUR 100 million, unless each of the undertakings concerned achieves more than two-thirds of its aggregate Community-wide turnover within one and the same Member State.'

Concentrations with a Community dimension must be notified to the EC and approved prior to their implementation. The EC must determine whether notified concentrations would 'significantly impede effective competition' in the EU or in a substantial part of it, 'in particular as a result of the creation or strengthening of a dominant position', in which case the EC must prohibit the transaction.

The interpretation and application of the EUMR have generated thousands of pages of commentary, and a full discussion of this topic is outside the scope of this chapter. I briefly discuss below three topics that are most likely to be of particular relevance to companies involved in blockchain applications: (i) the criteria for determining whether the formation of a new jointly owned blockchain will be considered 'full-function' and thus potentially as a concentration requiring EUMR review if the thresholds are met; (ii) actions that may be considered illegal implementation, or 'gun-jumping', if taken before approval is received under the EUMR; and (iii) the EC's evolving approach to assessing the competitive effects of combining big datasets, which may arise where two or more companies with existing blockchain applications merge.

[B] Full-Function Joint Ventures

The concept of full-functionality is discussed in Part IV of the CJN, paragraphs 91–109. The CJN clarifies that the formation of a full-function joint venture may constitute a notifiable concentration even where the joint venture is a 'greenfield operation' or the parties contribute their own assets to the joint venture, without the need for an acquisition of control over a company with pre-existing operations. The concept of full-functionality does not mean that the joint venture enjoys autonomy as regards the adoption of its strategic decisions. The issue is rather whether the joint venture is full-function in operational respects, i.e. it has sufficient resources to operate independently on the market; it performs activities beyond one specific function for the parents; it is not excessively dependent on sale/purchase relations with its parents beyond a start-up period; it is intended to operate on a lasting basis.

Where two or more companies cooperate in the establishment of a blockchain application, they will typically need to consider whether the blockchain (or a company formed to own and operate it) will give rise to a full-function joint venture. This may be the case, in particular, where a blockchain application is intended to provide services to third parties, not only to its parents, and will have sufficient resources (e.g., its own personnel) necessary to do so. If so, the EUMR thresholds can be met by the parents alone, even if the blockchain is created on a greenfield basis and has no turnover of its own. By contrast, a blockchain application that is owned and operated by one company, such as a supply chain management platform accessible to third-party suppliers, would normally not qualify as a full-function joint venture and would not be notifiable under the EUMR.

[C] Gun-Jumping

The term 'gun-jumping' is not clearly defined in the EUMR. In practice, it is used to indicate two distinct, but closely related, violations: (i) violation of the obligation under Article 4(1) EUMR to notify concentrations with a Community dimension and (ii) violation of the obligation under Article 7(1) EUMR not to implement a notifiable concentration either before its notification or until it has been approved by the EC. Similar provisions exist in most national merger control regimes.

In addition, if the parties to the transaction are competitors, inappropriate pre-closing conduct may be caught by Article 101(1) TFEU (and its national equivalents), which prohibits restrictive agreements, decisions and concerted practices. Competition authorities are often unclear about which rules to apply in a given case: gun-jumping or general antitrust rules. A 2018 judgment clarified that pre-approval actions contributing to a lasting change of control over the target can be sanctioned as gun-jumping, while conduct that falls short of contributing to such a change of control but constitutes anticompetitive coordination between the merging parties may be challenged under Article 101(1) TFEU.

The EC is demonstrating greater intolerance to breaches of procedural rules by merging parties, including in particular gun-jumping. The EC can impose fines up to 10% of companies' global group turnover for gun-jumping violations; in 2018, the EC imposed a fine of EUR 125 million on a French company, Altice.[38]

The clearest case of gun-jumping occurs where the parties implement a notifiable transaction without making a required notification. Such an error can be surprisingly easy to make under EU law, because some of the EUMR thresholds are relatively subjective or difficult to apply in practice, in particular in the case of minority investments in publicly listed companies and joint ventures, where it can be difficult to determine whether a transaction involves the acquisition of joint control or a creation of a full-function joint venture. So far, however, the EC has imposed fines in only four such cases.

Another form of gun-jumping occurs where a transaction is duly notified, but some form of premature implementation takes place prior to obtaining clearance. While most companies are aware of this prohibition, the line between legitimate preparatory measures and partial implementation is often unclear. Merging companies, therefore, often face questions about the exact extent of the standstill obligation.

38. Case M.7993 – Altice/PT Portugal, decision of 24/4/2018, available at: https://ec.europa.eu/competition/mergers/cases/decisions/m7993_849_3.pdf (accessed on 25 Feb. 2020)

Gun-jumping questions may arise in the context of mergers and acquisitions involving companies that operate blockchains, but in such cases, where the EUMR thresholds are met by the parties' turnover, those blockchain operations are less likely to be central to the gun-jumping issues. By contrast, gun-jumping issues may be critical where a blockchain, or company operating a blockchain, is being set up by two or more parents and the blockchain is likely to be full-function.

Merging companies, and companies creating a new joint venture must carefully assess their pre-closing actions on a case-by-case basis, particularly in relation to exchanges of competitively sensitive information, integration planning, management changes, coordination of competitive behaviour, and transfer of business risks associated with the target's business.

[D] Merger Control and Blockchain

The EC's substantive analysis of notified concentrations is, of course, highly fact-specific. It is not practical in this context to discuss all the substantive issues that typically arise in such review; such as the definition of the relevant markets; the assessment of the market positions of the parties and their competitors; and the assessment of the likely competitive effects of the combination of the parties' positions, whether they are direct competitors (horizontal issues) or have a customer-supplier relationship (vertical issues).

Given the role of blockchain in storing large quantities of data, however, one issue that has become increasingly important in recent years bears particular mention here: the EC's approach to analysing the effects of mergers resulting in the combination of big datasets.

The EC has a long track record of assessing the effect of notified mergers on data-related markets. The EC has analysed a wide range of data-related markets, from market research and marketing information services[39] to financial information,[40] to navigable digital map databases,[41] to online advertising.[42] In these cases, the EC's traditional tools for assessing the effects of a combination on horizontally and vertically affected markets can normally be applied in a straightforward way.

39. *See e.g.*, *VNU/AC Nielsen*, COMP/M.2291, dated 12.02.2001 available at: http://ec.europa.eu/competition/mergers/cases/decisions/m2291_en.pdf (accessed on 25 Feb. 2020) and WPP/TMS, COMP/M.5232, dated 23.09.2008, available at: http://ec.europa.eu/competition/mergers/cases/decisions/m5232_20080923_20212_en.pdf (accessed on 25 Feb. 2020).
40. *See e.g.*, *Thomson Corporation/Reuters*, COMP/M.4726, dated 19.02.2008, available at: http://ec.europa.eu/competition/mergers/cases/decisions/m4726_20080219_20600_en.pdf (accessed on 25 Feb. 2020).
41. For example, *TomTom/TeleAtlas*, Comp/M. 4854, dated 14.05.2008, available at: http://ec.europa.eu/competition/mergers/cases/decisions/m4854_20080514_20682_en.pdf (accessed on 25 Feb. 2020) and *Nokia/Navteq*, COMP/M 4942, dated 2.7.2008, available at: http://ec.europa.eu/competition/mergers/cases/decisions/m4942_20080702_20682_en.pdf (accessed on 25 Feb. 2020).
42. *See e.g.*, *Google/DoubleClick*, COMP/M.4731, dated 11.3.2008, available at: http://ec.europa.eu/competition/mergers/cases/decisions/m4731_20080311_20682_en.pdf (accessed on 25 Feb. 2020).

Recent debates on big data and antitrust, by contrast, focus on the antitrust implications of companies collecting and using big data that are not offered as a product on the market. The Franco/German Study opined that a combination of 'data troves could raise competition concerns if the combination of data makes it impossible for competitors to replicate the information (…)'[43] possessed by the merged entity.

In several recent decisions, the EC has elaborated on its approach to big data issues in merger review. These decisions help to illustrate the EC's approach and its attempts to fit big data issues into its traditional analytical frameworks, as set out in its Guidelines (the Horizontal Guidelines) on the assessment of horizontal mergers under the EUMR, its Guidelines (the Non-Horizontal Guidelines) on the assessment of non-horizontal mergers under the EUMR[44] and its Notice (the Remedies Notice) on remedies acceptable under the EUMR.[45] These decisions go a long way towards formalizing the EC's approach to assessing data-related aspects of notified mergers where the data are not themselves being offered to third parties as part of a product or service. This emerging approach is discussed below, first in relation to horizontal issues and then in relation to vertical issues.

In one leading case, *Verizon/Yahoo*, the EC noted[46] that '[a]ssuming data combination is allowed under the applicable data protection legislation, there are two main ways in which a merger may raise horizontal issues as a result of the combination, under the ownership of the merged entity, of two datasets previously held by two independent firms. First, the combination of two datasets post-merger may increase the merged entity's market power in a hypothetical market for the supply of this data or increase barriers to entry/expansion in the market for actual or potential competitors, which may need this data to operate on this market. Competitors may be required to collect a larger dataset in order to compete effectively with the merged entity than absent the merger. Second, even if there is no intention or technical possibility to combine the two datasets, it may be that pre-merger the two companies were competing with each other on the basis of the data they controlled and this competition would be eliminated by the merger.'

Concluding that the combination of the parties' data did not raise antitrust concerns, the EC noted the potential restrictions imposed by EU data protection rules and observed that the combination would not raise barriers to entry/expansion for other players since there would 'continue to be a large amount of internet user data that are valuable for advertising purposes and that are not within the Parties' exclusive control'. Indeed, the EC's market test confirmed that Yahoo's and Verizon's data were not 'unique'.

Since the EC has found no big data-related ground for concern as a result of the combination of big datasets, it has not been required to discuss potential theories of harm in detail.

43. Franco-German Study, *supra* n. 33.
44. OJ C 265/6, 18/10/2008, available at: http://eur-lex.europa.eu/legal-content/EN/TXT/PDF/?uri=CELEX:52008XC1018(03)&from=EN (accessed on 25 Feb. 2020).
45. OJ 267/1, 22/10/2008, available at: http://eur-lex.europa.eu/legal-content/EN/TXT/PDF/?uri=CELEX:52008XC1022(01)&from=EN (accessed on 25 Feb. 2020).
46. Paragraphs 81 et seq.

Compared to horizontal concerns, the EC's analytical framework appears better suited to dealing with big data concerns in a vertical context. Input foreclosure concerns are addressed in the Non-Horizontal Guidelines, and potential remedies for such concerns are discussed in the Remedies Notice. This is in line with the U.S. agencies' approach in focusing on vertical foreclosure issues where big data represented an important input to a downstream market.[47] The Franco/German Study also noted that a merger of companies holding 'strong market positions in separate upstream or downstream markets can foreclose these markets for new competitors', for instance, where an online service provider acquires 'producers of computers, smartphones or software in order to make sure to continue to access important amounts of data through users of these services'.[48]

According to the EC's Non-Horizontal Guidelines, a 'merger is said to result in foreclosure where actual or potential rivals' access to supplies or markets is hampered or eliminated as a result of the merger, thereby reducing these companies' ability and/or incentive to compete'. According to the EC, input foreclosure may occur in various forms. The merged entity may decide not to deal with its actual or potential downstream competitors, to restrict supplies, to raise prices to competitors and/or to otherwise make the conditions of supply less favourable (e.g., by degrading the quality of the input).

In assessing input foreclosure risks, the EC examines, first, whether the merged entity would have the ability to substantially foreclose access to inputs; second, whether it would have the incentive to do so; and third, whether a foreclosure strategy would have a significant detrimental effect on competition downstream. Concerns arise only if the input in question is important for the downstream product, for instance, because the input represents a significant cost factor or is important for other reasons.

According to the EC, a merged entity would only have the ability to foreclose if, by reducing access to its own upstream products or services, it could negatively affect the overall availability of inputs for the downstream market in terms of price or quality (e.g., because the remaining upstream suppliers are less efficient, offer less preferred alternatives, or lack the ability to expand output in response to the supply restriction) or due to the presence of exclusive contracts between the merged entity and independent input providers. Input foreclosure is only a concern where the merged firm has significant market power in the upstream market so that its conduct can be expected to significantly influence competition in the upstream market and thus, possibly, prices and supply conditions in the downstream market.

The incentive to foreclose depends on the degree to which foreclosure would be profitable. The merged entity faces a trade-off between the profit lost in the upstream market due to a reduction of input sales to (actual or potential) rivals and the profit

47. *See., e.g.*, Statement of the Fed. Trade Commission, in the Matter of Nielsen Holdings N.V. and Arbitron Inc., File No. 131-0058 at 1 (20 Sep. 2013); *see also*, Mc Sweeney, T. and O'Dea, B., *Data, Innovation, and Potential Competition in Digital Markets – Looking Beyond Short-Term Price Effects in Merger Analyst* (CPI Antitrust Chronicle, February 2018).

48. Franco-German Study, *supra* n. 33, at 16.

gain, in the short or long term, from expanding sales downstream or, as the case may be, being able to raise prices to consumers. Other things being equal, a merged entity is more likely to have an incentive to foreclose where the upstream margins are low, and the downstream margins are high. The merged firm's incentives also depend on the share of demand that may be diverted from downstream rivals to the merged entity.

In general, input foreclosure concerns may lead to a challenge when input foreclosure would lead to increased prices in the downstream market or raise barriers to entry to potential competitors, in particular, if input foreclosure would entail for such potential competitors the need to enter at both the downstream and the upstream level in order to compete effectively. Conversely, concerns may be rebutted if there are sufficient credible downstream competitors whose costs would likely not be raised, countervailing factors such as buyer power or the likelihood that entry upstream would maintain effective competition and efficiencies.

According to the Remedies Notice, concerns that competition may be significantly impeded by foreclosure can be addressed by 'commitments granting non-discriminatory access to infrastructure or networks of the merging parties' or 'information necessary for the interoperability of different equipment' where 'the control of key technology or IP rights may lead to concerns of foreclosure of competitors which depend on the technology or IP rights as essential input for the activities in a downstream market.'[49] Similarly, concerns that a merger may eliminate players' incentives to license patents may be eliminated by commitments to grant licenses on the same basis post-transaction to all third parties which depend on the IPRs or information for their activities.

In a number of recent cases, the EC has applied the analysis of input foreclosure effects to concerns about access to big data in the merger context. In *Microsoft/LinkedIn*, certain software solutions providers claimed that LinkedIn 'full data' would, in future, constitute an important input for the provision of advanced functionalities of customer relationship management (CRM) software. One complainant, in particular, argued that Microsoft could restrict access to LinkedIn full data, thereby making it harder for other providers to compete and to bring innovation in the market. The EC noted that LinkedIn did not generally make available LinkedIn full data to third parties pre-transaction, and the complaint assumed that, absent the transaction, LinkedIn would have started monetizing such data. The EC questioned that assumption but nonetheless analysed whether Microsoft would have had the ability and incentive to reduce competition by restricting access to LinkedIn full data to downstream competitors. Microsoft argued that LinkedIn full data were not an important input and that alternative data were available from other vendors.

The EC considered that the transaction would not have given Microsoft the ability to foreclose competition since reducing access to LinkedIn full data would be unlikely to negatively affect the overall availability of data needed by downstream competitors, in part because LinkedIn did not appear to have a significant degree of market power

49. *Supra* n. 45, paras 64–65.

in any potential relevant upstream market, which in this case would be a hypothetical market or segment for the provision of data.

In addition, the EC considered that LinkedIn full data could not be characterized as (and would not be likely to become in the next two to three years) an important input, since all major CRM vendors had already started offering advanced functionalities or planned to do so in the next two to three years, without access to LinkedIn full data. Furthermore, even if LinkedIn full data were to be used for that purpose, it would constitute only one of the many types of data needed and many other possible sources of data were already available.

Moreover, the EC considered that it was unclear whether Microsoft would have had the incentive to foreclose competing providers of CRM software solutions by restricting access to LinkedIn full data. The EC noted that the market investigation was inconclusive and that it was not clear to what extent any such foreclosing strategy would be profitable for Microsoft (since it was not possible to estimate what profits Microsoft would derive by licensing LinkedIn full data).

As regards the impact of a foreclosure strategy on the downstream market, the EC considered that the transaction was unlikely to have an overall negative impact on effective competition in the market for CRM software solutions, and any potential restriction of access to LinkedIn full data would be unlikely to lead to consumer harm since any impact would be felt in sub-segments representing less than 30% of the entire CRM software solutions market, and LinkedIn was only one of multiple data sources required. Therefore, it was unlikely that competing CRM software providers would be hampered in their ability to compete and innovate, or that the mere likelihood that Microsoft would carry out a foreclosure strategy would raise barriers to entry for potential competitors.

The analysis of big data-related input foreclosure concerns has tended to track the EC's traditional approach as set out in its Guidelines more closely than its analysis of horizontal issues. In *Microsoft/LinkedIn*, in particular, the EC closely tracked the Non-Horizontal Guidelines analysis of the merged entity's alleged incentive and ability to foreclose downstream competitors' access to data as an input, taking account of the parties' strength in upstream and downstream markets. The EC considered foreclosure effects in a 'hypothetical' market since the concerns were based on an unproven assumption that without the transaction LinkedIn would have attempted to monetize its full data by selling it to downstream competitors. The EC itself noted the theoretical difficulties with this approach; it is hard to see how the EC could meet its burden to show that a notified transaction would create the incentive and ability to foreclose the supply of data to competitors where the data have not been supplied by either merging party in the past, there is no course of dealing to measure the profitability of such a strategy, and the data in question has by definition not previously been a key input for competitors.

Future decisions may clarify how the EC will apply its analytical framework for vertical issues to big data, where the data are not already available as an input to competitors. The EC should also consider potential anticompetitive effects in view of the characteristics of the data in question. Again, the cases in which these issues have arisen involve first-party data (often personal data) collected by companies on their customers for use (or potential use) in online advertising. As noted, such data are the type most commonly considered to be non-rivalrous and ubiquitous, as acknowledged by the EC in calling such data a 'commodity.' Such data is also more likely – depending on the use case – to suffer from diminishing returns and to decline rapidly in value. Where the value of particular data is likely to be short-lived, it may be more appropriate to consider the potential foreclosure impact of the merging parties' sources for generating new data, as opposed to the combination of existing datasets. By contrast, where merging companies' data may have longer-lasting value, such as for developing and improving a platform's own online advertising algorithms or other products (e.g., spell-check programs or voice recognition software), incremental data may have decreasing marginal value, which would likely limit the competitive impact of combining the merging parties' data. The EC would also need to take account of non-data alternatives to address relevant needs. For example, if competitors can license a suitable algorithm from a software developer, access to a particular dataset to develop its own software may be less relevant.

In conclusion, though the EC has been less vocal on big data issues than some national authorities, it has developed a significant track record in examining big data-related concerns in the merger context. Most of the older decisions concerned data-related markets; i.e., markets in which the data in question were themselves the product market. More recently, the EC has started to explicate its approach to big data concerns where the merging parties collect large amounts of data in their business but do not offer such data to third parties as a product. Given the EC's focus on big data, future cases may delve into these issues in more detail. Novel issues are most likely to arise in relation to combinations of first-party data (i.e., data collected or inferred by the merging parties themselves), in particular data on consumers.

[E] Appropriate Safeguards

Once again, the EU and other merger review implications of a proposed transaction must be assessed on a case-by-case basis. EU and other antitrust authorities assess proposed mergers and acquisitions to estimate their likely impact on competition in relevant antitrust markets, i.e. the products and services offered by the parties. Whether, and if so, how those parties use blockchains will often be irrelevant to the review of a proposed transaction. However, the EU and other authorities are increasingly concerned about the competitive significance of data. Where merging parties control (or have access to) blockchains with significant datasets, authorities are likely to consider whether and to what extent the parties' combination is likely to affect others' ability to compete. Together with their antitrust counsel, merging parties should consider the potential competitive significance of their data along with their review of the market overlaps of their products and services.

FURTHER READING

Jacques Crémer, Yves-Alexandre de Montjoye and Heike Schweitzer, *Competition Policy for the Digital Era*, available at: https://ec.europa.eu/competition/publications/reports/kd0419345enn.pdf (accessed on 16 March 2020)

Digital Competition Expert Panel, *Unlocking Digital Competition – Report of the Digital Competition Expert Panel*, available at: https://assets.publishing.service.gov.uk/government/uploads/system/uploads/attachment_data/file/785547/unlocking_digital_competition_furman_review_web.pdf (accessed on 16 March 2020)

Ariel Ezrachi and Maurice E. Stucke, *Virtual Competition – The Promise and Perils of the Algorithm-Driven Economy* (Harvard University Press, 2016).

Renato Nazzini, *The Blockchain (R)evolution and the Role of Antitrust* (King's College London Law School Research Paper No. 2019-20, 28 September 2018), available at: https://ssrn.com/abstract=3256728 or http://dx.doi.org/10.2139/ssrn.3256728 (accessed on 16 March 2020)

Maurice E. Stucke and Alan Grune, *Big Data and Competition Policy* (Oxford University Press, 2016)

Bibliography

Akgiray, Vedat, *Blockchain Technology and Corporate Governance*, Report fort the Organisation for Economic Co-operation and Development, OECD doc. no. DAF7CA/CG/RD(2018)1/REV1 (6 June 2018) 12, available at http://www.oecd.org/officialdocuments/publicdisplaydocumentpdf/?cote = DAF/CA/CG/RD(2018)1/REV1&doclanguage = en

Alkhalifah, A., Ng, A., Kayes, A.S.M., Chowdhury, J., Alazab, M. and Watters, P., *A Taxonomy of Blockchain Threats and Vulnerabilities* (2019), available at https://www.preprints.org/manuscript/201909.0117/v1/download

American Bar Association, *Another Bad Blockchain Bill*, available at https://www.americanbar.org/groups/business_law/publications/committee_newsletters/cyberspace/2019/201905/blockchain

Arning, Alexander and Rothkegel, Tobias *Art. 4 DSGVO*, in *DSGVO, BDSG* (Taeger/Gabel eds, 3rd. ed., R&W, 2019)

Article 29 Data Protection Working Party, *Guidelines 04/2017 on Data Protection Impact Assessment (DPIA) and determining whether processing is "likely to result in a high risk" for the purposes of Regulation 2016/679* (WP 248, adopted on 04 April 2017)

Article 29 Data Protection Working Party, *Opinion 03/2013 on purpose limitation* (WP 203, adopted on 02 April 2013), available at https://ec.europa.eu/justice/article-29/documentation/opinion-recommendation/files/2013/wp203_en.pdf

Article 29 Data Protection Working Party, *Opinion 05/2012 on Cloud Computing* (WP 196, adopted on 01 July 2012), available at https://ec.europa.eu/justice/article-29/documentation/opinion-recommendation/files/2012/wp196_en.pdf

Article 29 Data Protection Working Party, *Opinion 05/2014 on Anonymisation Techniques* (WP 216, adopted on 10 April 2014), available at https://www.pdpjournals.com/docs/88197.pdf

Article 29 Data Protection Working Party, *Opinion 06/2014 on the notion of legitimate interests of the data controller under Article 7 of the Directive 95/46/EC* (WP 217, adopted on 14 November 2014)

Article 29 Data Protection Working Party, *Opinion 1/2010 on the Concepts of "Controller" and "Processor"* (WP 169, adopted on 16 February 2010), available at https://ec.europa.eu/justice/article-29/documentation/opinion-recommendation/files/2010/wp169en.pdf

Article 29 Data Protection Working Party, *Opinion 03/2010 on the principle of accountability* (WP 173 00062/10/EN, adopted on 13 July 2010), available at http://ec.europa.eu/justice/policies/privacy/docs/wpdocs/2010/wp173_en.pdf

Artzt, Matthias, *Is Blockchain Compatible with the GDPR?* (18 June 2019), available at https://platform.dataguidance.com/opinion/eu-blockchain-compatible-gdpr-part-1

Artzt, Matthias, *Territorial scope of the GDPR from the US Perspective* (26.06.2018), available at https://iapp.org/news/a/territorial-scope-of-the-gdpr-from-a-us-perspective/

Atzori, Marcella, *Blockchain Technology and Decentralized Governance: Is the State Still Necessary?* (University College of London, 2015), available at https://papers.ssrn.com/sol3/papers.cfm?abstract_id=2709713

Bacon et al., *Blockchain Demystified: A Technical and Legal Introduction to Distributed and Centralised Ledgers* (25 Richmond Journal of Law and Technology 1, 2018)

Badr, Shaimaa, Gomaa, Ibrahim, Abd-Elrahman, Emad, *Multi-tier Blockchain Framework for IoT-EHRs Systems* (141 Procedia Computer Science 159-166, 2018), available at https://www.sciencedirect.com/science/article/pii/S187705091831812X/pdf?md5=a019303c3f8b4d28728c53bbbe80807f&pid=1-s2.0-S187705091831812X-main.pdf

Balthazor, Andrew, *The Bona Fide Acquisition Rule Applied to Cryptocurrency* (Georgetown Law Technology Review, May 2019)

Basel Committee on Banking Supervision, *Discussion paper: Designing a prudential treatment for crypto-assets* (December 2019), available at https://www.bis.org/bcbs/publ/d490.pdf

Beck, Roman, Müller-Bloch, Christoph and King, John Leslie, *Governance in the Blockchain Economy: A Framework and Research Agenda* (19(10) *Journal of the Association for Information Systems* Article 1 1021, 2018), available *at: https://aisel.aisnet.org/jais/vol19/iss10/1*

Bekeschenko, Edward, Determann, Lothar, Perevalov, Vadim and Wood, Inna, *Keep Russian Data in Russia and Out of Clouds?* (32(6) Computer & Internet Lawyer 1, 2015)

Berberich M. and Steiner M. *Blockchain Technology and the GDPR – How to Reconcile Privacy and Distributed Ledgers?* (European Data Protection Law Review 422, 2016)

Berg, Alastair, *The Identity, Fungibility, and Anonymity of Money* (10 July 2018), https://ssrn.com/abstract=3211011 or http://dx.doi.org/10.2139/ssrn.3211011

Bericht und Antrag der Regierung an den Landtag des Fürstentums Liechtenstein betreffend die Schaffung eines Gesetzes über Token und VT-Dienstleister (Token- und VT-Dienstleister-Gesetz; TVTG) und die Abänderung weiterer Gesetze, Nr. 54/2019, 55; available at https://impuls-liechtenstein.li/wp-content/uploads/2019/12/Bericht-und-Antrag-TVTG.pdf

Bermuda Digital Business Act 2018, Section 2, available at http://www.bermudalaws.bm/laws/Annual%20Laws/2018/Acts/Digital%20Asset%20Business%20Act%202018.pdf

Bertram, Ute, *Smart Contracts – Praxisrelevante Fragen zu Vertragsabschluss, Leistungsstörungen und Auslegung* 1416 (MDR 2018)

Bill to amend the Code of Virginia by adding a section numbered 8.01-390.4, relating to business records electronically registered on a blockchain self-authenticating, A, available at https://leg1.state.va.us/cgi-bin/legp504.exe?191+ful+HB2415&191+ful+HB2415

Blockchain Bundesverband, *Blockchain, Data Protection, and the GDPR* (Blockchain Bundesverband e.V., v. 1.0, 25.05.2018)

Blockchain Bundesverband, *Statement on Token Regulation with a Focus on Token Sales* (2019), https://bundesblock.de/wp-content/uploads/2019/01/180209_Statement-Token-Regulation_blockchain-bundesverband.pdf

Blockchain Strategy of the Federal Government, *We Set Out the Course for the Token Economy* (18 September 2019) 4, available at https://www.bmwi.de/Redaktion/EN/Publikationen/Digitale-Welt/blockchain-strategy.pdf?__blob=publicationFile&v=3

Bont, Patrick, *Kryptowährungen – und was machen die Regulatoren?* (Handout to the speech held on 26 October 2017, Liechtenstein FMA, 2017), available at https://www.fma li.li/files/fma/fma-digital-banking-liechtenstein.pdf

Botschaft zum Bundesgesetz zur Anpassung des Bundesrecht an Entwicklungen der Technik verteilter elektronischer Register (2019), 7 (1.1.3, III.), available at https://www.newsd.admin.ch/newsd/message/attachments/59301.pdf

Boyd, Thomas M., *How a Rich Californian Hijacked the Legislature – Threatened with a Ballot Initiative, Lawmakers Pass a Ruinous Data-Privacy Law* (The Wall Street Journal, 04/07/2018), available at www.wsj.com/articles/how-a-rich-californian-hijacked-the-legislature-1530723133

Bremann, Nils Lennart, *Smart Contracts im Einsatz* (DSRITB 2019, 299)

Bullmann, Dirk and Klemm, Jonas & Pinna, Andrea, *In Search for Stability in Crypto-Assets: Are Stablecoins the Solution?*, 230 Occasional Paper Series of the European Central Bank (August 2019), available at https://www.ecb.europa.eu/pub/pdf/scpops/ecb.op230~d57946be3b.en.pdf

Buocz et al., *Bitcoin and the GDPR: Allocating Responsibility in Distributed Networks* (Computer Law & Security Review 2019)

Canadian Securities Administrators, *CSA Staff Notice* (46-307 Cryptocurrency Offerings, 2017), available at https://www.osc.gov.on.ca/documents/en/Securities-Category4/csa_20170824_cryptocurrency-offerings.pdf

CSA Staff Notice (46-308 Securities Law Implications for Offerings of Tokens, 2018), available at https://www.osc.gov.on.ca/documents/en/Securities-Category4/csa_20180611_46-308_implications-for-offerings-of-tokens.pdf

Chander, Anupam, *How Law Made Silicon Valley* (63 Emory Law Journal 639, 2014), available at https://ssrn.com/abstract=2340197

Commission Nationale de l'Informatique et de Libertés (6 November 2018) *Blockchain and the GDPR: Solutions for a Responsible use of the Blockchain in the Context of Personal Data*, available at https://www.cnil.fr/en/blockchain-and-gdpr-solutions-responsible-use-blockchain-context-personal-data

Communication from the Commission, FinTech Action plan: *For a more competitive and innovative European financial sector* COM(2018)109 final (8 March 2018), available at https://www.europarl.europa.eu/doceo/document/TA-8-2018-0373_EN.html?redirect

Communiqué of the G20 Finance Ministers & Central Bank Governors Meeting 22-23 February 2020, Riyadh, Saudi Arabia, at 3, available at https://g20.org/en/g20/Documents/Communique%CC%81%20Final%2022-23%20February%202020.pdf

Copeland, Rory, *FCA Final Guidance on Crytoassets: Jettisoning Tech-neutrality?*, Oxford Business Law Blog (23 September 2019), available at https://www.law.ox.ac.uk/business-law-blog/blog/2019/09/fca-final-guidance-cryptoassets-jettisoning-tech-neutrality

Crémer, Jacques, de Montjoye, Yves-Alexandre and Schweitzer, Heike, *Competition Policy for the Digital Era* (2019), available at https://ec.europa.eu/competition/publications/reports/kd0419345enn.pdf

Cusa, Emanuele, *Le quote di s.r.l. possono essere valori mobiliari* (Rivista delle societa, 4/2019, 675 - 694)

Solove, Dan and Schwartz, Paul, *Privacy Law Fundamentals* (IAPP, 2019)

Solove, Dan and Schwartz, Paul. *Information Privacy Law* (6th ed., Aspen Publishing Co., 2018)

De Filippi, Primavera and Hassan, Samer, Blockchain Technology as a Regulatory Technology: From Code Is Law to Law is Code, 12 First Monday 21 (2016) 1, available at https://arxiv.org/ftp/arxiv/papers/1801/1801.02507.pdf

De Filippi, Primavera and Wright, Aaron, *Blockchain and the Law – The Rule of Code* (2018) 193

Deloitte, *2019 Global Blockchain Survey*, available at https://www2.deloitte.com/content/dam/Deloitte/se/Documents/risk/DI_2019-global-blockchain-survey.pdf

Deloitte, *Blockchain @ Media – A New Game Changer for the Media Industry?*, available at https://www2.deloitte.com/content/dam/Deloitte/tr/Documents/technology-media-telecommunications/deloitte-PoV-blockchain-media.pdf

Determann, Lothar and Gupta, Chetan, *Indian Personal Data Protection Act of 2018: Draft Bill and Its History, Compared to GDPR and California Privacy Law* (Berkeley Journal of International Law 481, 2019)

Determann, Lothar and Lorenz, Manuel, *FinTech: Ground Rules and Checklist for Starting Up and Going Global* (BNA's Banking Report, 27/11/2017)

Determann, Lothar and Lorenz, Manuel, *Fintechs im Dschungel der Regulierungen* (Börsenzeitung, 01/04/2017)

Determann, Lothar and Sprague, Robert, *Intrusive Monitoring: Employee Privacy Expectations are Reasonable in Europe, Destroyed in the United States* (26 Berkeley Technology Law Journal 979, 2011)

Determann, Lothar and Weigl, Michaela, *Data Residency Requirements Creeping into German Law* (Bloomberg BNA Privacy & Security Law Report, 15 PVLR 529 - 03/14/2016)

Determann, Lothar and zu Guttenberg, Karl-Theodor, *On War and Peace in Cyberspace: Security, Privacy, Jurisdiction* (41 Hastings Constitutional Law Quarterly, 1, 13, 2014)

Determann, Lothar, *Adequacy of Data Protection in the USA: Myths and Facts* (International Data Privacy Law 2016)

Determann, Lothar, *Broad Data and Business Regulation, Applicable Worldwide* (IAPP Advisor, 02/07/2018), available at https://iapp.org/news/a/analysis-the-california-consumer-privacy-act-of-2018/

Determann, Lothar, *California Privacy Law, Practical Guide and Commentary – U.S. Federal and California Law* (IAPP 3rd ed. 2018)

Determann, Lothar, *Data Residency Rules Cutting Into Clouds: Impact and Options for Global Businesses and IT Architectures* (Bloomberg BNA Data Privacy & Security Law Report, 16 PVLR 496 - 04/03/2017)

Determann, Lothar, *Datenschutz auf Kalifornisch* (FAZ v. 11.7.2018)

Determann, Lothar, *Determann's Field Guide to Data Privacy Law – International Corporate Compliance* (Edward Elgar Publishing Ltd. 4th ed. 2020)

Determann, Lothar, *Healthy Data Protection*, 26 Michigan Technology Law Review (2020)

Determann, Lothar, *New California Data Security and Breach Notification Requirement* (Bloomberg BNA Privacy & Security Law Report, 15 PVLR 219, 02/01/2016)

Determann, Lothar, *No One Owns Data* (70 Hastings Law Journal 1, 2018)

Determann, Lothar, *Privacy and Data Protection.* ***КОНФИДЕНЦИАЛЬНОСТЬ И ЗАЩИТА ПЕРСОНАЛЬНЫХ ДАННЫХ*** (Moscow Journal of International Law 1, 2019)

Determann, Lothar, *Social Media @ Work 2014* (BNA/Bloomberg Social Media Law & Policy Report, 2 SMLR 49, 12/17/2013)

Determann, Lothar, *Social Media Privacy – A Dozen Myths and Facts* (2012 Stanford Technology Law Review 7, 2012)

Determann, Lothar, *US-Datenschutzrecht – Dichtung und Wahrheit* (Neue Zeitschrift für Verwaltungsrecht 2016, 561)

Determann, Lothar, *California Privacy Rights Ballot Initiative: Business, Watch this Space* (The Recorder, 22 May 2020)

Dewey, Josias N., *Blockchain & Cryptocurrency Regulation 2020* (Global Legal Insights, 23 October 2019)

Digital Competition Expert Panel, *Unlocking Digital Competition – Report of the Digital Competition Expert Panel* (March 2019), available at https://assets.publishing.service.gov.uk/government/uploads/system/uploads/attachment_data/file/785547/unlocking_digital_competition_furman_review_web.pdf

DiMatteo, Larry A., Cannarsa, Michel and Poncibo, Christina, *The Cambridge Handbook of Smart Contracts, Blockchain and Technology and Digital Platforms* (Cambridge, 2019)

Ekblaw, A. et al., *A Case Study for Blockchain in Healthcare: "MedRec" Prototype for Electronic Health Records and Medical Research Data* (IEEE Technology and Society Magazine, 2016)

Estonian Financial Supervisory Authority, *Information for Entities Engaging with virtual Currencies and ICOs*, available at https://www.fi.ee/en/investment/aktuaalsed-teemad-investeerimises/virtuaalraha-ico/information-entities-engaging-virtual-currencies-and-icos

Estonian Financial Supervisory Authority, *The Legal Framework of Initial Coin Offering in Estonia*, available at https://www.fi.ee/en/investment/aktuaalsed-teemad-investeerimises/virtuaalraha-ico/legal-framework-initial-coin-offering-estonia

Estonian Ministry of Finance, *Analysis for Developing a Policy for the Possible Recognition and Use of Virtual Currencies*, available at https://www.rahandusministeerium.ee/et/system/files_force/document_files/2016-vv_virtuaalvaaringute_analuus-22-07.pdf?download = 1

European Banking Authority, Discussion paper on the EBA's approach to financial technology (FinTech), EBA/DP/2017/02 (4 August 2017) n. 8, available at https://eba.europa.eu/sites/default/documents/files/documents/10180/1919160/7a1b9cda-10ad-4315-91ce-d798230ebd84/EBA%20Discussion%20Paper%20on%20Fintech%20%28EBA-DP-2017-02%29.pdf?retry = 1

European Commission, *Blockchain Now and Tomorrow – Assessing Multidimensional Impacts of Distributed Ledger Technologies* (Joint Research Center of the European Commission, July 2019)

European Commission, *Commission Consolidated Jurisdictional Notice under Council Regulation (EC) No 139/2004 on the Control of Concentrations Between Undertakings* (OJ C95, 16/4/2008, pp. 1-48)

European Commission, *Commission Notice – Guidelines on Vertical Restraints* (SEC, 2010, 411), available at https://ec.europa.eu/competition/antitrust/legislation/guidelines_vertical_en.pdf

European Commission, *Commission Regulation No 330/2010 on the application of Article 101(3) of the Treaty on the Functioning of the European Union to categories of vertical agreements and concerted practices* (Official Journal L102, 23/4/2010, pp. 1-7)

European Commission, *Communication from the Commission – Guidance on the Commission's Enforcement Priorities in Applying Article 82 of the EC Treaty to Abusive Exclusionary Conduct by Dominant Undertakings* (OJ C45, 24/0/2/2012, pp. 7-20)

European Commission, *Communication from the Commission — Guidelines on the Applicability of Article 101 of the Treaty on the Functioning of the European Union to Horizontal Co-operation Agreements* (OJ 54, 14/1/2011, pp. 1-70)

European Council, *Council Regulation (EC) No 139/2004 of 20 January 2004 on the Control of Concentrations Between Undertakings* (OJ L24, 29/1/2004, pp. 1-22)

European Data Protection Board, *Draft Guidelines 2/2019 on the Processing of Personal Data under Art. 6(1)(b) of the GDPR* (adopted on 9 April 2019)

European Data Protection Board, *Guidelines 4/2019 on Article 25 Data Protection by Design and by Default* (Plenary Meeting November 2019, adopted on 13 November 2019)

European Data Protection Supervisor and the Agencia espanola proteccion datos, *Introduction to the Hash Function as a Personal Data Pseudonymisation Technique* (October 2019), available at https://edps.europa.eu/data-protection/our-work/publications/papers/introduction-hash-function-personal-data_en

European Fintech Alliance, *Regulatory Sandboxes* (16 December 2018), available at https://fintech-alliance.eu/regulatory-sandboxes

European Parliament, Resolution of 3 October 2018 on distributed ledger technologies and blockchains: building trust with disintermediation, (2017/2772(RSP), n. 65 and 68), available at https://www.europarl.europa.eu/doceo/document/TA-8-2018-0373_EN.html?redirect

European Parliamentary Research Service, *Blockchain and the General Data Protection Regulation – Can Distributed Ledgers Be Squared with European Data Protection Law?* (Scientific Foresight Unit, July 2019)

European Securities and Markets Regulator, *Advice Initial Coin Offerings and Crypto-Assets* (2019), available at https://www.esma.europa.eu/sites/default/files/library/esma50-157-1391_crypto_advice.pdf

European Securities and Markets Regulator, *Guidelines on the Key Concepts of the AIFMD*, available at https://www.esma.europa.eu/sites/default/files/library/2015/11/2013-611_guidelines_on_key_concepts_of_the_aifmd_-_en.pdf

Federal Trade Commission, The Financial Privacy Requirements of the Gramm-Leach-Bliley Act, available at https://www.ftc.gov/tips-advice/business-center/guidance/brief-financial-privacy-requirements-gramm-leach-bliley-act

Felten, E., *Does Hashing Make Data 'Anonymous'* (22 April 2018), available at https://www.ftc.gov/news-events/blogs/techftc/2012/04/does-hashing-make-data-anonymous

Financial Conduct Authority, *Guidance on Cryptoassets* (Consultation Paper CP19/3 January 2019) para. 3.14, available at https://www.fca.org.uk/publication/consultation/cp19-03.pdf

Finck, Michèle, *Blockchain – Regulation and Governance in Europe* (Cambridge University Press, 2018)

Finck, Michèle, *Blockchains and Data Protection in the European Union* (Max Planck Institute for Innovation & Competition Research Paper No. 18-01, 30 November 2017), available at https://edpl.lexxion.eu/data/article/12327/pdf/edpl_2018_01-007.pdf

Finck, Michèle, Moscon, Valentina, *Copyright Law on Blockchains: Between New Forms of Rights Administration and Digital Rights Management 2.0* (ILC 2019, 50, 77–108)

Finnish Financial Supervisory Authority, Fintech Counsel, *Regulations and Guidelines 4/2019 – Virtual Currency Providers* (14 June 2019, FIVA 12/01.00/2019)

Fischer, Michael J., Lynch, Nancy A., Paterson, Michael S., *Impossibility of Distributed Consensus with One Faulty Process* (J. ACM 32, 2, April 1985), 374-382, available at http://dx.doi.org/10.1145/3149.214121

Fotiou, Nikos and Polyzos, George C., *Smart Contracts for the Internet of Things: Opportunities and Challenges* (Department of Informatics, School of Information Sciences and Technology Athens, University of Economics and Business, 23 January 2019), available at https://arxiv.org/pdf/1901.10582.pdf

Freiwald, Susan, *First Principles of Communications Privacy* (Stanford Technology Law Review 3, 2007)

FRS Energy Florence School of Regulation, *Blockchain meets Energy, Digital Solutions for Decentralized and Decarbonized Sector*, available at https://fsr.eui.eu/wp-content/uploads/Blockchain_meets_Energy_-_ENG.pdf

Fuchs, Andreas, *Wertpapierhandelsgesetz* (C.H. Beck, 2nd ed., 2016)

Gatteschi, Valentina et al., *Blockchain and Smart Contracts for Insurance: Is the Technology Mature Enough?*, available at https://www.the-digital-insurer.com/wp-content/uploads/2018/07/1243-futureinternet-10-00020-v2-1.pdf

Geis, George S., *Traceable Shares and Corporate Law* (Virginia Public Law and Legal Theory Research Paper No. 2018-13, 2-50), available at SSRN: https://papers.ssrn.com/sol3/papers.cfm?abstract_id = 3129042&download = yes

Gerard, David, *Attack of the 50-Foot Blockchain: Bitcoin, Blockchain, Ethereum & Smart Contracts* (2017)

German Federal Financial Supervisory Authority, *Initial Coin Offerings: Hinweisschreiben zur Einordnung als Finanzinstrumente* (WA 11-QB 4100-2017/0010, 2017), available at https://www.bafin.de/SharedDocs/Downloads/DE/Merkblatt/WA/dl_hinweisschreiben_einordnung_ICOs

German Federal Financial Supervisory Authority, *Merkblatt – Hinweise zu den Tatbeständen des Eigenhandels und des Eigengeschäfts* (2019), available at https://www.bafin.de/SharedDocs/Veroeffentlichungen/DE/Merkblatt/mb_110322_eigenhandel_eigengeschaeft_neu.html

German Federal Financial Supervisory Authority, *Prospektpflicht - Rechtslage seit dem 21.07.2019* (Verlautbarung, geändert am 5.8.2019), available at https://www.bafin.de/DE/Aufsicht/Prospekte/Wertpapiere/Prospektpflicht/prospektpflicht_node.html

German Federal Financial Supervisory Authority, *Zweites Hinweisschreiben zu Prospekt- und Erlaubnispflichten im Zusammenhang mit der Ausgabe sogenannter Krypto-Token* (2019), https://www.bafin.de/SharedDocs/Downloads/DE/Merkblatt/WA/dl_wa_merkblatt_ICOs.html

German Federal Ministry of Justice and Consumer Protection, *Eckpunkte für die regulatorische Behandlung von elektronischen Wertpapieren und Krypto-Token* (2019), available at https://www.bundesfinanzministerium.de/Content/DE/Gesetzestexte/Gesetze_Gesetzesvorhaben/Abteilungen/Abteilung_VII/19_Legislaturperiode/2019-03-07-Eckpunktepapier-Wertpapiere-Krypto-Token/2019-03-07-Eckpunktepapier-regulatorische-Behandlung-elektronische-Wertpapiere-Krypto-Token.pdf;jsessionid = D5779523DB71FD407E8FE439C0A5C0D3?__blob = publicationFile&v = 7

German Government, *Blockchain-Strategie der Bundesregierung* (2019), available at https://www.bmwi.de/Redaktion/DE/Publikationen/Digitale-Welt/blockchain-strategie.pdf?blob = publicationFile&v = 10

González-Meneses, Manuel, *Entender Blockchain. Una introducción a la tecnología de registro distgribuido* (Thomson Reuters Aranzadi, 2nd ed., 2019)

Government of Canada, *Regulations Amending Certain Regulations Made under the Proceeds of Crime (Money Laundering) and Terrorist Financing Act, 2019* (SOR/2019-240, 2019), available at http://www.gazette.gc.ca/rp-pr/p2/2019/2019-07-10/html/sor-dors240-eng.html

Government of Germany, *Gesetzesentwurf der Bundesregierung, Finanzmarkt-Richtlinie-Umsetzungsgesetz* available at (Drucksache 16/4028 53, 2007)

Government of Germany, *Regierungsentwurf eines Gesetzes zur Umsetzung der Änderungsrichtlinie zur Vierten EU-Geldwäscherichtlinie RL (EU) 2018/843* (2018), available at https://www.bundesfinanzministerium.de/Content/DE/Gesetzestexte/Gesetze_Gesetzesvorhaben/Abteilungen/Abteilung_VII/19_Legislaturperiode/2019-05-24-Gesetz-4-EU-Geldwaescherichtlinie/0-Gesetz.html

Government of Liechtenstein, *Bericht und Antrag der Regierung an den Landtag des Fürstentums Liechtenstein betreffend die Schaffung eines Gesetzes über Token und VT-Dienstleister (Token- und VT-Dienstleistergesetz; TVTG) und die Abänderung weiterer Gesetze, Bericht und Antrag Nr. 54/2019* (2019), available at https://impuls-liechtenstein.li/wp-content/uploads/2019/06/bua_054_2019_tvtg.pdf

Government of Liechtenstein, *Stellungnahme der Regierung an den Landtag des Fürstentums Liechtenstein zu den anlässlich der ersten Lesung betreffend die Schaffung eines Gesetzes über Token und VT-Dienstleister (Token- und VT-Dienstleistergesetz; TVTG) und die Abänderung weiterer Gesetze aufgeworfenen Fragen, Bericht und Antrag Nr. 93/2019* (2019), available at https://www.llv.li/files/srk/bua_093_2019_stellungnahme-tvtg.pdf

Governor Lael Brainard from the U.S. Federal Reserve System on '*Update on Digital Currencies, Stablecoins, and the Challenges Ahead*' (18 December 2019), available at https://www.federalreserve.gov/newsevents/speech/brainard20191218a.htm

Greenberg, Brad A., *Rethinking Technology Neutrality* (207 Minnesota Law Review, 1495 2016), available at https://www.minnesotalawreview.org/wp-content/uploads/2016/04/Greenberg_ONLINEPDF.pdf

Gresham, Josh, *Is Encrypted Data Personal Data under the GDPR?* (06 March 2019), available at https://iapp.org/news/a/is-encrypted-data-personal-data-under-the-gdpr/

Grinhaus, Aaron, *A Practical Guide to Smart Contracts and Blockchain Law* (LexisNexis Canada, 21 March 2019)

Gyr, Eleonor, *Blockchain und Smart Contracts – Die vertragsrechtlichen Implikationen einer neuen Technologie* (Dissertation, Basel, 2019), available at https://biblio.unibe.ch/download/eldiss/19gyr_e.pdf

Habersack, Mathias, *Münchener Kommentar zum Bürgerlichen Gesetzbuch* (C.H. Beck, 6 A, 7th ed. 2017)

Heckelmann, Martin, *Zulässigkeit und Handhabung von Smart Contracts* (NJW 2018, 504)

Hileman Garrick and Rauchs, Michael, *Global Blockchain Benchmarking Study* (2017) 20, available at https://www.ey.com/Publication/vwLUAssets/ey-global-blockchain-benchmarking-study-2017/$FILE/ey-global-blockchain-benchmarking-study-2017.pdf

Hinmann, Bill, *Statement on 'Framework for 'Investment Contract' Analysis of Digital Assets* (2019), available at https://www.sec.gov/news/public-statement/statement-framework-investment-contract-analysis-digital-assets

Hinmann, William, *Digital Asset Transactions: When Howey Met Gary (Plastic), Remarks at the Yahoo Finance All Markets Summit: Crypto* (2018), available at https://www.sec.gov/news/speech/speech-hinman-061418

Hirsch, R. and Deixler, H., Final HIPAA Omnibus Rule Brings Sweeping Changes to the Health Care Privacy Law: HIPAA Privacy and Security Obligations Extended to Business Associates and Subcontractors (BNA Privacy and Security Law Report, 12 PVLR 168, 2013)

Houben Robby and Snyers, Alexander, *Cryptocurrencies and Blockchain, Legal Context and Implications for Financial Crime, Money Laundering and Tax Evasion*, Study requested by the TAX3 committee (July 2018), 15, available at http://www.europarl.europa.eu/cmsdata/150761/TAX3%20Study%20on%20cryptocurrencies%20and%20blockchain.pdf

Ibáñez, L-D., O'Hara, K. and Simperl, E., *On Blockchains and the General Data Protection Regulation*, available at https://eprints.soton.ac.uk/422879/1/BLockchains_GDPR_4.pdf

Information Commissioner's Office, *Deleting Personal Data* (26 February 2014), available at https://ico.org.uk/media/fororganisations/documents/1475/deleting_personal_data.pdf

International Swaps and Derivatives Association, Legal Guidelines for Smart Derivatives Contracts (January 2019), available at https://www.isda.org/a/MhgME/Legal-Guidelines-for-Smart-Derivatives-Contracts-Introduction.pdf

Jentzsch, Christoph, *The History of the DAO and Lessons Learned* (slock.it Blog, 24 August 2016), available at https://blog.slock.it/the-history-of-the-dao-and-lessons-learned-d06740f8cfa5

Joint Canadian Securities Administrators/Investment Industry Regulatory Organization of Canada, *Consultation Paper 21-402 – Proposed Framework for Crypto-Asset Trading Platforms* (2019), available at https://www.osc.gov.on.ca/en/SecuritiesLaw_csa_20190314_21-402_crypto-asset-trading-platforms.htm

Jünemann, Michael and Wirtz, Johannes, *ICO: Legal Classification of Tokens: Part 1 – Utility Token* (2019), available at https://www.twobirds.com/en/news/articles/2019/global/ico-legal-classification-of-tokens-utility-token

Jünemann, Michael and Wirtz, Johannes, *ICO: Legal Classification of Tokens: Part 2 – Security Token* (2019), available at https://www.twobirds.com/en/news/articles/2019/global/ico-legal-classification-of-tokens-2

Jünemann, Michael and Wirtz, Johannes, *ICO: Legal Classification of Tokens: Part 3 – Currency Token* (2019), available at https://www.twobirds.com/en/news/articles/2019/global/ico-legal-classification-of-tokens-3

Kaal, Wulf A., *Blockchain-Based Corporate Governance* (University of St. Thomas/Minnesota, Legal Studies Research Paper No. 19-10, 1-43), available at SSRN: https://papers.ssrn.com/sol3/papers.cfm?abstract_id=3441904

Kalss, Susanne, Oppitz, Martin and Zollner, Johannes, *Kapitalmarktrecht* (2nd ed., 2015)

Kasprzyk, Karolina, *The Concept of Smart Contracts from the Legal Perspective* (Review of European and Comparative Law, No. 3, 2018)

Kaulartz, Markus and Heckmann, Jörn, *Smart Contracts – Anwendungen der Blockchain-Technologie* 618 (Computer Report 9/2016)

Koch, Philipp, *Die Tokenisierung von Rechtspositionen als digitale Verbriefung* 359 (ZBB 2018)

Koch, Rüdiger, *Neue Regeln für Wertpapierprospekte* (2019), available at https://www.bafin.de/SharedDocs/Veroeffentlichungen/DE/Fachartikel/2019/fa_bj_1906_Wertpapierprospekte.html

Kumpan, Christoph, *Kapitalmarktrecht* (4th ed., 2010)

Lafarre, Anne and Van der Elst, Christoph, *Blockchain Technology for Corporate Governance and Shareholder Activism* (SSRN Electronic Journal, January 2018) 1-26, available at https://www.researchgate.net/publication/324670400_Blockchain_Technology_for_Corporate_Governance_and_Shareholder_Activism

Lautennschläger, Sabine, *A Supervisory Perspective on 2019 and Beyond* (Speech in Dublin, Ireland, 17 January 2019), available at https://www.ecb.europa.eu/press/key/date/2019/html/ecb.sp190117.en.html

Lessig, Lawrence, *Code Version 2.0* 124-25 (2006), available at http://codev2.cc/download+remix/Lessig-Codev2.pdf

Liechtenstein FMA, *Faktenblatt 'Initial Coin Offering'* (2019), available at https://www.fma-li.li/files/fma/fma-faktenblatt-ico.pdf

Liechtenstein FMA, *FMA-Mitteilung 2019/2 – Pflichten für Emittenten von Wertpapieren und Security Token* (2019), available at https://www.fma-li.li/files/list/fma-mittteilung-2019-2-emittenten-wp-st.pdf

Liechtenstein FMA, *Liste gebilligte Prospekte bis 20. Juli 2019 and Liste gebilligte Prospekte ab 21. Juli 2019* (2019), available at http://register.fma-li.li/index.php?id=277

Lopez, David, and Farooq, Bilal, *A Multi-layered Blockchain Framework for Smart Mobility Data-Markets* (arXiv preprint arXiv:1906.06435, 2019), available at https://arxiv.org/pdf/1906.06435.pdf

Lorente Howell, Jose Luis, *Aprobado el Anteproyecto de Ley para la Transformación Digital del Sistema Financiero* (Actualidad Jurídica Aranzadi, 2019)

Lorente Howell, Jose Luis, *Una regulación flexible adaptada al entorno 'FinTech'* (Actualidad Jurídica Aranzadi, 2018)

Low, Kelvin and Mik, Eliza, *Unpicking a Fin(e)tech Mess: Can Old Doctrines Cope in the 21st Century?* (2019), available at https://www.law.ox.ac.uk/business-law-blog/blog/2019/11/unpicking-finetech-mess-can-old-doctrines-cope-21st-century

Lupu, Ruxandra, *Zulässigkeit, Handhabung und rechtliche Grenzen bei der Gestaltung von Smart Contracts* 209 (DSRITB 2019)

Magnier, Véronique, Barban, Patrick, *Blockchain et droit des sociétés* (2019)

Mann, Maximilian, *Die Decentralized Autonomous Organization – ein neuer Gesellschaftstyp?*, 1024 (NZG 2017)

Martini/Weinzierl, *Die Blockchain-Technologie und das Recht auf Vergessenwerden*, 1251 (Neue Zeitschrift für Verwaltungsrecht 2017)

Maume, Philipp and Fromberger, Mathias, *Regulation of Initial Coin Offerings: Reconciling U.S. and E.U. Securities Laws* (19(2) Chicago Journal of International Law 2019)

Mayer, R., Butler, J. and Molnia, D., *Das US-Patent: Erwirkung und Durchsetzung unter besonderer Berücksichtigung der Rechtsprechung* (Annex 8, 5th ed., 2017)

Mc Sweeney, T. and O'Dea, B., *Data, Innovation, and Potential Competition in Digital Markets – Looking Beyond Short-Term Price Effects in Merger Analyst* (CPI Antitrust Chronicle February 2018)

Mlynar, Theodore J., Fettman and Robert, M., *Blockchain and Smart Contracts Will Change the Face of Insurance in the U.S.*, available at https://www.lexology.com/library/detail.aspx?g=b119f47b-764b-464c-9090-89b8e6e58219

Moeslein, Florian, *Smart Contracts im Zivil- und Handelsrecht* 254 (ZHR 2019)

Momtaz, Paul P., Rennertseder Kathrin and Schröder, Henning, *Token Offerings: A Revolution in Corporate Finance?* (49 The Capco Institute Journal of Financial Transformation 2019)

Moro Visconti, Roberto, *Blockchain Valuation: Internet of Value, Digital Networks and Smart Transactions* (2019), available at https://www.researchgate.net/publication/329916782_Blockchain_Valuation_Internet_of_Value_digital_networks_and_smart_transactions

Myers, John, Ulloa, Jazmine, *California Lawmakers Agree to New Consumer Privacy Rules That Would Avert Showdown on the November Ballot* (Los Angeles Times, 21/06/2018), available at www.latimes.com/politics/la-pol-ca-privacy-initiative-legislature-agreement-20180621-story.html#

Nägele, Thomas, Bergt, Josef, *Kryptowährungen und Blockchain-Technologie im liechtensteinischen Aufsichtsrecht* (Liechtensteinische Juristenzeitung, Number 2, 2019)

Nakamato, Satoshi, *Bitcoin: A Peer-to-Peer Electronic Cash System*, available at https://bitcoin.org/bitcoin.pdf

Nisbet K, *The False Allure of Hashing for Anonymization* (30 April 2018), available at https://gravitational.com/blog/hashing-for-anonymization/

NIST, *Blockchain Technology Overview* (NISTIR 8202, 2018)

O'Hara, Claire, *High-Net-Worth Investors Now Able to Hold Bitcoin Fund in Registered Accounts*, The Globe and Mail (2018), available at https://www.theglobeandmail.com/investing/globe-wealth/article-high-net-worth-investors-now-able-to-hold-bitcoin-in-registered/

Olegario, Rowena, Credit-Reporting Agencies: Their Historical Roots, Current Status, and Role in Market Development, available at http://siteresources.worldbank.org/INTWDRS/Resources/477365-1257315064764/2429_olegario.pdf

Ontario Securities Commission, *Decision in the Matter of the Securities Legislation of Ontario and in the Matter of the Process for Exemptive Relief Applications in*

Multiple Jurisdictions and in the Matter of Token Funder Inc. (2017), available at https://www.osc.gov.on.ca/en/SecuritiesLaw_ord_20171023_token.htm

Ontario Securities Commission (40(34) OSC Bulletin 2017), available at https://www.osc.gov.on.ca/documents/en/Securities-OSCB/20170824_oscb_4034_toc.pdf

Onza, Maurizio and Salomone, Luigi, *Prodotti, strumenti finanziari, valori mobiliari, in Commentario del codice civile* (Delle promesse unilaterali, dei titoli di credito, 2015)

Oppenheim, Robert and Romba, Eric, *Initial Coin Offering (ICO) aus rechtlicher Sicht: Der Token als digitale Urkunde?* (IT Finanzmagazin, 2018), available at https://www.it-finanzmagazin.de/initial-coin-offering-ico-rechtliche-sicht-token-digitale-urkunde-65569/

Paech, Philipp, *Law and Autonomous Systems Series: What Is a Smart Contract?* (University of Oxford, 9 July 2018), available at https://www.law.ox.ac.uk/business-law-blog/blog/2018/07/law-and-autonomous-systems-series-what-smart-contract

Papadodimas, Georgios, Palaiokrasas, Georgios, Litke, Antonios and Vavarigou, Theodora, *Implementation of Smart Contracts for Blockchain Based IoT Applications* (Electrical and Computer Engineering Department, National Technical University of Athens, Greece), available at http://bloomen.io/wp-content/uploads/2018/11/ICCS-nof2018.pdf

Paulmayer, Stefan, *Die kapitalmarktrechtliche Einordnung von Token*, in: Kirchmayr-Schliesselberger, Sabine et al. (ed.), *Kryptowährungen* 317 (Nomos 2019)

Paulus, Christoph and Matzke, Robin, *Smart Contracts und Smart Meter – Versorgungsperre für Fernzugriff* 1905 (NJW 2018)

Paulus, David and Matzke, Robin, *Smart Contracts und das BGB – Viel Lärm um nichts?* 431 (ZfPW 2018)

Payne, Bryan D. and Edwards, W. Keith, *A Brief Introduction to Usable Security* (Georgia Institute of Technology Published by the IEEE Computer Society, May/June 2008)

Pekler, Florian, Rirsch, Ralph, *Ausgewählte kapitalmarktrechtliche Aspekte bei der Emission von Crypto-Assets*, in: Kirchmayr-Schliesselberger, Sabine et al. (ed.), *Kryptowährungen* 333 (2019)

Poldma, Jaak, *Dragged to the U.S: Courts (Part 1): Jurisdiction and the Location of Blockchain Nodes*, available at https://blogs.orrick.com/blockchain/dragged-to-the-u-s-courts-part-1-jurisdiction-and-the-location-of-blockchain-nodes

Popper, Nathaniel, *Digital Gold: The Untold Story of Bitcoin* (2016)

Prenafeta Rodríguez, Javier, *Debe cumplir la emisión de criptomonedas y tokens la normativa de mercado de valores?* (Colegio Universitario de Estudios Financieros, Trabaljo Fin de Grado, 2019), available at https://www2.abogacia.es/publicaciones/blogs/blog-nuevas-tecnologias/debe-cumplir-la-emision-de-criptomonedas-y-tokens-la-normativa-de-mercado-de-valores/

Pricewaterhouse Coopers, *Initial Coin Offerings, A Strategic Perspective* (2018), available at https://www.pwc.ch/en/publications/2018/20180628_PwC%20S&%20CVA%20ICO%20Report_EN.pdf

Prosser, William, Privacy (48 California Law Review 383, 1960)

Queen Mary University of London, Centre for Commercial Law Studies, *Triggering Innovation How Smart Contracts Bring Policies to Life,* available at https://www.lloyds.com/~/media/files/news-and-insight/risk-insight/2019/triggering-innovation---how-smart-contracts-bring-policies-to-life.pdf

Rappard, Matthew and Skeith, Zachary, *Smart Contracts 101 – From a Technical to a Legal Understanding* (2019)

Raskin, Max, *Realm of the Coin: Bitcoin and Civil Procedure* (20(4) Fordham Journal of Corporate and Financial Law 2015)

Raskin, Max, *The Law and Legality of Smart Contracts* (1 Georgetown Law Technology Review 304, 2017)

Reidenberg, Joel R., *Lex Informatica: The Formulation of Information Policy Rules through Technology* (76 Texas Law Review 553, 555, 1997-1998)

Report of the European Union Blockchain Observatory and Forum, *Blockchain and the GDPR* (16 October 2018), available at https://www.eublockchainforum.eu/reports

Report of the European Union Blockchain Observatory and Forum, *Legal and Regulatory Framework of Blockchains and Smart Contracts* (27 September 2019), available at https://www.eublockchainforum.eu/sites/default/files/reports/report_legal_v1.0.pdf

Reyes, Carla L., *Conceptualizing Cryptolaw* (96 Nebraska Law Review 384, 400 2017), available at https://digitalcommons.unl.edu/cgi/viewcontent.cgi?article=3121&context=nlr

Reyes, Carla L., *Moving Beyond Bitcoin to an Endogenous Theory of Decentralized Ledger Technology Regulation: An Initial Proposal* (61 Villanova Law Review 202-203, 2016)

Richter, Thomas, *Blockchain – Rechtliche Aspekte aus Sicht der Finanzindustrie* (DGRI Jahrbuch 2017, v. Briner, Robert G. and Funk, Axel (ed.) 2018) 165-178

Riehm, Thomas, *Rechtshandbuch Smart Contracts* (Tom Braegelmann and Markus Kaulartz, eds, C.H. Beck 2019)

Robinson II, Randolph *The New Digital Wild West: Regulating the Explosion of Initial Coin Offerings* (85 Tennessee Law Review 897 2018), available at: https://ssrn.com/abstract=3087541

Robinson, Jeffrey, *BitCon: The Naked Truth about Bitcoin* (Amazon Digital Services, 2014)

Rodrigues, Usha R., *Law and Blockchain* (104 Iowa Law Revew 679, 682, 2019), available at https://ilr.law.uiowa.edu/print/volume-104-issue-2/law-and-the-blockchain

Rulli, Edoardo, *Incorporazione senza res e dematerializzazione senza accentratore: appunti sui token, in Rivista Orizzonti del diritto commerciale* (La Rivista, 2019), available at http://www.rivistaodc.eu/incorporazione-senza-res-dematerializzazione-token

Saad, M., Spaulding, J., Njilla, L., Kamhoua, C., Shetty, S., Nyang, D. and Mohaisen, A., *Exploring the Attack Surface of Blockchain: A Systematic Overview* (arXiv preprint arXiv:1904.03487, 2019), available at https://arxiv.org/pdf/1904.03487.pdf

Safran and Desai, *Cybersecurity and the Human Element: We're All Fallible* (DarkReading, 12 February 2019), available at https://www.darkreading.com/careers-and-people/cybersecurity-and-the-human-element-were-all-fallible-/a/d-id/1333789

Saive, David, *Rückabwicklung von Blockchain-Transaktionen* 371 (DSRITB 2018)

Salmon, John and Myers, Gordnon, *Blockchain and Associated Legal Issues for Emerging Markets*, 4 (Emerging Markets Compass Note 63, January 2019), available at https://www.ifc.org/wps/wcm/connect/da7da0dd-2068-4728-b846-7cffcd1fd24a/EMCompass-Note-63-Blockchain-and-Legal-Issues-in-Emerging-Markets.pdf?MOD = AJPERES&CVID = mxocw9F

Saluste, Kadi, *Tokenite kvalifitseerimine Eesti õiguse alusel ning kehtiva õiguse sobivus ICO-de reguleerimiseks* (Juridica, June 2018), 390-399

Savelyev, A., *Contract Law 2.0: 'Smart' Contracts as the Beginning of the End of Classic Contract Law* (Information & Communications Technology Law, 116, 2017)

Sayeed, Sarwar an Marco-Gisbert, Hector, *Assessing Blockchain Consensus and Security Mechanisms Against the 51% Attack* (9 Appl. Sci. 1788, 2019), https://doi.org/10.3390/app9091788

Schäfer, Sernetz, *Kommentar zu Kreditwesengesetz, VO (EU) Nr. 575/2013 (CRR) und Ausführungsvorschriften* (1 A, 5th ed., 2016)

Schawe, Nadine, *Blockchain und Smart Contracts in der Kreativwitrschaft – mehr Probleme als Lösungen?* 218 (MMR 2019)

Schrepel, Thibaut, *Is Blockchain the Death of Antitrust Law? The Blockchain Antitrust Paradox* (3 Georgetown Law Technology Review 281, 2019), available at https://papers.ssrn.com/sol3/papers.cfm?abstract_id = 3193576

Schrey, Joachim, Thalhofer, Thomas, *Rechtliche Aspekte der Blockchain*, 1431 (NJW 2017)

Schwartz, Paul, *Preemption and Privacy* (118 Yale Law Journal 902, 910 *et seq.*, 2009)

Serwin, Andrew B. *Information Security and Privacy: A Guide to Federal and State Law and Compliance* (2019-2020 ed.)

Serwin, Andrew, *The Federal Trade Commission and Privacy: Defining Enforcement And Encouraging Adoption of Best Practices* (48 San Diego Law Review 809, 2011)

Sherborne, Andreas, *Blockchain Smart Contracts and Laywers* (International Bar Association, December 2017)

Shikai, Yuriko Mary, *Applying the California Translation Act to Consumer Agreements* (Los Angeles Lawyer September 2012, 11–15)

Siibak, Kadri, *Mõningad virtuaalrahaga seotud õiguslikud probleemid, Juridica* (2015)

Song, Alfred H., Oral History Interview (California State Archives State Government Oral History Program), available at http://archives.cdn.sos.ca.gov/oral-history/pdf/song.pdf

Spada, Paolo, *Introduzione al diritto dei titoli di credito* (Tesi in Diritto, Documenti circolanti, Turin, passim.), available at https://www.tesiindiritto.com/tesi-in-diritto/riassunti-diritto/pdf/introduzione_al_diritto_dei_titoli_di_credito_paolo-spada.pdf

Spanish Central Bank and Spanish Stock Market Commission, Joint press statement by CNMV and Banco de España on'cryptocurrencies' and 'initial coin offerings'

(2018), available at http://www.cnmv.es/Portal/verDoc.axd?t = {6f310cc7-6b39 -4405-a8f7-70d2b1e682d1}

Spanish Ministry of Economy, *Proyecto de Ley de medidas para la transformación digital del sistema financiero* (2019)

Spindler, Gerald and Schuster, Fabian (eds), *Recht der elektronischen Medien* (München, C.H. Beck, 4th ed. 2019)

Spindler, Gerald, *Initial Coin Offerings und Prospektpflicht und -haftung* 2109 (Wertpapier Mitteilungen 2018)

Swiss Federal Council, *Bericht des Bundesrates 'Rechtliche Grundlagen für Distributed Ledger Technologie und Blockchain in der Schweiz' (Federal Council report 'legal framework for distributed ledger technology and blockchain in Switzerland')* (2018), https://www.newsd.admin.ch/newsd/message/attachments/55153.pdf

Swiss Federal Council, *Botschaft zum Bundesgesetz zur Anpassung des Bundesrechts an Entwicklungen der Technik verteilter elektronischer Register (Report on the draft regarding amendments to Swiss federal law in connection with the developments with the distributed ledger technology)* (2019), available at https://www.admin.ch/opc/de/federal-gazette/2020/233.pdf

Swiss Financial Market Supervisory Authority (FINMA), *Circular 2018/1 'Organised trading facilities'* (2018)

Swiss Financial Market Supervisory Authority (FINMA), *Guidance 02/2019, 'Payments on the Blockchain'* (2019), available at https://www.finma.ch/en/news/2019/08/20190826-mm-kryptogwg/

Swiss Financial Market Supervisory Authority (FINMA), *Guidelines Regarding the Regulatory Framework for ICOs of 16 February* (2018), available at https://www.finma.ch/en/news/2018/02/20180216-mm-ico-wegleitung/

Swiss Financial Market Supervisory Authority (FINMA), *Supplement to the Guidelines for Enquiries Regarding the Regulatory Framework for Initial Coin Offerings (ICOs)* (2019), https://www.finma.ch/en/news/2019/09/20190911-mm-stablecoins/

Szczerbowski, Jakub, *Lex Cryptographia. Znaczenie prawne umów i jednostek rozliczeniowych opartych na technologii blockchain* (2018)

Tai, Stefan, Jacob Eberhardt, Klems, Markus. *Not ACID, not BASE, but SALT* (Proceedings of the 7th International Conference on Cloud Computing and Services Science, SCITEPRESS-Science and Technology Publications, 2017), available at http://www.ise.tu-berlin.de/fileadmin/fg308/publications/2017/2017-tai-eberhardt-klems-SALT.pdf

Tendon, Steve and Ganado, Max, *Legal Personality for Blockchains, DAOs and Smart Contracts* (1 RTDF 1 2018) 1, see n. 5

Teubner, Gunther, *Digitale Rechtssubjekte? Zum privatrechtlichen Status autonomer Softwareagenten*, 218 AcP 155-205 (2018)

The Financial Action Task Force (FATF), *FATF Recommendations* (2019), available at http://www.fatf-gafi.org/publications/fatfrecommendations/?hf = 10&b = 0&s = desc(fatf_releasedate)

The Monetary Authority of Singapore, *Guide to Digital Token Offerings* (2019), available at https://www.mas.gov.sg/regulation/explainers/a-guide-to-digital-token-offerings

The Monetary Authority of Singapore, *Guidelines on the Regulation of Markets Guideline No. SFA02-G01* (2005), available at https://www.mas.gov.sg/-/media/MAS/resource/legislation_guidelines/securities_futures/sub_legislation/Guidelines_Regulation_of_Markets.pdf

The Monetary Authority of Singapore, *Response to Feedback Received on the Proposed Payment Services Bill* (2018), available at https://www.mas.gov.sg/-/media/MAS/resource/publications/consult_papers/2017/Response-to-Feedback-Received-on-Proposed-Payment-Services-Bill-MAS-P0212017.pdf

The Spanish Stock Market Commission, *CNMV Considerations on Cryptocurrencies and ICOs Addressed to Market Professionals* (2018), available at http://www.cnmv.es/Portal/verDoc.axd?t={62395018-40eb-49bb-a71c-4afb5c966374}

The Spanish Stock Market Commission, *Criteria in Relation to ICO* (2018), available at http://cnmv.es/DocPortal/Fintech/CriteriosICOsEN.pdf

The Spanish Stock Market Commission, *Portal FinTech / Portal de Innovación* (2019), available at https://www.cnmv.es/portal/Fintech/Innovacion.aspx?lang=es

The Spanish Stock Market Commission, *Questions and Answers Intended for FinTech Companies on Activities and Services That May Be Related to the CNMV, Sec. 6.4* (2019), available at https://www.cnmv.es/docportal/Legislacion/FAQ/QAsFinTech_EN.pdf

Thematic Report of the European Blockchain Observatory and Forum, *Legal and Regulatory Framework of Blochains and Smart Contracts,* 7 (27 September 2019), available at https://www.eublockchainforum.eu/sites/default/files/reports/report_legal_v1.0.pdf

Timmons, John and Hickman, Tim, *Blockchain and the GDPR: Co-existing in contradiction* (Blockchain & Cryptocurrency Regulation, Global Legal Insights, 2nd ed., 2020)

Todd, Ross, *Courthouse Steps Listening Devices Not Illegal* (The Recorder, 25/07/2016)

Trail of Bits Blog, *Ten Rules for the Secure Use of Cryptocurrency Hardware Wallets* (27 November 2018), available at https://blog.trailofbits.com/2018/11/27/10-rules-for-the-secure-use-of-cryptocurrency-hardware-wallets/

Tulsidas, Tanash Utamchandani, *Smart Contracts from a Legal Perspective* (University of Alicante, Faculty of Law, 2018), available at https://pdfs.semanticscholar.org/370b/bc9f7af31fa01a8f61276d2a67591d22680e.pdf

U.S. Securities and Exchange Commission, *Framework for 'Investment Contract' Analysis of Digital Assets* (2019), available at https://www.sec.gov/corpfin/framework-investment-contract-analysis-digital-assets

U.S. Securities and Exchange Commission, *Release No. 81207, 2017 Report of Investigation Pursuant to Section 21(a) of the Securities Exchange Act of 1934: The DAO* (2017), available at https://www.sec.gov/litigation/investreport/34-81207.pdf

UK Government Chief Scientist Adviser, *Distributed Ledger Technology, beyond Blockchain* (2016), available at https://assets.publishing.service.gov.uk/government

/uploads/system/uploads/attachment_data/file/492972/gs-16-1-distributed-ledger-technology.pdf

UK ICO, *Anonymisation: Managing Data Protection Risk Code of Practice*, available at https://ico.org.uk/media/1061/anonymisation-code.pdf

UK Jurisdiction Taskforce, *Legal Statement on Cryptoassets and Smart Contracts* (The LawTech Delivery Panel, November 2019)

van Valkenburgh, Peter, *What Could 'Decentralization' Mean in the Context of the Law?* (15 June 2018), available at https://coincenter.org/entry/what-could-decentralization-mean-in-the-context-of-the-law

Vannini, Marco, Detotto, Claudio and Mccannon, Bryan, *Ransom Kidnapping* (2015)

Varul, Paul, Anu, Avi and Triin, Kivisild, *Restrictions on Active Legal Capacity*, Juridica International IX (2004), available at https://www.juridicainternational.eu/public/pdf/ji_2004_1_99.pdf

Veil, Rüdiger, *Token-Emissionen im europäischen Kapitalmarktrecht* 183 (Zeitschrift für das gesamte Handels- und Wirtschaftsrecht 2019)

Veil, Winfried, *The Emperor's New Clothes - On the Structural Shortcomings of Both the Old and the New Data Protection Law* 686 (Neue Zeitschrift für Verwaltungsrecht 2018)

Vidal, Maria, Olivares, Jose Maria, Gutierrez Campiña, Sara, Ferrer, Jorge, *FinTech. Chapter for Spain* (Chambers Global Practice Guide, 2019)

Völkel, Oliver, *Initial Coin Offerings aus kapitalmarktrechtlicher Sicht* 103 (ZTR 2017)

Vos Sir, Geoffrey, *LawTech, Smart Contracts and Artificial Intelligence* (Speech at the German Bundesministerium für Justiz und Verbraucherschutz at 14 May 2019), available at https://www.judiciary.uk/wp-content/uploads/2019/05/CHC-speech-LawTech-Smart-Contracts-and-Artificial-Intelligence.pdf

Wang, Gang, Zhijie Jerry Shi, Nixon, Mark and Song Han, *SoK: Sharding on Blockchain* (1st ACM Conference on Advances in Financial Technologies, 21–23 October 2019), available at https://doi.org/10.1145/3318041.3355457

Wehowsky, Ralf, *Becksche Kurz Kommentar* (Erbs/ Kohlhaas, ed., Strafrechtliche Nebengesetze, Band 1, 228th ed. 2020)

Weiß, Hagen, *Tokenisation* (BaFin Journal, 2019), available at https://www.bafin.de/dok/12477346

West, Katherine, *Where Is Blockchain: Jurisdictional Issues That May Affect Distributed Ledgers*, available at https://www.lexology.com/library/detail.aspx?g=35f40e2e-38d8-49d7-81ca-9872d8ab9532

Wilkens, Robert and Falk, Richard, *Smart Contracts – Grundlagen, Anwendungsfelder und rechtliche Aspekte* (Springer Gabler 2019)

Wilsch, Harald, *Die Blockchain-Technologie aus der Sicht des deutschen Grundbuchrechts* 761 (Deutsche Notarzeitung 2017)

Wilsch, Harald, *The German 'Grundbuchordnung': History, Principles and Future about Land Registry in Germany* 224 (Zeitschrift für Geodäsie, Geoinformation und Landmanagement, 2012)

Woebbeking, Maren K., *The Impact of Smart Contracts on the Traditional Concepts of Contract Law* (10, 2019, JIPITEC 105 paragraph 1), available at https://www.jipitec.eu/issues/jipitec-10-1-2019/4880

Zepf, Tobias, *Blockchain, Technologie, Innovationen und Anwendungen - oder eine Kette, die Ketten sprengt* (Bachelor Thesis, 2016)

Zickgraf, Peter, *Initial Coin Offerings - Ein Fall für das Kapitalmarktrecht?* 293 (Die Aktiengesellschaft 2018), available at https://doi.org/10.9785/ag-2018-630903

Zimmerman, Evan Joseph, *Machine Minds: Frontier in Legal Personhood* (12 February 2015) 35-41, available at https://ssrn.com/abstract=2563965

Zogg, Samuel, *Bitcoin als Rechtsobjekt - eine zivilrechtliche Einordnung 95* (recht, Zeitschrift für juristische Weiterbildung und Praxis 2019)

Electronic References

Chapter 1 (Understanding Blockchain)

http://www.bitcoinstrings.com/
https://2019.www.torproject.org/about/overview.html.en
https://arxiv.org/pdf/1802.07242.pdf
https://assets.ctfassets.net/r1dr6vzfxhev/2t4uxvsIqk0EUau6g2sw0g/45eae33637ca92f85dd9f4a3a218e1ec/iota1_4_3.pdf
https://bitcoin.org/bitcoin.pdf
https://bitcoin.org/en/download
https://bitcoinmagazine.com/articles/long-road-segwit-how-bitcoins-biggest-protocol-upgrade-became-reality
https://blog.cloudflare.com/a-relatively-easy-to-understand-primer-on-elliptic-curve-cryptography/
https://blog.iota.org/the-tangle-an-illustrated-introduction-79f537b0a455
https://blog.muun.com/the-inbound-capacity-problem-in-the-lightning-network/
https://bravenewcoin.com/insights/etc-51-attack-what-happened-and-how-it-was-stopped
https://coinmarketcap.com/rankings/exchanges/
https://cointelegraph.com/tags/zilliqa
https://cryptii.com/pipes/enigma-machine
https://csrc.nist.gov/csrc/media/publications/fips/180/4/archive/2012-03-06/documents/fips180-4.pdf
https://diar.co/volume-2-issue-22/#4
https://digiconomist.net/bitcoin-energy-consumption
https://digiconomist.net/bitcoin-energy-consumption
https://docs.ethhub.io/ethereum-basics/governance/
https://docs.ethhub.io/ethereum-basics/history-and-forks/
https://docs.oracle.com/javase/7/docs/api/
https://eips.ethereum.org/all
https://en.bitcoin.it/wiki/SegWit2x

https://en.wikipedia.org/wiki/Advanced_Encryption_Standard
https://en.wikipedia.org/wiki/Computational_complexity_theory#Intractability
https://en.wikipedia.org/wiki/Foreshadow_(security_vulnerability)
https://en.wikipedia.org/wiki/Hawala
https://en.wikipedia.org/wiki/Paxos_(computer_science)
https://en.wikipedia.org/wiki/SQL
https://eos.io
https://etale-cohomology.github.io/stellar-tutorials/blog1.html
https://etheroll.com/#/about
https://etherscan.io/blocks
https://ethersphere.github.io/swarm-home/
https://ethgasstation.info
https://events.static.linuxfound.org/sites/events/files/slides/%28OSF_Mr.%20Dan%20O%27Prey%29Hyperledger%20-%20Open%20Source%20Forum.pdf
https://fenix.tecnico.ulisboa.pt/downloadFile/1126518382178117/10.e-CAP-3.pdf
https://github.com
https://github.com/bitcoin/bips
https://github.com/bitcoin/bips/blob/master/bip-0002.mediawiki
https://github.com/bitcoin/bitcoin
https://github.com/EOSIO/Documentation/blob/master/TechnicalWhitePaper.md#governance
https://github.com/ethereum/EIPs
https://github.com/ethereum/solidity
https://github.com/ethereum/wiki/wiki/Whisper
https://github.com/features/project-management/
https://github.com/hyperledger/fabric
https://github.com/hyperledger/sawtooth-core
https://groups.csail.mit.edu/tds/papers/Lynch/jacm85.pdf
https://gwei.io
https://home.unicode.org
https://hyperledger-fabric.readthedocs.io/en/release-1.4/architecture.html
https://hyperledger-fabric.readthedocs.io/en/release-1.4/chaincode.html
https://icobench.com/
https://idex.market/eth/idex
https://launchpad.binance.com/
https://lightning.network/lightning-network-paper.pdf
https://lisk.io
https://lists.linuxfoundation.org/mailman/listinfo/bitcoin-dev
https://litecoin.org/
https://metamask.io/
https://minivalist.cinn.app/validators
https://mwhittaker.github.io/blog/an_illustrated_proof_of_the_cap_theorem/
https://napster.com
https://neo.org
https://pdfs.semanticscholar.org/938a/24139dbf089d4d8a4318445c471e1e7f0aee.pdf

https://people.eecs.berkeley.edu/~luca/cs174/byzantine.pdf
https://sawtooth.hyperledger.org/docs/core/releases/1.1/transaction_family_specifications.html
https://stratisplatform.com
https://tendermint.com/
https://tezos.com/static/white_paper-2dc8c02267a8fb86bd67a108199441bf.pdf
https://theethereum.wiki/w/index.php/ERC20_Token_Standard
https://tron.network
https://wavesplatform.com
https://wiki.p2pfoundation.net/Peer_Governance
https://www.bitaddress.org
https://www.bitcoincash.org/
https://www.blockchain.com/en/charts/n-transactions-per-block?timespan=all
https://www.chainalysis.com
https://www.coindesk.com/soon-chain-governance
https://www.coinwarz.com/difficulty-charts/bitcoin-difficulty-chart
https://www.computerworld.com/article/3334542/mit-stanford-and-others-to-build-blockchain-payments-network-to-rival-visanet.html
https://www.cpacanada.ca/en/business-and-accounting-resources/cpa-canada-handbook-the-standards-and-guidance-collection
https://www.cryptokitties.co
https://www.elliptic.co/
https://www.factom.com
https://www.fileformat.info/tool/hash.htm
https://www.goquorum.com/
https://www.hyperledger.org/
https://www.hyperledger.org/wp-content/uploads/2017/08/Hyperledger_Arch_WG_Paper_1_Consensus.pdf
https://www.ifrs.org/
https://www.independent.co.uk/life-style/gadgets-and-tech/news/bitcoin-price-fall-criminals-blockchain-anonymous-cryptocurrency-zcash-monero-dash-a8174716.html
https://www.iota.org/
https://www.javatpoint.com/java-data-types
https://www.metmuseum.org/art/collection/search/329081
https://www.mycryptoheroes.net
https://www.oreilly.com/library/view/mastering-bitcoin/9781491902639/ch08.html
https://www.peercoin.net/
https://www.peercoin.net/whitepapers/peercoin-paper.pdf
https://www.python.org/dev/peps/pep-0001/
https://www.ripple.com/
https://www.sec.gov/litigation/investreport/34-81207.pdf
https://www.stellar.org/
https://www.theregister.co.uk/2019/02/12/intel_sgx_hacked/
https://www.tools4noobs.com/online_tools/hash/

https://www.weusecoins.com/assets/pdf/library/Ethereum_white_paper-a_next_generation_smart_contract_and_decentralized_application_platform-vitalik-buterin.pdf
https://xrpl.org/img/ledger-changes.png
https://xrpl.org/payment-system-basics.html
https://zilliqa.com/

Chapter 2 (Information Security)

https://cointelegraph.com/news/six-tools-used-by-hackers-to-steal-cryptocurrency-how-to-protect-wallets
https://blog.chainalysis.com/reports/money-supply
https://www.theguardian.com/technology/2013/nov/27/hard-drive-bitcoin-landfill-site
https://nypost.com/2018/05/26/i-accidentally-threw-away-60m-worth-of-bitcoin/
https://www.theguardian.com/technology/2013/nov/27/hard-drive-bitcoin-landfill-site
https://www.wired.co.uk/article/bitcoin-lost-newport-landfill
https://germanlawarchive.iuscomp.org/?p = 615
https://www.forbes.com/sites/nathanvardi/2018/04/19/the-last-days-of-banking-heir-matthew-mellon/#74427ea75d52
https://www.nzherald.co.nz/world/news/article.cfm?c_id = 2&objectid = 12037373
https://www.ccn.com/humans-die-cryptocurrencies-dont-why-cryptocurrency-investors-need-to-begin-estate-planning-immediately/
https://www.americanbar.org/groups/real_property_trust_estate/publications/probate-property-magazine/2019/july-august/estate-planning-cryptocurrency/
https://www.thinkadvisor.com/2018/10/22/4-key-steps-for-estate-planning-with-cryptocurrenc/?slreturn = 20190913175124
https://www.natlawreview.com/article/cryptocurrency-current-investment-future-inheritance
https://www.foley.com/files/uploads/Foley-Cryptocurrency-Survey.pdf
https://hackernoon.com/common-mistakes-that-crypto-beginners-make-77b5a5b6d7ec
https://www.bleepingcomputer.com/news/security/clipboard-hijacker-malware-monitors-23-million-bitcoin-addresses/
https://youtu.be/Ty-_IjavYH4
https://www.docdroid.net/Jug5LX3/ledger-receive-address-attack.pdf
https://www.zdnet.com/article/cryptocurrency-wallet-caught-sending-user-passwords-to-googles-spellchecker/
https://www.justice.gov/sites/default/files/criminal-ccips/legacy/2015/01/14/ccmanual.pdf
https://www.cps.gov.uk/legal-guidance/cybercrime-prosecution-guidance
https://www.itpro.co.uk/it-legislation/28174/what-is-the-computer-misuse-act
https://www.defcon.org/html/defcon-23/dc-23-speakers.html#Castellucci

https://www.wired.com/2015/07/brainflayer-password-cracker-steals-bitcoins-brain/
https://tylermoore.ens.utulsa.edu/thesis/vasek.pdf
https://medium.com/taptrust/frozen-the-story-of-the-largest-wallet-burglary-in-ethereums-history-a-massive-mystery-and-a-1b0a81f3ee88
https://www.newsbtc.com/2018/02/02/hightech-kidnapping-botched-old-fashioned-stupidity/
https://fortune.com/2018/02/01/bitcoin-kidnapping-cryptocurrenccy/
https://www.manhattanda.org/da-vance-man-indicted-stealing-18-million-cryptocurrency/
https://fortune.com/2018/02/01/bitcoin-kidnapping-cryptocurrenccy/
https://coinmarketcap.com/
https://bitcoinist.com/bitcoin-rocked-exmos-pavel-lerner-kidnapped-kiev-update-ransom-paid/
https://www.dw.com/en/russias-bitcoin-expert-pavel-lerner-freed-after-kidnapping/a-41975644
https://exmo.me/en/news_view?id = 2031&year = 2017&month = 12
https://www.telegraph.co.uk/technology/2017/12/28/bitcoin-exchange-chief-executive-kidnapped-leaves-work/
https://bitcoinist.com/exmo-crypto-analyst-pavel-lerner-on-his-kidnapping-and-life-afterwards/
https://forklog.com/pervoe-intervyu-posle-pohishheniya-pavel-lerner-o-bezopasnosti-i-novoj-rabote/
https://www.fbi.gov/news/stories/how-the-fbi-responds-to-international-kidnappings-050119
https://www.theguardian.com/news/2019/jan/25/business-of-kidnapping-inside-the-secret-world-of-hostage-negotiation-ransom-insurance
https://hackernoon.com/sim-jacking-attacks-are-on-the-rise-for-crypto-holders-829899dab2f8
https://nypost.com/2019/04/13/hackers-are-stealing-millions-in-bitcoin-and-living-like-big-shots/
https://elpais.com/elpais/2019/06/04/inenglish/1559634688_625364.html
www.ogusers.com
https://www.vice.com/en_us/article/vbqax3/hackers-sim-swapping-steal-phone-numbers-instagram-bitcoin
https://nypost.com/2019/04/13/hackers-are-stealing-millions-in-bitcoin-and-living-like-big-shots/
https://www.lifewire.com/what-are-sim-cards-577532
https://www.digitaltrends.com/mobile/sim-swap-fraud-explained/
https://www.vice.com/en_us/article/d3n3am/att-and-verizon-employees-charged-sim-swapping-criminal-ring
https://www.sanjoseinside.com/2019/04/25/bitcoin-bandit-sentenced-to-a-decade-behind-bars-in-nations-first-sim-swap-conviction/
https://krebsonsecurity.com/2018/08/alleged-sim-swapper-arrested-in-california/#more-44746

https://www.zdnet.com/article/wave-of-sim-swapping-attacks-hit-us-cryptocurrency-users/
https://in.reuters.com/article/us-crypto-currency-lawsuit/u-s-investor-awarded-75-million-in-cryptocurrency-crime-case-idINKCN1SG2CO
https://mashable.com/article/sim-swap-cryptocurrency-theft-nicholas-truglia/
https://www.youtube.com/watch?v=dnC5mFaIW3Q
https://thenextweb.com/insider/2017/07/11/card-trading-site-became-center-bitcoin-embezzlement-scandal/
https://www.coindesk.com/poll-mt-gox-withdrawal-issues
https://fortune.com/longform/bitcoin-mt-gox-hack-karpeles/
https://cointelegraph.com/news/the-mess-that-was-mt-gox-four-years-on
https://www.coindesk.com/mt-gox-ceo-mark-karpeles-arrested-in-japan
https://fortune.com/longform/bitcoin-mt-gox-hack-karpeles/
https://gigaom.com/2014/05/26/bots-were-responsible-for-bitcoins-stratospheric-ascent-anonymous-report-claims/
https://news.bitcoin.com/btc-e-operator-alexander-vinnik-terminates-his-hunger-strike/
https://fortune.com/2018/06/22/bitcoin-price-mt-gox-trustee/
https://thenextweb.com/hardfork/2018/08/24/mt-gox-cryptocurrency-claims/
https://selfkey.org/list-of-cryptocurrency-exchange-hacks/
https://www.nytimes.com/2018/06/27/business/dealbook/crypto-industry-regulation.html
https://economictimes.indiatimes.com/magazines/panache/a-crypto-millionaire-loose-ends-a-dead-end-a-consignment-of-teddy-bears-before-gerald-cotten-died/articleshow/68804401.cms
https://www.scmp.com/tech/blockchain/article/2185120/quadriga-cryptocurrency-exchange-founder-filed-will-12-days-he-died
https://www.millerthomson.com/wp-content/uploads/2019/12/Cover-Letter-to-RCMP-Final.pdf
https://en.wikipedia.org/wiki/Gavin Wood
https://gavwood.com
https://www.jdsupra.com/legalnews/when-smart-contracts-are-outsmarted-the-12326/
https://www.gnu.org/licenses/gpl-3.0.en.html
https://www.parity.io/the-multi-sig-hack-a-postmortem/
https://www.coindesk.com/30-million-ether-reported-stolen-parity-wallet-breach
https://press.swarm.city/parity-multisig-wallet-exploit-hits-swarm-city-funds-statement-by-the-swarm-city-core-team-d1f3929b4e4e
https://cointelegraph.com/news/parity-hack-white-hat-group-drains-85-mln-as-company-fills-holes
https://www.parity.io/a-postmortem-on-the-parity-multi-sig-library-self-destruct/
https://medium.com/blockmatics-blog/legal-issues-surrounding-parity-wallets-kill-switch-c551f02247d3
https://www.ccn.com/330-million-eip-999-stokes-debate-over-eth-frozen-by-paritys-contract-bug/

https://medium.com/blockmatics-blog/legal-issues-surrounding-parity-wallets-kill-switch-c551f02247d3
https://www.coindesk.com/understanding-dao-hack-journalists
https://medium.com/ledger-on-security-and-blockchain/ledger-101-part-1-do-you-really-need-a-hardware-wallet-7f5abbadd945
https://www.capco.com/-/media/CapcoMedia/PDFs/Digital-Asset-Custodians-for-Institutions_2page_v7.ashx
https://medium.com/proofofcapital/digital-asset-custody-primer-and-landscape-a889 79e05115

Chapter 3 (Blockchain Regulation)

https://www.hyperledger.org
https://www.corda.net
https://www.multichain.com
https://corpgov.law.harvard.edu/2017/03/16/delaware-blockchain-initiative-transforming-the-foundational-infrastructure-of-corporate-finance
https://searchsecurity.techtarget.com/definition/sandbox
https://www.ledgerinsights.com/turkey-blockchain-regulatory-sandbox
https://www.bafin.de/SharedDocs/Veroeffentlichungen/EN/Meldung/2017/meldung_171109_ICOs_en.html
https://www.esma.europa.eu/press-news/esma-news/esma-highlights-ico-risks-investors-and-firms
https://www.sec.gov/news/press-release/2017-131
https://www.sec.gov/news/press-release/2019-202
https://www.mmlawus.com/newsitem/pdf/Blockchain_Litigation_2019_Year_in_Review_01232020_standard_4777137568842645468.pdf

Chapter 4 (Smart Contracts):

http://firstmonday.org/ojs/index.php/fm/article/view/548/469
http://www.fon.hum.uva.nl/rob/Courses/InformationInSpeech/CDROM/Literature/LOTwinterschool2006/szabo.best.vwh.net/smart_contracts_2.html
https://news.samsung.com/global/a-relaxing-weekend-with-samsungs-ai-enabled-and-smart-appliances
https://execed.economist.com/blog/industry-trends/5-applications-blockchain-your-business
https://ambisafe.com/blog/smart-contracts-10-use-cases-business/
https://arxiv.org/ftp/arxiv/papers/1806/1806.03693.pdf
https://www.technologyreview.com/s/612748/hate-lawyers-cant-afford-one-blockchain-smart-contracts-are-here-to-help/
https://www.digicatapult.org.uk/projects/smart-contracts-for-creative-ip-distribution/
https://www.taylorvinters.com/article/smart-contracts-a-boon-or-bane-for-the-legal-profession

https://www.lloyds.com/~/media/files/news-and-insight/risk-insight/2019/triggering-innovation---how-smart-contracts-bring-policies-to-life.pdf
https://www.the-digital-insurer.com/wp-content/uploads/2018/07/1243-futureinternet-10-00020-v2-1.pdf
https://link.springer.com/article/10.1007/s11276-019-01949-0
https://www.techopedia.com/definition/28247/internet-of-things-iot
https://medium.com/smartz-blog/how-blockchain-and-smart-contracts-can-impact-iot-f9e77ebe02ab
https://www.thebalancesmb.com/the-sharing-economy-and-how-it-changes-industries-4172234
https://thenextweb.com/cryptocurrency/2018/04/13/blockchain-and-the-sharing-economy-a-match-made-in-heaven-this-startup-plans-to-prove-it/
https://myownbook.newgen.co/auth_token_login/84525d76-9a1a-4f99-9580-fd3d3cb8655b
https://www.lawcom.gov.uk/electronic-signatures-are-valid-say-governments-legal-experts/
https://www.law360.com/articles/1010335/smart-contracts-need-smart-corporate-lawyers
https://www.scl.org/articles/10493-in-code-we-trust-trustlessness-and-smart-contracts
https://pdfs.semanticscholar.org/370b/bc9f7af31fa01a8f61276d2a67591d22680e.pdf
https://www.webopedia.com/TERM/A/API.html
https://blocktribune.com/smart-contracts-weighing-the-pros-and-cons/
https://101blockchains.com/smart-contracts/#7

Chapter 5 (Data Protection)

https://www.ftc.gov/tips-advice/business-center/guidance/brief-financial-privacy-requirements-gramm-leach-bliley-act
www.leginfo.ca.gov/pub/09-10/bill/sen/sb_0901-0950/sb_909_cfa_20100621_110753_asm_comm.html
http://www.leginfo.ca.gov/pub/13-14/bill/sen/sb_0201-0250/sb_233_cfa_20130621_120929_asm_comm.html
http://www.leginfo.ca.gov/pub/13-14/bill/sen/sb_0201-0250/sb_233_cfa_20130621_120929_asm_comm.html
www.ftc.gov/tips-advice/business-center/guidance/complying-coppa-frequently-asked-questions#Verifiable%20Parental
www.pcisecuritystandards.org/

Chapter 6 (Capital Markets)

https://blockchain.kdpw.pl/en/
https://news.coinsquare.com/investing/csa-authorizes-three-digital-currency-investment-funds/
https://www.newswire.ca/news-releases/coinsquare-ranks-2nd-on-linkedins-2018-list-of-canadas-top-startups-692686911.html

https://www.ivey.uwo.ca/scotiabank-digital-banking-lab/canada-fintech/blockchain-crypto/coinsquare/

https://crowdlitoken.com/wp-content/uploads/doc/prspct/CRT-Prospectus_EN_digital.pdf

https://www.fxstreet.com/cryptocurrencies/resources/what-are-cryptocurrency-forks

https://curioinvest.com/templates/assets/docs/CurioProspekt.pdf

https://www.enercom.ag/prospectus-approved-by-fma/

https://business.financialpost.com/pmn/press-releases-pmn/business-wire-news-releases-pmn/3iqs-the-bitcoin-fund-receives-favourable-ruling-from-ontario-securities-commission-panel

https://www.bundesfinanzministerium.de/Content/EN/Standardartikel/Topics/Financial_markets/Articles/2019-04-15-two-years-fintech-council.html

https://www.theguardian.com/technology/2018/nov/20/bitcoin-price-plunges-2018-low-cryptocurrency-value

https://www.globenewswire.com/news-release/2019/04/02/1794894/0/en/Chaineum-acts-as-STO-Advisor-for-Carthagea.html

https://www.coindesk.com/police-freeze-bank-accounts-seize-luxury-cars-in-probe-of-22-million-ico-promoter-vanbex

https://invao.org/ivo-bond/#downloads_block_5d88da8aa7ab0

https://www.osc.gov.on.ca/en/SecuritiesLaw_ord_20191023_tokengx.htm

https://www.knf.gov.pl/?articleId = 61228&p_id = 18

https://www.knf.gov.pl/dla_rynku/fin_tech/Innovation_Hub?articleId = 60603&p_id = 18

https://www.gov.pl/web/cyfryzacja/strumien-blockchain-dlt-i-waluty-cyfrowe

https://www.gpw.pl/aktualnosc?cmn_id = 107748&title = Porozumienie + Ministerstwa + Cyfryzacji + i + GPW + w + sprawie + wykorzystania + technologii + blockchain

https://www.obserwatorfinansowy.pl/forma/rotator/rok-2019-moze-byc-czasem-innowacji-na-gieldach/

https://www.reuters.com/article/us-quadrigacx-crypto-canada/ontario-securities-regulator-looking-into-digital-platform-quadriga-idUSKCN1PX26G

https://www.google.com/search?q = SINGAPORE + INTERNATIONAL + COMMERCIAL + COURT&sourceid = ie7&rls = com.microsoft:de-DE:IE-Address&ie = &oe = #spf = 1580923208236

https://www.societegenerale.com/en/newsroom/first-covered-bond-as-a-security-token-on-a-public-blockchain

https://www.stockwatch.pl/wiadomosci/gpw-zastosuje-blockchain-oraz-chce-byc-dostawca-infrastruktury-dla-crowdfundingu,akcje,240997

http://alevtina.io/blockchain-finality-explained-what-and-why/

Chapter 7 (Intellectual Property)

https://cointelegraph.com/news/is-blockchain-about-to-become-a-patent-war-battleground https://www.unifiedpatents.com/insights/2019/12/16/lighthouse-check-depositing-patent-challenged-as-likely-invalid

Chapter 8 (Anti Trust)

https://www.oecd.org/competition/blockchain-and-competition-policy.htm

Table of Cases

English Case Law

European Case Law

European Commission

German Case Law

US Case Law

Other Cases

Index

D

E

Q

R